A COOK'S TOUR OF AMERICA

You'll get a gourmet cook's tour of the U.S. with the unique approach of DINING OUT AT HOME. This unusual book shows you how to make the most fabulous dishes from this country's finest restaurants.

Start off with *Avocado à la Horcher's* (Ernie's, San Francisco)—it is served cold with giant scampi and tangy sauce laced with brandy. Second course is *Smoky Fish Chowder* (Louis Pappas Riverside Restaurant in Tarpon Springs, Fla.)—it takes only ten seconds to make. Follow this up with golden-brown *Baked Chicken Breast Almondine* (Towne Lyne House in Lynnfield, Mass.)—a magical dish made with pineapple, sausage and slivered almonds, then smothered in rich *Supreme Sauce*. And when you're ready for dessert, try *Beignets De Fraises* (Imperial House, Chicago)—it is made with fresh strawberries fried to perfection, and served with powdered sugar and creamy *Sabayon Sauce*, which is prepared from three kinds of wine.

These and hundreds of other delicious recipes are now being published for the first time in DINING OUT AT HOME, a treasury of great recipes for people who like to cook and love to eat.

OTHER AWARD COOKBOOKS:

AN1014 *The Something-Went-Wrong-What-Do-I-Do-Now Cookbook*, by John and Marina Bear

A913D *Cook Right—Live Longer*, by Lelord Kordel

A872Q *The Organic Health Food Cookbook*, by Rory Marcus

A850N *Everyday Macrobiotic Cookbook*, by Barbara Rossi and Tom Bieber

A808S *$2 Dinners for Four*, by Peg Coleman

A747N *The Unharried Hostess*, by Rebecca Reis

A590S *The Fast Gourmet Cookbook*, by Poppy Cannon

A566N *Annemarie's Personal Cookbook*, by Annemarie Huste

A371S *Eating European Abroad and at Home, vol. I*, by Poppy Cannon

A372S *Eating European Abroad and at Home, vol. II*, by Poppy Cannon

A283S *Secret Recipes from the French Cuisine*, by Bifrons

A231S *The Overseas Press Club Cookbook*, Sigrid Schultz, Ed.

DINING OUT
AT HOME

James Stroman

AWARD BOOKS
NEW YORK

TANDEM BOOKS
LONDON

Titles are also available at discounts in quantity lots for industrial or sales-promotional use. For details write to Special Projects Division, Award Books, 235 East 45th Street, New York, N.Y. 10017.

CONTENTS

FOREWORD   vii
APPETIZERS   9
SOUPS   20
FISH AND SHELLFISH   53
POULTRY   192
MEATS   298
VEGETABLES   418
SALADS AND SALAD DRESSINGS   449
PASTA, RICE, EGGS, CHEESE   483
BREADS   514
BEVERAGES   530
DESSERTS   534
SAUCES—FOR MEAT, FISH & VEGETABLES   640
SAUCES—FOR DESSERTS   658
MISCELLANEOUS   661

FOREWORD

Cooking is an art, whether it is being done in the family kitchen or in a luxurious restaurant. While it is a simple art, it can never be mastered without a strong love for good food.

Many travelers will be able to visit some of the outstanding restaurants whose prize recipes appear in this collection; others will not be so fortunate. But imagination is a gift that all can possess, and with that delightful tool, any restaurant in any place may be visited at any time desired simply by flicking a page.

The recipes in this book have been written in simple language and can be prepared with ease. Many of them have never before been published. So flip the pages and visit all of these romantic establishments, right in your own dining room.

* * *

APPETIZERS

AVOCADO Á LA HORCHER'S

Ernie's Restaurant
San Francisco, Calif.

1½ pounds frozen imported scampi (already cooked)
3 avocados
Cocktail sauce (see below)

Thaw frozen scampi in refrigerator 24 hours (or overnight). Mix with cocktail sauce. Make small balls of avocados with melon ball cutter. In six cocktail supreme dishes put layer of avocado balls, layer of scampi, and cover with cocktail sauce. Serve well chilled.

Cocktail Sauce

3 tablespoons wine vinegar
1½ teaspoons dry mustard
2 egg yolks
1 tablespoon finely chopped
celery
1½ tablespoons horseradish
1 tablespoon chopped
chives and parsley,
mixed

1 tablespoon chopped
shallots
salt and pepper
1 cup olive oil
2 ounces brandy
4 tablespoons chili sauce
juice of ½ lemon

Mix vinegar, mustard, egg yolks, celery, horseradish, chopped chives and parsley, chopped shallots, salt and pepper together and beat well. Add olive oil and mix thoroughly. Add brandy and chili sauce and mix thoroughly. Add juice of lemon and mix again.

HOT CANAPE

Old Adobe Patio Restaurant
Tucson, Arizona

½ pound chicken livers
2 tablespoons butter
½ pound chicken gizzards
1 scant tablespoon flour
1 link Polish sausage
  (thinly sliced)
4 cups tomato sauce

3 cups tomato purée
1 cup mushrooms, cut into
  small pieces
½ teaspoon salt
¼ teaspoon pepper
1 scant teaspoon oregano
1½ teaspoon sugar

Sauté chicken livers in butter and chop. Boil chicken gizzards, chop, and dredge lightly with flour. Skin and thinly slice the Polish sausage.

Mix tomato purée and all but ½ cup of tomato sauce, and heat. Add mushroom pieces, slices of sausage, chicken livers and gizzards, and seasonings.

Bring to a low boil and add slowly the ½ cup tomato sauce in which one tablespoon of flour has been well mixed. Simmer for about 30 minutes or until the mixture thickens slightly.

Serve from a chafing dish.

MUSHROOM CANAPE

Mirror Lake Inn
Lake Placid, New York

White bread
Butter
1 tall can button mush-
  rooms
2 egg yolks, beaten

2 4-ounce packages cream
  cheese
2 tablespoons mayonnaise
¼ teaspoon salt
grated onion to taste

Cut ¾-inch rounds of bread and toast about 18. Butter one side. On this side, slice one or two mushrooms. Cover with the rest of the ingredients which have been thoroughly mixed together.

Place in refrigerator until ready to serve; then put under the broiler until they are golden brown.

TRANCHES d'ESTURGEON SURPRISE

Four Seasons Restaurant
New York City

Pumpernickel bread
Caviar
12 slices sturgeon

1 cucumber, peeled and
   sliced
2 hard-cooked eggs
Chives

Place thin slices smoked sturgeon on small pieces of thinly sliced, buttered, pumpernickel bread. Top with caviar, another slice sturgeon and paper-thin slices of peeled cucumber. Sprinkle with chopped hard-cooked eggs (yolks and whites chopped separately) and chopped chives.

AGUACATES RELLENOS DE CAMERON

Cafe La Margarita
Chicago, Illinois

3 large avocados
1 pound shrimp, cooked
   and hulled
1 chili jalapeno, or any
   chili pepper, in vinegar
1 hard-cooked egg,
   chopped
24 green olives, chopped

¼ cup mayonnaise
salt and pepper
parsley
1½ pounds boiled potatoes
1 cup sour cream
Prepared mustard, to your
   taste
Sliced lime, to garnish

Halve the avocadoes and remove the seed. Carefully scrape out the pulp and save the shell. Mash the avocado and mix with shrimp, chili jalapeno, egg and olives (all finely chopped) and then blend in the mayonnaise. Add salt and pepper. Stuff the avocado shells with the paste and decorate the top of each with a whole shrimp tail and two sprigs of parsley. Arrange on a platter with potato salad between the avocados. To make the potato salad, cut the potatoes in small cubes, add salt and pepper, mix with sour cream and season with mustard. Serve with plenty of sliced lime.

CEVICHE ACAPULQUEÑO

Acapulco Hilton
Acapulco, Mexico

1 pound filet of red snapper
  or similar fish, raw
lemon juice
1 large onion
1 green chili

3 peeled tomatoes
coriander (optional)
oregano (optional)
2 cups tomato juice
1 cup catsup
6 ounces pitted green olives

Cut fish into little cubes and wash carefully. Cover fish with lemon juice, let stand for three hours, stirring occasionally. Finely chop onion, tomatoes, chili and add coriander and oregano. Then add tomato juice and catsup. Mix lightly. Add cubed fish to sauce, and garnish with olives.

CHOPPED CHICKEN LIVERS

The Greenbrier
White Sulphur Springs,
West Virginia

3 onions, chopped
½ cup butter
1 pound chicken livers
⅔ cup sherry

1 jigger (2 ounces) brandy
1 teaspoon salt
Freshly ground pepper

Chop onions and sauté in butter until golden. Add the chicken livers and the sherry and simmer with lid on for ½ hour, then set to cool.

Add the brandy, salt and pepper. Grind up and press through a colander. Or put all in a food blender.

(It is important to add the brandy and seasoning *after* the cooking. "Sherry to stew, brandy to finish" is the adage).

The sherry and brandy combine to take some of the sharpness from the chicken liver.

CHOPPED CHICKEN LIVERS, BLACKHAWK

Blackhawk Restaurant
Chicago, Illinois

1 onion, chopped fine	1 teaspoon salt
2 tablespoons chicken fat	½ teaspoon pepper
1 pound chicken livers	½ teaspoon seasoning salt
2 hard-cooked eggs	

Sauté onion in chicken fat until slightly brown. Add livers and cook until they are browned. Grind eggs and cooked livers together. Add seasonings. If mixture is too stiff, add a little chicken fat.

PÂTÉ LAURENT

Restaurant Laurent
New York City

(serves 12)

¾ pound fresh chicken livers	salt and pepper to taste
¾ pound calves' liver	3 ounces cognac
¾ pound lean piece of veal	1 ounce black peeled truffle
1 quart milk	aspic
4 ounces sweet butter	

Marinate livers and meat in milk for 24 hours and then pass through the finest blade of the meat grinder. Mix with butter and place mixture in a buttered cake pan and bake in a slow oven for 3 hours, with the pan set in boiling water. Remove from oven, allow to cool, then pass everything through a fine sieve. Add salt and pepper to taste and then add cognac. Place pâté in a rectangular mold in layers of pâté and truffles. Cool mold in refrigerator for several hours. Serve in slices with chopped aspic.

GRILLED GRAPEFRUIT WITH KIRSCHWASSER

Brennan's
New Orleans, Louisiana

3 grapefruit
sugar

Kirschwasser
Maraschino cherries

Remove the core from grapefruit halves. Loosen meat from skin and sprinkle top very heavily with sugar. Sprinkle with kirschwasser (be generous) and put the grapefruit under broiler until it starts to brown. Garnish with maraschino cherry and serve.

PICKLED TROUT

Sun Valley Inn
Sun Valley, Idaho

6 trout (about 4 ounces in size)
6 tablespoons butter
½ cup water
1 cup vinegar

2 medium onions, sliced
1 clove garlic, sliced
1 tablespoon whole pickling spice
2 tablespoons salt

Sauté trout in butter. Bring water, vinegar, onion, garlic, and pickling spices to boil. Cover trout with brine and simmer trout for 5 minutes. Cool. Serve 24 hours later. Serve as appetizer or entrée.

SAUERKRAUT BALLS

The Mohawk
Old Forge, New York

½ cup onion, chopped
3 tablespoons butter
6 tablespoons flour
1 cup lean ham
1 cup ground corned beef
2 cups sauerkraut
1 teaspoon dry mustard
1 tablespoon chopped parsley

2 cloves garlic
½ cup sherry
flour
1 egg
½ cup milk
bread crumbs
hot fat

Sauté chopped onion in the butter until soft. Add flour and cook until well blended. Add 1 cup each lean cooked ground ham and ground corned beef. Add Sauerkraut (ground and drained before measuring), sharp dry mustard, parsley, cloves of garlic put through garlic press.

Add sherry, and cook until mixture forms thick paste. Spread on platter to cool, and chill well for at least two hours. Shape mixture into balls the size of a walnut, roll in flour. Beat egg, add the milk, dip balls in egg mixture and roll in fine dry bread crumbs. Fry balls in deep hot fat (370°) to a rich brown. Drain on absorbent paper.

CANAPÉ MARQUIS

Restaurant Laurent
New York City

6 slices white bread	Tuna fish equal to the
sweet butter	weight of the eggs
2 hard cooked eggs	½ cup mayonnaise
½ large green pepper	¼ cup chili sauce
8 filets of anchovies	Worcestershire sauce
1 large peeled tomato	

Chop eggs, pepper, anchovies, tomato and tuna fish together.

Toast 6 slices of bread on one side, and spread the untoasted side with sweet butter, then toast the buttered side until crisp. Place chopped ingredients on top of each toast piece.

Add spoonful of Russian dressing (which is composed of mayonnaise and chili sauce). Add several drops of Worcestershire sauce. Serve immediately.

NEPTUNE'S SHRIMP COCKTAIL

Neptune's Table
Phoenix, Arizona

2 pounds fresh shrimp with shells which have been washed in cold water
3 cups water
3 tablespoons lemon juice

2 teaspoons salt
1 bay leaf
1 teaspoon pickling spice
1 tablespoon paprika
1 clove garlic

Bring the mixture to a boil and drop the shrimp into it. Cover tightly. Simmer 10 minutes or until shrimp are pink and tender. Drain and cover with cold water to chill. Drain shrimp again. Peel and place in refrigerator until ready to serve. Serve on shaved ice with cocktail sauce.

NEPTUNE'S FLAMING SEAFOOD APPETIZER

Neptune's Table
Phoenix, Arizona

1½ cups cooked shrimp
1½ cups crab meat
1 teaspoon shallots, chopped
1 teaspoon leeks, very finely chopped
2 tablespoons butter

4 tablespoons dry white wine
2 cups white sauce
salt and pepper to taste
3 cups rock salt
6 tablespoons denatured alcohol

Combine shrimp, crab meat, shallots and leeks. Sauté in butter. Add wine, white sauce and salt and pepper to taste. Take six scallop shells and under each shell, place ½ cup rock salt. Prior to serving, add 1 tablespoon denatured alcohol to rock salt. Add appetizer to shells and ignite.

GUACAMOLE

El Parador Cafe
New York City

2 avocados, mashed
2 cloves garlic, mashed, or
    4 teaspoons garlic juice
4 teaspoons minced onion

¼ teaspoon Tabasco or 2
    chile serrano peppers,
    finely chopped
salt and pepper to taste

Combine ingredients into a paste. Serve as a dip with tortillas, or serve as a salad on lettuce with Salad Dressing a la Parador. Yield: 1⅓ cup.

NOTE: Cubed fresh tomatoes may be added to above mixture, if desired.

ARTISCHOKENBODEN MIT HÜHNERLEBER

Host International Restaurant
Honolulu, Hawaii

12 artichoke bottoms
 1 cup chicken bouillon
white wine
 1 tablespoon butter
 6 chicken livers
 6 goose livers
salt and pepper
½ teaspoon thyme
 2 bay leaves
 3 tablespoons parsley

2 tablespoons onion
1 clove garlic
1 teaspoon ginger
1 lemon
white wine
olive oil
butter
flour
parsley
 1 pimento

Simmer 12 large artichoke bottoms in 1 cup chicken bouillon, with a dash of white wine and 1 tablespoon butter. Reduce the liquid entirely and put artichokes on plate, hollow side up. Keep warm.

Marinate for 3 hours or more, the chicken livers and goose livers in salt, pepper, thyme, bay leaves, chopped parsley, minced onions, garlic, ginger and sliced lemon, adding wine and olive oil, to cover. Dredge livers with flour and sauté in butter; moisten with a little white wine and chicken stock.

For each serving place 2 artichoke bottoms, hollow side up, in oblong casserole. Then put in each bottom one chicken liver and one goose liver. Cover with hollandaise sauce and sprinkle with chopped parsley and diced pimento. Put under broiler and bring to a rich glaze.

CROQUE MONSIEUR

Cafe Jardin Suisse
Roney Plaza Hotel
Miami Beach, Florida

6 slices Vollendam ham
6 slices Gruyere cheese
12 slices white bread
3 eggs, well beaten
Salt and pepper, to taste

12 asparagus spears
3 deviled eggs
1 large tomato, peeled and
   sliced
6 olives
6 radishes

Make a sandwich of the ham and cheese. Dip the sandwich into pan containing beaten eggs with seasonings as desired. Put the sandwich on a griddle until color is golden yellow and brown. Garnish with asparagus spears. Garniture on plate consists of ½ deviled egg, tomato slice, olive, radish.

CHEESE SPREAD

The Pantry
Portland, Oregon

(Makes 12 servings)

½ pound margarine
¼ pound sharp cheddar
   cheese
¼ pound grated romano
   cheese

1 teaspoon Worcestershire
   sauce
Scant ¼ teaspoon garlic
   powder
½ teaspoon paprika
Sourdough French bread

Combine margarine and cheese at room temperature with remaining ingredients. Whip slowly in mixer until fluffy. Spread on sourdough French bread and toast under broiler.

SID'S CAPTAINS COVE CHEESE SPREAD

Sid's Restaurant
Algonac, Michigan

1 pound New York
   cheddar cheese
½ cup soft creamery butter
2 teaspoons prepared
   mustard

1 cup medium cream
½ teaspoon sage
½ teaspoon thyme
1 scant tablespoon
   Tabasco sauce

Cut cheese into pieces and put through moistened meat grinder using small cutter. Lightly cream the butter. Blend cheese, butter and mustard together. Add remaining ingredients and mix until completely blended. Store in stone crocks tightly covered. Keep refrigerated.

TOMATO PUDDING

Hotel Dilworth
Boyne City, Michigan

1¼ cup brown sugar
1 cup boiling water
¼ teaspoon salt

1 pound can of tomato
   purée
2 cups bread, diced
¾ cup melted butter

Add sugar, water and salt to tomato purée. Boil 5 to 8 minutes. Place bread squares in casserole (with a cover) and pour melted butter over them. Add hot tomato mixture and place cover on casserole. Bake in a moderate oven, about 350°, for 30 minutes. This dish appears as an entrée condiment rather than as a dessert on the hotel's menu.

SOUPS

CREAM OF ALMOND SOUP

The Mohawk
Old Forge, New York

3 cups chicken stock
3 tablespoons onion, chopped
½ cup celery, chopped
2 cups milk
1 cup light cream
3 tablespoons butter
3 tablespoons flour

1 teaspoon salt
1 dash Tabasco
½ teaspoon almond flavoring
Whipped cream
Toasted almonds, chopped fine

Simmer chicken stock, onions and celery until vegetables are tender. Strain and discard vegetables.

Scald milk and cream. Melt butter, add flour, combine with cream mixture. Cook over low heat, stirring constantly, until mixture is smooth and thickened.

Blend with chicken stock. Season. Add flavoring if needed. Garnish individual servings with whipped cream and chopped almonds. Serve hot or chilled.

POTAGE AMBASSADOR

Le Cafe Arnold
New York City

2½ cups fresh peas
6 tablespoons butter
chiffonade
1 cup green part of leeks
chervil

salt, sugar
1 cup water
3 cups consommé
1 cup cooked rice

Stew fresh peas in 4 tablespoons of butter, a little lettuce chiffonade, 1 cup of the green part of leeks, cut into pieces, a pinch of chervil, a little salt and sugar, and ½ cup of water.

Mash the peas as soon as they are cooked, moisten the purée with 3 cups of consommé, and rub through a fine sieve. Bring the preparation to a gentle boil and add 2 tablespoons butter at last moment with a cup of cooked rice.

TOMATO PEPPER POT SOUP

Columbine Ranch
Estes Park, Colorado

2 cans tomato soup
1½ cans cold water
1 tablespoon Worcestershire sauce
Tabasco sauce

¼ to ⅓ cup sherry
Juice of ½ lemon
Parmesan cheese
Garlic toast

To concentrated tomato soup add water, Worcestershire sauce and 5 dashes Tabasco sauce. Bring to boil. Lower heat to warm; add sherry and lemon juice. Serve with Parmesan cheese and garlic toast strips.

GAZPACHO

Matador Restaurant
Los Angeles, California

1 tablespoon parsley, minced
1 teaspoon fresh tarragon, minced
1½ cups green pepper, chopped
½ cucumber, peeled and seeded
6 scallions or 1 medium onion, chopped
4 cups garden fresh tomatoes, peeled, seeded and diced, or 1 large can tomatoes

¼ cup olive oil
½ teaspoon salt, or to taste
1 teaspoon lemon juice or 1 tablespoon vinegar
6 ounces mixed vegetable juice (½ of a 12-ounce can)
2 cups clear fat-free chicken broth
Minced green pepper and cucumber for garnish

Add minced parsley and tarragon (crush until paste-like) to green pepper and cucumber, put in blender and run at low speed until puréed. Add scallions or onions and finally tomatoes. Blend until well puréed. Add olive oil while blender is in motion, then salt, lemon juice, vegetable juice, and, if a richer red color is desired, 2 tablespoons tomato purée or paste. Blend with chicken stock.

Chill for several hours, the longer, the better. Serve with an ice cube and sliced cucumber in each soup dish.

GAZPACHO ANDALUZ

Restaurant Laurent
New York City

Liquefy 1 garlic clove and 1 medium onion in a blender. Add: 5 very ripe tomatoes; 2 sprigs parsley; 2 tablespoons vinegar; 3 tablespoons olive oil; ¼ teaspoon paprika and 1 cup beef stock or consommé. Blend at high speed for 2 or 3 minutes. Season to taste with salt and pepper. Refrigerate.

Serve chilled with chopped cucumber, tomato, green pepper, green onions and croutons, as condiments.

RED BEAN SOUP

Dunbar's Restaurant
New Orleans, Louisiana

2 tablespoons butter
1 small onion, chopped
½ pound red kidney beans
2 cloves garlic, chopped
2 stalks celery, chopped
2 bay leaves
2 sprigs thyme

1 teaspoon Worcestershire sauce
½ pound ham, ground fine
Salt and pepper to taste
6 tablespoons claret wine
Garnish of sieved hard-cooked egg and lemon slice

Brown onion in butter. Simmer beans for about 3 hours in sufficient water to cover, with seasonings. Strain mixture through coarse strainer, or mash with a large spoon. Add ham, salt and pepper. Place 1 tablespoon Claret wine in bottom of each bouillon cup. Pour in soup. Garnish with sieved hard-cooked egg and lemon slice.

BACON AND GREEN PEPPER CHOWDER

Hotel Racine
Racine, Wisconsin

6 medium-sized potatoes, diced
2 medium-sized onions, diced
2 green peppers, diced

½ pound bacon, diced
1 to 1½ quarts milk
2 cups medium white sauce

Cover the potatoes, onions and green pepper with water and cook in a covered pan until soft. In another pan, cover the bacon with water and simmer. Stir the white sauce into the cooked vegetables with whatever water remains after cooking. Add the simmered bacon. Slowly pour in milk and cook ten minutes taking care not to burn.

BOUILLABAISSE À LA MARSEILLAISE

Place Pigalle
San Francisco, California

1 large onion (shredded)
1 large leek (julienne — about 2-inch lengths)
4 stalks celery (julienne — same as leek)
2 tablespoons olive oil
2 cups clam juice
3 cups fish stock
1 bay leaf
1 pinch thyme
1 teaspoon eschalot (chopped)
1 teaspoon lemon juice
Arrowroot
1 cup fresh tomatoes (chopped)

¼ teaspoon saffron
salt, freshly ground black pepper to taste
3 or 4 Parisian potatoes
Fresh fish (in season) — include 1 cup crabmeat, 1 dozen prawns, 1 dozen clams, 1 dozen shrimp, 1 lobster, and any or all of the following: salmon, halibut, eel, sole— 3 pounds of fish cut into 3-inch pieces
6 thick slices French bread

Heat a heavy iron pot, sauté onion, leek, and celery in olive oil stirring constantly for about 2 minutes. Add clam juice and fish stock. Season with bay leaf, thyme, eschalot and lemon juice. Allow to cook until vegetables are tender. Thicken slightly with arrowroot. Add tomatoes, saffron, salt and pepper. Then add Parisian potatoes and any fresh fish available and simmer until fish and potatoes are done. Serve large portions on top of toasted garlic French bread slices.

LOBSTER BISQUE

Rive Gauche
Washington, D. C.

Make a stock by cooking fish bones and spice, onion, parsley, bay leaves and thyme.

Mirepois is made by cubing and combining onions, carrots, celery, and shallots.

1 1½-pound chicken
  lobster, cut into 4 pieces
2 tablespoons oil
1 cup mirepois (½ cup
  onions, 1 small carrot,
  ¼ cup celery, 2 shallots)
1 clove garlic
3 tablespoons brandy

½ cup white wine
1 quart fish stock
2 sprigs tarragon
2 ripe tomatoes, cut up
Salt, pepper, cayenne
  pepper
½ cup rice
1 cup heavy cream

Sauté the lobster with oil on high heat until shells turn red, shaking pan occasionally. Add the mirepois, cook 5 minutes and add garlic. Flame with warmed brandy.

Put in the white wine, fish stock, tarragon, cut up tomatoes, salt and freshly-ground pepper. Simmer 10 minutes and take out the lobster. Shell it, keeping the tail. Pound the lobster shell in a mortar (finely), dice the meat, and put all back into the soup with the rice. Simmer about 1 hour. Add cream, for desired consistency of a cream soup.

CLAM BISQUE

Wharf Restaurant
Fishermen's Terminal
Seattle, Washington

1½ cups diced celery
1 cup diced onions
1 quart clam nectar
1 cup clams, finely
  chopped
3 ounces butter

⅓ cup flour
¾ quart hot milk
1 teaspoon salt
¼ teaspoon white pepper
½ teaspoon Ac'cent
  (M.S.G.)

Simmer vegetables in clam nectar until tender. Add chopped clams.

Make a cream sauce by simmering butter and flour for five minutes, stirring constantly. Do not brown. Add hot milk, salt and pepper. Stir the cream sauce into the cooked vegetables and nectar mixture. Add Ac'cent. Serve with toasted garlic bread.

NEW ENGLAND CLAM CHOWDER

Andover Inn
Andover, Massachusetts

¼ pound salt pork
1 tablespoon butter
3 small onions, finely chopped
3 cups raw potatoes, diced
2 cups boiling water

1 quart clams, chopped, or 2 cans minced clams
2 cups milk, scalded
1 cup cream
Salt and pepper

Dice the salt pork into small cubes and cook them slowly in a heavy saucepan or skillet until lightly browned. Add butter and onions and cook slowly until soft and golden. Add diced raw potatoes, salt and pepper and boiling water and cook until the potatoes are done but not too soft, about 10 minutes. Meanwhile, strain the clam liquor, then bring the chopped clams slowly to a boil in it. Add to the potatoes with scalded milk and set aside for an hour to ripen. Add 1 cup cream, bring slowly to a boil again, and serve hot.

CHESAPEAKE INN CLAM CHOWDER

Busch's Chesapeake Inn
Annapolis, Maryland

(6 to 8 servings)

2 ounces bacon
2 stalks celery, chopped
1 small onion, chopped
1 large carrot, diced
1 quart clams, chopped coarsely
3 cups water

½ bay leaf
Pinch thyme
1 teaspoon salt
2 medium potatoes, diced
⅛ teaspoon white pepper
½ cup flour
½ cup water

Chop bacon and fry until almost done, add celery, onions and carrots to pan, and sauté until soft. Place clams, water, bay leaf and salt in pot. Cook ½ hour and then add sautéed vegetables and bacon. Bring to a boil and add potatoes and thyme. When potatoes are done, add pepper and then thicken with flour that has been mixed with cold water. Cook another five minutes. If chowder is too thick, thin with clam juice. Yield, about 3 pints.

CLAM CHOWDER

Chez Pauzé
Montreal, Quebec

1½ cups cooked diced potatoes	1 quart scalded milk
1½ cups cooked little neck clams	1 tablespoon butter
	Paprika

Be sure all ingredients are very hot. When ready to serve, put 2½ tablespoons potatoes, 2½ tablespoons clams in each of 6 soup bowls. Fill with hot milk. Add ½ teaspoon butter to each soup bowl and a dash of paprika. Serve immediately.

LADY CURZON SOUP

London Grill
Portland, Oregon

Clam nectar	Curry powder
Double beef consommé	Heavy cream, whipped
Diced lobster	

Mix together half clam nectar and half double beef consommé. Add diced lobster and a touch of curry. Top with unsweetened whipped cream and glaze to a nice golden brown under broiler, watching carefully, so cream does not burn.

SHE CRAB SOUP

Henry's Restaurant
Charleston, South Carolina

1 tablespoon butter
1 green onion, chopped
1 teaspoon flour
1 quart milk (dry milk won't curdle)
2 cups crabmeat
¼ cup crab eggs (roe)

½ teaspoon salt
⅛ teaspoon mace
½ teaspoon black pepper
½ teaspoon Worcestershire sauce
4 tablespoons dry sherry

Melt butter in top of double boiler. Sauté chopped green onions and blend with flour until smooth. Add the milk, stirring constantly. To this add crabmeat, roe and all seasonings except sherry. Cook slowly over hot water for 20 minutes. Add sherry just before serving.

QUICK SHE-CRAB SOUP

Ocean Hearth Restaurant
Boca Raton Sun and Surf Beach Club
Boca Raton, Florida

1 can condensed tomato soup
1 can condensed split pea soup
2 cans milk
½ to ¾ pound crab flakes

4 tablespoons butter
1 small onion, minced
Salt
Pepper
Sherry

Blend together tomato soup, split pea soup and whole milk. Heat on stove. Sauté crab flakes in butter with minced onions, salt and pepper and add this to the soup after browning. Add a few drops of sherry while soup is cooking. On serving, add a tablespoon of sherry to each bowl.

BISQUE OF HAMPTON CRAB, BELVIDERE

Williamsburg Inn
Williamsburg, Virginia

2 quarts water
6 live, hardshell crabs
2 stalks celery, chopped
1 large onion, chopped fine
3 bay leaves
Pinch of thyme
1 tablespoon salt
¼ teaspoon white pepper
¼ pound butter

¾ cup flour
1 tablespoon Worcestershire sauce
2 tablespoons Maggi seasoning sauce
2 cups medium cream
½ cup pimentos, finely chopped
Whipped cream

Bring water to boiling point, then drop in live crabs. When water resumes boiling add chopped celery, onion, thyme, bay leaves, salt and pepper. Let simmer for 25 minutes until crabs are done. Strain through cheesecloth. Keep stock at boiling point.

Pick the meat from the crabs and mince. Melt butter in sauce pan. Add flour a little at a time, stirring well until mixture is smooth and creamy. Add Worcestershire and Maggi, crab stock and crab meat. Remove from fire. Heat cream slightly and stir in last. When ready to serve, top with whipped cream and finely chopped pimentos.

SKY LODGE SEA FOOD BISQUE

Skylodge
Moose River, Maine

¼ pound sea scallops, diced
¼ pound fresh or frozen crabmeat
¼ pound haddock, chopped
½ cup chopped clams
5 large shrimp, chopped
½ cup chili sauce
1 onion (medium), chopped fine

2 tablespoons butter
1 cup water
3 cups milk
1 cup cream
1 teaspoon monosodium glutamate
2 ounces Sherry wine
Salt and pepper to taste

Sauté onion in butter until soft; add scallops, crabmeat, haddock, clams and shrimp; add one cup of water and cook until done (about 10 minutes). Add milk and cream, monosodium glutamate, chili sauce; bring to simmer; then add Sherry, salt and pepper to taste. Again bring to simmer but do not boil. Serves 6 generously.

PROVENÇALE FISH SOUP

*Fleur de Lys
San Francisco,
California*

6 different sea fish
½ quart different shellfish
3 tablespoons olive oil
2 onions, chopped
Thyme
1 bay leaf
Fennel seeds
1 quart water
2 orange peels
Salt and pepper
Slices bread
1 cup Aïoli *

* Aïoli . . . 6 garlic cloves, peeled, chopped and mashed to a point where they are pulverized; 1 cup mayonnaise is then added and they are stirred together

Cut fish in large chunks. Sauté in a casserole with oil and onions; add spices and orange peel. Cover with water and cook uncovered for 15 minutes. Strain the bouillon. Keep fish separated.

Toast the sliced bread and line the individual tureens with the slices. Then moisten with part of the bouillon.

Make Aïoli. Then slowly pour the hot, strained bouillon over the Aïoli, stirring uninterruptedly with a wooden spoon. Transfer this mixture to a casserole over a low fire, stirring again continuously until the sauce thickens.

The sauce is poured over the bread and fish in individual tureens.

SMOKEY FISH CHOWDER

Louis Pappas Riverside Restaurant
Tarpon Springs, Florida

1½ pounds Finnan Haddie
2 cups cold water
2-inch cube fat salt pork
1 medium onion, sliced

4 cups potatoes, peeled
  and sliced
4 cups hot milk
1 tablespoon salt
⅛ teaspoon pepper

Put cut up fish in cold water; cook until done. Cut pork into tiny dices and fry to a light brown. Add fish liquor and potatoes to fat and onions, and enough water to cover potatoes. Boil until potatoes are nearly done; add fish and hot milk and seasonings. Simmer 10 minutes. Serve with sour pickles and crackers.

NEW ENGLAND FISH CHOWDER

Red Lion Inn
Cohasset, Massachusetts

2 pounds cod or haddock,
  with head
2 cups cold water
3 or 4 medium potatoes,
  cut in cubes
1 quart milk

1 tablespoon butter
2 slices fat salt pork, diced
1 onion
1 tablespoon flour
Pepper and salt to taste
Common soda crackers

Simmer fish in water, with head. Cut potatoes in cubes and parboil with onion in liquid left from cooking the fish. Heat the milk in a double boiler. Add the picked-over fish and potatoes, chopped onion and flour which has been mixed with a little milk. Add butter and pepper and salt to taste. Cook the salt pork slowly for 5 minutes and add to chowder at the last minute. Also add crackers which have been split and toasted.

NASSAU FISH CHOWDER

*Emerald Beach Hotel
Nassau, The Bahamas*

2 medium onions, diced
4 sweet green peppers,
 diced
4 stalks celery, diced
2 medium potatoes, diced
6 tablespoons butter

1 quart fish stock or
 clam juice
1 pound white meat fish,
 diced small
4 ripe red tomatoes, peeled
 and chopped fine
Salt, pepper, thyme to taste

Sauté onions, peppers, celery and potatoes in butter until partly cooked but do not brown. Add approximately 1 quart fish stock or clam juice. Bring to boil and add fish and tomatoes. Season with salt, pepper, thyme. Thicken lightly with flour and water. Cook slowly for 1 hour.

BEAN POT SOUP

*Tiffany's Restaurant
Cerrillos, New Mexico*

2 cups dried pinto beans
1 pound ham, cubed
1 quart water
22-ounce can tomato juice
2 cups chicken stock
3 onions, chopped
3 cloves garlic, minced
3 tablespoons parsley,
 minced
¼ cup green pepper,
 chopped

2 tablespoons brown sugar
1 tablespoon chili powder
1 teaspoon each: salt;
 crushed bay leaves;
 Ac'cent and oregano
¼ teaspoon each: rosemary
 leaves, crushed; celery
 seed; ground thyme;
 ground marjoram and
 sweet basil
1 cup sherry

Cover beans with water and soak overnight. Add remaining ingredients, except sherry. Bring to a slow boil and simmer for 3 hours or until beans are tender. Add sherry. Serve in generous soup bowls topped with chopped green onions.

HUNGARIAN GOULASH SOUP

Bayview Restaurant
Callander, Ontario

6 onions, chopped
3 cloves garlic, chopped
3 tablespoons butter
1 pound stewing beef
Salt, to taste
1 teaspoon pepper
2 tablespoons paprika
6 cups boiling water
6 fresh carrots, diced

4 stalks celery, diced
4 potatoes, peeled and cubed
2 tomatoes, diced
2 green peppers, diced
2 tablespoons butter
2 to 4 tablespoons flour
Pinch marjoram

Cut onions very fine, mix with garlic and fry in butter to golden brown. Cut meat into small cubes, and half cook in pot with onions, stirring frequently. Add salt, pepper, paprika. Add water, to cover meat, add diced vegetables, then add remaining water. Knead butter and flour together and add. Add pinch marjoram. Simmer slowly until meat is tender, about 1½ to 2 hours.

POTAJE DE GARBANZOS
(Spanish Bean Soup)

Las Novedades Spanish Restaurant
Tampa, Florida

¼ pound garbanzos
1 tablespoon salt
1 beef bone
1 ham bone
1½ quarts water
4 ounces bacon

1 onion, finely chopped
¾ pound potatoes, peeled
pinch saffron
1 chorizo (Spanish sausage)

Soak garbanzos overnight with salt in sufficient water to cover. Drain and put into soup pot with beef bone and ham bone and water. Cook 45 minutes over low heat. Fry bacon and finely chopped onion; add with diced potatoes, saffron and salt. When potatoes are done, remove from fire, add chorizo sliced thin.

POTAGE BONNE FEMME

Chateaubriand Restaurant
New York City

½ cup of the white part of
   leeks (shred finely)
8 tablespoons butter
6 cups consommé
1½ cups potatoes, peeled
   and sliced

salt
pepper
chervil leaves
French bread

Shred finely the white part of leeks and cook in 3 table-spoons butter in a covered pan. Moisten with 6 cups of consommé. Add peeled sliced potatoes, season to taste and simmer gently. At the last moment, add 4 or 5 tablespoons of butter and chervil leaves.

Serve with long French bread, thinly sliced and dried in the oven.

BORSCH

Chicken Villa
Canora, Saskatchewan

(6 to 8 servings)

1 pound soup meat with
   bone
10 cups cold water
1 tablespoon salt
1 medium onion, chopped
3 medium beets cut in thin
   strips
1 small carrot cut in thin
   strips

1 medium potato, diced
½ cup thinly sliced celery
2 cups cabbage, shredded
¾ cup strained tomatoes
1 tablespoon flour
Salt and pepper to taste
Chopped dill
½ cup sour cream

Cover meat and bone with cold water, add salt, bring slowly to the boiling point. Cover and simmer for 1½ hours. Put in all the vegetables except cabbage and tomatoes and cook for 10 minutes, then add cabbage and cook until tender. Stir in the tomatoes. Blend the flour with 3 tablespoons of cold water, spoon into it some soup liquid, and then stir into the borsch. Season to taste with salt and pepper and bring to boiling point. Flavor it with the chopped dill. When ready to serve, add the sour cream.

OLD DROVERS INN CHEESE SOUP

Old Drovers Inn
Drover Plains, New York

4 tablespoons butter
½ cup diced carrot
½ cup diced green pepper
½ cup diced celery
½ cup minced onion
⅓ cup flour
1 quart well-seasoned chicken stock
6 ounces young cheddar cheese, grated

6 ounces well-cured cheddar cheese, grated (processed cheese cannot be used)
3 to 4 cups very fresh milk
Salt and white pepper to taste

Melt butter in top of double boiler. Add vegetables and braise till tender, but not browned. Blend in flour. Cook, stirring one minute. Add stock and cook, stirring until thickened. Place over boiling water in lower part of double boiler, add cheese and cook, stirring until cheese has melted. Add enough milk to thin to consistency of cream. Season to taste with salt and pepper. Strain. Reheat in double boiler. Serve hot in cold weather or cold in hot weather. Makes two quarts, or six to eight servings.

CHEESE SOUP A LA RADELL

Sanford's
Oakland, California

4 tablespoons butter
1 tablespoon grated onion
4 tablespoons flour
4 cups stock, or 2 cans of consommé and 2½ cans water
2 cups milk, scalded

2 cups Cheddar cheese, grated
½ teaspoon salt
½ teaspoon pepper
Dash cayenne pepper
½ teaspoon Worcestershire sauce

Melt the butter in a saucepan, add the onion and sauté for 5 minutes. Add flour and stir until smooth. Gradually add the stock, stirring constantly until the boiling point is reached. Add the milk, cheese, salt, pepper, cayenne and Worcestershire sauce. Mix well. Cook over low heat until the cheese is thoroughly melted and the soup bubbles. Stir occasionally.

CHEDDAR CHEESE SOUP

Imperial Hotel
Cripple Creek, Colorado

2 cups medium white sauce (2 tablespoons butter, 2 tablespoons flour, 2 cups milk)
1 can cream of celery soup
1 can chicken broth
2 cups aged cheddar cheese, finely grated

1 bay leaf
Large pinch cayenne pepper
3 teaspoons Worcestershire Sauce
4 tablespoons cream sherry
3 to 4 ounces beer
Salt to taste
Toasted herb croutons

Combine white sauce, celery and chicken broth, cheese, cayenne and bay leaf. Simmer over low heat for ½ hour, stirring occasionally. Remove from heat and add Worcestershire sauce, sherry and beer, and salt to taste. Serve topped with toasted herb croutons.

ROYAL CHICKEN SOUP

Williams Wayside Inn
Berthoud, Colorado

2 tablespoons chicken fat
½ cup each carrots, onions,
   celery (ground)
½ cup flour
2 cups powdered milk

½ cup cooked chicken
   (diced)
1 pimento
Salt and pepper to taste

Braise together in the chicken fat: ½ cup each of ground carrots, ground onions and ground celery. Blend in flour, stirring constantly. Add chicken stock and boil gently 30 minutes. Then add powdered milk diluted with water, the diced cooked chicken, and chopped pimento. Season to taste with salt and pepper and heat but do not boil. Serves 6.

CHICKEN BISQUE SOUP

The Pantry
Portland, Oregon

(Serves 6 to 8)

3 pound fowl
Enough water to cover
3 tablespoons salt
4 celery stalks
2 carrots, skinned and
   diced
1 medium-sized onion,
   skinned and diced

⅜ pound butter
¾ cup flour
½ cup each pimentos,
   blanched peppers,
   chicken
1 teaspoon M.S.G.
½ teaspoon pepper
Yellow food coloring

Boil chicken with seasoning and vegetables until it is tender and can be pulled off bone. Remove chicken and strain off 6 cups of chicken stock. Make butter roux by melting butter, then adding flour, stirring constantly.

Bring chicken stock to a very low boil, then slowly add to butter roux, stirring constantly. Simmer about 15 minutes, until soup takes on glaze. Add ½ cup each of chopped pimentos, blanched chopped peppers, chopped chicken. Add M.S.G. and pepper. Stir constantly. Add a few drops of yellow food coloring.

CHICKEN OKRA SOUP

Petite Marmite Restaurant
Palm Beach, Florida

2 leeks (diced)
1 cup celery (diced)
1 onion (finely chopped)
1 cup okra (sliced)
4 tablespoons butter
1 fowl—3 to 4 pounds
4 cups boiling water
celery leaves

2 carrots
1 medium onion
1 can pimento (diced)
2 ripe tomatoes (peeled and diced)
½ cup boiled rice
Salt, pepper to taste

Dice leeks and celery, finely chop onion and slice okra. Place in soup pot and brown lightly in butter. In another pot cook the fowl in boiling water, together with some celery, carrots and onion. Cook until the fowl is tender.

Remove fowl and strain chicken stock into diced brown vegetables and reduce to half the quantity. Add 1 small can diced pimento, fresh ripe tomatoes peeled and diced, and the boiled rice. Dice fowl into large bite size pieces and add to soup. Season with salt and pepper to taste.

VICHYSSOISE

The Greenbrier
White Sulphur Springs,
West Virginia

1 tablespoon butter
2 small leeks, finely sliced
1 onion, finely sliced
2 cups chicken broth
2 medium potatoes

Salt, pepper to taste
1 cup scalded milk
1 cup cream
Chopped chives

Melt butter in saucepan. Add the leeks and onions and simmer gently on a slow fire for 10 to 15 minutes, stirring from time to time with wooden spoon until nearly cooked.

This is very important in order to produce the proper flavor of the Vichyssoise.

Add the chicken broth, potatoes, salt and pepper and let simmer for another 15 minutes.

Add milk, bring to a boil. Correct the seasoning (it must be well seasoned). Then pass through a very fine sieve.

Pour into a bowl and put in refrigerator. When soup is well chilled, stir in the cream. Pour into cold cups. Sprinkle with chives and serve.

Note: The consistency should be that of heavy cream.

CREAM VICHYSSOISE

Arizona Inn
Tucson, Arizona

1 medium onion, chopped	1½ quarts chicken broth
1 medium carrot, chopped	½ cup apple sauce
2 stalks celery, chopped	Pinch nutmeg
3 cups white part of leek, chopped	Pinch mace
4 tablespoons butter	Salt and white pepper to taste
1 thin sliver garlic	1 cup heavy cream, used as needed
2 tablespoons flour	4 tablespoons fresh chives, chopped
3 cups potatoes, peeled and thinly sliced	

Melt butter in large pot, add onion, celery, carrot, leek and garlic and sauté until golden; add flour and combine with the vegetables. Take off fire and let rest nearby. In another large pot, put ½ the chicken broth and bring to boil; add the thinly sliced potatoes, cover, let simmer slowly until done. Remove from fire. Drain surplus broth off potatoes into a container and retain. Run potatoes through grinder with fine blade, combine again with their broth and keep warm. Take the other half of the chicken broth, bring it to boiling point and add to the sautéed vegetables and flour, put on medium fire and stir until it comes to a boil. Lower fire and let simmer for 30 minutes, then add potato purée and combine the salt, pepper, nutmeg and mace and put them in the boiling base.

After 10 minutes, add the apple sauce. Let boil for 5 minutes. Taste to see if more salt is needed. Texture should be like a thin cream sauce. If too thick, add more chicken broth. Strain through medium strainer into a container or crock. When cold, add cream, cover and store in refrigerator overnight. After thorough chilling, it is ready to serve, sprinkled with chives.

AVOCADO VICHYSSOISE

*The Tides Hotel
St. Petersburg,
Florida*

1 onion, sliced	1 small bay leaf
4 leeks (white part) sliced	Pinch celery greens
¼ cup butter	Pinch parsley
5 raw potatoes, peeled and sliced	1 large avocado, puréed
	2 cups heavy cream
1 quart chicken bouillon	Salt, pepper to taste
Sweet basil	Dash Ac'cent

Slice onion and the white parts of leeks, then place in heavy pot and sauté in butter. Add raw diced potatoes and chicken bouillon, a sprinkle of sweet basil and a small bay leaf, celery greens and parsley. Slowly cook for two hours; then pass through a fine sieve. Cool. Stir in finely mashed avocado and heavy cream. Season with salt, pepper and a dash of Ac'cent. Serve in cups bedded in ice with homemade Melba Toast.

BOWL OF THE WIFE OF KIT CARSON SOUP

The Fort
Morrison, Colorado

2½ quarts chicken stock
1 teaspoon oregano
1½ cups cooked chicken
  meat
1½ cups cooked white rice
1½ cups cubed Monterrey
  Jack cheese (one-inch
  cubes)

1½ cups cooked garbanzos
  (chick peas)
1½ tablespoons chopped
  chipotles adobados
  (smoked chile peppers)
1½ avocados, sliced thin
  lengthwise
Bent's water biscuits

For each serving:

Place in large bowl or iron pot: ¼ cup each of chicken, rice, garbanzos, cheese; ½ teaspoon chile pepper. Add oregano to chicken stock and bring to fast boil. Pour stock over serving bowl with ingredients. Top with slices of avocado (¼ avocado per person). Float a Bent's water biscuit on top.

THICK TURTLE SOUP

Royal Orleans Hotel
New Orleans, Louisiana

1 pound turtle meat, diced
2 tablespoons oil
2 onions, chopped
6 stalks celery, chopped
1 green pepper, chopped
1 clove garlic, minced
1 cup tomato purée

4 cups chicken stock
4 cups beef stock
2 hard cooked eggs,
  chopped
1 lemon, diced small
Sherry to taste
Salt and pepper to taste

Dice turtle meat. Sauté in very hot oil. Make a roux of butter and flour and mix in vegetables thoroughly. Add tomato purée, chicken and beef stock, and simmer for about two hours. When cooked, add hard cooked eggs, which have been chopped very fine and lemons which have been cut in small diced pieces. Add dry sherry to each serving and season to taste.

GAUTREAU'S VEGETABLE SOUP

*Gautreau's
Chepachet,
Rhode Island*

1 cup carrots, diced
1 cup onions, diced
1 cup celery, diced
1 cup peppers, diced
1 cup cabbage, diced
1 cup fresh tomatoes,
    peeled and chopped

4 tablespoons butter
1 tablespoon sugar
1 tablespoon salt
½ teaspoon white pepper
½ teaspoon Ac'cent
8 cups rich chicken stock

Sauté the vegetables in butter. Stir frequently, cook for 15 minutes. Add the stock and seasonings and simmer for 1 hour, or until vegetables are tender. Makes six to eight cups.

GUMBO À LA CREOLE

*Brennan's
New Orleans, Louisiana*

4 tablespoons butter
2 onions, chopped
2 tablespoons flour
3 quarts stock
1 can tomatoes
¼ pound okra, finely cut
Salt, pepper, cayenne to taste
Pinch thyme
1 bay leaf

Parsley
24 shrimp, peeled and
    veined
3 hard shelled crabs
1 pint oysters
Rice
1 tablespoon gumbo filé
    powder

Heat butter and cook onions until well browned. Add flour and cook 5 minutes. Add 3 quarts of good, rich stock, tomatoes and okra. Season with salt, pepper and cayenne. Add a small quantity of thyme, bay leaf and parsley, tied in a bit of cloth. This is termed a "bouquet."

Now add large peeled shrimp, hard-shell crabs and oysters. Let the whole cook for 1½ to 2 hours on slow fire. Just before serving, stir in gumbo filé powder. Serve over a heaping tablespoon of rice per person.

HANGOVER SOUP

Three Coins Inn
Baton Rouge, Louisiana

Vegetables as desired—
  potatoes, carrots, celery,
  peppers, etc.
1½ pounds beef, with fat
  2 cups cooking oil

1 10-ounce can sauerkraut
  juice
2 tablespoons rice
Water
  2 tablespoons sour cream
  Minced Parsley, optional

Cut vegetables in small pieces and brown them with the meat in cooking oil. Add sauerkraut juice, rice and five 10-ounce cans of water (use the juice can for measurement). Boil for 2 hours. Add water if necessary. Just before serving, add sour cream. Minced parsley may be added last, if desired.

GERMAN LENTIL SOUP

The Red Star Inn
Chicago, Illinois

  2 cups lentils
  1 onion, diced
  1 carrot
Stalk celery
  1 leek, halved and chopped
½ pound raw ham, cut up
¼ pound butter

1 tablespoon flour
1 potato, diced
3 quarts beef stock
Ham shank
Salt, pepper, to taste
Frankfurters, sliced (as
  garnish)

Soak lentils in cold water overnight. Drain. Cut into small cubes the onion, carrot, celery, leek and raw ham. Place butter in a casserole and simmer the vegetables and ham until they take on a slightly brown color. Add flour, potato, and the soaked lentils. Then add beef stock and ham shank. Cook slowly until the lentils are soft; season with salt and pepper. Before serving, add some sliced frankfurters.

ROLF'S GERMAN LENTIL SOUP

Rolf's
San Francisco, California

1½ cups dried lentils
2 ounces butter
3 slices bacon, chopped
1 onion, chopped
1 teaspoon salt
Flour

2 to 3 quarts water (in which lentils have soaked)
Ham bone
¾ cup sour cream
2 tablespoons vinegar
6 skinless frankfurters, diced

Wash dried lentils well and soak overnight in water to cover. Drain them, reserving the water. Melt butter in deep kettle and add chopped bacon. Fry lightly. Add chopped onion and cook until golden. Add salt, sufficient flour to bind the fat, lentils, 2 to 3 quarts water in which lentils have been soaked, and a ham bone. (Diced salt pork or diced fat ham can be substituted.) Bring to boil. Reduce heat and simmer until lentils are soft. Remove from fire and let cool. Then stir in ¾ cup sour cream and 2 tablespoons vinegar.

Boil diced frankfurters in 2 cups water and add to soup, including liquid. Season to taste with salt, pepper and Ac'cent. Simmer until well blended.

MULLIGATAWNY

The Greenbrier
White Sulphur Springs,
West Virginia

1 cup onions, chopped
4 tablespoons butter
⅓ cup flour
1 teaspoon curry powder
1½ quarts chicken broth
½ cup shredded coconut

½ cup apples (peelings and diced fruit)
1 cup cream
½ cup eggplant, diced
1 cup cooked chicken, diced

Sauté onions in butter until brown. Add flour. Simmer for 20 minutes. Add curry powder, mixing in well. Add broth and heat to boil. Add coconut and applepeelings and let simmer for 1 hour. Strain.

Bring to a boil again and add diced apples, and eggplant which has been sautéed in butter until soft. Add chicken. Season to taste.

TOKLAT'S WILD MUSHROOM SOUP

Toklat Restaurant
Ashcroft, Colorado

¼ pound dry wild mushrooms—Colorado Mountain Bolitas, Chilean or Polish
2 bunches scallions
1 cup hulled millet seed *

3 tablespoons oil—soy preferable
1 chicken bouillon cube
2 beef bouillon cubes
1 quart cultured buttermilk

* Millet seed is seldom used, but grows in United States and is obtainable in specialty food shops

Mix all ingredients, blending thoroughly. Heat, and serve piping hot.

FRENCH ONION SOUP

Craftwood Inn
Manitou Springs, Colorado

1 pound onions, peeled and sliced
1 tablespoon flour
⅛ pound butter

1½ quarts stock (½ beef, ½ chicken)
½ ounce dry sherry wine
Salt and pepper to taste
Gruyère cheese, grated

Sauté onions in butter until brown. Sprinkle flour over onions and stir. Add stock slowly, stirring until smooth. Add seasoning and let stand a few hours to improve the flavor. Place slice of Melba toast in bowl and pour hot soup over it. Sprinkle with cheese.

WHITE TURKEY ONION SOUP

The White Turkey Restaurants
New York City

6 large Bermuda or Spanish type onions
Beef suet
2 quarts rich beef stock (8 cups)
1½ teaspoons Worcestershire sauce

Pique seasoning (or Kitchen Bouquet)
Salt and pepper to taste
Parmesan cheese, powdered
6 slices French bread, toasted

Peel onions, slice very thin. Sauté until brown with beef suet in an iron skillet. Use no seasoning for this. The onion should be very brown but not burned.

Now add salt, pepper, Pique seasoning and Worcestershire sauce to taste. Add to beef stock and simmer for two hours. If served in a tureen or a flat soup plate, oven-toast slices of French loaf bread and float on top at last minute and sprinkle them with cheese. Serve additional powdered Parmesan cheese at the table.

If served in bouillon cups, cut the bread in 1-inch squares before toasting and float these on top.

ANDERSEN'S SPLIT PEA SOUP

Andersen's Restaurant
Buellton, California

2 quarts water
1 pound green split peas
1 carrot, diced
1 medium onion, diced
1 medium stalk celery, diced

1 medium bay leaf
¼ teaspoon thyme
1 teaspoon salt
Dash pepper
Small pinch cayenne

Put all ingredients into cold water. Bring to a hard boil for about 15 minutes; then simmer until peas are soft. When peas are soft, pick out the bay leaf and pass soup through a coarse collander.

Can be served with croutons.

CREAM OF PEANUT SOUP

King's Arms Tavern
Williamsburg, Virginia

1 stalk celery, chopped fine	4 cups chicken stock
1 small onion, minced	6 tablespoons peanut butter
2 tablespoons butter	Salt and pepper to taste
2 tablespoons flour	2 cups cream

Braise celery and onion in butter. Add flour and cook until well blended. Add chicken stock and bring slowly to a boil. Stir in peanut butter until well blended. Add cream, heat, and serve.

SOUTHERN PEANUT SOUP

The Mimslyn Inn
Luray, Virginia

½ cup celery, chopped fine	4⅓ cups hot milk
½ cup onions, chopped fine	¾ cup peanut butter
½ cup carrots, chopped fine	1 teaspoon sugar
¼ cup margarine	Worcestershire sauce to taste

Sauté celery, onions and carrots in margarine. Add to hot milk. Strain through china cup strainer and add peanut butter. Stir thoroughly and add a dash of Worcestershire sauce and a teaspoon of sugar.

NEW ENGLAND CORN CHOWDER

Publick House
Sturbridge, Massachusetts

4 slices bacon	Salt, pepper
1 medium onion, thinly sliced	2 cups cream-style corn (1 1-pound can)
2 cups water	2 cups rich milk, scalded
2 cups potatoes, diced	1 tablespoon butter

Cook bacon in a saucepan until some of the fat is fried out. Add the onion and cook until the bacon is crisp and the onion lightly browned. Take out the bacon and drain it on absorbent paper. Put water and diced potatoes into the pan with salt and pepper. Simmer covered for about 20 minutes, until potatoes are tender. Add cream-style corn and milk and simmer another 5 minutes. Just before serving, add butter and the bacon crumbled into bits.

COCK-A-LEEKIE SOUP

Crystal Room
Pick-Fort Hayes Hotel
Columbus, Ohio

1 fowl
2 quarts cold water
1 large teaspoon salt
6 shredded leeks
2 tablespoons rice

1 tablespoon chopped parsley
12 prunes (optional)
Salt and pepper to taste

Place fowl in large saucepan in the cold water. Wash giblets thoroughly and add, with salt. Bring to boil. Skim thoroughly. Simmer gently for 2 hours, skimming as necessary. Add leeks and rice. Continue to simmer until the fowl is tender. Remove fowl and giblets and any grease from the soup. Add parsley and salt and pepper to taste. Half an hour before serving, add a dozen prunes, unbroken, if desired. Serve fowl as a separate course.

ROLF'S POTATO LEEK SOUP

Rolf's
San Francisco, California

¼ pound butter
1 onion, chopped
4 leeks, diced ½ " in length
Flour
2 quarts beef stock
1 pound potatoes, diced ½ " long

Bouquet garni *
Salt, pepper, nutmeg to taste
Chopped parsley
4 frankfurters, diced
Dash Ac'cent

* Bouquet garni consists of a bunch of assorted herbs (such as parsley, marjoram, thyme and bay leaf) tied up in a piece of cheesecloth and cooked in soup or poultry for flavor.

Melt butter in saucepan. Add chopped onion and diced leeks. Simmer until soft and golden brown. Add sufficient flour to bind butter, beef stock, raw diced potatoes and Bouquet garni. Bring to boil, reduce heat and simmer until potatoes are soft. Season to taste with salt, white pepper, little nutmeg, and chopped parsley.

Boil skinless diced frankfurters in 2 cups water. Then add the frankfurters, including their liquid, and a dash of Ac'cent to the soup. Simmer until well blended.

POTATO AND WATERCRESS SOUP

The Lord Jeffrey Inn
Amherst, Massachusetts

1 medium onion, peeled and sliced thin
3 large potatoes, peeled and sliced
3 tablespoons butter
½ cup water
Salt, pepper
1 bunch watercress or parsley
2 cup chicken stock
1 cup light cream

Peel and thinly slice the onion and potatoes. Melt butter in a medium-size saucepan. Add the sliced vegetables, water, salt, and pepper. Cover and cook very slowly until the vegetables are soft and mushy, 20 to 30 minutes. Roughly cut up the bottom half of the watercress (the stems) and add it to the vegetables with 2 cups of chicken stock. Stir over the fire until the soup comes to a boil. Then put it through a strainer or food mill. Reheat, add cream, and just before serving, add the watercress leaves finely chopped.

This soup is also excellent cold.

SANCOCHO

El Panama Hilton
Panama City, Panama

1 small fowl
½ pound fresh pork
½ pound brisket of beef
4 onions, chopped
½ pound otoe root
½ pound yuca root
½ pound ñame root

1 plàtano (green banana)
  sliced
1 corn on the cob
2 culantro leaves—chopped
1 green pepper, chopped
Salt, to taste

Cut all ingredients into fairly large pieces (at least 6). First cook the meats, with the spices, in water to cover until almost done, about 1½ hours. Then add the vegetables and cook for ½ hour more or until done. Add banana slices, salt to taste. Serve in deep soup plates.

COLD SENEGALAISE

Jack & Charlie's "21" Club
New York City

4 cups chicken stock
1½ cups cooked chicken,
  finely chopped
½ teaspoon curry powder

6 egg yolks, well beaten
2 cups cream
Salt and pepper to taste

Boil chicken stock and add cooked chicken meat and curry powder (more or less to taste).

Beat yolks, stir in a little of the hot stock and blend in cream. Add this to the chicken stock, stirring constantly over low heat until soup is just thickened, being careful not to allow the eggs to curdle. Taste for seasoning, cook, and chill in the refrigerator.

EGG DROP SOUP

New China Inn
Baltimore, Maryland

6 cups chicken broth
2 eggs
2 teaspoons cornstarch

½ teaspoon MSG flavoring
powder
Salt, to taste

Beat the eggs and pour gradually into slowly boiling chicken broth, and stir while pouring. Add salt and MSG powder. Dissolve cornstarch in ¼ cup cold water and thicken broth with it.

FRENCH COUNTRYMAN'S SOUP

The Shed
Santa Fe, New Mexico

3 large potatoes, peeled and
grated
1 large turnip, peeled and
grated
1 leek, minced

4 carrots, grated
6 cups water or stock
⅛ pound butter
Salt, pepper to taste

Boil vegetables until soft, add salt, pepper, and put in blender or strain through soup mill or sieve. Add butter, the size of an egg, just before serving.

CREAM OF ISLAND COCONUT SOUP

Kahala Hilton
Honolulu, Hawaii

1 onion, cut up fine
2 leeks, halved and sliced
1 celery stalk, diced
4 ounces butter
2 cloves
1 bay leaf

2 ounces rice flour
3 pints chicken stock
1 pint coconut milk
¼ cup heavy cream
Salt, pepper and nutmeg
to taste

Sauté cut vegetables in butter without coloring it. Add cloves and bay leaf. Add rice flour, mix well with butter and vegetables. Add boiling chicken stock and coconut milk. Stir well and simmer for approximately 30 minutes. If soup gets too thick, add some chicken stock. Strain the soup and add the cream. Heat over low flame, do not allow to boil.

GUMBO Z'HERBES

Dunbar's Restaurant
New Orleans, Louisiana

1 pound boiled ham, diced	1 green cabbage
1 pound lean veal, diced	½ bunch scallions
2 tablespoons shortening	3 quarts water
1 bunch collard greens	1 large white onion, chopped
1 bunch mustard greens	
1 bunch turnip greens	2 bay leaves
1 bunch spinach	4 sprigs thyme
1 bunch watercress	1 tablespoon parsley, chopped
1 bunch beet tops	
1 bunch carrot tops	2 whole cloves
1 bunch chicory	2 whole allspice
1 bunch parsley	Cayenne, to taste
1 bunch radish tops	Salt and pepper, to taste

Wash all greens thoroughly; remove all stems or hard centers of leaves. Boil greens together for about two hours. Strain greens and save water. Chop greens finely.

Simmer ham and veal in shortening for about 10 minutes in deep iron skillet. Add onion and chopped parsley until onion is brown. Add greens and simmer 15 minutes. Add skillet contents back to water from greens. Add bay leaves, thyme, cloves, allspice, salt, pepper, cayenne. Simmer for one hour over low flame.

FISH AND SHELLFISH

BAKED STUFFED CLAMS

The Penthouse Club
New York City

12 clams
½ cup water
1 pound Boston scrod
1 very small onion,
  finely chopped
3 fresh mushrooms, finely
  chopped
1 small green pepper,
  finely chopped

¼ pound butter
1 cup flour
1 teaspoon curry powder
1 teaspoon Robert sauce
Dash cayenne pepper
3 tablespoons chili sauce
Salt, pepper to taste
Mornay sauce (see recipe
  under sauces)

Steam clams with water until opened. Strain clam broth through fine cloth. Remove meat from clams. Add scrod to broth and let simmer gently for 10 minutes. Remove scrod from broth and mince together with clams. Set aside.

Mix chopped onions, mushrooms and green peppers and place in a heavy-duty saucepan with butter. Let simmer but do not brown. Add flour, curry powder and blend together with clam broth to a very thick consistency. Add scrod and chopped clams. Add Robert sauce, Worcestershire sauce, cayenne and chili sauce and season to taste. Let simmer gently for 10 minutes, stirring constantly.

Place mixture in well scrubbed clam shells, cover evenly with Mornay sauce (see under sauces) and quickly brown under broiler. Serve very hot.

CALIFORNIA CLAM CHOWDER

Stacey's Round House Restaurant
San Francisco, California

1 onion, chopped
1 leek, halved and sliced
1 stalk celery
1 green pepper, chopped
¼ pound salt pork, cut in small pieces
1 ounce butter
5 cups stock or fish broth
3 potatoes, cut in half-inch pieces

Salt, pepper, paprika, to taste
1 teaspoon sugar
½ teaspoon thyme
Chopped parsley
4 tomatoes, peeled and cut in small pieces
40 little neck clams
½ cup cracker meal

Chop onion, leek, celery and green pepper in small pieces. Cut salt pork into small pieces. Put all together in a vessel with 1 ounce butter and simmer until well done. Add stock or fish broth, potatoes cut in half-inch squares, salt, pepper, a little paprika, sugar, thyme, parsley, and tomatoes cut in small dices (canned tomatoes may be substituted but won't be as good).

Bring to a boil and let cook until vegetables are tender.

Put 40 well washed little neck clams in a separate vessel and put on fire with 1 cup water and boil 10 minutes. Strain the broth and add to the chowder. Remove the clams from shells cut in 4 pieces, and add to the chowder with cracker meal and boil for 4 minutes. Use canned clams if fresh clams are not available.

Serve with chowder biscuits or pilot crackers.

CLAMS IN WHITE WINE

Chez Yvonne
Mountain View,
California

3 quarts clams	5 tablespoons butter
1½ cups white wine	2 teaspoons flour
6 shallots, finely chopped	Salt, pepper to taste
1 clove garlic, finely chopped	1 tablespoon parsley, finely chopped

Wash and scrub clams. Place in a saucepan or kettle with white wine, shallots and garlic. Cover and cook over a brisk flame for 6 to 8 minutes, or until the shells open. Remove the clams from the saucepan and, if desired, take off one shell from each clam. Arrange the clams in a heated, large, deep platter and keep them warm by covering with a towel soaked in hot water then wrung out.

Reduce the cooking liquor to ⅓ its original volume and thicken by adding beurre manie, made by creaming together butter and flour. Taste for seasoning, add parsley, and pour the sauce over the clams. Serve immediately in a deep soup plate and eat directly from the shell.

The clam broth may be served without reducing or thickening.

SAUTÉED SOFT CLAMS ON TOAST

Beau Sejour
Bethpage, New York

4 dozen raw fresh steamer clams (about 3 or 4 quarts)	8 tablespoons butter
	6 squares toast (white bread trimmed of crust)
1 cup thin batter—egg, flour and milk	Juice of 1 lemon
2 cups fine bread crumbs	2 teaspoons parsley, chopped
4 tablespoons cooking oil (preferably corn oil)	1 lemon, cut into 6 wedges, for garnish

Open clams with a sharp knife, being careful not to cut into the clam belly. Discard shells, juice, skirts and necks. Remove the center (clam belly), rinse away any sand, drain dry. Dip clams in batter, and then dip and toss in bread crumbs. Heat cooking oil with 4 tablespoons butter in a skillet, and fry clams until golden brown on all sides. Place a square of toast on each serving dish. Drain cooked clams of oil and place 8 clams on each square of toast. Sprinkle each with a little lemon juice, a pinch of parsley, a little melted butter and a wedge of lemon. Serve hot.

CLAMS CASINO

The Lamp
Valley Stream, New York

24 cherrystone clams
1 cup green pepper, finely
   chopped

Paprika
8 slices bacon, cut in thirds
Shredded lettuce

Wash and scrub clams very thoroughly. Open, reserving the juice. Arrange clams, on the half shell, in a skillet. Cover each clam with green pepper, sprinkle with paprika and place bacon on top. Pour reserved juice into skillet. Bring to a boil; place under broiler until bacon is crisp. Serve in the shells on a bed of shredded lettuce.

CRAB IMPERIAL

Harbour House
Annapolis, Maryland

3 pounds crabmeat
4 tablespoons butter
4 tablespoons flour
1¾ cup milk
1 teaspoon salt
½ teaspoon Ac'cent
½ teaspoon dry mustard
2 teaspoons lemon juice

2 teaspoons green pepper,
   chopped
½ teaspoon Worcestershire
   sauce
1 teaspoon onion, chopped
Dash of mace
2 eggs

Melt butter in saucepan, stir in flour, add milk, and cook over low heat until thick. Add remaining ingredients, except crabmeat and eggs. Remove from heat and stir in beaten eggs, then gently fold in crabmeat. Place mixture in clam shells, brush with mayonnaise and sprinkle with paprika. Bake in 350° oven for 20 minutes or until hot and desired color is attained.

CRAB IMPERIAL

The Thomas Jefferson Inn
Charlottesville, Virginia

1 pound fresh backfin crabmeat	½ cup mayonnaise
	1 teaspoon dry mustard
1 tablespoon green pepper, diced	½ teaspoon salt
	¼ teaspoon freshly ground black pepper
1 tablespoon pimento, diced	Paprika
1 tablespoon butter	

Carefully remove any pieces of shell from crabmeat. Sauté green peppers and pimento in butter until peppers are somewhat soft (don't brown). Mix all ingredients together and fold in crabmeat. Fill crab shells or scallop shells, molding it high. Spread more mayonnaise generously over all sides of crabmeat. Sprinkle with paprika. Bake in 400° oven until brown (15 to 20 minutes).

CRAB IMPERIAL

The Occidental Restaurant
Washington, D. C.

½ green pepper, diced	1 tablespoon (heaping) mayonnaise
¼ Italian onion (red), chopped	Salt and pepper to taste
1 tablespoon pimento, diced	Worcestershire sauce, to taste
1 tablespoon butter	Old Bay Seafood Spice, to taste
1 pint cream sauce (see recipe below)	2 1-pound cans lump crab meat
2 egg yolks	

Smother green pepper, onion and pimentos in butter for 8 to 10 minutes. Cool the mixture and add cream sauce, egg yolks, mayonnaise, salt and pepper, Worcestershire sauce and spice to taste. Fold crab meat into mixture very lightly, so that lumps do not break.

Form into equal parts, 6 or 12 balls, as you prefer. Insert them in crab shell or aluminum foil. Sprinkle white bread crumbs over each and bake at 400° for 15 to 20 minutes.

Cream Sauce
(Recipe for 1 quart. For above recipe use one-half amount)

⅛ pound butter
Flour—enough to absorb all fat

1 quart milk, heated
Salt and pepper to taste

Melt butter, gradually add enough flour to absorb all fat. Pour in heated milk; season lightly with salt and pepper. Simmer for 15 minutes. Use wire whip and stir frequently. If sauce is lumpy, strain through sieve.

CRABMEAT GUMBO IMPERIALE

Imperial House
Chicago, Illinois

1 cup celery, diced
1 cup onions, diced
1 cup leeks, diced
1 cup green pepper, diced
4 tablespoons butter
½ pint fish stock or clam juice
2 cups stewed tomatoes
2 cups beef or chicken broth

3 bay leaves
3 cloves
Pinch rosemary
½ cup okra
¼ teaspoon Ac'cent
Salt and pepper to taste
1 pound fresh crabmeat
1 cup cream
2 ounces Madeira or Sherry wine

Sauté vegetables in butter. Add fish stock, tomatoes and broth. Tie spices in a small sack (such as a tea bag) and add spice bag to other ingredients; simmer for 45 minutes.

Five minutes before removing from stove, add okra,

Ac'cent, salt and pepper. Just before serving add crabmeat, cream and Maderia or Sherry.

SOFT-SHELL CRABS SAUTÉED MEUNIÈRE

Chateaubriand
New York City

12 soft-shelled crabs (live)	Broth
Salt and pepper to taste	Juice of 1 lemon
Milk	Parsley, chopped
Flour for dredging	¼ pound butter, melted
6 tablespoons oil for frying	

Clean fresh, live soft-shell crabs. Season with salt and pepper, sprinkle with milk and roll in flour. Heat frying pan with cooking oil and a little broth; when hot place crabs in it, brown on both sides over moderate heat. Remove the crabs and place them on a serving dish; squeeze lemon juice over them and sprinkle with parsley. Melt butter in the cooking pan, and when hot pour over the crabs in the serving dish.

SOFT-SHELL CRABS SAUTÉ, GRENOBLOISE

The Voisin Restaurant
New York City

3 to 5 crabs per serving	6 lemon wedges
Salt, pepper to taste	Capers, to taste
Flour for dredging	Lemon juice
½ cup butter	

Allow 3 to 5 crabs per person, depending upon the size. Clean the crabs, season with salt and pepper, then flour them. Sauté in clarified butter until golden brown on both sides. Place the crabs on a serving dish and garnish with lemon wedges. Add more butter to the pan, heat to a light brown, put in some capers and lemon juice and pour this over the soft-shell crabs.

CRAB SOUFFLE

The Buttery
Midland, Texas

1 pound crab meat
3 tablespoons butter or
other fat
¼ cup flour
1½ teaspoons salt
½ teaspoon powdered
mustard

1 cup milk
3 egg yolks beaten
2 tablespoons parsley,
chopped
2 teaspoons onion, grated
1 tablespoon lemon juice
3 egg whites, beaten

Remove any shell from crab meat. Melt butter, blend in flour and seasonings. Add milk gradually and cook until thick and smooth, stirring constantly. Stir a little of the hot sauce into egg yolks, add to remaining sauce, stirring constantly. Add parsley, onion, lemon juice and crab meat. Fold in egg white. Place in well-greased 1½ quart casserole. Place in a pan of hot water. Bake in moderate oven, 350°, for 1 hour or until souffle is firm in the center. Serve immediately.

CRABMEAT REMICK

The Caribbean Room
The Pontchartrain Hotel
New Orleans, Louisiana

1 pound lump crab meat
6 crisp bacon strips
1 scant teaspoon dry mustard
1 teaspoon paprika
½ teaspoon celery salt

3 drops Tabasco sauce
½ cup chili sauce
1½ teaspoons tarragon
vinegar
1½ cups mayonnaise

Pile crab meat into 6 buttered individual shells or ramekins. Heat in the oven and top each with a bacon strip. Blend together dry mustard, paprika, celery salt and a few drops Tabasco sauce. Add chili sauce and tarragon vinegar. Mix well, and add mayonnaise. Spread the warm crab meat with sauce and glaze under the broiler flame.

CRAB RAVIGOTE

Christiana Campbell's Tavern
Williamsburg, Virginia

1 pound fresh backfin
  crabmeat
6 natural crab shells
1 tablespoon onion,
  chopped fine
1 tablespoon red pepper,
  chopped fine
1 tablespoon green olives,
  chopped fine
¾ tablespoon dill pickle,
  chopped fine

2 tablespoons whipped
  cream
⅓ cup mayonnaise
1 teaspoon Worcestershire
  sauce
2 hard cooked eggs
3 sprigs parsley
6 tomato slices
6 lemon wedges

Mix together all the ingredients, except eggs, parsley, tomato and lemon slices, with mayonnaise which has been lightened with whipped cream. Fill crab shells and decorate with chopped parsley, chopped egg white, and chopped egg yolk. Serve in a lettuce cup with slice of tomato and lemon wedge.

CRAB SUPRÊME AU CHABLIS

Cafe Johnell
Fort Wayne, Indiana

1½ pounds Alaskan King
  crab meat
6 ounces mushrooms, sliced
4 or 5 whole peppercorns
1 sprig tarragon
1½ cups Chablis wine

2 tablespoons butter
Salt
Freshly ground black pepper
¼ pint cream
1 teaspoon parsley, chopped

Cut crab in bite-size pieces and place in well-buttered fire-proof dish. Add mushrooms. Flavor with peppercorns and tarragon. Pour wine over all. Bake in a moderate hot oven, 350°, for 15 minutes. Remove crabmeat, place on a hot serving dish, and keep warm. Reserve liquid, reducing it to about ¾ cup. Melt butter in a pan with salt and black pepper. Add cream and slowly beat in the wine liquid from the crab. Bring slowly to a boil and simmer to the consistency of cream. Add parsley. Pour over crabmeat and serve very hot.

KING CRAB PLATE

Pine Cone/Branding Iron
Restaurant
Merced, California

6 12-ounce King Crab legs in shell
3 avocados, cut in half
1½ heads butter lettuce, cut into quarters (or use fig leaves)

3 tomatoes, cut in half and sliced
1 cup Louis dressing (see recipe below)
1 cup cocktail sauce

Arrange lettuce or fig leaf garnish on a large round plate. Leave King crab legs in shell and cut in approximately 3-inch pieces. Place sliced tomatoes, avocado and King Crab pieces on plate. Pour Louis dressing over lettuce and avocado. Serve cocktail sauce on the side.

Louis Dressing

½ cup mayonnaise
¼ cup French dressing
¼ cup chili sauce
1 tablespoon olive, chopped

1 teaspoon horseradish
Dash Worcestershire sauce
Salt, pepper to taste

Blend all ingredients well; serve cold.

CRAB PATTIES

The Pirate's House
Savannah, Georgia

1½ pounds crab meat
3 eggs
3 cups soft bread crumbs
1½ teaspoons dry mustard
1½ teaspoons Worcestershire
  sauce
3 tablespoons lemon juice
¾ teaspoon pepper

¾ teaspoon salt
½ teaspoon Tabasco
6 tablespoons melted butter
1½ tablespoons vinegar
Cracker meal
2 eggs, beaten with a
  little milk

Mix crab meat, eggs and bread crumbs. Blend all seasonings, melted butter and vinegar and add to crab mixture. Divide into 12 patties. Roll in cracker meal. Beat eggs with a little milk; dip patties in egg and back in cracker meal. Chill about 1 hour before cooking. Fry in hot deep fat, 375° till brown. Drain on absorbent paper.

CRAB MADAGASCAR

The Red Knight
San Francisco, California

6 5-inch crêpes
1 cup crab meat
½ cup cream sauce
1 teaspoon curry powder

½ cup Hollandaise sauce
½ cup heavy cream,
  whipped
Truffle slices, optional

Prepare crêpes and set aside. Mix crab meat with cream sauce (made of ½ cup milk, 1 teaspoon butter and 1 teaspoon flour) and curry powder. Roll an equal portion of mixture in each crêpe and flood all with a glazing mixture of equal parts Hollandaise sauce and unsweetened whipped cream. Glaze under broiler and serve with bit of truffle or other garnish.

SAUTÉED FRESH DUNGENESS CRAB LEGS

John Franco's Hidden Harbor
Seattle, Washington

1½ pounds crab legs
1½ green peppers, diced
2 hearts of celery, diced
½ onion, diced
⅛ pound butter

3 ounces Sauterne wine
½ teaspoon salt
¼ teaspoon black pepper
⅛ teaspoon thyme

Sauté vegetables in butter for 5 minutes. Add crab legs and sauté the mixture an additional five minutes. Add wine, salt, and black pepper and thyme. Cover the pan and sauté over a very slow fire for about 10 minutes.

CRAB LEGS GOURMET

London Grill
Portland, Oregon

6 Dungeness crab legs
6 artichoke hearts
12 slices avocado

2 tomatoes, cut into strips
6 celery hearts
Sprigs parsley

Place crab legs on top of artichoke hearts and decorate with avocado slices, tomato strips, celery hearts and parsley. Serve with Gourmet dressing (see recipe below).

Gourmet Dressing

½ cup tarragon vinegar
Lemon juice
1½ cups olive oil
1 teaspoon soy sauce
Ac'cent to taste

2 teaspoons dry mustard
2 teaspoons scallions,
    chopped
Salt, pepper to taste

Place all ingredients in a jar and shake to blend well.

DUNGENESS CRAB LEGS FLAMBÉE

London Grill
Portland, Oregon

6 6-ounce crab legs
2 tablespoons butter
12 medium mushrooms, sliced
1 tablespoon green peppers, chopped

¾ cup ketchup
3 ounces brandy
1½ cups light cream
Dash Ac'cent
Dash Tabasco
Salt and pepper to taste

Preheat the flaming pan, melt butter until golden brown, add mushrooms and green peppers, and sauté for 2 minutes. Add ketchup, let simmer for a minute or two (do not stir). Pour brandy in and flame; simmer for one more minute, stirring constantly, and finally add cream, seasonings and crab legs. Boil for 3 or 4 minutes and serve with Pilaff rice (see under rice recipes).

BAKED COQUILLE OF CRAB LEGS WITH WILD RICE, ST. DENIS

The Holiday Hotel
Reno, Nevada

2 pounds Dungeness crab legs
3 shallots, finely chopped
1 cup dry sherry wine
¼ pound butter
1 teaspoon Worcestershire sauce

4 ounces cream sauce
4 tablespoons Hollandaise sauce
4 tablespoons unsweetened whipped cream
Dash cayenne pepper
Pinch chives

Heat butter in a large skillet and sauté shallots. Add crab legs and sauté few minutes. Add sherry wine and Worcestershire sauce and allow to reduce by half.

Place crab shells on baking sheet pan and arrange a border of wild rice dressing (see recipe below) around the edges of the shell. Fill the center with crab legs and pour drippings from sauté pan on top.

Mix cream sauce, Hollandaise sauce, whipped cream, cayenne and chives. Coat the crab legs with this glazage and bake in very hot oven, 450°-475°, or in broiler, until golden brown.

Wild Rice Dressing

1 pound wild rice, boiled	¼ pound ham, diced
1 small onion, very finely chopped	2 tablespoons butter
½ pound mushrooms, finely chopped	6 ounces cream sauce
	Dash ground thyme
	1 teaspoon Ac'cent

Sauté onions, mushrooms and ham in butter. Add boiled wild rice, cream sauce, dash of thyme, Ac'cent and cook together for 15 minutes.

CRAB VALENCIA

Harbor Restaurant
Santa Barbara, California

2 cups crabmeat	3 tablespoons butter
3 tablespoons red peppers, diced	Cayenne pepper, dry mustard to taste
3 tablespoons green peppers, diced	Worcestershire sauce, to taste
1 small onion, finely chopped	Mornay sauce (see recipe for sauce)
½ pound mushrooms, sliced	½ cup Parmesan cheese, grated
1 clove garlic, crushed	

Toss crabmeat, red and green peppers, onions, mushrooms and garlic in butter. Season with cayenne pepper, mustard powder and Worcestershire sauce. Fill 6 crab shells. Cover with Mornay sauce. Dot with butter. Sprinkle with Parmesan cheese and bake at 375° until crab is thoroughly hot.

CHESAPEAKE INN CRAB CAKES

Busch's Chesapeake Inn
Annapolis, Maryland

8 tablespoons butter, melted
1 teaspoon Worcestershire sauce
2 eggs
5 tablespoons mayonnaise
5 slices fresh bread, chopped fine
½ teaspoon dry mustard

2 teaspoons salad mustard
½ teaspoon white pepper
¼ teaspoon red pepper
2 teaspoons salt
½ teaspoon Ac'cent
1 teaspoon parsley, chopped
2 pounds lump crab meat

Combine all ingredients, except crab meat, in bowl of electric mixer. Put wet items in first. Mix until you have a smooth batter. Carefully fold in the crab meat, without breaking the lumps. When well mixed, place in refrigerator until cold. Form into 12 cakes, handling the mixture as little as possible. Deep fry at 300° to 325° until golden brown.

BOOKY BAKED CRAB

Bookbinders Seafood House
Philadelphia, Pennsylvania

3 eggs
2 pounds large lump crabmeat (preferably backfin)
¾ cup mayonnaise

Pinch salt, pepper, dry mustard
1 teaspoon Worcestershire sauce

In mixing bowl, add eggs to crabmeat and stir in ¾ cup mayonnaise. Season with pinch of salt, pepper, dry mustard, and Worcestershire sauce. Form into 6 molds. Bake in moderate oven, 350°, for 15 to 20 minutes.

CRAB À LA KING

The Pirate's House
Savannah, Georgia

¼ cup pimentos, chopped
¼ cup bell peppers,
　chopped
1 quart milk
5 tablespoons flour
1 teaspoon salt
¼ teaspoon pepper

4 tablespoons butter
Juice of 1 lemon
1 tablespoon Worcester-
　shire sauce
1½ pounds fresh or canned
　crab meat

Add peppers and pimentos to 2 cups of milk. Combine flour, salt and pepper and mix into a paste with 2 cups of milk. Add to milk and peppers mixture and cook until thickened. Add butter, lemon juice, Worcestershire sauce and crab meat. Simmer until hot. Serve on toast.

LUMP CRAB AU GRATIN

Victoria House Restaurant
Victoria, Texas

2 pounds lump crab meat
½ pound butter
2 tablespoons sherry wine
2 cups Mornay sauce (see
　recipe under sauces)

1 cup Parmesan cheese,
　grated
6 slices white bread,
　toasted

Sauté lump crab meat in butter. Add sherry to Mornay sauce. Place in individual casseroles, sprinkle with grated Parmesan cheese, small amount of paprika for color, a little melted butter, and brown slightly under broiler. Cut toast slices in triangles and dip two pieces in paprika (points only) and two in parsley. Serve hot.

ALIOTO'S CRAB MORNAY EN CASSEROLE

Alioto's
San Francisco, California

3 cups rich cream sauce
3 cups fresh cooked crab
  meat
3 tablespoons sherry wine

3 slices American cheese
Paprika, as needed
Melted butter, as needed

Pour layer of cream sauce on bottom of 6 individual casseroles. Into each put ½ cup crabmeat, ½ tablespoon wine, ½ cup cream sauce. Top with ½ slice cheese. Sprinkle with paprika and butter. Bake in a moderate oven, 350°, for 10 minutes. Serve hot.

MRS. TRAUB'S CRAB CASSEROLE

The Pirate's House
Savannah, Georgia

3 cups milk
6 tablespoons butter
6 tablespoons flour
1 teaspoon nutmeg
2 tablespoons parsley,
  chopped
Grated rind of 2 lemons
4 tablespoons lemon juice
4 tablespoons Durkees
  Dressing

2 teaspoons Worcestershire
  sauce
½ teaspoon salt
¼ teaspoon pepper
6 tablespoons sherry
2 pounds crabmeat, picked
  over
2 eggs, beaten lightly
Bread crumbs

In a saucepan, melt butter, flour and part of the milk, stirring continuously until well blended. Add remaining milk and seasonings. Cook until thick and smooth. Add sherry, crabmeat and eggs. Pour into buttered casserole, cover with buttered bread crumbs and bake at 375° for 30 minutes.

CRAB CROQUETTES

Shady Nook Inn
Salmon, Idaho

1 large can shredded crab
1½ cups thick cream sauce
Salt, pepper, paprika, to
  taste
1 tablespoon Worcester-
  shire sauce

4 tablespoons butter
1½ cups stale bread
  crumbs
2 eggs, beaten

Add crab to cream sauce, season with salt, pepper and paprika. Add Worcestershire sauce and butter. Add 1 cup bread crumbs, allow to cool. Roll into croquettes about three inches long. Dip alternately in crumbs and beaten egg. Place in refrigerator and let stand overnight. Cook in deep fat, 375° to 385° until golden brown. Drain on absorbent paper. Serve with tartar sauce.

CRAB AND SHRIMP AU GRATIN

The Pirate's House
Savannah, Georgia

4 tablespoons flour
½ teaspoon salt
Pepper, to taste
2 cups milk
½ cup Kraft's Cheese Whiz

¼ teaspoon Tabasco
¾ pound cooked shrimp
½ pound crab meat
1 cup cheese, grated

Mix flour, salt and pepper with part of the milk. Beat until smooth. Add Cheese Whiz to rest of milk in a double boiler. When Cheese Whiz has melted, add flour mixture and Tabasco. Stir until smooth and thickened. Add shrimp and crab meat. Pour into casserole. Top with grated cheese. Bake at 350° for 20 minutes.

ESCARGOTS EN POTS
(Snails in Pots)

Four Seasons Restaurant
New York City

2 cloves garlic, cut
½ pound butter
4 shallots, finely chopped
1 tablespoon parsley, finely
 chopped
1 tablespoon chives, finely
 chopped

½ cup white Burgundy
 wine
1 tablespoon Pernod
Pinch salt
Juice of ½ lemon
2 cans snails and shells
Bread crumbs for topping
Toasted bread sticks

Rub bowl with garlic. Add soft butter, shallots, parsley, chives, wine, Pernod, pinch salt, lemon juice. Knead all together with fingers until butter is very creamy. Drain 2 cans snails (about 36); rinse in cool water; drain. Place each snail in a tiny pot (or each in a shell). Press butter mixture over top of each pot or into each snail shell. Sprinkle tops with fine bread crumbs. Bake 5 to 7 minutes at 350°, or until butter bubbles. Serve with seasoned, toasted bread sticks.

ESCARGOTS BOURGUIGNONNE

Chateaubriand
New York City

6 dozen escargots (snails),
 canned, with shells
2 cloves garlic, finely
 chopped
2 tablespoons shallots,
 finely chopped

1½ ounces Pernod
Salt and pepper to taste
2 tablespoons fresh parsley,
 finely chopped
1¼ cups butter
Dry white wine

Mix garlic, shallots and parsley very well and remove all moisture by squeezing through a cloth. Add Pernod. Salt and pepper to taste. Add the butter and mix well. Let cool.

Place some of this butter mixture into each snail shell. Then drain snails and put them into prepared shell. Place more of the butter over escargots, until shells are filled. Place on special escargot dish, being sure that the opening of the shell is on top. Bake in hot oven, 375°, until butter is sizzling. Remove and sprinkle with dry white wine. Serve very hot.

SNAILS FORESTIERE

Kahala Hilton
Honolulu, Hawaii

1¼ cups sweet butter
1 cup white wine
2 cloves garlic, chopped
½ cup parsley, chopped
Juice of 1 lemon
Salt, white ground pepper
  to taste

2 tablespoons shallots,
  chopped
½ teaspoon Ac'cent
5 to 6 dozen canned snails
5 to 6 dozen mushroom
  caps
¼ pound butter

Mix butter, white wine, garlic, parsley, lemon juice, salt, pepper, shallots and Ac'cent in a blender or bowl to a smooth paste. This amount is sufficient for 5 to 6 dozen snails. Place one snail in each mushroom cap, which have been sautéed in butter. Fill mushroom caps with the paste (snails have to be covered). Bake in hot oven, 400°, for about 6 minutes, until snails are heated and butter is melted.

ESCARGOTS À LA BOURGUIGNONNE

Jenny Lake Lodge
Grand Teton National Park,
Wyoming

3 dozen canned snails and
  shells
1 cup red wine
1½ ounces Cointreau
½ pound butter
6 cloves garlic, finely
  chopped

1 large Spanish onion,
  finely chopped
Pinch salt and pepper
Small bunch parsley,
  chopped

Combine red wine and Cointreau in sauce pan. Heat over a slow fire, bring to a boil, until both liquids are half evaporated. Add butter and simmer for 5 minutes; add garlic, chopped onions, salt and pepper, simmer over low fire for about 20 minutes. Remove from stove, stir in chopped parsley and chill to room temperature. When cool, refrigerate. The sauce then becomes a paste.

Stuff each spiral shell with the paste and snail, alternating a layer of paste, the snail, and paste. Bake in a moderate oven, 350°, for about 8 to 10 minutes, until snails are heated and paste is melted.

SHELL-FISH CRÊPES "AMBASSADEURS"

Ambassadeurs Restaurant
Mexico City

3 eggs, beaten
1 pint milk
1½ cups sifted flour
½ teaspoon salt and
  tarragon
6 cooked shrimp, cleaned
  and finely sliced
6 cooked crawfish, cleaned
  and finely sliced
6 moro-crab legs, cleaned
  and finely sliced

Meat of 1 lobster, finely
  sliced
½ pound mushrooms, sliced
¼ pound butter
Cognac
 1 cup cream sauce
 1 cup sweet cream
Pinch tarragon, chopped
Salt and cayenne
Sauce—see recipe below

Stir 3 eggs, milk, flour, salt and tarragon well with a wire whisk. In a middle-sized frying pan prepare 6 large crêpes with the batter. Set aside.

Sauté the seafood and mushrooms in ¼ pound butter. Flame with cognac. Add cream sauce, sweet cream, tarragon, salt and cayenne.

Distribute the filling in the middle of the crêpes. Roll them. Place the crêpes on a fireproof platter. Pour the sauce over the crêpes. Sprinkle some grated Parmesan cheese and crumbs, minced parsley and paprika over all. Broil until it begins to brown.

Sauce

8 egg yolks
¾ pound butter
2 cups cream sauce

Garnish of Parmesan
cheese, grated; parsley,
minced; bread crumbs
and paprika

Whip egg yolks in top of double boiler over hot water.
Gradually stir in butter, then cream sauce.

GRENOUILLES À LA POULETTE
(Frogs' Legs)

*Chateaubriand
New York City*

18 jumbo frogs' legs
1 cup white wine
4 tablespoons butter
1 tablespoon lemon juice
Salt, pepper to taste
1 small onion, finely
minced
Bouquet garni (1 bay leaf,
1 sprig thyme, 6 sprigs
parsley, 3 sprigs green
celery tops)

½ pound mushrooms,
peeled and sliced
½ cup light cream
3 egg yolks, slightly
beaten
1 tablespoon sweet butter
1 tablespoon parsley,
chopped
1 tablespoon lemon juice

Cook frogs' legs gently in white dry wine with butter and
lemon juice. Season with salt and pepper. Add a small
onion and a bouquet garni. As soon as the liquid comes to
a boil, add mushrooms. Cover and simmer gently for 15
minutes.

Drain the frogs' legs and the mushrooms; strain the stock
and boil it down. Thicken with cream and egg yolks. This
sauce should be fairly thick. Put the frogs' legs and mushrooms back in the sauce and heat. At last minute, add butter,
parsley and another squeeze of lemon juice. Serve immediately. May be served in a pie crust or a vol au vent (patty).

CUISSES DE GRENOUILLES À LA PROVENÇALE

Cafe Johnell
Fort Wayne, Indiana

36 frogs' legs (use baby
  legs only)
Lemon juice
½ cup flour
Salt and pepper
 8 tablespoons butter
 2 garlic cloves, crushed

6 slices white bread,
  toasted
2 tablespoons fresh parsley,
  finely chopped
Watercress
 6 lemon wedges
Tomato sauce

Wash frogs' legs very well in lemon juice and water. Dry and dust with flour lightly seasoned with salt and pepper. Put butter in a pan, heat to foaming and add crushed garlic cloves. Cook for 1 minute, put in frogs' legs and shake until golden brown on each side. Stack frogs' legs pyramid shape on toast points and pour butter from pan over frogs' legs. Sprinkle with parsley. Garnish with watercress and lemon wedges. Serve with tomato sauce flavored with a touch of garlic.

FROGS' LEGS À LA SIBIRIENNE

The Red Onion
Aspen, Colorado

18 pairs frogs' legs
Lemon juice
Salt, pepper
 2 tablespoons oil
 2 tablespoons butter
1½ ounces vodka
 2 tablespoons onion,
  finely chopped
1½ ounces dry white wine
 2 tablespoons natural
  beef gravy

4 tablespoons cream
1 tablespoon ketchup
Few drops Tabasco sauce
Few drops Worcestershire
 sauce
1 tablespoon parsley,
  finely chopped
Lemon rind, grated
1 clove garlic, crushed
Leek seasoning
Pinch thyme and rosemary

Season the frogs' legs with lemon juice, salt and pepper. Sauté in butter and oil, until golden brown on both sides. Add vodka and set aflame. Sauté onions until wilted and add to frogs' legs. Add white wine, beef gravy, cream and ketchup. Simmer together until sauce is slightly thickened. Add mixed seasonings (lemon rind, crushed garlic, leek seasoning, thyme and rosemary), totalling about a tablespoon all together; add a few drops Tabasco and Worcestershire sauce and chopped parsley. Simmer all ingredients together for just one minute. Serve with rice.

FROGS LEGS "GISELLE"

Fleur de Lys
San Francisco, California

Use legs from small frogs, if possible from Texas or southern states. 10 to 12 pairs of legs to each serving.

6 dozen frogs legs	¼ cup parsley, finely chopped
4 ounces butter	
Salt	Juice of 3 lemons
Ground black pepper	1½ lemons, quartered
¼ cup fresh fennel, finely chopped	Parsley, for garnish

Clean frogs' legs and soak in cold water for several hours. Dry well. Season with salt and pepper. Sauté in frying pan in very hot butter. Cook approximately 10 minutes, turning once, until golden brown. Arrange the frogs' legs on platter; keep hot. To the frying pan drippings add chopped parsley and fennel, and lemon juice. Cook two minutes at high heat and pour over the legs. Serve right away, garnished with parsley and quartered lemons.

COQUILLE DE HOMARD À LA SAINT CAST

La Bourgogne
San Francisco, California

4 pounds lobsters
1 quart court bouillon
½ pound mushrooms
2 tablespoons butter

3 egg yolks
Salt, pepper to taste
½ cup Madeira wine

(Court bouillon is fish stock well flavored with vegetables, herbs and 1 pint white wine.)

Boil whole lobsters in court bouillon 25 minutes. When lobsters are cool enough to handle, lift from liquid and remove flesh from shells. Slice tails and claws, pound remainder of lobster to a paste and strain.

Sauté mushrooms in butter until tender, blend with egg yolks and add to the puree of lobster. Salt and pepper to taste. Moisten to a paste form with court bouillon and Madeira.

Fill scallop shells with a layer of lobster paste, then a layer of the lobster slices arranged evenly, then top with another layer of the lobster paste. Glaze under broiler and serve hot.

BROILED LIVE LOBSTER

Johnson's Hummocks Restaurant
Providence, Rhode Island

For Each Individual Serving

Live 1¼ to 1½-pound
    lobster
1 cup bread crumbs
½ teaspoon onion, grated
1 tablespoon lemon juice

¼ teaspoon salt
4 tablespoons butter,
    melted
2 tablespoons butter
¼ lemon

Live lobster should be a mottled bluish-green color and should be active in the movement of its tail and claws. Select a live lobster, 1¼ to 1½ pounds for each serving. Kill lobster by placing it on its back and inserting a sharp knife where tail and body come together. Make deep incision through chest to its mouth then split lengthwise to the end of the tail. Spread open and remove stomach near mouth of lobster and intestinal vein running the length of the body. Crack the claws with knife but do not crush. Spread lobster as flat as possible.

Make stuffing by combining bread crumbs, grated onion, lemon juice, salt and melted butter, lightly but thoroughly. Stuff into chest cavity of lobster. Place lobster in wire rack or on baking sheet; if using sheet, put small weight at extreme end of tail to keep the lobster flat. Cook in 375° to 400° oven for approximately 15 minutes or until tail meat can be easily separated from its shell. Remove and serve with melted butter and lemon quarters.

BROILED LIVE LOBSTER, TRINKAUS

Trinkaus Manor
Oriskany, New York

6 live 2-pound lobsters	¾ cup heavy cream
3 cups cracker crumbs	1 cup dry sherry
1½ cups Alaska King	Paprika
crab, chopped	⅜ pound butter
¾ pound butter, melted	

Split open lobsters with a sharp knife through the middle, removing veins and stomach and tomalley. Place in dish. Mix cracker crumbs, crab, melted butter, cream and sherry with the tomalley. Stuff lobsters and sprinkle paprika over top. Put two tablespoons butter over each lobster and bake in very hot oven, 425°, for 20 minutes.

BAKED MAINE LOBSTER LUCULUS

Essex House
New York City

3 Maine lobsters, 3 pounds
each, cooked in Court
Bouillon
1½ tablespoons shallots,
chopped
6 ounces butter
1½ cups white wine
1½ cups fish veloute

Salt and pepper
¾ cup thick tomato sauce
3 ounces Brandy
3 tablespoons Hollandaise
sauce
6 large mushroom caps,
sliced thick

Cook the lobsters in court bouillon. (The court bouillon
is made with 2 carrots, sliced, 2 onions, sliced thin, parsley,
1 sprig thyme, 2 bay leaves, salt and pepper, boiled in 1½
to 2 quarts water). Let lobsters cool off in their own cooking juice.

Simmer chopped shallots in 1 tablespoon butter for about
10 minutes. Add white wine and reduce almost completely.
Add fish veloute and tomato sauce. Sauté mushrooms in
butter. Cut the lobster in two lengthwise; remove the flesh
carefully and crack the claws. Remove the meat. Slice tails
(about ¼ inch thick); warm all the meat in 5 ounces butter
and flame it with brandy. Add Hollandaise to the resulting
sauce and taste for correct seasoning. Put part of the sauce
on the bottom of lobster shell, arrange carefully lobster
slices and mushrooms in the shell. Pour the rest of the sauce
over and glaze under broiler. Serve very hot.

BAKED LOBSTER WITH CLAM DRESSING

*Boone's Restaurant
Portland, Maine*

6 small live lobsters
1½ pints clams with juice
6 scant cups cracker
  crumbs
Salt and pepper to taste
1½ teaspoons dry mustard
1½ teaspoons poultry
  seasoning

2 large eggs
Lobster livers (tomalley)
1½ cups cream or undiluted
  evaporated milk
3 ounces sherry
½ pound butter

Boil live lobsters. Beginning at the mouth make a deep incision and with sharp cut draw knife quickly through body and entire length of tail. Remove stomach, intestinal vein and liver. Save livers for dressing. Put clams through meat grinder, saving juice. Mix together cracker crumbs, salt, pepper, mustard, poultry seasoning. Add eggs, lobster livers, cream, sherry and clams. Mix well. Add clam liquor. Mixture should be quite moist. Cover lobsters with clam dressing and dot with 6 tablespoons butter. Place in 400° oven and bake until shells are pink. Place under broiler until stuffing is brown. Serve with drawn butter.

Drawn Butter

⅓ cup butter
3 tablespoons flour
½ teaspoon salt
⅛ teaspoon black pepper

1½ cups hot water or
  fish stock
1 teaspoon lemon juice

Melt half the butter, add flour, salt and pepper, stirring continuously until smooth. Add water or stock, stirring continually and boil for 5 minutes. Add lemon juice and remaining butter.

BAKED STUFFED LOBSTER IN CASSEROLE

Yankee Pedlar Inn
Holyoke, Massachusetts

1½ pounds fresh lobster
  meat
6 tablespoons Parmesan
  cheese, grated

⅜ pound melted butter
2 cups fresh bread crumbs
Paprika

Place lobster meat in casserole. Sprinkle the grated cheese over the lobster meat. Place bread crumbs evenly over all. Spoon melted butter over the bread crumbs. Dust with paprika, and bake in 350° oven for 15 minutes.

BAKED STUFFED LOBSTER IN CASSEROLE

Asticon Inn
Northeast Harbor, Maine

1 pound fresh lobster meat
6 ounces tomalley (liver)
2 cups fresh bread crumbs
2 teaspoons chives,
  chopped

4 tablespoons lemon juice
Salt, pepper
Melted butter
Dry sherry

Make dressing of the bread crumbs, tomalley, chives, lemon juice, salt, pepper and enough melted butter to make a "moist" filling. Mix well. Place 2½ ounces lobster meat in each casserole. Fill casserole with dressing, press down gently. Sprinkle tops with a very dry sherry and a little more melted butter. Bake 10 minutes in a hot, hot oven, 500°.

MAINE LOBSTER BISQUE

Old Mill Inn
Bernardsville, New Jersey

1 pound lobster meat,
   diced
6 tablespoons butter or
   margarine
¼ cup flour

1½ quarts milk
Salt, pepper, M.S.G.,
   to taste
Sherry to taste

Sauté lobster and tomalley in 2 tablespoons butter. Set aside. Melt ¼ cup butter, stir in ¼ cup flour and blend well over medium heat. Add hot milk gradually, stirring continuously until sauce thickens slightly. Season to taste. Add diced lobster meat and sherry to taste.

LOBSTER THERMIDOR

Flamingo Hotel
Las Vegas, Nevada

3 Maine lobsters or
   crawfish
¾ cup mushrooms, diced
3 shallots, or large onions,
   chopped fine
2 tablespoons butter

Salt and white pepper
   to taste
1½ teaspoon dry mustard
½ teaspoon dry tarragon
   leaves, crushed
¾ cup Sherry wine

Boil the lobsters or crawfish for 15 minutes. Remove the meat from the shell, cut lengthwise and crosswise to dice meat. Save the shells and wash them; use as baking dishes for the thermidor. Sauté shallots and mushrooms in butter. Add lobster meat and brown lightly. Season the mixture with salt and pepper, dry mustard and tarragon leaves. Add wine and simmer slowly. Fill lobster shells with mixture and bake in hot oven, 375° to 400° till bubbly, about 8 or 10 minutes.

LOBSTER THERMIDOR

Comet Restaurant
Grand Rapids, Michigan

3 lobsters, about
   1½ pounds each
3 shallots, chopped
4 ounces butter
½ cup Sauterne
⅜ cup heavy cream
¾ cup Bechamel sauce

Salt, pepper to taste
¾ teaspoon chervil,
   chopped
3 ounces cheese, grated
3 ounces bread crumbs
1½ teaspoons powdered
   mustard

Boil lobsters for 20 minutes in salt water. Remove, cut them in half, and break off claws. Remove all meat from claws and bodies without spoiling shells. Reserve shells. Dice lobster meat.

Brown shallots lightly in butter. Add Sauterne, reduce liquid, add cream and Bechamel sauce, season with salt and pepper. Add chervil, and cook to reduce well until sauce coats the spoon. Add lobster meat to sauce, and cook slowly for about 2 minutes. Remove from fire, and fill lobster shells with mixture.

Mix grated cheese and bread crumbs with mustard, sprinkle over lobster and glaze in very hot oven, 450°.

LOBSTER À LA DANNY

Danny's Hide-a-Way
New York City

6 1-pound boiled Maine
   lobsters
1 pound fresh crabmeat
1 cup additional lobster
   meat

1½ cups Mornay sauce
   (see recipe under sauces)
Brandy, to taste
Bread crumbs

Split lobster. Put crabmeat, additional lobster meat, Mornay sauce and a dash of brandy in a bowl and mix well.

Spread these ingredients on top of the split lobster. Sprinkle with bread crumbs and bake in moderate oven, 350°, for 20 minutes.

LOBSTER VITRE—FIVE CHATEAUX

Charter House Hotel
Cambridge, Massachusetts

6 1½-pound lobsters, boiled
¼ pound butter
¾ cup sherry
Parmesan cheese, grated

Vitre stuffing (see recipe below)
Fish sauce (see recipe below)

Remove the claws and slice the back of boiled lobsters. Take all the meat out and reserve the shells. Cut lobster meat into 1-inch pieces and sauté in 5 tablespoons butter. Add sherry; add ⅓ of the Vitre stuffing. Stir until all the juices have been absorbed.

Sauté the remaining ⅔ Vitre stuffing in 3 tablespoons butter and stir until the scallops are cooked.

Line the bottom of the lobster shells with the stuffing and add the lobster. Cover with fish sauce, sprinkle top with grated Parmesan cheese and place in hot oven, 400°, until the sauce becomes golden brown.

Vitre Stuffing

3 cups white bread crumbs
3 cups boiling milk
1 tablespoon salt
¾ pound fresh sea scallops, finely sliced or chopped
6 ounces mushrooms, sliced and cooked
2 tablespoons chives, chopped
2 tablespoons shallots, chopped and cooked
1½ teaspoons garlic, chopped
1½ teaspoon salt
Pinch pepper
¾ cup white wine

Make a bread panada (a binder) by adding bread crumbs and salt to boiling milk and beating briskly over fire until mixture does not cling to the spoon. Let this cool. When cool add the remaining ingredients, mix together very well; let stand for four hours. This completes the stuffing.

Fish Sauce

6 tablespoons butter	½ cup white wine
¾ cup flour	Pinch nutmeg
3 cups fish stock	Salt and pepper to taste
¾ cup cream	

Melt butter; add flour and stir until the flour does not stick to the spoon. Add boiling fish stock and let cool for 10 minutes. Add cream, white wine and nutmeg. Season to taste. Strain.

LOBSTER, ARCHIDUC

*The Open Range
Jackson, Wyoming*

4 boiled lobsters, 1½ pounds each	Salt, white pepper to taste
1 large onion, thinly sliced	6 egg yolks, well beaten
6 ounces canned mushrooms	Bread crumbs, for topping
3 ounces brandy	Parmesan cheese, grated
3 tomatoes, diced	Dash paprika
1½ cups heavy cream	6 thin slices butter
	Lemon wedges
	Parsley sprigs

Dice meat of cooked lobsters into one-inch cubes. Sauté with onions and mushrooms, well drained. Add brandy and fresh tomatoes. Add cream and cook for 5 minutes. Season to taste with salt and white pepper. Bind with the egg yolks.

Stuff lobster shells and top with bread crumbs, Parmesan cheese and paprika. Place butter slices on lobsters and bake in hot oven, 375°, for 10 to 15 minutes or until golden brown. Garnish with lemon wedges and parsley sprigs.

LOBSTER OREGANATO

Camillo Restaurant
New York City

For each individual serving

Split one 2-pound lobster in half. Broil 15 minutes, then cover with the Oreganato (see recipe below) and broil 5 minutes longer.

Oreganato (for each serving)

1 cup bread crumbs	Pinch Ac'cent
Olive oil	1 bay leaf
Pinch oregano	Salt and pepper to taste
Pinch thyme	

Sprinkle bread crumbs with olive oil and add remaining ingredients. Toss lightly.

LOBSTER À LA ABSINTHE

Club Domino
San Francisco, California

⅜ pound butter	½ cup Pernod or Absinthe
8 small shallots, chopped very fine	6 tablespoons Hollandaise sauce
1½ pounds lobster meat	6 tablespoons whipped cream
Salt and pepper to taste	
3 cups half and half (or light cream)	6 tablespoons Parmesan cheese, grated
4 egg yolks, lightly beaten	

In saucepan, heat butter and shallots and cook. When shallots start to turn transparent, add lobster meat. Cook for about 3 minutes. Add salt and pepper, and half and half. Let simmer a while in order to reduce; add egg yolks and Pernod. Take lobster meat from pan and place in lobster shell. Add Hollandaise sauce and whipped cream to the mixture in the saucepan. Blend well. Pour entire mixture over lobster meat; see that it is well covered in the lobster shell. Glaze under flame for about 7 minutes or until brown. Top with Parmesan cheese.

CAPON AND LOBSTER MADEIRA

The Lord Simcoe Hotel
Toronto, Ontario

¼ pound butter
 1½ pounds cooked capon, diced
1½ pounds lobster pieces
⅜ cup Madeira wine
 2 cups heavy cream
 6 ounces cold fresh butter, mixed with enough flour to make a fairly stiff paste

Salt, to taste
 4 egg yolks
 3 cups cooked rice
 ½ cup almonds, blanched and chopped
 1 teaspoon butter

Melt butter. Sauté together in hot pan capon and lobster pieces. Pour in Madeira wine; add cream and bring to a boil. Thicken with the butter and flour paste, but do not let it become too thick. Season with salt to taste. Bring to boil. At the last, just before serving, add egg yolks, stirring in quickly so that they mix in smoothly. Serve with rice topped with almonds which have been sautéed in butter.

LOBSTER IN WHISKEY

Fleur de Lys
San Francisco, California

 6 live lobsters, 1½ pounds each
Salt
Pepper
Dash cayenne, thyme, laurel to taste
 1 cup oil for frying

¾ pound butter
10 shallots, chopped
 3 cloves garlic, crushed
 2 cups whiskey
 1 tablespoon paprika
1½ pints heavy cream

Cut live lobsters in pieces. Season. Sauté rapidly in frying oil until red. Take off the fire, drain oil. Add butter, shallots, garlic and 1 cup whiskey. Cook 20 minutes. Keep lobster pieces warm separately. Strain cooking sauce. Heat strained sauce, add 1 cup whiskey, paprika and cream. Stir, do not boil. Place lobster pieces in a hot casserole and cover with cream sauce. Garnish preferably with Indian rice.

CANTONESE STYLE LOBSTER

Jimmy Wu's New China Inn
Baltimore, Maryland

4 live chicken lobsters, 1 pound size	4 cups chicken broth
4 tablespoons oil or shortening	4 eggs
1 teaspoon salt	4 tablespoons corn starch (dissolved in water)
Dash pepper	2 tablespoons soy sauce
1 pound lean pork, coarsely ground or chopped	½ teaspoon Chinese seasoning powder M.S.G. (Ac'cent)
4 cloves garlic, crushed	1 onion, chopped fine
	3 cups boiled rice

Clean and cut lobsters into big pieces by first removing the head, shell and legs. Use a heavy cleaver or heavy knife and split lobster into halves and cut each half into 3 or 4 sections with the shell attached; split claws lengthwise.

Put oil or shortening into pre-heated frying pan over a moderate flame. Add salt, coarsely ground pork and garlic. Sauté for 2 minutes. Add lobster and chicken broth. Cover pan tightly and cook for 5 minutes. Crack eggs and put in center of frying pan. Cook for a minute or two without cover. Add cornstarch together with soy sauce, Chinese seasoning powder and chopped onion. Stir constantly until juice thickens.

Serve hot with boiled rice.

FISHERMAN STYLE LOBSTER

Great House Restaurant
Warwick, Rhode Island

6 live lobsters
4 cups bread crumbs
  with melted butter
Pinch thyme

Freshly ground pepper
  to taste
Water
Garnish of lettuce, parsley
  sprigs, lemon wedges

Use live lobsters. Lay them on their back in pan and insert sharp knife from mouth to end of tail. Remove vein and stomach. Remove liver and coral and save for stuffing. Break off claws and boil for 10 minutes. Remove meat from claws and use in stuffing. Spread lobsters as flat as possible. Spread upper body with crumbs, thyme, pepper, liver and coral, and meat of claws. Add water to cover bottom of pan. Cover pan and bake in very hot oven, 550°, for 15 to 20 minutes. Serve on platter garnished with lettuce, parsley and lemon wedges.

GALA WITH THE CARDINAL OF THE SEA

Le Provençal Restaurant
Toronto, Ontario

6 1½-pound live lobsters
Court bouillon
24 medium mushrooms,
  cut up
3 tablespoons butter
3 ounces truffles, peeled

1½ ounces brandy
2 cups heavy cream
Salt, pepper to taste
Hollandaise sauce
Marinade—see recipe below

Poach lobsters in court bouillon for 20 minutes. With scissors cut the top part of the shell in a 2-inch rectangle from tail to the middle of the head. Marinate lobster tails and heads in the mixture given below. Use half of tail meat to slice 24 medaillons. Dice the rest of meat, including claws. Reserve shells.

Sauté mushrooms in butter. Add lobster meat and truffles.

Flame with brandy. Add heavy cream and stir until thick. Season with salt and pepper. Fill the marinated shells with this preparation, setting the medaillons on top. Spread with Hollandaise sauce and glaze.

Marinade

¼ cup lemon juice
¼ cup salad oil
 1 teaspoon salt and
   paprika

¼ teaspoon shallots,
   minced

Mix all ingredients together.

LOBSTER À LA NEWBURG

*Testa's Restaurant
Bar Harbor, Maine*

6 Maine lobsters (boiled)
  1¼ pounds each
½ pound butter
2 cups heavy cream
6 egg yolks, slightly beaten

1 cup sherry wine
Salt, pepper to taste
3 slices white bread,
  toasted and cut into
  wedges

Remove cooked meat from lobster. Cut meat in good sized pieces. Melt butter in heavy skillet. Add lobster meat and cook until the lobster turns the butter bright red. Combine cream and egg yolks. Cook until thickened, add lobster meat, sherry and seasoning. Allow to stand over very low heat 5 minutes for lobster flavor to penetrate the sauce. Serve with toast wedges.

LOBSTER À LA NEWBURG

Cape Cod Room
The Drake Hotel
Chicago, Illinois

1½ pounds Maine lobster
  meat, cooked, diced
⅜ pound butter
2 tablespoons sherry wine
1½ teaspoons flour

2 tablespoons paprika
2 cups cream
6 egg yolks, beaten lightly
Salt and pepper to taste

In skillet, melt butter over low flame. Add lobster meat and sauté lightly. Add paprika and flour; stir until smooth and well mixed. Add sherry and cream; let mixture come to a boil. Add egg yolks slowly, stir until well mixed and to desired thickness. The egg yolks should be added just before serving. Do *not* cook. This is to prevent egg from becoming scrambled.

LOBSTER TAILS THERMIDOR

Seafare Restaurant
Nags Head, North Carolina

6 large frozen lobster tails
4 tablespoons butter
1 cup mushrooms, sliced
4 tablespoons flour
1 teaspoon dry mustard
1 teaspoon salt
Dash cayenne
2 cups milk
2 egg yolks, slightly
  beaten

1 tablespoon lemon juice
2 tablespoons sherry
¼ cup fine bread crumbs
2 tablespoons Parmesan
  cheese, grated
2 tablespoons melted
  butter

Boil lobster tails; remove meat and dice; save shells. Melt 4 tablespoons butter in saucepan; add mushrooms and sauté until lightly browned. Blend in flour, mustard, salt, cayenne. Gradually add milk. Cook over medium heat, stirring constantly until mixture thickens and comes to boil. Stir small amount of hot mixture into egg yolks; add to sauce. Remove from heat; stir in lemon juice, sherry and lobster meat. Spoon into shells. Combine bread crumbs, cheese, melted butter, sprinkle over lobster. Bake in hot oven, 400°, for 15 minutes.

SCHULER'S IMPERIAL BROILED LOBSTER TAILS

Win Schuler's
Marshall, Michigan

6 8-9 ounce African
　　lobster tails
⅜ pound butter, melted
2 tablespoons lemon juice
6 tablespoons crushed
　　garlic croutons:
　　　2 slices white bread,
　　　cubed

1 tablespoon butter
½ clove garlic, sliced
Paprika, to taste
3 tablespoons butter
Lemon juice
Garnish of parsley sprigs,
　　melted butter, 6 lemon
　　wedges

Split African lobster tails down the back. Lift the meat out of the shells and turn it over. Place meat back into shells. This will result in a beautiful raised appearance when the tails are served.

Broil 20 to 25 minutes, brushing generously with a butter-lemon juice combination throughout the cooking time.

Toast slices of day-old bread in garlic butter. Crush the resulting croutons and sprinkle 1 tablespoon on each tail about 5 minutes before lobsters are done. Sprinkle tails liberally with paprika; dot or brush with butter. A dash of lemon juice is the crowning touch.

Serve garnished with parsley sprigs, an ample supply of melted butter and lemon wedges.

LOBSTER MENZIES

Host International Restaurant
Honolulu, Hawaii

6 12-ounce Rock lobster
  tails
¾ cup butter
3 quarts court bouillon
1½ cups white wine
¼ pound butter
¾ cup onions, minced
1 clove garlic
1 cup flour
1½ tablespoons dry
  mustard
3 tablespoons honey
5 tablespoons tarragon
  vinegar
3 tablespoons English
  fish sauce

1⅓ tablespoons
  Worcestershire sauce
1½ tablespoons Maggi
  sauce
1½ tablespoons lemon
  juice
Salt, white pepper,
  to taste
¾ cup dark rum
1½ cups heavy cream
1½ cups bananas, diced
1½ cups pineapple cubes
Hollandaise sauce,
  to cover
3 limes, cut in half
Sprigs watercress

Cut lobster tail from back. Boil in court bouillon for 12 minutes. Put lobster in cold water and cool. Remove lobster meat from shell and cut into cubes. Reserve shells. Sauté lobster cubes in ¾ cup butter. Set aside. To 3 quarts court bouillon, add 1½ cups white wine and reduce to half.

Melt ¼ pound butter and sauté onions and garlic. Add flour and simmer for 5 minutes at reduced heat to make roux (do not brown roux). Add stock and mustard, honey, vinegar, sauces, lemon juice, salt and pepper. Simmer all ingredients for ½ hour under slow fire. Adjust seasoning of salt and pepper to taste. Add dark rum and simmer for 5 minutes.

Blend in heavy cream, stirring continuously. When well blended, add lobster cubes, diced bananas and pineapple cubes. Fill each lobster shell with mixture and place on hot plate. Cover with Hollandaise sauce and place under broiler for a rich glaze. Garnish each with ½ lime and sprig of watercress.

LOBSTER CREOLE IN CASSEROLE

The Sea Shell
Halifax, Nova Scotia

1 pound cooked lobster
  meat (fresh or canned)
2 tablespoons butter
1 large onion, diced
1 green pepper, diced
4 cups tomatoes, fresh
  or canned
¼ teaspoon salt

1 teaspoon sugar
2 bay leaves
1 cup mushrooms,
  sautéed
Dash Tabasco
Dash Worcestershire
  sauce

Cut lobster meat into large pieces. Melt butter in sauce-pan, add onion, green pepper, tomatoes, salt, sugar and bay leaves, and simmer for 10 minutes. Remove bay leaves, add mushrooms, Tabasco, Worcestershire sauce and lobster meat, simmer until lobster is heated and serve at once with steamed rice.

LOBSTER OR CRABMEAT CASSEROLE

Meyer's
Greensboro, South Carolina

1 pound lobster or
  crabmeat, cooked and
  drained
1 cup water or milk
2 cans concentrated
  cream of mushroom
  soup

¼ cup celery, finely
  chopped
1 bay leaf
Salt and pepper
2 cups cooked rice
Hard-cooked egg yolks,
  crumbled
Paprika

Dice the lobster or crabmeat. Blend water or milk and mushroom soup until smooth. Add celery, bay leaf, salt and pepper. Add shellfish meat and rice and mix thoroughly. Turn into individual casseroles and sprinkle with egg yolks and paprika. Bake in 350° oven for 20 minutes.

CREAMED LOBSTER AND MUSHROOMS
WITH NOODLES IN CASSEROLE

The Williams Inn
Williamstown, Massachusetts

½ pound mushrooms
¼ pound butter,
approximately
3 quarts water
½ pound medium noodles
1 pound lobster meat
¼ cup sweet sherry

1 scant teaspoon lemon
juice
½ scant cup flour
¼ teaspoon paprika
1½ cups light cream
½ cup heavy cream
Salt, white pepper
6 to 8 Ritz crackers

Slice mushrooms and sauté in 4 tablespoons butter over a gentle fire until very lightly browned. Meanwhile, boil 3 quarts of water, add salt and cook the noodles for 10 minutes, stirring them occasionally with a long fork to keep them from sticking to the bottom of the pan. When done, rinse with warm water and drain thoroughly in a colander. Cut lobster meat into large dice. Put lobster meat into a double boiler with 1 tablespoon butter, sherry and lemon juice to get thoroughly heated.

Make a sauce by draining butter from mushrooms and adding enough additional butter to make ½ cup. Blend in flour and paprika. Pour on light cream, season with salt and white pepper, and stir until the sauce comes to a boil. Add heavy cream and bring to a boil again. Simmer for about 5 minutes. Add mushrooms and the lobster with all the juices. Stir only until blended, as too much stirring can toughen the lobster. Taste for seasoning.

Make 3 alternate layers of the noodles and lobster mixture in a buttered 2-quart casserole. Coarsely crush Ritz crackers, mix with melted butter, and sprinkle over the top. Bake uncovered in a moderate oven, at 350°, for 20 to 30 minutes, until thoroughly heated and the top is lightly browned. Longer baking doesn't matter; just cover casserole so that the top won't get too brown.

LOBSTER IN PUFFED PASTE

Kahala Hilton
Honolulu, Hawaii

1 pound lobster meat, diced ½" x ½"
1 tablespoon butter
1 shallot, finely chopped
Pinch paprika
2 ounces sherry
½ cup heavy cream

1 teaspoon tarragon, chopped (use fresh or preserved)
Lemon juice to taste
Pinch salt—use very little
½ ounce Pernod
6 baked patty shells

Melt butter in saucepan, add shallot. Add lobster meat. Sprinkle with pinch of paprika and sauté for about 2 minutes. Pour sherry over mixture and set aflame. When spirit has burned out, add cream and tarragon. Bring to a boil and simmer for another 5 minutes. Add lemon juice, salt, and Pernod. By then, the cream should be reduced to a smooth sauce.

This sauce is sufficient for 6 appetizer portions, to be filled in freshly baked patty shells.

TREADWAY INN LOBSTER PIE

The Williams Inn
Williamstown, Massachusetts

Filling: Lobster Newburg

6 tablespoons butter
¾ cup sherry
1½ pounds lobster meat, coarsely chopped

3 tablespoons flour
2¼ cups light cream
Salt, white pepper
3 egg yolks, beaten

A true Newburg is thickened only with egg yolks, but it is a tricky sauce to make and to keep from curdling, so a little flour is added in this recipe to stabilize the sauce.

Melt 3 tablespoons butter in the top of a double boiler. Add sherry and lobster meat. Let stand over simmering water while you make the sauce. Melt 3 tablespoons butter.

Blend in flour, pour on 1 cup cream, and stir until the mixture comes to a boil. Season with salt and white pepper and simmer for 5 minutes to cook the flour, stirring continuously. To beaten egg yolks add 1¼ cups cream. Pour a little of the hot sauce over the yolks, stir, and blend the egg-cream mixture into the sauce. Stir until the sauce thickens, but do not let it boil.

Add to lobster, stir lightly (stir lobster meat as little as possible to keep it from getting tough) and let stand over simmering water at least 10 minutes to blend the flavors. Remove from the fire. Put into 6 small deep individual casseroles or 1 large one. Sprinkle with lobster pie topping (see recipe below). Bake for 15 to 20 minutes in a moderate oven, 350°, or brown immediately under the broiler.

Lobster Pie Topping

6 tablespoons butter	3 tablespoons crushed potato chips
¾ teaspoon paprika	1½ tablespoons Parmesan cheese, grated
¾ cup cracker meal or finely crumbled stale bread crumbs	⅜ cup sherry

Melt butter with paprika and let stand over a very low fire for about 5 minutes to cook the paprika a little. Blend with cracker meal or finely crumbled crumbs, potato chips, Parmesan cheese and sherry. It will not need any salt; the potato chips supply this.

BAKED LOBSTER PIE

*Colonial Inn
Concord, Massachusetts*

1½ pounds lobster meat	2 ounces sherry
6 tablespoons butter	3 cups hot milk
1 tablespoon paprika	Salt and pepper
1½ heaping tablespoons flour	1 large pinch Ac'cent

Sauté lobster meat in butter, with paprika, until it crackles. Add flour and cook about 1 minute. Add sherry and milk, bring to a boil and simmer for a few minutes. Season with salt and pepper and Ac'cent.

Put in casserole and top with fresh bread crumbs and melted butter (see recipe below). Put in 400° oven until crumbs brown.

Topping

1 cup bread crumbs	Sherry to taste
Salt, pepper, Ac'cent to taste	Juice of ½ lemon
1 teaspoon paprika	Dash Worcestershire sauce

Mix fresh bread crumbs with remaining ingredients.

LOBSTERS, SCALLOPS AND MUSHROOMS AU GRATIN

Viking Hotel
Newport, Rhode Island

6 tablespoons butter	1½ cups scallops
½ pound mushrooms, sliced	3 cups medium white sauce
1½ cups lobster meat	American cheese, grated

Melt butter; sauté mushrooms until nearly done. Add lobster and scallops and stir lightly to cook slightly. Scallops need very little cooking. Blend with white sauce and season well. Fill 6 large scallop shells and make a border with Duchess potato (about 2 cups) around edge of shells. Sprinkle with grated cheese. Place in 450° oven to heat through and brown.

CAPON AND LOBSTER CURRY WITH RICE PILAFF

Imperial House
Chicago, Illinois

¼ pound butter
1 apple, cored, peeled and sliced
1 large onion, sliced
1 stalk celery, cut up
2 bay leaves
3 ounces flour
2 ounces curry powder
1 quart chicken broth
1 cup cream
1 fresh coconut—milk and meat

1 pound cooked lobster meat
1½ pounds white meat of chicken or capon, cooked
Salt and pepper to taste
Rice pilaff (see recipe below)
6 heaping tablespoons chutney

Melt butter in a very large skillet. Add apple, onion, celery, and bay leaves and smother mixture for 15 minutes. Then sprinkle flour and curry powder in the mixture; stir well and cook slowly for another 15 minutes. Add chicken broth, cream and the milk and shredded meat from a fresh coconut and again cook slowly for 15 minutes.

Remove from the fire and strain the sauce through a coarse piece of cheesecloth or a fine sieve into a large saucepan; add cooked lobster and chicken or capon meat. The pieces of both lobster and chicken should be cut 1 inch square. Season to taste with salt and pepper and heat thoroughly over a very low flame. Serve over rice pilaff and put a generous tablespoon chutney over each serving.

Rice Pilaff

3 tablespoons olive oil or fat
2 tablespoons onion, chopped
1 cup raw rice

Salt and pepper to taste
Consommé to cover
Small amount cheese, grated

Put olive oil or other fat in a heavy pan and add chopped onion. Cook briskly for 1 minute, then add raw rice and salt and pepper to taste. Cook very slowly for 3 minutes, stirring all the time. Cover the rice with enough consommé to reach ½ inch above the rice, cover the pan with wax paper, put on the lid, and cook in a 375° oven for 20 to 25 minutes. Remove the lid, stir in a very little grated cheese.

PAELLA "VALENCIANA"

Columbia Restaurant
Tampa, Florida

("Valenciana"—a dish made in large quantities)

1 scant cup olive oil
1 onion, peeled and chopped
2 cloves garlic, peeled and minced
¼ pound pork, cubed
1 pound chicken, cut into medium-sized pieces
1 green pepper, seeded and chopped
½ pound crawfish
½ pound shrimp, shelled and deveined
¼ pound oysters
¼ pound scallops
6 cups seafood stock
2½ cups rice, washed and drained
2 bay leaves
Pinch saffron
Pinch yellow coloring
Salt, pepper to taste
1 cup petit pois
1 cup pimientos
White wine

Pour olive oil in casserole; when hot add minced garlic and sauté for 15 minutes. Braise the pork and chicken with the garlic until brown and tender. Add onions and green peppers and the seafood.

When seafood is almost done add seafood stock and rice. Bring it to a boil, add bay leaf, saffron, coloring, and salt and pepper to taste. When rice begins to thicken, cover and bake for 15 minutes at 350°. Garnish with petit pois and pimientos, and sprinkle with white wine.

PAELLA À LA VALENCIANA

*Matador Restaurant
Los Angeles, California*

1 large white onion,
 chopped
1 green onion, peeled
 and chopped
1 shallot finely chopped
1 broiler chicken, cut up
6 ounces olive oil
2 rock lobster tails,
 cut up in thick slices
½ pound large shrimp
1 bay leaf
Salt, pepper to taste
2 cups long grain rice
1 can green peas
¼ pound string beans,
 cut

1 large Chorizo (Spanish
 sausage), sliced
1 thick slice ham,
 cut in squares
2 ripe tomatoes, peeled
 and sliced
1 pinch saffron
4 cups stock
1 seven-ounce can red
 pimientos
2 hard cooked eggs,
 sliced
Black and green olives
Canned clams

Sauté chicken in oil with onions and shallots in large paella pan (any large pan will do) and cook until golden. At the same time, in a smaller sauce pan, combine lobster, shrimp, bay leaf, salt and pepper, and sauté in olive oil for 20 minutes. Pour this seafood into the large pan, which contains the chicken, and add rice, peas, beans, Chorizo, ham and tomato. Add salt, pepper and saffron. Cover pan with stock and let cook over medium fire until rice is almost done, but still very moist. Decorate with pimientos, sliced hard cooked egg, black and green olives and clams. Place the paella for 4 minutes in a preheated 350° oven.

LOBSTER AND CHICKEN COSTA BRAVA
WITH THREE COLORED RICE

Casa de Piedra
Cuernavaca, Mexico

6 chicken breasts	¼ pound butter
Salt, pepper to taste	4 tablespoons flour
⅜ cup cooking oil	3 tablespoons concentrated
6 lobster tails	tomato paste
15 almonds, blanched	3 ounces brandy
2 cloves garlic	1½ ounces Pernod
¼ teaspoon saffron powder	Parsley chopped

Salt and pepper the chicken breasts. Sauté in oil no more than five minutes. Add lobster tails in their shells and sauté another five minutes. Pour off the oil, reserve and keep it warm.

Add water to cover the chicken breasts and lobster tails and boil 15 minutes on a low flame. Remove from flame. Strain the broth and keep it warm.

In a small saucepan, and in a small amount of oil, sauté almonds and garlic until golden. Remove from flame and add saffron (which must only be warm to give off its perfume).

Crush almonds and garlic in a mortar; wash off what adheres to the sides with some of the broth. Reserve.

Strain oil used to sauté the chicken breasts and lobster tails. (If there is not enough, add butter.) Add flour and cook over low flame for 10 minutes, stirring continuously. Add tomato concentrate and, little by little, broth from the chicken-and-lobster. Stir steadily to avoid lumps. This must turn out to be a light sauce. Add the crushed almonds, garlic and saffron.

In an earthenware or enamel casserole, arrange the chicken breasts and peeled lobster tails. Pour brandy and warmed Pernod over all and set aflame. When the flame has died down, pour sauce over all. Keep on a low flame until all is properly cooked. Check for salt and pepper. Just before serving, sprinkle with chopped parsley.

The best accompaniment to lobster and chicken Costa Brava as made at Casa de Piedra is colored rice (see recipe below).

Colored Rice

1½ cups rice
3 sweet red peppers

3 sweet green peppers

On an open flame, toast green and red peppers, turning them so they do not burn. Remove and fold into a warm cloth; while warm, peel off the thin outer skin, split and remove the seeds and inner ridges.

In the blender, mash up red peppers with 1 cup of water. Use this mash to cook your red rice. Use the same method for the green peppers and green rice. Cook white rice as usual. Three cooking pots are needed and the three rices must be cooked simultaneously.

Arrange the three rices on a platter to set off their colors, and serve.

COQUILLES SAINT-JACQUES CHAPON FIN

The Mohawk
Old Forge, New York

(Scallops in Wine Sauce with Tomatoes and Mushrooms)

1 cup clam juice, fish stock, or water
1 small bay leaf
2 sprigs parsley
3 tablespoons onion, chopped
1 cup dry white wine
1½ pounds scallops, rinsed
½ cup light cream
3 tablespoons butter

3 tablespoons flour
Salt to taste
1½ cups fresh mushrooms (whole if small, cut in pieces if large)
2 ripe tomatoes, peeled, seeded and cut into pieces
Buttered crumbs
Paprika
Fresh parsley, chopped

Combine clam juice, fish stock or water with bay leaf, parsley sprigs and onion, and cook until reduced by half. Strain and reserve the liquid.

Add white wine to reserved liquid, salt if needed, and heat. Add scallops and cook gently for a few minutes until scallops begin to turn white. Remove scallops from liquid, cut into quarters or halves, depending on size. Add cream to liquid and heat. In another pan, melt butter, add flour, blend slowly. Add cream and liquid mixture and cook over low heat, stirring constantly until sauce is smooth and thick. Sauté mushrooms in butter until no moisture remains. Add tomatoes and cook until tomatoes are soft. Mix sauce with scallops, tomatoes and mushrooms. Fill buttered scallop shells or individual casseroles with the mixture. Sprinkle with buttered crumbs and dust with paprika. Brown in hot oven or under broiler. Garnish with chopped parsley.

COQUILLES ST. JACQUES

Maison Gerard
Beverly Hills, California

1 pound washed scallops
½ pound fresh mushrooms, sliced
1 cup dry white wine
½ teaspoon salt
Pinch white pepper
½ bay leaf

2 tablespoons minced shallots
Sauce—see recipe below
6 tablespoons Swiss cheese, grated
3 tablespoons butter

Mix wine, salt, pepper, bay leaf, shallots in a saucepan and simmer for 5 minutes. Add scallops and mushrooms and pour in enough water barely to cover ingredients. Bring to simmer stage. Cover, and simmer slowly for 5 minutes. Remove scallops and mushrooms with a slotted spoon and set aside in a bowl. Reserve liquid.

Cut the scallops into crosswise pieces about ⅛ inch thick. Blend ⅔ of the sauce with the scallops and mushrooms. Butter 6 scallop shells. Spoon the scallops and mushrooms into them, and cover with rest of the sauce. Sprinkle with grated Swiss cheese and dot with 2 tablespoons butter. Arrange the shells on a broiling pan and broil in 400° oven until brown (about 8 minutes).

Sauce

3 tablespoons butter
4 tablespoons flour
¾ cup milk
2 egg yolks
½ cup heavy cream

Salt and white pepper
  to taste
Few drops of fresh
  lemon juice
Liquid in which scallops
  have cooked

Melt the butter and add the flour slowly; cook for 2 minutes. Remove from heat, blend in boiling cooking liquid and milk. Boil 1 minute. Blend the egg yolks and cream in a bowl, then beat the hot sauce into them very slowly. Return the sauce to the pan and boil, stirring for 1 minute. Thin out with cream if necessary. Season to taste with salt, pepper and lemon juice. Strain.

CHUPE DE MARISCOS
(Shellfish Stew)

The Restaurant Internacional
Hotel Carrera
Santiago de Chile

1 pound shrimp, peeled
  and cleaned
1 pound scallops, or clams,
  or lobster
1 cup water
1 onion, finely chopped
¼ pound butter
Dash paprika
1½ cups bread crumbs

1 cup milk
4 tablespoons soft cheese
1 tablespoon butter
2 egg yolks
Salt, pepper, cayenne
  to taste
2 hard-cooked eggs,
  quartered
Mashed potatoes

Boil the various shellfish in water for 30 minutes and reserve the water in which they were cooked. Fry onion in butter with a dash of paprika. Add soft bread crumbs, milk and a little of the broth. Simmer until it has the consistency of a sauce. Add soft cheese, butter, egg yolks, salt, pepper and cayenne. Lay the shellfish at the bottom of a clay dish, pour the sauce over, cover and bake in a moderate oven, 350°, for 40 minutes. Uncover and place under broiler for 10 minutes to brown. Serve with hardcooked eggs and mashed potatoes.

CIOPPINE À LA CATHERINE
(Italian Fish Stew)

Anthony's Fish Grotto
La Mesa, California

2 to 3 pounds scallops,
  icelandic lobster meat,
  King crablegs
4 tablespoons butter

Pepper and Ac'cent to taste
1 cup boiled rice
3 cups tomato sauce
  (see recipe below)

Sauté scallops, lobster meat and crablegs in butter seasoned with pepper and Ac'cent for about 5 minutes. Add boiled rice and tomato sauce. Simmer 5 minutes longer and serve immediately in individual heated casseroles. Any type seafood may be substituted.

Tomato Sauce

2½ tablespoons olive oil
  or vegetable oil
1 medium onion, minced
2 cloves garlic, minced
2 sprigs parsley, minced
2 ounces sherry
½ can tomato paste
  (about 3 tablespoons)

1 #2 can whole tomatoes,
  chopped
¼ teaspoon pepper
Salt to taste
Pinch thyme
1 cup water (for thicker
  sauce, use less water)

Heat oil in saucepan. Add onion, garlic, parsley and sauté until brown. Add sherry and cook a little longer. Add tomato paste and tomatoes. Cook about 15 minutes. Season to taste. Add water and cook 35 minutes longer. For a smoother sauce, strain before adding to seafood.

FRUIT DE MER AU WHISKEY

Grand Motor Hotel
Montreal, Quebec

½ cup scampi
½ cup lobster, cut into
  pieces
½ cup shrimp, cut into
  pieces
½ cup scallops
½ cup oysters
½ pound butter

2 tablespoons shallots,
  finely chopped
Whiskey for flaming
Fish veloute (see
  recipe below)
½ cup Hollandaise sauce
½ cup heavy cream,
  whipped

Heat butter in sauté pan and cook scampi, lobster, shrimp, scallops and oysters just enough to take color. Add chopped shallots and flame with whiskey. Add fish veloute to seafood mixture and finish with a touch of Hollandaise sauce and whipped cream. Brown under the broiler.

Fish Veloute

⅓ cup butter
⅓ cup flour

3 cups fish stock
Salt, pepper to taste

Melt butter, add flour and cook over low flame, stirring continuously. Add fish stock gradually, stirring continuously. Cook for 15 to 20 minutes; strain through a fine sieve.

TUNA FISH MOLD, KNUDSON HOUSE

*The Knudson House
Ephraim, Wisconsin*

1 package lemon gelatin
1 cup boiling water
1 cup cold water
Pimiento strips
Green pepper strips
Sliced stuffed olives
Sliced hard cooked eggs
Celery strips
1 package lime flavored
   gelatin
1 cup boiling water
½ cup cold water
1½ tablespoon vinegar

½ teaspoon salt
Dash pepper
1 cup shredded cabbage
1 cup shredded carrot
¼ cup finely diced
   cucumber or celery
¼ cup finely chopped
   green pepper
1 tablespoon minced
   onions
1 can (7 ounces) tuna
   fish, drained and flaked

Dissolve lemon gelatin in boiling water, add cold water and pour half in bottom of a 2-quart fish mold. Chill until slightly thickened. Arrange fish design in thickened gelatin, alternating pimiento strips and green pepper strips for the tail, sliced pimiento and stuffed olives for backbone, slices of hard cooked eggs for eyes, and celery strips or half egg slices for ribs. Carefully add the remaining gelatin to cover the design. Chill until almost firm.

Meanwhile, dissolve lime-flavored gelatin in 1 cup boiling water, add ½ cup cold water, vinegar, mayonnaise, salt and pepper and blend with rotary beater. Beat until fluffy. Fold in vegetables and tuna. Carefully pour mixture over the thickened lemon gelatin.

Chill until firm. Unmold on a bed of lettuce and garnish with Norwegian sardines.

Note: Shrimp or lobster may be substituted for tuna.

TUNA FISH AND EGG CASSEROLE

Purefoy Hotel
Talladega, Alabama

2 7-ounce cans (2 cups) tuna fish
2 tablespoons lemon juice
4 hard cooked eggs, sliced
1 cup cooked peas
4 tablespoons butter or margarine
4 tablespoons flour

2 cups milk
½ teaspoon salt
⅛ teaspoon pepper
1 cup American cheese, grated
1 teaspoon Worcestershire sauce
1 cup fresh bread crumbs

Drain the oil from the tuna fish and reserve. Flake the fish and add lemon juice. Arrange the fish, eggs, and peas in alternate layers in a greased 1½ quart casserole. Melt butter in a double boiler. Add flour, then blend. Add the milk, seasonings and cheese, and cook over boiling water, stirring constantly until thick. Pour over casserole mixture, and top with bread crumbs to which the tuna-fish oil has been added. Bake in a moderately hot oven, 375°, about 30 minutes or until the crumbs are a golden brown.

TUNA-OLIVE TOWERS

Colonial Room
Peabody Hotel
Memphis, Tennessee

1 7-ounce can tuna
2 hard-cooked eggs, chopped
1 cup stuffed green olives, chopped
½ cup cucumber, finely chopped
½ cup celery, finely chopped
¼ cup sweet pickle, finely chopped
¼ cup mayonnaise

1 tablespoon lemon juice (fresh)
¼ teaspoon Lowry's seasoned salt
12 slices white bread, trimmed
6 slices whole wheat bread, trimmed
6 stuffed olives
6 leaves lettuce
6 slices fresh tomato

Toss together flaked tuna, eggs, celery, cucumbers, sweet pickle and mayonnaise. Add lemon juice and salt. Spread slices of bread with butter (butter prevents sogginess). Spread with tuna mixture. Add whole wheat bread slices, buttered side up, spread with olives. Top with lettuce, then with remaining white bread.

Place slice of tomato in center of sandwich. Cut diagonally in half. Top with ½ stuffed olive on tomato slice using a colored cello frill pick. Garnish with potato chips and parsley.

OYSTERS À LA HARLEQUIN

The Caribbean Room
The Pontchartrain Hotel
New Orleans, Louisiana

3 dozen oysters	3 ounces butter
1½ cups water	1½ tablespoons flour
2 whole allspice	6 artichokes, cooked
1 bay leaf	Bread crumbs
3 shallots, chopped	

Place oysters in water. Add whole allspice and bay leaf. Bring to boil, let simmer and skim scum. Sauté shallots in butter until tender. Add flour, blend well, add oysters and oyster liquor; stir to a smooth sauce. Take outer leaves of artichoke, scrape and add to sauce. Place each artichoke heart in an individual casserole and put oysters around. Sprinkle with bread crumbs, brown under broiler flame and serve.

OYSTERS ROFFIGNAC

Brennan's
New Orleans, Louisiana

½ pound butter
Scant ½ cup cooked
 mushrooms, finely
 chopped
Scant ½ cup shallots,
 finely chopped
¾ cup onion, finely
 chopped
¾ cup boiled shrimp,
 finely chopped

3 tablespoons garlic,
 minced
3 tablespoons flour
¾ teaspoon salt
¼ teaspoon pepper
Dash cayenne
1½ cups oyster liquid
¾ cup red wine
3 dozen oysters

Fill 6 pie pans with rock salt and place in hot oven to preheat salt. While salt is warming, make sauce: In a 9-inch skillet melt butter and lightly sauté mushrooms, shallots, onion, shrimp, and garlic. When onion is golden brown, add flour, salt, pepper and cayenne. Brown well, about 7 to 10 minutes. Blend in the stock and wine and simmer over low heat for 15 to 20 minutes. Place 6 half shells on each pie pan and place an oyster in each. Put stuffing in pastry bag and cover each oyster. Bake in 400° oven for 10 to 12 minutes or until edges of oyster begin to curl.

OYSTERS ROCKEFELLER: ANTOINE'S

Antoine's
New Orleans, Louisiana

36 freshly opened oysters
 on the half shell
6 tablespoons butter
6 tablespoons finely
 minced raw spinach
3 tablespoons onion,
 minced
3 tablespoons parsley,
 minced

3 tablespoons celery,
 minced
5 tablespoons bread
 crumbs
Tabasco sauce
½ teaspoon Herbsaint
½ teaspoon salt

Melt butter in saucepan. Add all the rest of the ingredients except the oysters. Cook, stirring constantly, for 15 minutes or until soft. Press through sieve or food mill. Cool. Place rock salt in pie tins. Set oysters on half shell on top and put a spoonful of sauce on each oyster. Broil under medium heat until sauce begins to brown. Serve immediately in the pie tins.

The exact recipe of Antoine's oysters Rockefeller is a secret of the house. Owner Roy Alciatore gives this as a close facsimile.

OYSTER FRITTERS

The Pirate's House
Savannah, Georgia

2 eggs, beaten
1 cup milk
1 tablespoon melted
 butter
2 cups sifted flour

3 teaspoons baking
 powder
1½ teaspoons salt
1 pint oysters, drained
 and chopped
Fat for deep frying

Mix eggs, milk and butter. Sift dry ingredients and add to mixture. Stir until smooth. Add oysters and drop into deep fat, 350° to 360°. Cook until brown, about 5 minutes. Drain on absorbent paper.

ESCALLOPED OYSTERS

King's Arms Tavern
Williamsburg, Virginia

½ cup butter
¾ cup flour
3 teaspoons paprika
1 teaspoon salt
½ teaspoon black pepper
2 tablespoons cracker
 crumbs
4 tablespoons onion,
 chopped fine

4 tablespoons green
 pepper, chopped fine
½ teaspoon garlic, chopped
2 teaspoons lemon juice
1 tablespoon Worcestershire
 sauce
1 quart oysters
Cracker crumbs

Melt butter, add flour and cook for 5 minutes or until dark brown. Stir constantly. Add paprika, salt, black pepper. Cook for 3 minutes. Add onion and green pepper; add garlic. Cook slowly for 5 minutes. Take from fire and add lemon juice, Worcestershire sauce and oysters (which have been picked over and heated in own liquor). Pour into baking dish, sprinkle cracker crumbs over the top and bake in oven at 400° for 30 minutes.

MAYLIE'S OYSTERS ST. JACQUES

Maylie's Club Restaurant
New Orleans, Louisiana

3 dozen large oysters
3 tablespoons shallots, minced
2 tablespoons garlic, minced
¼ cup green peppers, finely chopped
2 tablespoons lard
Sprig parsley, minced
Sprig thyme, minced

Dash Tabasco
Salt and pepper to taste
3 thick slices stale French bread
2 eggs
Bread crumbs
2 tablespoons butter
Asparagus and drawn butter

Drain and wipe oysters and place in skillet, in their liquid, on slow fire until the edges begin to curl; keep liquid to soak bread. Chop oysters. Cook shallots, green peppers, garlic in lard until tender. Add chopped oysters, all other seasonings, and bread which has been soaked in oyster liquid and squeezed thoroughly. Simmer all until well blended. Remove from fire and stir well; then beat in eggs, one at a time. Stuff shells, sprinkle with bread crumbs and dot with butter. Bake 15 to 20 minutes in hot oven, 375°. Serve with drawn butter and asparagus.

OYSTERS DIABLO

The Pontchartrain Hotel
New Orleans, Louisiana

3 dozen oysters— reserve
   shells
3 shallots, finely chopped
1 tablespoon butter
2 tablespoons flour
⅛ teaspoon nutmeg
Few grains cayenne
½ teaspoon salt

½ teaspoon prepared
   mustard
1 tablespoon
   Worchestershire sauce
1 can small mushrooms,
   chopped
½ teaspoon chopped parsley
2 egg yolks
Buttered cracker cumbs

Wash and chop oysters. Cook shallots in butter, add flour and brown. Add the rest of the seasoning, oysters and mushrooms. Cook a few minutes. Remove from fire and add egg yolks. Put mixture in deep halves of oyster shells, cover with crumbs and bake 15 minutes, in 350° oven.

CURRIED PACIFIC OYSTERS

London Grill
Portland, Oregon

3 pints oysters
3 teaspoons butter
1 tablespoon onion,
   chopped
3 small garlic cloves,
   crushed
2 tablespoons
   Worchestershire sauce

3 tablespoons dry white
   wine
Freshly ground pepper
Dash Ac'cent
6 tablespoons sour cream
1 teaspoon curry powder
   (or more, to taste)
Few drops lemon juice

Melt butter to golden brown, add onions and garlic. Add oysters and let simmer for a minute or two. Then work in the remaining ingredients one by one, stirring constantly. Boil the mixture until oysters are cooked, then take the oysters out; place them in serving dish. Boil the sauce down to desired consistency. Pour sauce over the oysters and serve with pilaff rice.

BAKED OYSTERS BAROQUE

The Baroque Restaurant
New York City

4 ounces butter, softened
½ green pepper, chopped fine
2 pimentos (canned) chopped fine
1 clove garlic, minced
2 shallots, chopped fine

Juice of ½ lemon
1 teaspoon chives, chopped
1 cup white bread crumbs
Salt and pepper to taste
36 oysters
5 or 6 strips bacon

Make a paste with the soft butter and pepper, pimento, garlic, shallots, chives, bread crumbs and lemon juice. Put approximately 1 teaspoon of paste on each oyster on the half shell. On top of paste place a bit of bacon. Put the prepared oysters on the half shell in a baking dish that has been filled with hot rock salt. Bake for approximately 15 to 20 minutes, until cooked.

OYSTERS A LA FINELLIA

Michael's Fine Food
Cleveland, Mississippi

24 large oysters, opened on the half shell
⅜ pound butter
1 cup flour
3 cups milk
2 teaspoons Worcestershire sauce
2 tablespoons sherry

Salt and pepper to taste
Paprika (used in sauce for color)
1½ cups lobster meat, cubed
24 thin small slices sharp Cheddar cheese

Bake oysters in the half shell until edges curl. Melt butter, blend in flour. Add milk very slowly to form smoth sauce. Add seasonings and lobster meat. Divide sauce and lobster in each oyster; put cheese slice on top. Sprinkle with paprika. Bake in hot oven, 400° until cheese melts.

ANGELS ON HORSEBACK

*Fleur de Lys
San Francisco, California*

36 Eastern oysters	6 ounces butter
9 slices bacon	Salt, pepper
6 slices toasted bread	1½ lemons, quartered
3 ounces bread crumbs	Parsley sprigs

Cut each slice of bacon in four. Pull oysters from shells and wrap each oyster in bacon. File oysters on skewers (six on each). Grill 4 minutes and place on toast. Sprinkle with bread crumbs. Cover with butter and season. Broil.

Serve on hot platter, garnished with quartered lemons and parsley sprigs.

TORTUE AU XERES

(Turtle with Sherry)

*Fleur de Lys
San Francisco,
California*

8-inch green turtle, cooked in bouillon —use only the fins	Pepper
	¼ pound butter
	1 cup sherry wine
Salt	

Bone the fins. Cut turtle meat in 2-inch squares. Braise in butter; season to taste. Add sherry; simmer.

Sauce

2 cups sherry	Black pepper
2 slices ham, minced	Dash cayenne
Salt	2 cups turtle consommé
1 pimento, minced	1½ cups tomato purée
2 shallots, finely chopped	

Heat one cup sherry. Add ham, pimento, shallots, pepper, cayenne, turtle consommé, tomato purée. Heat until well blended. Add second cup of sherry. Heat. Place turtle pieces in casserole. Pour sauce over the meat.

SAUTÉED SCALLOPS HARBORSIDE

Harborside Inn
Edgartown, Massachusetts

1½ pounds Cape scallops
   (Small sea scallops may
   be substituted)
1 cup dry white wine—
   Chablis preferred
1½ teaspoons salt

2 or 3 dashes Tabasco
Roux—a paste of equal
   parts butter and flour
Paprika
Toast points

In a large sauté pan, place undrained scallops and pour in wine; add salt and Tabasco. Bring quickly to a rolling boil. Scallops should almost immediately turn white and smooth. At this point, remove from the fire, do not overcook. Remove scallops and place in individual warm baking dishes lined with toast points. Place pan with drained liquid back on a medium high flame and when just under boil, stir in enough roux to thicken. Continue stirring over flame, stirring constantly for a smooth sauce; taste to correct seasoning, then pour equal amounts over scallops in casseroles. Garnish with paprika and serve immediately.

SAUTÉED SCALLOPS EN COQUILLE

The Sea Shell
Halifax, Nova Scotia

2 pounds scallops
1 medium onion, chopped
   fine
1 green pepper,
   chopped fine

3 tablespoons butter
½ teaspoon salt
½ teaspoon pepper
Parsley, chopped

Wash scallops and cook quickly in a small amount of water for 5 minutes. Drain and dry. Sauté onion and green pepper in butter until tender, add scallops and cook until lightly brown. Season and sprinkle with chopped parsley. Serve in individual scallop shells.

BAKED SCALLOPS HEARTHSIDE

Royal's Hearthside
Rutland, Vermont

1½ pounds sea scallops, sliced in half, flat
¾ pound melted butter
3 ounces sherry wine

1 to 2 cups fresh bread crumbs
Salt and pepper

Butter bottom of a casserole, and put in the sliced scallops. Season with salt and pepper. Pour the sherry wine over the scallops. Pour half the butter over the scallops. Cover with the bread crumbs and pour remaining butter over the crumbs. Bake in hot oven, approximately 375°, for 15 minutes.

Alaskan King crab meat or cooked lobster meat may be substituted for scallops.

COQUILLES SAINT JACQUES

The Mad Hatter
Nantucket Island, Mass.

1 pound fresh scallops
1 cup dry white wine
3 shallots
½ cup butter
1 pound cooked lobster
1 pound cooked, cleaned shrimp
½ pound fresh mushrooms
1 tablespoon chopped chives
1 tablespoon chopped parsley

1 tablespoon brandy
1 teaspoon ginger
Few grains cayenne pepper
1 tablespoon salt
1 tablespoon dry mustard
1 quart light cream
4 tablespoons cornstarch, moistened
3 eggs, beaten
Grated Parmesan cheese

Poach scallops in the wine for 5 minutes. At same time sauté the shallots in ¼ cup butter until transparent. Add the cooked lobster and the cooked shrimp to shallots. In another pan sauté ½ pound fresh mushrooms in ¼ cup butter. To this add the chopped chives and parsley. When mushrooms are cooked add the brandy and flambé the mixture. Add scallops to lobster and shrimp mixture. Season with the ginger, cayenne pepper, salt and dry mustard. Scald the light cream and thicken with the moistened cornstarch and cook until thick. Slowly add the beaten eggs to cream, then add mushrooms and cook for 5 minutes over low fire, stirring constantly. Fold this sauce into fish mixture. Place in large casserole or individual ramekins. Cover with the grated cheese and brown under broiler. Serves 6.

SCAMPI O SOLE MIO

Terry and Jerry's O Sole Mio
Bay City, Michigan

36 large shrimp, shelled and deveined	6 ounces dry white wine
2 tablespoons butter	¾ cup water
2 tablespoons capers	6 parsley sprigs
2 tablespoons meatless chicken base (Sexton's)	Powdered garlic to taste

Clean and devein shrimp. Split shrimp down the back so they will curl when cooked. Place all ingredients in small covered sauce pan. Bring to boil. Simmer for 4 or 5 minutes. Do not overcook. Dust lightly with powered garlic and serve in small casseroles.

BROILED STUFFED SCAMPI

Chez Pauzé
Montreal, Quebec

36 large shrimp, cleaned and deveined	1½ cups butter, melted
3 cups fine bread crumbs	¾ cup dry white wine
	1 tablespoon mustard

Split shrimp. Make dressing of bread crumbs, melted butter, wine and mustard. Spread each shrimp with dressing and cook under broiler at 500° for 7 minutes until brown. Serve with cole slaw, French fries and melted butter.

SCAMPI PIEMONTESE

Grand Motor Hotel
Montreal, Quebec

2 pounds large shrimp,
   peeled and deveined
Thin slices Prosciutto ham
Milk
Salt, pepper to taste
Flour for dredging

6 tablespoons butter
Butter, to taste
1 clove garlic, crushed
   very fine
Parsley, minced
1 teaspoon lemon peel

Wrap shrimp in very thin slices of Prosciutto and marinate them for a minute in seasoned milk. Drain well, roll shrimp in flour and sauté them in butter in a pan.

Serve with a mixture of butter and garlic, parsley and lemon peel.

SCAMPI OR JUMBO SHRIMP À LA TANTALO

Tappan Hill
Tarrytown, New York

2 pounds shrimp
   or scampi
4 tablespoons shallots,
   chopped
1 red onion, finely
   chopped

Finely chopped parsley
1 small can anchovy filets
1 can tomato purée
¼ cup white wine
½ cup drawn butter

Lightly brown shallots in 6 tablespoons butter; add shellfish and cook slowly until well browned. Add one tablespoon per portion of the following special tomato sauce:

Brown onion in 2 tablespoons butter. Add mashed anchovies and tomato purée, diluted with white wine. Cook until sauce thickens. Just before using add sprinkle of parsley.

SHRIMP NORFOLK

*O'Donnell's Sea Grill
Washington, D. C.*

2½ to 3 pounds Gulf
   shrimp (26 to 30 count)

¼ pound sweet butter
Tarragon vinegar, to taste

Thaw, peel and devein frozen shrimp. Cook for 3 minutes only in just enough salted water to cover. Heat sweet butter in a heavy skillet, and when the butter starts to sizzle, add cooked shrimp, stirring lightly while sautéing. When slightly brown season with a few dashes tarragon vinegar and serve quickly in 6 heated individual shallow casseroles.

SHRIMP DE JONGHE

*The Garden Seat
Clearwater, Florida*

2 pounds shrimp (20 to
   25 count), cooked,
   peeled, deveined and
   split
1 cup butter
1 cup bread crumbs
2 cloves garlic,
   chopped fine

Pinch thyme
Pinch ground cloves
Salt, pepper to taste
½ cup dry sherry
Buttered bread crumbs
   for topping

Soften butter and work into it bread crumbs, garlic, thyme and cloves. Blend thoroughly. Season to taste with salt, pepper. Add sherry. Arrange shrimp in 6 individual well-buttered ramekins and spread the mixture over them. Sprinkle buttered bread crumbs over the top and put under broiler for about 6 or 7 minutes, or until lightly browned. Do not cook too rapidly as the butter sauce will burn.

BUTTERFLY SHRIMP

New China Inn
Baltimore, Maryland

2 pounds fresh jumbo shrimp, shelled and deveined
6 slices bacon; each slice cut into 3 pieces
2 eggs, beaten
1 onion, sliced
4 tablespoons tomato sauce
2 teaspoons Worcestershire sauce
Tabasco sauce, to taste
½ teaspoon M.S.G.
3 cups chicken broth or water
2 teaspoons cornstarch dissolved in ½ cup water
6 scallions, chopped fine
Toasted almonds, slivered

Split shrimp open from back, but don't cut all the way through. Make three slits on inside of shrimp. Slip bacon pieces into slits. Dip each shrimp in eggs. Place shrimp in skillet, bacon side down. When bacon becomes crisp, turn shrimp and cook for 7 to 9 minutes. Remove shrimp and keep warm.

In fat, sauté onions. Add seasonings and broth. Cover skillet and cook 3 to 5 minutes. Thicken with cornstarch. Pour gravy on shrimp. Top with scallions and almonds.

BAKED STUFFED SHRIMP

Grey Gull Inn
Nantucket, Massachusetts

3 pounds jumbo shrimp, shelled and deveined
1½ cups bread crumbs
¾ cup melted butter
¾ cup ground cooked lobster, scallops or crabmeat
Salt and pepper to taste
1 teaspoon paprika
Dash cayenne
½ to ¾ cup dry sherry
Melted butter and lemon wedges

Split raw shrimp from back, leaving tail on. Cut through back to make pocket for the stuffing. Combine bread crumbs and ground seafood and stir in melted butter. Add seasonings and enough sherry to hold mixture together. Stuff each shrimp pocket and place shrimp in a shallow pan, back up to prevent curling. Cook in a very hot oven, 450°, about 4 minutes or until shrimp are white. Do not overcook. Serve in individual bowls with melted butter and lemon wedges.

GOLDEN PARROT BAKED STUFFED SHRIMP

Golden Parrot Restaurant
Washington, D. C.

1½ pounds fresh or
    frozen shrimp (about
    10 shrimps)
¾ cup milk
1 egg
¾ cup bread crumbs
Salt and pepper
½ teaspoon paprika
1½ pounds lump
    crabmeat
1½ teaspoons
    Worcestershire sauce

Salt, pepper
Dash Tabasco
1½ teaspoons prepared
    mustard
2 tablespoons mayonnaise
2 slices fresh bread,
    crusts removed and
    cubed
1 onion, minced
¾ green pepper,
    finely chopped
¾ cup melted butter

Peel uncooked shrimp, leaving tail shell on. Split shrimps down the back and spread butterfly fashion. Dip uncooked shrimps into milk and egg mixture. Then in bread crumps and paprika which have been combined. Combine crabmeat, Worcestershire sauce, salt, pepper, Tabasco, mustard, mayonnaise and bread cubes. Sauté onion and green pepper in 3 tablespoons melted butter and add to crabmeat. Firmly stuff breaded shrimp with crabmeat mixture. Place shrimp tail side up on a greased shallow baking dish. Baste shrimps with melted butter. Bake in 400° oven until brown. Serve piping hot.

BAKED STUFFED SHRIMP DE JONGHE

The Ropewalk
Nantucket, Massachusetts

1¼ cups bread crumbs
¼ cup chives, chopped
¼ cup parsley,
  finely chopped
¾ teaspoon garlic,
  minced
1 teaspoon salt
½ teaspoon ground pepper

¼ pound butter
½ cup water
½ teaspoon pickling spice
1 bay leaf
1½ pounds jumbo shrimp,
  boiled and deveined
¼ cup Marsala wine

Blend all ingredients together, except shrimp and wine. Remove shells from shrimp up to tail. Leave tail on. Split open in half. Stuff shrimp with mixture and place in well greased casserole. Heap mixture high. Bake at 350° for 15 to 20 minutes. Sprinkle with paprika and wine and continue to bake 10 minutes longer.

PUBLICK HOUSE BAKED STUFFED SHRIMP

Publick House
Sturbridge, Massachusetts

18 jumbo shrimp (about
  5 inches long) washed
  and deveined
¾ pound scallops
6 tablespoons butter
½ teaspoon paprika
3 tablespoons crushed
  potato chips

½ cup cracker meal
5 tablespoons Parmesan
  cheese, grated
2 to 3 tablespoons
  sherry, optional
Lemon wedges

With a sharp knife cut the shrimp from the underside through the meat but not through the shell. Put a toothpick under the meat but over the shell at both ends to keep the shrimp flat; otherwise they will curl when they are baked.

Chop raw scallops and fill into the shrimp. Melt butter in a small saucepan, add paprika, and cook over very slow heat for 10 minutes to take the raw taste out of the paprika. Combine with potato chips, cracker meal and Parmesan cheese. Cover the shrimp with mixture and place them in a shallow baking dish with a little water in the bottom to prevent shrimp from drying out. Bake for about 20 to 25 minutes in a moderate, 350° oven; sherry may be sprinkled over the shrimp if desired just before removing them from the oven. Serve with lemon wedges. Shrimp baked this way have a lovely fresh flavor and a nice moist texture.

SHRIMP IN PINK SAUCE

The Pirate's House
Savannah, Georgia

2 pounds raw shrimp, peeled	¼ cup catsup
½ cup butter	1 cup milk
1 4-ounce can pimentos, drained	1½ tablespoons cornstarch
1½ teaspoon salt	½ cup milk
	2 tablespoons sherry
	3 cups boiled rice

Sauté raw shrimp in butter in saucepan for 3 minutes. Add pimentos and salt. Cook covered for 3 minutes. Stir in catsup and 1 cup milk. Blend cornstarch and ½ cup milk. Stir into shrimp mixture. Cook, stirring until mixture boils and thickens slightly. Stir in sherry. Serve over hot rice.

SHRIMP GIOUVETSAKI TOURKOLIMANO

Tino's Continental
Washington, D. C.

1 onion, chopped fine
½ cup olive oil
3 cloves garlic,
   chopped fine
1½ teaspoon oregano
1 quart canned plum
   tomatoes
½ cup tomato purée
3 heaping teaspoons
   parsley, chopped

1½ cups water
3 pounds shrimp
   (small: 20 to 25 per
   pound) cooked, peeled
   and deveined
Salt, pepper to taste
⅜ pound Feta cheese
   (semi-soft cheese)

Sauté onion in ¼ cup olive oil until soft. Add garlic and sauté very lightly. Add oregano, sauté for a few minutes; add tomatoes and tomato purée. Sauté until tomatoes start cooking, add parsley and water. Season with salt and pepper and simmer for 45 minutes. Add more water if too oily.

Sauté shrimp in ½ cup oil until shrimp turn pink. Place tomato sauce in earthen shallow pot, mix in shrimp with sauce. Sprinkle small pieces Feta cheese on top. Bake for 20 minutes at 375°.

NEW ORLEANS SHRIMP CREOLE

Jack Tar Hotel
San Francisco, California

3 pounds medium shrimp,
   peeled, cooked and
   deveined
3 medium onions,
   coarsely chopped
1 stalk celery, cut up
3 green peppers,
   coarsely chopped
5 tablespoons bacon fat
   or other shortening
2 tablespoons flour

2 cups consommé or
   other stock
Salt and pepper to taste
1 teaspoon chili powder
1 teaspoon vinegar
2 teaspoons sugar
3 cups tomatoes, peeled
   and cooked
½ pound rice
Pinch saffron
8 slices bacon

Brown onions, celery and green peppers slowly in bacon fat. Blend in flour. Add consommé and stir until smooth. Add seasoning (salt, pepper, chili powder, vinegar and sugar) and simmer about 15 to 20 minutes. Add tomatoes and shrimp and simmer until shrimp are thoroughly heated.

Boil rice until tender, drain and wash clean. Fry bacon until crisp. Cut up and add rice and saffron, mix thoroughly until rice is hot. Serve with shrimp creole.

SHRIMP PILAU

The Pirate's House
Savannah, Georgia

6 slices bacon
½ cup onions, chopped
2 cups canned tomatoes
½ teaspoon salt
¼ teaspoon black pepper

⅛ teaspoon Tabasco
2 cups uncooked rice
1½ cups raw shrimp,
    peeled and deveined

Fry bacon. Remove and save. In the bacon grease, fry onions until transparent. Add tomatoes and cook for a few minutes. Add seasonings, rice, shrimp and crumbled bacon. Pour into 1 quart casserole with cover. Bake in 350° oven for 45 minutes. Stir with fork two or three times.

SHRIMP WIGGLE ESCHE PUDDLE

Water Gate Inn
Washington, D. C.

½ pound butter
1 cup flour
1 quart milk
2 cups (½ pound)
    Wisconsin cheese,
    grated
1 tablespoon salt
¼ tablespoon white
    pepper

3 egg yolks or 2 drops
    yellow food coloring
3 ounces dry sherry wine
3 cups cooked shrimp
5 cups cooked rice
1 cup frozen green peas
Cheese, grated, for
    topping
Paprika

To make cream sauce, blend flour with melted butter; add boiling milk and when mixture comes to boil again, add seasoning, egg yolks and sherry.

In a casserole or skillet, put rice, shrimp and peas. Pour sauce over top. Top with cheese and paprika and bake in 400° oven for 10 minutes.

SHRIMP MARINARA À LA PUNJAB

Punjab Restaurant
New York City

2 cloves garlic, chopped
1 onion, chopped
½ cup olive oil
1 teaspoon oregano
2 pounds raw shrimp
1 can Pastene brand
  tomatoes

Salt, pepper, Ac'cent
  to taste
Tabasco, optional
3 cups boiled rice
  or spaghetti

In a skillet sauté garlic and onions in olive oil. Add oregano. When onion is soft, add raw shrimp; mix well. Add tomatoes. Cut tomatoes with fork while cooking. Add salt, pepper and Ac'cent. Also Tabasco, if desired. Cook over low flame for 25 to 30 minutes. Serve with Rice a la Punjab or spaghetti.

CANLIS' SHRIMP

Canlis' Charcoal Broiler
Seattle, Washington

2 pounds large prawns
  in shell
1 ounce butter
1 ounce olive oil
½ teaspoon salt

½ teaspoon fresh ground
  black pepper
2 ounces dry Vermouth
Juice of ½ lemon

Into a large skillet place olive oil and butter and allow to blend over a medium fire. Add shrimp, salt, and pepper. When you think you have too much salt, add more. This is one dish where you cannot use too much salt. Cook shrimp until golden red. When done, raise fire to very hot. Add lemon juice and Vermouth and cook for about 1 minute, constantly stirring or shaking over a very high fire.

SHRIMP, ANDRE STYLE

Gourmet Restaurant
Terrace Hilton Hotel
Cincinnati, Ohio

4 tablespoons shallots, minced
½ pound mushrooms, peeled and sliced
⅓ cup sweet butter
1½ pounds jumbo shrimp, split
2 cloves garlic, finely chopped

2 tablespoons parsley, finely chopped
Juice of ½ lemon
¼ cup sherry wine
Meat stock
1 loaf French bread, toasted

Sauté shallots and fresh mushrooms in sweet butter. Add jumbo shrimp, garlic and parsley. Turn shrimp quickly for a few minutes. Add lemon juice, sherry wine and a few drops of meat stock. Add more butter if too dry.

Serve very hot with toasted French bread.

SHRIMP PANAMA

Kendall Inn
Indianapolis, Indiana

¼ pound smoked bacon
⅛ pound butter
⅓ cup onions, chopped
1 teaspoon Worcestershire sauce
2 cups tomato catsup

36 shrimp
Beer, to cover
2 bay leaves
2 teaspoons vinegar
½ teaspoon celery salt
1 red pepper pod

Fry bacon and remove from the skillet. Add butter to bacon grease. Sauté chopped onions in this mixture until golden. Remove from stove and stir in Worcestershire sauce. Add tomato catsup.

Steam shrimp in beer with bay leaves, vinegar, celery salt and red pepper pod. Use care and do not overcook.

Remove shrimp from liquid. When cool, peel and devein, then wrap with enough bacon to go around shrimp once. Hold bacon on with toothpick. Place 6 shrimp per serving in shallow casserole and lightly cover with sauce. Place in oven and heat until the sauce bubbles for 3 to 5 minutes (375°). Remove and serve immediately.

SHRIMP FANTASY

Royal Scots Grill
Pick-Congress Hotel
Chicago, Illinois

36 shrimp, cooked, peeled and deveined	Pickle relish
Lettuce leaves	White French dressing— see recipe below
6 slices tomato	

Marinate shrimp in White French Dressing for 24 hours. On a plate, place a thick tomato slice on a bed of lettuce and pyramid the shrimp, 6 to a serving. Garnish with pickle relish.

White French Dressing—makes 1 pint

¾ tablespoon brown sugar	1 teaspoon mustard
½ tablespoon salt	1 teaspoon horseradish
1 teaspoon Worcestershire sauce	2 cups oil
	⅓ cup vinegar
1 egg yolk	1½ tablespoons lemon juice

Place brown sugar, salt, Worcestershire sauce, egg yolk and mustard in bowl and beat with mixer for 3 minutes. Mix horseradish, oil, vinegar and lemon juice together, and add to first mixture, one cup at a time.

FRIED SHRIMP POLYNESIAN

Kahiki Supper Club
Columbus, Ohio

Batter

1 cup all purpose flour
1 cup cornstarch
1 teaspoon baking powder
Pinch salt
Pinch sugar

2 eggs, well beaten
Milk
2 pounds shrimp,
   peeled and deveined

Combine all the dry ingredients. Add sufficient milk until the mixture is of pancake batter consistency. Add eggs. Using index finger, thumb and middle finger, separate the body of the shrimp into three prongs. Dip in batter. Fry in deep hot fat, at 375°, until golden brown. Serve with Kahiki sauce.

Kahiki Sauce

1 cup catsup, best
   quality
1 cup chili sauce
1 tablespoon sugar
Juice of ½ lemon

1 teaspoon mustard
   powder
1 teaspoon prepared
   horseradish
1 tablespoon
   Worcestershire sauce

Mix all ingredients well. Refrigerate until used.

SHRIMP CASSEROLE À LA MONTEMAR

Hotel Montemar
Aguadilla, Puerto Rico

¾ pound egg noodles
¾ pound sweet corn,
   whole kernel
2 pounds shrimp, peeled,
   cooked and deveined
1½ pounds mushrooms,
   sliced

2 ounces butter
2 teaspoons flour
1½ cups milk
6 ounces strong
   American cheese,
   grated
Salt and pepper to taste

Cook noodles until tender in boiling, salted water. Drain and place in casserole. Arrange whole kernel corn, shrimp and mushrooms over the noodles. Melt butter in frying pan. Add flour and stir until smooth. Add milk, shrimp and mushrooms and cook until thick and smooth, stirring constantly. Add cheese, seasoning (salt and pepper) and pour sauce over noodle mixture. Mix gently. Sprinkle cheese over top. Bake in 400° oven for 30 minutes.

For variety, use carrots instead of corn.

SHRIMP AND SAUTÉED CRAB FLAKES NORFOLK

The Occidental Restaurant
Washington, D. C.

½ ounce olive oil
2 ounces butter
1 red onion, chopped fine
1 green pepper, diced
1 clove garlic, chopped fine
1½ pounds shrimp, cooked, peeled and deveined
1 pound crab flakes

2 ounces Virginia ham, thinly sliced
½ teaspoon salt
⅛ teaspoon black pepper
Few drops Worcestershire sauce
2 to 3 slices white bread, toasted
Parsley or chives, chopped

Heat oil and butter. Add onion and green pepper. Smother for 4 to 5 minutes. Add garlic and shrimp and heat thoroughly. Add crab flakes, Virginia ham and seasonings. Sauté for a few minutes, until the mixture is well heated. Put in shallow casserole with toast in bottom. Sprinkle with parsley or chives and serve.

SHRIMP AND CRABMEAT GUMBO

The Tides Hotel
St. Petersburg, Florida

½ cup bacon fat
2 cups flour
½ cup celery, diced
½ cup green peppers, diced
½ cup onions, diced
1 pound raw shrimp, peeled
1 pound Alaskan King crabmeat
Salt and pepper
1 tablespoon gumbo filé

1 bay leaf
3 or 4 cloves
1 teaspoon pickling spice
2 cloves garlic, crushed
1 tablespoon Worcestershire sauce
Dash Tabasco
1 pint canned okra
2 pints canned tomatoes
1 cup cooked rice

Blend bacon grease and flour and brown lightly. Add diced vegetables and brown well. Add shrimp and crabmeat. Add spices. Cook slowly; then add okra and tomatoes. Bring the whole mixture to a boil and as the very last thing, add cooked rice. Serve in abalone shells.

SZECHUEN PRAWNS

The Golden Pavilion
San Francisco, California

2 pounds Prawns, uncooked, cleaned and deveined, fresh or frozen
10 green onions in ¼″ slices
6 cubic inches ginger root, minced
3 cloves garlic, minced
6 tablespoons cooking oil
1 tablespoon Szechuen Pepper Sauce or

Chinese Pepper Oil (recipe below)
1 cup catsup
Salt to taste
¼ teaspoon monosodium glutamate
2 ounces Vodka or bourbon
1 teaspoon sugar
2 egg whites
1 tablespoon cornstarch

Marinate prawns in egg whites, cornstarch and pinch of salt for 10 to 15 minutes. Marinate ginger root in vodka or bourbon for same length of time. Place cooking oil in a Dutch oven, add 1 teaspoon of salt and heat to smoking temperature. Add ginger, ginger marinade, garlic, green onions and pepper sauce (or pepper oil), stirring constantly for one to two minutes. Add prawns, monosodium glutamate, sugar and stir for one minute or until the prawns begin turning pink. Quickly add catsup, stirring until thoroughly blended. Remove from pan and serve immediately.

Chinese Pepper Oil

Gently simmer 6 chopped and dried red chili peppers in ¼ cup cooking oil until the oil is red, approximately 30 to 45 minutes. Use only 1 tablespoon of this pepper oil. The rest may be stored for future use.

JUMBO PRAWNS WITH GARLIC BEAN SAUCE

Bamboo Terrace
Vancouver, British Columbia

2 tablespoons salted
 black beans
2 cloves garlic, crushed
2 tablespoons soy sauce
2 tablespoons peanut oil
½ teaspoon salt
2 pounds prawns or
 jumbo shrimp, shelled
 and deveined

⅔ cup chicken stock
½ teaspoon M.S.G.
1 tablespoon cornstarch
 dissolved in ¼ cup
 cold water
Scallions and parsley
 for garnish

Rinse salted black beans (available at Chinese food stores) in hot water. Drain and dry well. Combine beans with garlic and soy sauce.

In a large saucepan, heat peanut oil, stir in salt and add whole prawns or shrimp. Sauté the prawns until golden brown on both sides.

Add bean mixture to prawns; toss well and cook for 2 or 3 minutes. Add chicken stock and M.S.G. and cook, covered, for 3 minutes. Add cornstarch paste and cook the mixture, stirring continuously, for 1 minute. Arrange prawns on a heated platter and pour sauce over them. Garnish the platter with green onions and parsley.

BOUILLABAISSE MAISON

Rib Room
Hotel America
Hartford, Connecticut

1 whole live lobster, cut into pieces
Water
12 small sea scallops
12 raw shrimp, shelled and deveined
12 ½-ounce strips halibut
12 1-ounce pieces of eel (if available)
12 cherrystone clams
3 pounds sole bones
1 carrot, cut into small pieces
1 onion, chopped
1 leek, cut into small pieces
1 stalk celery, cut up

1 stalk fennel (if available)
2 cloves garlic, minced
3 tomatoes, peeled, seeded and chopped
6 sprigs parsley, chopped
2 tablespoons tomato purée
2 tablespoons butter
2 tablespoons olive oil
2 cups white wine
Tarragon, ¼ teaspoon thyme, 1 bay leaf, whole black pepper, very little saffron
Garlic croutons

Boil lobster for 15 minutes in water with sole bones added. Remove from pot and cook all the other fish in the same stock. Sauté vegetables in butter and oil until lightly browned. Add tomato purée, white wine and spices. Add the stock. Bring to a boil and simmer for 20 to 30 minutes. Strain. Place fish in chaffing dish and pour hot stock over it. Serve with garlic croutons.

BOUILLABAISSE MARSEILLAISE

The Boar's Head Inn
Charlottesville, Virginia

1 carrot, peeled and
  chopped
1 onion, peeled and
  chopped
3 stalks celery, chopped
Sufficient oleo to cover
  bottom of pan
1 pinch garlic
3 pounds mixed fish:
  black bass, skate, eel,
  halibut, red snapper
1 lobster

½ pound sea scallops
8 clams
10 mussels
1 pinch pure Italian
  saffron
1 cup white wine
Enough water to cover
  the mixture well
2 tomatoes, peeled
  and cut up
6 slices garlic bread
Parsley, chopped

Heat oleo with garlic and add celery, carrots and onion. Brown well. Add fish and shell fish. Cook 10 minutes. Add saffron, wine, water, tomatoes. Cook 15 to 20 minutes, until fish is done. Strain the liquid, add the fish pieces. Sprinkle with chopped parsley. Serve very hot with French garlic bread.

MUSSELS GLAZED

Cafe Chauveron
New York City

6 pounds mussels
6 shallots, chopped
3 cups dry white wine
Salt and pepper
3 cups light cream

1½ cups thick cream
  sauce
3 tablespoons butter
6 tablespoons whipped
  cream
3 egg yolks

Clean the shells of the mussels very thoroughly. Place in a pan with shallots, white wine, salt and pepper, and cover. Cook for 10 minutes until they open. Drain. Remove the upper shell from each mussel and place mussels in a separate bowl, piled on top of each other.

Cook the sauce left in the first pan on a slow fire for about 20 minutes, adding light cream and thick cream sauce, then butter, a little at a time, stirring constantly. When the sauce is cooked, take it off the fire and add whipped cream and egg yolks (mix into the sauce slowly). Pour the finished sauce over the mussels and place the dish under the grill until the mussels are well browned.

MOULES MARINIÈRES
(Stewed Mussels)

The Greenbrier
White Sulphur Springs, West Virginia

36 mussels	2 teaspoons parsley, very finely chopped
1½ tablespoons shallots, very finely chopped	6 tablespoons butter
1½ tablespoons onion, very finely chopped	2 teaspoons flour
	¾ cup dry white wine
	Salt, freshly ground pepper

Wash mussels thoroughly, scraping with a knife and changing water several times. Remove any that are dead. (These will be either heavier, being full of sand; or very light, empty, or open.)

Place in saucepan with shallots, onion, parsley, and 1 tablespoon butter. Cover tightly and steam over a good fire until shells open; then pour into a colander over a bowl. Put mussels in the dish in which they will be served and keep warm.

Pour cooking juice back into sauce pan, taking care not to include the sediment which may have been deposited in the bottom of the bowl. Reduce this juice to ⅓ its volume. Thicken by adding "beurre manie", (made by creaming together 5 tablespoons butter and 2 teaspoons flour) stirring continuously. Correct seasoning. Pour juice over mussels and serve in deep soup plates.

CREOLE SEAFOOD GUMBO

Motor House Cafeteria
Williamsburg, Virginia

1 cup medium shrimp, peeled, deveined and diced—reserve hulls
3½ quarts water
Celery tops
½ cup onions, diced
½ cup celery, diced
½ cup green pepper, diced
1 clove garlic, diced
¼ pound butter
4 cups canned tomatoes
1 cup canned tomato purée

3 ounces flour
½ cup scallops, diced in quarters
1 cup fresh okra, chopped
Dash Tabasco
1 teaspoon Worcestershire sauce
1 bay leaf
1 tablespoon gumbo filé
½ cup Alaskan crabmeat
½ cup whole oysters
¼ pound rice, cooked

To the reserved hulls of the cleaned shrimp add water and a few celery tops. Cook over medium heat for 15 minutes.

Sauté onions, celery, green pepper and garlic in 7 tablespoons butter, until tender, but not brown. Add tomatoes, tomato purée and the stock from the shrimp hulls. Let simmer for 25 minutes.

Make a roux by melting 1 ounce butter and adding flour. Mix thoroughly and cook 3 or 4 minutes (do not brown). Fold roux into stock and cook for 5 minutes.

Add shrimp, scallops, okra, Tabasco, Worcestershire sauce and bay leaf to stock and simmer 20 minutes. Add ½ cup of the stock to gumbo filé and whip until thickened. Return to stock and simmer 5 minutes.

Remove from heat. Fold in crabmeat and oysters last. Heat thoroughly. Serve on platter or in casserole, with or without rice.

CIOPPINO À LA CATHERINE
(Italian Fish Stew)

Anthony's Fish Grotto
La Jolla, California

Tomato Sauce

2½ tablespoons olive oil
   or vegetable oil
1 medium onion, minced
2 cloves garlic, minced
2 sprigs parsley, minced
2 ounces sherry
½ can tomato paste,
   about 3 tablespoons

Pinch thyme
1 #2 can whole
   tomatoes, chopped
1 cup water (for
   thicker sauce, use
   less water)
¼ teaspoon pepper
Salt to taste

Prepare the tomato sauce in advance of the stew. Heat oil in sauce pan. Add minced onion, garlic, parsley and sauté until brown. Add sherry and cook a little longer. Add tomato paste, thyme and chopped tomato, cook about 15 minutes. Add water and cook 35 minutes longer. For a smoother sauce, it may be strained before adding to seafood. Season to taste.

Cioppino a la Catherine

2 pounds bay scallops
1 pound lobster meat
2 King crab legs
4 tablespoons butter

Salt, pepper to taste
M.S.G.
1 cup boiled rice

Sauté scallops, lobstermeat and King crab legs in butter that has been seasoned with pepper and M.S.G., for about 5 to 10 minutes.

Add 1 cup boiled rice and 3 cups of the prepared tomato sauce. Simmer an additional five minutes and serve in individual casseroles.

If the above seafood is not available, any seafood may be substituted.

LA PECHE DES CARAIBES

El Panama Hilton
Panama City, Panama

6 ounces butter
1 pound shrimp, shelled
  and deveined
1 pound lobster meat
6 to 8 shallots, minced
1 green pepper, seeded
  and cut up

Native herbs
Salt and pepper
½ pound mushrooms,
  sliced
¼ cup Cognac
½ cup white wine

In butter, sauté fresh shrimp and lobster meat with shallots, green pepper, native herbs, salt, pepper and mushrooms. Flavor with Fundador Brandy and white wine, and blend with butter sauce (see recipe below). Serve with pilaff rice and salad.

Butter Sauce

6 ounces butter
6 tablespoons onion,
  sliced

½ cup flour
6 ounces white wine
Salt and pepper to taste

Sauté onion in butter; add flour, stirring continuously. Add wine and stir until smooth. Season to taste.

SEA FOOD "LORD CALVERT"
(Tender Lobster Morsels, Crabmeat and Pink Shrimp Under a Cheese Canopy)

Miller Brothers
Baltimore, Maryland

6 to 8 filets of sole
12 shrimps, peeled,
  deveined, cooked
  and diced
½ pound crabmeat

½ pound lobster meat
3 to 4 tablespoons butter
6 to 8 slices American
  cheese
Newburg sauce

Cut filets of sole in half lengthwise. Form into 6 to 8 rings, fastening with toothpicks. Arrange in well buttered baking dish. Fill center of rings with diced shrimp, crabmeat and lobster. Dot with butter. Bake in moderate oven, 325°, for 20 minutes. When ready to serve, top with cheese slice and reheat for 5 minutes. Pour on Newburg sauce.

SEAFOOD SHELBURNE

The Shelburne Hotel
Atlantic City, New Jersey

1 stalk celery, cut up	½ pound Maine lobster meat
1 small onion, sliced	½ pound shrimp
3 bay leaves	¼ pound scallops
2 small carrots, sliced	½ pound crabmeat
1 small tomato	8 ounces Sherry wine
3 cups cold water	Cream sauce—see recipe below
1 pound filet of flounder—6 pieces	

In a saucepan, place celery, onion, bay leaves, carrots, tomato and water. Heat over moderately high flame until it comes to a boil. Strain off broth. Add to the broth the flounder, lobster meat, shrimp, scallops and 5 ounces of the wine. Bring to a boil. Add crabmeat, place cover on pan and allow to boil until practically all the broth has evaporated. Fold in cream sauce, add balance of wine. Serve in hot chafing dish.

Cream Sauce

6 ounces butter	1¼ quarts milk
¾ cup flour	½ pint light cream

Melt butter, mixing in the flour and stirring until it is a golden color. Gradually add milk and cream until mixture is smooth. Stir with a fine whisk at all times.

BAKED SEAFOOD CASSEROLE, GRANVILLE CHEESE

Yankee Pedlar Inn
Holyoke, Massachusetts

1 pound Cape scallops
(raw)
Butter
⅔ pound fresh crabmeat
½ pound lobster meat

⅔ quart Velouté Sauce
(see recipe below)
⅓ pound Granville cheese,
diced
Fresh bread crumbs
Paprika

Broil Cape scallops in enough hot butter to brush each one. Set aside. Put lobster meat, crabmeat and scallops in a casserole and cover with Velouté Sauce. Sprinkle diced cheese over sauce, and add enough bread crumbs to cover. Sprinkle with paprika for color. Bake 10 minutes in 400° oven. Serve immediately.

Velouté Sauce

2 cups cream
2 cups fish stock

Chianti, to taste

Blend ingredients, simmer for 5 minutes. Set aside till ready to use.

INDIVIDUAL SEAFOOD PIES

Christiana Campbell's Tavern
Williamsburg, Virginia

½ pound scallops, cut
  in quarters
12 oysters
½ pound shrimp, peeled
  and deveined
½ pound lobster meat,
  diced
3 quarts court bouillon
Roux made of 3 tablespoons
  butter and 3 tablespoons
  flour
2 tablespoons onion,
  chopped

1½ tablespoons celery,
  chopped
2 tablespoons green
  pepper, chopped
1 tablespoon pimento,
  chopped
2 tablespoons mushrooms,
  sliced
3 tablespoons butter
Salt, pepper, cayenne,
  pinch nutmeg, to taste
2 tablespoons Sherry wine
6 individual pie shells
Additional dough to cover

Cook seafood in court bouillon for 5 minutes. Drain and save stock. Thicken stock with roux. Sauté vegetables in butter, stirring continuously. Add prepared seafood and vegetables to sauce. Season to taste. Add Sherry wine. Turn the mixture into 6 pie shells. Cover the pies with thin crust. Bake in hot oven, 400°, for 25 to 30 minutes.

BROILED SEAFOOD GRILL ASTOR

Hotel Astor
New York City

4 ounces filet of sole
6 fresh jumbo shrimp
12 deep sea scallops
Olive oil to cover
Salt and pepper
3 tomatoes cut in half,
  stuffed with crab meat
6 fresh open clams,
  topped with shallots
  and bacon, chopped

6 cooked lobster tails,
  removed from shell
½ pound sweet butter,
  melted
Lemon juice and melted
  butter
Parsley, chopped

Dip filet of sole, shrimp and scallops in enough oil to cover. Drain well, season with salt and pepper. Place in a flat pan and add stuffed tomatoes, clams and lobster tails. Sprinkle the seafood with melted sweet butter. Broil the whole combination for 15 to 20 minutes. Serve with lemon juice and melted butter, with chopped parsley over the fish.

ITALIAN FISH RAGOUT

Harbor Restaurant
Santa Barbara, California

2 pounds assorted fish
1 onion, chopped fine
1 cup tomato purée
¼ teaspoon rosemary
¼ teaspoon oregano
1 bay leaf
Salt and pepper
2 cups fish stock

Sauté small pieces of a variety of salt water fish. Add onions, tomatoes (or purée) and fine herbs. Add fish stock to moisten and cook slowly until fish flakes easily. Garnish with croutons and serve with Polenta.

BRODETTO DI PESCE
(Fish Broth)

Gurney's Inn
Montauk, New York

1 chicken lobster, split in half, claws cracked
6 large shrimp, cleaned and deveined
8 bay scallops or 5 sea scallops
6 cherrystone clams
6 soft shell clams
2 plum tomatoes, chopped
5 tablespoons olive oil
2 cloves garlic, minced
2 white scallions, cut in 2-inch pieces
1 bay leaf
Salt and pepper
Oregano
4 cups water
2 cups white wine
Chopped parsley
1 lemon, sliced

Sauté lobster, cut side down, shrimp, scallops, clams in olive oil with minced garlic for 5 minutes. Add other ingredients and bring to a boil. Reduce heat and cover. Simmer until the clams are opened. Serve with lemon slices.

BAHAMIAN GROUPER
(Fish Chowder)

The Sheraton British Colonial Hotel
Nassau, Bahamas

2 pounds grouper or
  jackfish, boned
Dash salt and cayenne pepper
Juice of 2 lemons
2 large onions, cut in fine
  strips
1 large potato, cut in small
  thin slices

1 cup butter or oil
3 tablespoons flour
5 tablespoons tomato
  purée
1 teaspoon thyme leaves
6 cups water
Boiled rice

Cut grouper or jackfish, which has been boned, into 6 pieces. Sprinkle with salt and cayenne pepper and marinate in lemon juice for 1 hour. Cut onions in fine strips and potato in very small thin slices. Heat butter or oil in skillet, dip fish in flour, fry golden brown on both sides. Take fish out. In the same fat sauté onions and potatoes for 5 minutes, sprinkle flour over and allow to cook for 1 minute more. Add tomato purée, thyme leaves, fill with water and put fish in skillet. Let simmer for 15 to 25 minutes. Serve with boiled rice.

PACIFIC ABALONE CHOWDER

Jack Tar Hotel
San Francisco, California

1½ to 2 pounds abalone
   steak
¼ cup celery stalks,
   diced
1 onion, diced
½ cup green peppers,
   diced
2 tablespoons oil or
   butter
5 to 6 cups stock
   or water

1 cup tomatoes, peeled,
   seeded and chopped
Clam nectar
Worcestershire sauce,
   to taste
Chili powder, to taste
Pinch thyme
Pinch oregano
3 medium potatoes,
   diced
Arrowroot flour
Sherry, to taste

Sauté celery, onions and peppers in oil or butter. Grind abalone coarsely and add to the sautéed ingredients. Add stock (if not available, use water). Add tomatoes, clam nectar and all seasonings. Boil for approximately 30 minutes, then add diced potatoes. Simmer until potatoes and abalone are tender. Mix arrowroot flour with water and use as a thickener, but thicken mixture slightly. Bring back to a boil, add sherry and serve.

ABALONE GOURMET

Anthony's Fish Grotto
La Jolla, California

1 large abalone
2 eggs, beaten lightly

2 tablespoons water
Cracker meal

Pound through one large (2 to 2½ pound) pink abalone. Pat dry. Sprinkle with salt and pepper. Dip in egg and water mixture, then in cracker meal. Broil on grill, four minutes on each side.

ABALONE STEAK

Anthony's Fish Grotto
San Diego, California

2 pounds abalone, sliced
2 eggs, beaten lightly
2 tablespoons water

Cracker crumbs, to cover
 fish slices
Oil
Salt, Ac'cent to taste

Pound fish slices with a wooden mallet. Dip in egg and water mixture, then in cracker meal, then dip in an oil prepared with salt to taste, and Ac'cent. Allow oil to drip off. Broil on hot grill, one minute on each side. Do not cook longer.

CANADIAN FISH TIMBALE

Chateau Frontenac
Quebec, Canada

¾ cup cooked salmon
¾ cup cooked shrimps
½ cup cooked halibut
3 teaspoons soft butter
Salt, pepper and cayenne
 to taste
2 ounces dry sherry
1 teaspoon pistachios,
 finely chopped (for
 halibut)

1 teaspoon truffles, diced
 small (for shrimps)
1 teaspoon green and
 red peppers, diced small
 (for salmon)
2 cups heavy cream,
 whipped
2 cups fish aspic

Pass the fish through fine sieve, each separately. Add 1 teaspoon butter to each; season to taste; divide sherry wine evenly; add other ingredients as indicated, then finish one fish at a time by folding in whipped cream and aspic. Place fish in layers in aspic lined mold. Keep under refrigeration until used.

STEAMED ARCTIC CHAR
(Alaskan Fish)

The Moorings Restaurant
Toronto, Ontario

1 whole char (5 to 6 pounds)

2 tablespoons onion, chopped

2 tablespoons celery, chopped

Salt and pepper to taste

Measure thickness of fish. Wipe and place on aluminum foil. Add chopped onion and celery; wrap securely in foil, making sure the package is watertight.

Boil whole package in covered pot, 10 minutes per inch of thickness if the fish is fresh; 20 minutes per inch thickness if fish is frozen.

BROILED FILET OF ARCTIC CHAR, CHATEAU

Chateau Laurier Hotel
Ottawa, Ontario

6 filets arctic char (8 ounces each)

2 teaspoons salt

2 teaspoons pepper

2 teaspoons paprika

1 cup olive or cooking oil

4 lemons cut in half

12 slices ripe tomato

24 small mushroom caps, peeled

24 anchovy strips

4 ounces butter

3 ounces sauterne

½ cup chopped parsley

Baste the filets with olive or cooking oil and sprinkle with salt, pepper and paprika. Broil 15 to 20 minutes at 400° until fish is golden brown.

On each filet place two slices of tomato and garnish crosswise with four filets of anchovy, topped with four cooked mushroom caps.

Squeeze over all the juice of half a lemon, sprinkle with sauterne and chopped parsley, dot each piece of fish with butter and return to broiler until butter has melted.

Serve with lemon halves and parsleyed potatoes.

COD TONGUES "SAUTEES MEUNIÈRE"

Hotel Madeline Sur Mer
Riviere Madeleine, Canada

Allow ¼ pound per serving. Prepare and wash in cold water medium size cod tongues. Drain in a piece of cloth. Dip the tongues in flour, then into eggs beaten lightly. This method seals up the tongues, keeping oil or butter out and retaining flour.

Use heavy iron skillet with about ½ inch of cooking oil. Have oil good and hot but not smoking. This will quickly form a crust on tongues resulting in a nice golden brown. Turn tongues over individually; then put in a 350° oven for about 10 minutes. Serve with tartar sauce.

COD FISH BALLS

Cobb's Mill Inn
Weston, Connecticut

8 ounces salt codfish
8 ounces mashed potatoes
2 egg yolks

2 tablespoons cream
Black pepper
Fat for frying

Soak dry salted filets of codfish overnight. Drain. Place in boiling water and simmer for about 10 to 15 minutes. Drain. Put through a fine grinder. Add an equal amount of dry mashed potatoes. Add egg yolks. Add medium or heavy cream to moisten. Add black pepper to taste. Shape into balls and fry in deep fat, 375°, until golden brown.

MAINE CODFISH CAKES SUPREME

Boone's Restaurant
Portland, Maine

2 cups salt codfish
2 cups hot mashed potatoes
1 tablespoon butter
1 egg

1 cup milk
½ teaspoon baking powder
⅛ teaspoon pepper
Bacon

Soak the codfish in cold water for several hours. Drain and cover with fresh cold water and simmer until fish is tender. Remove any bones and chop the codfish. Combine all ingredients except the bacon, and beat until light. Cover and let stand overnight. In the morning, mold the cakes about ½ inch thick. Fry 2 strips of bacon for each person. Fry fish cakes in bacon fat and serve with the crisp bacon.

These are nice for lunch served with a Tomato Cream Sauce made as follows:

Tomato Cream Sauce

2 cups canned tomatoes or 6 fresh tomatoes	1 cup celery, cut in pieces
1 onion, chopped	½ teaspoon salt
1 teaspoon sugar	1½ tablespoons flour
1 bay leaf	1½ tablespoons butter

Combine all the ingredients except the flour and butter. Cook for 15 minutes, then strain. Melt the butter and stir in the flour, then add the strained tomato juice and cook until the mixture thickens.

SALT FISH CAKES

La Boucan Restaurant
Trinidad Hilton Hotel
Port of Spain, Trinidad

1 pound salted cod	3 cups mashed potatoes
3 large onions, chopped	Flour
3 eggs, beaten	Oil for frying
1 teaspoon Ac'cent	

Soak cod overnight, drain, and place in boiling water. Simmer 15 minutes. Drain and mince finely. Add mashed potatoes, onions, Ac'cent and the beaten eggs. Shape into balls, dust with flour. Fry in deep fat, 375°, quickly, until golden brown. Serve piping hot.

BOILED SALT COD WITH BROWNED PORK SCRAPS AND BAKED POTATO

The Holderness Inn
Holderness, New Hampshire

1½ pounds salt cod
Salt pork
  6 baked potatoes

3 tomatoes, peeled and
  sliced

Cut salt cod in one inch pieces and soak in water for 12 hours. Add fresh water and bring to a boil. Dice salt pork in amount desired and fry crisp. Drain on paper. Pour top from fat. Toss drained fish in remainder of fat. Heat and drain. Top fish with pork scraps and serve with hot baked potato and sliced tomatoes.

FILET OF FLOUNDER EN PAPILOTTE

Clarksville Inn
West Nyack, New York

For each serving:
  6 ounces flounder
Milk, flour and enough
  beaten egg to moisten
  4 ounces butter
  2 shrimps, chopped fine

2 langonstinos, chopped
  fine
1 shallot
Wine
Salt, pepper
12-inch square of white
  paper

Fold paper in half. Cut a curve on each side from the end of the fold to a point 4 inches in from the corners of the paper. Unfold the paper and set aside. Prepare a sauce by combining shrimp and langonstinos, all chopped fine, with a shallot, a dash of wine, salt and pepper. Sauté the mixture for a few minutes in 2 ounces butter. Set aside. Dip flounder in milk, then in flour, then in egg, and sauté in 2 ounces melted butter on a hot skillet, browning for a few minute on each side. Cover with the shrimp and langonstine sauce, and lay the fish on one side of the fold in the paper. Cover with the other side of the paper and seal by folding down the edge in overlapping sections 1½″ wide and ½″ deep. Bake in shallow pan in 300° oven for ½ hour. Serve in the paper, which will be puffed up from the baking.

FILET OF FLOUNDER À LA PARKER

Parker House
Boston, Massachusetts

6 filets of flounder, about 7 ounces each	Pinch chopped chives
6 ounces cooked lobster meat, diced small	Juice of 1 lemon
½ pound butter	Flour
	Salt and pepper

Dip flounder in flour, season with salt and pepper. Sauté in frying pan with 4 ounces of butter until golden brown, which will be about 12 minutes.

Sauté lobster meat in 4 ounces of butter. Add chives. Place fish on platter and squeeze the juice of the lemon over it while hot. Cover flounder with sautéed lobster meat. Serve with parisienne potatoes.

STUFFED FLOUNDER

Commander's Palace
New Orleans, Louisiana

¼ cup white onions, minced	½ cup boiled shrimp, chopped
1 cup celery, minced	½ cup lump crabmeat
½ cup shallots, minced	3 tablespoons parsley, chopped
3 cloves garlic, minced	½ cup bread crumbs
½ pound margarine	Salt and pepper to taste
2 tablespoons flour	6 1-pound flounders
½ cup milk	
1 cup dry white wine	

Sauté onions, celery, shallots and garlic in margarine until tender. Add flour and blend. Add milk and white wine, cook until thick. Add shrimp and crabmeat, parsley, and finish thickening with bread crumbs.

Stuff flounders loosely. Arrange on a buttered pan, season to taste. Broil slowly on both sides until golden brown, adding butter if necessary.

STUFFED FLOUNDER

Brennan's
New Orleans, Louisiana

1 bunch green onions, finely chopped
1 large Bermuda onion, finely chopped
¼ pound butter
1 cup flour
2 quarts fish stock
2 dozen oysters—scald (do not boil)— finely chopped
½ pound boiled shrimp, finely chopped
½ pound fresh mushrooms, finely chopped
Salt, cayenne pepper to taste
6 1-pound flounders

Sauté onions in butter, blend in flour thoroughly. Add fish stock and boil for 5 minutes. Add oysters, shrimp, and mushrooms. Season to taste with salt and cayenne pepper.

Remove backbone from flounder and fill loosely with the above stuffing. Broil slowly on both sides until golden brown.

STUFFED FLOUNDER WITH CRABMEAT

Gurney's Inn
Montauk, New York

6 flounders, 1½ to 2
pounds each, cleaned,
heads and tails off,
with pockets on each
for stuffing *
1 pound crabmeat
1 small onion,
chopped fine
2 eggs, beaten
½ cup flour

⅓ cup mayonnaise
2 teaspoons lemon juice
1 teaspoon Ac'cent
Salt and pepper
2 tablespoons baking
powder
Oil
1½ lemons, cut into
quarters

* To make pocket for stuffing, with a sharp boning knife make a deep slit 4 inches long on the dark side of the flounder along the line of the backbone, leaving an inch uncut on both head and tail sections. Slant the knife toward the side in the slit and scrape along the bone to loosen the meat from the bone on both sides.

Mix crabmeat with remaining ingredients and divide into 6 parts. Stuff into the flounder pockets and brush with oil. Bake in hot oven, 450°, for 20 minutes or until done. Serve with lemon quarters.

FRIED CATFISH AND HUSH PUPPIES

Smith's Cross Lake Inn
Shreveport, Louisiana

6 medium-sized catfish
Dill

Yellow and white cornmeal
Fat for frying

Thoroughly clean catfish and remove collar bones. Wash in dill sauce (dill and water). Pat dry. Dip each piece of fish into a mixture of salted yellow and white corn meal (equal parts). Fry in deep fat at 450° for 15 minutes until brown. Serve on warm platter with fried potatoes, cole slaw, tartar sauce and Hush Puppies.

Hush Puppies

2 cups white corn meal	2 cups boiling water
1 teaspoon salt	or milk
¼ cup onions,	1 egg, well beaten
finely chopped	(if desired)

Add salt to meal and finely chopped onions. Mix thoroughly. Scald meal with boiling water, making stiff batter. Add beaten egg if desired. Mold into small round balls. Drop into deep hot fat, 370°, and fry until golden brown on both sides. Time same as catfish and serve immediately.

FILET OF HALIBUT WALESKA

The Tidewater Inn
Easton, Maryland

6 filets of halibut	1 pound lobster meat,
6 ounces butter	cut up
4 shallots, thinly sliced	2 tablespoons flour
8 ounces chablis	Truffles or chives, chopped

Wipe fish with a damp cloth. Place in shallow pan with Chablis, butter and shallots. Bring to a boil and cover, lower the heat. When the halibut is cooked, add lobster, cut in small square pieces, bring to a boil and boil for five minutes. Remove to a chafing dish.

Add 2 tablespoons flour to the sauce and simmer just under the boiling point until the sauce is reduced to a thick liqueur. Pour sauce over the filets and garnish with truffles or, if you prefer, chopped chives.

ANGEL FISH LOAF WITH LOBSTER SAUCE

*Boone's Restaurant
Portland, Maine*

1⅓ cups soft bread crumbs	1 teaspoon celery salt
1 cup hot milk	1 teaspoon salt
1½ pounds raw halibut, ground	1 tablespoon pimento, minced
1 teaspoon baking powder	2 egg whites, stiffly beaten

Make a paste of the bread crumbs and hot milk. Add the halibut, baking powder, celery salt, salt and pimento. Mix well. Fold in the beaten egg whites. Turn into a small bread tin, which has been lined with waxed paper and well greased. Place the tin in a shallow pan of water and bake at 350° until firm and lightly browned, about 45 minutes.

Serve in slices, with lobster sauce:

Lobster Sauce

Meat from 1¼ pound lobster	1½ cups medium white sauce, well seasoned
2 tablespoons butter	¼ teaspoon paprika

Sauté lobster meat in the butter, in a heavy skillet. Add cream sauce and paprika. Heat thoroughly.

FINNAN HADDIE À LA ANTHONY

*Anthony's Pier 4
Boston, Massachusetts*

1 large haddock (5 pounds) smoked with bone and skin, cut into 6 equal parts	½ pound butter
	½ pound flour
	Pinch white pepper
1 quart milk	Parsley, for garnish

Place fish in casserole and cover with one quart milk. Bake at 450° for 35 minutes. Strain milk. Remove bones from fish and serve with cream sauce. Garnish with parsley.

Cream Sauce

Melt butter and gradually add flour. Cook mixture for two minutes, stirring constantly. Slowly add the strained milk and boil for 10 minutes. Season with white pepper. Serve the sauce separately.

TETSU-YAKI

Yamato Sukiyaki Restaurant
San Francisco, California

2 pounds halibut, or sea
   bass, or salmon,
   or chicken
1½ tablespoons salt
⅓ cup soy sauce
⅔ cup sweet sherry wine
⅓ cup sugar

⅓ cup sake (sherry can
   be substituted)
1½ pints green onions,
   cut in 2-inch pieces
2 teaspoons salad oil
Lemon slices

Cut fish into 3½ to 4½ inch pieces and ¾ inch thick. Salt fish generously. Let stand 3 hours. Combine soy sauce, sherry, sugar and sake; marinate fish in this mixture overnight, or in the refrigerator for 4 hours. Place marinated fish on a bed of green onions. Sprinkle salad oil over fish to keep it from drying. Broil in hot oven 4 minutes per side. Pour over the marinade and serve with lemon slices.

COLD KENNEBEC SALMON EN GELEE

Louis & Armand Restaurant
New York City

1 6-pound salmon	3 hard cooked eggs,
Cold water to cover	sliced
Pinch mixed spices	Pimentos
1 carrot, diced	Ripe olives
1 stalk celery, chopped	Truffles, sliced
1 bay leaf	Gelee (see recipe below)
¼ teaspoon vinegar	

Place whole salmon in an oblong boiling pan, add sufficient cold water to cover it. Add a pinch mixed spices, carrots, celery, bay leaf and vinegar. Bring to a boil and let simmer until well done (a 6 to 8 pound salmon would take about 8 to 10 minutes per pound). Remove fish carefully from pan, and place on a flat tray.

Use a spatula to divide the fish in half, lengthwise, and remove center bone. Use a second tray to turn fish over, then remove the skin from both halves.

Decorate the salmon with slices of hard cooked eggs, pimentos, ripe olives, truffles, etc. Cover both halves with the Gelee, place in refrigerator. When the Gelee is solid, cut the salmon into horizontal slices and serve with a mixed vegetable salad.

The Gelee

3 cups consommé or	1 ounce cognac
beef broth	1 ounce sherry
3 egg whites	2 envelopes granulated
Pinch mixed spices	gelatin
2 ripe tomatoes, chopped	½ cup cold water

Soften gelatin in cold water. Add broth, then add other ingredients. Use a heavy pot, with a heavy bottom. Place pot on fire; if open flame is used, the mixture must be constantly stirred until it comes to a boil, then lower the flame and let the mixture simmer for about 30 minutes—

without moving or stirring—otherwise it will turn cloudy. Strain, without disturbing, through a very fine cloth; season to taste and let cool off. The Gelee should be very clear at all times.

POACHED SALMON AROMATIC

John Bartram Hotel
Philadelphia, Pennsylvania

2 quarts water	¼ stick cinnamon
1 cup vinegar	½ medium onion
2 bay leaves	½ small carrot,
2 cloves	cut in four
¼ teaspoon oregano	½ celery stalk,
½ teaspoon thyme	cut in four
¼ teaspoon basil	1 clove garlic
1 pinch nutmeg	6 salmon steaks
¼ teaspoon rosemary	

Cut a 6-inch square piece of cheese cloth and place all spices in the center of cloth and tie into a little bag. Place water, vinegar, spice bag and cut vegetables in a pot large enough to hold the salmon. Allow it to boil for 10 minutes, then place salmon in the boiling contents. Allow to simmer for 12 minutes. Remove the salmon from bouillon and serve with Hollandaise sauce.

POACHED SALMON WITH SAUCE

Hotel Madeleine Sur Mer
Riviere Madeleine, Canada

4 pound piece of	½ lemon, sliced
salmon	½ raw onion
Hot water (amount	½ teaspoon salt
depending on size	
of pan)	

Wipe salmon with a damp cloth. Put fish in the hot liquid with lemon, onion and salt, and reduce the flame. Let simmer slowly until fish is done, about 25 to 35 minutes.

Sauce

1 cup milk	1 tablespoon cornstarch
1 onion, minced	¾ cup cold water
½ teaspoon salt	Paprika

Mix together milk, onion and salt, and bring to a boil. Remove from heat. Add cornstarch mixed with cold water. Stir until well blended and serve on salmon. Sprinkle with paprika.

DECORATED SALMON

The Wharf Restaurant
San Francisco, California

Clean a fresh salmon, leaving on head. Place fish upright on rack, or line bottom of pan with dry bread slices. Grease outside of fish lightly and put in moderate oven (375°) for 45 to 60 minutes for a 6-pound fish.

After fish is baked, cool and chill in refrigerator before trying to decorate. Place fish on serving board, platter or tray. Cut skin around head and tail with sharp knife and lift off.

Decorate with a gelatin glaze. This is helpful in keeping the fish from drying out and in keeping the decorations in place. A glaze can be made by mixing a concentrated gelatin, using less water than called for on box directions.

For decorations you may use various items, such as red pimento, green peppers, lemons, oranges, green onions, red and green cherries, ripe and green olives, hard cooked eggs, romaine, endive, parsley, and mayonnaise applied with a pastry bag.

RED SALMON PATTIES

Vick's Continental Restaurant
Dallas, Texas

1 can #1 Red
  Sockeye salmon
1 7 ounce can tuna
2 stalks celery, chopped
1 green bell pepper,
  chopped

2 teaspoons onion, chopped
1 clove garlic, chopped
2 eggs, well beaten
⅓ cup cracker crumbs
Salt and pepper to taste

Put fish in a bowl. Add chopped vegetables, mix well. Add eggs and cracker crumbs, salt and pepper and mix well. Shape the mixture into patties and roll in cracker crumbs. Fry in deep fat at 375° until brown on both sides. Drain on absorbent paper.

DARNE DE SALMON ALA NATIONAL

Sheraton-Brock Hotel
Niagara Falls, Ontario

3 pound salmon steak
  (tail piece)
1 carrot, thinly sliced
1 turnip, thinly sliced
1 small piece celery
1 onion, thinly sliced
Salt
6 peppercorns
Bouquet of herbs
1 pint fish stock
½ cup Chablis

3 or 4 potatoes, peeled
2 small cucumbers,
  peeled (reserve
  peelings)
3 ounces butter
1 ounce flour
½ cup milk
Salt, pepper, to taste,
  grate nutmeg
1 tablespoon cream
Parsley

Cut the fish into slices about ½ inch thick. Line a buttered pan with carrots, turnip, celery and onions. Put in the fish, season with salt, cover with the remainder of the vegetables. Add the peppercorns, savory herbs, moisten with fish stock and Chablis. Cover with a buttered paper and cook in a slow oven for about 30 minutes, 300°.

Scoop out as many round balls of potatoes and cucumber as possible, blanch them separately, drain. Cook them in some white stock or salted water until tender, then drain and keep till wanted.

Remove salmon from oven, cover, and keep it hot. In the meantime prepare a white sauce:

Melt 1½ ounces butter, add the flour, stir well; strain in the stock left from the fish, add the milk (boiling), also the trimmings of the cucumbers which have been blanched in salt water. Bring to a boil and simmer for 20 minutes adding more stock as the sauce reduces. Pass through a fine sieve, return to the saucepan, add cream, season with a pinch of white pepper and a grate of nutmeg.

Pour the sauce over the slices of fish so as to mask them completely. Sprinkle with chopped parsley, garnish the sides with groups of the prepared potatoes and cucumbers and serve.

SALMON PARISIENNE

Cafe Chauveron
New York City

1 salmon (4 to 5 pounds) sliced thick	2 stalks celery
½ cup vinegar	2 bay leaves
1 large onion, sliced	½ teaspoon thyme
1 large carrot, sliced	1 tablespoon salt
2 sprigs parsley	8 peppercorns
	1 lemon, sliced

Place salmon in a large saucepan, add the remaining ingredients with water to cover. Simmer until boiling. Remove from the fire and let cool.

When cool, remove salmon from the pan and take out the bone and remove the skin. Place the salmon on a large platter, then place lemon slices and parsley around the platter for decoration. Serve cold with any kind of vegetable salad.

Dressing: Mayonnaise, tartar sauce or Russian dressing.

FILET OF BASS À "LA RAVIGOTA"

Hotel Arizpe-Sainz
Satillo, Mexico

2½ pounds filet of sea bass   Salt, juice of lemon to taste
4 tablespoons butter

Cut each filet in half lengthwise, roll half and encircle with the other half filet, fastening them with toothpicks. Place in a small shallow ovenproof dish in a hot (375°) oven for 15 minutes. Cover with butter, salt and juice of lemon to taste.

Remove from oven and add sauce (see recipe below), garnish with lettuce, mint, beets, jello, slices of lemon, small gherkin and a cherry in the center.

Sauce

2 hard cooked eggs
1 small bottle pickled
  onions
1 small bottle sweet
  pickles
1 small bottle capers

1 tablespoon parsley,
  chopped
Vinegar
Oil
Salt and pepper to taste

Chop all ingredients finely; add vinegar and oil, salt and pepper to taste.

ROBALO À LA VERACRUZAN
(Sea Bass—Veracruz Style)

Acapulco Hilton
Acapulco, Mexico

2½ pounds sea bass
  in filets
½ onion
1 bay leaf
8 ounces butter
1 pint white wine
4 onions, sliced

6 fresh sweet red peppers,
  cut in thin strips
2½ pounds tomatoes,
  diced
8 ounces green olives,
  chopped

Simmer fish in a little water with onion and bay leaf. Dot with 4 tablespoons butter, season to taste. Add white wine to fish broth and cook until fish is tender.

Sauté in butter sliced onions, sweet red peppers, diced tomatoes and olives. When cooked, pour sauce over fish and serve with rice pilaff or steamed potatoes.

BROILED SCAMP OR RED SNAPPER
SOUTHERN STYLE ALA MIRABELLA

Mirabella's
Tampa, Florida

2 pounds scamp or
  red snapper, cut into
  filets
2 cups water
Juice of 3 lemons
¼ cup onion, chopped
2 cloves garlic, minced
Salt, pepper to taste
1 tablespoon olive oil

¼ pound butter
Paprika
2 fresh tomatoes, sliced
1 Spanish onion
1 green pepper
2 hard cooked eggs
Small can pimentos
1 lemon, cut into wedges
Lemon butter sauce *

* To make lemon butter sauce, add lemon juice and chopped parsley to brown butter.

Marinate fish filets for at least three hours before broiling. Use water with lemon juice, chopped onions and clove of garlic, minced. Add salt and pepper to taste and olive oil to mixture.

After filets have marinated for at least three hours, remove from pan, drain, and sprinkle with salt and pepper. Brush broiler pan with butter before placing fish on pan. Then sprinkle fish with paprika and brush filets with lemon butter sauce. Make sure you place fish flesh side up on pan and place broiler rack about 6 inches from flame. This should require about 10 to 15 minutes, according to thickness of filets.

While fish are broiling, slice tomatoes, Spanish onion and green pepper. Just before removing fish from broiler brush with lemon butter sauce and place two slices of tomato with onion and green pepper on each filet. Return to broiler and let cook for another 3 minutes.

Remove from broiler and serve hot with lemon wedge and garnish with olives, strips of pimentos and hard cooked eggs.

BROILED FILET OF RED SNAPPER

Ambassadeurs Restaurant
Mexico City

6 filets of red snapper	¼ cup olive oil
Salt, pepper	Flour for dredging
Juice of 1 lemon	

Wipe filets of red snapper with a damp cloth. Season with salt, pepper, juice of lemon and olive oil and marinate for 10 minutes. Remove from marinade; drain well. Sprinkle filets with flour. Broil them for 12 minutes. Serve with slices of lemon and boiled potato.

FILET OF RED SNAPPER POACHED WALESKA

Hotel Tropicana
Las Vegas, Nevada

6 filets of red snapper
Mornay sauce (see
  under sauces)

2 egg yolks, well beaten
Butter
  6 slices lobster
  6 slices truffle

Poach the filets in a fish stock with white wine (see recipe below). Remove from stock when done and put them on serving platter. Add Mornay sauce to the stock in pan and let simmer for a while. After the sauce is smooth, add egg yolks and cook at low heat for a few minutes, incorporating little by little a few cubes of fresh butter.

Place a slice of lobster and a slice of truffle on each filet. Cover with sauce and glaze under broiler.

Fish Stock Ingredients

Bones and trimmings
  of fish
1 onion, minced
¼ cup mushroom parings
1 sprig thyme

Parsley
  1 bay leaf
Salt, to taste
Water to cover
½ cup white wine

RED SNAPPER "ALICANTE"

Columbia Restaurant
Tampa, Florida

1 3-pound red snapper
  steak, cut into
  8-ounce slices
1 onion, sliced
½ cup brown gravy
⅔ cup Spanish olive oil
1 teaspoon salt
3 green peppers,
  cut into rings

Pinch of white pepper
½ cup white wine
24 almonds, grated
12 shrimps
12 rings of breaded
  eggplant
Parsley

Place red snapper steaks on top of onion slices, which have been spread over the bottom of a casserole.

Over the fish pour olive oil, brown gravy, white wine, salt, white pepper, grated almonds, and green pepper rings. Bake at 350° for 25 minutes.

Garnish with breaded eggplant rings and shrimps.

BONELESS BAKED CAROLINA SHAD

Evans Farm Inn
McLean, Virginia

3 or 4 pounds shad
1 quart water
1 tablespoon vinegar

Salt and pepper to taste
4 or 5 strips bacon

Boil shad in water and vinegar with seasonings for 20 minutes. Drain off water; put in a heavy, tightly covered roaster and cook in oven slowly (200°) for 5 or 6 hours. Add roe about 30 minutes before fish is done. Put strips of bacon across the shad and place under broiler for bacon to brown. When done, the bones are completely dissolved.

FILETS DE SOLE PIERRE LE GRAND
(Poached filets of sole with wine sauce)

O'Neil's Restaurant
Akron, Ohio

4 ounces cooked Holland
  ham, cut in julienne
  strips
1 truffle, julienne
2 hard cooked eggs
6 filets of sole
Butter
  1 cup dry white wine
½ cup water
½ teaspoon salt

Pinch pepper
  2 tablespoons butter
  3 tablespoons flour
½ teaspoon salt
⅛ teaspooon white
  pepper
1 cup hot milk
½ cup Hollandaise
½ cup whipped cream

Cut ham, truffle and the whites of the eggs into julienne strips. Press yolks of eggs through a coarse sieve and reserve for garnish.

Arrange 6 filets of sole in buttered skillet. Add wine, water, salt and pepper. Simmer for 8 to 10 minutes. Transfer filets to shallow casserole. Sprinkle 2 filets with ham, 2 with truffles, and 2 with egg whites. Use sieved yolk for garnish.

Cook liquid in which fish were cooked over high heat to reduce to ½ cup.

In sauce pan melt butter, stir in flour, salt and white pepper. Cook, stirring, for 5 minutes. Add hot milk, and continue cooking, stirring rapidly, until smooth and thick. Stir in the fish liquid.

Add Hollandaise and whipped cream. Pour over filets and brown under broiler.

FILET OF SOLE À LA BONNE FEMME

Rickey's Studio Inn
Palo Alto, California

6 filets of sole, 6 to 7
    ounces each
1 green onion, finely
    minced

3 tablespoons mushrooms,
    sliced
Salt and pepper
Wine
Water

Place 6 filets of sole in buttered saucepan. Sprinkle with green onions, mushrooms, salt and pepper. Cover the fish with equal parts dry white wine and water. Cover saucepan with a piece of buttered wax paper and place in medium hot oven, 350°, until cooked.

Sauce

2 tablespoons butter
1½ tablespoons flour
Fish broth

Salt, pepper, lemon juice
    to taste
Heavy cream (if needed)
Parsley, chopped

Melt butter in saucepan, add flour, stir well. Pour the broth of the fish into the flour and butter, mix well and season to taste. Add heavy cream if sauce is too thick. Add chopped parsley to taste.

Place the fish on a platter, pour the sauce over the fish, and glaze under the broiler. Serve with boiled potatoes and lemon.

ENGLISH DOVER SOLE PENROSE

The Penrose Room
The Broadmoor
Colorado Springs, Colorado

6 English Dover sole,
  1 pound size
1 quart white wine
1 pint water
½ teaspoon thyme
2 stalks celery, chopped
1 medium onion, chopped
½ teaspoon salt
Parsley
  6 ounces butter
  6 ounces flour
  1 pound shrimp, peeled
    and deveined

12 ounces raw lobster tail
  4 ounces sherry
  1 pint heavy cream
¼ teaspoon white pepper
  4 shallots
  1 pint Hollandaise sauce
  1 pint heavy cream,
    whipped
24 pieces fleurons (small
    flaky pastry forms,
    used for decorations)

Remove filets from sole. Use skin and bones to make fish broth using 1 pint white wine, 1 pint water, seasoned with thyme, chopped celery, onion, salt and parsley. Bring to boil and simmer slowly for 10 minutes; strain liquid through cheese cloth and save (1 quart).

Prepare roux with butter and flour; bake in oven at 350° for 10 minutes.

Make fish veloute using broth and roux. Simmer slowly for 30 minutes.

Grind shrimp and lobster through fine blade and beat into sherry and cream to make a smooth paste; salt and pepper.

Take filets which have been cut into 24 pieces and flatten without breaking them by using a smooth, wet towel folded over the filet and hitting gently with flat part of cleaver. Then spread smooth paste on top of filet and roll into cylindrical shape. Poach in remaining white wine with shallots. Remove cooked filets from liquid and arrange on silver platter. Reduce liquid to ¼ cup and add to fish veloute; pour over filets saving one pint to mix with Hollandaise sauce and whipped cream. Cool this mixture and pour over veloute. Place platter under broiler until golden brown. Decorate platter with puff pastry fleurons, cut in crescent shapes.

DOVER SOLE PROPELLER

Open Hearth Restaurant
Boca Raton Sun and Surf Beach Club
Boca Raton, Florida

6 fresh Dover sole, fileted (if Dover sole is not available, any sole will do)	1½ cups bread crumbs
	¼ pound butter
	Mayonnaise
	1½ cups medium white sauce
¾ pound lump crab meat	Fish stock
1 tablespoon onions, finely chopped	12 mushroom buttons

Sauté crab meat in butter with finely chopped onions. Add bread crumbs to the crabmeat and continue to sauté until the crumbs turn deep brown. Make sure there is sufficient butter in pan to keep the mixture moist. Spread equal amounts of stuffing on top of the raw sole to make a layer about ¼ inch thick. Bake for 20 minutes at 250° in baking pan with a little water (uncovered). Remove from oven and lay a strip of mayonnaise on top of the crabmeat. Put under broiler for 2 minutes until brown. Make mushroom cream sauce by flavoring medium white sauce with fish stock and sautéed mushroom buttons. Ladle sauce onto serving platter and serve fish on top of sauce.

DOVER SOLE MARIE ANTOINETTE

Le Chateau Richelieu
New York City

2 pounds Dover sole,
  cut into 6 filets
Milk
Flour for dredging

4 tablespoons butter
1 or 2 apples, sliced
Parsley sprigs

Bone sole, making 6 filets. Dip filets in milk, sprinkle with flour. Sauté in 2 tablespoons butter until very brown, 5 minutes on each side.

In another pan, sauté in 2 tablespoons butter apple slices, until golden brown. Place apple slices in a regular row on top of the filets, garnish the platter with a sprig of parsley and serve piping hot.

SUPRÊMES OF DOVER SOLE AMANDINE

The Fox and Crow Restaurant
Montgomery, Ohio

6 filets of sole
Salt and pepper
Flour
¾ cup sweet butter

½ cup almonds, blanched
  and slivered
2 tablespoons parsley,
  chopped
Juice of 1 lemon

Wipe filets of sole with damp cloth. Salt and pepper the suprêmes and dust lightly with flour. Sauté in clarified butter until lightly golden, about 3 to 4 minutes. (Use about ½ cup butter.) Remove to a silver platter, sprinkle with lemon juice and keep warm.

Heat the remaining butter in a separate skillet and stir the slivered almonds until nut brown and the butter begins to foam. Shake the skillet in a circular motion until the foaming butter begins to subdue and takes a noisette color. Add the chopped parsley and pour this mixture over the suprêmes.

Decorate with sprigs of parsley and lemon quarters.

WHOLE DOVER SOLE ALA MEUNIÈRE

Old Mill Inn
Bernardsville, New Jersey

6 1-pound whole sole
Milk for dipping
Salt, pepper to taste
Lemon juice

½ pound butter
½ cup almonds, blanched
   and sliced

Wash and clean whole sole. Dip in seasoned milk (seasoned with salt, pepper, and a squirt of lemon juice). Dip in flour (some salt may be added to flour). Sauté fish in clarified butter until golden brown on both sides. When cooked, transfer to serving platter. To the clarified butter remaining in the saucepan, add lemon juice and sliced almonds. Heat slightly and pour over fish (this will give you an ala Meunière Almandine).

WHOLE DOVER SOLE COLBERT

London Grill
Portland, Oregon

1 large sole
Salt, pepper to taste
Flour for dredging
2 eggs, well beaten

Bread crumbs—enough
   to coat fish
6 tablespoons butter

Skin the sole on both sides. Add salt and pepper to taste; dip in flour, next in well beaten eggs and then in fresh white bread crumbs. Fry in butter at medium heat for 4 minutes on each side. When serving, top the sole with Colbert butter (recipe follows).

Colbert Butter

½ pound butter
1½ teaspoon parsley, chopped
1 teaspoon tarragon, chopped
1½ teaspoon lemon juice

1 teaspoon tarragon vinegar
½ teaspoon Worcestershire sauce
Salt and pepper to taste

Mix all ingredients together until well blended. Serve over hot sole (or other fish).

POACHED FILET OF NATIVE SOLE, DUGLERE

Mayfair Farms
West Orange, New Jersey

3 tablespoons butter
4 shallots, finely chopped
6 filets of sole
Juice of 1 lemon
1 cup white wine
2 whole firm tomatoes, peeled, seeded and chopped

Pinch salt
Dash cayenne pepper
Parsley, chopped
¾ cup heavy cream
3 tablespoons Hollandaise
1½ tablespoons whipped cream

Place butter in skillet with shallots, filets of sole, lemon juice, wine and tomatoes, cover and bring to a boil. Then place in hot oven and bake for 10 minutes, at 400°. Remove the sole and tomatoes, place in ramekins, and keep warm. Reduce sauce to half the amount, then add heavy cream and reduce a little more. Remove from fire, add a little chopped parsley, a dash cayenne pepper, and blend in Hollandaise and whipped cream. Pour over fish and glaze under broiler for a minute or two. The glaze is optional; if not desired, omit whipped cream.

FILET OF SOLE CORONADO

Hotel Del Coronado
Coronado, California

6 filets of Dover sole	¼ pound sweet butter
Vermouth	3 shallots
Salt, pepper	Juice of 1 lemon
Flour for dredging	

Season filets lightly with salt and pepper and marinate overnight in Noilly Pratt Vermouth. Remove from Vermouth, wipe dry, dredge with flour and sauté in hot sweet butter until brown.

Sauté shallot until lightly brown. Add lemon juice and 1 cup of the Vermouth used as marinade. Cook until reduced to one-half. Pour over fish when serving.

DOVER SOLE AU VERMOUTH

Chez Desjardins
Montreal, Quebec

6 Dover sole, 14 ounces per fish	1½ cups French vermouth
6 ounces butter, flaked	6 ounces whipping cream
6 dried shallots, finely chopped	Salt and pepper to taste
	1½ cups Bechamel sauce

In a shallow baking dish, place sole, butter, dried shallots, salt, pepper and vermouth. Simmer uncovered in 375° oven for 10 to 15 minutes. When cooked, take fish from liquid and remove all bones. Place fish on warm service platter. Mix remaining liquid in pan with Bechamel Sauce and whipping cream; pour mixture over sole. Before serving, glaze swiftly under broiler. Serve with tossed salad and parsley boiled potatoes.

Bechamel Sauce

Make a roux of 3 tablespoons melted butter and 3 tablespoons flour. While beating vigorously, add 1½ cups scalded milk, all at once. When it comes to a boil, lower heat and simmer 5 minutes. Season to taste with salt, pepper and pinch of nutmeg.

SOLE À LA VERONIQUE

The Three Fountains
St. Louis, Missouri

6 filets of lemon sole
¼ cup butter, melted
2 shallots, chopped or
½ small onion, chopped
⅜ cup white wine
⅜ cup fish stock or
water

Juice of 1 lemon
Salt and white pepper,
to taste
½ pint cream
4 dozen seedless
grapes (canned)

In cold sauté pan, place half of melted butter, add chopped shallots, or onion. Place in filets by folding each in half. Add white wine, fish stock or water, juice of lemon. On top, pour remainder of butter, add salt and white pepper to taste.

Cover pan and bake in 400° oven no more than 15 minutes. Remove filets, reduce fish stock in pan, add cream and further reduce until creamy. Pour cream over filets, glaze in broiler. Remove and garnish with seedless grapes.

STUFFED BOSTON SOLE

Le Cafe
Hotel Pontchartrain
Detroit, Michigan

8 Boston yellow tail
sole, 1½ pounds each
1½ shallots
3 tablespoons butter
3 pounds King crabmeat,
broken
1½ tablespoons flour

1½ cups cream
White pepper
Salt
5 tablespoons dry
white wine
Melted butter
Paprika

Skin both sides of sole. Cut pocket along backbone. Chop shallot and sauté in 3 tablespoons butter. To this add crab-meat, broken up with a fork, and 1½ tablespoons flour. Cook for 2 minutes. Add cream and mix well. Season with salt, white pepper and white wine. Stuff sole with crab mixture; sprinkle each fish with salt and paprika. Brush with ⅓ cup melted butter and bake 20 minutes at 350°. Serves 8.

DOVER SOLE BAROQUE

*The Baroque Restaurant
New York City*

For each serving:

1 Dover sole—1 to
1½ pounds
2 large mushrooms,
minced
½ cup white wine
1 cup veloute of fish
(butter, flour, fish
stock)

½ cup heavy cream,
whipped
1 shallot, finely chopped
Butter
Salt and pepper

Filet a Dover sole (making four pieces), and arrange the filets in a buttered skillet. Add chopped shallot, wine, salt and pepper to taste. Cover; let poach about 10 minutes.

Remove the filets from the skillet; add 1 cup veloute to ingredients still on the fire. Let simmer very slowly.

Place two filets on a serving dish, cover them with mushrooms, then add the other two filets on top of the mushrooms.

When the ingredients in the skillet are cooked (about 3 minutes) remove from fire and beat until smooth. Add the whipped cream, folding lightly. Pour over the sole and put under open flame until glazed, or until the sauce has turned brown.

BRAISED TURBOT MIRABEAU CAFE BONAPARTE

Sheraton-Blackstone Hotel
Chicago, Illinois

1 4-pound turbot
Salt, pepper to taste
1 pint dry red wine
1 bunch herbs
3 shallots, sliced

½ pint demi-glace
1 tablespoon anchovy
   paste
2 ounces butter
16 anchovy filets

Clean turbot and season lightly. Place in pan and add wine, herbs and sliced shallots. Braise slowly in medium oven, basting often. Braising time is about 50 minutes. When done, remove from pan, strain and add demi-glace to stock. Reduce to desired thickness. Whip in the anchovy paste and butter. Cover turbot with sauce. Decorate with a lattice of anchovy filets and serve the rest of the sauce on the side.

POMPANO TOULOUSE

Brennan's
New Orleans, Louisiana

¼ cup butter
4 shallots, finely
   chopped
2 green peppers,
   chopped
2 tablespoons flour
3 cups white wine

1 medium size can
   pimentos, chopped
2 tablespoons Worcestershire
3 tablespoons capers
   sauce
4 cloves garlic, chopped
6 filets of pompano

Sauté in butter shallots and green peppers. Add flour and blend, then blend in white wine. Add pimentos, capers, including the juice, Worcestershire sauce and garlic. Sauté 6 filets of pompano, cover with sauce and serve.

PESCADO EN PAPILLOTE
(Fish in Paper Bag)

Cafe Renaissance
New York City

6 filets—pompano, red snapper, or striped bass	1 tablespoon parsley, finely chopped
1 onion, finely chopped	4 tablespoons butter
2 cloves fresh garlic, pressed	2 tablespoons flour
	1 cup fish stock

Bone and cut fish into filets, allowing one large filet per person.

Saute onion, garlic and parsley in butter, 10 to 15 minutes. Add sifted flour and fish stock. Allow to simmer while preparing paper.

Use ordinary brown wrapping paper cut into squares large enough to cover filets. Fold in half. On bottom half of paper spread one tablespoon of sauce, which by now should be fairly thick. Place filet on sauce, in bias form. Spread more sauce on filet and repeat layers of filet and sauce. Fold other side of paper over and crinkle-fold edges airtight. Bake for 15 to 25 minutes, at 375°.

To serve, cut with scissors close to edges around top of paper. Serve piping hot, in paper.

POMPANO Á LA SHERADI

Henry's Restaurant
Charleston South Carolina

3½-pound pompano	6 strips bacon
Salt and pepper	Chopped olives

Select firm whole fish. Remove heads and split down flat side removing center bone structure to provide pocket. Salt and pepper, then stuff with the following stuffing, topping opening with shrimp, chopped olives and bacon strip. Place in covered dish and bake 15 minutes in hot oven, 450°.

Stuffing

¾ pound cooked shrimp, minced
½ pound white crabmeat
1½ cups bread crumbs
½ bunch scallions
Sherry, to moisten

½ cup butter, melted
2 tablespoons parsley, chopped fine
2 eggs, well beaten
Salt and pepper to taste

Mix above ingredients well. Cook slowly to prevent scorching.

POMPANO LOUISIANA

*River Queen Restaurant
St. Louis, Missouri*

6 1-pound whole pompano
Salt and pepper
1 pound butter

Juice of 1 lemon
¼ pound toasted almonds, slivered

Clean and score pompano. To score, make diagonal slashes along dorsal fin area. Broil fish with full heat, five inches from heat until outer skin is charcoaled and meat is white and sweet—13 to 15 minutes. Lavish with drawn butter and toasted almonds. Serve immediately.

Drawn butter: Melt slowly 1 pound butter and lace with lemon juice.

POMPANO PAPILLOTE

Cape Cod Room
Drake Hotel
Chicago, Illinois

1 cup dry red wine
¼ cup butter
¼ cup cooked lobster,
  diced
¼ cup mushrooms, cut
  julienne

1½ teaspoon shallots,
  chopped
½ cup water
6 8-ounce selected
  pompano filets
Arrowroot or cornstarch
Salt to taste

Combine the red wine, butter, lobster, mushrooms, shallots and water. Bring to a boil. Reduce heat and add pompano. Poach fish in this mixture for 20 minutes. Remove pompano and thicken sauce with arrowroot or cornstarch to desired consistency. Season with salt.

Place pompano filets with equal amount of sauce on individual sheets of paper,* wrap to form paper bags, clamping all edges so that no air is allowed to escape. Bake at 350° until bags begin to puff up.

Serve in the paper bags or remove to a hot platter, as preferred.

* Heavy brown paper, parchment, or foil may be used.

BAKED TIGER MUSKY

Lost Lake Resort
Sayner, Wisconsin

1 6-pound muskellunge
Oil
1 potato
Salt, pepper to taste
1 lemon, sliced
2 tomatoes, cut into
  wedges

1 cup wild rice
¼ cup butter
1 clove garlic, minced
1 onion, chopped
2 strips bacon, cut up

Skin fish, leaving heads, tail and fins on. Grease body with oil. Cover head, tail and fins with heavy foil to prevent burning. Prop mouth open with potato. Season with salt and pepper. Tie heavy string from head to tail to produce curved effect, as in swimming. Stuff with wild rice dressing (below). Bake in 325° oven 1 hour. Serve on platter garnished with lemon slices, tartar sauce, and tomato wedges. Place tomato in open mouth, pimento olive slices for the eyes.

Wild Rice Dressing

Cook wild rice in salt water and blanch. Sauté in butter, adding garlic, onions and bits of bacon.

MERLITON FARCI
(Stuffed Merliton)

Dunbar's Restaurant
New Orleans, Louisiana

6 merlitons	2 sprigs thyme
¼ pound butter	2 bay leaves
½ pound ham, finely chopped	1 tablespoon parsley, chopped
1 pound shrimp, boiled and ground	⅓ loaf stale French bread
1 small onion, ground	Salt and pepper to taste
2 cloves garlic, ground	Pimento strip and parsley sprig to garnish

Wash merlitons well. Parboil until tender. Halve, scoop out center and save shells. Mash inner pulp well. Place in skillet with melted butter. Add ham, shrimp and seasoning. Simmer 20 minutes.

Soak bread and press dry. Add to mixture. Add salt and pepper. Cook 10 minutes over low flame, stirring constantly. Fill shells with stuffing. Sprinkle with bread crumbs and dot with butter. Bake in 375° oven. Serve with pimento strip and parsley sprig on top.

LES OEUFS D'ALOSE A L'OSEILLE
(Shad Roe with Sorrel)

Chateaubriand
New York City

6 pairs fresh shad roe
1 pound butter
Salt and red pepper, to taste
3 tablespoons shallots,
  chopped

8 ounces dry white wine
2 cups fresh sorrel,
  chopped
1 pint heavy cream

For 6 servings have 6 pairs fresh shad roe; butter pan generously and place shad roe in it. Dust with salt and red pepper;
add shallots, wine, and sorrel. Cover pan and simmer over low
heat for about 20 minutes. Drain off liquid and add to this
heavy cream and let cook down to thickness of sauce; add
to the hot shad roe just before serving.

MAHI MAHI OAHU
(Ma-hēē Ma-hēē)

Host International Restaurant
Honolulu, Hawaii

6 pieces 8-ounce
  Mahi Mahi filet
Lemon juice
Salt and pepper
Flour for dredging
¾ cup butter
¾ cup white wine
1½ cups court bouillon,
  well seasoned

3 tablespoons tomato
  sauce
3 tablespoons pineapple
  juice
¼ lemon, sliced
Hollandaise sauce
Sliced almonds

Garnish

Glazed pineapple spear
Baked banana
Toasted coconut chips

Lime halves
Watercress

Rub each filet with lemon juice and season with salt and pepper. Dredge in flour. Put clarified butter in pan and sauté filets on both sides until golden brown. Reduce heat and pour over filets the white wine, court bouillon, tomato sauce, pineapple juice and lemon slices. Cover and simmer until filets become flaky.

Place each filet on hot serving plate, cover with Hollandaise sauce and sprinkle with sliced almonds. Garnish around the filet with glazed pineapple spear, baking banana, and toasted coconut chips. Glaze under broiler. Garnish with ½ lime and watercress spray.

OVEN FRIED HIGH COUNTRY TROUT

Hotel Splendide
Empire, Colorado

6 ½-pound trout	Salt, pepper to taste
⅜ pound butter	6 lemon wedges

Place three pats of butter under each head, middle and tail of 6 trout, on aluminum steak platter. Place in pre-heated oven, 475°, and cook 10 minutes. Remove from oven, salt and pepper trout and turn over with a spatula. Return to oven and cook ten more minutes. Remove platter to wooden tray and serve trout with a lemon wedge placed at the tail.

Sliced cucumbers marinated in well-seasoned oil and vinegar dressing, and hashed brown potatoes are splendid accompaniments for this dish.

POACHED TROUT MARINIÈRE

Brennan's
New Orleans, Louisiana

½ cup butter	½ cup white wine
1 cup shallots, finely chopped	6 ½-pound filets of trout, poached * in salted water
4 tablespoons flour	
2 cups milk	3 egg yolks, beaten
½ teaspoon salt	Paprika
¼ teaspoon cayenne	

* Poached differs from boiling in that very little water is used, barely covering fish. Wine vinegar or lemon juice may be added.

In a 9-inch skillet melt butter. Sauté shallots until tender. Blend in flour and cook slowly 3 to 4 minutes, stirring constantly. Stir in milk until smooth. Add salt, pepper, and wine. Cook about 10 minutes more. Add poached trout and heat through. Remove from heat and stir in egg yolks. Place pieces of warm poached trout in serving dish and spoon hot sauce over top. Sprinkle with paprika and heat under broiler flame until piping hot.

RAINBOW TROUT MARINA

Edgewater Inn
Marina Hotel
Long Beach, California

6 8-ounce Rainbow trout	½ cup butter
Seasoned flour	¼ pound King crab
3 eggs, well beaten	Potatoes for frying

Bone trout. Dip in seasoned flour, then in egg. Sauté in butter. Place 2 ounces King crab down center of each trout. Cover crab with béarnaise sauce.* Place in oven, at 375° for 10 minutes. Serve with cottage fried potatoes.
* See under sauces.

TROUT BLANC

Brennan's
New Orleans, Louisiana

½ cup butter
2 tablespoons garlic, minced
1 cup raw shrimp, peeled
1 cup raw oysters
¾ cup cooked mushrooms, sliced
½ teaspoon Spanish saffron
2 cups whole canned tomatoes
1½ cups fish stock
1½ teaspoon salt

¼ teaspoon cayenne
2 tablespoons cornstarch
¼ cup water
Parsley
3 trout (2 pounds each) cleaned, boned (save heads, skin and bones for making stock)
2 cups seasoned mashed potatoes
12 whole small mushrooms
2 tablespoons butter
12 shrimp, peeled

In a 10-inch skillet, melt butter and sauté garlic, shrimp, oysters, mushrooms and saffron. Add tomatoes, fish stock, salt and cayenne. Simmer 15 to 20 minutes. Combine cornstarch and water, add to sauce to thicken. When desired consistency is obtained, remove pan from heat; add parsley. Keep warm.

Grill or broil trout and remove to warm serving platter. Place mashed potatoes in pastry bag, flute extreme edge of platter. Cover fish with sauce; garnish with whole mushrooms and shrimp sautéed in butter. Dust paprika on potatoes, then place under broiler until potatoes brown.

TROUT VERONIQUE

The Pontchartrain Hotel
New Orleans, Louisiana

6 filets of trout from 1½ pound trout
2 pints white wine
1½ cups heavy cream sauce

1½ cups very rich Hollandaise sauce
8 seedless grapes for each trout

Poach trout in white wine in pan that will cover trout, about 7 minutes. Remove from poaching liquor and drain well, then place on plate. Reduce liquid over fast fire to about ¾ cup of liquid. Add cream sauce and Hollandaise sauce and stir briskly. Place grapes on trout, then sauce and glaze quickly under the broiler.

FRESH TROUT STRASBOURGOUIESE

Hotel Tropicana
Las Vegas, Nevada

6 trout, cleaned	Cream, to barely cover
Cream for dipping	Salt, pepper to taste
Flour	¾ cup almonds, blanched
4 tablespoons butter	and sliced
1 cup brandy or cognac	

Dip trout in cream and then in flour. Heat a frying pan with butter and brown the fish quickly on both sides. Add brandy or cognac and it will flame for a few seconds. When the flame is out, add enough cream so that the trout is partly covered, and let it simmer slowly for a while.

In about five minutes the fish will be done. Put it on a serving platter and keep hot. In the meantime, reduce the sauce, season, and strain. Cover the trout with the sauce, sprinkle sliced almonds over the trout, and put under the broiler just long enough to give the almonds color. Serve hot.

TRUITES DE LAC FARCIES À LA CREME DE PORTO
(Stuffed Salmon Trout in Port Wine and Cream)

Four Seasons Restaurant
New York City

¾ filet of trout
½ pound filet of pike
¼ cup cold water
¼ pound butter
3 egg whites
1½ eggs
½ teaspoon salt
Pinch white pepper
Salmon trout—about
    3½ pounds
¾ cup celery, chopped
¾ cup onions, chopped

¾ cup carrots, chopped
⅓ pound butter, melted
¾ cup dry white
    Burgundy
¾ cup fish stock
    (see below)
1 tablespoon cornstarch
    mixed with a little
    water
2 cups heavy cream
5 ounces port wine
Salt and pepper to taste

Grind in food grinder or in blender the fish filets with cold water. Mix with soft butter (use wooden spoon or mixer). Blend slowly with 3 egg whites. Then blend in 1½ eggs and beat with wooden spoon until fluffy. Add salt, pepper; cover and chill mixture until firm.

Fill the salted cavity of a 3½ pound salmon trout, or substitute same size fresh salmon or trout (boned from back and fins removed) with the fish mixture. Tie string four or five times around body of fish to hold filling in cavity.

Cover bottom of roasting pan with chopped vegetables; place fish on vegetables. Baste with melted butter. Add Burgundy and fish stock. Bake uncovered at 400° 45 to 50 minutes, until fish is done. Remove fish to warm platter. Discard string.

Strain pan juices into saucepan; bring to boil. Add cornstarch which has been mixed with water. Stir in heavy cream, port wine, salt and pepper to taste. Serve sauce with slices of fish.

Fish Stock

Bones, heads and tails of
    fileted trout and pike
2 cups water
2 cups dry white wine
1 bay leaf
Pinch thyme

2 stalks parsley
¼ cup carrots, chopped
¼ cup onions, chopped
¼ cup celery, chopped
Salt, white pepper

Place all ingredients in saucepan, cover and simmer 30 minutes. Strain out fish bones, reserve stock for sauce.

STUFFED BAKED TROUT

The Harrison Hotel
Vancouver, B. C.

6 1½ pound trout,
    cleaned
6 tablespoons butter
Dash nutmeg, oregano,
    ground fennel, English
    mustard, curry
Juice of 1 lemon

¾ cup oil
3 cups shrimp, cleaned
3 hard cooked eggs,
    chopped
Salt and pepper to taste
Parsley and lemon
    slices for garnish

Make a spicebutter with the following spices: nutmeg, oregano, fennel, English mustard, curry and lemon juice. Stuff the cleaned fish with the spicebutter. Place fish in frying pan in which the oil has been heated in advance. Brown nicely on both sides. Cover and place in oven and bake at 350° for 15 minutes.

Remove and place fish in serving dish. Put the frying pan back on the stove and add the shrimp and chopped egg. Simmer for few minutes, then place the shrimp and egg garnish over the fish and decorate with lemon slices and parsley.

TROUT ALMONDINE

The San Marco Dining Room
The Brown Palace Hotel
Denver, Colorado

6 trout—8 to 10 ounces
    each—cleaned
Salt and pepper to taste
Flour

Oil about ¼ inch deep
    for frying
Butter
Egg batter—see recipe
    below

Dip trout, which has been boned and seasoned, in flour; then in egg batter. Fry in pan in mixture of oil and butter until golden brown on both sides. Serve with Almondine Sauce—recipe below.

Egg Batter

3 whole eggs, beaten
½ cup cream

Mix eggs and cream and beat well.

Almondine

½ cup blanched almonds,
    slivered

¼ cup butter
Juice of ¼ lemon

Melt butter, add almonds and stir until golden brown. Take off fire and add lemon juice. Pour sauce over trout.

TRUITE BRAISEE AU CHAMPAGNE

Place Vendome
Washington, D. C.

For 6 persons, 6 fresh
trout, 10 to 12
ounces each
½ pound sweet butter
3 tablespoons shallots,
chopped
3 cups champagne
3 cups fish stock (made
with fish bones, onion,
celery, parsley, leeks,
thyme, bay leaves,
whole black pepper,
white wine and
water)

1 cup fish veloute or
regular white sauce
1 cup Hollandaise sauce
6 mushrooms
Salt and pepper
12 slices truffle
12 fleurons—flaky pastry
shaped in small crescents

In a pan put 3 tablespoons butter and chopped shallots.
On top of this place the trout. Season with salt and pepper.
Add champagne and fish stock. Bring to a boil, then let
simmer slowly for 20 minutes, covered. Remove the trout
from pan, add the fish veloute, and reduce the cooking juice
to ⅓.

While sauce is cooking, peel the trout. Add to the sauce
the rest of the butter and Hollandaise sauce. Adjust seasoning.

To serve, place mushroom heads on the trout. Stir the
sauce through a sieve. On top of the trout place truffle slices
and fleurons for decorations.

TROUT ALMENDRA

Spanish Park Restaurant
Tampa, Florida

6 speckled trout—
1 pound each
6 large shrimp, cooked
and chopped very fine
½ pound cooked lobster
meat, chopped
very fine
1 large onion, chopped
very fine
¼ pound toasted almonds

1 cup milk
2 tablespoons butter
¼ cup flour
4 egg yolks
6 filets of anchovies
Cracker meal
4 eggs, beaten
¼ pound butter
½ cup sherry
Juice of 1 lime

Take filets from each trout, being careful to remove *all* bones and skin. Chop shrimp and lobster meat and onion as fine as possible. Wrap almonds in cloth and beat until broken in fine pieces. Boil milk. In a separate pan fry onion in butter until golden brown, then add chopped shrimp, lobster, and flour. Add boiling milk and stir until creamy; add egg yolks and keep stirring until mixture thickens. Divide this mixture into 6 parts, and add 1 anchovy filet to each part. Place mixture between 2 filets of trout. Roll in cracker meal, then in beaten eggs, and again in cracker meal. Place fish in pan and bake for 20 minutes at 350°, 10 minutes on each side. Melt ¼ pound butter in sherry, and add lime juice and crushed almonds. Keep hot and pour over fish when ready to serve.

POULTRY

BAKED CHICKEN WITH ROSEMARY

Old Adobe Patio Restaurant
Tucson, Arizona

2 2¼ pound broilers,
   quartered
Flour for dredging
Salt and pepper, to taste

Paprika
8 teaspoons butter
2 teaspoons rosemary

Dredge quarters with flour, salt and pepper. Lay the chicken skin side down in a roaster containing enough water to cover well the lower half of the quarters. Dust with paprika. On each quarter put one teaspoon butter. Sprinkle with rosemary.

Cover and bake in oven preheated to 325° for ½ hour. Uncover and turn quarters over and continue baking for another ½ or ¾ hour, or until done.

Very frequent basting (it's a bore, but rewarding) is mandatory during this last half hour to produce chicken rich in flavor, brown and beautiful to behold.

BAKED CHICKEN DANISH FASHION

Jul's Danish Farm
Rock Falls, Illinois

6 chicken halves
1½ teaspoons salt
1½ teaspoons pepper
1 teaspoon Alamo
   zestful seasoning
1 cup carrots, coarsely
   chopped
1 cup celery, coarsely
   chopped
6 small onions

¾ cup butter, melted
1 pint water
1½ cups chicken stock
   (from baked chicken)
1 pint half and half
   or light cream
6 tablespoons flour
¼ cup oil
¾ cup lingonberries

Mix salt, pepper and seasoning powder, and rub inside of chickens with mixture. Stuff chickens with vegetables. Sprinkle remaining seasoning over chickens. Pour melted butter over chickens. Place in roasting pan breast side down and add water. Bake in a moderate oven, 350°, 1 hour. Turn chicken over and bake at 425° for 30 minutes. Bring chicken stock and cream to a boil. Stir in roux of flour and oil to make a smooth sauce. Cook until thickened. Stir in lingonberries. Season if needed. Serve sauce over chicken halves.

WHOLE ROAST STUFFED SPRING CHICKEN ON PLANK

Arrowhead Lodge
Lake Ozark, Missouri

½ cup melted chicken fat or oil
1 cup celery, finely chopped
1 onion, finely chopped
2 cups white bread, diced
1 cup corn bread, diced
Chicken stock
Sage, to taste
2 teaspoons salt
1 teaspoon black pepper
3 eggs, well beaten
2 teaspoons sweet basil, coarsely chopped
1 4½ to 5 pound roasting chicken
Garnish: Fresh vegetables Tomatoes, peeled and quartered

Sauté celery and onion in chicken fat or salad oil until tender. Add chicken stock to diced breads to moisten. Add sautéed vegetables, sage, salt, black pepper, eggs; mix well. Stuff chicken. Season with salt, white pepper, sweet basil. Bake in oven at 325° for 1 hour. Serve on plank, with potatoes, mashed and put through pastry bag. Garnish with fresh vegetables and tomato.

OVEN BROILED CHICKEN WITH CRANBERRY FRITTERS

*The Holderness Inn
Holderness, New Hampshire*

Chicken

3 broilers, halved or
   quartered
Seasoning salt
½ cup flour

½ teaspoon poultry
   seasoning
Onion salt, to taste
Celery salt, to taste
¼ pound butter

Halve or quarter broilers, wash and dry. Dust with seasoning salt and shake in paper bag containing flour and remainder of seasoning ingredients. Place in roasting pan, dot with butter. Cover and cook at 375° until almost done. Uncover, baste and brown.

Cranberry Fritters

2 cups griddle cake batter
½ cup drained cranberry sauce

Fat, for frying

Combine griddle cake batter with cranberry sauce. Spoon into hot deep fat, 375°, and fry to golden brown.

Sauce

1 cup cranberry sauce
1 cup hot water

Dash lemon juice
Sugar to taste

Combine ingredients, stirring well. Add cornstarch to give a creamy base, if desired. Serve hot on fritters.

MENNONITE BAKED CHICKEN

Water Gate Inn
Washington, D. C.

2 2-pound frying chickens,
   disjointed
Salt and pepper to taste

6 tablespoons butter
2 cups sour cream
Milk
Chopped parsley

Disjoint chickens, season with salt and pepper and sauté pieces in butter until golden brown. Put pieces in baking pan, cover with sour cream thinned with some sweet milk. Bake until chicken is tender and has been thoroughly permeated with the sour cream-seasoned gravy. Whenever, during the cooking, the sour cream thickens too much, add some milk. Serve in flat casserole with sour cream gravy all around and sprinkled with chopped parsley.

PENN-DAW FRIED CHICKEN

Penn-Daw Restaurant
Alexandria, Virginia

3 2-pound chickens
Flour for dredging

Salt, pepper to taste
⅜ pound shortening

Mix salt and flour together and place chicken in mixture until covered lightly. Place in pan of shortening and fry for about 20 to 30 minutes, or until done. Pour off shortening and add a little water. Place over fire and steam for a minute or two. Chicken is ready to serve.

OVEN FRIED HALF SPRING CHICKEN PAPRIKA

Hotel Splendide
Empire, Colorado

3 2½-pound frying
   chickens, cut in half
6 ounces butter

Salt, pepper
Paprika

Put six pats butter in baking pan and place over it, skin side up, the chicken halves. Place in pre-heated oven, 475°, and cook for 30 minutes. Remove from oven, turn chickens, and cook about 15 more minutes. Salt and pepper chicken on both sides and return to original position in pan and cook 15 minutes longer. Sprinkle with paprika, remove to dinner plates, and serve.

Red currant jelly spooned into the cavity of a melba peach half makes a tasty and colorful decoration.

POULET À L'ESTRAGON

Le Valois Restaurant
New York City

3 2½-pound broilers
¼ pound butter
1 tablespoon fresh
    tarragon, chopped
3 tablespoons butter

3 tablespoons vegetable
    fat
Mirepoix: Carrots, celery,
    onion, finely diced
1½ cup chicken broth

Garnish

1 tablespoon fresh tarragon, chopped
1 ounce hazelnuts, roasted and grated
4 tablespoons butter, melted

Wash chickens and dry. Mix butter with fresh tarragon and rub the mixture heavily inside the chickens. Tie chickens with white twine and place them in roasting pan with butter and vegetable fat. Roast in a very hot oven (450°) about 25 minutes, to get them nice and brown. Sprinkle chickens with salt and mirepoix.

Return chicken to oven, lower heat, and simmer for about 10 minutes more. When chicken is done, drain butter from pan, add chicken broth and let reduce to ¾ cup.

Melt butter with grated hazelnuts. This is noisette butter. Put chickens on serving platter, strain the gravy on top, sprinkle with fresh chopped tarragon and cover with small amount of noisette butter.

HEN AND BEANS

*The Inn Unique
Hart's Location
New Hampshire*

1 5-pound chicken,
cut up
2 large cans
baked beans
Salt pork as desired
(3 inches square used
at The Inn Unique)
Sweetening (molasses or
brown sugar) as desired

2 stalks celery, or 1
teaspoon celery seed
1 large onion, chopped
fine
⅛ teaspoon pepper
2 teaspoons salt
1 teaspoon dry mustard

Cover bottom of large casserole with beans. Arrange cut up chicken over beans. Add more beans to cover chicken. Place the pork in small squares, add all other seasonings. Fill up dish with remaining beans. Cover and bake 1 hour in low oven or until chicken is done. Serve with corn muffins.

POULET DE GRAIN MASCOTTE ONDINE

*Ondine
Sausalito, California*

2 2½-pound broilers
or caponettes
¼ pound butter, melted
24 potato balls (size of
hazelnuts)
4 artichoke hearts

2 shallots, chopped
½ cup sauterne
2 cups brown sauce
1 large truffle, thinly sliced
Salt and pepper

To melted butter in a heavy casserole add the broilers, potato balls and sliced and parboiled artichoke hearts.

Sauté the chickens for a few minutes on each side, until they are uniformly golden. Remove the potatoes and artichoke hearts and keep warm. Cover the casserole and cook the chickens over low heat for 35 minutes or until done. Add more butter if necessary.

Remove chickens to a warm platter and pour the pan juices over them. Add chopped shallots and sauterne to casserole and cook the mixture over high heat for 5 minutes. Add brown sauce and simmer for 1 minute more. Strain the sauce over the potatoes and artichoke slices and reheat them. Add salt and pepper to taste and 1 large truffle, thinly sliced.

Cover the chicken immediately. Arrange a garnish of potatoes and artichoke heart slices around each serving and pour sauce over the vegetables.

CHICKEN À LA RALPH WALDO EMERSON

The Ralph Waldo Emerson
Rockport, Massachusetts

2 broiling chickens, quartered (about 3½ pounds weight)	2 stalks celery, chopped
	4 chicken bouillon cubes
	2 cups water
1 carrot, sliced	Flour, paprika, salt
1 onion, sliced	Salad oil

Dust chicken in mixture of flour, paprika and salt. Brown in heavy skillet half filled with salad oil. Put browned pieces in baking pan. Add carrot, onion and celery and sauté in oil in which chicken was fried. Dissolve bouillon cubes in water. Pour sautéed vegetables, oil and bouillon over chicken and bake in 325° oven for 90 minutes. Thicken stock with flour and water mixture and pour over chicken as served. Leftover pieces are even better when reheated in the gravy.

CHICKEN 21

Café Martin
Montreal, Quebec

Place a few sprigs of parsley and a bay leaf inside a 5 or 6 pound stewing chicken. Place bird in deep kettle and cover with boiling water. In addition to salt you may add onions, celery, carrots, bay leaves, thyme and parsley. Simmer chicken until tender. Remove chicken to hot platter. Strain broth through a fine sieve.

Make a Bechamel Sauce by melting 3 tablespoons butter in a saucepan over moderate heat without letting it brown. Add 3 tablespoons flour and stir until it is well blended. Whip in 1 egg yolk, then slowly add chicken broth, stirring constantly until thickened.

Remove meat (white meat preferably) from bones and cut into large pieces. Add meat to the sauce and let simmer for a while. Place in ovenproof casserole with cooked wild rice—chicken at one end and rice at the other end of the casserole. Sprinkle with Parmesan cheese and bake in 450° oven for 5 minutes.

CHICKEN MERINGUE

King's Inn
Highlands, North Carolina

1 4-pound fowl	4 eggs, well beaten
Water to cover	1 teaspoon salt
Salt, 4 or 5 peppercorns	½ teaspoon paprika
2 cups bread crumbs	1¼ pints chicken broth
1 cup cooked rice	Mushroom sauce (see recipe
¼ cup butter, melted	below)
¼ cup pimento	

Cook chicken in water with salt and peppercorns, until meat leaves the bones .Dice and mix with the above ingredients, in the order listed. Pour into a greased pan and bake 1¼ hours. If baked in ring, fill center with mushroom sauce when done. Cut in blocks and serve with mushroom sauce.

Mushroom Sauce

1 cup cream sauce
½ cup mushrooms, thinly sliced
2 tablespoons butter

To cream sauce add mushrooms cooked in butter and well drained. Before serving add 1 tablespoon butter.

FRIED CHICKEN À LA FLORENTINE

Tappan Hill
Tarrytown, New York

2 2½-pound chickens,   1½ or 2 ounces dry white
  each cut into 8 pieces   wine
1 medium onion, diced   Flour for dredging
1 large carrot, diced   2 eggs, well beaten
1 stalk celery, diced   Salt and pepper to taste
1 bay leaf   ¾ cup olive oil
Juice of lemon

Cut each chicken into eight pieces. Prepare a marinade with onion, carrot, celery, bay leaf, lemon juice, white wine. Place chicken pieces in marinade and keep in refrigerator for at least six hours. Remove chicken from marinade, drain well, dredge with flour and coat with beaten egg. Salt and pepper the pieces to taste. Fry in olive oil until brown and tender.

Serve immediately with fried zucchini, cut in 2-inch long and ½-inch thick sticks.

POULET SAUTE AUX MORILLES (Morels)

Rive Gauche
Washington, D. C.

3 2-pound chickens,   3 cups morels or other
  quartered   small mushrooms
Salt and pepper   1½ cups white wine
¾ cup butter   6 tablespoons butter

Season chicken pieces with salt and pepper and sauté in butter for 20 minutes, browning lightly on all sides. Add mushrooms, cover and simmer gently for 10 minutes longer. Remove chicken and mushrooms and keep hot. Add wine to pan, reduce slightly, add butter and stir to combine. Correct seasoning, add mushrooms and put sauce over the chicken. Serve very hot with Pommes de terre à la Parisienne (see recipe below).

Pommes de Terre à la Parisienne

5 large potatoes
2 tablespoons butter

With a round vegetable scooping spoon, scoop out pieces the size and shape of hazelnuts, from potatoes. Sauté potatoes in butter until golden all over. Season to taste.

CHICKEN WITH WHITE GRAPES

The Elms Inn
Ridgefield, Connecticut

2 2½-pound chickens, cut up
Flour for dredging
¼ pound butter
4 ounces sherry
2 tablespoons red currant jelly
1 cup brown sauce
White seedless grapes
Mandarin oranges
Grand Marnier

Bone and skin breast and leg of chicken, dip lightly in flour. Sauté in butter until light brown, drain butter from pan. Add sherry, cook slowly to reduce wine. Add red currant jelly and brown sauce, cook slowly until sauce is reduced to half. Remove chicken and place in ovenware dish, strain sauce over chicken, add white grapes and cook slowly for 5-8 minutes. Garnish chicken with Mandarin oranges and a few drops of Grand Marnier.

BONELESS CHICKEN FLORENTINE

Viking Hotel
Newport, Rhode Island

3 2½-pound broilers
4 eggs, beaten
Salt
Pepper
Flour
¼ pound Parmesan cheese, grated
⅜ pound butter
1 pint chicken stock
6 ounces white wine

Remove all bones from chicken except shoulder wing bones. Dip chicken in flour and egg batter and fry golden brown in butter. (Egg batter consists of eggs, salt, pepper, flour and 4 tablespoons Parmesan cheese). When chicken is brown, remove from pan and place in moderate oven to finish cooking.

For sauce, combine 2 ounces butter with 2 tablespoons flour to make a roux. Add hot chicken stock and wine. Reduce to heavy creamy consistency. Strain and mix in remainder of grated cheese. When serving, place sauce on platter with the chicken on top, and serve additional sauce on the side.

CHICKEN DIVAN

Divan Parisien Restaurant
New York City

1 4 to 5-pound chicken	1 cup Parmesan cheese, grated
Water to cover	
3 teaspoons salt	¾ cup Hollandaise sauce
½ cup melted butter	½ cup heavy cream, whipped
½ cup flour	
2 cups milk	1 teaspoon Worcestershire sauce
2 bunches broccoli	
Salt, to taste	1 jigger sherry

Place chicken in a large pot with enough water to cover. Add salt. Bring to a boil and simmer until tender. When chicken is cool, remove skin and slice. Prepare a sauce. To melted butter, slowly add flour, stirring constantly. Add milk, stirring until the sauce is thickened and smooth. Set aside and keep hot.

Chicken Divan

Boil broccoli in salted water until tender. Drain well. Cover a heat-proof serving platter with broccoli. Cover broccoli with layers of sliced chicken. Combine Hollandaise sauce with cream sauce. Add whipped cream, sherry, Worcestershire sauce. Cover broccoli and chicken slices with combined sauce. Sprinkle with Parmesan cheese. Place under broiler until cheese is well browned.

HALF BONED CHICKEN IN ALMOND CHILE SAUCE

*Hotel Arizpe-Sainz
Satillo, Mexico*

3 small fryers
Salt and pepper to taste

Split fryers in half. Cook in water to cover, until chicken is tender, for about 1 hour, adding salt and pepper to taste. When cooked add the following sauce:

Sauce

1 tablespoon Gebhart's chili powder or any similar powdered chile
6 cloves garlic
3 cloves
2 slices bread, toasted
2 squares sweet chocolate
¼ cup almonds, toasted
1 small bottle catsup
Salt and pepper to taste
½ cup oil
3 cups chicken broth

Put all ingredients, except oil and broth in blender and grind fine. Sauté mixture in oil, stirring constantly. Add chicken broth and heat. Cover the chicken with sauce. Decorate the dish with toasted tortillas.

POULET MICHELINE

*Robaire's French Cuisine
Los Angeles, California*

3-pound chicken
Water to cover
½ teaspoon salt
½ teaspoon pepper
½ bay leaf
Broth chicken was boiled in
4 tablespoons flour
6 tablespoons butter
½ pound fresh mushrooms, sliced
Salt, pepper to taste
2 cups cooked rice
½ pound ham, cooked and sliced
½ pound Swiss cheese, grated

Boil chicken with seasoning. Let it come to a full boil. Remove skin and bones after 10 minutes. Let broth boil for additional 5 minutes, then simmer. Add flour and 3 tablespoons butter until the soup thickens. Sauté mushrooms in 3 tablespoons butter for 10 minutes. Season with salt and pepper.

Cover bottom of a casserole with cooked rice. Place boned chicken on the rice. Add three quarters of the cream sauce, then add mushrooms. Cover this mixture with thin sliced ham and Swiss cheese. Cover with remaining cream sauce. Bake in 350° oven for 15 minutes, until brown.

CHICKEN À LA JOHNNIES

Johnnie's Italian Cuisine
New York City

1, 3 to 3½-pound chicken, cut into pieces
6 potatoes, peeled and cut into thin slices
2 onions, peeled and cut into thin slices
Butter

½ cup Sauterne
Juice of ½ lemon
Salt, pepper, oregano to taste
Parmesan cheese
Olive oil
2 very ripe tomatoes

Wash chicken in salted water. Dry with cloth. Butter pan. Place chicken in center, surround with sliced potatoes and onions. Pour Sauterne and lemon juice over all. Add salt, pepper, oregano, Parmesan cheese, and sprinkle with olive oil. Squeeze very ripe tomatoes over all and bake in 350° oven until chicken is tender.

CHICKEN COVEY

Covey's Weatherpane Restaurant
Seagoville, Texas

2 frying chickens, cut into
  serving pieces
6 potatoes, peeled and
  sliced
2 onions, peeled and sliced
Butter
1 cup dry white wine

Juice of 1 lemon
Salt and pepper, to taste
Pinch oregano
Parmesan, grated
2 fresh tomatoes
Olive oil

Wash chicken in salt water. Dry with cloth. Butter pan. Put chicken in center, surround with sliced potatoes and onions. Pour over dry white wine and lemon juice. Add salt, pepper and oregano. Sprinkle with Parmesan cheese and with olive oil. Squeeze fresh tomatoes over all. Bake in moderate oven (350°) until chickens are tender.

PANNED CHICKEN

The Dinner Bell Inn
Dover, Delaware

3 2-pound chickens, split
  in half
Salt, white pepper, paprika

¼ pound butter
Water

Place chicken in a 2-inch deep pan, bone down. Sprinkle with salt, white pepper and paprika. Cut butter in pats and place on top. Cover three-quarters with water. Cover loosely with a cookie sheet. Bake in 400° oven for 1 hour and 15 minutes. Chicken should be very tender. Remove cookie sheet last 15 minutes to brown

CHICKEN SAUTÉ SEC

Villa Venice
Tulsa, Oklahoma

1 3½-pound frying
chicken, cut in pieces
Salt and pepper to taste
4 tablespoons oil
4 scallions
2 tablespoons parsley,
chopped

2 twigs rosemary
1 cup mushrooms, sliced
½ teaspoon garlic, minced
1 cup chicken broth or beef
bouillon
½ cup sherry wine

Heat oil in a large heavy skillet. Season the chicken pieces with salt and pepper and add to oil; sauté until they are golden brown. Cook thoroughly. Add scallions, parsley, rosemary and mushrooms. When the ingredients are soft but not brown, add minced garlic. Cook for ½ minute and pour chicken broth or beef bouillon over the chicken. Simmer 5 minutes. Then add sherry. When the liquid is evaporated, serve piping hot.

CHICKEN PORTOLLA

The Lord Simcoe Hotel
Toronto, Ontario

1 large chicken or fowl
(about 4 pounds)
2½ teaspoons salt
½ pound butter
6 coconuts, cut in half
Coconut meat
3 green pimentos, diced
1 medium onion, chopped
fine

3 cups sliced mushrooms
1 cup red pimento, diced
3 cups kernel corn, cooked
1 cup sherry
1 cup white wine
4 cups curry sauce
1 cup cream

Boil chicken in salted water. When cooked, remove skin and dice the meat of the chicken in ½ inch cubes.

Place ¼ pound butter in a large skillet or thick bottomed frying pan. When hot put in diced coconut meat, green pimento, the onions and the sliced mushrooms. Stir them for

2 minutes, then put in the chicken and let cook slowly for 5 to 6 minutes; then add the red pimento and kernel corn. Mix everything together with a wooden spoon, then pour in sherry and white wine, curry sauce and finish with cream. Let simmer for 10 minutes. Add salt, pepper to taste, and a drop of lemon juice.

While the chicken is cooking, prepare one coconut shell for each person to be used as a serving dish, sawing off the bottom so that it will stand on the table, and saw off enough from the top to make a cover.

When the chicken has finished cooking, pour into the coconuts, which have been warmed, put the cover on the top, and seal with a paste made with flour and water or any leftover dough. Place in oven at 350° for 15 minutes. Serve.

CHICKEN PORTOLLA CURRY SAUCE (about 4 cups)

2 medium onions, chopped
2 cloves garlic, chopped
2 tart apples, diced
1 stalk celery, chopped
½ cup butter
1 cup flour
1 pound fresh tomatoes
2 tablespoons tomato purée
⅛ teaspoon each mixed
   spice, cinnamon, ginger,
   thyme

1 bay leaf
½ cup raisins
½ cup almonds, chopped
1½ tablespoons curry
   powder
1½ tablespoons chutney
Salt, pepper, lemon juice
Cream, to taste

Take the first 4 ingredients and place in a saucepan with butter. Cook over low heat, stirring occasionally, until soft. Add flour and let it become slightly brown.

Add the remaining ingredients, mix together and let cook for 5 minutes on a very slow fire with the pan covered. After 5 minutes, moisten with water until the sauce is beginning to thicken, but not too much, and let it simmer for another 30 minutes.

When cooked, drain the sauce into another saucepan and finish with cream and lemon juice if you find the sauce too sharp.

CHICKEN PONTALBA

Brennan's French Restaurant
New Orleans, Louisiana

2 2½-pound broilers,
boned and cut into
pieces
¼ pound butter
1 cup onions, sliced

1 cup deep fried potatoes,
diced
Salt and pepper, to taste
¾ pound mushrooms,
sliced
Dry white wine, to moisten

Broil 12 chicken pieces in butter. Set aside and prepare onion, potato, mushroom mixture. Lay pieces of chicken on base and top with Bearnaise Sauce. Heat and serve.

Sauté onions in butter, add deep fried potatoes. Season to taste. Add mushrooms and sauté for 5 minutes. Add dry white wine to moisten mixture.

CHICKEN AND DUMPLINGS À LA LAURETTA

The Ropewalk
Nantucket, Massachusetts

1 4-5 pound roasting
chicken
1 Spanish onion, chopped
2 celery stalks, chopped

½ teaspoon salt
½ teaspoon pepper
½ teaspoon poultry
seasoning

Boil chicken and remaining ingredients together for 1¼ hours, or until tender.

Dumplings

2 cups flour
4 teaspoons baking
powder
½ teaspoon salt

1¼ cups milk
2 tablespoons parsley,
chopped

Mix ingredients to form soft dough. Drop with tablespoon into cooked chicken broth. Cook uncovered for 20 minutes.

CHICKEN KAMEHAMEHA IV

Kahala Hilton Hotel
Honolulu, Hawaii

3 2½-pound chickens,
  cooked and diced
¾ pound butter
2 ounces sherry
¾ cup heavy cream
1½ cups chicken sauce
Salt, pepper to taste

Juice of ½ lemon
3 tablespoons Hollandaise
  sauce
½ cup whipped cream
3 pineapples, cut in half
  lengthwise and partly
  scooped out

Sauté cooked chicken lightly in butter. Add sherry and reduce to half. Add heavy cream and reduce to a thick cream. Fill pan with chicken sauce. Season to taste. Squeeze lemon juice into the sauce. Before serving, blend with Hollandaise sauce and whipped cream. Place in pineapple shells and put under broiler for a few minutes. Serve pilaff rice on the side.

BLUEBERRY HILL CHICKEN WITH CAPERS

Blueberry Hill Farm
Brandon, Vermont

3 2½-pound broilers
2 cloves garlic, minced
Salt, pepper

½ pound butter
2 tablespoons capers

Split 3 broilers with backbone removed all the way down to the neck. Salt and pepper well and add a little minced garlic. Lay on pans, skin side down, and dot the cavity with butter. Broil under very high heat for 10 minutes, turn and broil another 10 minutes, skin side up. Remove chickens to a hot platter, after first cutting them with a poultry shears into serving size pieces.

Keep chicken pieces in a warm place and add 2 tablespoons butter to the butter in the broiling pan, scrape it all around, getting up the brown bits; add capers, and pour brine of capers into the butter sauce. Pour the caper sauce over the chicken.

BONELESS CHICKEN SAUTÉ ANDALUZA

La Zaragozana
San Juan, Puerto Rico

3 2½-pound chickens,
  boned and halved
3 cloves garlic, peeled
Parsley, chopped
½ cup orange juice
1 cup flour for dredging
½ cup Spanish oil
¼ pound butter

½ cup Spanish manzanilla
  (dry Sherry wine)
4 tablespoons raisins
4 tablespoons almonds,
  sliced
3 ounces small Spanish
  olives
Salt to taste

Cut the chickens in half and take all the bones out. Be sure to put the raisins in the manzanilla at least two hours before cooking in order that they will be very soft.

Crush garlic, parsley and orange juice in a mortar. Soak chickens in mixture. Dry chickens, then dredge in flour. Fry them in Spanish oil until brown on both sides. Remove oil from pan; add butter and Spanish manzanilla. Heat it until a glaze forms. Add raisins, almonds, olives and the chickens. Fry everything on a low fire for 15 minutes until it is ready to serve. Serve with Spanish fried potatoes.

CHICKEN GOURMET

Doc's Airpark Restaurant
Quincy, Illinois

3 2-pound chickens
1 cup wild rice
½ cup almonds,
  blanched and slivered
1 tablespoon butter
18 chicken livers
  (precooked or raw, as
  desired) diced

1 small can mushrooms,
  diced
3 onions finely chopped
2 tablespoons butter
Salt, pepper
Thyme

Remove all bones except drumsticks and tips of wing bones from chickens, without breaking skin. Fill with a stuffing made as follows:

Prepare wild rice by placing in boiling water for 20 minute periods until done (total one hour). Do not boil rice, just place in boiling water. Set rice aside. Sauté slivered almonds in 1 tablespoon butter and set aside. Sauté onions in 2 tablespoons butter and season with salt, pepper and a little thyme. Add almonds, chicken livers, mushrooms and onions to wild rice and stuff cavities of chickens until they are their original shape (before de-boning). Fry in deep fat for 26 minutes at 325°. Each chicken will serve 2 people.

CHICKEN SAUTÉ, LIVERMORE

San Francisco Commercial Club
San Francisco, California

2 fryers, cut into pieces, 2¼ pounds each	1 cup tomatoes, peeled, seeded and diced
Salt, white pepper, monosodium glutamate	1 cup California Riesling or other white wine
½ cup oil	¾ cup brown chicken sauce
½ tablespoon shallots, finely chopped	4 tablespoons butter
2 cups mushroom caps, quartered	¾ cup seedless grapes

Season chicken pieces with salt, pepper and monosodium glutamate. Sauté in shallow pan in hot oil until golden brown. Pour off excess fat and add shallots, mushrooms and tomatoes; cook until liquid from mushrooms and tomatoes is reduced. Add wine and cook slowly until chicken is done and wine is reduced; add chicken sauce, bring to a boil, check for seasoning and serve in the center of an unmolded Polenta ring. Top with seedless grapes sautéed in butter, or serve on plate with individual molds.

POLENTA (yellow cornmeal mush)

1 pint water	1 cup yellow cornmeal, coarse
1 teaspoon salt	
¼ pound butter	

Bring water, salt and butter to a boil, pour in cornmeal while stirring with a wooden spoon; cook for 2 minutes and let stand covered on low heat for 10 minutes before molding.

CHICKEN SAUTÉ AU MIEL

*The Royal Orleans Hotel
New Orleans, Louisiana*

2 2½-pound chickens
½ cup oil
1 onion, finely chopped
8 large mushrooms, sliced
½ pound pork brisket, diced

4 large tomatoes, peeled and chopped
3 green peppers, seeded and quartered
6 tablespoons golden honey
White wine
2 cups demi-glace

Cut chickens into serving pieces. Sauté the pieces in a casserole in oil with onion, mushrooms and pork brisket.

Sauté tomatoes and peppers in oil. Remove the garnishes from the casserole. Add golden honey and deglace with white wine and fond de veau lie (demi-glace). Put the tomatoes in a covered terrine. Put the chicken with garnishes in, next the green peppers and the sauce on top. Cover and cook in an oven from 25 to 30 minutes at 350° F. Serve with rice pilaf à la menthe.

CHICKEN AMANDINE—POLLO ALMENDRADO

*Acapulco Hilton
Acapulco, Mexico*

3 chickens, 1½ to 2 pounds each
Salt, pepper to taste
Flour, for dredging
½ cup vegetable oil
¼ cup cognac, warmed
1 cup white wine

1 pint sweet cream
1 pint brown sauce
6 tablespoons butter
Juice of ½ lime
Almonds, toasted and blanched

Cut chickens into halves. Season with salt and pepper. Dip chicken halves into flour. Place a saucepan over fire and heat vegetable oil. Fry floured chickens until golden brown, then flame them with cognac, and then add white wine.

Add 1 pint sweet cream and 1 pint demi-glace (brown sauce). When chickens are cooked, take out of saucepan and add butter and lime juice to sauce. Pour sauce over chickens. Garnish with toasted almonds. Serve hot with any green vegetable and potato croquettes.

POULET RICHELIEU

Le Chateau Richelieu
New York City

3 small chickens	1 can truffles
1½ pounds cooked noodles	12 chestnuts
3 tablespoons butter	¾ pound chicken
1½ cups champagne	livers

Note: poele is a kitchen utensil used for frying food.

Stuff pullets with cooked noodles which have been lightly tossed in butter, and *poele* (sauté) them.

Swirl champagne into the pan. Surround the pullet with medium-sized truffles, cooked in champagne. Alternate these with little heaps of cooked and glazed chestnuts, and place a few chicken livers between each heap.

Serve separately a brown sauce flavored with truffle essence and combined with the reduced champagne-liquor.

CHICKEN CYNTHIA À LA CHAMPAGNE

Ernie's Restaurant
San Francisco,
California

2 chickens (approximately 2½ pounds each)	1½ cups consommé or bouillon
Salt and flour for dredging	1½ cups sliced mushrooms
2 tablespoons butter	2 tablespoons butter
2 tablespoons oil	¾ cup heavy cream
1 jigger Curaçao	Orange wedges
6 ounces dry champagne	Seedless grapes, skinned

Disjoint chickens. Set wings and legs aside and bone remaining parts. Salt and flour chicken. Sauté chicken parts in butter and oil for 10 minutes on each side. Remove from frying pan and continue browning in moderate oven (350°) for 20 minutes. Remove from oven and pour on Curaçao and champagne. Then cover with bouillon or consommé and let chicken simmer on top of stove until tender, approximately 20 minutes. Sauté mushrooms in butter, add mushrooms and cream to chicken. Serve in chafing dish. Decorate with orange wedges and skinless grapes.

WHOLE BONELESS CHICKEN, AU CHAMPAGNE, WILD RICE

Junco's Stone Ends Restaurant
Glenmont, New York

6 whole small boneless chickens	3 jiggers sherry
4 cups wild rice	½ cup butter, melted
6 large orange slices	2 cups champagne (use more for stronger flavor)
Juice of 2 lemons	Rosemary leaves

Stuff the cavity of the boneless chickens with cooked wild rice and place in roasting pan. Place an orange slice on each and pour lemon juice, sherry, melted butter and champagne over top. Sprinkle breasts with rosemary leaves. Bake in moderate oven (350°) for 35 to 40 minutes. Brown top under broiler if necessary.

CHICKEN CHAMPAGNE "POUCETTE"

Fleur de Lys
San Francisco, California

1 roasting chicken, 3½ pounds, cut in serving pieces	⅜ cup cognac, warmed
Salt, pepper	⅜ cup tomato, purée
½ pound butter	One fifth champagne, brut
4 shallots, finely chopped	½ pint heavy cream
	½ teaspoon nutmeg

Season chicken with salt and pepper. Sauté shallots with butter to a golden color. Add chicken and sauté till golden brown. Flame with cognac. Add tomato purée and champagne. Cover and cook rapidly for 20 to 25 minutes.

Place chicken parts on platter. Strain sauce, add cream and nutmeg to sauce, heat and stir 2 to 3 minutes. Pour sauce over chicken.

COQ AU VIN

Chateaubriand
New York City

½ cup fat salt pork
  or bacon, diced
2 tablespoons butter
2 to 3½ pound chicken,
  cut into 8 pieces
1 teaspoon salt
Dash of pepper
12 small white onions
12 small mushrooms
2 tablespoons flour
2 or 3 shallots (small
  sweet onions)

1 clove garlic, crushed
2 cups red wine
  (Burgundy)
1 bunch herbs (3-4 sprigs
  parsley, 1-2 stalks
  celery, 1 leek, 1 bay
  leaf, few sprigs
  fresh or dried thyme,
  tied in a bunch)
Parsley, chopped

Parboil pork or bacon for 5 minutes. Drain. Melt butter in saucepan. Add pork or bacon and cook until golden brown. Remove from fat and set aside. Wash chicken, season with salt and pepper. Sauté in fat in saucepan until golden brown on all sides. Add onions and mushrooms. Cover and cook over low heat until onions are slightly tender and lightly browned.

Pour off half of the fat, place in small pan, and blend in flour. Add shallots and garlic. Cook over low heat, stirring constantly, until well blended and thickened. Remove from heat. Gradually stir in wine. Add bunch of herbs. Bring to a boil, stirring occasionally. Add pork. Pour over chicken in pan. Cover and simmer over moderate heat 35 to 40 minutes, or until chicken is tender.

Skim fat from gravy in pan. Remove herbs. Add additional salt and pepper to taste.

Arrange chicken, mushrooms, onions and pork on hot platter. Cover with sauce. Sprinkle with chopped parsley.

COQ AU VIN MARNAZIENNE

The Penrose Room
The Broadmoor
Colorado Springs, Colorado

3 2½-pound chickens
1 quart white wine
1 medium onion, chopped
3 celery stalks, chopped
1 carrot, chopped
1 cup flour
1 quart red wine
1 quart chicken broth
¼ teaspoon thyme leaves
2 bay leaves
½ teaspoon crushed white pepper
1 bouquet garni
Salt, pepper
Dash nutmeg
Flour for dredging
½ pound butter
1½ pounds fresh mushrooms
24 small baby onions

Remove breast and legs from carcass (cut legs in two, leave breast in one piece). Place in crock, cover with white wine and soak overnight. Then cut up the carcass and roast the bones until golden brown.

Add onion, celery and carrot and continue roasting until vegetables are golden brown. Add flour, mix well with vegetables and bones and roast for 10 minutes. Add red wine and chicken broth; mix until smooth and add thyme, bay leaves, crushed pepper, bouquet garni; bring to boil, cover and simmer for 2 hours. Add more liquid if needed during cooking. Strain through cheese cloth and save for next day.

About 1½ hours before serving, remove chicken pieces from crock and save the white wine; season with salt, pepper and dash of nutmeg. Roll chicken in flour and sauté in clarified butter until golden brown. Remove chicken and deglace pan with white wine in which chicken was soaked. Add sauce that was prepared day before; bring to boil and add chicken; cover and cook for 35 minutes in 350° oven. When chicken is done place in cocotte; strain the sauce, reduce it and pour over chicken.

Garnish top with mushrooms, glazed onions and bacon slab which has been cut into small sticks, all sautéed together. Serve with rice pilaf or creamed whipped potatoes.

COQ AU VIN DE BOURGOGNE

Restaurant Laurent
New York City

2 frying chickens, cut in serving pieces	5 tablespoons butter
¼ pound butter	18 small onions
Salt, pepper to taste	6 slices salt pork, diced
4 ounces cognac	12 mushroom caps
Bouquet garni	Bread
Red Burgundy	

In a large skillet or Dutch oven, heat butter and brown chicken until pieces are brown on all sides. Sprinkle the chicken with salt and pepper, pour warm cognac over chicken, and set the cognac aflame. When the flame burns out, add a bouquet garni and enough red Burgundy to just cover the chicken. Cover the skillet and simmer the chicken gently for about 40 minutes or until tender.

In 3 tablespoons butter, sauté onions and salt pork until onions are brown. Cover and cook until the onions are tender. Add mushroom caps and continue to cook until the mushrooms are tender. Arrange onions, mushrooms and salt pork on a warm serving platter. Place the chicken on top and strain sauce over chicken.

Serve with triangles of bread sautéed in 2 tablespoons butter.

COQ AU VIN À LA GENEVOISE

Swiss Chalet
San Juan, Puerto Rico

1 5-pound chicken, disjointed	1 bay leaf
1 cup cooking oil	Sprinkle of rosemary
Salt and pepper	½ cup tomato purée
Flour	3 cups red wine
2 onions, diced	1 cup chicken stock
1 clove garlic, chopped	½ pound mushrooms
	12 to 18 pearl onions

Fry disjointed chicken, which has been seasoned with salt and pepper and dusted with flour, in hot oil until brown. Add onions, garlic, bay leaf and rosemary, tomato purée and sprinkle with flour. Add wine and chicken stock, mix well and cook on low flame, covered, for about 20 minutes. Remove chicken, strain sauce and add some sautéed mushrooms and pearl onions to the sauce. Serve in casserole, very hot, with buttered rice.

CHICKEN IN RED WINE

Chateau Laurier Hotel
Ottawa, Ontario

1 3-pound frying chicken, disjointed	12 small mushroom caps
4 tablespoons flour	2 cups red wine
4 tablespoons butter	2 ounces cognac
1 bouquet garni (thyme, celery tops, bay leaf, garlic, all tied in cheese cloth)	Salt and pepper to taste
	12 triangular shaped pieces of white bread
12 small shallots or pickling onions	2 tablespoons garlic flavored butter (melted butter flavored with a little sliced garlic)
½ cup diced cooked salt pork or bacon	

Dredge chicken pieces in flour and sauté in butter until well browned on all sides. Sprinkle with salt and pepper and turn gently. Pour cognac over and ignite. When flame has subsided, add bouquet garni and red wine. Cover and cook until tender.

In a separate saucepan, sauté the onions with the salt pork until onions are golden and transparent. Add the mushroom caps and continue cooking until the mushrooms are tender. Place onions, mushrooms and salt pork on the bottom of serving dish. On top of this place the chicken pieces. Strain the sauce over the chicken and serve with triangular shaped croutons, sautéed in garlic flavored butter.

CHICKEN IN WINE

Chez Bruchez
Daytona Beach, Florida

2 3-pound chickens
¼ pound butter, melted
Salt and pepper
Oregano

1 cup dry white wine
2 shallots, peeled and
   crushed

Rub chickens well with butter and roast. Salt and pepper. Add a little oregano inside each bird. In a saucepan, cook the white wine with crushed shallots until it is reduced to one-third. Add some of the chicken juice. Pour over chicken.

Serve with tiny canned French peas whipped in creamed potatoes.

French Peas

1 can tiny green peas
Lettuce leaves, shredded

1 medium onion,
   finely sliced

Cook juice from canned peas with lettuce and onions. Add to peas.

BREAST OF CAPONETTE SOUFFLE

The Occidental Restaurant
Washington, D. C.

3 2½-pound chickens,
  boned (except the
  wings)
1½ teaspoon salt
1 pinch pepper
1 pinch mace
3 ounces sherry
1½ pint heavy cream
Flour
Eggwash—2 eggs whipped
  with 1 tablespoon
  salad oil

White breadcrumbs
English mustard
 4 to 5 ounces
  clarified butter
6 slices Smithfield ham
5 shallots, chopped
2 small truffles, chopped
8 ounces white wine (dry)
1½ pints chicken stock
2 cups heavy cream

Grind all dark meat very fine through meat-grinder twice, using the finest blade. Keep it very cool by placing it in bowl, on shaved ice. Mix in salt, pepper, mace, sherry and cream. Stir until fluffy.

Flatten breasts with cleaver. Place dark meat mixture in center and roll or cover with the overlapping parts of the breast. Dust with flour, dip in eggwash and roll in white breadcrumbs seasoned with a little English mustard.

Sauté breasts in clarified butter on all sides until golden brown. Then place them in oven for about 45 minutes at moderate heat (375°). Place breasts on Smithfield ham slices.

Sauté chopped shallots and truffles in left-over butter, just a little. Add a little flour to absorb butter, add white wine and chicken stock. Reduce to one-half and add heavy cream. Season sauce to taste and pour over breasts.

BREAST OF CHICKEN "ALMENDRADA"
(Almond Sauce)

Ambassador Restaurant
Mexico City

6 whole chicken breasts,
  boned
Salt and pepper
½ cup butter
1 large onion, chopped
1 carrot, cut into pieces
1 tomato, cut into pieces

Paprika, to taste
¼ cup dry white wine
½ cup almonds
  blanched
1 tablespoon butter
1 cup heavy cream

Bone and skin large chicken breasts. Season to taste. Spread with butter and bake them for half an hour with onions and carrots. Add tomato and paprika. Add white wine and bake until chicken breasts are tender. Brown almonds in butter, stir in the cream, heat but do not boil, and pour the sauce over the chicken. Add some chilis "gueros."

BREAST OF CHICKEN, VALDOSTANA

Louis & Armand Restaurant
New York City

3 whole chicken breasts,
  boned and halved
3 slices Prosciutto ham,
  cut in julienne
6 narrow slices mozzerella
  cheese (thickness of a
  half dollar)
3 ounces white truffles,
  sliced

Flour for dredging
2 eggs, beaten
White bread crumbs
  (no crust)
Parmesan cheese, grated
4 tablespoons butter
Marsala or white wine,
  optional

Bone the chicken breasts. Remove the skin and pound the breasts as thin as possible. Cut the Proscuitto ham in julienne. Place ham in center of breasts; place mozzerella over ham. Place sliced truffles over the cheese. Take each breast and fold toward center, then take bottom and fold toward center. Press lightly together to form cushion effect. Roll in flour, then dip in beaten egg. Dip in bread mixture (consisting of 3 parts bread crumbs and 1 part grated Parmesan). Sauté in butter using a heavy skillet. Cook slowly on each side until brown (always over a slow fire). Remove chicken from skillet. If desired, a dash of Marsala or white wine can be added to gravy and poured over the whole.

SUPRÊME OF CHICKEN CARDINAL MERCIER

The Music Center
Los Angeles, California

6 chicken breasts, boneless
½ cup clarified butter
½ cup chicken fat
Lemon juice
4 shallots, peeled and chopped
1 small clove garlic
2 tablespoons butter
Paprika, to taste
Sauterne
¼ cup heavy cream
Truffle slices
12 walnut halves

Make a good risotto (rice) sauce, lightly colored with paprika, and keep ready. Sauté boneless chicken breasts without browning in clarified butter and chicken fat, with a little lemon juice added to keep chicken white. Set the breasts aside in warm place, covered with wax paper. Sauté shallots and garlic in butter, but keep white, and add a little paprika. Deglaze with lemon juice and Sauterne and heavy cream and let reduce. On a large platter, dress each Suprême on a mound of risotto, 1½ inches apart. Strain the sauce over the Suprêmes and top each with a slice of truffle and two sautéed walnut halves. Serve with asparagus tips.

BREAST OF CHICKEN À LA DOMINO

Club Domino
San Francisco, California

12 chicken breasts, boned
Salt and pepper to taste
12 small slices Virginia ham
12 small slices
　Gruyere cheese
Flour for dredging
　1 cup butter
　2 tablespoons shallots,
　　finely chopped
　1 pound mushrooms,
　　thinly sliced

½ cup dry white wine
　2 large fresh tomatoes,
　　peeled and chopped
1 cup heavy cream,
　or half and half
Chives, chopped fine,
　to taste
Parsley or watercress
　to garnish
Parmesan cheese, grated

Pound chicken breasts as thin as possible between sheets of wax paper. Sprinkle with salt and pepper. Put a slice of Virginia ham and Gruyere cheese on each chicken breast. Cover and dredge with flour.

Sauté shallots and mushrooms in butter. Add chicken breasts and cook each side for six minutes. Then add wine and tomatoes. Add cream and chopped fresh chives. Season to taste.

Place chicken in casserole, blend sauce well, and bake in 375° oven until chicken is tender. Serve with saffron rice. Top with grated Parmesan cheese.

BREAST OF CHICKEN WITH GNOCCHI MONTPENSIER

Hotel Tropicana
Las Vegas, Nevada

3 whole chicken breasts
¾ cup bread crumbs
Salt, pepper to taste
　4 tablespoons butter

Sauce Italienne (see
　recipe below)
Gnocchi (see recipe below)

Bread chicken breasts, season with salt and pepper and sauté in butter until brown on both sides. Serve with Sauce Italienne and Gnocchi.

Sauce Italienne

1 cup dry wine
1 cup mushrooms, finely chopped
4 tablespoons onions, chopped
4 tablespoons ham, chopped
2 cloves garlic, finely chopped
2 cups brown sauce
½ cup tomato purée
2 tablespoons parsley, chopped
Salt, pepper to taste

Add mushrooms, onions, chopped ham and garlic to wine. Add brown sauce, tomato purée and let simmer for about 15 minutes. Add parsley at the last moment and season to taste.

Gnocchi

2 pounds Idaho potatoes (dry, meal type must be used)
½ teaspoon salt
Water
3 egg yolks
¾ cup flour
½ cup butter, melted
Salt, pepper to taste
Nutmeg, optional
Melted butter, for topping
½ cup or more Parmesan cheese, grated

Boil potatoes in salt water, drain and dry in oven. Rice the potatoes while still hot; add egg yolks, flour, melted butter, salt, pepper and a pinch of nutmeg. Cut this mixture in pieces, roll them out in small balls and flatten against the back of a fork.

Cook in boiling water 5 to 10 minutes. Do not cook too many at a time. Drain. Place in dish with melted butter and sprinkle with Parmesan cheese.

CHICKEN PAGAN

Camillo Restaurant
New York City

3 chicken breasts, boned
6 slices Procesiotto
  (Italian ham)
6 bay leaves
6 teaspoons chicken liver,
  chopped
6 to 8 tablespoons
  Parmesan cheese,
  grated

¼ pound butter
Flour for dredging
Juice of 1 lemon
1½ cups Chablis
½ pound mushrooms,
  sliced

Flatten chicken breasts and place one slice of Procesiotto on each portion, a bay leaf and spread one teaspoon chicken liver on ham. Sprinkle with grated Parmesan cheese and roll tight.

Place butter in saucepan. Dip rolled chicken in flour and sauté in saucepan until golden brown. Take out and place in oven and bake, at 350°, 35 to 45 minutes. In the same pan, add more butter, lemon juice and Chablis, and mushrooms. Simmer for 15 minutes. When chicken is done, pour mushroom sauce over chicken breasts, and serve hot.

CHICKEN À LA KIEV

Seven Continents Restaurant
O'Hare Field
Chicago, Illinois

Champagne Sauce

4 ounces butter
3 ounces flour
1½ quarts chicken stock
1 cup cream

1 cup California
  champagne
Salt, pepper

Prepare roux of melted butter and flour. Blend over medium flame for approximately 1 minute. Add chicken stock; boil for 30 minutes, stirring occasionally. Remove from fire—add cream and champagne. Season with salt and pepper to taste. Strain before serving.

Chicken Breasts—Step 1

2 ounces butter
1 shallot, chopped fine
½ cup mushrooms,
    chopped fine
1 pound butter

½ pound French bread
    crumbs
1 tablespoon parsley,
    chopped
Salt and pepper to taste
½ cup brandy

Sauté mushrooms and shallots in butter and let cool. Cream the pound of butter in electric mixer and add mushroom/shallot mixture. Add bread crumbs, parsley, salt, pepper and brandy. Refrigerate the mixture until gently firm but not brittle.

Chicken Breasts—Step 2

Boneless breasts of 3 chickens (3 to 3⅓ pounds)

Leave skin on chicken and flatten breasts (meat side up) by pounding with mallet.

Chicken Breasts—Step 3

Flour for dredging
2 eggs, slightly beaten
1 pound French bread crumbs

Lay chicken, flat, skin side down, and fill with refrigerated butter mixture. Roll up tightly. Be sure to keep butter mixture inside the rolled up chicken. Dredge pieces in flour, dip in egg, then roll in French bread crumbs.

Chicken Breasts—Step 4

Deep fat for frying

Fry chicken in deep fat, at 375° until golden brown (about 5 minutes). Place in shallow baking dish or roasting pan, uncovered, and finish in 400° oven, approximately 10 to 12 minutes. Serve with Champagne Sauce.

BREAST OF CHICKEN, CHAMPAGNE

Mediterrania Restaurant
Beverly Hills, California

6 chicken breasts (from 2½ pound chickens)
1 pound fresh mushrooms, sliced
12 shallots, finely chopped
Salt and M.S.G.

1 pint heavy cream
1 pint champagne
2 ounces butter
1 teaspoon cornstarch, with 1 teaspoon water

Butter the bottom of a cooking utensil. Sprinkle shallots over the surface. Place chicken breasts side by side and cover with mushrooms. Season with salt and M.S.G., douse with champagne. Cover and cook until chicken is done (approximately 15 minutes). Remove the chicken breasts and reduce liquid to one half. Add cream, bring to boil, and thicken with cornstarch. Ladle sauce over chicken.

BREAST OF CHICKEN À LA MARSALA

Piety Corner Gardens Restaurant
Waltham, Massachusetts

3 chicken breasts
½ cup olive oil
⅓ cup water
1 teaspoon salt

Pepper to taste
½ cup Marsala wine
1 cup mushrooms, sliced
Parsley, chopped

Cut chicken breasts in half. Pat dry. Sauté in olive oil until brown, then drain off all oil. Add water, salt, pepper and wine. Cook until tender. Then add mushrooms and cook a few minutes longer. Sprinkle with chopped parsley just before serving.

BREAST OF CHICKEN PERIGOURDINE

Red Lion Inn
Stockbridge, Massachusetts

3 chicken breasts, boned and halved	Flour
	½ cup dried mushrooms
Salt and freshly ground pepper	½ cup chicken broth
	¼ cup light cream
½ pound butter	2 cups Hollandaise sauce
10 mushrooms, finely sliced	¼ cup sherry

Melt 6 tablespoons butter in a large skillet. Brown chicken breasts on both sides, adding more butter as needed. Remove, add more butter to skillet and sauté mushrooms; remove mushrooms. Into butter, stir flour, salt, dried mushrooms (which have been soaked in water for 1 hour), broth, and light cream.

Cook, stirring over medium heat until thickened and smooth. Place chicken in sauce and simmer gently for 20 minutes. Meanwhile, make Hollandaise sauce (see sauces) and refrigerate it. When chicken is tender, add sherry and sautéed fresh mushrooms. Spread cold Hollandaise over chicken and place under broiler for 1 minute or until just golden. Serve at once.

BONELESS BREAST OF CHICKEN ARISTOCRAT

Schine Queensbury Inn
Glens Falls, New York

6 chicken breasts, split	½ cup bread crumbs, toasted
½ pound sausage meat	
4 strips bacon, chopped fine	⅓ tablespoon onion flakes
	1 tablespoon parsley, chopped
¼ pound mushrooms— chopped fine	Salt and pepper
2 tablespoons butter	1 cup sherry
	6 bacon strips

Split chicken breasts. Sauté sausage meat and drain thoroughly. Fry bacon until crisp, drain thoroughly. Sauté mushrooms in butter. Combine sausage, bacon pieces, sautéed mushrooms, bread crumbs, onion flakes and parsley. Season with salt and pepper, add sherry to moisten. Stuff chicken breasts with sausage mixture, wrap each with a bacon strip, fasten with toothpick. Bake in a moderate oven, 325°, 25 to 30 minutes or until brown.

SUPRÊME DE POULARDE BAROQUE

The Baroque Restaurant
New York City

6 chicken breasts
1 cup white wine
1 stalk celery
½ carrot
½ onion
½ cup butter
1 bay leaf
2 cloves garlic
Salt and pepper to taste
1½ tablespoons flour

1½ cups light cream
½ cup Hollandaise sauce
½ cup heavy cream, whipped
Parmesan cheese, grated
4 ounces medium noodles
1 ounce butter
6 asparagus tips per person

Braise chicken breasts in white wine with vegetables, butter, bay leaf and cloves garlic. When cooked (light brown) remove chicken and add flour and light cream to sauce. Strain.

Add Hollandaise sauce, whipped cream and sprinkling of grated Parmesan cheese. Mix together. Season to taste.

Boil noodles, strain, and sauté in 1 ounce butter. Season and place noodles on platter molded individually. Place chicken breasts on top of noodles and place on top of each a slice of foie gras. Pour sauce over all and place in oven, at 350° for 10 minutes.

Serve with asparagus.

BAKED CHICKEN BREAST ALMONDINE

Towne Lyne House
Lynnfield, Massachusetts

6 chicken breasts, skinned,
   boned, and cooked
3 cups wild rice
24 mushrooms
6 pineapple rings

6 sausages, cooked
3 cups Suprême sauce
   (see under sauces)
Slivered almonds

Place chicken breasts on bed of wild rice in casserole. Cover with Suprême sauce. Garnish each chicken breast with a ring of pineapple that has been browned in a skillet, 1 sausage and 4 mushrooms. Sprinkle with almonds. Brown in 450° oven for 10 minutes. Serve piping hot.

SUPRÊME DE POULET VIENNOISE

Restaurant Laurent
New York City

3 breasts of chicken
2 eggs, beaten
Milk
Salt, pepper to taste
Crumbs

6 tablespoons butter
6 lemon slices
12 anchovy filets
Capers
2 hard-cooked eggs

Flatten breasts of chicken as thin as possible without breaking. Dip them lightly in egg thinned out with milk. Season with salt and pepper. Sprinkle with white bread crumbs on both sides. Cook lightly in butter until golden brown. Place on a platter dressed with lemon slices and filet of anchovies crossed on top of the breasts. On the sides of the breasts, place separately a bouquet of capers, chopped egg white and egg yolk. As a garniture, serve string beans separately.

COTELETTE KIEV BOUQUETIERE

Embassy Club and Knight Box
Sheraton-East Hotel
New York City

3 chicken breasts, skinned,
  boned, and halved
⅓ pound butter

2 cups white bread crumbs
Fat for deep frying

Use half of a breast of chicken (1½ pounds) for each serving. Remove the "filet" of the breast and put to one side. Flatten breast with even, easy strokes (with help of a few drops of water) as thin as possible without damaging breast. Flatten the filet and lay on breast to even out cotelette.

Shape butter into six cones, place 1 cone in center of each breast. Season with salt and pepper. Roll breast evenly around butter. Refrigerate for ½ hour or longer. Bread twice with crumbs. Deep fry in hot fat (360°) for 7 to 8 minutes to a golden brown. Place on platter and surround with a garnish of varied small vegetables.

FILET DE POULET À LA SANFORD

Sanford's
Oakland, California

4 breasts of chicken,
  about 10 ounces each
Salt, Pepper, Ac'cent
Flour
¼ pound butter
1 pound fresh mushrooms,
  sliced
3 shallots, or 1 small
  white onion, finely
  chopped

1 cup canned chicken
  broth
¾ cup dry white wine
1 cup heavy cream
1 8-ounce package frozen
  artichoke cups, cooked
  and quartered
½ cup coarsely chopped
  walnuts, toasted
Steamed rice

Cut chicken breasts into halves; remove bone. Season with salt, pepper and Ac'cent; dust lightly with flour. Brown chicken on both sides in butter in large skillet. When browned, add mushrooms, shallots, chicken broth and wine; season; cover and simmer for 25 minutes or until chicken is tender. Add cream and artichokes. Cover and simmer 8 to 10 minutes longer. Remove chicken to hot serving platter. Thicken sauce with 3 tablespoons flour; season to taste, then spoon over chicken. Garnish with walnuts. Serve with steamed rice.

STUFFED BREAST OF CHICKEN, ANGOSTURA

"La Boucan" Restaurant
Trinidad-Hilton Hotel
Port-of-Spain, Trinidad
West Indies

6 pieces breast of chicken (skinless and boneless)
1 tablespoon salt
1 tablespoon curry powder
3 bananas, cut in half
6 teaspoons Angostura Bitters

6 slices of cooked ham
1 cup flour for dredging
2 eggs, beaten
3 cups shredded coconut
Oil for frying

Flatten chicken breast with a cleaver, like you do for a veal cutlet. Season with salt and curry powder. Top with a half banana which has been turned in Angostura Bitters and wrapped in ham slice. Roll chicken breast and carefully seal the edges. Keep under refrigeration for 2 to 3 hours.

To finish, dip chicken breast in flour, in egg, and bread with shredded coconut. Fry in hot oil (367°) and finish in moderate oven, 350°, until cooked through, for about 15 minutes.

This dish can be served with a Bigarde sauce (see sauces) rum and diced pineapples, and a Spanish rice (Valencia), green peas, saffron and red pimento.

CHICKEN PRYZYPZNY (Cha-peas-knee)

France's Restaurant
Washington, D. C.

3 chicken breasts, about
  2½ pounds each, boned
Water or white wine

⅛ pound butter
Stuffing (see recipe below)

Stuff breasts and bake in pan with about ½ inch water or white wine and ⅛ pound butter, at 325° for 45 minutes, or until browned. Set aside until ready to serve.

Stuffing

1½ cups wild rice,
  cooked and seasoned
¼ cup shallots, chopped

½ cup mushrooms,
  chopped and sautéed
Salt and pepper

Put all ingredients in a bowl, toss lightly until well mixed.

Sauce

Chicken stock
Light cream
Sherry

Sautéed mushrooms
Parmesan cheese, grated

Prepare medium cream sauce made with equal parts chicken stock and light cream. Add sherry to taste. Add ½ cup sliced sautéed mushrooms and ½ cup grated Parmesan cheese per quart of sauce. Stir until smooth.

Sauce may be poured over breasts of chicken, or poured on plate first and the breasts laid on top. Top each breast with mushroom cap, garnish with chopped parsley.

BONELESS BREAST OF CHICKEN, COLBERT

Williamsburg Lodge
Williamsburg, Virginia

3 whole chicken breasts,
  boned and halved
Salt and pepper, to taste

¼ cup butter
2 cups chicken broth

Salt and pepper breasts of chicken. Broil lightly (baste with butter). Place chicken breasts skin side up, in a covered baking pan containing chicken broth. Bake at 325° for 20 minutes or until ready to serve.

Sauce Colbert

3 to 4 tablespoons beef extract
½ cup boiling water
¼ pound butter, softened
Juice of 1 lemon

Few grains nutmeg
2 tablespoons sherry
1 teaspoon tarragon leaves, finely chopped

Dissolve beef extract in boiling water and let boil for 2 minutes. Remove from fire. Add butter, beating constantly with wire whip, until thoroughly blended. Add lemon juice, nutmeg and sherry, stirring continuously. Strain through a fine sieve and add tarragon leaves.

BREAST OF CHICKEN BARCELONETTE

*The Voisin Restaurant
New York City*

½ pound medium noodles
⅜ pound butter
Salt and pepper
6 chicken breasts
1 pound mushrooms, chopped
2 tablespoons onion, chopped
1 cup bread crumbs

2 tablespoons parsley, chopped
2 tablespoons flour
3 cups boiling milk
2 egg yolks
½ cup heavy cream, whipped
¾ cup Parmesan cheese, grated

Cook the noodles in salted boiling water. Mix with 2 tablespoons butter and season with salt and pepper. Sauté the breasts of chicken in 4 tablespoons butter slowly, for about 15 minutes, until light in color. Place the chicken breasts on the noodles. Sauté the chopped mushrooms and chopped onion in 2 tablespoons butter for 15 minutes, add the bread crumbs and parsley.

Season mushroom mixture with salt and pepper and mix well. Place mixture in mounds on the chicken breasts. Heat together the remaining butter and flour. Add milk, stirring constantly, and boil for 10 minutes. Add egg yolks, stirring, and bring to a boil, then add the whipped cream. Season with salt and pepper. Pour this mixture over the stuffed chicken breasts. Sprinkle with Parmesan cheese and glaze under the broiler until brown.

BREAST OF CHICKEN VERSAILLES

The Lord Simcoe Hotel
Toronto, Ontario

6 large chicken breasts
Madeira wine to cover
4 teaspoons lemon juice
2 bay leaves
8 peppercorns
1 clove garlic, crushed
½ cup butter
4 tablespoons chicken fat or margarine
4 tablespoons flour
1 cup meat broth

½ teaspoon monosodium glutamate
4 teaspoons tomato paste
1 teaspoon Worcestershire sauce
Salt
½ pound mushrooms
2 tablespoons butter
1 cup green peas (cooked)
1 tablespoon butter

Remove all skin and bone from chicken breasts, flatten a little, place in bowl and cover with Madeira wine, crushed garlic and peppercorns for at least 4 hours. Remove from marinade, dry, and fry in butter in hot skillet, after browning well on both sides (about 10 minutes). Remove chicken, keep it in warm place and use the same skillet to make the basic sauce.

Heat chicken fat or margarine and add flour and the marinade from the chicken and a little chicken broth (or water and chicken base or cube) boiled together. Add Worcestershire sauce, tomato paste and check for thickening. Sauce should simmer for at least 10 minutes. In the meantime, sauté mushrooms in butter. Add green peas and make ideal potatoes or substitute with straw potatoes. Use your favorite serving dish, preferably skillet or casserole.

Place in bottom the potatoes, place chicken breast on top, mushrooms on top of the chicken, and strain the thickened Madeira sauce over all.

Place in hot (400°) oven for another 10 minutes and just before serving sprinkle with the hot buttered green peas.

Ideal Potatoes

Cut a potato in match sticks and fry in skillet seasoning with salt and pepper. Add sliced truffles if desired.

MIGNON OF CHICKEN AND VEAL, ITALIENNE

Mayfair Farms
West Orange, New Jersey

3 8-ounce chicken breasts,
  cut in 1½ inch cubes
¾ pound veal, sliced
  thin and cut in 2
  inch pieces

1 pound mushrooms,
  sliced
½ pound sweet pimentos
2 cloves garlic
1 cup olive oil

Combine chicken, veal, mushrooms and garlic and sauté in olive oil. Before serving, remove garlic and add sweet pimentos.

CHICKEN LEG FOLIES BERGERES

Hotel Astor
New York City

6 chicken legs
Flour for dredging
3 ounces butter or
  shortening
3 carrots, sliced
  ¼-inch thick
3 leeks, sliced
  ¼-inch thick

6 stalks celery, sliced
  ¼-inch thick
6 whole mushrooms
Chicken stock
1 cup chicken veloute
2 cups light cream
Chives, chopped

Dredge the chicken legs in flour. Place in a heavy pan and sauté in shortening until lightly colored on both sides. Place in 375° oven for 10 minutes. Then add vegetables. Allow to simmer an additional 10 minutes, then add a little chicken stock. Continue cooking until the legs are done.

Remove the legs and thicken pan drippings with chicken veloute. Add light cream, replace chicken legs, and sprinkle with chives.

STUFFED CHICKEN WINGS

La Boucan Restaurant
Trinidad Hilton Hotel
Port of Spain, Trinidad

12 boned chicken wings
Salt and pepper
Vinegar
Garlic
Bamboo shoots, cut
  into strips
 1 cup cold roast pork,
  cut up

½ pound mushrooms,
  sliced
¾ cup melted butter
 1 onion, chopped
 3 tablespoons chives,
  chopped
 2 stalks celery, chopped
Soy sauce

Season chicken wings, stuff with strips of bamboo shoots, pork, and mushrooms. Close the opening with poultry pins. Brush with melted butter. Place in baking dish with onion, chives and celery to give additional flavor, with a touch of Soy sauce. Bake in 350° oven, covered, until tender, about 20 to 30 minutes.

CHICKEN LIVERS, AU SHERRY

Jack Tar Hotel
San Francisco, California

1½ pounds chicken
  livers
 2 medium onions,
  diced fine
 1 pound fresh mushrooms,
  sliced

2 to 3 tablespoons sherry
 1 tablespoon bacon fat
  or other shortening
 1 tablespoon flour
 1 cup chicken consommé
Pinch salt and pepper

Clean and wash chicken livers, removing all bile. Dice onions very fine and slice mushrooms. Sauté chicken livers in shortening until brown, over a low flame. Add sherry. Sauté onions and mushrooms in separate pans, blend in flour, add consommé and stir constantly until smooth. Blend chicken livers with sauce, bring to a boil, add seasoning, simmer for 15 to 20 minutes and serve.

CHICKEN LIVERS, CARUSO

Motor House Cafeteria
Williamsburg, Virginia

2 pounds raw chicken livers
¼ pound butter
½ pint chicken stock
½ cup flour
½ cup red wine
¼ teaspoon butter with chopped shallots

1 tablespoon pimento, chopped
1 teaspoon parsley, chopped
¼ teaspoon Ac'cent
4 ounces spaghetti

Heat ⅛ pound butter in frying pan until hot, but not brown. Sauté chicken livers for 3 or 4 minutes in butter, then add red wine and bring to simmering point.

Make a brown sauce by melting the other ⅛ pound butter (do not brown) and adding flour, mixing thoroughly. Add chicken stock and simmer for five minutes.

Melt a very small amount of butter in another pan and add shallots. Sauté but do not brown.

Add to chicken livers the brown sauce, shallots, pimentos, parsley, and Ac'cent.

Boil water to which a little salt has been added and add spaghetti. Cook for approximately 20 minutes, until tender, drain water, and wash with very warm water. Mix a little butter into spaghetti.

Serve spaghetti on plate, place chicken livers over spaghetti and garnish with chopped parsley.

CHICKEN LIVERS EN CASSEROLE

London Inn
Tulsa, Oklahoma

¾ cup olive oil
8 cloves garlic, minced
  fine
1½ pounds chicken livers
Flour for dredging
Salt and pepper, to taste

1½ cups mushrooms,
  chopped
Parsley
6 ounces Madeira
  (or Muscatel)
Toast points

Place olive oil and garlic in a sauce pan. Heat till very hot. Dredge chicken livers in flour until they are well covered and add them to the oil and garlic. Season to taste with salt and pepper while cooking. Sauté the livers golden brown and well done, but do not let them get to the over-cooked stage.

One minute before removing from the fire add chopped mushrooms, parsley and wine. Blend together well and serve en casserole with toast points.

CHICKEN RARITONGA

Bali Hai Restaurant
Dallas, Texas

Chicken Salad served in Pineapple Boats, Garnished with a Fruit Salad with Fresh Fruit Glace.

Salad Mixture

4 cups chicken or turkey
  breasts, cooked
1 cup French dressing
2 cups celery, finely diced
2 teaspoons salt

½ teaspoon white pepper
Curry, to taste
1 teaspoon lemon juice
1 cup mayonnaise

Cut cooked chicken (or turkey) breasts into ¾-inch cubes. Marinate in French dressing at least 2 hours. Add celery, salt, white pepper, curry. Add lemon juice to mayonnaise and fold this carefully into chicken and celery mixture.

Pineapple Boats

2 pineapples
Pistachio nuts

Cut fresh No. 16 pineapples lengthwise, stem to stern, into quarters. Remove fruit and trim fronds. Fill pineapple boats with chicken salad, mounding and molding to shape. Sprinkle with pistachio nuts.

Fresh Hawaiian Fruit Lei

Pineapple scooped from shells
Fresh fruits in season

Mix ingredients. Pour on fresh fruit glace (see recipe below).

Fresh Fruit Glace

½ cup water
2 cups sugar
4 tablespoons lemon juice
Grated rind of ½ lemon
2 tablespoons lime juice
Grated rind of 1 orange
¼ cup maraschino juice

Add boiling water to sugar. Stir in fruit juices and rinds. Bring to boil and simmer 5 minutes.

Pour fresh fruit glace over Hawaiian fruit salad, and arrange on platter surrounding the pineapple boats.

NEW ENGLAND CHICKEN PIE
(For 6 Individual Pies)

The White Turkey Restaurants
New York City

4 tablespoons chicken fat
4 tablespoons flour
2 cups chicken stock
Salt and pepper
3 cups cooked chicken
   meat, equal parts white
   and dark, cut in large
   pieces

¾ cup cooked peas
¾ cup cooked carrots,
   diced
Basic pie pastry

Melt the fat, stir in the flour and when smooth add the stock, stirring constantly. Add salt and pepper, using less salt if butter is used instead of fat. Boil 2 minutes, continuing to stir and when thick remove from the stove. Cut the cooked chicken into large cubes. Divide the chicken, peas and carrots between individual casseroles. Pour sauce over this. Roll the pastry, made by pie recipe, and cut to fit tops of casseroles. Lay these on casseroles with 4 small slits in each pastry to allow steam to escape. Bake in hot oven (400°) for 10 to 15 minutes; reduce heat to 350° and bake 15 to 20 minutes longer. The important feature is to cut your chicken in large pieces.

CHICKEN CACCIATORE

Agostino's Restaurant
Chicago, Illinois

3½ to 4 pound chicken,
   cut into pieces
½ cup olive oil
½ cup butter
2 cups onion, finely
   chopped
1 green pepper, finely
   chopped

3 cloves garlic, crushed
Pinch basil
1 teaspoon salt
Pinch red pepper
1 cup tomatoes
Italian noodles

Warm olive oil in a heavy skillet. Add butter and allow it to melt. Sauté onion until brown. Add chicken and sauté with the giblets and the onion. Add green pepper, garlic, basil, salt, red pepper and cook slowly for 5 minutes. Finally add tomatoes and cook with a cover for 30 minutes over very low heat. Serve with Italian noodles.

CHICKEN CACCIATORE

Marchio's Italian Cafe
Omaha, Nebraska

1 onion, coarsely chopped
½ cup olive oil
2 chickens, cut into
   serving pieces
⅛ teaspoon sweet basil
Pinch nutmeg, cloves and

2 bay leaves
3 cups canned tomatoes
½ cup Sauterne
Mushrooms—optional
Salt and pepper to taste

Brown onions in olive oil. Remove onions. Brown chicken on all sides in oil. Add onions, spices, tomatoes, mushrooms, wine, and simmer over low flame until chicken is done. Add salt and pepper to taste.

POLLO ALLA CACCIATORA
(Chicken Hunter Style)

Como Inn
Chicago, Illinois

1, 3 to 3½-pound roasting
   chicken, cut into
   serving pieces
2 tablespoons olive oil
1 small onion, chopped
1 tablespoon celery,
   minced
1 clove garlic, chopped

1 cup mushrooms, sliced
Salt, pepper to taste
Pinch rosemary
1 cup wine
3 tomatoes, peeled,
   seeded, coarsely
   chopped
Chicken broth

Brown the chicken pieces on all sides in 4 tablespoons olive oil heated in heavy pan. After about 10 minutes add onion, celery, clove of garlic, mushrooms, salt and pepper and a pinch of rosemary. When the vegetables are slightly browned, add wine, cover and cook 5 minutes. Add tomatoes, cover the pan, and simmer the chicken slowly for 25 to 35 minutes, or until it is almost tender, adding a small amount of chicken broth should this be necessary.

CHICKEN CREOLE

Antoine's
New Orleans, Louisiana

3½-pound frying chicken
¼ cup olive oil
1 No. 2 can tomatoes
2 tablespoons butter
1 teaspoon salt
Few grains pepper
Few grains cayenne
1 sprig thyme
1 tablespoon minced
    parsley

1 bay leaf
3 cloves garlic, minced
1 tablespoon flour
6 shallots, chopped or
    ⅓ cup onion, minced
5 tablespoons green
    pepper, chopped
½ cup white wine
Garnish of avocado slices
    and parsley

Disjoint chicken, wipe pieces with clean damp cloth. Sauté crisply in olive oil, turning to brown both sides. Combine tomatoes and 1 tablespoon butter. Simmer 10 minutes, stirring occasionally. Add salt, pepper and cayenne. Cook 10 minutes. Add thyme, parsley, bay leaf and garlic. Cook 15 minutes or until sauce is thick. Melt 1 tablespoon butter, blend in flour, cook until brown. Add chopped shallots or onion, green pepper and brown slightly. Add wine, stirring constantly, until slightly thickened. Add chicken. Cover. Simmer 45 minutes or until chicken is tender. Serve on hot cooked rice, garnish with avocado slices and parsley sprigs.

CHICKEN FRICASSEE GRAVY

Hotel Astor
New York City

2 tablespoons butter	1 teaspoon salt
2 tablespoons chicken fat	¼ teaspoon pepper
½ cup flour	2 egg yolks, beaten lightly
1 quart chicken stock— rich, and reduced to half amount of chicken broth	Egg coloring, optional

Melt butter and chicken fat together. Add flour and cook 5 minutes without browning, stirring constantly. Stir in the rich chicken stock. Cook slowly to boiling point, stirring frequently. Add seasonings. Add a little sauce to egg yolks and mix. Then add the egg yolk mixture to sauce. Add enough egg coloring (if desired) to give a pleasing light yellow color.

Note: When making sauce to cook fluffy dumplings in, omit the egg yolks until after the dumplings have been cooked.

OLD FASHIONED STEWED CHICKEN

Parry Lodge
Kanab, Utah

1 stewing chicken, cut into pieces	1 bay leaf
3 stalks celery	Salt, pepper
1 large onion, sliced	2 tablespoons butter
	1 to 2 tablespoons flour

Place chicken in a stewing pan. Add 3 cups water, celery, onion and bay leaf. Simmer over a low flame until chicken is tender. Remove the chicken. Strain the stock and thicken with butter and flour. Add chicken to gravy. Serve with freshly made dumplings, cooked in about 2 inches gravy.

BRUNSWICK STEW

Purefoy Hotel
Talladega, Alabama

1 medium onion,
 chopped fine
3 tomatoes, peeled
 and chopped
1 stewing chicken,
 cut in pieces
2 slices bacon, cut in
 small pieces
3 to 4 cups boiling water
1 cup corn, cut from cob

2 cups rich chicken stock
1 cup bread crumbs,
 grated fine
½ teaspoon brown sugar
1 teaspoon salt
½ teaspoon white pepper
½ pod red pepper
1 teaspoon Worcestershire
 sauce

Place onions, tomatoes and chicken into a large soup pot. Add bacon. Cover with water let simmer until tender. Remove chicken from the liquid when cool enough to handle. Cut meat from bone into small pieces. Return to kettle, add corn, stock, bread crumbs, sugar, salt, pepper and pepper pod, and Worcestershire sauce. Cook 20 minutes. Serve in soup plates.

CHICKEN BRUNSWICK STEW

The Carriage House Restaurant
Norfolk, Virginia

1 3-pound chicken
2 #303 cans tomatoes
1 medium onion, sliced
1 box frozen butterbeans

1 box frozen corn
1 box frozen okra
2 cups potatoes, diced

Cook chicken. Strip meat from bones. Save stock.

To chicken stock add tomatoes and sliced onion, and cook slowly 15 to 20 minutes. Add butterbeans, corn, okra, potatoes and chicken, and cook an additional 20 minutes. If too thin, thicken slightly. Serve in individual casserole dishes, with complement of fresh Chef's salad.

A MOROCCAN CHICKEN STEW
(A Hot, Spicy Dish)

Fleur de Lys
San Francisco, California

2 live young chickens
Water to cover
6 ounces olive oil
6 fresh tomatoes, cut in
  large pieces
6 zucchinis, cut up
6 large onions, cut in
  large pieces
6 green and sweet red
  peppers, cut in large
  pieces
Thyme, laurel, salt, pepper,
  cayenne, cumin
4 green walnuts

Kill the chicken and retain the blood separately. Pluck the feathers and eviscerate. Then place the whole chickens, not cut, in an earthenware casserole. Add oil, vegetables cut in large pieces, and spices; add the walnuts and cover with water. To the blood, in a separate cup, add more cumin and red pepper. Stir and add this to your casserole. Put on a medium fire, preferably a wood fire—cover and cook slowly five hours.

Sit on the floor in a circle—take the cover off the casserole and use a wooden spoon to dish out. The chicken should be almost melted. If one of your guests is Moslem it would be correct for the host and guests not to use silver but strictly the right hand (left hand is reserved for ablutions).

CHICKEN AND YELLOW RICE "VALENCIA STYLE"

Columbia Restaurant
Tampa, Florida

3 2½ pound fryers
1 cup Spanish olive oil
2 onions, sliced thin
4 cloves garlic, chopped
1 green pepper, cut up
½ cup tomatoes
6 cups chicken broth
2 tablespoons salt
Pinch Spanish saffron

Pinch egg coloring
½ pound Spanish Valencia rice
1 cup small green peas
Parsley
Spanish pimiento
2 hard-cooked eggs, quartered
Asparagus tips

Cut chicken in quarters, simmer in olive oil until brown. Remove from cooking pot, and in the same olive oil braise the onions, garlic, green pepper and tomatoes. Place the browned chicken in the casserole, add chicken broth and set over medium heat. When boiling, add salt, saffron, yellow coloring and rice. Bring to boil again, cover casserole and place in 350° oven. Bake for 20 minutes.

Garnish with small peas, pimiento, parsley, eggs and asparagus tips.

ARROZ CON POLLO

Las Novedades Spanish Restaurant
Tampa, Florida

1 4-pound fryer, disjointed
½ cup olive oil
2 cloves garlic, minced
1 onion, finely chopped
3 fresh tomatoes, chopped
2 cups stock, or 1 can consommé and ½ can water

1 bay leaf
2 tablespoons salt
2 cups raw rice
1 pinch saffron
2 green peppers, finely sliced
1 2-ounce can Petit Pois (small size)
2 pimentos, sliced

Cut chicken in quarters. Heat olive oil. Fry chicken in oil until lightly browned. Add onions and garlic. When onion is tender, add tomatoes and liquid. Boil 5 minutes. Add bay leaf, salt, rice, saffron and green peppers. Stir thoroughly. Cover and bake in moderate oven, 350°, for 20 to 25 minutes. Add petit pois and pimentos, and water if the rice is dry; cover, and bake 10 minutes longer. Serve hot.

CHICKEN SAUTÉ NEW ORLEANS

The Blue Room
The Roosevelt Hotel
New Orleans, Louisiana

3 chickens, halved	3 cups chicken broth or
½ cup flour	consommé
½ pound butter	1½ cups dry white wine
12 large, fresh mushrooms	2 bay leaves
1 large green onion, chopped	1 teaspoon crushed thyme
1 clove garlic, chopped fine	Salt and pepper to taste
	8 to 10 fresh oysters

Dust chicken with about half the flour. Melt butter in a deep skillet and sauté chicken to golden brown. Remove chicken to a deep pot. Sauté mushrooms in remaining butter until delicately browned and place over chicken. Add onions and garlic to the skillet and sauté them until tender but not browned; remove and place over chicken. Blend remaining flour with butter left in the skillet, making a roux. Gradually add consommé and wine and stir over low heat until smooth. Add bay leaves, thyme, salt, pepper; stir well and heat; correct for seasoning and pour mixture over chicken. Rotate pot gently to blend; bring to a boil, cover pot closely and simmer 30 to 40 minutes. Put oysters in the pot the last ten minutes.

CHICKEN CURRY NEW DELHI

Punjab Restaurant
New York City

1, 3 to 4-pound stewing
   chicken
Water to cover
4 carrots
4 stalks celery
2 teaspoons salt
4 peppercorns
2 cloves garlic, chopped
2 onions, peeled
   and chopped

¼ cup vegetable
   or corn oil
2 tablespoons flour
1 tablespoon curry powder,
   or more, to taste
Accent
Tabasco
Salt and pepper to taste

Boil chicken in water, adding fresh carrots, celery, salt and peppercorns. When chicken is tender, remove chicken meat from bones. Save chicken broth, celery and carrots. In a pot sauté garlic and onions in oil. When soft, add flour and curry powder. Make paste. Add chicken meat, stirring gently. Then add chicken stock, the amount determined by the desired thickness of the sauce. Add Accent, Tabasco, salt and pepper to taste.

Serve with Rice a La Punjab, carrots and celery. Condiments optional: raisins, shredded coconut, and cashews.

CHICKEN CURRY

East Indian Kitchen
Hotel Pierre
New York City

½ cup oil or butter
3 or 4 cloves garlic,
   chopped
4 onions, chopped
1 bay leaf
1 teaspoon cinnamon
5 whole cloves
3 pounds chicken meat

3 cups hot water
1½ tablespoons salt
1 teaspoon black pepper
1 teaspoon cumin
1 teaspoon coriander
1 tablespoon paprika
2 tablespoons curry powder

Heat oil or butter in stew pot. Add garlic and onions and brown together for a few minutes. Add bay leaf, cinnamon and cloves, cover and cook for 5 minutes. Add chicken meat, cover with water, and when water from meat has steamed off, add salt, pepper, cumin, coriander, paprika and curry powder. Stir carefully to avoid burning. Cook until chicken is tender.

TAHITIAN BARBECUED CHICKEN

The Captains' Inn
Long Beach, California

6 broiler halves, split
 down back
1 cup dry Vermouth
1 pound butter
1 tablespoon rosemary
 leaves
1 teaspoon curry powder

1 tablespoon soy sauce
1 teaspoon Worcestershire
 sauce
2 dashes Tabasco
Salt and pepper to taste
Barbecue spice

Prepare basting sauce by simmering (do not boil) Vermouth, butter, rosemary, curry, soy sauce, Worcestershire sauce and Tabasco. Let simmer for 30 minutes.

Brush broilers with basting sauce and season heavily with salt, pepper and any standard barbecue spice. Barbecue over charcoal, turning every 10 minutes. Baste each time just before turning. Cook for approximately 45 minutes.

CHICKEN PRINCE OF THE ISLAND

Stardust Hotel
Las Vegas, Nevada

2 young spring chickens,
 cut in pieces
Chinese rice wine
Salt, pepper
Flour for dredging
Almond oil for frying
6 mushrooms, sliced
2 tablespoons butter

2 tablespoons shallots,
 chopped
1 teaspoon ginger root,
 slivered
2 tablespoons butter
Pineapple chunks
Mandarin orange sections
3 cups cooked rice

Marinate young spring chickens in Chinese rice wine for about 2 hours and season with salt and pepper. Dip in flour and sauté in almond oil until golden brown. Slice mushrooms and saute in 2 tablespoons butter with shallots. Put in a dash of rice wine and ginger root. Pour mushroom-shallot mixture over chicken; cover, and simmer for 15 minutes in a 375° oven. Arrange chicken on serving platter. Sauté pineapple chunks and mandarin sections in 2 tablespoons butter for 2 minutes, then pour over the chicken.

Serve with long grain rice.

BAMBOO TERRACE PINEAPPLE CHICKEN CUBES

Bamboo Terrace
Vancouver, British Columbia

1 to 1½-pound boned
  breast of chicken meat,
  cut in 1 inch cubes
2 tablespoons soy sauce
3 tablespoons vegetable oil
¾ teaspoon salt
2 cloves garlic, crushed
½ teaspoon M.S.G.
  (optional)
2 stalks celery,
  sliced in ½ inch pieces

1 medium onion,
  cut in 6 sections
1 medium green pepper,
  sliced in ½ inch strips
1 can mushrooms,
  drained (reserve liquid
  for use)
1½ cups pineapple cubes
1 tablespoon cornstarch

Marinate chicken cubes in soy sauce. Heat oil very hot in large frying pan. Add half of the salt and half of the garlic. Add marinated chicken and M.S.G. Sauté 4 or 5 minutes, or until chicken is slightly browned. Remove chicken meat from pan and set aside. Using same frying pan and oil, add remainder of garlic and salt, add celery, onions, green pepper, mushrooms and pineapple. Cover and cook 3 to 4 minutes. *Do not overcook vegetables.* Return chicken meat to pan, add cornstarch mixed smooth with ½ cup mushroom and pineapple liquid; stir and mix well. Cook until gravy is thickened.

CHOP SUEY

The Nankin
Minneapolis, Minnesota

2 cups chicken meat,
cut up
3 tablespoons
peanut oil
2 cups celery,
cut in strips
1 cup bamboo sprouts,
cut in strips
1 cup bean sprouts

1 cup water chestnuts,
sliced thin
1 cup mushrooms,
peeled and sliced
1½ cups chicken broth
½ teaspoon salt
Sugar
Soybean sauce
2 teaspoons cornstarch
Chinese molasses

Chop meat and vegetables separately. Fry meat in hot peanut oil. Add chopped vegetables and chicken broth. Boil for 10 minutes. Add gravy made of ½ teaspoon salt and 1 teaspoon sugar, 2 tablespoons soybean sauce, cornstarch and ½ teaspoon Chinese molasses. Dissolve these in ½ cup water, let entire mixture come to a boil. Serve with side dish of rice.

Special Chop Sueys may be made by adding ingredients such as green peppers, beef, black mushrooms, etc.

RUBY CHOW'S ALMOND OR SESAME FRIED CHICKEN

Ruby Chow's
Seattle, Washington

3 pound fryer, boned and
cut into pieces and
scored lightly
2 cups chicken stock
1 teaspoon salt
½ teaspoon M.S.G.
½ teaspoon sugar

⅛ teaspoon caramel
coloring
Cornstarch thickening
¼ cup crushed, blanched
and toasted or deep-fried
almonds, or ¼ cup
toasted sesame seeds
½ head lettuce, shredded

Dip chicken into egg batter (see recipe below). Drop chicken into hot, deep fat, 375°. Fry until golden brown. Meantime, prepare sauce as follows: Heat chicken stock, salt, M.S.G. and sugar to boiling. Add caramel coloring and stir. Add cornstarch thickening to make sauce the consistency of thin cream sauce. Place shredded lettuce on platter. Top with drained fried chicken. Pour hot sauce over the chicken and sprinkle with sesame seed or crushed almonds. Serve immediately.

Egg Batter—for dipping

1 egg
½ cup water (part or all milk may be used)

½ cup flour
½ teaspoon salt
½ teaspoon M.S.G.

Combine ingredients and beat to blend thoroughly. Two eggs may be used and more or less liquid to make the batter thinner or thicker, as desired.

Steamed Rice—Chinese method

Use Texas extra-fancy patna rice. Briskly wash rice, rubbing between hands. Drain. Repeat the washing twice. Put rice in heavy saucepan and add enough water so it comes over the rice to the first joint of the thumb. Cover tightly and bring to boil. Reduce heat and cook over low heat until all the water is absorbed and rice is tender. Rice will require no stirring and will be in fluffy, white, separate kernels.

ROYAL HAWAIIAN CHICKEN IN COCONUT

Royal Hawaiian Hotel
Honolulu, Hawaii

6 spring chickens,
   1½ pounds each (boned)
3 young green coconuts
Wild rice stuffing
Parchment paper
Oil

6 pineapple rings (canned)
6 large mushrooms
Demi-glace
Duchesse potatoes for borders
1 fresh grated coconut

Bone chickens. Saw coconuts into halves crosswise, trim the edges with a sharp knife, so that they are clean and smooth. Pipe a border of Duchesse potatoes around the edges of the coconut, with a pastry bag through a star tube. Set aside.

Now stuff the chickens with wild rice stuffing, then fold them together so that the legs will stand upright. Wet with oil 6 strips of parchment paper about 18 inches long and 2 inches wide, and tie the stuffed chicken into a ball, leaving its legs and top uncovered. Place chickens in a lightly oiled roasting pan and bake in moderate oven at 350° for 25 minutes. Remove from the oven, take off the paper strips and set the chickens in the coconuts. Place on top of each one a pineapple ring and mushroom in the center, return to the oven for 5 minutes, just enough to let the heat penetrate through the coconut and brown the potatoes and mushroom. Remove from oven, pour over each some demi-glace sauce. Sprinkle with fresh grated coconut.

The Royal Hawaiian adds "Serve on a silver platter with a napkin underneath."

Wild Rice Stuffing for Chicken in Coconut

1½ cups wild rice, raw	1 tablespoon or more
1½ teaspoons salt	curry powder
½ cup butter	Little pepper
2 tablespoons shallots, chopped	Pinch rosemary
1 cup diced pineapple (canned)	½ cup Demi-glace sauce, to moisten

Wash the wild rice thoroughly in a colander with cold water. Place in a pan deep enough for the water to extend at least 1 inch over the rice, cover with boiling water and let stand until the water cools. Drain, then cook the rice with salt, adding enough water to extend 1 inch over the rice. Boil 35 to 40 minutes. Drain well.

Heat butter in a saucepan, add shallots and simmer for two minutes. Add the wild rice, the pineapple, and blend well. Add curry powder, salt to taste, pepper, rosemary and demi-glace. Blend well. When the rice is well heated, remove from fire. Then stuff the chickens with the rice.

MARENGO CHICKEN SAUTÉ

Rimrock Room
Hotel Palliser
Calgary, Alberta

2 2-pound chickens,
  cut into pieces
Salt and pepper
4 tablespoons oil
2 cloves garlic, crushed
3 tomatoes, peeled
  and chopped

1 cup white wine
18 mushrooms,
  cut into quarters
Few slices truffles
Croutons
Parsley, chopped

Season chicken pieces with salt and pepper. Heat oil in heavy saucepan. Brown chicken on all sides, turning frequently. Remove chicken to flameproof casserole. Add garlic, tomatoes and wine. Cover casserole and cook over low flame until chicken pieces are almost tender. Add mushrooms. Cook 10 to 12 minutes more, until chicken is tender. Sprinkle with parsley, truffles and garnish with croutons. Serve in casserole.

PEDRO'S BARBECUE CHICKEN

South of the Border Restaurant
South of the Border, South Carolina

3 frying chickens, 2½ pounds each
Barbecue Mix
Barbecue sauce

Dip chickens into barbecue mix and cook slowly for 3 hours over charcoal or hickory embers, or in the oven at 250°. Serve with a pitcher of heated barbecue sauce.

Barbecue Mix

½ pound brown sugar
4 tablespoons paprika
2 tablespoons salt

2 tablespoons ground
  black pepper

Combine all ingredients and mix well.

Barbecue Sauce

4 tablespoons butter	2 tablespoons Worcestershire sauce
2 medium onions, chopped fine	2 tablespoons brown sugar
½ cup celery, chopped fine	1 teaspoon dry mustard
1 cup water	1 teaspoon salt
1 cup catsup	½ teaspoon black pepper
4 tablespoons lemon juice	2 tablespoons M.S.G.
	1 teaspoon oregano

Combine all ingredients and simmer for about 30 minutes. Serve hot.

PAELLA "GOOD FRIEND"

Granada Grill
Century Plaza Hotel
Century City, California

½ cup olive oil	4 ounces blanched slivered almonds
1 4-pound roasting chicken	¾ cup stuffed olives, chopped
Salt and pepper to taste	12 medium mushrooms, sautéed
6 small onions, chopped	2 ounces butter
½ garlic clove, crushed	2 tablespoons chives, chopped
2½ cups raw rice	Generous pinch of saffron
1 bouquet garni	
1 cup dry white wine	
5 cups chicken broth	
1 teaspoon oregano	

Heat oil. Cut chicken into serving pieces and season with salt and pepper. Sauté until browned, add onions, garlic and raw rice. Mix well and add bouquet garni. Add white wine, most of chicken broth, saffron and simmer 45 minutes. Sprinkle with oregano, blanched almonds and minced olives. Add remaining stock if too dry, remove bouquet garni and sprinkle with mushrooms and chives.

CHICKEN NERONE

Restaurant Elite
New York, New York

3 1½-pound broilers	6 to 8 ounces brandy
6 tablespoons olive oil	Flour
¾ pound butter	6 laurel leaves
Lemon juice	Kirsch
White wine, to cover	Salt, pepper

Clean broilers, cut from belly down and flatten (like an open book). Place chicken in heavy-bottomed frying pan, pour in olive oil, place a 15 pound weight on top of chickens and cook till brownish in color. Remove chicken from pan and discard oil.

Place chicken back in pan, add butter and lemon juice and cook over slow fire until tender. Then pour white wine over chickens and continue cooking until wine evaporates. Remove chicken and add brandy and flour to sauce in pan. Saturate laurel leaves in small amount of Kirsch, ignite leaves. With two forks, hold chickens over flaming leaves to absorb aroma.

Remove bones and cut into pieces. Add salt and pepper. Douse with brandy sauce from pan. Serve hot.

CHICKEN MOLE

El Parador Cafe
New York City

1 3½ to 4-pound broiler-fryer, cut up, or the equivalent in chicken parts	1⅓ cups canned tomatoes, drained
½ cup almonds, blanched	2 teaspoons vinegar
2 tablespoons peanuts or peanut butter	2 tablespoons chili powder
1½ tablespoons olive oil	¾ cup onion, chopped
1½ tablespoons flour	1 clove garlic, mashed
2 cups beef or chicken broth	1 square (1 ounce) unsweetened chocolate, grated
	½ teaspoon cinnamon
	Salt and pepper to taste

Broil or roast chicken until tender. Sauté almonds and peanuts, or peanut butter, in olive oil. Add flour and stir until browned. Add broth, tomatoes, vinegar, and chili powder; stir until smooth. Add onion, garlic, chocolate, and cinnamon; stir until sauce comes to a boil. Cover. Simmer, stirring occasionally, for about 45 minutes, or until sauce is thick. Add cooked chicken and simmer until chicken is hot.

GALLINA EN MOLE POBLANO
(Chicken with Mole)

Patio Mexicano Santa Rosa
Monterrey, Mexico

1 large chicken, cut into
  serving pieces
½ cup lard
2 cups mole sauce
  (see recipe below)

3 cups meat stock
Salt, to taste
2 tablespoons sesame seed,
  toasted (for garnish)

Brown the chicken pieces in lard in a large earthenware casserole. Add one-half of the mole sauce and let simmer until almost dry. Add 1 cup stock and salt to taste. Continue cooking. Add other half of mole sauce and cook until done. Sauce should be well thickened. Serve on a platter and sprinkle with toasted sesame seed. Also, may be garnished with pepper and onion rings, tomato with parsley, carrots and radishes cut in strips.

Mole Sauce

2 green peppers
6 cloves garlic
1 slice dry white toast
½ cup almonds
6 tomatoes
½ teaspoon cinnamon
¼ teaspoon pepper

Salt
1½ tablespoons chili
  powder
2 ounces unsweetened
  chocolate, grated
¼ cup oil
Meat stock

Grind together peppers, garlic, toast, almonds and tomatoes. Add cinnamon, pepper, salt, chili powder and chocolate.

Heat oil and add mixture with 2 cups meat stock. Cook over flame for 5 to 10 minutes, stirring constantly.

CHILES RELLENOS DE POLLO
(Green Peppers Stuffed with Chicken)

Beverly Wilshire Hotel
Beverly Hills, California

6 large chiles (green peppers) peeled
1 pound chicken meat, chopped very fine
¼ pound raisins
¼ pound almonds, chopped
1 tomato, chopped
1 tablespoon parsley, chopped

Salt, cumin, pepper
2 eggs, separated
Flour, enough to make thin batter
Hot oil for frying
Parmesan cheese, grated
Tomato Salsa (see recipe below)

Combine chicken, raisins, almonds, tomatoes, parsley, salt, cumin, pepper. Stuff each green pepper with the mixture. Beat egg whites until stiff but not dry; add flour and egg yolks. Coat peppers with egg flour, then fry in hot oil, 375°, until golden brown. Drain. Top with grated cheese and serve with Tomato Salsa (sauce).

Tomato Salsa

3 ripe tomatoes, chopped fine
3 green peppers, chopped
1 to 2 cloves garlic, minced
1 tablespoon parsley, chopped

1 onion, chopped
1 tablespoon vinegar
3 tablespoons tomato juice
Olive oil
Salt, pepper to taste

Chop all the vegetables very fine. Add the liquids and season to taste. Serve hot with Chiles Rellenos de Pollo and other Mexican meat dishes.

CHICKEN CHILAQUILES

Restaurant Embassy
Mexico City

6 tortillas
⅛ pound lard
2 green tomatoes
1 green chili pepper
1 branch coriander leaf
1 onion, minced
3 ounces Philadelphia
  cream cheese

¼ chicken, cooked and
  cut up
1 cup chicken broth
2 hard-cooked eggs,
  minced
4 chives
2 radishes, minced
Oil for frying

Cut tortillas in quarters (4 pieces) and fry them, removing from oil before they brown. Make sauce as follows:

Cook tomatoes and mash them with chili pepper, coriander and onion. Fry in small amount of oil until very hot through and through. Add chicken broth. Spread lard in baking pan, put half of the tortillas in, half the cream cheese, the chicken, half the sauce. Cover it again with tortillas, cheese, chicken and remaining sauce. Bake at low heat, 325°, for about 30 minutes.

When ready to serve, decorate with the minced boiled egg, chives and radishes.

CAZUELA DE AVE

The Cooper Room
Hotel Carrera
Santiago de Chile

1 stewing hen, cut into
  serving pieces
Water to cover
2 onions, left whole
12 medium potatoes
2 cups string beans, sliced
2 cobs corn, sliced into
  rounds 1 inch thick

1 green or red pepper,
  sliced
Cumin, to taste
Marjoram, to taste
½ cup rice, cooked
1 egg yolk, beaten
Parsley, chopped
2 tablespoons white wine

Cut a stewing hen into serving pieces. Cover with water and boil until tender. Remove scum as it forms. Add onions, potatoes, string beans, corn rounds, pepper, cumin and marjoram. 20 minutes before serving, add rice. Just before serving, add beaten egg yolk, chopped parsley and white wine.

CREAMED CHICKEN CANNELLONI AU GRATIN STONEHENGE

Stonehenge
Ridgefield, Connecticut

Creamed Chicken

4 cups cooked chicken, minced	Salt and pepper to taste
12 large mushrooms, sliced	½ cup sherry
2 tablespoons butter	2 cups cream sauce

Mince the cooked chicken. Sauté mushrooms in butter. Add chicken. Add salt and pepper to taste. Then stir in sherry and mix regularly prepared cream sauce.

Hollandaise Sauce

3 egg yolks	2 tablespoons cream sauce
½ pound butter, melted	
Pinch salt	

Beat egg yolks over a hot fire until half cooked, then add melted butter and pinch salt. Add about 2 tablespoons cream sauce to prevent curdling.

Pancake Batter

2 eggs	1 cup milk
1 cup flour	Butter to fry

Beat eggs, flour and milk to a smooth batter. Pour very small quantity in hot buttered frying pan; tip pan so that batter forms a very thin coating. Pour off excess. Cook until golden brown, very light in color. Turn and brown on other side.

To Assemble

Creamed chicken
Pancakes

Hollandaise sauce
Parmesan cheese, grated

Spread creamed chicken on pancakes; roll up. Cover with Hollandaise sauce, sprinkle lightly with grated cheese and place under broiler for a few minutes to brown.

CHICKEN LOAF

The Pirate's House
Savannah, Georgia

2 cups soft bread crumbs
2 egg yolks, beaten
1 cup cream
1½ cups cooked chicken, minced
1½ cups cooked green peas

1 tablespoon onion, minced
1½ cups cooked carrots, diced
Salt and pepper to taste
3 egg whites, beaten

Mix in order listed, adding egg whites last. Pour into greased loaf pan. Bake in moderate oven (325°) for 1½ hours.

GUSSIE'S CHICKEN CASSEROLE

The Pirate's House
Savannah, Georgia

4 cups cooked spaghetti
2 cups chicken stock
½ cup butter
½ cup flour
1 tablespoon salt
2 cups milk
3 cups cooked chicken, diced

1½ pounds mushrooms
½ cup sliced almonds
1 tablespoon grated onions
½ cup bread crumbs
⅓ cup stuffed olives
½ cup cheese, grated

Put chicken stock in a 2-quart sauce pan. Add butter. Mix flour and salt with milk and stir into chicken stock. Continue stirring until thickened. Add all the remaining ingredients except olives and cheese. Place spaghetti into bottom of casserole. Add chicken mixture. Top with cheese and olives and bake for 30 minutes in a moderate oven, 350°.

CHICKEN AND HAM

The Homestead Inn
Lake Placid, New York

½ small Bermuda onion,
   minced
¼ cup butter
½ cup mushrooms, sliced
1 teaspoon paprika
1 teaspoon salt
¼ teaspoon nutmeg

6 slices chicken,
   white meat
6 slices boiled ham
1¾ cups cream, heated
3 or 4 tablespoons
   Parmesan cheese,
   grated

Sauté onion in butter until tender. Add mushrooms and seasonings, then cook for 5 minutes. Arrange chicken and ham slices in alternate layers in a 1½ quart casserole; add enough cream to cover. Place in 400° oven for 10 minutes. Cover with cheese and return to oven to brown. When bubbly, serve.

CHICKEN CROQUETTES

The Pirate's House
Savannah, Georgia

3 tablespoons butter
4 tablespoons flour
½ cup milk
½ cup chicken stock
½ teaspoon salt
   (if stock is not salty)
1 egg

2 cups cooked chicken,
   cut up
Fat for deep frying
1 egg mixed with
   3 tablespoons water
Bread crumbs

Melt butter. Stir in flour until smooth. Add milk and chicken stock. Cook until very thick. Add seasonings and beat in egg. Blend well. Add chicken and cool. Shape into croquettes. Dip croquettes in egg lightly beaten with water. Roll in bread crumbs. Fry in deep fat (375°). Drain on absorbent paper. Makes 10 or 12.

CHICKEN JUBILEE

The Beverly Hills Hotel
Beverly Hills, California

1 5-to-6-pound capon, cut into pieces	3-4 ounces sherry
Salt, pepper	1 cup chicken broth or consommé
3 tablespoons butter	36 cherries
2 tablespoons oil	3 tablespoons cognac
1 onion, coarsely chopped	½ ounce Kirschwasser
2 carrots, sliced	

Season capon and saute in butter and oil. As soon as the pieces are nicely browned on both sides, add onions and carrots, sherry and chicken broth or consommé. Cover and bake at 375°, until brown. Strain sauce and keep warm.

In a separate casserole heat cherries, reduce the juice and flame with cognac. Add Kirschwasser. Mix this with the chicken and serve with rice, prepared to your liking.

POULET SAUTÉ MARENGO

The Alouette Restaurant
San Francisco, California

1 capon, cut into pieces	1 small bunch bay leaves, parsley, thyme, celery leaves
8 tablespoons olive oil	
1 large onion, chopped	
1 clove garlic, crushed	¼ pound small white onions
1 cup white wine	
1 cup chicken base	¼ pound mushrooms
¼ cup tomato sauce	½ pound French bread
2 tablespoons flour	Parsley, coarsely chopped

Brown chicken pieces in 6 tablespoons oil. When half cooked, add chopped onions and garlic. Add white wine and stir it with whatever is left of the gravy. Mix chicken base with tomato sauce and flour and add this to the gravy. Add small bunch of mixed herbs and cook over low heat for 45 minutes.

Brown small onions and mushrooms in 2 tablespoons oil.

After chicken has cooked for 45 minutes, remove from pan, strain the gravy. Now put everything (chicken, gravy, browned onions and mushrooms) into a frying pan, mix, and simmer over low flame for 15 minutes.

Fry in oil a few slices of diced French bread. Place the pieces of chicken on a platter, as well as the garniture of onions, mushrooms and fried bread. Sprinkle with coarsely chopped parsley.

BONELESS CAPON, TICONDEROGA

Edgewater Inn
Marina Hotel
Long Beach, California

1 4-pound capon	½ cup mushrooms,
1 cup cooked wild rice	sliced thin
½ cup carrots,	Sherry wine
finely chopped	Salt, pepper, paprika
½ cup onion,	6 slices brown bread
finely chopped	Sauce suprême

Remove bone from leg and thigh of a 4-pound capon. Flatten out and stuff with wild rice, fine chopped carrots, onions, celery, mushrooms. Moisten with sherry. Mold into dome shape and wrap it with 1½-inch strips of waxed paper dipped in oil. Sprinkle top with salt, pepper and paprika. Roast in 400° oven for 35 minutes. Place capon on steamed brown bread sliced ½ inch thick and cover with sauce suprême.

BREAST OF CAPON CAPRICCIO

Mario's Villa d'Este
New York City

6 capon breasts
Flour for dredging
Herbs (optional)
Salt, pepper to taste
2 eggs, beaten
¼ pound and 6 tablespoons
  butter

½ pound mushrooms,
  sliced
2 bay leaves
½ cup dry white wine
6 slices liver pâté

Coat capon breasts in flour (seasoned with your favorite herbs) plus salt and pepper. Dip in beaten eggs and again in flour. Sauté in 6 tablespoons butter on both sides. Melt ¼ pound butter in another saucepan; sauté mushrooms with bay leaves until mushrooms are tender, add dry white wine, simmer about 5 minutes. Remove bay leaves. Arrange capon in baking dish. Top each breast with a thin slice of liver pâté and pour mushroom-wine sauce over all. Bake in 350° oven until tender, 45 minutes to 1 hour.

BREAST OF CAPON

Four Chimneys
Old Bennington, Vermont

1 4-5 pound capon
1 slice Vermont cheese
1 slice Polish ham
Flour for dredging

2 eggs, beaten
½ cup light cream
Bread crumbs
¼ pound butter

Bone capon except for wing bones. Remove skin. Split breasts in half but not completely through. Flatten gently with wooden mallet. Roll Vermont cheese and Polish ham into cavity of the breast. Fold breast over. Dust in flour, then dip into mixture of eggs beaten with light cream. Roll in bread crumbs. Place in sauté pan and sauté on top of stove, in butter, until lightly brown on one side. Turn and brown other side. Place in oven at 425° until done. The capon is done when drumsticks move.

SUPRÊME DE VOLAILLE "TRIANON"

Le Trianon Restaurant Français
San Francisco, California

Breasts of 3 young capons
Salt, pepper to taste
Grey Poupon mustard
6 ounces Roquefort cheese

½ pound Swiss cheese
¾ to 1 pound butter
Lemon juice

Bone the capon breasts, lay the flesh of each side apart and pound thin. Sprinkle with salt and pepper and spread with a thin layer of Grey Poupon mustard. Blend Roquefort and Swiss cheese and butter and form into 6 balls. Place a cheese ball into the center of each breast and fold the meat well over the cheese. Roll lengthwise into a firm roll, making sure the ingredients are well sealed inside.

In a small skillet place butter (enough to cover ¾ the capon rolls) and melt over a slow flame. Place the rolls in the melted butter on top of stove 2 or 3 minutes, then in oven at 325° for 20 to 25 minutes.

Top with melted butter and a squeeze of lemon. Garnish to taste.

BREAST OF CAPON POLIGNAC

Fleur de Lys
San Francisco, California

3 breasts of capon
Salt and pepper
2½ pounds goose liver
  (Alsace)
6 whole peeled black
  truffles (Perigord)

2 egg whites, lightly
  beaten
Flour
Bread crumbs
6 ounces sweet butter
2 ounces cognac or brandy
Hearts of artichoke

Skin and bone the breasts, and divide them, so you have six pieces of meat. Place them between pieces of waxed paper and flatten them. Take out all the nerves. Season with salt and pepper. Cover truffles with goose liver and roll the white meat of the chicken delicately around so that it takes the shape of an egg. Season again with salt and pepper. Coat the oval-shaped breasts in the beaten egg whites and then roll in flour and then in bread crumbs.

To cook, heat the butter in a frying pan and sauté the rolled chicken breasts until slightly brown. Pour the cognac and flame. Finish by placing in a 350° oven for approximately 12 minutes.

Set on fried slices of bread. Garnish with goose liver and a slice of truffle and hearts of artichoke.

PIGEONNEAUX ROYALE: ANTOINE'S

Antoine's
New Orleans, Louisiana

6 royal squabs	1 cup chopped celery
Salt	1 cup chopped carrot
Freshly ground black pepper	⅓ cup chopped onion
¼ cup butter	Sauce Paradis

Wipe squabs inside and out with damp cloth and sprinkle inside and out with salt and pepper. Rub with butter. Combine celery, carrots and onion and spread on bottom of roasting pan. Place squabs on vegetables. Roast in a slow oven, 325°, for 30 minutes. Remove squabs. Arrange them in a deep casserole. Pour sauce Paradis over them, cover and bake for 15 minutes. Serve immediately.

Sauce Paradis

¼ cup butter	2 tablespoons
¼ cup flour	red currant jelly
2 cups double strength	2 cups seedless
veal or chicken stock	white grapes
½ cup Madeira wine	2 large truffles, sliced

Melt butter, add flour and stir until smooth. Add veal stock, cook, stirring constantly until slightly thickened. Add wine and jelly and cook, stirring until jelly is melted. Add grapes and truffles.

BOK OPP SOONG
(Diced Squab Tumble in Lettuce Cups)

Kan's
San Francisco, California

2 large squabs
1 pound water chestnuts,
 peeled and diced
 (use canned if fresh are
 not available)
6 dried Chinese black
 mushrooms (softened
 in water), diced
⅓ cup celery,
 finely chopped
2 tablespoons lean
 raw pork, diced
2 teaspoons smoked
 Chinese duck liver
 (Opp Geok Bow),
 optional, chopped

½ cup bamboo shoots,
 diced
4 tablespoons
 vegetable oil
Pinch salt
1 cup chicken stock
1 teaspoon any type sauce
Dash ground pepper
½ teaspoon M.S.G.
1 tablespoon cornstarch
 mixed with 1 tablespoon
 water
1 head lettuce
 leaves, crisped

Completely bone 2 large uncooked, dressed squabs. With a Chinese chopping cleaver, mince squab meat very fine. Finely dice water chestnuts, mushrooms, celery, pork, liver, and bamboo shoots.

In a preheated skillet place vegetable oil and salt. Add meat of squab and diced ingredients. Stir and mix at medium heat for 2 minutes. Add chicken stock, sauce, pepper and M.S.G. Stir and mix, then cover skillet and cook at medium heat for 10 minutes. Remove cover. Add paste made of cornstarch and water. Cook at medium heat, tossing and mixing constantly until very hot. Transfer to serving compote or platter.

Have prepared crisped leaves of one head lettuce on platter. Each guest takes a lettuce leaf and places two tablespoons of Soong on it and eats it with his hands.

ROYAL SQUAB BAROQUE

*The Baroque Restaurant
New York City*

6 squabs, 1¼ pounds each
Salt and pepper to taste
2 carrots, chopped
4 celery stalks, chopped
1 onion, chopped
2 bay leaves
1 cup butter
6 ounces champagne

6 medium potatoes
24 small white onions
12 ounces salt pork
12 ounces fresh mushrooms
1 pint brown sauce
6 slices foie gras
1 pony brandy

Wipe the squabs inside and out with a damp cloth. Rub with salt and pepper to taste. Braise the squabs in ½ cup butter with carrots, celery, onions and bay leaves. When golden brown on each side, reduce the remaining gravy, add champagne, and cook for a few minutes.

Cut potatoes in shape of orange sections and roast in butter. Braise the onions in ¼ cup butter. Cut salt pork in large dices and boil, then fry it and pour off excess fat. Add mushrooms and simmer for a few minutes and add brown sauce, roasted potatoes and braised onions.

Add champagne gravy to the salt pork mixture and add flaming brandy.

Place squabs in casserole with a slice of foie gras on top. Pour the champagne gravy with the added ingredients over the top of the birds and put in oven until well heated for serving.

BONED SQUAB CHICKEN FLAMBÉ

Stuft Shirt Restaurant
Pasadena, California

6 1½-pound squab
  chickens, eviscerated
6 ounces butter
Salt and pepper
1 cup long grain rice
¾ cup onions,
  finely chopped
¾ pound chicken
  livers

2 cups chicken broth
½ cup cashew nuts
3 ounces dry vermouth
1 piece lemon peel
Pinch of M.S.G., tarragon,
  celery salt
3 ounces cognac

Bone chickens, leaving only leg bones. Rub inside and out with a little butter. Lightly salt and pepper inside and out. In covered pot, sauté raw rice in rest of butter. Add chopped onions, chicken livers and all other ingredients except cognac. Bring to boil. Put cover on pot and reduce flame to simmer. Cook for 30 minutes. Stuff chickens with this mixture, and truss and skewer with small skewers. Roast chickens in 350° oven until tender. Place on garnished serving platter. Pour warm cognac over the birds and ignite at table. Serve immediately.

SQUAB CHICKENS MAISON
(Boneless or With Bone)

Imperial House
Chicago, Illinois

6 squab chickens
1 large onion,
  chopped fine
¾ pound mushrooms,
  diced
6 ounces sweetbreads,
  diced
6 ounces chicken livers,
  diced

¾ pound butter
2 eggs
6 ounces minced meat
3 ounces sausage meat
3 cups risotto
  (see recipe below)
Nutmeg, salt, pepper to taste
¾ cup sherry
¼ pound butter

Bone the chickens. Sauté onion, mushrooms, sweetbreads and chicken livers in skillet in butter. Simmer until cooked. Remove from fire. Allow to cool. Then add eggs, minced meat, sausage meat, risotto. Season with a dash of nutmeg, salt and pepper. Mix well.

Fill boned chickens with stuffing. Roast in casserole dish in oven at 375° for 25 minutes. Remove chickens. Strain gravy and reheat with sherry and ¼ pound butter. Pour over chicken just before serving.

Risotto

1 onion, cut fine	Dash saffron
¼ pound butter	1 bay leaf
1 cup uncooked rice	Salt and pepper
3 cups chicken broth	Parmesan cheese

Place 4 tablespoons butter in shallow pan. Fry onions in butter until light brown. Add rice and chicken broth, saffron and bay leaf. Boil for 2 minutes. Cover and simmer gently until rice is tender and liquid mostly absorbed. Add salt and pepper. Mix with 4 tablespoons butter and sprinkle with Parmesan cheese.

SQUAB CORNISH GAME HEN
À LA CHATEAUBRIAND

Chateaubriand
New York City

6 1¼-pound birds	¼ cup brandy
2 cups cooked wild rice	3 chopped truffles
2 ounces foie gras, diced	¼ cup dry sherry
1 teaspoon nutmeg, ground	¼ cup port wine
1 cup brown sauce	2 ounces sweet butter

Prepare this stuffing: Wild rice, seasoned with salt, pepper and a little nutmeg; add foie gras and 2 ounces chopped truffles.

Bone the birds and stuff. Place them in a buttered pan and roast until well browned in 350° oven, 35 to 45 minutes, until tender. When cooked remove and place on serving dish and keep warm. In pan where birds were cooked, deglace with brandy, sherry and port; add 1 ounce chopped truffles and brown sauce. Let reduce and at last minute add butter. Pour over the birds.

DUAZ—FENJO ALA TUNISIA

La Tunisia Restaurant
Dallas, Texas

6 Cornish game hens,
  1 pound each
Melted butter
  3 apples, peeled and diced
  2 stalks celery, diced
  1 onion, chopped fine
  6 cups cooked saffron rice

Pinch cardamon
Pinch curry powder
Salt and pepper
Honey for glazing
Almonds, blanched and
  sliced

Clean Cornish game hens and brush with melted butter. To prepare stuffing, sauté apples, celery and onion for about 5 minutes. Add saffron, cardamon and curry powder, and sauté for 3 minutes more. Salt and pepper to taste.

Stuff hens and cook for about 1 hour at 400°, or until done. Glaze with honey and almonds. Serve on a bed of saffron rice.

SQUAB STYLE CORNISH HEN

House of Gong
Dallas, Texas

3 Cornish hens
1½ quarts water
  1 cup soy sauce
  1 tablespoon salt
½ cup sugar
Peel of ¼ Chinese dried
  orange
¼ stalk leek or
  ¼ clove garlic
1 clove

2 scallions
2 slices fresh ginger
  1 teaspoon Ac'cent
Pepper as needed
  3 tablespoons vinegar
2 stalks anise
Waterchestnut flour or
  corn starch as needed
Cooking oil for deep frying

Combine all ingredients except Cornish hens and flour or cornstarch. Bring to a boil and let boil for 5 minutes. Put in the Cornish hens and let come to a boil again. Turn the heat low and cook for 20 minutes. Remove the hens and let cool and dry.

Heat oil in deep vessel to 350°. Roll Cornish hens in the flour and fry until brown. Cut into quarters, or smaller pieces if desired, and serve hot.

COUNTRY INN ROCK CORNISH GAME HENS

Edith Palmer's Country Inn
Virginia City, Nevada

Herb Fruited Pilaf Dressing

1 cup wheat pilaf,
  uncooked
2 tablespoons butter
1 small white onion,
  finely chopped

½ tart apple, peeled
2 cups fresh strained
  chicken broth
1 teaspoon Greek oregano
Salt, to taste

Sauté onion, celery, apple and pilaf in butter until pilaf is golden brown. Add chicken broth and seasoning. Cover, bring to boil, reduce heat and simmer for 15 minutes. Cool to room temperature.

Country Inn Special Herb Mix

4 tablespoons dried
  imported Greek oregano
2 teaspoons white pepper

2 tablespoons sweet basil
2 teaspoons dried mint

Mix ingredients and pulverize with mortar and pestle.

Rock Cornish Game Hens

6 Rock Cornish hens
Juice of 3 lemons, strained
¼ to ½ pound butter,
  melted
Salt to taste

Country Inn Special Herb
  Mix (see recipe)
Paprika
1 cup dry sherry wine
½ cup water

Prepare Rock Cornish game birds by removing giblets and neck from the birds. Rinse in cold water. Thoroughly wipe the cavity with paper toweling. Tie wings close to the breasts and the legs close together with heavy white thread. Fill each cavity with 1½ tablespoons pilaf (do not pack). Sprinkle birds with strained lemon juice (½ lemon to each bird). Brush birds with melted butter. Use a pastry brush and be generous. Salt to taste. Sprinkle generously with Country Inn Special Herb Mix. Touch lightly with sweet paprika (for color).

Butter roasting pan, put in 1 to 1½ cups water. Place birds breast up in pan, uncovered. Preheat oven to 450°. Put roaster in oven. Baste birds with wine sauce made of 1 cup sherry and ½ cup water. Baste throughout the cooking. Roast until light golden. Turn birds breast down and roast again until light golden. Turn back breast up, basting constantly, and reduce heat to 300°; cook for 1¾ hours. Remove from roaster and place in warm oven. Remove trussing from birds. Add ½ cup water to drippings in roaster. Scrape pan juices. Heat thoroughly. Pour through a fine strainer into another vessel. Put back on stove and add remaining wine sauce left over from basting.

Grape Sauce

Pan juices   Seedless grapes
Wine sauce

Heat the sauce (pan juices plus wine sauce). Drop in white seedless grapes, 1 tablespoon per serving. Canned grapes may be used. Heat only, do not cook.

Garnish

Endive   6 orange slices
Parsley   12 unpeeled red apple slices

Place birds on garnished, piping hot plate, breast up. Pour heated grape sauce over birds. Garnish with sprig of endive, touch of fresh parsley, choice orange slice, red apple slices.

Note: Constant basting is essential for the success of this recipe.

LE GRAND DUKE PHEASANT

Le Chateau Richelieu
New York City

3 pheasants (use breasts, split in half, and drumsticks)	4 ounces butter
	6 medium sized apples
	6 tablespoons light cream
Salt and pepper to taste	

Season pheasants and brown them in 3 ounces butter, in a heavy skillet. Meanwhile, quarter, peel, mince and lightly toss in the remaining butter the six apples.

Garnish the bottom of a terrine with a layer of apples and place the browned pheasant on top. Arrange around it the remainder of the apples and sprinkle the whole with cream.

Now cover the terrine and bake at 375° for 35 to 45 minutes. Serve the pheasant in the terrine.

ROAST STUFFED PHEASANT WITH WILD RICE À L'ANGOUMOISE

The Holiday Hotel
Reno, Nevada

3, 2–3-pound pheasants	Carrots, sliced
Wild Rice dressing (see below)	Celery, diced
12 slices bacon	1½ bay leaves
Onions, sliced	Rosemary, to taste
	6 ounces brandy

Stuff pheasants with a preparation of wild rice dressing. The birds should be highly seasoned before roasting. Wrap the birds in bacon (4 slices for each pheasant) and roast in 350° oven for one hour on a bed of fresh vegetables (onions, carrots, a little celery, bay leaves and rosemary), basting frequently.

Remove bacon and roast 10 minutes more to allow the outside of the pheasant to brown.

Sprinkle heated brandy over the birds. Remove from pan and serve with a Madeira Sauce (see sauces) on the side, made with brai██████████les and game stock.

Wild Rice Dressing

Note: 1 cup raw wild rice = 3 to 3½ cups cooked wild rice.

3 to 3½ cups wild rice, boiled	4 ounces diced ham
1 small onion, very finely chopped	¼ cup butter
½ pound mushrooms, finely chopped	1 cup cream sauce
	Ground thyme
	1 teaspoon Ac'cent

Sauté onions, mushrooms, and ham in butter. Add boiled wild rice, cream sauce, dash ground thyme, Ac'cent and cook together for 15 minutes.

SALMIS OF DISJOINTED CHUKKAR WITH RED WINE
(Partridge)

The Holiday Hotel
Reno, Nevada

2 chukkar (partridge)	2 teaspoons butter mixed with 2 teaspoons flour
Hot Marinade (see recipe below)	
Flour for dredging	1 cup chicken broth or water
6 tablespoons butter	4 teaspoons butter
4 ounces brandy	2 teaspoons parsley, chopped

Cut 2 chukkar in four pieces: 4 breasts, 4 legs and thighs; and marinate for three hours in hot marinade.

To cook, remove from marinade, drain well, and flour each piece lightly. Pan fry in hot butter until both sides are golden brown. When golden brown, drain the fat and add brandy. Flame the brandy and then add marinade plus butter roux and chicken broth or water. Cover and braise in the oven at 400° for 45 minutes or until done.

When done, remove chukkar from the pan and lay in chafing dish. Strain gravy through ███████ and add 2 ounces butter and chopped parsley. ███████ seasoning if necessary. Pour gravy on chukkar and serve piping hot.

Hot Marinade

2 medium onions, diced	Salt
4 carrots, diced	Crushed black pepper
2 celery stalks, diced	Pinch thyme
Olive oil	Pinch rosemary
2 cups dry Burgundy wine	2 bay leaves

Sauté onion, carrots and celery in olive oil until golden brown. Add Burgundy, and seasonings. Boil for 10 minutes and pour on chukkar parts.

TOURTE FEUILLETÉE AUX CAILLES
(Pâté of Quail)

Four Seasons Restaurant
New York City

Pâté Croustade (for bottom of pan) (see recipe below)	6 quail breasts, boned and skinned
Forcemeat (see recipe below)	Feuilletée (puff paste) (see recipe below)

Place pâté croustade over bottom and sides of 6 x 8 x 2½ inch loaf baking pan, securing pastry under outside rim of pan. Fill with forcemeat and top with 6 boned, skinned quail breasts, which have been stuffed with forcemeat. Top each quail with feuilletée, pressing dough under rim to seal; brush with beaten egg yolk. Bake 1¼ to 1½ hours at 350°.

Pâté Croustade

3 cups flour
6 ounces soft butter
1 teaspoon salt

1½ eggs, beaten
4⅓ tablespoons cold water

Mix all ingredients together, roll out to ¼ inch thickness.

Forcemeat

Legmeat from 6 quail
1 pound boneless pheasant meat
½ pound pork neck
¼ pound goose or pheasant liver (or ¼ pound chicken livers)

3 ounces Madeira wine
2 eggs
⅛ teaspoon marjoram
⅛ teaspoon pepper
½ teaspoon salt

Grind together meats and livers, with Madeira wine. Stir in eggs and seasoning.

Feuilletée

4 ounces butter
4 cups flour (3 cups pastry, 1 cup all-purpose)

2 teaspoons salt
8 to 10 tablespoons water
10 ounces butter

Mix butter, flour, salt and water together to firm dough; let stand 30 minutes. Roll out dough; put 10 ounces butter in center. Fold dough over butter in envelope shape, seal. Roll dough out 4 times, refrigerate 1 hour between each rolling. Roll to ¼ inch thickness.

QUAIL WITH GRAPES

Fleur de Lys
San Francisco, California

½ pound salt pork, sliced
6 quail
½ pound butter
1 pound ripe white grapes
  (preferably muscat type)

Salt and pepper
½ cup dry white wine
 4 ounces Madeira wine
Juice of 1 lemon
 2 ounces cognac

Pluck the quail, eviscerate and wrap in salt pork. Sauté in butter then season and bake 18 to 20 minutes in hot (400°) oven. Skin and pit the grapes, add them to the casserole; add the wine and Madeira and simmer another 20 minutes.

Remove from oven, add the juice of a lemon, and serve in the casserole. Flame with cognac. Quail should be eaten with fingers.

BRANDIED QUAIL

John Bartram Hotel
Philadelphia, Pennsylvania

6 quail
Salt and pepper to taste
½ pound sweet butter
1 cup brandy

½ cup claret port wine
1 cup rich chicken or
  veal stock
1 tablespoon currant jelly

Clean and singe 6 quail. Rub birds inside and out with salt and pepper. Place quail in small roasting pan. Add sweet butter and roast in 375° oven for 20 minutes or until tender. Remove from oven. Add brandy, wine, stock and jelly. Cover tightly and place back in oven for 15 minutes more. Remove from oven. Remove quail from roasting pan. Put sauce back on the stove and allow to simmer for 5 minutes.

Serve on a bed of wild rice with bread sauce on the side.

Bread Sauce

8 slices bread	1 teaspoon butter
1½ cups cream	1 teaspoon sugar
2 pinches nutmeg	

Boil all ingredients together for two minutes. Remove from fire and serve.

BOHEMIAN PHEASANT

Le Chateau Richelieu
New York City

3 2½-pound pheasants	1 cup Madeira
Foie gras (goose liver)	6 tablespoons butter
Salt, paprika	1 cup brandy, heated
3 raw truffles, quartered	

For each pheasant, season a small foie gras with salt and paprika. Stud the foie gras with truffles, and poach in Madeira for 20 minutes. When foie gras is cold, insert into the pheasant, which should be highly seasoned. Truss the birds and cook in butter in a saucepan or a cocotte for 45 minutes. When ready to serve, remove some of the butter used in cooking. Sprinkle the birds with hot brandy and add a few tablespoons of reduced game gravy to the cooking liquor. Serve pheasants in their cooking utensil.

PHEASANT EN CASSEROLE, VALLÉE D'AUGE

Gourmet Restaurant
Terrace Hilton Hotel
Cincinnati, Ohio

3 pheasants, 2½ to 2¾ pounds	4 cups apples, diced
Salt and pepper to taste	6 tablespoons avocado, sliced
Salt pork, sliced	2 cups sour cream
6 to 8 tablespoons butter	

Season birds lightly with salt and pepper. Wrap each in salt pork and tie securely. Brown pheasants in butter in deep casserole. Cover and let simmer over low heat until tender. Add apples, avocado, cream, and cook over slow heat until ready to serve.

TURKEY CORDON BLEU

Hilton Inn
San Francisco, California

6 turkey thigh cutlets, about 5 ounces each
6 1½-ounce slices ham
6 ½-ounce slices Swiss cheese
Salt, pepper, Ac'cent

1 generous cup bread crumbs
Flour for dredging
2 eggs, lightly beaten
Fat for deep frying

Place cutlets between pieces of waxed paper and pound until thin. Put slice of ham and slice of Swiss cheese in the center of each cutlet. Season with salt, pepper and Ac'cent. Fold cutlets and dredge in flour, dip into beaten egg and roll in bread crumbs.

Put in freezer about one hour. Deep fry at 360° until light brown, then put in 400° oven for 20 minutes. Place on rice dressing, well garnished, and topped with Sauce Bordelaise (see under Sauces).

Garnish generally consists of minced ham and shallots in an Espagnole or brown sauce that is flavored with garlic, thyme, mace and claret wine, and slices of beef marrow.

TURKEY IN SHROUD

Fleur de Lys
San Francisco, California

Stuffing

½ pound chicken meat, chopped
½ pound goose liver

1 pint heavy cream
Salt and pepper
1 ounce cognac

Mix all ingredients well, and use to stuff turkey.

Turkey

1 small turkey— 10 or
    12 pounds maximum
1½ pounds ham, sliced
12 truffles, sliced
Salt, pepper, laurel and
    thyme as needed

6 shallots
6 ounces butter
½ pound salted pastry
    dough

Stuff turkey. Cover the entire turkey with slices of ham —then cover entirely with slices of truffles. Use bits of thyme branches to place the truffles on the ham. The turkey must be entirely covered with the truffles.

Place the turkey in a deep earthenware casserole. Add seasoning, shallots and butter. Cover the top of the casserole with pastry dough, making sure to prick openings in dough with fork, to enable steam to escape. Bake in a medium oven, 375°, for 2½ hours.

Present the casserole as it comes out of the oven and then cut off the pastry crust at the table. Only the turkey is to be served.

TURKEY CUTLETS MIRZA

The Canadiana Hotel
Toronto, Ontario

12 3-ounce turkey cutlets
Salt, freshly ground white
    pepper
Flour
  3 ounces butter
1½ cups Rhein wine
  1 teaspoon meat glaze
  2 cups heavy cream
Lemon juice

6 medium tart apples,
    peeled and cut in half
White wine
  2 tablespoons butter
¼ cup sugar
  8 ounces fresh cranberries
Syrup for cranberries—
    1 cup sugar with enough
    water to cover berries
Parsley

Cut 12 3-ounce cutlets from raw turkey breast. Season with salt and freshly ground white pepper. Dip in flour and sauté in clarified butter. Remove cutlets, add Rhein wine and meat glaze. Reduce to one third. Add cream. Reduce to desired thickness and add few drops of lemon juice.

Cut peeled apples in half, using parisienne cutter for removing core. Poach in white wine with 2 tablespoons butter and sugar. Fill apples with fresh cranberries which have been poached in syrup.

Dress turkey cutlets on hot platter. Coat with sauce. Arrange apples around, alternating with whole parsley.

BREAST OF TURKEY BERNICE

Tail o' the Cock
Los Angeles, California

2 ounces butter, melted
¼ cup shallots, finely
  chopped
3 pounds turkey breast,
  sliced
2 ounces sherry wine
1 quart cream sauce or
  bechamel sauce

Salt and white pepper
  to taste
Juice of ½ lemon
1 egg yolk
2 cups cream
⅛ pound butter

Sauté together shallots and butter in heavy pot. Add turkey and wine and simmer together for 5 minutes. Add cream sauce and seasoning and simmer until very hot. Add lemon juice and finish with cream, egg yolk and butter.

SLICED BREAST OF TURKEY SUPRÊME AU GRATIN

The Black Steer
West Allis, Wisconsin

Sliced breast of cooked
  turkey, enough for 6
  servings
Butter

Cooked broccoli
Parmesan cheese, grated
Sauce Suprême (see
  recipe below)

Place cooked broccoli in buttered casserole, cover with sliced turkey. Cover with Suprême sauce, sprinkle with grated Parmesan cheese and bake in oven for 15 minutes at 300°.

Suprême Sauce

½ pound warm butter
3 egg yolks

1 cup heavy cream, whipped
Salt, pepper to taste

Mix whipped cream into butter and egg yolks. Season to taste.

WILLIAMS INN TURKEY NEWBURG

The Williams Inn
Williamstown, Massachusetts

4 tablespoons butter
½ pound mushrooms, sliced
3 tablespoons flour
1 cup chicken or turkey stock
1 cup light cream

Salt, cayenne
3 cups cooked turkey, diced
2 egg yolks
2 to 3 tablespoons sherry
Toast, cut into triangle shapes

Melt butter in the top of a double boiler over direct heat. Add the sliced mushrooms and cook slowly for 8 to 10 minutes. Blend in flour. Pour on chicken or turkey stock and light cream and stir until the sauce comes to a boil. Season with salt and cayenne, and simmer for about 10 minutes over gently boiling water. Add cooked turkey and cook until the meat is thoroughly heated. Just before serving, beat egg yolks slightly with sherry. Add a little of the hot sauce, blend, then stir into the turkey mixture. Cook for a minute or two, just until the yolks have thickened the sauce. Serve in individual casseroles with toast points.

SLICED TURKEY CASSEROLE

Meyer's
Greensboro, North Carolina

Turkey dressing
Cooked turkey, sliced,
   enough for 6 servings
 1 pound frenched string
  beans, cooked

1 cup almonds, blanched
  and slivered
Gravy

In greased individual casseroles arrange layers of dressing, cooked french style green beans, sliced turkey, and cover with gravy. Sprinkle almonds on top. Place in medium oven, 350°, until thoroughly heated through.

TURKEY DRESSING

Vick's Continental Restaurant
Dallas, Texas

Cornbread

1 cup flour
1 teaspoon salt
3 teaspoons baking powder
2 teaspoons sugar

¾ cup corn meal
 2 eggs, well beaten
 1 cup milk
 ¼ cup shortening, melted

Sift flour, salt, baking powder and sugar. Mix with cornmeal. Combine eggs, milk and shortening and add to dry ingredients. Mix until moistened, pour in greased 9-inch square pan. Bake 20 to 30 minutes in 400° oven.

Dressing

Cornbread (see above)
¼ cup celery, chopped
¼ cup onion, chopped

Salt, pepper to taste
 2 eggs, well beaten
2½ cups turkey stock

Crumble cornbread. Add chopped celery and onions, salt and pepper to taste. Add eggs, mix well. Add turkey stock, mix well. Put in baking dish overnight. Bake at 400° for 30 minutes before serving. Sage may be added to taste, if desired.

ROAST DUCK

Latham's on Cape Cod
Brewster, Massachusetts

1 6-pound duck	Salt
1 large onion, peeled	Black pepper
Flour for dredging	

Select a duck weighing six pounds or slightly larger. Wash inside and out, removing excess fat and wipe quite dry. Place a large onion in the cavity. Rub flour all over the duck, massaging it to rub it into the skin thoroughly. Sprinkle with salt and black pepper. Grease a roasting pan with some of the duck fat removed from the duck. Place the duck, back down, in the pan and bake uncovered, in a 400° oven for 1½ hours. Increase the heat to 450° and continue cooking for 30 minutes longer. Remove onion, carve duck into serving pieces, and serve.

ROAST FARM POND DUCKLING

Evans Farm Inn
McLean, Virginia

3 2-pound ducklings	1½ cups currant jelly
Juice of 2 oranges	2 ounces Grand Marnier
Rind of 1 orange, sliced thin	Garnish of spiced prunes, crabapples, orange slices

Place ducklings in open roasting pan on rack and roast in moderate oven, 350°, for 45 minutes or until tender. Cook sliced orange rind in boiling water for 5 minutes until slightly tender. Add currant jelly and orange juice. Stir until blended. Add Grand Marnier to sauce, blend. Serve duckling garnished with spiced prunes, crabapples, and orange slices, with sauce all over.

ROAST DUCKLING WITH CHERRIES AND WILD RICE

Le Chambertin Restaurant
New York City

1 5–6-pound duck	1 large can dark, sweet
½ teaspoon salt	pitted cherries
⅛ teaspoon pepper	2½ tablespoons cornstarch
¼ cup sugar	2 tablespoons cognac
2 tablespoons wine vinegar	3 tablespoons sherry
1 cup sherry	1 tablespoon Grand
2 cups duckling stock	Marnier (orange liqueur)
1 lemon, cut into cubes	1 tablespoon Cointreau

Clean a 5 to 6 pound duck. Season inside with salt and pepper. Lay it on its side on a rack in a shallow roasting pan. Roast at 350° for 1¾ hours or until it is well browned, turning it from side to side and basting it every 15 minutes. Put it on its back for the last 30 minutes to brown the breast.

Carve duck into serving pieces. Keep in warm place. Add the bones left from carving to the giblets and trimmings and prepare a stock to be used in preparing the sauce and wild rice.

In a large heavy saucepan combine sugar and wine vinegar. Heat over a low flame until edges of mixture turn golden brown. Add sherry, duckling stock and lemon cubes. Bring to low boil; simmer covered for 1 hour. Drain juice from large can of cherries and add juice to sauce. Add cornstarch, cognac and sherry, stirring sauce constantly until thickened. Strain sauce and add Grand Marnier and Cointreau. Sprinkle the reserved cherries with sugar and sherry and place under broiler for a few minutes. Broil until cherries are covered with thin crust. Serve carved duckling with broiled cherries and spoon hot sauce over individual servings to glaze duckling and cherries.

Serve with wild rice.

ROAST LONG ISLAND DUCKLING NORWIGANO WITH WILD RICE

Thunderbird Inn
North Wildwood, New Jersey

2 3½-pound ducklings
Kitchen bouquet
Salt
Pepper

Garlic salt
Caraway seed
Paprika

Split ducklings, coat with kitchen bouquet, season with salt, pepper and garlic salt, sprinkle generously with caraway seed, and dust with paprika.

Bake slowly in a moderate (350°) oven until golden brown and crispy.

Wild Rice

1½ cups wild rice
3 quarts boiling water
1 tablespoon salt
3 tablespoons onions,
  finely chopped
3 tablespoons mushrooms,
  finely chopped
3 tablespoons shallots,
  finely chopped

4 tablespoons butter
1½ cups chicken or
  beef stock
2 tablespoons parsley,
  chopped
2 tablespoons chives,
  chopped

Boil rice in boiling salted water, uncovered, for 5 minutes. Drain.

Sauté the rice in duck fat.

Sauté chopped onions, mushrooms and shallots in butter. Transfer rice and vegetables to a roasting pan and add rich chicken or beef stock, chopped parsley, and chives. Cook slowly until rice is tender and dry.

ROAST DUCK NORMANDY

Frenchy's
Milwaukee, Wisconsin

2, 2½ to 3-pound ducks	2 carrots, sliced
Bread stuffing	2 leeks, sliced
1 cup almonds, sliced	2 turnips, sliced
and blanched	4 small onions, cut in half
1 cup seedless raisins	2 oranges, sliced
1½ cups sliced apples	
(seeded and peeled)	

With boning knife or poultry shears, reach into ducks and remove all the fine bones that make up the rib cage. Do not remove the breast bone. Wash birds thoroughly and drain.

To your favorite bread stuffing add almonds, raisins and apples. Stuff the birds with this mixture, truss well and place in a roasting pan which has been lined with carrots, leeks, turnips and onions. Roast for 45 minutes at 350° turning every half hour. Reduce heat to 325° and continue roasting until tender, basting frequently with orange sauce. When duck is golden brown remove and serve on heated platter. Garnish with sliced oranges and plenty of hot orange sauce in a side dish.

Orange Sauce

1 cup sugar	¼ cup Madeira wine
1 tablespoon butter	⅛ teaspoon vanilla
1 cup orange juice	½ teaspoon salt
Juice of ½ lemon	1 tablespoon cornstarch
Grated rind of 1 orange	Water
2 tablespoons Marsala wine	

In a heavy saucepan, slowly heat sugar and melted butter until it caramelizes. Add all other ingredients, except cornstarch, and simmer, stirring all the while, until caramel is dissolved and then thicken with cornstarch dissolved in water. Sauce should be as thick as heavy cream and fairly sweet. Add more sugar if necessary.

DUCK À LA THREE COINS

Three Coins Inn
Baton Rouge, Louisiana

2 4-pound Long Island
  ducklings
3 pounds sauerkraut,
  squeezed of all juice

6 medium apples, cut in
  very small pieces
Salt, pepper and paprika
  to taste

If duck is frozen, defrost completely. Bring to boil a large pot of salted water. When boiling briskly, add the duck and boil for 10 minutes after water comes to boil again. In a large baking pan, spread the sauerkraut mixed with apples. Rub ducks inside and out with salt, pepper and paprika. Set ducks on top of sauerkraut. Bake for 40 minutes in 400° oven. Turn ducks and bake again for 30 to 40 minutes, allowing about 20 minutes per pound. Baste occasionally with juice from the pan. Whole potatoes may be added to bake at the same time, if desired.

LONG ISLAND DUCKLING FLAMBÉ AUX CERISES

Seven Continents Restaurant
O'Hare Field
Chicago, Illinois

1, 5 to 6-pound duckling
Salt, pepper, paprika
  (1 teaspoon of each
  mixed together)
2 carrots, diced large
2 onions, diced large

1 cup white wine
¾ cup Campari
1 cup chicken stock
40 black cherries
¼ cup brandy

Put seasonings inside and outside duckling and roast in 400° oven for 1 hour, uncovered. Reduce oven to 300°, add carrots and onions and cook for 45 minutes more. Baste the duckling 3 or 4 times during roasting process. Remove duckling from oven and strain off fat. To residue, add white wine and ½ cup Campari, and reduce over heat to ½ the quantity. Then add chicken stock, boil 2 or 3 minutes, and strain. Save the liquid, adding the cherries to it.

Cut the duckling into serving pieces and place in a *very hot* skillet. Flambé by pouring over it brandy and ¼ cup Campari. While it is flaming, add the liquid and cherries.

For sure success, the secret is in the Campari.

DUCK WITH ORANGE

The Williams Inn
Williamstown, Massachusetts

1 6-pound duck	1½ cups orange juice
Salt, pepper	½ cup red wine or
2 large oranges	Grand Marnier
1 small onion	3 tablespoons red currant
2 teaspoons potato flour	jelly

Season the duck lightly with salt and pepper. Stuff it with a quartered orange and small onion, and tie the legs together. Place in a roasting pan breast side up, and roast in a moderate oven, 350°, for 20 to 25 minutes to the pound. Keep pouring off the fat as it accumulates, so that when the duck is cooked, there are only about 2 to 3 tablespoons of fat in the pan with all the brown glaze. Meanwhile remove thin slices of the peel from an orange, using a vegetable peeler, and cut them in small julienne strips. Cover with cold water, bring to a boil, and drain. Section the orange.

Place the cooked duck on a hot serving platter and keep it warm. Make the following sauce in the roasting pan: Blend potato flour into the pan juices. Pour on orange juice and red wine or Grand Marnier and bring to a boil, stirring constantly. Add red currant jelly and the drained rind and taste for seasoning. Simmer for a few minutes. Just before serving, add the orange sections. Spoon a little of the sauce over the duck and serve the rest separately.

DUCK WITH ORANGE

Thwaites Inn
City Island, New York

4 carrots, sliced
6 stalks celery, chopped
4 oranges, sliced into
  segments
1 large duck, cut into
  8 pieces
1 teaspoon salt
4 tablespoons butter
3 tablespoons sherry
  or brandy

½ cup currant jelly
Rind of 1 orange
2 tablespoons potato
  flour
1 teaspoon meat glace
1 teaspoon tomato paste
½ cup red wine
1 cup stock

In a baking pan, place the carrots and chopped celery and cover with orange slices. On top place well cleaned large duck, boned, cut into 8 pieces, meat side down. Sprinkle with salt.

Place in a 400° oven and roast for 1½ to 2 hours. Baste every 10 minutes with Burgundy until well browned and crisp.

In a skillet, heat butter, place the pieces of duck in foaming butter and flame with sherry or brandy. Remove duck and add orange rind and cook for 2 minutes. Remove from fire, add potato flour, meat glace, tomato paste, red wine, stock and currant jelly, and a little more salt if desired. Place duck in the pan and keep in warming oven. Take the sections of 3 oranges as garnish. Place duck on serving dish, pour over the sauce and neatly place the orange segments down the center of the dish. Serve hot.

CANARD À L'ORANGE, GOURMET STYLE

The Gourmet Restaurant
Terrace Hilton Hotel
Cincinnati, Ohio

5 to 6-pound duck
Salt and pepper to taste
1 cup dry white wine
1 tablespoon sugar
1 tablespoon vinegar
Juice of 4 oranges
Juice of 1 lemon

2 tablespoons Grand
  Marnier
Peels of 4 oranges, blanched
  and cut julienne
Garnish of orange wedges
  and watercress

Wipe duck with a damp cloth and truss it. Rub it with salt and pepper. Roast in a hot oven, 450°, for 15 minutes. Reduce the heat to moderate, 350°, and continue to roast, allowing 20 minutes to the pound. Baste several times during the cooking period with a cup of dry white wine.

In a small pan melt 1 tablespoon sugar and blend in 1 tablespoon vinegar until it caramelizes. Remove the roasted duck from the oven and set it aside to keep warm. Remove excess fat from roasting pan and to the approximately 1 cup of white stock remaining add orange and lemon juice and Grand Marnier. Scrape bottom of pan well, and blend juices and stock well. Add the caramel-vinegar and cook sauce for 10 minutes more, very slowly.

Carve the duck, arrange it on a hot platter, sprinkle with julienne of blanched orange peels, surround the platter with orange wedges and watercress. Pass the sauce through a fine sieve and serve it very hot on the side.

Suggested accompaniments are a slice of fried hominy and wild rice.

BRAISED DUCK À L'ORANGE

Hotel Astor
New York City

6 pound duck
Salt and pepper
2 stalks celery, sliced
1 onion, sliced

1 carrot, cut in pieces
1 bay leaf
3 ounces shortening

Clean duck well, wash in salt water and season. Place shortening and duck in roasting pan and bake in 400° oven for 30 minutes. Reduce heat to 350° and continue roasting for 1 hour. Baste during roasting time. Drain fat. Add sliced carrots, onions, celery and bay leaf after draining and cook slowly for an additional 30 minutes.

Gravy

4 tablespoons sugar
½ cup orange juice
Juice of 1 lemon
4 cups light brown sauce
Salt, pepper to taste

2 oranges, peeled and diced
Rind of 2 oranges, cut into thin strips

Slice duck, using bones and vegetables for gravy. Place into deep pot, large enough to hold a quart, add sugar and bring to golden color. Add orange juice and lemon juice, stir slowly. Add light brown sauce, season to taste and simmer for 1⅓ hours. Strain gravy and add diced oranges. Place orange rind julienne in boiling water to remove bitter taste, drain and add to gravy. Pour gravy over duck and serve hot.

DUCKLING FLAMBÉ BIGARADE

King Henri IV
New York City

2 4-pound Long Island
  ducklings
Salt and pepper, to taste
1 cup water or stock
3 tablespoons sugar
4 large oranges: Remove
  peel of 2, cut in very
  thin strips
  Juice of 2
  Sections of 2

2 tablespoons currant jelly
2 ounces Curacao
1 tablespoon arrowroot
  or cornstarch
4 ounces Triple Sec
3 cups cooked wild rice

Season ducklings with salt and pepper. Roast 40 minutes, 10 minutes at 450° and remainder at 400°. Remove ducklings and discard fat. Add 1 cup water or stock to pan. Cut ducks in half, saving pieces. Remove breastbone and put in pan with stock. Bring to a boil and simmer for 5 minutes.

Place sugar in a small pan, add a few drops of water and allow to caramelize. Add strained stock to it. Add juice of 2 oranges, currant jelly, and peel of 2 oranges which have been boiled and drained. Add Curacao and thicken with arrowroot or cornstarch.

Place pieces of duckling in serving platter, decorate with orange sections. Heat in oven, add Triple Sec and light with match. Serve with sauce and wild rice.

ROAST DUCKLING WITH BING CHERRY SAUCE

Sheraton-Wayfarer Motor Inn
Manchester, New Hampshire

3 4-pound ducklings
Stuffing for ducklings
1 No. 2½ can pitted
  bing cherries

¾ cup red port wine
1½ tablespoons cornstarch

Stuff ducklings with favorite stuffing. Roast in 325 degree oven on racks for 2½-3 hours, or until tender. Drain cherries, reserve juice, add wine to liquid. Bring liquid to boil and thicken with cornstarch which has been mixed with cold water. Return cherries to sauce and bring to a boil. Split roasted ducklings in halves, lengthwise. Top with hot cherry sauce.

BREAST OF DUCKLING WAIALAE

Kahala Hilton
Honolulu, Hawaii

3 breasts of young ducks
¼ pound butter
½ cup cognac
2 bananas, sliced
Lychee nuts
1 can mandarin orange slices
2 ounces Grand Marnier
3 cups cooked wild rice

Sauté breast of duckling for 15 to 20 minutes in butter. Drain off fat. Flame with cognac. Remove duckling and add to the pan the banana slices, mandarin orange slices and some lychee nuts. Add Bigarade sauce (see recipe below). Let simmer until tender. When ready to serve, add Grand Marnier to the sauce, and pour over the duckling. Serve with wild rice.

Bigarade Sauce

Peel of 2 oranges, cut in julienne
4 tablespoons sugar

Peel oranges and cut in fine julienne (long, thin strips). Boil this peel for 2 minutes and drain well. Place sugar in a small pan and let it come to a light caramel color. Moisten with duck gravy which has been put through a fine sieve. Add the julienne of orange.

MEATS

CHATEAUBRIAND À LA PRESIDENT KENNEDY

Bar Harbor Motor Inn
Bar Harbor, Maine

6 Chateaubriand
3 cloves garlic, chopped
  very fine
4 to 6 shallots, chopped
  very fine
1 pound fresh mushrooms,
  chopped very fine
1 cup butter

1½ cups bread crumbs
2 cups sherry wine
1 pound French (puff)
  pastry
1 egg, well beaten, diluted
  with 2 tablespoons water
Pinch salt
Pinch pepper

Chop garlic, shallots, mushrooms as fine as possible. In a skillet melt 1 cup butter. When the butter starts to smoke, add the chopped vegetables and reduce the fire. Cook gently until done, pour in sherry, and continue to cook until it is reduced to ⅓ its original volume.

Remove pan from fire and cool. Combine with breadcrumbs and make a paste. Next, broil or roast the Chateaubriand rare and set it aside. Roll the pastry dough to ⅛ inch thick and make squares big enough to cover the Chateaubriand.

Paint the dough with the beaten egg and spread the paste evenly over it. Place the Chateaubriand in the center and close it in by joining two opposite ends, and again the other two opposite ends.

Paint the outside of the dough with the egg and bake for 10 to 12 minutes, or until golden brown.

Serve on a platter bordered with chain or Parisien fried potatoes and bouquetière * of assorted vegetables. This dish should be served with red table wine.

* Bouquetière: various vegetables arranged in bouquets.

MIGNON DE BOEUF DUGLERE

Grand Motor Hotel
Montreal, Quebec

12 mignon of beef,
   3 ounces each
2 tablespoons butter
1 tablespoon oil
1 cup tomato purée

Onion rings, fried
Asparagus tips
   1 cup red wine
   1 cup brown sauce
Sauce Bearnaise as garnish

Sauté beef in sauté pan in butter and oil. Arrange on tomato purée and garnish with fried onion rings and sautéed asparagus tips.

Add wine and brown sauce to frying pan and reduce. Pour sauce over mignon and top with Bearnaise sauce.

FILET À LA GRAND VENEUR

The Red Onion
Aspen, Colorado

6 beef filets—6 ounces
   each
Salt
   3 ounces butter
1 tablespoon peppercorns,
   crushed

5 tablespoons whole
   cranberries
3 ounces cognac
6 ounces dry white wine
1 cup natural beef gravy
1 cup cream

Pound filets to approximately one inch in thickness. Sprinkle lightly with salt and broil lightly on both sides. Remove from broiler and set aside. Heat butter in chafing dish, add filets, and cook to desired taste. Add pepper and cranberries around filets and flambé with cognac. Put filets on serving platter and keep them warm. Next add white wine, beef gravy and cream to chafing dish and cook all together until of a creamy consistency. Pour sauce over filets and serve while hot.

Serve with rice, buttered noodles, or your favorite potatoes.

DU BARRY FILET OF BEEF

Farm Fare
Lucerne, Colorado

3 pounds U.S. Top Choice
 filet of beef
Salt and pepper
½ pound butter

1 cauliflower, cut into
 flowerettes
2 cups cheese sauce
Parmesan cheese, grated

Baste filet with melted butter on the top and sides. Sprinkle the whole with salt and white pepper. Place the meat on a rack and roast in a 325° oven to a medium-well doneness. (Internal meat temperature, 160°). Remove filet from oven and let stand at room temperature for 10 minutes.

Cut the filet into ½ pound steaks (against the grain). Place these steaks on a platter and surround them with small mounds of cauliflower flowerettes coated with a heavy cheese sauce and sprinkled with Parmesan cheese.

BEEF TENDERLOINS FLAMBÉS (Filets Mignons)

Motel de Ville
Ottawa, Canada

6 filet mignons,
 1 inch thick
1 teaspoon salt
¾ teaspoon freshly
 ground pepper
6 tablespoons butter
¼ cup shallots, minced
¾ teaspoon dried
 rosemary, crushed
4 tablespoons cognac

1½ teaspoons mild
 mustard
1¼ cup Pinot Noir
 red wine
6 tablespoons dry Madeira
½ pound mushrooms,
 sliced
1 cup heavy cream
3 tablespoons parsley,
 chopped

Sprinkle the filets with salt and pepper on both sides. Heat 5 tablespoons butter in a large heavy skillet. Add filets, shallots and rosemary, cook over high heat 1 minute on each side. Add cognac and flame. When the flame has died down, transfer filets to a heated plate. Spread on each side with a little mild mustard. Keep warm. Pour red wine and Madeira into skillet liquid. Meanwhile, sauté mushrooms in remaining 1 tablespoon butter for about 2 minutes. Add mushrooms, cream and parsley to reduced skillet liquid. Correct seasonings. Return filets to the skillet and cook them uncovered over medium heat for 4 to 6 minutes, or to desired doneness, turning once.

Serve with rice and salad, or Parisienne potatoes and watercress dressed with oil and lemon juice.

FILET "ARIZPE SAINZ" SPECIAL

Hotel Arizpe-Sainz
Saltillo, Mexico

6 filets mignon, approximately ½ pound each
6 slices bacon

Sauce

1½ tablespoon Kitchen Bouquet	1 tablespoon sugar
1½ tablespoons Worcestershire sauce	1 tablespoon mustard
	Agi-No-Moto, salt and pepper to taste

Flatten filets on a chopping board with a meat cleaver or rolling pin to desired thickness. Place slices of bacon on top of each filet, forming a cross. Secure with toothpicks. Put them on a grill or thick frying pan for 5 minutes—3 minutes on one side and 2 minutes on the other.

In an ovenproof shallow plate put the filets and pour over the sauce. Leave the dish in the oven, at 350° for about 5 minutes.

Garnish to taste with Parmesan cheese, grated; radishes; hard-cooked egg; quartered pickled onions; asparagus; hearts of artichokes, grilled; pineapple, lettuce and parsley.

FILET OF BEEF PERIGUEUX

Cafe Renaissance
New York City

6 prime or top choice filets of beef, cut to desired
medaillon size, broiled to your preference.

Sauce Perigueux

1 cup beef stock	2 tablespoons foie gras
¼ cup Madeira wine	2 to 4 truffles, minced
2 tablespoons cognac	

Purée the foie gras in beef stock, adding wine and cognac.
Add truffles and sauté for 5 minutes. Pour sauce over filets
at serving. Serve with petit pois and potatoes varié.

POLYNESIAN DELIGHT

The Castaway
Burbank, California

6 4-ounce filet mignon steaks	6 mushroom caps
6 slices bacon	3 bananas
	3 tomatoes

Wrap one slice bacon around edge of each steak and
secure with toothpick. Broil or sauté to taste. Top cooked
steak with Bearnaise sauce, then a sautéed mushroom cap.
Garnish each filet with one-half baked banana and one-half
broiled tomato with special topping.

Topping for Tomatoes

1 cup bread crumbs	Salt and pepper to taste
3 fresh shallots, chopped	¼ pound butter
3 cloves garlic, chopped	1 teaspoon parsley, chopped
Pinch thyme	

Mix all ingredients together thoroughly and spread on
tomatoes.

FILETS OF BEEF AUX BANANES

Sheraton-Brock Hotel
Niagara Falls, Ontario

2 pounds filet of beef
Salt, pepper to taste
4 ounces butter
1 small onion, sliced
1 cup cream
2 egg yolks
4 bananas

Meat glaze
Horseradish
Flour for dredging
1 egg, beaten
Breadcrumbs
Fat for frying
Brown sauce

Trim the filet and cut into 6 even-sized slices. Season with pepper and salt. Sauté in butter over a quick fire for about 8 minutes. Remove and keep hot. Fry onion, without browning, in butter in which the filets were cooked, add cream, stir until hot not boiling, then add egg yolks and blend. Rub sauce through a strainer and keep hot.

Peel bananas, slice each in two and divide in halves crosswise, dip in flour, egg and breadcrumbs and fry in hot fat. Place the filets on a hot dish, mix some finely grated horseradish with the sauce and put a spoonful of it on top of each filet. Sprinkle with liquid meat glaze and parsley; garnish with fried bananas and serve with brown sauce.

TENDERLOIN OF BEEF À LA LOUIS & ARMAND

Louis and Armand Restaurant
New York City

Dough

1½ pounds flour
¾ pound butter
Pinch salt

Mix ingredients well. Add enough water (about 1 cup) to make a stiff dough. Keep in refrigerator.

Stuffing

¾ pound veal, cut
in small pieces
½ pound ham,
cut in small pieces
½ pound larding pork,
cut in small pieces
1 onion, finely chopped
4 tablespoons Sherry

2 tablespoons stock
6 stalks spinach leaves
2 bay leaves
Salt and pepper to taste
2 egg yolks
⅓ cup Parmesan cheese,
grated

Combine meats and onion and brown in a skillet. Add sherry, stock, spinach, bay leaves and seasoning, and cook over low heat until the meat is done. Put through a food chopper. Then stir in egg yolks and grated cheese.

Filet

Filet of beef, 3½ to 4 pounds

Brown a whole filet of beef on all sides over high heat and allow to cool. Roll out the dough into a rectangle shape, large enough to enclose the filet. Spread dough with a thin layer of stuffing and wrap it around the filet, turning in the ends securely. Bake the whole on the rack of a roasting pan in a moderate oven, 350°, for about 20 minutes. Remove the pan from the oven and let it stand for 10 minutes. With a large spatula, carefully transfer the loaf to a serving platter, taking care not to break the pastry. Serve with Perigourdine Sauce (see below).

Perigourdine Sauce

2 ounces truffles, chopped
3 slices dry mushrooms,
chopped

½ cup Madeira wine
2 cups brown sauce
Salt and cayenne to taste

Chop truffles with mushrooms and cook in a small pan with Madeira wine until the liquid is reduced almost to nothing. Add brown sauce. Season with salt and cayenne to taste.

MEDAILLON HELDER

Eugene's
Reno, Nevada

2¼ pounds filet of beef
3 strips lard
Salt, pepper to taste
Flour for dredging
4 tablespoons butter
¾ cup Madeira

¾ cup Périgourdine
  sauce
1 cup Béarnaise sauce
3 tablespoons stewed
  tomatoes, chopped
6 truffle slices

With special needle, insert small strips of lard inside filet. Divide into six equal slices. Salt and pepper to taste; dredge lightly with flour. Sauté in butter to desired taste (rare, medium, etc.). Remove from skillet and drain off fat. Deglaze with Madeira and Périgourdine sauce (brown sauce with truffle peels and chopped mushrooms) and reduce to half. Take sauce off the fire and put Medaillon of filet back in it. Cover each with a tablespoon of Béarnaise sauce. In the center place a teaspoon of chopped stewed tomatoes, and top all with truffle slice. Place on serving platter, with crouton underneath. With the remaining sauce, whip in remaining Béarnaise sauce, and serve on the side.

This dish should be served with a green vegetable (broccoli or asparagus) and with a basket made of shoestring potatoes (bird nest) filled with small glazed carrots and button mushrooms.

ROAST FILET OF BEEF—COBB'S MILL

Cobb's Mill Inn
Weston, Connecticut

Filet of beef
Olive oil
Salt and pepper to taste

Trim fat and ends from a filet of beef. Rub with olive oil and let stand a few minutes. Season lightly with salt and pepper. Preheat oven to 500°. Reduce heat to 350° and put meat in oven; roast 20 to 25 minutes for medium rare—longer for well done.

Serve in natural gravy or with Mushroom sauce.

BEEF TENDERLOIN SHISH-KEBAB

The Millstone Restaurant
North Attleborough,
Massachusetts

3 pounds choice tenderloin	3 large onions
6 to 8 sweet green peppers	8 medium, firm tomatoes
	3 tablespoons oil

Cut tenderloin into 1½ inch cubes. (Do not marinate.) Cut peppers into quarters and cut onions so that there will be twice the number of pieces as peppers. All should be as equal in size as possible. Select the thick sweet bell peppers, if possible, and large Bermuda onions are preferred.

Precook both the peppers and onions in a skillet with oil, over a low flame, before skewering the Kebabs.

Place at least 5 cubes of beef on each skewer, alternating with tomato, pepper and onion. Two halves of tomato on each skewer is usually ample and it is best to have a cube of meat at both ends of the skewer with the other items in the center, for better broiling. Season to taste and broil over an open flame as you would an ordinary steak. Once on each side brings best results and total average cooking time is approximately 10 minutes.

Serve on a bed of beef-flavored fluffy rice pilaff immediately after broiling.

SPANISH MONDIGILLAS

Fleur de Lys
San Francisco, California

1 whole choice beef filet
  (6 pounds)
½ pound salted pork
Salt
Cayenne
  2 garlic cloves,
  chopped

4 whole eggs
3 egg whites, beaten
Bread crumbs
Frying oil, as necessary
1 pound tomato purée

Trim all fat and fibrous parts from the filet. Use only lean meat. Chop finely together with pork. Season with salt, cayenne pepper and garlic. Then add 4 whole eggs. Form into patties the size of hamburgers. Dip each patty into white of eggs, roll in bread crumbs and deep fry quickly in very hot oil, 375° to 385°. Take out immediately and place them in pan. Cover with tomato purée. Let simmer for ½ hour.

Arrange on platter. Cover with remaining sauce from pan and serve with chopped parsley on top. Garnish with branches of parsley.

COEUR DE FILET PERIGOURDINE
(Heart of Beef Filet Perigourdine)

Fleur de Lys
San Francisco, California

A choice filet of an Eastern
  steer (about 6 pounds)
1½ pounds goose liver
  (foie gras d'Alsace)
1 pound truffles
  (truffles du Périgord)
4 ounces butter—
  for the sauce

1 pint beef glaze sauce
Salt, pepper, thyme
1 laurel leaf
2 ounces fresh mushrooms,
  finely chopped
1 ounce cognac
3 ounces tawny port wine
4 ounces truffles, chopped

Trim beef filet, denerved. It must be entirely lean. Pierce hole in middle all through the filet. Stuff alternately with one slice goose liver, one whole truffle. Season and roast with butter in very hot oven to a rare state, 10 to 12 minutes per pound.

Sauce: Use lean gravy from the roast (separate the fat, which is not to be used). Add spices and mushrooms. Cook 10 minutes. Add cognac, port and chopped truffles. Warm up, but do not boil.

Slice thick slices from the roast. Serve covered with sauce.

FILET OF BEEF WELLINGTON

The Penrose Room
The Broadmoor
Colorado Springs, Colorado

8-9 pound tenderloin
1 pound fresh mushrooms, sautéed in butter
6 shallots, finely chopped

1 pound chicken meat, cooked
Salt, pepper to taste
Puff pastry
1 egg yolk, beaten

Remove fat, chainette and silver skin from tenderloin. Roast for 15 minutes in 500° oven.

Smother and cook mushrooms, shallots and chicken meat together for five minutes; grind through fine blade to make purée; season with salt and pepper. Cover top of filet with this mixture (about ½ inch thick).

Fold over and under a puff pastry cover; decorate top with puff pastry cutouts; brush with egg yolks and bake for 20 minutes (rare) or 30 minutes (medium) at 375°.

TOURNEDOS CORDON ROUGE
with Marchand de vin Sauce

Center Club
Kirkeby Center
Los Angeles, California

8 eight-ounce filets of beef, split horizontally
Strips of bacon
Salt and pepper

Butter
Rounds of bread
8 slices ham
foie gras, sliced

Split the filets of beef horizontally. Wrap each half in a strip of bacon. Season lightly with salt and pepper. Saute in butter to desired degree—rare, 3 minutes; medium, 5; well, 6. Prepare rounds of bread the same size as tournedos. Toast on both sides in butter. Place slice of ham on each piece of toast, top with beef, a half dollar size slice of foie gras, and sauce marchand de vin. Serve with broiled tomatoes and fresh green beans. Serves 8.

Sauce Marchand de vin

Saute ⅓ cup finely chopped shallots in 4 tablespoons butter until brown. Add ¾ cup dry red wine and cook until reduced by half. Add 1½ cups brown sauce and cook over high heat 8 to 10 minutes, stirring occasionally. Strain through a sieve and bring to a boil. Turn off heat and stir in 2 tablespoons cold butter to thicken. Yields 2 cups.

TOURNEDOS OF BEEF

*Club Domino
San Francisco,
California*

Goose liver paste
  6 slices toasted bread
  6 filet mignon
    (the tournedo)
  6 thick slices tomato,
    breaded

Sauce Bearnaise
  (see sauces)
Salt and pepper
  3 zucchini, cut in half
  12 small artichoke hearts

For each serving, spread goose liver paste on one slice of toast. Place one broiled filet mignon on the toast. Then place one breaded, fried slice of tomato on the beef. Pour over Bearnaise sauce. Taste for seasoning.

Stuffed zucchini and artichoke hearts are served on the side.

TOURNEDOS DOMINIQUE

Dominique
Dallas, Texas

6 3-ounce tenderloin
  steaks
6 large mushroom caps,
  sliced
3 ounces roasted peppers,
  chopped

1 cup white
  Burgundy wine
1½ ounces brandy
½ pound butter

Sauté steaks in butter until rare to medium rare. Remove from pan, and to the butter in pan add mushrooms, roasted peppers and Burgundy. Simmer 5 minutes. Return steaks to sauce, add brandy, and flame. Serve at once with wild rice.

TOURNEDOS ROSSINI

The Pickfair Tavern
Toronto, Ontario

6 tournedos (8-ounce
  steaks cut from the filet
  of beef)
6 thin slices
  larding pork
2 to 3 tablespoons
  clarified butter

6 rounds of white bread,
  crusts removed, toasted
6 slices foie gras
6 mushroom caps, sautéed
6 slices truffle
Madeira sauce
  (see under sauces)

Cut steaks from the filet about 1½ inches thick. Tie a thin slice of larding pork (salt pork) around each steak. Sauté in clarified butter over a brisk fire, then set on a round piece of toast. Place a slice of foie gras, slightly smaller than the steak, on top of each steak. Top with a sautéed mushroom cap and garnish with a truffle slice. Place under broiler to quickly heat foie gras. Serve with Madeira sauce.

TOURNEDOS ST. LAURENT

La Saulaie Restaurant des gourmets
Boucherville, Quebec

6 beef filet mignons, 8 ounces each	3 tablespoons oil
3 tablespoons shallots, cut fine	8 tablespoons butter
3 tablespoons parsley, cut	Salt and pepper to taste
	20 ounces canned white asparagus

Heat oil and 3 tablespoons butter in a frying pan. Sear meat on both sides over a very hot fire, then reduce heat for 4-5 minutes additional cooking, for rare. Drain cooking grease, then put remaining butter in pan and heat until golden brown. Remove frying pan from fire, add shallots, salt, pepper and parsley; shake pan to mix. Cut each filet slantwise in 4 pieces and place on hot plate in overlapping slices. Pour hot butter sauce over meat and garnish with hot asparagus spears.

TOURNEDOS NANCY

The Alouette Restaurant
San Francisco, California

6 tournedos, 1 to 1½ inches thick (round, thick cut of filet of beef)	1 package frozen artichoke hearts
6 small new potatoes, peeled	6 small tomatoes, peeled
4 tablespoons butter	Pepper, to taste
Salt	⅜ cup white wine
Ac'cent	⅜ cup bouillon or rich beef stock
	Parsley, chopped

In skillet, sauté potatoes in 1 tablespoon butter until golden brown; sprinkle with salt and Ac'cent. Cover and simmer until almost tender. Add artichoke hearts; season; continue cooking until potatoes and artichokes are done, about 10 minutes. Add whole tomatoes, just long enough to heat through but not cook. Season tournedos with salt, Ac'cent and pepper. Brown quickly on both sides in 3 tablespoons butter, cooking to desired doneness; set aside to keep hot. Pour fat from pan, add wine and bouillon, simmer until reduced to half. To serve, arrange a potato, tomato, tournedo, and artichoke heart on each plate. Spoon sauce over all; sprinkle tomato with chopped parsley or chive.

TOURNEDOS À LA MAISON

Sanford's
Oakland, California

12 slices tenderloin
   of beef
Salt and pepper to taste
 6 tablespoons butter
 6 English muffins
 3 ounces brandy
 1 teaspoon beef extract
¾ cup brown stock

12 canned artichoke
   bottoms
 1 3-ounce can pâté
   de foie gras
Garnish of glazed carrots
   and asparagus
   Hollandaise

Cut slices of tenderloin 2 ounces each. Flatten slices to ¼ inch thick. Salt and pepper and pan fry in butter over brisk flame for about 2 minutes on either side for medium rare. Place tenderloin slices on halves of English muffins arranged on a serving dish. Place frying pan back on flame and add brandy, beef extract and brown stock; stir and let simmer.

Stuff artichoke hearts with pâté, place on tenderloin slices. Pour sauce over each artichoke. Serve with glazed carrots and asparagus Hollandaise.

COEUR DE BOEUF MAISON

Leonello Restaurant
Shaker Heights, Ohio

 6 individual tenderloin
   steaks
⅜ pound butter
Chives, minced, to taste
 6 teaspoons dry

English mustard
Salt, pepper to taste
Juice of 1 lemon
Dash of Worcestershire
   sauce

In a heavy skillet put 1 tablespoon butter for each steak, chives to taste, and dry English mustard. Add salt and pepper to taste. Cook steaks to doneness desired. Remove meat from pan and keep hot. Make sauce by adding 6 tablespoons butter to juice in pan, lemon juice, dash of Worcestershire sauce, and simmer for a few minutes. Pour sauce over meat and serve.

STEAK DIANE FLAMBÉE

Danny's
Baltimore, Maryland

6 filets of beef, 8 ounces each	1½ tablespoons Worcestershire sauce
½ pound butter	6 tablespoons Sauce Robert (Escoffier)
1 pound mushrooms, sliced fine	1½ teaspoon salt
¾ cup shallots, chopped fine	2 teaspoons freshly ground pepper
2 tablespoons chives, chopped	1 cup beef stock
2 tablespoons parsley, chopped	1¼ cup cognac
	¾ cup dry Sherry
	3 cups cooked wild rice

Melt butter in the top pan of a chafing dish. Add and sauté mushrooms and shallots. Sauté for 5 minutes. Add chopped chives and parsley. Add Worcestershire sauce, Sauce Robert, salt and pepper and simmer well over the flame for 15 minutes.

In another skillet sauté beef in butter. When done to a medium turn add cognac and set aflame. When the flame is extinguished, add sherry.

Serve Steak Diane on a heated platter and spoon sauce on top. Ring platter with wild rice and serve.

STEAK DIANE IMPERIALE

Imperial House
Chicago, Illinois

For each Individual Serving:

5 to 6 tablespoons butter
4 drops Worcestershire sauce
2 ounces red or white wine
1 teaspoon prepared mustard
1 tablespoon Escoffier Sauce Diable

1 tablespoon A-1 sauce
½ teaspoon shallots, chopped
2 pinches chives, chopped
Salt and freshly ground pepper to taste
1 8-to-10-ounce minute steak

In a pan, smother shallots and chives in 2½ tablespoons butter. Add the wine and reduce it by half. Then add the mustard, Escoffier Sauce Diable and A-1 sauces, mix the ingredients thoroughly and bind the sauce with 1½ tablespoons butter.

Take a regular minute steak and pound it very thin. Fry the steak in a very hot flat pan, in 1½ tablespoon butter for 2 minutes on each side. Put steak on a very hot plate and pour sauce over it. Add salt and freshly ground pepper to taste.

TERIYAKI STEAK

Pieces of Eight Restaurant
Marina Del Rey, California

6 12-ounce filet mignon steaks
1½ ounces fresh ginger, chopped

1 cup soy sauce
1 cup Worcestershire sauce
½ cup sherry wine

Marinate steaks in marinade, made up of ginger, soy sauce, Worcestershire sauce and sherry, for 24 hours; then broil to desired doneness. Serve with Teriyaki Sauce (see below).

Teriyaki Sauce

1 cup honey
½ cup corn syrup

2 ounces fresh ginger,
   chopped
Cornstarch

Boil honey, corn syrup and ginger together for five minutes, thickening slightly with cornstarch.

GRENADINE OF BEEF TENDERLOIN
SAUCE BEARNAISE

Ernie's Restaurant
San Francisco, California

2½ to 3 pounds filet
  (already cleaned, use
  either head or tail)
12 small strips lard
Salt and pepper
3 tablespoons butter
 1 cup sauce Chasseur
  (see recipe under sauces)

4 tablespoons butter
2 tablespoons parsley,
  chopped
1 cup Bearnaise sauce (see
  recipe under sauces)
6 mushroom caps
Glace de viande *

Divide beef in 12 parts around 3 ounces each. Flatten, pound to resemble scallopine. Insert 1 strip of lard in each piece of beef. Salt and pepper; then sauté quickly in butter, approximately 1 minute each side, depending upon individual taste. Put cup Chasseur sauce on serving tray with 3 tablespoons butter and 1 tablespoon parsley. Place Grenadine of Beef on top individually. Top Grenadine with Bearnaise Sauce and top again with mushroom cap sautéed in 1 tablespoon butter; then with glace de viande (brown stock).

* Glace de viande can be bought commercially. It is a meat extract.

SLICED BEEF TENDERLOIN SAUTÉ
WITH BLACK MUSHROOMS

London Chop House
Detroit, Michigan

2 ounces butter
2 cloves garlic
Salt
1 medium onion, very
  finely chopped
¼ pound dried black
  Chinese mushrooms

2 ounces butter
1 to 1½ pounds beef
  tenderloin (sliced in 12
  2½ inch squares
Salt, pepper and paprika to
  taste
3 tablespoons dry Sherry

Melt 2 ounces butter in sauté pan over low heat; add garlic cloves, finely mashed with salt, and very finely chopped onion. Cook until onion is transparent, about 7 minutes.

Add dried black Chinese mushrooms which have been soaking overnight in water and then drained on absorbent paper (save liquid for soups). Tough stems are removed and the large mushrooms cut in two with kitchen shears. Lower flame to less than medium and cook 10 minutes.

In another sauté pan, melt 2 ounces butter over medium high flame. Sauté beef tenderloin slices, which have been seasoned with pepper, salt and paprika.

When meat is browned on both sides, add and combine the mushroom mixture. Cook three minutes. Add 3 tablespoons dry sherry. Blend and cook two minutes.

TENDERLOIN OF BEEF KIMBERTON

The Kimberton Country House
Kimberton, Pennsylvania

12 slices filet mignon, 2½
  inches thick
¼ pound butter
6 pieces toast
½ pound mushrooms,
  sliced

2 tablespoons butter
¾ cup beef stock
2 ounces Burgundy
Salt, pepper to taste

Medium sauté in butter slices of filet mignon. Season to taste. Place in casserole dish on toast slices, using two slices of filet to each slice of toast. Add mushroom and Burgundy sauce, piping hot, and serve.

Mushroom and Burgundy Sauce

Sauté mushrooms in butter to a golden brown. Add beef stock and Burgundy wine. Season to taste. Heat thoroughly.

MEDALLIONS DE BOEUF SAUTÉS, AMBASSADEUR

Place Pigalle
San Francisco, California

12 slices beef filet, cut about ¾ inch thick
¼ to ⅓ cup butter

Pan sauté filet of beef. When done to individual tastes, serve on bed of wild rice a la Place Pigalle * and top with Bearnaise Sauce.**

* See wild rice recipe
** See Bearnaise sauce recipe

MEDALLIONS OF FILET MIGNON

Chart Room
Anchorage-Westward Hotel
Anchorage, Alaska

For each Individual Serving:

2 slices of filet mignon, about 1¼ inch thick and slightly larger than a silver dollar (about 2¼ inch)
4 tablespoons butter (plus 1 tablespoon for each additional slice)
Fresh ground black pepper
Salt, to taste

Juice of ½ lemon
1½ tablespoons Claret
1 tablespoon Worcestershire sauce
½ tablespoon A-1 sauce
1 tablespoon chopped mushrooms
2 whole mushroom caps
Watercress, for garnish
Chopped parsley

Use meat from the long tenderloin of the filet mignon. Cut pieces approximately 1¼ inch thick and slightly larger than a silver dollar. Form into a round shape like a silver dollar. Use a crêpes pan or other similar sautéing pan. Preheat pan, add to hot pan butter, 4 tablespoons, with an additional tablespoon for each additional filet. While butter is melting, sprinkle the raw meat with fresh ground pepper and rub into meat with the back of a tablespoon. Place meat into pan, add salt to taste, then cook to order. Remove meat from pan and place on an oval platter.

Into pan add juice of ½ lemon, drip juice into pan slightly so that it will ignite and flame slightly. Hold the hands approximately 1½ to 2 feet above the pan. Add Claret, and more butter if necessary but not more than 4 additional tablespoons. Add Worcestershire and A-1 sauce, 1 tablespoon chopped mushrooms per serving, and sauté in mixture. Put meat back into pan and reheat with the mushrooms and sauce. Add 2 whole mushroom caps per serving to sauce.

After reheating, place 2 slices Medallions on each entree plate garnished with a sprig of watercress. Spoon the chopped mushrooms and sauce over the Medallions and place one large mushroom cap on each piece of meat. Sprinkle lightly with chopped parsley. Serve immediately.

MEDAILLONS OF BEEF TENDERLOIN FORESTIERE

The Macdonald Hotel
Edmonton, Alberta

6 ½-inch thick slices beef tenderloin
Salt, pepper to taste
1 cup diced bacon
½ cup onions, diced

2 cups mushroom caps, quartered (cepes if available)
3 tablespoons butter
2 cups diced potatoes
Parsley, chopped
Demi-glace

Cut ½-inch thick slices of tenderloin from the center of a filet of beef. Season with salt and pepper and sauté 30 seconds on each side in a very hot cast iron sauté pan. Have the following garnish ready and serve immediately:

Sauté until golden brown, 1 cup largely diced bacon with ½ cup diced onions. Add quartered mushroom caps. In another pan sauté in butter diced potatoes, until brown and cooked and mix with other ingredients. Place this garnish alongside the medaillons and sprinkle with chopped parsley. Accompany with demi-glace* in a sauce boat on the side.

* Demi-glace—see recipe under sauces

SCALLOPED BEEF TENDERLOIN À LA DEUTSCH

The Macdonald Hotel
Edmonton, Alberta

1½ pounds beef tenderloin (scalloped)
2 cups mushrooms, sliced
1 green pepper, cut into large dice
1 large onion, cut into large dice
¾ cup red pimento, cut into large dice
6 tablespoons clarified butter
1 cup tomatoes, peeled and diced
Salt, pepper
4 ounces red wine
1 cup brown sauce
Chopped parsley

Sauté mushrooms, onions, green peppers, in half the butter until transparent or limp, then add the tomatoes and red pimento. Toss lightly for approximately one minute.

In a separate frying pan over a very hot fire, heat the remaining butter to the smoke point and quickly toss the beef tenderloin for one or two minutes, adding salt and freshly ground pepper to taste. Pour on red wine, tossing lightly again and adding brown sauce, then immediately place on a hot platter. Place the sautéed vegetable garnish on top and sprinkle with chopped parsley; serve immediately.

Can be served with rice.

BROCHET OF BEEF ON WILD RICE

Barney's
Calgary, Alberta

Brochets

Center cut beef tenderloins, sliced in half lengthwise

Cut brochets approximately 6 ounces each; broil or grill as you would a Chateaubriand.

Wild Rice

1 cup wild rice
6 cups warm water
1 teaspoon salt

Wash wild rice several times in cold water; drain. Cover with 6 cups warm water and 1 teaspoon salt. Bring to a boil, then simmer until tender, approximately 20 to 30 minutes. Rinse rice with cold water and drain. Makes about 3 cups.

Fried Wild Rice

3 cups cooked wild rice
¾ cup butter
1 green pepper, chopped
1 onion, chopped
¼ pound mushrooms, chopped
¼ cup almonds, blanched and slivered
Salt and pepper to taste

Place butter in frying pan, add peppers, onions, mushrooms and almonds and fry until tender. Add wild rice and spices. When wild rice is hot, remove from heat.

Place wild rice in middle of plate. Place brochet on top and garnish with parsley.

BEEF À LA FRENCH MARKET

Hotel Blackstone
Omaha, Nebraska

2½ pounds sliced beef
   tenderloin tips
2 tablespoons oil
4 tablespoons flour
2 cups tiny whole carrots
2 cups fresh or frozen peas

1 cup mushrooms, sliced
½ cup shallots
6 cups cooked egg
   noodles
½ cup red wine
Salt and pepper to taste

Sauté beef tips in cooking oil, quickly so they remain rare. Remove from pan. Stir flour into the drippings, then add water to make thick sauce.

Add red wine and vegetables and let simmer until the vegetables are done. Put beef back in the pan. Pour over the previously cooked noodles and serve hot.

TENDERLOIN TIPS IN BURGUNDY WINE

Hotel Severin
Indianapolis, Indiana

6 tablespoons butter
1½ pounds beef tenderloin,
   cut in very thin 2-to-3-
   inch strips
½ teaspoon salt
2 medium onions, chopped

2 green peppers, chopped
1¼ cups brown beef gravy
   or 1 can brown gravy
1 cup red Burgundy wine
2 tablespoons cornstarch

Melt two tablespoons butter in skillet. Sprinkle beef with salt. Sauté one-third of meat at a time, browning strips quickly all over; then remove from pan, adding two tablespoons more butter as needed. Add remaining butter to empty skillet; sauté vegetables for about 3 minutes. Add gravy. Slowly stir wine into cornstarch, then into gravy mixture. Cook and stir until mixture bubbles; cook and stir 2 minutes longer. Season with salt and pepper. Add browned beef; heat thoroughly.

SAUTÉ BEEF TENDERLOIN

The Garden Seat
Clearwater, Florida

2½ pounds beef tenderloin trimmed of all fat and cut into ½ to ¾ inch squares
4 ounces butter
¼ cup olive oil
Salt, pepper to taste

1 tablespoon onion, minced
2 to 3 tablespoons dry white wine
2 cups heavy cream
Flour
Buttered egg noodles

Sizzle the meat in butter and oil combined, salt and pepper to taste. When lightly browned, drain off the oil and butter. Cook onions in lightly greased pan until soft, add wine, the oil and butter that the meat was browned in, cook for 3 or 4 minutes more. Add cream and cook until thickened, adding a little flour if you desire a thicker sauce. Add browned beef and cook over low heat for 10 to 15 minutes. Serve on buttered egg noodles, adding wine before serving; 2 or 3 tablespoons is usually enough. Prime tenderloin is desirable for this dish as the cooking time is short, and tender meat is necessary.

BEEF TENDERLOIN TID-BITS

Arrowhead Lodge
Lake Ozark, Missouri

2¼ to 2½ pounds beef tenderloin
Flour for dredging
3 tablespoons butter
1 pint brown sauce
1 medium onion, sliced

1 medium bell pepper, sliced
8 mushrooms, sliced
¼ cup Burgundy
4 tablespoons catsup
3 to 4 ounces Sherry

Cut beef tenderloin into 12 pieces, roll in flour, and sauté in butter until medium done. Add brown sauce. Sauté onion, pepper and mushrooms in butter. Add Burgundy, catsup and Sherry. Blend all together and serve.

GRENADINE OF BEEF MEXICAINE

Beverly Hilton Hotel
Beverly Hills, California

12 thin slices beef
   tenderloin
Salt and pepper
½ cup clarified butter
 1 green pepper, seeded,
   diced and cooked in
   butter until tender

1 cup sliced mushrooms,
   cooked in butter until
   wilted
½ cup brown sauce

Sprinkle meat with salt and pepper and cook in butter to desired degree of doneness. Add the pepper, mushrooms and brown sauce. Serve hot.

BEEF TIPS BURGUNDY

Lazarus
Columbus, Ohio

 5 pounds beef cubes (1
   inch)
10 tablespoons flour
½ cup shortening
 3 cups tomato soup
   (undiluted)
 3 cups water
 2 tablespoons salt

½ teaspoon thyme
 1 tablespoon Worcester-
   shire sauce
 1 bay leaf
¾ cup Burgundy wine
 1 pound (raw weight)
   broad noodles

Dust meat cubes with flour and brown in shortening. Add tomato soup, water, salt, thyme, Worcestershire sauce and bay leaf to browned beef cubes. Braise in 350° oven until tender, approximately 1½ hours. Add Burgundy wine when finished cooking. Let stand ½ hour before serving to blend wine flavor. Serve over buttered broad noodles.

BEEF BOURBONNAISE

*The Mount Kineo
Kineo, Maine*

2 pounds sirloin tips (or cubed top round)
1 medium onion, finely chopped
½ green pepper, finely chopped
¼ pound butter

1 tablespoon flour in ¾ cup water
1 tablespoon parsley, chopped
½ teaspoon garlic powder
½ pint sour cream
2 ounces Burgundy
Dash Worcestershire sauce

Sauté onion and pepper in butter in hot pan. Add beef and allow to brown quickly. Add flour mixture and stir constantly until desired thickness occurs. Add salt, parsley and garlic powder. Taking care not to overcook beef (center of cubes should be slightly red), add sour cream and wine. Serve shortly after adding sour cream and wine.

A vintage Bourjolais is suggested with this dish, together with a simple green salad and wild rice.

BARBECUED STEAK SUN VALLEY STYLE

*Sun Valley Inn
Sun Valley, Idaho*

6 New York sirloin steaks, or 6 club steaks (14 ounces per steak. Use prime or choice)
1 small clove garlic, rubbed well into steak
Small amount dry mustard

Small amount barbecue spice
4 drop liquid smoke to each steak
Salt and pepper to taste
Enough oil to cover steaks
Onion slices
12 large mushrooms

Rub garlic, dry mustard, barbecue spice and liquid smoke into each steak, season to taste and marinate in olive oil. Broil over charcoal. Serve with grilled onion slices and large mushrooms.

ENTRECOTE SAUTÉ "MARCHAND DE VIN"
(Ribs of Beefsteak - Sirloin Steak)

Essex House
New York City

6 sirloins of prime beef,
  trimmed (12 ounces
  each)
Salt, pepper
6 tablespoons butter
6 ounces marrow, sliced
1½ tablespoons shallots,
  chopped

2 tablespoons butter
1 pint red wine
6 ounces Fond de Veau
  (gravy made with veal,
  onions, carrots and
  herbs)
1½ teaspoons parsley,
  chopped

Cook the shallots lightly in 2 tablespoons butter, then add red wine. Reduce almost to a glaze. Add the fond de veau—let simmer lightly for about 30 minutes and drain the resulting sauce.

Season the steaks with salt and pepper. Sauté the steaks in 3 tablespoons butter as desired, rare or medium-rare. Remove the steaks and add the red wine mixture to pan and simmer gently. Add the remaining 3 tablespoons butter while stirring the sauce. Check the seasoning and drain this sauce again.

In the meantime, poach the marrow in salted water. Drip the sliced marrows dry and place them carefully on the steaks, spread the sauce over the steaks. Garnish with chopped parsley.

Note: Serve the above very hot, but avoid overheating of the platter as this hardens the steaks.

GERMAN RHEINEBRATEN

Santa Barbara Inn
Santa Barbara, California

6 10-ounce sirloin steaks
Salt and pepper to taste
Flour for dredging
5 tablespoons lard
2 large onions, sliced
3 large apples, diced
1 tablespoon paprika

3 tablespoons flour
1 quart consommé or chicken broth
24 whole stewed prunes, pitted
1 pint sour cream

Season steaks with pepper and salt, roll in flour, brown in 2 tablespoons lard until almost done, put aside. Sauté, in 3 tablespoons lard, onions and apples until golden. Add paprika and 3 tablespoons flour, cook for 5 minutes. Add hot consommé or chicken broth, simmer for 10 minutes. Add prunes and steaks, simmer for 20 minutes. Add salt and pepper to taste. Before serving, fold in sour cream. Serve with buttered noodles Polonaise (see below).

Buttered Noodles Polonaise

1 pound noodles
¼ cup bread crumbs
1 tablespoon butter

1 hard cooked egg, chopped fine
1 tablespoon parsley, chopped

Cook noodles, wash off starch. Sauté bread crumbs in butter until brown. Add finely chopped hard cooked egg, chopped parsley, mix well with buttered noodles.

PYRAMIDES DE BOEF TASTEVIN

Four Seasons Restaurant
New York City

2 pounds boneless sirloin beef
6 thin slices beef suet

6 slices beef
Sauce Garniture (see recipe below)

Have butcher cut sirloin beef into boneless piece about 1¾ inches thick, weighing 2 pounds. Cut beef into 6 individual pieces, pyramid shaped. Cover each piece with paper thin layer sliced beef suet, then paper thin slices of any boneless beef. Place meat in roasting pan; roast about 25 minutes at 350° for rare. Remove fat and meat layers; discard fat. Serve beef with sauce garniture.

Sauce Garniture

6 shallots, chopped
6 ounces red Burgundy wine
6 ounces beef gravy
½ ounce Marc (or brandy)
¼ pound butter, softened
24 tiny pearl onions, peeled
1 tablespoon butter
1 tablespoon sugar

2 ounces dried currants (soaked 1 hour in warm water and vinegar)
¼ pound fresh red currants (or 1 3-ounce jar red currants in sugar syrup)
10 ounces canned French cèpes (mushrooms) drained
½ teaspoon salt
¼ teaspoon pepper

Place shallots and Burgundy in sauce pan. Simmer slowly until reduced by half. Add beef gravy, Marc (or brandy). Stir in soft butter, strain. Set sauce aside.

Boil tiny peeled pearl onions until tender; drain. Sauté with 1 tablespoon each butter and sugar. Add dried currants, which have been soaked in warm water and vinegar, and fresh red currants or canned red currants, in sugar syrup. If canned currants are used, omit sugar.

In another pan, sauté canned French cèpes. Add to cèpes the reserved sauce, the onion currant mixture. Simmer all ingredients together a few minutes. Season with salt and pepper.

BUTTER-YAKI

Yamato Sukiyaki Restaurant
San Francisco, California

2 cups mushrooms, sliced
2 cups scallions, cut in 1½ inch pieces

½ cup melted butter
2 pound sirloin steak, cut into ½" x 2" strips

Sauce

¾ cup Shoyu sauce
Juice of 1 lemon

1 teaspoon Japanese wasabi (horseradish may be substituted)

Pan fry mushrooms and scallions in butter until tender. Add meat and cook to desired doneness. Make sauce by combining Shoyu sauce and lemon juice, add wasabi to desired taste. Sauce should be served in individual bowls as a dip for the butter-yaki.

SUKIYAKI

Miyako Sukiyaki Restaurant
Pasadena, California

1 small piece beef suet
1½ pound top sirloin or rib steak, sliced bacon thin
1 cup celery, sliced
2 bunches scallions, cut 2 inches long
¾ cup fresh mushrooms, sliced

¾ cup bamboo shoots, sliced
¾ cup fresh bean sprouts
4 medium onions, sliced
4 cups partially boiled spinach leaves
3 cups boiled rice
Sukiyaki cooking sauce (see recipe below)

Arrange vegetables and meat in groups on a large platter, and place near charcoal hibachi or electric skillet. Preheat iron pan or 12-inch skillet, rub bottom with suet and heat until bottom is coated with fat. Remove suet, and add vegetables, keeping them in separate groups. Add meat and cooking sauce. Turn vegetables and meat over once during cooking. Serve while vegetable is still crisp, with hot rice. Sugar and more sauce can be added if necessary.

Sukiyaki Cooking Sauce

2 ounces Japanese wine (Sake)
4 teaspoons sugar
1½ teaspoons M.S.G.

¾ cup Japanese soy sauce
1 cup consommé or beef stock

Heat ingredients and blend until sugar dissolves.

CANTON GREEN PEPPER MUSHROOM STEAK CUBES

Bamboo Terrace
Vancouver, British Columbia

1 2-pound sirloin steak, 1-inch thick, marinated in
2 tablespoons soy sauce
1 cup celery, slant-sliced ¾-inch long
1 medium onion, cut in 6 sections, separated

2 medium green peppers, sliced in 1-inch strips
1 can mushrooms (drain and retain liquid for use)
2 cloves garlic, crushed
2 tablespoons corn starch
½ teaspoon M.S.G.
4 tablespoons vegetable oil

Heat oil very hot in large skillet. Quickly sear both sides of steak brown. Remove meat to a dish. When cooked, cut in 1-inch cubes. Sprinkle salt and pepper over meat. Using same hot skillet and oil in pan, add garlic and vegetables and fry for 3 minutes. Add salt, M.S.G., soy sauce and half of mushroom liquid. Cover and cook 3 minutes. Add cubed steak. Mix well in skillet. Do not overcook vegetables. Make a smooth paste with remaining mushroom liquid and cornstarch. Add to meat mixture, stirring until gravy thickens.

RAGOUT OF BEEF

Corinne Dunbar's
New Orleans, Louisiana

2 pounds beef sirloin, cut
  in 6-inch squares ½
  inch thick
1½ tablespoons shortening
2 tablespoons flour
1 onion, chopped
1 clove garlic, minced

4 sprigs thyme, chopped
2 bay leaves
1 bell pepper, chopped
4 sprigs parsley, chopped
2 tomatoes, chopped
2 cups water
Salt and pepper to taste

Brown beef in shortening and remove from skillet. Add flour and all seasonings to fat in skillet and brown thoroughly to make a dark roux. Add tomatoes and water. Cover and simmer mixture for about 30 minutes. Add beef and simmer until meat is tender. Serve gravy with the beef.

BIFTEC CASSERO

Gaucho Steak House
Americana Hotel
Bal Harbour, Florida

1 pound prime sirloin
  steak for each serving
Olive oil, mildly spiced
Shallots, finely chopped

Onions, finely chopped
Pinch marjoram
Red Burgundy wine

For each serving, marinate one pound prime sirloin steak in mildly spiced olive oil, and broil to the individual's liking. Place on a bed of fine shallots and onions, delicately flavored with a pinch of marjoram and sweetened with vintage red Burgundy wine.

ENTRECOTE KALAKAUA

Kahala Hilton
Honolulu, Hawaii

For each individual serving

1 12-ounce New York
  Steak
1 clove garlic, finely
  chopped
1 shallot, finely chopped

French mustard
2 ounces butter
1½ ounces brandy
½ cup red wine sauce

Sauté steak in skillet over high fire to almost the desired cooking point. In second skillet, sauté shallot and garlic in butter. Put steak in and coat both sides with very little French mustard. Pour brandy in and set aflame. Take steak out and pour wine sauce in skillet to blend with first ingredients. Simmer 3 minutes. Then pour sauce over the steak. Raisin noodle cake is served with this dish.

Raisin Noodle Cake

Cooked noodles, about 1½
  cups
1 cup milk
2 eggs, beaten

Salt and pepper
Ground cinnamon
Dry raisins

Mix cooked fine noodles with milk and remaining ingredients. Fill small ovenproof dishes with mixture and bake approximately 10 minutes at 350°.

STEAK AU POIVRE À LA NORMAN

Thunderbird Inn
North Wildwood, New Jersey

6 club steaks, or boneless
  New York strip steaks
2 tablespoons coarsely
  ground black pepper

2 tablespoons butter
Chablis
Watercress

Sprinkle steaks with pepper. Sauté in butter until they reach desired doneness. Transfer to platter. Flame pan with Chablis. Reduce one-third. Pour over steak and garnish with watercress.

ENTRECOTE MINUTE À L'AIGLON

L'Aiglon Restaurant
New York City

6 14-ounce steaks, pounded to ⅛ inch
½ pound butter
4 tablespoons olive oil
6 teaspoons chives, chopped very fine

Salt
Black pepper
6 tablespoons Worcestershire sauce
6 teaspoons English mustard

Put butter, oil and chives in a fairly large frying pan. Cook over a very strong fire until almost black—chives should be almost consumed.

Add steak which has been salted and peppered, and cook two minutes on each side. Add Worcestershire sauce and mustard to sauce. Serve immediately on warm platter.

BEEF STROGANOFF
(Beef in Sour Cream)

Cafe Jardin Suisse
Roney Plaza Hotel
Miami Beach, Florida

2 pounds beef filet, cut into thin strips
Salt and pepper
1 tablespoon flour
2 tablespoons butter
2 cups beef stock

3 tablespoons heavy sour cream
2 tablespoons tomato juice or paste
3 tablespoons butter
3 tablespoons onion, grated

Cut filet of beef into thin strips, sprinkle freely with salt and pepper, and let stand for two hours in a cool place or in the refrigerator.

Make a roux by blending 1 tablespoon flour with two tablespoons butter over low heat until the mixture bubbles and is smooth. Gradually stir in beef stock and cook until the mixture begins to thicken. Boil for 2 minutes, then strain through a fine sieve into a saucepan. Add sour cream alternately with tomato juice or paste, stirring constantly. Simmer very gently, without boiling.

Meanwhile, fry the beef in 3 tablespoons butter with grated onion. When the meat is brown, pour the meat, onion, and butter into the sauce, taste for seasoning, and simmer gently, or cook in a double boiler over hot water for 20 minutes.

Serve at once with a side dish of boiled rice or potato balls and thin slices of dark bread generously buttered.

BEEF STROGANOFF

Schine Queensbury Inn
Glens Falls, New York

3 tablespoons flour
1½ pounds round or
    tenderloin steak, cut
    ½ inch thick
¼ cup butter or margarine
¼ cup onion, chopped fine
½ pound mushrooms,
    peeled and sliced

1 teaspoon soy sauce
¼ teaspoon Worcestershire
    sauce
1 cup sour cream
2 cups beef broth
Salt and ⅛ teaspoon black
    pepper

Pound flour well into beef until steak is about ¼-inch thick. Then cut into ¼-inch wide strips. Add beef strips to butter which has been heated in a heavy skillet, and brown on all sides, turning frequently. Remove to bowl and cover to keep hot. Add onion and mushrooms to pan, cover and cook slowly 5 minutes, stirring occasionally. Return meat to skillet, stir in Worcestershire sauce, soy sauce, sour cream and beef broth, cover and reheat to boiling. Season with salt and pepper and serve at once with hot fluffy boiled white or wild rice.

BEEF STROGANOFF SHERATON-BLACKSTONE

Sheraton-Blackstone Hotel
Chicago, Illinois

1½ pounds beef filet, cut
  in thick strips
2 large onions, diced
3 ounces butter
¼ pint demi-glace

Salt, pepper
¼ pint sour cream
1 teaspoon mustard
Juice of ½ lemon

Remove all skin and fat from meat. Cook onions in 1 ounce butter until almost done. Add demi-glace and finish cooking. Heat the remainder of butter and add meat, seasoned with salt and pepper, a little at a time, so that it browns immediately on all sides. Place meat in collander so it drips. Save the drippings. Add sour cream to the demi-glace and onions. Add the drippings from meat. Season with mustard and lemon juice. Add the browned meat to sauce and heat to boiling point but do not boil.

BEEF STROGANOFF

Ruth Woodward's House by the
Side of the Road
Dallas, Texas

1 cup butter
¾ cup flour
1 teaspoon salt
¼ teaspoon pepper
Dash cayenne
2½ cups milk, scalded
1 medium onion, sliced
  thin
1 pound mushrooms,
  sliced thin
Juice of 2 lemons

1 cup dry white wine
3 tablespoons tomato paste
1 tablespoon dry English
  mustard
2 tablespoons water
2 cups sour cream
2½ pounds beef tenderloin
  cut in 2-inch strips
1½ teaspoons salt
¼ teaspoon pepper

Melt ¼ cup butter and blend in flour and seasonings. Add milk and cook until thick and smooth. Simmer 10 minutes on low heat. Sauté onion and mushrooms in another ¼ cup butter. Add juice of lemons and wine and reduce the liquid by at least half. Add tomato paste and simmer 5 minutes. Stir in mustard blended with water. Simmer 5 minutes longer. Remove from heat; blend in sour cream and white sauce. Sauté meat in remaining butter and season with salt and pepper. Blend in sour cream sauce. Heat through but do not boil.

BEEF STROGANOFF

The Ranchhouse Restaurant
Estes Park, Colorado

1½ pounds beef tenderloin, sliced in 1½ inch strips
½ cup scallions, chopped
½ cup mushrooms, chopped
3 tablespoons butter

Salt and pepper to taste
1½ cups brown gravy
¼ cup sour cream
¼ cup Burgundy wine
2 cups hot noodles

Sauté beef, onions, mushrooms, in skillet with butter until meat is a light brown. Add salt and pepper. Stir in gravy and sour cream, and stir frequently, cooking over low fire for 5 minutes. Add wine to suit individual taste. Serve over noodles in a casserole.

SAUERBRATEN

Mader's Restaurant
Milwaukee, Wisconsin

4 pounds beef rump, chuck, or sirloin
1 cup vinegar
3 cups water
1 medium onion, cut in slices
3 tablespoons whole mixed spice

2 tablespoons salt
1 carrot, sliced
2½ tablespoons shortening
½ cup flour
2 ginger snaps
¼ cup sugar, white or brown
½ cup red wine

Mix vinegar, water, onions, spice, salt, carrots. Pickle meat in this brine for 3 to 4 days, turning once in a while. Save brine for making gravy later. Grease heavy roasting pan with shortening. Roast meat in 300° heat for 2 hours or wait until meat is brown on both sides and almost done. Sprinkle sugar over meat and roast for 5 to 10 minutes more, turning meat while roasting until sugar is dissolved and meat is nice and brown.

Take all brine meat was pickled in and add flour, ginger snaps; mix well and pour over meat. Roast meat for ½ hour more or until gravy is creamy and thick. Take out meat. Stir wine into gravy and then remove grease from gravy and strain. During roasting, if meat looks too dry, baste with the pickling brine. Serve with potato dumplings or noodles.

OX YOKE SAUERBRATEN

Ox Yoke Inn
Amana, Iowa

4 pounds beef, chuck or sirloin	2 teaspoons salt
3 cups vinegar	3 whole peppercorns
3 cups water	5 lemon slices
1 onion, sliced	½ cup flour
3 bay leaves	6 ginger snaps
3 cloves	2 tablespoons sugar
	½ cup red wine

Mix liquids and spices and let meat stand in it for 3 days. Turn once a day, and save vinegar broth.

On third day, remove meat from marinade; brown on both sides in heavy kettle. Remove meat from pan and brown flour. Add vinegar broth, boil until thick. Add meat to this gravy and cover. Bake in 325° oven 2½ to 3 hours. Turn and baste meat several times. Add ginger snaps and sugar.

About 30 minutes before meat is done, add red wine. Skim all grease off gravy and strain. Serve with potato dumplings or noodles.

SAUERBRATEN

Johnny Cake Inn
Ivoryton, Connecticut

5 pounds bottom round
beef (tied in 5-inch
diameter)
1 quart cider vinegar
1 quart water
2 tablespoons mixed whole
pickling spices
1 cup sugar

2 lumps sour salt
2 large unpeeled onions,
quartered
2 large scrubbed carrots,
cut into one inch pieces
½ bunch celery (include
leaves) cut into
one-inch pieces

Mix ingredients until sugar dissolves, add meat, let stand at room temperature for four hours; put into refrigerator, let stand two to three days, turning completely submerged meat twice daily.

To cook, remove meat from marinade, strain liquid, place meat in cooking pot, add vegetables and spices, add enough liquid to cover meat halfway. Save balance of liquids to add to sauerbraten while cooking if necessary, to maintain to half-way level. Brown meat in 450° oven, turn until all sides are browned. Remove from oven and cook on top of stove for two hours. Remove from stove and cook in cooking pot placed on wire rack.

When done, let cool, and when cool, remove sauerbraten from pot and refrigerate. Strain liquids, divide into two portions, one for making gravy, one for heating sauerbraten.

Gravy

2 peeled apples, grated
36 ginger snaps
Strained liquid saved for gravy

To make gravy, add grated apple to liquid, simmer until apple is transparent, add approximately 36 ginger snaps to thicken gravy.

To serve sauerbraten, cut into ¼-inch slices. Place in portion of strained liquid saved for heating and simmer until hot. Potato pancakes and applesauce, sweet and sour red cabbage should accompany this entree.

GERMAN SAUERBRATEN

Schweizer's
Detroit, Michigan

4 pound beef roast, lean
1 cup vinegar
3 cups water
2 cloves garlic, bruised
2 onions, sliced
1 carrot, cut
Salt and pepper to taste
1 bay leaf

1 heaping tablespoon
   pickling spices
Flour
3 tablespoons olive oil
1 teaspoon sugar
1 tomato, diced
4 or 5 gingersnaps,
   crumbled

Cover roast with a marinade made up of vinegar, water, garlic, onions, carrot, salt and pepper, bay leaf and pickling spices. Marinate for five days in the refrigerator. Remove meat from marinade, drain, then dust with flour and brown on all sides in olive oil. When roast is brown, add 1½ to 2 cups of the marinade (depending on pan size), and vegetables, 1 teaspoon sugar and diced tomato. Braise until the meat is tender. Strain the gravy left in the pan, thicken with crumbled ginger snaps and correct the seasoning. Roast should be sliced thin, about five slices per person, topped with the gravy, garnished with potato pancakes.

SCHROEDER'S SAUERBRATEN

Schroeder's Cafe
San Francisco, California

5 pounds beef
2 cups vinegar
4 cups water
1 large onion, sliced
¼ cup whole mixed spices

Salt to taste
2 tablespoons shortening
3 tablespoons flour
2 tablespoons sugar
½ cup red wine

Use rump or top round of beef. Make a pickling solution of the vinegar, water, onions, spices and a little salt; soak the meat for two or three days, turning frequently. At the end of the time, remove from the solution, place meat in hot fat in a heavy pot. Brown meat on all sides, remove to tray or plate. Brown flour in the fat, add spices from the pickling solution, a little water, sugar and simmer a few minutes. Place the browned meat in roasting pan, add the sauce, cover pan and bake the meat from 2½ to 3 hours in moderate oven, 350°. Turn and baste frequently. One half hour before meat is done, add the red wine.

When meat is done, lift to hot platter, add water and flour paste to make gravy, straining it into a gravy boat. If sauce is not sour enough, add a little more vinegar to it.

SAUERBRATEN MIT KARTOFFEL KLÖSSE
(Pot Roast with Potato Dumplings)

Luchow's
New York City

3 pounds round steak	2 bay leaves
1 tablespoon salt	2 tablespoons kidney fat
½ teaspoon pepper	6 tablespoons butter
2 onions, sliced	5 tablespoons flour
1 carrot, sliced	1 tablespoon sugar
1 stalk celery, chopped	8 or 10 gingersnaps,
4 cloves	crushed
4 peppercorns	Potato or bread dumplings
1 pint red wine vinegar	

Wipe steak with damp cloth; season with salt and pepper. Place in earthen, glass or enamelware bowl. Combine onions, carrot, celery, cloves, peppercorns, vinegar and bay leaves and 2½ pints water, or enough to cover meat. Cover and put in refrigerator 4 days.

On fifth day, remove from refrigerator, drain meat, sauté in kidney fat and 1 tablespoon butter in enamelware, glass or earthenware utensil, until seared on all sides. Add marinade liquid and bring to a boil, then lower heat and let simmer about 3 hours.

Melt remaining 5 tablespoons butter in a pan. Stir flour smoothly into it. Add sugar, blend, and let brown to nice dark color. Add to simmering meat mixture. Cover and continue cooking until meat is tender, about 1 hour longer.

Remove meat to a warmed serving platter. Stir crushed gingersnaps into the pot juices and cook until thickened. Pour this special sauerbraten gravy over meat. Serve with potato or bread dumplings.

POT ROAST

Shoyer's Restaurant
Philadelphia, Pennsylvania

5 pounds beef
2 carrots, sliced
1 onion, quartered
1 small bay leaf

¼ ounce garlic powder
1½ ounces salt
¼ ounce black pepper
Water, as required

Note: We recommend and have always used choice brisket meat, as best suited for pot roast.

Place meat in roasting pan with carrots, onion, bay leaf, garlic powder, salt and pepper.

Add sufficient water to prevent meat from burning. It may be necessary to add more water as the roasting process continues.

Roast at 350°. Baste at intervals. Roast should be finished in about 2½ to 3 hours.

LONDON INN'S POT ROAST

London Inn
Tulsa, Oklahoma

4 to 5 pounds choice arm
   roast with bone left in
2 tablespoons olive oil
2 teaspoons salt
1 teaspoon sugar
   (optional)
1 teaspoon black pepper

4 tablespoons flour
4 cups water or beef stock
4 medium potatoes, peeled
   and quartered
3 large onions, quartered
6 large carrots, peeled and
   cut about 2 inches long

Braise the roast in oil in a cast iron Dutch oven, until both sides are well browned. Add salt, sugar, black pepper. Mix flour with cold water or beef stock and add. Cover tightly and place the roast in a moderate, 325° to 350°, oven, and cook for 1½ hours. Add the vegetables and cook for 1 hour more, until vegetables are tender.

BEEF STEAK PIE LONDON HOUSE

Hotel Astor
New York City

1 pound round steak, cut into 1-inch cubes
¼ cup shortening
2 cups potatoes, peeled, cooked and cubed
1 cup green peas, cooked
1½ cups carrots, cut 2 inches long, cooked
12 medium mushrooms, cooked

2 cups brown sauce
½ cup Bordelaise or Claret wine
6 small onions, glace
1 Bouquet garni (parsley, thyme, bay leaf, celery stalk, tied together)
Pastry for single crust pie

Heat shortening in a skillet and brown the meat. Place the pieces in a heavy pot with the bouquet garni. Add wine and brown sauce; cook about 2 hours.

Remove steak pieces when cooked and place in 1½ quart casserole. Mix with vegetables. Strain gravy and pour over the prepared dish. Cover with regular pastry dough, slash top so steam can escape, and bake in hot, 425° oven, for 30 minutes or until crust is done.

BEEF STEAK PIE, COUNTRY STYLE

*Patterson's Supper Club
Sturgin, Michigan*

2 pounds round steak, cut in 1-inch cubes
2 tablespoons shortening or beef fat
1 cup onions, sliced
Salt, pepper, M.S.G. to taste
1 tablespoon Worcestershire sauce
2 tablespoons parsley, chopped
Water
2 cups potatoes cubed
1 tablespoon butter
2 tablespoons flour
2 cups biscuit dough

Brown round steak pieces in hot fat. Add onion slices seasoned with salt, pepper, M.S.G., Worcestershire sauce and parsley. Brown lightly. Cover with boiling water and simmer slowly for 30 minutes Add diced potatoes and cook 45 minutes. Melt butter over low fire and blend flour into it until it is a smooth paste. Add to beef mixture. Stir well until thickened. Pour entire mixture into deep baking dish and let cool slightly. Cover with a thin layer of biscuit dough. Cut gashes in top to permit steam to escape, and bake in 400° oven for 15 to 25 minutes, until crust is golden brown.

STEAK AND KIDNEY PIE

*King Arthur's Pub
Chicago, Illinois*

2 pounds round steak
2 teaspoons salt
½ teaspoon white pepper
¾ cup oil
1 pound beef kidneys
½ pound onions, chopped
1 cup flour
3 cups beef stock
1 small bay leaf
¼ teaspoon chevril
½ teaspoon dry English mustard
½ cup carrots, diced
½ cup celery, chopped
½ pound mushrooms, chopped

Cut beef into ¾ inch squares, season with salt and white pepper, place in heavy skillet, in ½ cup oil, and brown. Cut kidneys into ¾ inch squares and blanch in boiling salted water. Strain and rise. Place beef and kidneys in large cooking pot.

Sauté onions in ¼ cup vegetable oil, and brown. Add onions to beef and kidneys. Add flour to ingredients, stir in beef stock, and add bay leaf, chevril and dry mustard. Let these ingredients boil on a slow fire until meat is almost done. Add carrots, celery and mushrooms. Simmer until meat is tender.

Crust

2 cups flour	⅓ to ½ cup water
⅔ cup shortening	1 egg yolk
Salt to taste	

Mix flour, shortening, salt and water. Knead and let dough rest ½ hour.

Place steak and kidney stew in a casserole. Flatten out dough and shape it to just overlap casserole. Rub egg yolk around edge of casserole, place dough on top and press overlapping dough around the casserole. Brush top of crust with egg yolk. Place in 350° oven and bake for 10 to 15 minutes.

BEEF STEAK AND KIDNEY PIE

Williamsburg Inn
Williamsburg, Virginia

1⅛ pounds top sirloin of beef	2 tablespoons shortening
1 pound lamb kidneys, trimmed	1 quart beef stock or beef consommé
1 large onion, sliced very thin	4 bay leaves
½ teaspoon salt	1 teaspoon Flavor Glow or Ac'cent seasoning
¼ teaspoon black pepper	4 hard cooked eggs
½ teaspoon paprika	8 mushrooms
¼ cup flour	Pastry for single crust pie (see recipe below)

Cut beef into 1-inch cubes. Remove tissue from kidneys and cut into slices about ⅛-inch thick. Slice onion very thin. Place beef, kidneys and onion in a pan; season with salt, pepper and paprika. Then add flour, mixing well so that beef and kidneys are well coated with flour. Put shortening in a braising pan or dutch oven. Let it get very hot, then add beef, kidneys, onions and any remaining flour. Use spoon and continue to stir until meat is brown. Add stock, bay leaves and other seasonings. Cover and let simmer on slow heat for one hour or until beef is tender. Remove from fire and let cool. Place in a baking dish, top with sliced eggs and mushrooms. Cover with pastry and bake about 20 minutes in 350° oven or until crust is brown.

Pastry Cover

2 cups bread flour	1 teaspoon salt
⅔ cup shortening	1 egg, beaten with a little
⅓ cup ice water	milk

Sift flour and salt together and add shortening. Rub together until well blended, then use wooden spoon and mix gently. Add ice water a little at a time until thoroughly mixed. Handle very gently and make a ball. Place on a floured board. Roll out thin, cover pie, tuck edge, and brush top with a little milk mixed with beaten egg.

BAR X MEAT PIE

Bar X Bar Ranch
Crawford, Colorado

1 quart cooked or canned meat—beef, venison, or elk	3 cups water
	1 cup tomato sauce
½ cup onion, diced	3 stalks celery, diced
2 medium carrots, diced	3 drops Tabasco sauce
1 teaspoon salt	½ cup tomato paste
⅛ teaspoon pepper	½ cup flour, mixed with ½ cup cold water

In small roasting pan bring meat, onion, carrots, salt, pepper and water to boil. Then add remaining ingredients. Cover with small biscuits and bake in 450° oven until biscuits are golden brown, about 15 minutes.

SUPRÊME OF BEEF RAPA-NUI

Stardust Hotel
Las Vegas, Nevada

3 pounds choice aged
   sirloin steak
½ cup olive oil
2 tablespoons soy sauce
Garden herbs, to taste

2 cups red wine
Freshly ground pepper
Garnish of Chinese snow
   peas
3 tomatoes, halved

Marinate steak in a mixture of olive oil, soy sauce, herbs, red wine, pepper. Let stand for 2 hours. Broil the steak slowly over a charcoal fire to your taste. Serve with sautéed Chinese snow peas and broiled tomatoes.

The perfection of this steak is the slow process in cooking it.

BOEUF BOURGUIGNON

Gautreau's
Chepachet, Rhode Island

2 pounds top round steak
   cut in 1½ inch cubes
2 to 3 tablespoons oil
½ pound onions, chopped
½ tablespoon salt
¼ teaspoon white pepper
1 bay leaf

½ pound fresh mushrooms,
   cut in half
1½ cups rich beef stock
1 cup Burgundy wine
1 tablespoon flour
1 tablespoon butter
Pinch M.S.G.

Braise beef in oil in roasting pan in oven at 350° for 15 minutes, stirring often. Add onions, salt, pepper, bay leaf and mushrooms. Braise for 5 more minutes. Add beef stock and wine. Cover again. Cook until meat is tender. Pour off the gravy and skim off the fat. Thicken gravy slightly with a flour and butter roux. Pour back on beef. Cover. Cook 15 minutes. Add M.S.G.

ROLLADEN

*Sandy's Oak Ridge Manor
Kansas City, Missouri*

3 pounds round steak,
  ½ inch thick, cut in 6
  portions
2 tablespoons French
  mustard
1½ teaspoons white pepper
1½ teaspoons salt
1½ tablespoons bacon,
  chopped
1½ tablespoons onion,
  chopped
4 tablespoons butter
3 tablespoons flour
1 cup water
1 cup sherry
1 can mushrooms

Spread meat with mustard, pepper and salt. Add bacon
and onions, roll up, fasten with toothpick on each end. Fry
in butter in skillet until all sides are a golden brown. Simmer
in oven for 1 hour. Remove meat and add flour, let brown,
add water, sherry and mushrooms. Heat well. Pour over meat
and serve. Very delicious!

DANISH BIFF

*King Oscar's Smorgasbord
Seattle, Washington*

2 pounds round steak
4 tablespoons butter
1 large onion, finely
  sliced
2 tablespoons flour
Milk
Pinch of salt, white pepper
  and sugar
Sherry
Boiled potatoes

Grind the round steak three times and shape into 1-inch
thick small patties. Fry patties in butter until brown and
still rare in center. Remove patties from pan, add onion to

drippings and cook until light brown. Add flour and stir continuously until brown. Then add enough milk to make gravy desired thickness. Add seasonings to taste and sherry wine last. Put the meat patties into the gravy and simmer for 2 or 3 minutes. Serve with boiled potatoes.

BRACINOLINI ALLA SICILIANA

Luigi's Sphaghetti House
Boynton Beach, Florida

6 slices top choice round
   steak, cut thin and
   approximately 8 inches
   square
3 hard cooked eggs
6 slices prosciutto cheese
6 slices Italian salami

3 slices Provalone cheese
   (imported) cut in half
1 clove garlic, finely
   chopped
Parsley, salt and pepper to
   taste
Tomato sauce

Coarsely chop eggs, cheese, salami and mix with garlic and seasonings. Place mixture on top of steak and roll. Hold rolled meat secure with toothpicks, or tie with string. Place in casserole and cover with tomato sauce. Cover casserole with foil, and bake in 375° oven for 45 minutes.

STUFFED BEEF ROULADES

Eberhard's Restaurant
Columbia, Illinois

12 beef slices, ⅛ inch thick
Mustard
Salt and pepper
24 strips crisp fried bacon
   (save bacon fat)

3 dill pickles, quartered
1 onion, sliced
2 bay leaves
Salt, pepper, Ac'cent to
   taste

Brush beef slices with mustard, sprinkle with salt and pepper. Top each slice with two bacon strips and one pickle slice. Roll up and fasten with toothpick. Brown on all sides in hot bacon fat, using Dutch oven. Cover meat with water, add sliced onion, bay leaves, seasonings. Cover tightly and simmer for 2½ hours, adding water if necessary.

Gravy

¾ cup heavy cream
1 cup sour cream
  3 tablespoons flour
Salt, pepper, Ac'cent to
  taste

3 bay leaves
2 teaspoons sugar
½ cup Rhine wine

Remove the tender meat from the juice. Mix cream, sour cream and flour well, add to the juice, stir constantly until boiling. Add sugar and wine. Strain and pour over meat.

BEEF KA TIKI

Kahiki Supper Club
Columbus, Ohio

1 medium yellow onion,
  sliced fine
1 clove garlic, chopped
2 pounds cut cross grain
  lean beef, sliced
¼ cup oil
1 pound precooked green
  pepper, cut up
1½ pounds tomatoes,
  cut up
2 stalks celery, cut into
  pieces

2 tablespoons cornstarch,
  dissolved in ½ cup
  water
1 cup tomato catsup
1 tablespoon soy sauce
1 teaspoon salt
1½ tablespoons sugar
1 teaspoon seasoning
  powder (Ac'cent
  preferred)

Heat oil in skillet; sauté onion, garlic and meat. Add green pepper, tomato, celery and remaining ingredients. Bring to a boil. Simmer until the water has been absorbed and the mixture thickened.

BURGUNDY OF BEEF

Miller Brothers
Baltimore, Maryland

4 pound rump roast
½ cup carrots, coarsely cut
½ cup onions, coarsely cut
½ cup leeks, coarsely cut
½ cup celery, coarsely cut

Salt, pepper to taste
6 tablespoons butter
2 tablespoons flour
1½ cups beef stock
Burgundy wine to taste

Place beef on a bed of coarsely chopped carrots, onions, leeks and celery.

Rub beef with seasoning and 3 tablespoons butter. Put in very hot oven and sear the meat well. Then put in Dutch oven. Add 3 tablespoons butter and 2 tablespoons flour to pan, stir until brown and add beef stock. Pour gravy over beef in Dutch oven. Add Burgundy wine to taste and simmer, covered, until meat is tender.

CANTERBURY BEEF
WITH ENGLISH PARSLEY SAUCE

Win Schuler's
Marshall, Michigan

3 to 4 pound chuck steak or brisket of beef
1 cup Whitbreads Ale—or any full bodied beer or ale
½ cup sour cream

Braise pot roast at 200° for several hours, until meat thermometer thrust into center registers 140°. Enclose the meat and pan during the roasting period in a brown paper bag to retain moisture and develop flavor.

Blend ale and cream lightly. Baste roast with the ale-cream mixture.

When roast has reached 140° internal temperature, allow to cool in its juices, turning occasionally. To finish the roast, broil it for 15 minutes on a rack as near the heat source as possible, turning often to prevent burning. Use the natural juices to prepare the English parsley sauce served with roast.

English Parsley Sauce

2 tablespoons butter
1 tablespoon shallots, finely chopped
2 tablespoons flour
1 cup hot beef broth
½ cup hot chicken broth

¼ cup parsley, finely chopped
2 tablespoons Major Grey chutney, coarsely chopped

Melt butter in a saucepan. Add shallots, sauté until tender. Stir in flour and blend thoroughly over the heat until the mixture bubbles and begins to brown. Gradually add hot beef broth drippings from Canterbury beef roast mixed with hot chicken broth, stirring constantly. Cook gently until the mixture thickens, stirring constantly. Season to taste with salt and pepper, and just before serving, stir in parsley and Major Grey chutney. Taste for seasoning and serve at once over Canterbury beef.

SWEDISH MEAT HASH

Emerson's Smorgasbord
Newcastle, Maine

4 cups cooked beef, ground (use left-over roast beef or pot roast and include fat)

2 cups cooked potatoes, ground
½ cup onions, chopped
Salt and pepper to taste

Mix all together and cook in skillet over low heat until well browned. This takes about 45 minutes.

Note: The included fat makes a moist hash without any additional liquid.

TOKLAT'S ALASKAN MEAT BALLS

Toklat Restaurant
Ashcraft, Colorado

Meat Balls

1 pound choice lean beef, ground
1 pound choice lamb shoulder, ground
3 cups sourdough bread crumbs
1 cup parsley, chopped
1 cup scallions, chopped
2 large cloves garlic, mashed

4 cups spinach or beet tops, chopped
6 eggs
1 cup sharp Cheddar cheese, grated coarse
1 teaspoon salt
Good dash coarse ground pepper
Oil for frying

Sauce

Tomato juice
½ cup grated sharp cheddar cheese
½ cup chopped parsley

Mix well the meats, bread crumbs, parsley, onions, garlic, chopped greens, eggs, cheese, salt and pepper. Form into balls the size of golf balls. Brown in heavy skillet, with ample oil, over hot flame. Place in baking dish two layers deep, cover with sauce of parsley and cheese and tomato juice. Bake uncovered in 350° oven for ½ to ¾ hour, till sauce bubbles heavily. Serve at once.

SWEDISH MEAT BALLS

King Oscar's Smorgasbord
Seattle, Washington

1 pound beef
¼ pound pork
1 small onion
1 cup bread crumbs
¼ cup flour
½ teaspoon allspice

¼ teaspoon black pepper
¼ teaspoon white pepper
2¼ teaspoons salt
1 cup milk
2 to 3 tablespoons butter

Grind meat three times, adding onion on last grind. Add all dry ingredients, then add milk and mix immediately until mixture no longer sticks to fingers. Roll into small meat balls and fry in about 2 to 3 tablespoons butter over medium heat until done. Serve with or without sauce as desired.

CANTONESE SWEET AND SOUR MEAT BALLS

Dines Restaurant
Lansing, Michigan

1 small onion, diced
1 small green pepper, diced
2 tablespoons butter
1½ pounds lean ground beef
2 eggs, well beaten

2 cups white bread crumbs
Cold milk (to soften crumbs)
Salt, pepper to taste
1 teaspoon beef base
1 teaspoon fresh parsley, chopped

Saute onion and green pepper in butter until golden brown and tender. Add to ground beef. Add eggs, bread, seasonings and parsley. Mix well. Form balls about one inch in diameter. Bake on sheet pan, in 350° oven, for 30 to 40 minutes. Serve with sauce below.

Sauce

½ cup apricot nectar
¾ cup pineapple juice
½ cup water
½ cup white sugar
1 tablespoon Ac'cent
½ cup cider vinegar

¼ stick cinnamon
Pinch salt
Grated peel from ½ fresh lime
3 tablespoons corn starch and ½ cup cold water

Mix all ingredients together and boil for 20 minutes, before adding cornstarch. Mix cornstarch and cold water and add to mixture, stirring constantly, and continue cooking until medium thick.

DANISH MEAT BALLS

Jul's Danish Farm
Rock Falls, Illinois

1 pound beef	3 eggs
1 pound pork	¾ pound flour
2 medium onions, cut in pieces	Salt and pepper to taste
	⅛ teaspoon ground ginger
1 celery stalk	1 cup milk

Grind beef, pork, onions and celery three times through fine grinder. Combine with remaining ingredients and mix well. Shape into 1 ounce balls. Place on baking sheets. Bake in moderately hot oven, 425°, for 35 minutes.

MEAT BALL LASAGNE

Villa Venice
Tulsa, Oklahoma

Meat Balls

1 pound chopped beef	3 tablespoons Parmesan cheese, grated
½ pound lean pork, ground	6 tablespoons olive oil
3 eggs, beaten	4 slices stale French bread
1 clove garlic, minced	
3 tablespoons parsley, finely chopped	3 tablespoons oil (for cooking)

Combine meat, eggs, garlic, parsley, grated cheese and 6 tablespoons olive oil. Soak stale bread in water for 5 minutes; squeeze out bread and blend in with meat mixture. Form into small balls and fry in 3 tablespoons hot oil until brown on all sides.

Sauce

1 No. 2 can Italian pear tomatoes	2 bay leaves
1 cup tomato paste	Salt and pepper to taste

Combine the ingredients, heat to just below boiling. Then add the meatballs and simmer the sauce for 1½ hours. Remove bay leaves.

1½ pounds Lasagne noodles	Italian sausage, sliced
1 tablespoon olive oil	Ricotta cheese
Mozarella cheese, sliced	Parmesan cheese, grated

Add 1 tablespoon oil to a large pot of rapidly boiling salted water, to prevent noodles from sticking. Cook Lasagne until tender. Drain.

Pour 1 cup tomato sauce in which the meatballs were cooked into a baking dish. Over it arrange a layer of noodles, a layer of sliced Mozarella cheese, a layer of sausage and a layer of meatballs. Over the meatballs spread a layer of Ricotta cheese and sprinkle generously with grated Parmesan and tomato sauce. Repeat the layers until all the ingredients have been used, finishing with tomato sauce and grated Parmesan cheese. Bake in moderate oven, 350°, 20 to 30 minutes.

SMALL MEAT BALLS WITH ONION SAUCE

Ola Restaurant
Boston, Massachusetts

2 pounds bottom round of beef	1 tablespoon sugar
½ pound pork	1 tablespoon mace
2 cups bread crumbs	Salt, pepper to taste
3 eggs, well beaten	Butter or shortening for frying
2 cups stock	

Grind meats, putting them through the grinder twice; add bread crumbs, eggs, stock, sugar, mace and salt and pepper to taste. Mix ingredients thoroughly by hand (the more kneading the better), make into small balls the size of a large marble. Fry in butter or shortening, shaking pan to turn the meat balls rather than using a knife or fork. After each batch has been fried, rinse out pan with small amount of water or beef stock and save the stock in a dish.

Onion Sauce for Meat Balls

3 large onions, sliced very
   thin
2 tablespoons butter
½ cup strong black coffee

Salt and pepper to taste
Stock (saved from meat
   balls)

Fry onions in butter. When nicely browned, add coffee, stirring constantly. Let simmer for a few minutes. Salt and pepper to taste. Then add stock saved from meat balls. Let simmer for another 5 minutes and pour over meat balls just before serving.

BELGIAN MEAT BALLS

Brooks Hotel
Corvallis, Montana

1½ pound chopped beef
2 tablespoons onion, finely
   chopped
2 tablespoons green
   pepper, chopped
¼ cup corn meal
1 teaspoon chili powder
1½ teaspoons dry mustard
1 teaspoon salt

⅛ teaspoon pepper
½ cup milk
1 egg
¼ cup flour
¼ cup shortening
1½ cup canned or cooked
   tomatoes, or tomato
   juice

Combine chopped beef, onion, green pepper, corn meal, seasoning, milk and egg, and blend thoroughly. Form into 12 balls. Roll in flour and brown in hot fat in skillet. Add remaining flour and tomatoes, cover and bake in hot oven (450°) 35 to 45 minutes.

MEAT LOAF

The Coffee Pot
Luverne, Alabama

1½ pounds ground round
  steak
1 bell pepper, chopped
1½ large onions, chopped
½ cup cracker crumbs or
  toasted bread, chopped
  and moistened

1 cup catsup
½ cup mustard
1½ teaspoons salt
2 eggs

Mix all ingredients, shape into loaf. Top with 3 strips of bacon. Bake 35 minutes at 375°. Make sauce by adding 1 small can tomato paste to drippings and pour over meat loaf.

SPICY MEAT LOAF

Bar X Bar Ranch
Crawford, Colorado

1 pound ground meat
½ pound sausage
1 cup milk
1 cup bread crumbs
½ cup catsup

1 egg
1 medium onion, chopped
1 teaspoon salt
½ teaspoon black pepper

Mix all ingredients together and shape into loaf. Cover with two strips of bacon. Bake in 350° oven 1½ hours.

BOILED SHORT RIBS OF BEEF
WITH HORSERADISH SAUCE

Old Farms Inn
Avon, Connecticut

6 pounds short ribs of
beef, cut into serving
pieces
1 tablespoon salt
1 tablespoon pickling
spice
1 tablespoon Ac'cent

½ cup vinegar
½ clove garlic
1 onion, cut up
2 stalks celery, cut
coarse
2 carrots, chopped coarse

Tie each short rib with a piece of butcher's twine. When this is done, place them in a heavy pot. Add pickling spice, vinegar, garlic, and ¼ tablespoon each salt, Ac'cent, onion, celery and carrots. Add enough water to cover. Bring to a boil and let simmer 1½ hours. Drain and cover with fresh water. Add remaining salt, Ac'cent, onions, carrots and celery. Bring to boil and simmer another hour. Drain. Serve with horseradish sauce.

Horseradish Sauce

1 cup horseradish
Water
¼ cup flour

Take 1 quart stock from the shortribs and strain. Bring to boil and thicken with the flour and an equal amount of water. To this add horseradish, stir well.

BAKED SHORT RIBS OF BEEF WITH SUPER
BAR-B-QUE SAUCE

Johnny's Cafe
Omaha, Nebraska

6 pounds lean short ribs
Salt and pepper

Wipe meat with a damp cloth. Salt and pepper well on both sides. Place on a rack in a roasting pan and put into a pre-heated 350° oven for 25 minutes or until ribs have started to cook. Then pour the sauce over and bake for 1 hour covered and ½ hour uncovered. Baste occasionally during last part of cooking.

Sauce

2 tablespoons smoked salt
½ teaspoon red pepper
2 tablespoons paprika
1 teaspoon cumin seed, ground
2 cups tomato purée
4 tablespoons Worcestershire sauce

4 cups juice from roast beef
1½ tablespoon cider vinegar
4 stalks celery, cut fine
1 medium onion, diced fine

Place all ingredients in a large skillet and simmer for 30 minutes. Then pour over the short ribs and bake as directed.

ESTOFADO DE RES

Cafe La Margarita
Chicago, Illinois

1 pound lean beef, in cubes
2 teaspoons cooking oil
1 large onion, sliced thin
Salt and pepper
1 bay leaf
½ teaspoon each thyme, marjoram, and oregano

2 cups broth
2 large sweet peppers, chopped
3 large tomatoes or one can of tomato sauce
6 medium potatoes, peeled and quartered

Sauté the meat in oil, then the onion, and cook lightly. Add salt, pepper, herbs and broth. Cover and cook until the meat is tender. Add peppers and tomatoes and cook another half hour before adding the potatoes. Cook for 40 minutes until the liquid is thickened.

BEEF TURNOVER

Piety Corner Gardens Restaurant
Waltham, Massachusetts

1½ pounds ground beef
2 medium onions, chopped
    fine
2 tablespoons oil
3 large potatoes, peeled

1½ teaspoons salt
Pepper to taste
Pie crust
1 egg, beaten

Mix onions with beef. Cook in oil until well done. Cook potatoes in salted water, then mash. Add potatoes to meat mixture with salt and pepper. Set aside to cool.

Make up pie crust. Roll out and cut out six 5-inch circles. When filling is cool, divide in six portions, putting a portion on each circle. Fold over pie crust and seal edges with fork. Prick the top with a fork and brush with beaten egg. Bake in 350° oven for 40 minutes. Serve hot.

GAH MING YEONG
(Mock Lamb)

Kan's
San Francisco, California

1 cup raw beef, finely
    sliced
3 cups bamboo shoots,
    finely sliced
1 cup Chinese dried
    mushrooms (pre-
    soaked), finely sliced
2 cups celery, finely
    sliced
⅔ cup dried onion, finely
    sliced

Oil for frying
3 cups rice sticks (Mai
    Fun)
2 teaspoons salt
1 cup chicken stock
1 teaspoon M.S.G.
2 teaspoons soy sauce
1 teaspoon sugar
3 teaspoons cornstarch
3 teaspoons water

Prepare the finely sliced ingredients; set them aside.
In deep fat fryer cook in oil, at 350° the rice sticks. Remove when crisp and light. Set aside.

In a preheated wok or skillet place 4 tablespoons vegetable oil. Bring oil to sizzle at high heat and add sliced beef. Toss and turn rapidly for 1 or 2 minutes and remove from pan when half cooked. Add salt and the remaining sliced ingredients to the same pan, bring to medium heat. Toss and turn all ingredients for about 2 minutes. Add chicken stock combined with M.S.G. Cover and continue cooking at medium heat for 3 minutes. Remove cover. Add soy sauce, sugar and the half-cooked sliced beef. Increase to high heat and continue to toss while cooking. When all ingredients are thoroughly blended, immediately add a paste made of cornstarch and water. Continue to toss and cook until sauce has thickened (about 1 minute, no longer).

Place on service dish, top with the crisped rice sticks.

CRYSTAL RESTAURANT PASTITSIO

The Crystal Restaurant
Reading, Pennsylvania

Ground Beef

3 small onions, chopped
4 cloves garlic, chopped fine
½ cup olive oil
2 pounds ground beef
1 cinnamon stick (3 inch)
5 cloves
½ cup sherry
1 cup Italian tomato paste
6 cups water
Salt and pepper to taste

Sauté and brown chopped onions and garlic in olive oil. Add ground beef, cinnamon stick and cloves and cook until meat is golden brown. Add sherry, tomato paste and water, and cook over slow fire for 1½ hours. Add salt and pepper for proper seasoning.

Cream Sauce

½ pound butter
1 cup flour
2 quarts milk
3 eggs, well beaten
¼ pound Italian Romano cheese, grated

Melt butter, add flour, gradually stir in milk until smooth. Remove from fire (about 10 minutes). Add 3 eggs and cheese and stir well, until smooth.

Macaroni

1¼ pound Italian macaroni ziti #2
3 eggs, well beaten

¼ pound Italian Romano cheese, grated
Paprika

Boil macaroni in salted water until medium done. Drain. Place macaroni in large container. Add 3 eggs and cheese, mix well. Add the cooked ground beef and mix well with macaroni. Place this mixture in baking casserole (11" x 16") and arrange macaroni in layer to cover entire casserole. Add cream sauce, covering all the macaroni. Sprinkle with paprika. Bake at 350° for approximately 1¼ hours. Serve hot.

HUNGARIAN GOULASH

Pals Cabin
West Orange, New Jersey

2 pounds steak and trimmings, cubed
1 pound onions, sliced
4 tablespoons butter
2 tablespoons paprika (sweet Hungarian type)
1 clove garlic
Pinch caraway seed

Slice lemon peel, finely chopped
Salt and pepper, to taste
1 cup stewed tomatoes (not too much juice)
Beef stock, to cover
¼ cup flour
1 tablespoon butter
1 tablespoon lard

Melt butter in heavy pot. Put in meat, paprika and onions. Simmer until onions have disintegrated. Add garlic and lemon peel to meat mixture with caraway. Season. Add tomatoes and beef stock to cover and simmer until meat is tender, about 1½ hours. Thicken gravy with a roux of flour and half butter, half lard.

HUNGARIAN BEEF GOULASH

Henrici's
O'Hare Inn
Des Plaines, Illinois

2 tablespoons melted
  shortening
3 pounds lean beef stew
  meat cut in large
  uniform pieces
3 large onions, diced
3 stalks celery, diced
½ clove garlic
¼ cup flour
2 tablespoons paprika
  (Hungarian sweet
  variety)
2 cups hot beef stock

½ cup tomato puree
⅛ teaspoon thyme, ground
⅛ teaspoon marjoram,
  ground
⅛ teaspoon red pepper,
  ground
½ bay leaf
½ tablespoon Worcester-
  shire sauce
1 tablespoon salt and
  pepper mixed
⅛ cup Sherry wine

Heat fat in large kettle. Add the beef. Place in preheated oven at 350°. Braise until light brown. Add the onions, celery and garlic. Sauté until transparent. Sprinkle the flour and paprika over meat. Stir and cook for 15 minutes. Add the beef stock slowly while stirring. Add the tomato purée. Add the spices. Cover. Simmer until meat is tender, about 1½ to 2 hours. Remove bay leaf. Add Worcestershire sauce. Add salt and pepper and sherry.

AMERICAN GOULASH

The Glen
Aspen, Colorado

8 slices bacon
2 pounds ground beef
1 onion, chopped
1 sweet pepper,
  chopped
2 large cans tomatoes

1 large can red
  kidney beans
1 can tomato sauce
Salt and pepper to taste
Chili powder (optional)

Cut bacon in small pieces and cook slowly until brown. Remove from pan and drain bacon well. Brown two pounds ground beef in same pan. Combine bacon, ground beef, onion, pepper, tomatoes, kidney beans and tomato sauce; add salt and pepper to taste. Simmer 1 hour.

BEEF STEW IN BEER

Walper Hotel
Kitchener, Ontario

3 pounds short ribs
½ pound onions, diced in large pieces
4 ounces lard
⅓ ounce salt
Pinch of paprika

1¼ pounds peeled and pressed tomatoes
1 cup water
1¼ pounds potatoes, sliced
6 ounces beer

Cut beef into half-inch slices. Combine meat and onions and saute over moderate fire until onions are golden. Season with salt and paprika. Add tomatoes and ⅓ cup water. Cover and cook in oven for 1½ hours. Add remaining water and potatoes. Continue to cook in oven, basting often. Do not stop basting until the liquid is entirely reddened. When finished, add beer.

HUNTERS BEEF STEW

1000 Acres Ranch Resort
Stony Creek, New York

2½ pounds top or bottom round choice lean meat, cut in 2-inch squares
1 teaspoon salt
½ teaspoon black pepper
½ cup oil
2 pounds small white onions

4 cloves garlic, sliced
1 bay leaf
2 whole cloves
1 No. 2½ can first quality tomatoes (crushed well)
2 quarts beef stock
6 ounces white wine

Place meat with salt, pepper and oil in hot skillet; braise until meat is golden brown on all sides. Add onions, simmer on low heat until onions are half done. Add the garlic, bay leaf, cloves and crushed tomatoes. Simmer 10 minutes, add beef stock and wine. If you don't have stock available, you may use 3 beef bouillon cubes or 1 tablespoon beef base. Cook until meat is tender. May be served with small white potatoes and green beans.

MRS. KNOTT'S OLD FASHIONED PIONEER BEEF STEW

Knott's Berry Farm
Buena Park, California

2 pounds stew meat, cubed
1 cup flour
3 cups fresh carrots, diced
2 cups fresh onion, diced
1 No. 2 can green
  lima beans

1 No. 2 can tomatoes
¾ teaspoon white pepper
½ teaspoon garlic powder
1 teaspoon M.S.G.
1 teaspoon celery salt
1 tablespoon salt

Roll meat in flour and steam in pressure cooker for 2 hours. In a separate container cook fresh vegetables together until tender. Add lima beans and tomatoes to steamed meat. Combine all cooked ingredients. Add seasonings and simmer a few minutes.

If a pressure cooker is not used, brown meat in 3 tablespoons hot oil and simmer all ingredients together until beef is tender.

PIONEER BEEF STEW

Westward Ho Steak House
Pasadena, California

2 pounds lean beef
2 tablespoons bacon fat
1 onion, chopped
1 cup tomatoes or purée
Salt, pepper
2 tablespoons Ac'cent
4 cups water

2 tablespoons cornstarch
2 stalks celery, diced
3 potatoes, cut in quarters
2 carrots, diced
1 cup fresh peas
18 pearl onions

Cut lean beef into one-inch cubes, braise in bacon fat until brown, using fast fire. Add onion, tomatoes or purée to beef, and brown. Add seasonings. Add water, let boil, and add cornstarch to thicken, stirring constantly. Boil all vegetables and add to beef mixture.

ENCHILADAS

Cafe La Margarita
Chicago, Illinois

12 tortillas
Oil for frying
1 can mole sauce
1 pound longhorn cheese
  (shredded)

1 cup chicken or beef for
  filling, shredded
1 cup sour cream

Fry each tortilla lightly in oil before filling with meat or chicken. Roll. Then heat the mole sauce and pour over the enchiladas, top with shredded cheese, heat in a warm oven for five minutes, and garnish with sour cream.

TACOS

Cafe La Margarita
Chicago, Illinois

12 tortillas
1 onion, chopped
½ green pepper, chopped
1 tablespoon corn oil
1 pound ground beef
1 can tomato sauce
2 solid packed tomatoes

1 teaspoon chili powder
Salt and pepper
1 head lettuce, shredded
2 tomatoes, sliced
Small bowl sharp grated
  cheese
Hot oil for frying

Sauté the onion and green pepper in corn oil until they are limp. Then add meat and mix and crumble. Brown for five minutes and pour in tomato sauce, tomatoes, chili powder, salt and pepper. Simmer over a low heat for two hours until the meat is crumbly and fairly dry. Just before you are ready to serve, prepare bowls of shredded lettuce and grated cheese.

Then double the tortillas, add in the meat filling, hold with tongs and fry quickly in hot oil. The tacos should be golden and slightly firm, but not hard. Ordinarily, one next adds the tomato, then lettuce, and then cheese is sprinkled over the entire serving.

TAMALE PIE

The Mountain Home Cafe
Grand Lake, Colorado

Filling

2 tablespoons shortening	½ cup celery, chopped
1 pound ground beef	2 cups canned tomatoes
1 cup green peppers, chopped	1 cup cream style corn
	1 clove garlic, crushed
1 cup ripe olives, sliced	1 tablespoon chili powder
	2 teaspoons salt
1 large onion, chopped	1 cup grated cheese

Melt shortening in skillet. Brown meat, add remaining ingredients except cheese. Simmer 20 minutes. Place in casserole lined with corn meal mixture (recipe below). Top with remaining corn meal cut in squares. Sprinkle with grated cheese. Bake in 350° oven for 45 to 60 minutes.

Corn Meal Mixture

2½ cups yellow corn meal	2 teaspoons salt
4 cups water	1 teaspoon chili powder.

Combine ingredients in saucepan, and cook over medium heat until thickened, about 15 minutes, stirring frequently. Line the sides and bottom of two buttered 2-quart rectangular casseroles with ⅔ of this mixture. Retain other ⅓ for topping.

WALT DISNEY CHILI

Disneyland Hotel
Disneyland, California

2 pounds dry pink beans
2 onions, sliced
2 pounds coarse
   ground beef
2 cloves garlic, minced
½ cup oil
1 cup celery, chopped
1 teaspoon chili powder
1 teaspoon paprika
1 teaspoon dry mustard

1 large can solid pack
   tomatoes
Pinch of each of the
   following: coriander
   seeds, tumeric, chili
   seeds, cumin seeds,
   fennel seeds, cloves,
   cinnamon, dry ginger
1 small yellow Mexican
   chili pepper
Salt to taste

Soak beans overnight in cold water. Drain. Add fresh water to cover 2 inches over beans. Simmer with onions until tender (about 4 hours). Meanwhile prepare sauce by browning meat and garlic in oil. Add remaining ingredients and simmer for one hour. When beans are tender, add sauce to beans and simmer ½ hour longer.

CHILI CON CARNE, À LA VICKS

Vick's Continental Restaurant
Dallas, Texas

1½ pounds chopped beef
1 large onion, chopped
   very fine
1 tablespoon salt
1 tablespoon black pepper
2 large cloves garlic,
   chopped fine

1 tablespoon powdered
   cumin seed
4 cups beef broth
1 tablespoon paprika
½ teaspoon cayenne
2 tablespoons chili powder

Mix beef, onion, salt, pepper and garlic up thoroughly, and braise in pan. Add powdered cumin seed and stir while cooking for 5 minutes. Add beef broth and cook another 15 minutes. Add paprika, cayenne and chili powder and cook 25 minutes, until meat is tender and sauce is thick as desired.

PEDRO'S CHILI CON CARNE

*South of the Border Restaurant
South of the Border,
South Carolina*

2 pounds ground beef
4 tablespoons butter or oil
2½ cups tomato sauce
½ cup celery, chopped fine
1 tablespoon onion, minced
1 bouillon cube
1 tablespoon parsley flakes

½ tablespoon light brown sugar
½ tablespoon Worcestershire sauce
½ tablespoon garlic powder
1 cup water
1 teaspoon M.S.G.
2 teaspoons chili powder
2 cups cooked pinto beans

Brown beef in a skillet in butter or oil. Combine all ingredients except the cooked pinto beans, chili powder and M.S.G. Simmer for 1½ hours, then add remaining ingredients, bring to a boil and simmer for 5 more minutes.

ESCALOPE CORDON BLEU
(Gruyere cheese and Ham Stuffed Veal Cutlet)

*Chalet Suizo de Mexico
Mexico City*

12 thin slices of veal cutlet
Salt, pepper
6 slices Gruyere cheese
6 slices cooked ham

Flour for dredging
2 eggs, well beaten
½ pound butter, melted
1 pint oil

Salt and pepper each cutlet. Place one slice of Gruyere and one slice of ham on each and cover with another cutlet, salt and pepper. Dip cutlet in flour, then in beaten egg, and again in flour. Heat oil, add the cutlets and cover. Turn so that both sides will be brown. This will take about 5 minutes total time. Do not overcook. Then, in another frying pan put the browned cutlets with melted butter. Turn them to butter on both sides. Serve with fried potatoes.

MIGNON DE VEAU MARAMÊ

Grand Motor Hotel
Montreal, Quebec

12 veal mignon or scallops, flattened to ¼-inch thickness
12 bread croutons
2 tablespoons butter
1 tablespoon oil
½ cup white wine
1½ cups creme sauce

Paprika to taste
Curry to taste
3 tablespoons red pimentos
3 tablespoons green pimentos
1 cup cream
Salt, pepper to taste

Sauté veal mignon in butter and oil until brown on both sides. Place them on bread croutons.

Add white wine to the sauté pan, and the creme sauce, paprika, curry, pimentos, cream and reduce. Season to taste. Cover veal with sauce. Serve with Pilau Rice (see below).

Rice Pilau

¼ pound butter
½ clove garlic, chopped
1 onion, chopped
1½ cups rice

Cloves, allspice or cinnamon, to taste
Salt, to taste

Melt butter in a deep pan. Add chopped garlic and onion and cook until soft. Add rice and cook 5 to 8 minutes, stirring occasionally. Season to taste with ground cloves, allspice or cinnamon, and salt. Cover rice with boiling water and simmer until rice is tender and water is absorbed.

ESCALOPES DE VEAU, ST. HELENA

World Trade Club
San Francisco, California

Portion: 2 veal cutlets
per person
Thinly sliced veal cutlets,
2 to 3 ounces each
Salt, pepper, flour
2 ounces butter
1 tablespoon shallots,
chopped
½ pint fresh mushrooms,
sliced
¾ cup California white
dinner wine, such as
Sauterne or Chablis

1¼ cups heavy cream
1¼ cups supreme sauce
Dash cayenne
2 medium tomatoes, cut
in half
15 Jumbo asparagus spears,
cooked and cut in half
25 Parisienne potatoes,
roasted
Parsley for garnish

Pound veal slices with cleaver, season with salt and pepper; dredge lightly in flour. Sauté in butter for approximately two minutes on each side. Remove veal and place on serving platter; keep warm.

To the pan sauce, add shallots and mushrooms and sauté for 30 seconds. Deglaze pan with wine and cook for 5 minutes. Add cream and supreme sauce: boil 5 minutes. Correct seasoning and finish with a dash of cayenne.

Garnish platter with broiled tomatoes topped with asparagus and potatoes on the side. Slightly mask veal escalopes with sauce and serve remainder on side. Add chopped parsley on each cutlet.

VITELLO ALL' UCCELLETTO
(Sautéed Veal Scallops)

Enrico & Paglieri
New York City

1½ pounds veal	½ teaspoon dried sage,
Flour for dredging	or 3 leaves fresh
Salt, pepper to taste	½ teaspoon meat glaze
3 tablespoons butter	⅜ cup white wine
1½ tablespoons oil	1½ teaspoon sweet butter
1 bay leaf, broken in bits	1½ teaspoon parsley, finely
	chopped

Cut tender veal into small, very thin slices. Flatten them with the side of a cleaver. Dust very lightly with flour and shake off the excess. For 6 people, use 12 or more little slices.

Season veal with salt and pepper, and brown quickly 2 to 3 minutes on each side in butter and olive oil, melted and sizzling hot in your frying pan. Add bay leaf and dried or fresh sage. Stir in meat glaze blended with white wine. When all is well blended and the sauce reduced to just enough for a good spoonful for each slice of veal, add at the last minute butter that has been creamed with parsley. The whole should be rapidly done and served at once.

VEAL CUTLET CORDON BLEU

Eugene's
Reno, Nevada

6 large and 6 small	1 cup light cream or
veal cutlets	half and half
Salt, pepper	Flour to dredge
6 slices ham	3 tablespoons butter
(boiled or prosciutto)	2 tablespoons oil
12 very thin slices	2 tablespoons melted
Swiss cheese	butter
2 eggs	

Salt and pepper veal cutlets. Place on top of each large cutlet one slice Swiss cheese, one ham slice, then another slice of cheese, and cover with small cutlet. Break egg and mix with same quantity of half and half or cream. Beat and spread this mixture around sides of small cutlet. Then bring edges of larger cutlet up and fold over. This mixture will act as sealer. Dredge with flour very lightly and place in skillet with butter and oil to sauté *very gently* for 6 or 7 minutes each side. Place on serving dish, melt 2 tablespoons butter until hazelnut color and pour over meat.

Serve with grilled tomatoes, see recipe below.

Grilled Tomatoes

6 tomatoes	Salt and pepper to taste
Bread crumbs	Butter

Cut tomatoes in half, sprinkle with bread crumbs, salt and pepper to taste and dot with small pieces of butter. Grill under broiler, and serve on platter with the meat.

GRENADINE OF VEAL GENTILHOMME

Ondine Restaurant
Sausalito, California

2 tablespoons butter	3 tablespoons sherry
2 tablespoons flour	3 avocados, cut in half
1 cup chicken broth	lengthwise
1 chicken bouillon cube	3 shallots, chopped very
6 6-ounce veal cutlets,	fine, or 3 tablespoons
pounded lightly	finely chopped scallions
Salt, white pepper, Ac'cent	2 tablespoons cognac
Flour for dredging	1 cup light cream
6 tablespoons stewed	½ teaspoon
tomatoes	Worcestershire sauce

Bake Bechamel sauce: Melt butter in saucepan, stir in flour, slowly, stirring constantly. Heat chicken broth in separate saucepan; add bouillon cube and stir until dissolved. Add chicken broth mixture to butter and flour; cook over medium heat until sauce is thickened and comes to a boil. Cover and set aside.

Flour cutlets and brown on both sides in butter. Season with salt, pepper, and Ac'cent. Put a tablespoon stewed tomatoes on each cutlet. Add sherry; cover and simmer until veal is tender.

Sprinkle avocado halves on both sides with salt and Ac'cent. Place one, cut side down, on each cutlet. Cook, covered, 10 minutes longer. Remove veal to serving dish and set aside to keep hot.

Cook down liquid in skillet until almost gone; add shallots and cognac. Cook until shallots are golden. Stir in Bechamel sauce and light cream. Heat, stirring constantly, until sauce comes to a boil. Season to taste with salt, pepper, Ac'cent and Worcestershire sauce. Serve over veal cutlets.

COTELETTES DE VEAU DU PATRON LEON

Sooke Harbour House
Sooke, British Columbia

6 veal chops, ½-pound each, ¾-inch thick
6 thick slices cooked ham
6 thick slices old Dutch cheese
Pepper and salt
3 egg whites, lightly whipped
Bread crumbs
½ pound butter
1½ teaspoons paprika
6 dashes Worcestershire sauce
1 pint heavy cream
1½ pounds fresh cooked asparagus

Cut the cutlets to the edge and fold open like envelope. Fold in ham and cheese. Close tight. Pepper and salt. Roll in egg whites and bread crumbs. Fry until light brown on both sides, in butter. Sprinkle with paprika and Worcestershire sauce stirred in butter. Top with cream and asparagus.

PICCATE DI VITELLO ALLA GABRIELLA

Mercurio Restaurant
New York City

2 pounds veal scallops
   (6 scallops) pounded
   very thin
Flour seasoned with
   salt and pepper
¼ cup olive oil

½ cup white wine
Juice of 2 lemons
1 cup mushrooms, sliced
1 cup cooked artichoke
   hearts, sliced
3 tablespoons butter

Coat veal with flour. Sauté the scallops in hot olive oil for about 2 minutes on each side or until they are just tender. Remove from pan and keep warm. Pour off any oil in the pan and add white wine and the juice of 2 lemons. Bring the mixture to a boil, stirring and scraping up all the brown bits that cling to the pan and cook the sauce until it thickens slightly. Return the scallops to the pan and add sliced mushrooms and cooked artichoke hearts, sautéed in 3 tablespoons butter until browned. Simmer the mixture for three minutes and serve immediately.

VEAL CUTLET GABRIELE

Caproni's
Cincinnati, Ohio

1 pound veal, cut in six
   slices and pounded thin
   with flat side of cleaver
1 cup fresh bread crumbs
   (use Italian bread if
   possible)
Ground mixed spices

2 teaspoons Parmesan
   cheese, grated
Salt and pepper to taste
1 egg, well beaten
Flour for dredging
1¼ cup butter
Juice of ½ lemon for
   each slice

Mix bread crumbs with pinch ground mixed spices, 1 teaspoon grated cheese and salt and pepper to taste. Set aside. Mix well beaten egg with pinch ground mixed spices, 1 teaspoon grated cheese and salt and pepper to taste. Set aside.

Each slice of veal should just about cover the bottom of a medium-sized skillet. Dust each piece with flour and dip first in the egg batter and then in the breadcrumb mix. Melt butter in a very hot skillet, and fry cutlet over a medium flame until golden brown; turn and fry the other side. When finished, squeeze juice of half a lemon over the meat and add any drippings from the pan.

VEAL CUTLET MONTEREY

Bantam Cock
Los Angeles, California

6 5-ounce veal cutlets
1 cup bread crumbs
2 eggs well beaten, and diluted with 4 tablespoons water
6 tablespoons butter
3 tomatoes, peeled, sliced vertically

2 avocados, peeled and sliced
4 cups Mornay sauce (see under sauces)
¼ pound Parmesan cheese, grated

Bread veal cutlets by dipping in bread crumbs, then in egg mixture then again in bread crumbs. Fry in butter until brown on both sides. Place on cookie sheet. Top with slices of tomato and avocado, three slices each, alternately over the cutlet. Top with Mornay sauce. Sprinkle with grated Parmesan cheese and brown under broiler.

VEAL CUTLET À LA PARMIGIANA

Bruno's Little Italy
Little Rock, Arkansas

1½ pounds baby veal
  (6 slices)
8 ounces flour
1 cup cracker meal
1 egg
2 ounces cream
Deep fat for frying
2 cans Hunt's tomato
  sauce

1 shaker Parmesan
  cheese, grated
½ pound American or
  Mozzarella cheese
Salt and pepper to taste
Parsley, chopped
Pimento

Roll veal slices in flour, then in a combination of beaten egg and cream before dredging in cracker meal. Salt and pepper to taste. Fry in deep fat until brown on both sides and drain. Place in individual casseroles and cover with heated tomato sauce and grated cheese. Cut solid cheese in strips and make a Christmas tree design on top of each casserole. Sprinkle with parsley and pimento and bake in 450° oven for 10 minutes.

SCALLOPINI

Marchio's Italian Cafe
Omaha, Nebraska

6 4-ounce veal steaks
1 large onion, sliced
2 bay leaves
Pinch nutmeg, clove,
  sweet basil
⅓ cup Sauterne wine

3 cups canned tomatoes
1 cup water
½ cup oil
Parsley, chopped
Garlic salt, to taste
Salt, pepper to taste

Brown onion in oil. Add spices. Fry meat which has been seasoned with parsley and garlic. Put onion mixture over meat, add wine, tomatoes and water and cook until meat is tender, approximately 1 hour. Add salt and pepper to taste.

VEAL SCALLOPINI ALLA FERRANTE

Ferrante's Restaurant
Plainville, Connecticut

1½ pounds Italian style
  veal cutlets
Flour for dredging
Salt and pepper to taste
⅜ cup olive oil
  1 clove garlic, minced
  6 to 8 green frying
    peppers, quartered

8 button mushrooms
½ small onion, chopped
2 cups Italian plum
  tomatoes (pulp only)
1 tablespoon parsley,
  chopped

Cut veal into 3 inch pieces and dredge in seasoned flour. Put olive oil in large frying pan and heat. Brown garlic and remove. Sauté veal over very low flame and remove when brown on both sides. Sauté peppers. Just before peppers are done add mushrooms and onion, continue to sauté until onion becomes transparent. Add tomato pulp, salt and pepper to taste, simmer for 10 minutes. Return veal to pan and simmer for another 10 minutes. Remove from pan to large platter and sprinkle parsley over the top.

VEAL BRACIOLETTE SICILIANA

Tappan Hill
Tarrytown, New York

2 pounds veal
Salt, pepper
  1 cup queen olives, diced
  2 cups cooked ham, diced
  2 tablespoons butter
1 cup Swiss cheese,
  diced

White bread squares
⅔ cup white wine
  2 tablespoons olive oil
Melted butter (enough
  to dip skewers)

Pound veal scaloppini into very thin slices, using three slices per portion. Season with salt and pepper. Sauté ham and olives in oil and fill each scaloppini with the ham and olive mixture and with uncooked Swiss cheese. Roll the slices and place on skewer, alternating veal roll and white bread squares. Dip entire skewer in melted butter and put in medium hot oven, 350°. When brown and cooked, place in serving dish. Swish cooking pan with white wine, after removing cooking fat. Allow resulting sauce to thicken and pour it over meat.

Serve immediately with your favorite vegetable and potato.

VEAL ALL'AGRO DI LIMONE

Amelio's
San Francisco, California

1½ pounds veal	1 tablespoon parsley,
Flour for dredging	chopped
1 tablespoon olive oil	2 ounces white wine
1 tablespoon butter	1 tablespoon butter
Juice of 1½ lemons	1 lemon, sliced

Cut veal in slices, pound them thin to the size of 3 x 4 inches. Dip in flour. Place in a frying pan a tablespoon each of butter and olive oil, and when this is sizzling hot, fry the veal in it until brown on both sides.

Now remove pan from fire, sprinkle with lemon juice, chopped parsley and white wine. While shaking the pan, gradually add another tablespoon butter until it is completely blended with all ingredients to serve as a sauce.

Arrange the veal slices on a hot platter, and pour the sauce over them. Place a slice of lemon on top of each veal slice, and serve with whatever vegetables and/or potatoes you desire.

NOISETTE DE VEAU OSCAR

Sanford's

Oakland, California

6 6-ounce veal steaks	Bearnaise sauce
Flour for dredging	(see under sauces)
4 tablespoons butter	Glazed carrots as
30 asparagus spears	garnish
30 crab legs	

Dust veal steaks with flour and pan fry in butter until golden brown. Place on warm serving dish. Arrange 5 warm asparagus spears on each veal steak. Place 5 warm crab legs across the asparagus spears. Cover top of each steak with 3 tablespoons of Bearnaise sauce. Serve with glazed carrots or any other colorful vegetable.

ESCALOPES DE VEAU FLAMBEES HENRI

The Gourmet Restaurant
Terrace Hilton Hotel
Cincinnati, Ohio

6 escalopines of veal,
sliced very thin
Flour for dredging
4 tablespoons butter
2 tablespoons shallots,
chopped
⅜ cup mushrooms, sliced

1½ ounces cognac
Salt and pepper
3 tablespoons heavy
cream
2 teaspoons parsley,
chopped

Place the meat between two sheets of waxed paper and flatten with a mallet or the flat side of a knife. Remove paper and dredge meat in flour. Heat butter in a skillet and brown the meat on both sides. Add shallots and mushrooms to the skillet. Cook until the mushrooms are wilted.

Warm the cognac, add it to the pan and ignite.

Sprinkle with salt and pepper. Transfer meat to a hot platter and keep warm. Add cream to skillet. Stir to blend the sauce and add the chopped parsley. Pour over the escalopes.

Serve with rice flavored with saffron.

VEAL MARY C

Windham Hill Farm
West Townshend, Vermont

1¾ pounds veal scallops
Flour, salt, pepper
Butter
1 large onion, chopped
¾ cup chicken broth

¾ cup Chablis or other
   dry white wine
1½ teaspoons caraway
   seeds
Salt and pepper to taste

Veal scallops are made by pounding thinly sliced veal between wax paper with side of wooden mallet or potato masher. Cut veal into dollar size pieces or thin strips, then shake in seasoned flour. Sauté in heavy skillet in butter until browned. Remove and drain excess butter. In heavy casserole with cover sauté 1 large chopped onion in butter until tender. Add browned veal, ¾ cup chicken broth, ¾ cup chablis wine, the caraway seeds and simmer covered until meat is tender and gravy thickens, about 1 hour. Season with salt and pepper to taste.

Serve with rice. Serves 6.

AIGUILLETTES OF VEAL NORMANDE

Malmaison Restaurant
New York City

2 to 2½ pounds veal, cut
   into thin slices
   2 slices per serving

Flour for dredging
¼ cup oil

Dry veal, dredge it with flour. In a skillet heat oil, add veal and brown on both sides. Set aside and keep hot.

Sauce Normande

½ pound mushrooms,
   sliced
3 tablespoons butter
½ cup Sauterne

1½ cups heavy cream
Cayenne pepper
Tarragon leaves, chopped

Sauté fresh mushrooms gently in butter; do not allow mushrooms to become brown. Pour some Sauterne over the mushrooms. Boil for one minute, mix together with the juices of veal and remainder of wine, and the cream. Mix well and allow the sauce to soften by blending. Season with a dash of cayenne pepper and some chopped fresh tarragon leaves.

Place the 12 aiguillettes on a hot silver platter and cover generously with the Sauce Normande. Serve with a garniture of rice pilaff.

BAKED VEAL CUTLET AND COTTAGE CHEESE

Jack Tar Hotel
San Francisco, California

2 cups stewed tomatoes
½ cup onion, finely diced
2 tablespoons parsley, chopped
Mint, chopped, to taste
1 pound cottage cheese
4 egg yolks
4 ounces Parmesan

cheese, grated
6 6-ounce veal cutlets
Salt, pepper
Flour for dredging
2 eggs, well beaten
2 teaspoons water
1 cup breadcrumbs
¼ cup butter

Flavor stewed tomatoes, canned or fresh, with onions, parsley and fresh mint. Cook until most of the juice has evaporated.

Pass cottage cheese through fine sieve. Add yolks and Parmesan cheese and blend together to form a smooth spread.

Tenderize veal cutlets with cleaver. Bread lightly (flour, eggs mixed with water, and breadcrumbs). Heat butter in skillet and sauté meat until brown on both sides. Spread cottage cheese mixture ¼ inch thick on top of veal cutlets. Cover the bottom of a small casserole with tomato mixture. Place cutlets on top of tomatoes. Bake in 350° oven until cheese is golden brown.

HUNTER STYLE ESCALOPES DE VEAU

Hickey's Hyatt House Hotel
Palo Alto, California

6 veal cutlets, 5 to 6
  ounces each
Salt, pepper
Flour for dredging
¼ cup butter
¼ cup oil
2 shallots, chopped fine

½ pound raw mushrooms,
  sliced
½ cup white wine
½ cup demi-glace
2 teaspoons tomato purée
2 tablespoons butter
Parsley, chopped

Season and flour the veal cutlets. Sauté them in half oil and half butter. Remove them from pan. Sauté the shallots in the frying fat, add mushrooms and brown them quickly. Reduce the white wine to half, boil up with demi-glace and tomato purée, and remove from heat. Add 2 tablespoons butter and a little chopped parsley to sauce and pour over the cutlets on a heated serving platter.

VEAL SCALOPPINI ALLA MARSALA

Augustine's Restaurant
Belleville, Illinois

6 6-ounce veal cutlets
  (preferably from loin,
  filet or top of leg)
1 cup clarified butter
Parmesan cheese, grated
1 cup fresh mushrooms,
  thinly sliced

Salt and pepper to taste
1 teaspoon extract of
  beef (commercial)
2 tablespoons hot water
1 tablespoon sweet butter
4 tablespoons Marsala
  wine

Dip each escalope (cutlet) into clarified butter, then into finely grated Parmesan cheese. Heat ⅓ to ½ cup clarified butter and sauté prepared escalopes until brown on both sides. In separate pan cook 2 tablespoons butter over low flame, add mushrooms, toss and turn frequently. When escalopes are tender and well browned season to taste with salt and pepper. Arrange on a hot platter, having them overlap each other.

Mix beef extract with hot water, sweet butter and Marsala wine; add mixture to mushrooms. Bring all to a boiling point, but do not actually boil. Pour the mushroom-wine sauce over hot escalopes. Serve immediately.

EMINCÉ OF VEAL ZURICHOISE

Swiss Chalet
San Juan, Puerto Rico

½ cup clarified butter	2 tablespoons flour
2¼ pounds thinly sliced lean veal	1 cup dry white wine
	2 cups heavy cream
¼ pound butter	Salt, pepper
1 onion, finely chopped	Parsley, chopped
6 ounces fresh mushrooms, sliced	

Heat frying pan with clarified butter, sauté veal over high flame to a light brown. Remove meat from pan, add some butter, onions, mushrooms, sprinkle with flour, white wine and heavy cream, and cook until sauce is thick; add sautéed veal, salt to taste. Do not boil. Sprinkle with chopped parsley when served.

SCHNITZEL À LA LÜCHOW

Luchow's
New York City

6 8-ounce veal cutlets	1½ teaspoons salt
8 tablespoons butter	½ teaspoon pepper
1½ cups stock	10 medium fresh mushrooms, sliced
6 eggs	
2 tablespoons chives, chopped	24 stalks hot cooked fresh asparagus

Wipe cutlets with damp cloth; pound. Cook in 6 table-spoons butter until golden on both sides and cooked through. Remove cutlets to warmed serving dish and keep hot.

Stir stock into pan gravy and cook until smooth and slightly thickened.

Beat eggs; add chives, salt, and pepper. Sauté mushrooms in remaining butter 3 or 4 minutes. Add egg and chive mixture to mushrooms; cook over moderate heat, stirring like scrambled eggs. Pour this mixture over cutlets. Streak with a little hot gravy. Garnish platter with asparagus.

VEAL CHOP À L'AIGLON

*L'Aiglon Restaurant
New York City*

6 6-ounce veal chops	1 cup breadcrumbs
Salt and pepper	⅜ cup butter
1 egg, beaten	¾ pound green noodles
1 tablespoon water	Melted butter

Pound veal chops until thin—about ⅛-inch. Season with salt and pepper. Dip chops in egg and water mixture and coat with bread crumbs. Cook in clarified butter until golden brown. Boil green noodles, strain them dry and then mix in melted butter.

Place chops on top of green noodles and cover with Mornay sauce. Broil until golden brown.

Mornay Sauce

6 tablespoons butter, melted	3 egg yolks
6 tablespoons flour	½ to 1 cup Parmesan cheese, grated
1 pint milk	¼ cup heavy cream, whipped
Salt and pepper	

Melt butter over moderate heat. Add flour and stir until well blended. Cook 10 minutes, stirring constantly. Add boiling milk and stir with whisk until creamy—about 8 minutes. Remove from fire, add the egg yolks and stir for 4 minutes. Cook 15 minutes. Add cheese and whipped cream.

VEAL SAVOYARD

London Chop House
Detroit, Michigan

12 6-ounce veal chops
Salt, pepper
  4 tablespoons butter
  1 large onion, chopped
½ cup celery, diced
  1 green pepper, diced
  2 carrots, sliced

  1 clove garlic, chopped
  1 bay leaf
  3 fresh tomatoes,
    chopped
Pinch oregano
  3 medium potatoes,
    diced

Season veal chops with salt and pepper. Sauté lightly in butter. Place in earthenware casserole. Add remaining ingredients, bake in oven, at 350°, for 45 minutes. (Add a little broth to cover, if needed).

MINCED VEAL, ZURICH STYLE

Motel de Ville
Ottawa, Canada

1½ pounds boneless veal
  6 tablespoons butter
  3 tablespoons shallots,
    minced
  3 tablespoons cognac
  4 tablespoons flour
½ teaspoon salt

¼ teaspoon white pepper
⅓ cup dry white wine
½ cup brown gravy
  1 cup fresh mushrooms,
    sliced
  1 cup heavy cream

Trim meat of all fat. Cut against the grain into 1-inch thin pieces. Heat butter in a large skillet, add shallots and cook 2 minutes. Add veal, cook for 1 minute. Flame with cognac.

Meanwhile, sauté mushrooms in remaining 1 tablespoon butter for about 2 minutes; mushrooms must be still white and firm.

When flame has died down, sprinkle flour over veal. Stir in salt, pepper and mushrooms. Add white wine, gravy and cream. Cook over low heat, stirring constantly, until mixture comes to a boil and thickens.

MEDAILLONS DE VEAU POMPADOUR

King Cole Restaurant
Dayton, Ohio

Loin of veal, about 4
    pounds
Salt and pepper to taste
Flour for dredging
¼ cup butter
  1 pound mushroom
    buttons

½ pound artichoke hearts,
    quartered
¼ cup butter
  1 cup veal juice
Parsley, chopped
Watercress
Croutons

Remove the tenderloin and eye of a medium veal loin, about 4 pounds. Cut tenderloin and eye in pieces one inch thick and flatten slightly. Season the medaillons with salt, pepper and flour lightly, then sauté in ¼ butter until medium well done.

For the garnish, sauté in butter the mushrooms and artichoke hearts. Add veal juice and bring to a boil.

Place medaillons on shaped croutons with garnish on top. To decorate, sprinkle with chopped parsley and add a small bouquet of watercress. Serve with either pommes chateau or pommes parisienne.

VEAL À LA SWISS

Swiss Tavern
Pompton Lakes, New Jersey

2 pounds veal filet, cut in
  small pieces
4 shallots, chopped
4 tablespoons butter

Flour
½ cup white wine
  1 cup beef stock
Salt

Simmer shallots in butter. Add veal and sprinkle a little flour over veal. Sauté quickly in large frying pan over hot fire. Add wine and beef stock. Cook 5 minutes. Serve in casserole with hash brown potatoes and mixed green salad.

GERMAN VEAL ROULADES
(Veal Birds)

The Tides Hotel
St. Petersburg, Florida

1½ pounds veal, cut into
    thin even slices
Carrot strips
Dill pickle slices
Ham strips
Knob celery, sliced
Salt, pepper to taste
  6 tablespoons butter

1 onion, finely chopped
2 tablespoons flour
1 teaspoon mustard
½ pound mushrooms,
    sliced
2 cups chicken stock
¼ cup Burgundy

Flatten veal slices with a meat cleaver to the size of a small hand.

Spread slices with meat farce (see recipe below) about ⅛ inch thick. Place on one end strips of carrots, dill pickle, ham and knob celery about a quarter inch thick cut. Roll veal so the stuffing is on the inside. Tie with a light string. Season with salt and pepper and brown lightly in butter, in a heavy pan. Take roulades out and in same pan sauté diced onions; then add flour, mustard, sliced mushrooms. Add chicken stock and Burgundy. Simmer for one hour and serve with Spaetzles.

Meat Farce

½ pound lean pork
½ pound veal
1 tablespoon parsley,
    finely chopped
2 rolls, soaked in milk

½ onion, sautéed in butter
2 eggs, well beaten
Salt, pepper, sweet basil,
    garlic, nutmeg, to taste

Run through fine blade of grinder pork, veal, parsley, softened rolls and onions. Add eggs and seasoning. Mix well. Cook in butter for 5 to 10 minutes and cool.

MEDAILLONS OF VEAL OSCAR

*Hotel Benson
Portland, Oregon*

3 medium-size veal
   tenderloins, well trimmed
Salt and pepper to taste
½ cup flour
18 Dungeness crab legs
2 eggs, well beaten

1 cup white bread crumbs
½ cup Chablis wine
¾ pound butter
Bearnaise sauce (see recipe
   under sauces)

Cut veal tenderloins into pieces of 2½ ounces each (three per person). Pound them down a little. Add salt and pepper on both sides and dip in flour. Dip crab legs in flour, next in well-beaten egg, and then in bread crumbs.

Preheat the frying pan to high temperature; put 4 tablespoons butter into pan and cook the veal until golden brown, approximately 10 minutes. Meanwhile, deep-fry the crab legs in the remaining butter which has been pre-heated in a sauce pan, and put aside.

Place the cooked medaillons on a platter and flash the pan with the Chablis; simmer for one minute and pour over the meat. Put one teaspoon of Bearnaise Sauce over each medaillon and top each piece with a fried crab leg.

OSSO BUCO
(Braised Veal Knuckle)

*Cafe Jardin Suisse
Roney Plaza Hotel
Miami Beach, Florida*

3 pounds veal knuckles,
   sawed into 2½-inch
   pieces
Flour for dredging
Salt, pepper to taste
6 tablespoons butter
1 clove garlic, finely
   chopped

1 carrot, thinly sliced
Rind of ½ lemon, grated
6 tablespoons parsley,
   finely chopped
1 cup white wine
Meat stock
2 tablespoons tomato
   purée (optional)

Roll the veal knuckles in seasoned flour. Sauté in butter in a large skillet. When well browned on all sides, add garlic, carrot, grated lemon rind, 3 tablespoons parsley, white wine, and enough meat stock to cover the knuckles halfway. Tomato purée may be added.

Bring the mixture to a boil, reduce the heat, and simmer gently, covered, for about one hour, or until the meat is tender but not falling from the bones, turning the pieces once while cooking. Remove the lid for the last few minutes of cooking to allow the sauce to reduce and become slightly thickened. Taste for seasoning and remove to a large heated platter. Sprinkle with 3 tablespoons finely chopped parsley and serve with hot boiled rice.

VEAL GOULASH WITH FRIED SPATZEN

Sun Valley Inn
Sun Valley, Idaho

3 pounds veal, cut into
  2-inch squares
2 teaspoons paprika
2 large onions, minced fine
2 cloves garlic, minced
  fine
Flour for dredging

Salt, pepper to taste
  3 thyme leaves
  1 bay leaf
½ cup tomato juice
½ cup bouillon
  3 cloves
¼ cup butter

Mix a little flour, salt, pepper and paprika. Dust the veal with the mixture. In a heavy sauce pan, heat butter. Add the veal, onion and garlic, and sauté until meat is golden. Add bouillon and tomato juice, enough to cover all the veal. Cover and simmer until the veal is tender, about 1 to 1½ hours. The thyme, bay leaf and cloves should be tied in a cloth and put into the sauce pan while it is simmering.

Spatzen (or Spaetzle)

2 eggs, well beaten
½ cup cream
½ teaspoon salt

1½ cups flour
2 tablespoons parsley,
  chopped

To the eggs add cream, salt, flour and chopped parsley. This mixture should be harder than dumpling mixture. Have boiling salted water and put mixture, through a colander into the boiling water. Simmer for 5 to 10 minutes. When tender, drain and fry lightly in hot butter. (This step may be omitted). Serve with veal goulash.

ESCALOPE DE ROGNONS DE VEAU DIJONNAISE

La Bourgogne
San Francisco, California

6 ounces butter
6 veal kidneys, sliced into small escalopes
Paprika and salt to taste
12 button mushrooms
3 shallots, finely chopped
2 ounces brandy

½ cup cream
2 teaspoons Dijon mustard
Pinch tarragon, chopped
1 teaspoon fines herbs (chives, or parsley) chopped

Heat butter in pan, add seasoned kidney escalopes, button mushrooms and finely chopped shallots. Toss over hot flame for 1 minute. Pour brandy over kidneys and flambé, tossing over hot flame for 2 more minutes. Remove pieces of kidneys and mushrooms from pan. Keep warm.

To the shallots add fresh cream, allow to cook over hot flame 1 minute to reduce. Add the kidneys and mushrooms. Blend in Dijon mustard. Check the seasoning. Sprinkle with chopped tarragon and fines herbes before serving.

TRIPE À LA CRÉOLE

Maylie's Club Restaurant
New Orleans, Louisiana

2 pounds tripe, partially pre-cooked
½ tablespoon lard
1 sliver fat salt pork
1 onion, minced
2 tomatoes, coarsely chopped

1 small green pepper, finely sliced
1 tablespoon garlic, minced
1 tablespoon parsley, minced
Thyme
1 pint beef broth

Rinse the tripe well in several changes of cold water and dry thoroughly. Cut into narrow and short strips or dice. Melt lard and fry salt pork. Place tripe in hot fat, frying well; then add onion, tomatoes, green pepper and garlic. Simmer, then add other seasonings. Add beef broth and let simmer for 1 hour. When tender, sprinkle with parsley.

CERVELLI DIVITELLO, VILLA BETACCI

The Greenbrier
White Sulphur Springs, West Virginia

3 calves brains	2 eggs, well beaten
2 tablespoons vinegar	1 tablespoon heavy cream
1 onion, halved	½ cup butter
1 bay leaf	6 artichoke hearts
2 cloves	1 tablespoon butter
Salt, pepper, flour	6 slices truffle

Soak brains in water. Remove skin between crevices. Put brains in small casserole, cover with cold water. Add vinegar, onion, bay leaf and cloves. Bring slowly to a boil. Simmer for 10 to 15 minutes, then remove from fire. When cool, take brains out and put on a napkin.

Cut brains in half. Season with salt and pepper and powder with flour. Then dip completely in egg batter (eggs and heavy cream beaten together). Put in clarified butter to brown on both sides.

Serve with quartered artichoke hearts sautéed in butter and slices of truffles.

BROILED HONEYCOMB TRIPE À LA PARKER

Parker House
Boston, Massachusetts

3 pounds honeycomb tripe	2 lemons, cut in quarters
Salt, pepper to taste	Parsley sprigs
Flour for dredging	Garnish of French fried
½ cup melted butter	eggplant
Bread crumbs	Mushrooms

Wash 3 pounds of thick fresh honeycomb tripe in cold water, trim, divide into 6 pieces and wring water out with clean towel. Season with salt and pepper, dredge in flour thoroughly. Then dip in melted butter or vegetable oil and bread crumbs. Place in a hot charcoal broiler, if possible, and let cook for about 6 minutes on one side; turn over, repeat until done, taking about 12 minutes in all. Arrange on platter, spread with melted butter, garnish with lemon and parsley. Serve very hot with french fried egg plant and fresh mushrooms.

HASENPFEFFER
(Rabbit Stew)

The Red Star Inn
Chicago, Illinois

2 rabbits, cut up	1 teaspoon juniper berries, crushed
4 cups red wine	
1 cup wine vinegar	1 tablespoon salt
1 carrot, sliced	⅜ cup butter
1 onion, sliced	1 cup flour
2 stalks celery, cut up	1 cup sour cream
2 parsley roots	½ cup water
3 bay leaves	24 small onions
3 cloves	Salt pork, cut in large dice
Thyme	Seasoning to taste
1 teaspoon pepper	

Cut up two rabbits, about 4 pounds. Leave shoulders and legs whole. Save blood and liver in separate dish. Put cut up meat in an earthen pot and cover with red wine and wine vinegar. Add carrot, onion, celery, parsley roots, bay leaves, cloves, thyme, black pepper, juniper berries and salt. Let stand in refrigerator for two days.

Strain the marinade and dry the meat. Put butter in a casserole and when hot, add flour, allow to become golden brown, stirring all the while to prevent its burning. Add the cut up meat and simmer for five minutes. Add the drained marinade, sour cream and water. Cover pot and simmer about 45 minutes, until meat is tender.

Parboil and fry small onions. Parboil and fry diced salt pork. When stew is about three-quarters cooked, add onions and pork and cook until done. Chop the liver fine, mix with the blood and stir into the stew just before removing from the fire. Do not let boil after adding the liver. Season and serve in earthen casserole.

VEAL KIDNEY FLAMBÉ

Beverly Hilton Hotel
Beverly Hills, California

6 veal kidneys
6 tablespoons clarified
  butter
¼ cup armagnac or cognac
½ cup sherry wine

1 cup mushrooms, sliced
  and cooked in butter
  until wilted
¾ cup brown sauce
Salt and pepper to taste
Parsley, chopped

Cut the kidneys in half and remove center core and excess fat. Cook kidneys in butter until medium done. Pour off butter from the skillet and add armagnac or cognac. Set it aflame and pour in sherry. Add brown sauce, stir in the mushrooms, and season to taste with salt and pepper. Serve sprinkled with chopped parsley.

TOURNEDO ROYAL

Brennan's
New Orleans, Louisiana

½ cup butter
¾ cup onions, chopped
½ cup breadcrumbs
1½ teaspoons paprika
1½ teaspoons capers
1½ teaspoons truffles,
  chopped
Pinch powdered thyme

1 cup sweetbreads,
  parboiled and chopped
  fine
6 artichoke hearts
6 filets mignon, 12 to 14
  ounces each
Pepper, salt
½ cup Bearnaise sauce (see
  under sauces)

In a small skillet melt butter and sauté the onions, bread crumbs, paprika, capers, truffles and thyme until done. Add sweetbreads and heat through. Remove pan from heat. sweetbreads and heat through. Remove from heat. Form mixture into 6 balls. Place each ball in an artichoke heart. Season filets and grill to taste. Place on serving plate. Pour 1 tablespoon Bearnaise over filet and place stuffed artichoke heart on top.

BRAISED OXTAIL, GLAZED VEGETABLES

Place Pigalle
San Francisco, California

4 to 5 pounds oxtail, disjointed	Salt, black pepper
6 tablespoons fat	Thyme and rosemary
1 medium onion, chopped	½ cup red wine
1 large carrot, chopped	1½ cups tomato juice
2 stalks celery, chopped	½ cup tomato purée
1 bay leaf	4 cups consommé
	Arrowroot or cornstarch

Brown oxtail in fat in very hot heavy skillet. When brown on all sides, transfer to a casserole. To pan add onion, carrot, celery and seasonings. Cook for 5 to 10 minutes and add red wine. Add tomato juice, tomato purée and consommé. Strain liquid through very fine sieve. Return liquid to fire and allow to come to full boil. Remove excess fat which comes to top of pot. Thicken slightly with arrowroot or cornstarch. Then pour over oxtails, cover and bake 2½ to 3½ hours, until meat is tender, at 350°. Add desired vegetables: (include small pearl onions, carrots, green beans and potatoes). Cook until vegetables are tender.

RACK OF LAMB, SARLANDAISE

Essex House
New York City

2 single racks of spring lamb, trimmed	3 pounds new potatoes, peeled
Salt and pepper	3 truffles, sliced thin
10 ounces butter	4 ounces roast gravy (juice of roast)
2 ounces white wine	

Note: Sarlandaise means potatoes, sliced thin and layered with truffles

Season the racks of lamb. Roast them with 4 ounces butter in oven at 375°. Baste them frequently in their own juice and add a few drops of water once in a while to prevent burning of the butter. Roasting time: 25 to 30 minutes, until meat is medium rare, pink, and juicy. Remove the racks and the juice of the meat gravy. Eliminate some fat and mix the gravy with white wine and continue cooking, reducing it to about one half. Strain the resulting gravy and add one ounce butter Noisette (brown butter). Check the seasoning to your taste.

Cut potatoes to thickness of a half dollar and season with salt and pepper. Sauté in a saucepan over a high flame with 6 ounces butter, and add the truffles. Put meat, potatoes and truffles in a big earthen platter, not too deep, and cook in oven, 350°, for about 25 minutes.

Carve the racks. Line up the slices of lamb on the potatoes sarlandaise. Place in oven again for about three minutes and serve immediately.

RACK OF LAMB PARSLEY

L'Aiglon Restaurant
New York City

1 large loaf white bread, crusts removed, grated into crumbs
1 pound butter, soft but not melted
½ cup shallots, chopped
2 cloves garlic, chopped
3 cups fresh parsley, chopped
2 teaspoons Worcester-shire sauce
Salt and pepper, to taste
Rack of lamb—5 to 6 pounds

Mix white bread crumbs, butter, shallots, garlic and parsley and Worcestershire sauce in a bowl with salt and pepper to taste. Mix well, until lumps of butter disappear, mixture should resemble dough. Place in refrigerator; this will keep safely for one week under refrigeration.

Season lamb with salt and pepper. Roast rack at 350°, 12 minutes per pound for rare, 18 minutes for well done. Cut the dough-like mixture into thin slices and cover the outside of the lamb with it. Put the roast back into the oven for 10 more minutes—longer if desired well done. The bread will be brown. Serve with lamb gravy.

RACK OF LAMB BOUQUETIERE

Ernie's Restaurant
San Francisco, California

3 rack of lamb (approximately 1½ pounds each when cleaned)
Salt and pepper
1 onion, sliced
1 teaspoon thyme
1 bay leaf
1 cup white wine
1 cup brown sauce
½ cup baby carrots

3 tablespoons peas
3 tablespoons green beans, diced
2 tablespoons butter
6 artichoke bottoms
2 cups new potatoes, peeled
3 tomatoes
Watercress

Salt and pepper the lamb and place in 400° oven for approximately 1½ to 2 hours, depending on how well done you want it (18 minutes per pound for well done, 12 for rare). Put sliced onion, thyme, bay leaf with meat and roast for five more minutes. Take meat out of oven and drain fat from pan. Deglace with white wine and add brown sauce. Then let simmer for 5 minutes. In the meantime, sauté the vegetables in butter. Put the smaller vegetables inside the artichoke bottoms. Sauté the potatoes in butter and grill the tomatoes in halves. Drain sauce. Use a little sauce to glaze the rack of lamb and serve the rest on the side. Put rack on serving tray and garnish with artichoke bottoms, tomatoes and potatoes alternately around the meat. Add bouquet of watercress here and there for color.

LAMB CHOP BRAISED WITH SLICED POTATOES AND TOMATOES

Hotel Astor
New York City

6 5-to-6-ounce shoulder
   lamb chops
Salt, pepper
1 onion, sliced
4 tablespoons butter
2 pounds raw potatoes,
   peeled and sliced

½ to ⅔ cup stock
1 small can tomatoes,
   including juice
1 clove garlic, mashed
Chives, parsley, chopped

Season chops with salt and pepper. Brown on both sides in frying pan in 3 tablespoons butter.

Remove and place in single layer in shallow baking pan. Pour drippings over chops. Smother onions in 1 tablespoon butter; do not brown. Mix onions with potatoes, season with salt and pepper. Cover lamb chops with potatoes and onions. Moisten slightly with stock. Cover and bake 30 minutes, at 350°. Then add tomatoes and garlic, and bake one hour longer, or until chops are done.

Serve in oval shirred egg dish with chop on the bottom and potatoes on top. Garnish with chopped chives or chopped parsley.

CASSEROLE OF BAKED LAMB CHOPS, CHAMPVALLON

Hotel Tropicana
Las Vegas, Nevada

3 onions, sliced
6 double lamb chops
Salt, pepper to taste
2 pounds potatoes, peeled
   and sliced

10 tablespoons butter
2 cloves garlic, crushed
1 bouquet garni
2 cups beef broth

Sauté onions slightly in 2 tablespoons butter. Spread them evenly on the bottom of a casserole and keep them hot. Season the chops and sear them quickly on both sides in 4 tablespoons butter. Lay them on top of the onions.

Place potatoes on top of the chops, add 4 tablespoons butter, garlic cloves, the bouquet garni, and pour broth over all. Season lightly and put in 350° oven. Baste frequently during cooking process until meat and potatoes are cooked. Serve in casserole. Cooking time, about 30 minutes.

SADDLE OF LAMB

Quo Vadis
New York City

5-pound saddle of lamb	½ teaspoon thyme
1 large onion, quartered	½ teaspoon rosemary
2 carrots, sliced thick	1 clove garlic
2 celery stalks	1 cup dry white wine
Salt, pepper	1 cup beef stock
1 bay leaf	

Trim, skin saddle, season with salt and pepper and set in roasting pan. When roasting for half an hour, at 350°, add spices and diced vegetables. Roast for another 20 minutes for rare or 25 minutes for medium done. Remove saddle, pour out all fat, pour wine over vegetables, let cook and reduce 5 minutes. Add beef stock, season to taste. Strain sauce into a bowl.

ROAST LEG OF SPRING LAMB

The Crystal Restaurant
Reading, Pennsylvania

1 leg of spring lamb, 5 to 6 pounds	Salt and pepper
3 cloves garlic, sliced lengthwise	4 tablespoons melted butter
	Juice of 1 lemon

Wipe leg of lamb with a damp cloth. Make slits with a sharp knife in various places and on both sides of lamb.

Insert pieces of garlic in slits made in lamb. Season with salt and pepper and brush with melted butter. Squeeze lemon juice over lamb and place in preheated oven, 450°, about ½ hour. Lower heat to moderate, 350° to 375° and add 2 cups hot water. Bake slowly, 20 to 25 minutes per pound, adding more water if needed.

Gravy can be made in same pan by removing most of the fat and serving the lamb with its natural gravy.

SHISH KEBAB

London Grill
Portland, Oregon

1 leg of lamb, shank off (approximately 2½ to 3 pounds) boned, trimmed, and cut in one-inch cubes
1 cup olive oil
1 cup dry sauterne wine
1 teaspoon turmeric
1 teaspoon Ac'cent
1 teaspoon curry powder
1 teaspoon ginger powder
3 teaspoons salt
1 medium onion, grated
1 garlic clove, crushed
Onions, sliced in one-inch cubes
Green peppers, cubed
Zucchini, cubed
Mushrooms
¼ pound butter melted

Cut lamb in one-inch cubes. Prepare a marinade of olive oil, sauterne, turmeric, Ac'cent, curry powder, ginger powder, salt, grated onion and garlic. Marinate lamb in this for 24 hours.

Alternate the meat cubes on the skewers with cubes of onion, green pepper, zucchini, mushrooms and broil, turning to brown on all sides and basting with butter. Serve with rice.

SHISH KEBAB

Barberian's Steak House
Toronto, Ontario

Lamb
 1 cup red wine
 1 cup tomato juice
 ¼ cup olive oil
 3 cloves garlic, crushed
 1 teaspoon oregano
 1 tablespoon salt

Black pepper, to taste
 1 small leg of lamb, cut
 into 2-inch cubes
 8 or 10 small onions,
 quartered
Small tomatoes (optional)
Green peppers (optional)

Prepare a marinade of red wine, tomato juice, olive oil, garlic, oregano, salt and pepper. Figure about ¾ pound lamb per person. Cut into 2-inch cubes, trim away fat and sinew. Place meat and quartered onions in marinade overnight in a cool place.

Alternate the meat and onions and, if desired, add small tomatoes and quartered green peppers, on skewers. Place skewers over low charcoal fire. Cook until outside is brown and inside pink. Serve on onion roll or French stick.

SHASHLIK CAUCASIAN
(with cold mustard sauce)

Embassy Club and Knight Box
Sheraton-East Hotel
New York City

1 leg of lamb, 8 to 10
 pounds, diced
Juice of 2 lemons
 1 onion, chopped
 1 lemon, sliced

 1 teaspoon salt
 1 teaspoon freshly ground
 black pepper

Bone the lamb and dice into 1½ inch cubes. Add lemon juice, onions, sliced lemon, salt and pepper. Marinate in a stone pot for 24 hours. Place cubes of lamb on skewers and broil, to taste. (For serving, string beans and wild rice are suggested.) Serve the mustard sauce separately.

Mustard Sauce
(to be served cold, separately)

1 teaspoon English mustard	1 tablespoon heavy cream
1½ cups brown sauce	1 cup Chablis wine

Blend ingredients well; serve cold.

CORDERITO COLUMBINE

Columbine Ranch
Estes Park, Colorado

Leg of lamb	Salt
Sauterne wine	Pepper
Garlic powder	Honey
Nutmeg	Grated orange rind

Remove the gland kernel from a leg of lamb (this kernel is just above the shank). Marinate lamb overnight in Sauterne wine. Remove, retain wine, and cover lamb generously with garlic powder, nutmeg, salt, pepper, honey and grated orange rind. Cook 25 minutes per pound in 350° oven. Baste with wine left over from marinating, adding more if necessary. Make gravy from wine drippings by adding a small amount of water.

IRISH LAMB STEW

The Matador Room
Davenport Hotel
Spokane, Washington

3 pounds lean lamb stew meat	3 carrots, sliced thick
1 onion, sliced	3 potatoes, sliced thick
¼ head cabbage	Salt, pepper
	Parsley, cut coarse

Bring lamb to a boil, drain and wash through collander. Return lamb to roaster that can be covered tightly. Cover with onion, cabbage, carrots and potatoes, in this order. Barely cover with water and season with salt and white pepper. Do not mix.

Cover tightly and put in 400° oven approximately 2 hours or until lamb is tender. *Do not stir.*

Lift out meat and vegetables with skimmer. Thicken juice to light gravy consistency and strain. Pour back over stew, add parsley and mix lightly.

IRISH STEW

Miller Brothers
Baltimore, Maryland

3 pounds lamb and veal, cut in 2-inch pieces
Cold chicken stock, to cover
Carrots, cut in 2-inch pieces
Leeks, cut in 2-inch pieces
Celery, cut in 2-inch pieces
Salt, pepper

Kitchen Bouquet to taste
3 tablespoons flour
Water
1 tablespoon parsley, chopped
1 tablespoon Worcestershire sauce

Put meat in heavy kettle with cold chicken stock and bring to boil. Add carrots, leek, celery (as much as desired). Add salt and pepper and Kitchen Bouquet, and cook until meat is tender. Mix flour and cold water and strain into boiling stew. Before serving, add parsley and Worcestershire sauce.

LAMB STEW WITH GREEN BEANS

Middle East Restaurant
Philadelphia, Pennsylvania

2 pounds stewing lamb, with or without bones
2 tablespoons olive oil
2 medium onions, coarsely chopped
2 pounds fresh green beans, cut in half

1¼ teaspoon salt
1 large can whole tomatoes
¼ teaspoon black pepper
¼ teaspoon allspice (optional)
1 clove garlic (optional)

Clean meat well, removing all excess fat. Place in a medium size heavy pot with the olive oil and brown on all sides. Add the onions and fry to a golden brown, stirring often to keep from burning. Then add the well-washed green beans and salt. Mix together well. Cover tightly and steam over a low flame for 30 minutes or until beans have begun to wilt. Add tomatoes and black pepper. Stir a few times. Raise the flame until stew begins to boil. Then lower the flame, stir again and cover, and cook for another 30 minutes. Taste for seasoning. Add more if necessary. Stir again. Cover and cook until sauce has thickened and beans are done. Serve with rice.

Note: Beans cooked this way taste even better the following day.

LAMB KIDNEY À LA BERRICHONNE

The Lodge at Smuggler's Notch
Stowe, Vermont

9 lamb kidneys, finely sliced
3 shallots, chopped
1 teaspoon butter
6 ounces red Burgundy

9 medium mushrooms, sliced
3 ounces boiled lard, diced
Salt, pepper to taste
2 tablespoons parsley, chopped

Put kidneys with shallots in *hot* pan with very hot butter. Cook for 2 minutes. Remove kidneys and put aside. Add Burgundy. Reduce to half. Put kidneys, mushrooms and lard in pan. Let boil for 2 minutes. Remove from heat and add seasoning, butter and parsley.

WAIOLI MEAT PASTRIES

Waioli Tea Room
Honolulu, Hawaii

½ pound ground round
¼ pound pork sausage
1 small onion, grated
¾ teaspoon sage
1¼ teaspoons salt
⅛ teaspoon pepper

1½ teaspoon Ac'cent
1 cup potatoes, boiled and cut in very small pieces
½ cup potato water
Pie or biscuit dough
Milk

Mix all ingredients, except pie dough, together till well blended. Cut pie crust in 2½ inch circles and put 1 teaspoon of mixture on each circle. Brush edge with milk, fold over, and seal. Pierce the top with a fork. Bake at 350° for 25 to 30 minutes.

Mixture must be soft; add milk if necessary.

Note: For piecrust, use the water from the boiled potatoes.

BEEF WELLINGTON

The Tides Hotel
St. Petersburg, Florida

8 ounces pork
8 ounces beef
8 ounces veal
½ cup bread crumbs
4 eggs, well beaten
2 tablespoons parsley, chopped

Salt, pepper, garlic salt, marjoram, nutmeg, to taste
3 to 4 pound beef tenderloin
Puff paste

To avoid going through an hour long preparation of the puff paste, buy this at a pastry shop.

Make a meat farce by grinding pork, beef and veal. Mix all in a bowl with bread crumbs, eggs, chopped parsley and seasonings to a smooth consistency. Wipe a whole, well trimmed beef tenderloin, season it well with salt and pepper, and sear it in a pre-heated pan on all sides. Let it cool.

Roll out puff paste to ⅛ inch thickness, spread on meat farce and lay the filet in the center. Then roll paste around; close the ends by putting overlapping paste tight together. Lay the filet on a baking pan and brush with water. Bake in an oven at 400° for 30 minutes, until crust is golden brown.

MAPLE BAKED HAM

The Little House and Pantry
Northfield, Vermont

1 canned 5-pound ham
Cloves
1 cup or more dark maple syrup

Bake a canned ham in a slow oven, 325°, for 1 hour. Pour off the salty broth to use in pea soup. Score the fat top of ham and stick with cloves. Over this, pour at least 1 cup of dark maple syrup and bake for another hour, basting frequently. To glaze nicely boil down the maple syrup in the pan.

BAKED HAM MOHAWK

The Mohawk
Old Forge, New York

1 6-to-7-pound sugar
   cured, fully cooked ham
Water—about 1 quart
Whole cloves
1½ tablespoons dry
   mustard

Worcestershire sauce, to
   taste
Tabasco, to taste
Brown sugar
Fruit syrup or juice

Put ham in roasting pan with water, cover, and cook for about 2 hours at 375°, or until tender. Cool and remove bone, and tie. Put ham in shallow pan, large side up. Score fat in about ½ inch squares, stick whole clove in each square. Cover top with dry mustard, add Worcestershire sauce and Tabasco. Pour over ham syrup from spiced fruits (syrup from spiced watermelon, peaches, etc.), or pineapple juice or orange juice. Have enough juice around ham to cover pan for about ½ inch. Place brown sugar over ham to cover top, packing it firmly. Put in oven at 375°. Baste frequently until brown, about one hour.

MARYLAND HAM

Olney Inn
Olney, Maryland

1 country ham	1 cup dry wine (Sherry,
½ cup maple syrup, honey	Burgundy or Claret)
or brown sugar	1 cup fine bread crumbs
1 teaspoon whole cloves	½ cup brown sugar
¼ teaspoon whole allspice	Sherry
4 bay leaves	Whole cloves

Soak ham overnight in cold water. Drain off the water. Place in deep kettle with fresh cold water to cover. Add maple syrup (or honey or brown sugar), whole cloves and allspice, bay leaves and wine. Cider may be substituted for wine, if desired. Cover kettle tightly. Bring very slowly to boil, then turn fire very low and let simmer until ham is very tender—about 20 minutes per pound. Let cool in water in which ham was cooked. Remove skin.

Cover fatty top ¼ inch thick with mixture of fine bread crumbs, brown sugar and sherry, using 1 cup crumbs to ½ cup brown sugar and enough sherry to hold mixture together, so that it may be patted in shape without running. Stick with whole cloves one inch apart. Brown in hot oven, 400°, until sugar has glazed and fat is crisp. Serve cold.

PENNSYLVANIA DUTCH SCHNITZ UN KNEPP

Walps Restaurant
Allentown, Pennsylvania

4 pounds ham end	Pinch cinnamon
½ cup brown sugar	2 cups biscuit mix
6 ounces dried apples	¾ cup milk
(Schnitz)	

To make dried apples, cut the whole apple in wedges and remove core—(about six wedges from each apple). Put apples in uncovered roasting pan and place in 200° oven for two hours.

Soak dried apples overnight in enough water to cover. Simmer ham for 3 hours in small amount of water. Add brown sugar, cinnamon, dried apples and water in which they had been soaked to the ham. Simmer for another hour. Remove ham. Mix biscuit mix and milk (this is the knepp) and drop by tablespoonfuls into rapidly boiling ham broth. Cover the kettle and simmer for 15 minutes. Serve hot with ham.

HAM ROLLS

Lake Breeze Resort
Three Lakes, Wisconsin

6 slices boiled ham,
⅛-inch thick
6 slices Swiss cheese
Asparagus spears, canned or frozen, and cooked
2 tablespoons butter or margarine

¼ cup onion, chopped
¼ cup green pepper, chopped
1 8-ounce can tomato sauce
½ cup chili sauce
½ cup water

Top each ham slice with Swiss cheese. Arrange 3 or 4 spears of asparagus at end of slice and roll up. Fasten with tooth pick. Arrange in flat baking dish.

Melt butter in skillet. Add onion and green pepper. Cook about 5 minutes. Stir in remaining ingredients. Pour over ham rolls. Cover and bake in 350° oven about 30 minutes.

BAKED HAM LOAF WITH YORKSHIRE SAUCE

Comet Restaurant
Grand Rapids, Michigan

2 pounds smoked ham, ground
1 cup fine bread crumbs
3 eggs, slightly beaten
2/3 cup milk
1/3 cup green peppers, chopped

1/3 cup onions, chopped
2 teaspoons mustard
2/3 teaspoon allspice
1/3 cup sweet pickle relish
12 whole cloves
2/3 cup tomato juice

Combine all ingredients except cloves and tomato juice in a large bowl. Blend well, and press into loaf pan. Insert cloves in ham loaf, pour tomato juice over meat. Bake in 350° oven for 45 to 50 minutes. Allow loaves to set in pans five minutes before serving.

Yorkshire Sauce

1/3 quart brown sauce
1/6 cup currant jelly
1/6 cup port wine

2/3 cup orange juice
1/3 teaspoon grated orange rind

Work currant jelly into brown sauce, add port wine, orange juice and grated rind. Simmer gently until flavors are blended.

BANANA HAM NUTWICH

Hilton Inn
San Francisco, California

1 Pullman-style loaf
bread, unsliced
1⅓ cups soft cream cheese
(4 3-ounce packages)
½ cup soft butter or
margarine
1 tablespoon lemon juice
1 tablespoon horseradish
1 tablespoon salt
1 teaspoon Worcestershire
sauce
¼ teaspoon white pepper

¼ teaspoon Tabasco
2 cups chopped baked
ham
1½ cups mashed ripe
bananas
¾ cup chopped pecans
6 lettuce leaves
Potato chips or shoestring
potatoes
18 slices orange (about 3
oranges)
Parsley sprigs

Trim all crusts from loaf of bread. Then slice loaf length-wise into six horizontal slices, ¼ inch thick. Blend together cream cheese, butter or margarine, lemon juice, horseradish, salt, Worcestershire sauce, white pepper and Tabasco. Spread each slice with cream cheese mixture. Combine ham and bananas. Spread ham mixture over cream cheese mixture. Sprinkle nuts evenly over ham mixture.

Starting at narrow end, roll up each spread slice jelly roll fashion. Wrap in waxed paper and place in refrigerator for at least 30 minutes. When ready to serve, remove from re-frigerator and cut into ½-inch slices. Serve on lettuce leaf with potato chips or shoestring potatoes, orange slices and parsley sprigs.

This recipe makes 36 ½ inch slices.

HAM AND PINEAPPLE ROLL

Mac's Restaurant
Jamestown, North Dakota

8 slices ham
8 pineapple spears
3 tablespoons butter

1 cup whipping cream
Flour

Flour 8 pineapple spears, then brown in the butter. Roll each spear in a ham slice and secure with a toothpick. Bake in 350° oven for 30 minutes. Pour 1 cup whipping cream over dish and bake for another 15 minutes, basting once.

GRANDMA'S HAM LOAF

Smith Farm
Falmouth, Maine

2 cups bread crumbs
½ teaspoon salt
¼ teaspoon black pepper
½ teaspoon dry mustard
2 eggs, beaten
1¼ cups milk

1 pound smoked cooked ham, ground
1 pound hamburger
½ cup brown sugar
¼ teaspoon ground cloves
Pineapple slices

Make dressing of crumbs, salt, pepper, mustard, eggs and milk. Add ham and hamburger. Grease loaf pan. Mix brown sugar and ground cloves and place in bottom of pan. Arrange pineapple slices on brown sugar, turn ham loaf mixture into pan, and press down. Bake at 350° for 1½ hours.

HAM FRIED RICE

Kahiki Supper Club
Columbus, Ohio

2 tablespoons butter
½ yellow onion, chopped
1 cup cooked diced ham
2 cups precooked rice

Soy sauce mixture (see recipe below)
2 eggs, beaten
2 stalks scallions, chopped

Melt butter in heavy skillet and sauté onion and ham. Add rice and soy sauce mixture. Add eggs. Mix well. Add chopped green onions. Serve piping hot.

Soy Sauce Mixture

¼ teaspoon salt
1 teaspoon sugar
2 tablespoons soy sauce

Mix ingredients well.

ROAST PORK

Vasata Restaurant
New York City

4 pound loin of pork   1 teaspoon cornstarch
Salt   Water
Caraway seeds

Preheat oven to 400°. Wash a loin of pork in cold water.
Rub in salt to taste and sprinkle with caraway seeds. Place
some pork bones and a few pieces of fat in roasting pan.
Place loin on top. Add a little warm water and roast 2 to
2½ hours, turning meat every 30 minutes. Add more water
if necessary. When meat is done, remove it from pan. Mix
cornstarch in a little cold water and add to gravy. Turn oven
to 500° and cook gravy for about 15 minutes. Strain, add
salt to taste and serve over pork.

HUNGARIAN LECCHO WITH RICE

Bayview Restaurant
Callander, Ontario

6 lean center cut pork   Salt and pepper, to taste
  chops   3 tomatoes, sliced
3 tablespoons butter   1 tablespoon paprika
4 large onions, sliced   2 tablespoons ketchup
2 medium green peppers,   1½ cups rice
  sliced

Fry the chops in butter, browning them on both sides.
Remove chops, add onions and peppers, salt and pepper.

Cover and cook for seven minutes, until almost done. Add sliced fresh tomatoes and paprika, and continue to cook for three minutes. Add ketchup. Place chops in sauce and simmer until chops are tender and sauce is well blended.

Cook rice in rapidly boiling salted water. Drain. Place chops on bed of rice and pour gravy over all.

BUTTERFLY PORK CHOPS, SOUTH SEA ISLAND

Crystal Room
Pick-Fort Hayes Hotel
Columbus, Ohio

6 8-ounce pork chops
Salt, pepper
Dash paprika
  3 slices toast, halved
  2 tablespoons peanut
    butter
  6 pineapple rings, glazed
    in butter

1 cup melted butter
  6 small broccoli flowers,
    cooked
Fresh peas, cooked
12 kumquats
24 small sweet potato balls
    (from 4 whole sweet
    potatoes)

Split the pork chops and flatten down with a cleaver so they will remain open. Season with salt, pepper and a little paprika. Broil or grill until nicely brown. Spread each piece of toast with peanut butter and place a chop on each half slice. Top each chop with a pineapple ring glazed in butter and place a broccoli flower in the center of the ring. Put fresh peas and kumquats around pineapple ring as a garnish. Serve with sweet potato balls sautéed in butter.

PORK TERIYAKI

4 B's Cafe
Missoula, Montana

3 pounds fresh pork, cut
  in cubes
6 tablespoons butter
2 cups turkey stock
1 teaspoon ginger
⅓ cup soy sauce
2 cups pineapple juice
½ cup brown sugar

2 tablespoons cornstarch
1¾ cups pineapple chunks
3 cups celery, chopped
1½ large onions, chopped
3⅓ cups bean sprouts
5 cups steamed rice
Green pepper strips and
  carrot slices

Braise pork cubes in 3 tablespoons butter until well browned. Make sauce by heating together stock, ginger, soy sauce, pineapple juice and brown sugar. Heat well, then thicken slightly with moistened cornstarch. Simmer for a few minutes. Add pineapple chunks and braised meat. Braise celery, onions and bean sprouts together in remaining butter until just tender. Serve hot meat and sauce over steamed rice. Border with braised vegetables. Garnish with raw green pepper and carrot slices. Serves 8.

STUFFED PORK SPARE RIBS WITH BAKED APPLE

The Holderness Inn
Holderness, New Hampshire

Salt, pepper, paprika, to
  taste
6 to 8 pounds spare ribs
Flour for dredging
Bread dressing with apple

1 tomato, peeled and
  sliced
1 large onion, cut in 6
  rings

Season spare ribs to taste. Cut each slab in two and dust with flour. Add chopped apple to bread dressing and spread over ribs. Top with tomato slices and onion rings. Cover the pan and bake at 325° until nearly done, about 2½ hours. Uncover, baste, and brown as desired, baking about 30 minutes more.

Serve with baked apple made as follows:

Baked Apple

6 medium apples, cored   Raisins
Sugar, cinnamon, to taste   Lemon juice

Core apples and fill cavity with raisins, sugar and cinnamon. Bake in pan with small amount of water. Remove apples when baked and make heavy syrup of drippings to pour over apples, adding extra sugar, lemon juice and cinnamon as needed.

NEW ENGLAND STYLE ROAST SPARE RIBS

Hotel Astor
New York City

4 pounds fresh spare ribs —3 inches wide, 6 inches long   2 tablespoons onion, chopped
4 cups bread crumbs   ½ teaspoon sage
Milk to moisten   Salt, white pepper to taste
1½ tablespoons shortening   ½ teaspoon marjoram
    ½ cup water

Pour milk over stale bread crumbs and let stand. Cook onions in shortening until tender. Mix onions, sage, salt and moistened crumbs together to make a fairly moist stuffing.

Crack spare ribs across the middle and place the stuffing on one half; then fold over and sew or tie together.

Cover bottom roasting pan with ½ cup water and place the ribs on a rack in the pan. Roast in hot oven, 375°, turning once, until the ribs are brown and crisp.

NEW ORLEANS JAMBALAYA

Mickelberry's Log Cabin Restaurant
Chicago, Illinois

½ pound fresh pork,
  shredded
2 tablespoons shortening
½ pound fresh pork
  sausage
1 medium onion, chopped
2 cloves garlic, minced
½ pound raw smoked ham,
  coarsely diced
1 cup tomatoes, cut up

1 quart stock
1 tablespoon mixed
  pickling spices
1 tablespoon parsley,
  chopped
1 teaspoon chili powder
1½ pounds shrimp, cooked
3 cups cooked rice

Sauté pork in shortening about 15 minutes. Add sausage and cook 10 minutes. Stir in onion, garlic, ham and tomatoes. Simmer for 10 minutes. Add stock, spices and parsley and cook for 30 minutes over a low fire. Add shrimp and simmer for a few minutes. Serve on bed of rice.

PORK PIE

Smith Farm
Falmouth, Maine

Double recipe rich pie
  crust
Apples, peeled and sliced
1 pound fat salt pork,
  diced very fine

Raisins
Cinnamon
Molasses

Make a rich pie crust. Line a deep dish with a thick crust.

Make a layer of sliced apples mixed with diced salt pork, raisins, cinnamon (be generous); add about 1 cup of molasses per layer. Top with crust.

Continue with layers of apple-salt pork mixture and pie crust until dish is full. Be sure to cut slits in each crust layer so steam may escape. Bake in a slow, 300° oven, all day.

RAGOUT FIN IN NOODLE NEST

Three Coins Inn
Baton Rouge, Louisiana

3 ounces fresh lean pork, cubed small
3 ounces beef, cubed small
3 ounces lamb, cubed small
3 ounces ham, cubed small
3 ounces chicken, cubed small
3 tablespoons butter
½ small onion, minced
2 tablespoons flour
4 tablespoons water
1 egg, separated
Salt, pepper to taste
2 ounces mushrooms, stems and pieces
2 tablespoons parsley, minced
Basil leaves to taste
Very thin egg noodles
3 4-inch baking shells
Parmesan cheese, grated
Paprika

Sauté all meats in butter until golden brown on outside. Add onions and stir constantly for 3 minutes. In a cup, mix flour with water, egg yolk, and salt and pepper. Add this, together with mushrooms and parsley to the meat and mix in 2 pinches of basil leaf. Beat egg white. Dip noodles into egg white and set in baking shells; bake for 10 minutes in 350° oven. Take out and fill with meat mixture. Bake again for 20 minutes at 350°. Sprinkle grated cheese (Parmesan or American), paprika over top, and serve.

CASSOULET MONTALBANAIS

La Bourgogne
San Francisco, California

½ pound salt pork, sliced lengthwise in 4 equal pieces
1 pound haricots beans (white beans)
1 pound bacon rind, cut in small pieces
1 pound garlic sausages, cut in ½ inch slices
2 medium onions, sliced
3 cloves garlic
1 bay leaf
Sprig thyme
2 pounds goose, cut in pieces
1 tablespoon tomato puree
Salt and pepper

Soak sliced salt pork overnight. Drain, add fresh water and boil gently for 1 hour.

Soak white beans in water overnight, then bring to a boil for 30 minutes. Drain, rinse and put them in a casserole.

Lightly brown bacon rind and sliced onions. Add garlic, bay leaf, thyme, goose pieces (previously browned in pan), sliced garlic sausage, tomato puree and parboiled salt pork. Pour this mixture over beans, arranging salt pork evenly on top, cover level with water, season with salt and pepper. Cover dish tightly and bake in a slow oven, 300°, 2 to 3 hours. Serve in casserole.

ROAST VENISON

Le Chateau Richelieu
New York City

6 pound leg, loin or rib of venison	Pepper
Salt pork, cut in strips	Flour
Garlic salt	¼ cup melted bacon fat

Use a tender cut from the leg, loin, or rib. Lard with strips of salt pork and sprinkle with garlic salt, pepper and flour. For accurate judging of cooking time, insert meat thermometer into center of roast, being careful not to let it touch a bone. Roast in 350° oven until rare or medium rare, which gives the best flavor and most tender meat. Use readings on thermometer for beef or allow 20 to 25 minutes per pound. Bast frequently with melted bacon fat.

Serve with buttered noodles, chesnut purée, buttered peas and tart jelly.

VEGETABLES

STUFFED BAKED ARTICHOKES

The Ropewalk
Nantucket, Massachusetts

1 cup bread crumbs
2 cloves garlic, chopped
2 teaspoons parsley,
chopped
½ teaspoon salt

½ teaspoon pepper
1 teaspoon oregano
2 tablespoons melted
butter
6 artichokes

Mix together thoroughly the bread crumbs, garlic, parsley, seasonings and melted butter.

Cut about 1 inch off tops of artichokes and remove the tough outside leaves. Boil, covered, in salted water for 20 to 30 minutes or until tender. Remove from water, spread leaves, and with a spoon, scrape and take out the fuzzy portion from the heart of the artichoke. Stuff with bread crumb mixture.

Place the artichokes in a baking dish. Pour boiling water around them to the depth of one inch. Bake, covered with aluminum foil, in moderate 350° oven, for 20 to 25 minutes.

BOSTON BAKED BEANS

Durgin-Park
Boston, Mass.

2 cups beans
1 teaspoon baking soda
4 cups cold water
¾ pound salt pork, diced
1 medium onion, peeled

½ cup molasses
½ teaspoon dry mustard
1 teaspoon salt
½ teaspoon pepper

Soak beans overnight. In the morning, drain the beans, then parboil them for 10 minutes with baking soda. Then run cold water over the beans in a colander or strainer. Dice rind of salt pork in inch squares. Put half on bottom of bean pot with whole onion. Put beans in pot. Put rest of pork on top. Mix other ingredients with hot water and pour over beans. Cover the pot and bake in 300-degree oven for six hours. Add water as necessary only to keep beans moist. Do not add too much water to flood the beans.

HOMEMADE BAKED BEANS

Stan Hack's Landmark
Dixon, Illinois

2 pounds Great Northern
   White Beans
Salt
1½ cups catsup
 3 cups brown sugar
½ teaspoon dry mustard
3 tablespoons Worcester-
   shire Sauce
Dash powdered garlic
2 cups uncooked diced
   bacon squares

Cook beans in salted water until done. Mix all ingredients and add to cooked beans. Bake for three hours in very slow oven, 275°. Can be stored.

HOME BAKED BEANS

Lambertville House
Lambertville, New Jersey

2 cups dried pea beans
2 tablespoons molasses
½ cup brown sugar
Salt and pepper
1 whole onion
1 tablespoon dry mustard
¼ pound salt pork, diced

Soak beans overnight. Drain the beans. Cover with cold water and boil one hour. Drain the beans and add remaining ingredients. Cover with plenty of boiling water. Bake beans, covered, for 6 to 9 hours in 275° oven, adding boiling water as necessary. Uncover the beans the last hour of cooking.

BAR X BAKED BEANS

Bar X Bar Ranch
Crawford, Colorado

1 large can (1 lb. 14
   ounces) pork and beans
¼ pound bacon, diced
1 cup catsup
½ cup brown sugar
¼ teaspoon cinnamon
¼ teaspoon cloves
¼ teaspoon ginger
little water

Mix all together and bake in casserole dish for 1½ hours
at 300°.

MARINATED STRING BEANS IN SOUR CREAM SAUCE

Menemsha Inn
Menemsha, Massachusetts

2—#2 cans whole green
   beans
1 onion thinly sliced
⅓ cup Italian salad dressing
1 cup sour cream
¼ cup mayonnaise
1 teaspoon lemon juice
1 tablespoon horseradish
¼ teaspoon onion juice
¼ teaspoon dry mustard
¼ teaspoon tarragon

Marinate green beans and onion in Italian dressing overnight. Drain and cover with mixture of the other ingredients.

EL RANCHO MARINATED BEANS

El Rancho Inn
St. Albans, West Virginia

1 small can green beans
1 small can wax beans
½ teaspoon salt
½ teaspoon garlic powder
2 tablespoons salad oil
1 cup sugar
½ cup vinegar
1 small onion (cut in
   rings)
1 pimento or 1 green
   pepper (cubed)

Drain juice from canned beans. Add all other ingredients to beans in large salad bowl. Mix well and allow to marinate overnight or all day in refrigerator. Serve with garnish of pimento or green pepper, cubed.

CABBAGE ROLLS

Chicken Villa
Canora, Saskatchewan

1 cup rice
1½ cups boiling water
1 teaspoon salt
1 medium onion, chopped fine

4 tablespoons butter
Salt and pepper to taste
1 large cabbage

Wash the rice well. Add to boiling water. Stir in the salt and bring to a brisk boil and let cook for one minute. Cover, turn off the heat and allow it to stand until the water is absorbed. The rice will be only partially cooked. Cook the onion in 1 tablespoon butter until it is golden brown. Mix with the rice and season to taste with salt and pepper.

Remove core from large cabbage head by cutting around it with a sharp pointed knife. Place the cabbage in a deep utensil and pour boiling water into the hollow of the core to cover head completely. Let it stand until the leaves are soft and pliable. Drain the cabbage and take the leaves apart carefully without tearing them. Cut off the hard center rib from each leaf. Cut the large leaves into 2 or 3 sections. Place a generous spoonful of the rice filling on each leaf and roll lightly. Arrange the rolls in layers in a casserole. Sprinkle each layer with some salt. Pour a cup of water over the rolls and put 3 tablespoons butter over them. Protect the top from scorching by covering it with a few large leaves. Cover the cabbage rolls tightly and bake in moderate 350° oven for 1½ to 2 hours until the cabbage and rice are cooked. Serve hot.

SWEET AND SOUR RED CABBAGE

Johnny Cake Inn
Ivoryton, Connecticut

2 large red cabbages
4 slices bacon, cut into ¼
 inch squares
2 apples, peeled, cored
 and thinly sliced

1 cup water
1 teaspoon salt
½ cup red wine vinegar
½ cup brown sugar

Strip outer leaves of cabbage, cut in two. Cut away hard core. Shred or cut fine strips. Soak in cold water.

In heavy dutch oven, fry out bacon that has been cut into squares. Add cabbage, removing from water direct to cooking pot; add apples. Add water, salt, cover and cook over low heat until apples are transparent (about 1 hour). Add vinegar and brown sugar. Cook 20 minutes longer, lifting cabbage frequently until sugar dissolves. This may be prepared in advance, the day before serving. To reheat, use double boiler.

RED CABBAGE GERMAN STYLE

Schroeder's Cafe
San Francisco, California

1 red cabbage, 3 to 4
 pounds
2 cups boiling broth
4 tablespoons bacon fat
2 tablespoons vinegar
2 peeled, cut apples

2 whole cloves
½ glass red wine
1 tablespoon sugar
Salt and pepper to taste
½ stick cinnamon

Remove wilted leaves from cabbage. Cut head in half and remove center. Shred cabbage very fine, pour boiling broth over it, add bacon fat and cook for 1 hour; then add remaining ingredients and continue cooking for ½ hour, turning it frequently. Ten minutes before serving, add ½ glass red wine and finish cooking. The cooked cabbage should be neither too sour nor too sweet.

STUFFED CABBAGE WITH SWEET
AND SOUR SAUCE

London Chop House
Detroit, Michigan

 1 head cabbage
½ pound beef, chopped
½ pound lamb, chopped
½ cup raw rice
 1 onion, chopped fine

Salt and pepper to taste
2 cups broth (canned
   chicken or beef broth
   can be used)

Remove core from cabbage and parboil a few minutes to wilt leaves. Separate leaves carefully. Mix meat, rice, onion and salt and pepper together. Put two tablespoons of mixture on wilted cabbage leaves and roll, enclosing ends. Place in baking pan and cover with broth. Bake for 1 to 1½ hours in 350° oven. Serve with sweet and sour sauce. Allow 2 or 3 stuffed leaves for each serving.

Sweet and Sour Sauce

⅓ cup raisins
 1 small onion, chopped
 2 tablespoons butter
 1 green pepper, chopped
 1 tablespoon brown sugar

½ cup wine vinegar
2 tablespoons cornstarch,
   mixed with 2
   tablespoons cold water

Simmer raisins in water for 30 minutes. Sauté onion in butter till transparent. Add chopped pepper and cook 2 more minutes. Add raisins, sugar, vinegar and bring to a boil. Thicken with cornstarch.

CARROTS VICHY

Chez Bruchez
Daytona Beach, Florida

 3 cups carrots, peeled
   and sliced
¾ cup boiling water
1½ tablespoons sugar

¼ teaspoon salt
3 tablespoons butter
Parsley, chopped

Place carrots in boiling water, with sugar and salt. Cover the pot with a tight cover and cook until water evaporates. Brown carrots in butter. Sprinkle with chopped parsley.

CELERY AU GRATIN, WITH ALMONDS

Latham's on Cape Cod
Brewster, Massachusetts

4 cups celery, cut in one-inch pieces
½ cup blanched almonds, chopped

½ cup American cheese, grated
½ cup bread crumbs

Sauce, made of the following:

2 tablespoons butter or margarine
2 tablespoons flour

1 cup rich chicken stock
¼ cup light cream
Salt and pepper to taste

Parboil celery and drain. Place a layer of celery in a baking dish or casserole. Sprinkle with some of the chopped almonds. Pour half of the sauce over all. Repeat the process. (Use only two layers of each ingredient.) Sprinkle the top with cheese and crumbs. Bake at 350° for 30 minutes or until slightly brown.

CELERY CASSEROLE

Colonial Inn
Blackfoot, Idaho

4 cups celery, diced
⅓ cup almonds, slivered
¾ cup water chestnuts
6 tablespoons butter
4 tablespoons flour

1½ cups chicken broth
1 cup half-and-half cream
¾ cup mushrooms
¾ cup Parmesan cheese
¾ cup bread crumbs

Parboil diced celery for 5 minutes. Drain and put in casserole with almonds and water chestnuts. Heat in 4 tablespoons butter and make smooth paste with flour. Slowly stir in broth and cream. Simmer over slow fire for 5 minutes. Add mushrooms to sauce just before pouring over celery. Sprinkle with cheese, butter dots and bread crumbs. Bake in 350° oven until bubbly. Serves 8. (This recipe can be used with green or lima beans as the main ingredient.)

CORN CABBAGE

Colonial Room
Peabody Hotel
Memphis, Tenn.

5 to 6 strips of crisp
  dry bacon
4 cups cabbage, shredded
1½ cups fresh corn
1 medium green pepper,
  minced

1⅓ teaspoons salt
2 tablespoons brown sugar
1 cup water

Fry bacon until crisp, set aside. Cook together all other ingredients. Just before serving, crumble crisp bacon over cabbage.

CORN FRITTERS

Imperial Hotel
Cripple Creek, Colorado

1 tablespoon sugar
1 cup sifted all-purpose
  flour
1 teaspoon salt
1 tablespoon salad oil

2 eggs, beaten
1 teaspoon baking powder
1 cup milk
1 cup whole kernel corn,
  canned

Mix all ingredients together and drop by small spoonsful into deep hot oil or fat heated to 360°. Fry until golden-brown, drain on paper towels and serve with honey. Makes about 12 fritters.

CORN PUDDING

King's Arms Tavern
Williamsburg, Virginia

6 ears of corn
2 eggs, slightly beaten
¼ cup flour
1 teaspoon salt

½ teaspoon pepper
2 cups milk
1½ tablespoons melted butter
    (for baking dish)
3 tablespoons butter

Take large, tender, milky ears of corn. Split the corn down the center of each row, cut off the top, and then scrape the cob well. Add eggs and stir them into the corn. Add flour, salt and black pepper. Stir in milk and mix all together thoroughly. Put into a buttered baking dish about 4 inches deep. Cover the top with butter cut into small pieces. Bake in a moderate oven, 350°, about 1 hour. Serve hot.

CHILE RELLEVOS CON QUESO

Old Adobe Patio Restaurant
Tucson, Arizona

12 chiles
6 eggs
6 tablespoons hot water
Salt, to taste

Flour, to make thin batter
4½ cups Cheddar cheese,
    grated

Parch the chiles over an open flame, on the grill, or in a dry iron skillet, turning as they begin to blister. When the skin is evenly blistered and puffed away from the pulp, lay the chiles on a cloth and sprinkle with water. Cover with another cloth to steam. The skins may then be pulled off. Remove all seeds, if possible.

Beat eggs to a froth, gradually add water, salt and flour; a thin batter will be formed.

Fill chiles with grated cheese. Dip each chile into the batter and place in frying pan containing hot oil (370°) about 1½ inches deep. Fry until golden brown. Drain the chiles and set aside where they will stay hot.

Prepare the following sauce:

2 cups fresh stewed
  tomatoes, or 1 No. 2 can
2 cups chicken stock
1 scant teaspoon oregano,
  rubbed between the hands
1 large onion, chopped fine

2 or 3 cloves garlic
3 tablespoons butter
3 tablespoons flour
1 teaspoon salt
⅛ teaspoon pepper
Parmesan cheese, grated

Cook tomatoes, chicken stock and oregano 15 minutes. Rub through colander. Brown onion and garlic in butter. Sprinkle flour into onion and garlic, add salt and pepper. Cook for three minutes, then add to tomato and chicken stock mixture.

Pour over stuffed chiles. Sprinkle grated cheese on top. Allow two peppers per portion.

CHILES RELLENOS

Cafe La Margarita
Chicago, Illinois

6 large bell peppers
1 small package cream
  cheese
3 eggs, separated

Pinch of salt
1 cup flour
Oil for frying

Sauce

4 tablespoons onion,
  chopped
2 tablespoons corn oil

1⅓ cups tomato sauce
¼ teaspoon oregano
Salt and pepper to taste

Slit the peppers at the lower end and remove the seeds and pulp, but leave on the stems. Boil in water until tender, drain, and stuff each pepper with pieces of cheese. Separate the eggs and beat the whites until they are like snow, then add the yolks and continue beating until uniform and fluffy. Add salt. Heat the oil in a pan (370°) roll the peppers in flour, then dip in the egg mixture and fry until golden. Pour sauce over each relleno and serve. To make the sauce, sauté the onions in oil and add tomato sauce, salt and pepper, and oregano. Simmer for ten minutes.

TROPICAL EGGPLANT CASSEROLE

*The St. Croix by the Sea
Christiansted, St. Croix,
Virgin Islands*

1 large eggplant, peeled
and diced
Boiling water
½ teaspoon salt
½ cup butter
3 large onions, finely sliced
4 stalks celery, cut in strips

½ pound fresh mushroom
caps, cut up
2 green peppers, seeded
and cut into strips
¼ cup bread crumbs
1 cup Parmesan cheese,
grated
Paprika, to taste

Cover eggplant with boiling water, add salt and simmer 8 to 10 minutes. Drain.

Braise onions, celery, mushrooms, green peppers in ¼ cup butter. Combine with eggplant and place in casserole. Brush the top with ¼ cup melted butter and sprinkle bread crumbs or cracker crumbs over it. Add grated cheese and paprika. Place casserole in moderate oven, 350°, for 20 to 25 minutes, until cheese melts. Serve very hot.

EGGPLANT BOURBONNAISE

*The Mohawk
Old Forge, New York*

1 cup onion (chopped
fine)
3 tablespoons butter or
margarine
1 No. 2½ can tomatoes, or
3 cups fresh tomatoes,
cut into pieces
1 medium clove garlic
(minced fine or put
through garlic press)

1 teaspoon salt
4 drops Tabasco
1 large eggplant, peeled
and cut into 15 slices
¼ inch thick
1½ cups milk
1½ cups flour
Salt and pepper to taste
Fat or oil for frying
Parsley, chopped

Melt butter, add onion, cook until soft and yellow. Add pulp of tomatoes, cut into small pieces, and juice. Add garlic and seasonings. Cook over low heat until thick, stirring occasionally. This makes the sauce.

Dip eggplant slices in milk, then in seasoned flour. Sauté in fat or oil in frying pan until brown on both sides. Place slices of eggplant into a baking dish, overlapping the slices, and pour sauce over all. Place in moderate oven, 350°, for five to ten minutes, or until heated through. Sprinkle with chopped parsley.

EGGPLANT PROVENCALE

Testa's Restaurant
Palm Beach, Florida

1 large eggplant
1 cup olive oil
4 cloves garlic, crushed
2 large cans Italian style
  tomatoes, peeled

Oregano, to taste
Salt and pepper, to taste
¼ cup capers

Wash and trim a large, perfect eggplant. Cut the eggplant in six parts and make several small incisions in the flesh with a sharp paring knife "to let the fruit breathe." Dip the pieces in olive oil and arrange them on a large, flat baking pan, cut side up. Bake the eggplant in a very hot oven (400°) for 20 minutes or until tender.

Crush garlic and brown lightly in olive oil. Add Italian style tomatoes and simmer the mixture for 1½ hours. Remove the sauce from the heat and season it to taste with oregano, salt and pepper. Pour the sauce over eggplant, sprinkle with capers. Serve hot or cold.

This makes a wonderful vegetable or a nice appetizer or an addition to an antipasto.

BAKED EGGPLANT

*Vick's Restaurant
Dallas, Texas*

1 large eggplant
¾ cup salt
2 eggs
6 tablespoons butter or
margarine

½ cup onion, chopped fine
Pepper, to taste
6 or 8 crackers, crushed
½ cup cheese, grated

Pare and cut one large eggplant in ½ inch slices. Place in large bowl and cover with water; sprinkle salt over top and let stand for 1 hour. Drain off salt water, put in sauce pan and parboil eggplant until tender, about 15 minutes.

Drain off all water, mash well. Beat eggs and add to mashed eggplant. Add butter, or margarine, stirring well. Add onion, pepper to taste and crushed crackers, and stir well. Put in buttered baking dish and bake in moderate oven, 350°, about 30 minutes. When done, sprinkle grated cheese on top, put back in oven until cheese is melted.

GUINEA SQUASH PIE

*The House by the Road
Ashburn, Georgia*

1 eggplant, medium size
3 slices white bread,
toasted
Milk
2 eggs, beaten slightly
1 onion, chopped

3 tablespoons melted
butter
1 teaspoon salt
Pepper to taste
2 tablespoons cream

Peel eggplant, and boil in salted water. When done drain and mash.

Soak bread until soft. Mix with mashed eggplant. Beat eggs with a little milk and add to eggplant mixture. Sauté onions in butter, add to the egg plant mixture with salt and pepper, and place in buttered casserole. Pour cream over top and bake in 350° oven for 25 minutes until golden brown.

FRIJOLES REFRITOS
(Refried Beans)

Cafe La Margarita
Chicago, Illinois

2 cups beans
1 onion, finely chopped
½ pound fresh ham, or
½ pound bacon

2 tablespoons corn oil
½ cup Parmesan cheese,
grated

Soak the beans overnight. Cook beans with chopped onion, and ham or bacon. When the beans are done, lower the flame, and add corn oil. Then mash the mixture with a potato masher. Sprinkle the mixture with Parmesan cheese and continue mixing until thoroughly blended.

GARNACHAS

Cafe La Margarita
Chicago, Illinois

12 tortillas
½ onion, chopped fine
½ green pepper,
chopped fine
1 large tomato, peeled
and chopped

Oil
Refried beans
Tomato sauce
Longhorn cheese, shredded

Sauté the onion, green pepper and tomato in oil until cooked. Cut the tortillas in quarters and brown in deep fat. Spread each tortilla very lightly with refried beans and tomato sauce and top with cheese. Then heat in a hot oven or broiler until the cheese is melted.

FRIJOLES NEGROS
(Black Beans)

Las Novedades Spanish Restaurant
Tampa, Florida

¾ pound black beans
1½ quarts water
1 large onion, peeled
  and sliced
3 green peppers, seeded
  and sliced
1 clove garlic

½ cup olive oil
1 tablespoon salt
2 ounces bacon
¼ pound ham bone
3 bay leaves
½ cup vinegar

Soak beans in water overnight. Drain beans and reserve water. Fry onion, green peppers and garlic lightly in olive oil, stirring frequently. Combine all ingredients except vinegar, including water in which beans were soaked, and simmer until beans are tender and liquid is of thick consistency. Add vinegar a few minutes before serving.

HUMMOS BI TAHEENI
(Chick Peas with Sesame Oil Sauce)

Middle East Restaurant
Philadelphia, Pennsylvania

In the Pressure Cooker

1 pound hummos
  (chick peas)
½ teaspoon soda
1 teaspoon salt
¼ cup taheeni (sesame oil)

4 tablespoons lemon juice
2 cloves garlic, minced
2 tablespoons chopped
  parsley
Olive oil

Wash peas well, remove imperfections, and soak overnight with soda. Place in pressure cooker with water to cover and salt. Cook 20 minutes under pressure. Press cooked peas through sieve. Set some aside for topping. To the pea purée slowly add sesame oil and lemon juice, alternately. Add garlic, crushed with salt. Purée should be thick and smooth but if it seems too thick, thin with water. Pour onto serving platter. Garnish with parsley and a few whole cooked peas. Pour a little olive oil over the purée.

In an Open Pan

Use same ingredients as above. Boil soaked peas in fresh water until very tender, adding more water if necessary. Purée the cooked peas and combine with remaining ingredients, as above. Peas will require several hours cooking to become tender.

LIMA BEAN CASSEROLE

Hotel Racine
Racine, Wisconsin

1 pound large lima beans	1½ cups brown sugar
2 large Bermuda onions, sliced	1 cup liquid in which the beans have cooked
1 pound salt pork (or smoked bacon)	Salt and pepper to taste

Soak the beans overnight. The next morning, drain carefully and cover again with fresh boiling water. Cook for 30 minutes. Drain. Reserve one cup of liquid. Place a layer of beans in the bottom of a small casserole with cover. Cover with onion slices, salt pork or bacon slices, and brown sugar.

Repeat until beans and salt pork are used. You should end with salt pork or bacon on top. Sprinkle with brown sugar and pour the cup of liquid over the top. Bake at 350° until done. Beans and ovens vary. Two hours or more should do it! Remember to keep tightly covered while baking.

STUFFED BAKED MUSHROOMS

The Ropewalk
Nantucket, Massachusetts

18 large fresh mushrooms
4 tablespoons oil
1 cup bread crumbs
2 cloves garlic, chopped
3 teaspoons parsley,
    finely chopped

1 teaspoon oregano
Salt and pepper to taste
6 tablespoons melted
    butter

Cut off and chop stems of mushrooms and sauté in oil for 10 minutes. Mix with other ingredients, stirring until mixture is well heated. Spoon mixture into buttered mushroom caps. Place in buttered pan. Bake 20 minutes at 350°.

BAKED STUFFED MUSHROOMS WITH KING CRAB MEAT

The Bahia Restaurant
San Diego, California

1 pound crab legs,
    chopped
1 bell pepper, finely
    minced
1 medium size onion,
    finely minced
¾ pound butter

Juice of ½ lemon
1 quart milk
1 cup sherry
Salt and pepper to taste
1 cup flour
1 bunch fresh asparagus
18 large mushroom caps

Prepare filling first to chill. Combine crab legs chopped with finely minced bell pepper and onion. Sauté in ¼ pound butter and add lemon juice. Add 1 quart of milk, 1 cup of sherry and season to taste. Thicken with roux (equal parts of flour and butter—approximately 1 cup of each mixed together). Cool the mixture.

For each serving, place 4 pieces of fresh asparagus in a long casserole, two on each side, and place three large mushroom caps in the center. Fill each cap with crab filling. Heat 20 minutes in 350° oven. Top with Hollandaise sauce (see sauces). Place under broiler until golden brown.

ONIONS AU GRATIN

The Pirate's House
Savannah, Georgia

4 cups cooked onions,
drained and chopped
4 cups grated Cheddar
cheese
1 cup self-rising flour

¼ teaspoon black pepper
½ teaspoon salt
4 tablespoons melted
butter

Mix 3 cups of the cheese and all of the other ingredients together and pour into a one-quart casserole. Sprinkle the remaining cup of cheese on top and bake at 350° for 30 minutes.

FRENCH FRIED ONIONS

General Wayne Inn
Merion, Pennsylvania

3 Spanish onions,
peeled and sliced
Flour
2 eggs, lightly beaten

2 tablespoons milk
¾ teaspoon salt
1 cup bread crumbs

Slice onions into rings ¼ inch thick. Place in ice cold water for 20 minutes. Drain the onions and dry on absorbent paper. Beat eggs with milk and salt. Dip onions in flour, then in egg mixture, return to flour, then to egg mixture again. Roll in fresh bread crumbs. (Dry bread crumbs may be used, but fresh ones are better.) Fry in deep fat or oil (370°). Drain on absorbent paper.

STUFFED GREEN PEPPERS WITH RICE

Bayview Restaurant
Collander, Ontario

6 large green sweet
  bell peppers
6 tablespoons shortening
3 medium onions,
  finely chopped
1 12-ounce bottle catsup

or 6 ounces tomato
  paste
2 cups water
3 teaspoons paprika
Pinch each pepper, cayenne
  pepper and salt

Cut off the stem ends from the peppers. Remove the seeds and pith. Sauté onions in shortening until transparent. Stir in the rest of the ingredients, mixing thoroughly. Let simmer. This is the sauce.

Filling

1 pound lean minced
  beef
1 raw egg
1 chopped onion

Salt, pepper
Pinch of majoram
Clove of garlic, minced
2 cups cooked rice

Mix beef, egg, onion, seasonings and rice together to make the filling.

Stuff the peppers with the filling. Place in baking dish and pour the sauce around them. Bake for 30 to 40 minutes, until peppers are tender, at 350°.

POTATO DUMPLINGS

Mader's Restaurant
Milwaukee, Wisconsin

6 Idaho potatoes in
  jackets
1 to 1½ cups flour,
  sifted
1 egg, well beaten

1 tablespoon salt
Pinch pepper
1 teaspoon grated onion
2 pieces white bread
  toast, cut into croutons

Boil potatoes a day in advance. Peel and grate fine (or use food chopper or ricer). Mix ground potatoes with flour, egg, seasonings and onion until consistency of soft, smooth dough.

Form dough into balls the size of an egg, flatten, and fill center with 3 or 4 croutons. (Make croutons out of toast cut in small squares.) Work dough around croutons and roll in form of a dumpling. Cook dumplings in boiling salted water 8 to 10 minutes. Take out of water immediately, drain well, and pour butter topping over dumplings.

Butter Topping

4 tablespoons butter
½ cup bread crumbs

Melt butter, add bread crumbs, and stir well.

POTATO PANCAKES

Schroeder's Cafe
San Francisco, California

3 pounds raw potatoes
4 eggs, well beaten
1¼ cups flour
½ tablespoon salt
Pepper

½ teaspoon onion, grated
1 large sour apple,
  peeled and grated
Lard for frying

Peel potatoes, wash and let stand 30 minutes in cold water. Remove from water and grate quickly, let drain. Then mix in eggs, flour, pepper, salt, grated apple and onion. Shape into patties, ¼ inch thick and 4 inches in diameter. Heat lard very hot and fry 3 to 4 pancakes in the pan at one time. Potato pancakes should be brown and crisp. Do not cover them before serving.

POTATO PANCAKES

Eberhard's Restaurant
Columbia, Illinois

6 medium potatoes, pared and grated coarsely
1 small onion, grated
3 eggs, well beaten
1 teaspoon salt

1½ tablespoon flour
1 dash freshly ground pepper
1 dash nutmeg
Hot fat for frying

Extract moisture from grated potatoes. Add onion. Stir in eggs, salt, flour and pepper and nutmeg. Shape into patties. Sauté in ½ inch hot fat. Turn and brown other side until crisp. Drain on absorbent paper. Serve hot.

POTATO PANCAKES

Johnny Cake Inn
Ivoryton, Connecticut

4 large potatoes or 2 cups grated potatoes
3 eggs, lightly beaten
3 tablespoons flour

Oil
1 teaspoon salt
1 large onion, grated

Peel potatoes, grate on fine grater. Press the grated potatoes and pour off the liquid. Add eggs, flour, onion, salt. Stir briskly.

Using heavy skillet, melt your favorite shortening or oil to a depth of ¼ inch. When fat is smoking hot, drop a large spoonful of batter into skillet and flatten with spoon. Cook over gentle flame until golden brown, turn and brown other side. Remove and drain on absorbent paper.

PUMP ROOM POTATO ROYAL

The Pump Room
Hotel Ambassador
Chicago, Illinois

6 sliced Idaho potatoes
  (one potato per person)
Butter

Salt and pepper to taste
Roquefort cheese
Sprigs of parsley

Slice the peeled Idaho potato into ⅛-inch thick slices. Melt enough butter to cover the bottom of a large skillet; when the butter is hot, line the bottom of the skillet with the sliced potatoes. Sprinkle with salt and pepper, then add another layer of sliced potatoes. Fry over a medium flame until the bottom is brown and crisp. In frying, the two layers will stick together so that it will be easy to flip the potatoes over to fry on the other side. When both sides are done, remove potatoes and circle with small pieces of Roquefort cheese, placing a larger piece of cheese in the center. Set beneath broiler until cheese starts to melt. Garnish with parsley and serve piping hot.

POMMES SALARDAISE

Quo Vadis
New York City

4 large Idaho potatoes,
  peeled and sliced

Salt and pepper to taste
4 tablespoons butter
4 black truffles, thinly sliced

Slice potatoes, season with salt and pepper. Butter a frying pan, set one row of potatoes in the bottom, overlapping slices to make a design over potatoes, add sliced truffles, cover with another row of potatoes. Pour 1 ounce melted butter over all and cook in a 350° oven for 40 minutes. When done, turn over onto a serving dish.

HEREFORD HOUSE POTATOES

Hereford House Restaurant
Hotel Gramatan
Bronxville, New York

6 large Idaho potatoes, · 1 cup melted butter
  peeled · Parmesan cheese

Peel and thinly slice (not quite through) large Idaho potatoes. Press tightly together to form the natural shape of the potato. Then use a pan small enough to press the potatoes close together. Fill the pan half full of water and add melted butter. Sprinkle the potatoes with plenty of Parmesan cheese. Bake slowly in 350° oven for about 1½ hours, basting regularly with own juice. It is most important to keep the potatoes moist as they will absorb the water and will not turn out dry.

POMMES SOUFFLÉES

Antoine's
New Orleans, Louisiana

8 California Burbank, or 8 mature potatoes
Fat for frying

Note: It is very important to use the right potatoes.

Peel California Burbank or mature potatoes, and cut in ⅛ inch slices, lengthwise.

Place potatoes in wire basket and run cold water over them to remove any excess starch. Dry thoroughly.

Have two kettles of fat. Have fat in one kettle at a moderate temperature (275°) and fat in other kettle at a very hot temperature (400°).

Cover bottom of frying basket with layer of potatoes. Do not crowd. Place basket in kettle of moderately hot fat.

Cook until potatoes rise to the surface, and edges show signs of puffing. (If the puff does not develop, start again with a new batch of sliced potatoes).

When faint puffing appears, drain them on absorbent paper and cool. Then transfer to the very hot kettle of fat, a few at a time. Cook until fully puffed and browned.

Drain on absorbent paper. Salt. Serve immediately.

POTATO FILLING

Boone's Restaurant
Portland, Maine

6 potatoes	1 tablespoon parsley, chopped
1 onion, cut fine	1 tablespoon salt
2 tablespoons butter	¼ teaspoon pepper
½ cup bread crumbs	3 cups milk
2 eggs, well beaten	

Boil potatoes and mash.

Brown the onion in butter, add bread crumbs to the browned onions. Mix this together with the eggs, parsley, salt and pepper. Add the mashed potatoes. Heat milk and add gradually in small amounts to the mixture, while mixing the ingredients. Pour into casserole and bake ½ hour in 400° oven. Serve hot.

POTATO DUMPLINGS

Eberhard's Restaurant
Columbia, Illinois

3 boiled medium sized potatoes	¼ pound butter
4 raw potatoes	2 eggs, beaten
1 medium onion, grated	Salt, pepper, Ac'cent, to taste
2 cups bread cubes	¾ cup cornflake crumbs
	Cornstarch

Pass boiled potatoes through ricer. Set aside in large mixing bowl. Grate raw potatoes and onions together and squeeze through kitchen towel until dry. Fry bread cubes in butter until brown. Mix boiled and raw potatoes with breadcubes, eggs and seasonings. Add crumbs and mix well.

Form potato balls, and roll them in cornstarch. Drop the dumplings in boiling salted water, turn down heat to simmer. Cook the dumplings, *uncovered,* for about 10 minutes. Sprinkle with cornflake crumbs.

POTATO DUMPLINGS

Ox Yoke Inn
Amana, Iowa

4 cups boiled potatoes, diced	2 slices bread, cubed and browned in butter
2 eggs, slightly beaten	½ cup flour
Salt to taste	Parsley, chopped
1 medium onion, cut fine and browned in butter	½ cup bread crumbs
	¼ cup browned butter

Mix potatoes, eggs, salt, onion, bread cubes, flour and parsley together and form into balls the size of an egg. Boil in salted water for 15 minutes. Skim the dumplings from water and drain. Sprinkle with bread crumbs which have been browned in ¼ cup butter.

SWEET POTATOES

King's Arms Tavern
Williamsburg, Virginia

½ teaspoon nutmeg	2½ pounds sweet potatoes, mashed
¼ teaspoon cinnamon	
¾ cup sugar	¼ pound butter, melted
1 scant teaspoon salt	2 cups milk

Mix together nutmeg, cinnamon, sugar and salt. Add mashed sweet potatoes, melted butter and milk. Bake in hot oven, 400°, until glazed on top.

CANDIED SWEET POTATOES

Publick House
Sturbridge, Massachusetts

6 medium size sweet
  potatoes, boiled
¾ cup brown sugar

1 teaspoon salt
4 tablespoons butter
Marshmallows, optional

Peel boiled sweet potatoes after they have cooled and cut them into slices about ½ inch thick. Butter a baking dish or casserole that can be used for serving. Place a layer of potatoes in the bottom, sprinkle with brown sugar and salt, and dot with butter. Continue these layers until you have used up all the potatoes. Be sure to have some sugar and butter on top. Bake uncovered in a moderate oven (375°) for about 30 minutes, or until the potatoes are glazed on top. (The potatoes can also be cooked on top of the range in a large skillet—cover for the first 20 minutes.) A layer of marshmallows can be put on top of the potatoes just before they are taken from the oven and cooked for 5 minutes or so, or until they have melted a little and the top is lightly browned.

SWEET POTATO PUFF

The Lodge at Steinhart Park
Nebraska City, Nebraska

1 large can sweet potatoes
1 teaspoon salt
Small marshmallows

Cornflakes, finely crushed
Oil

Drain can of sweet potatoes well, add salt, and mash. Take tiny marshmallows and mold the potato around until ball is about 3 inches in diameter. Roll these potato balls into finely crushed corn flakes. Deep fry in 350° oil until light brown and crispy. Drain on absorbent paper. Serve piping hot with meat dishes.

SWEET POTATO SOUFFLE

The House by the Road
Ashburn, Georgia

6 sweet potatoes,
    medium size
2 egg yolks, beaten
½ cup milk
½ cup sugar
½ cup raisins
1 teaspoon nutmeg

3 tablespoons melted
    butter
2 egg whites, beaten
4 tablespoons sugar
1 teaspoon lemon juice or
    orange juice

Peel potatoes and boil in salted water until tender. Put through a potato ricer and mash thoroughly.

Mix egg yolks, milk, sugar, raisins, nutmeg and butter and stir in mashed potatoes. Put in buttered casserole and bake 350° oven for 30 minutes until light brown on top and bottom. Make a meringue of the egg whites and sugar, and the juice and place on top of potatoes. Put under broiler a few minutes to brown.

CREAMED SPINACH

Blackhawk Restaurant
Chicago, Illinois

2 ounces salt pork
2 tablespoons bacon
    drippings
4 tablespoons onion,
    chopped fine

3 pounds frozen spinach,
    finely ground
Salt, pepper to taste
1 cup cream sauce

Grind salt pork fine and sauté until brown. Add bacon drippings, and chopped onion, and sauté 20 to 30 minutes until brown. Add finely ground frozen spinach, salt and pepper to taste, and let come to a boil, stirring occasionally. Add cream sauce and cook 15 to 30 minutes, stirring frequently.

CREAMED SPINACH

Shoyer's Restaurant
Philadelphia, Pennsylvania

1 large onion,
  finely chopped
4 tablespoons shortening
4 tablespoons flour
2 cups milk, scalded

2 pounds spinach,
  finely chopped
1 teaspoon salt
½ teaspoon pepper

Sauté onions in the shortening until they are tender. Stir in flour. Add milk, stirring constantly to avoid scorching. Add the spinach, salt and pepper, stirring constantly.

Spinach should be finished in 20 to 25 minutes, using a slow flame. It may be thinned by adding more milk.

CREAMED SPINACH À LA LAWRY'S

Lawry's The Prime Rib
Beverly Hills, California

1½ packages frozen
  chopped spinach
3 slices bacon, finely
  chopped
½ cup onion, finely
  chopped
3 tablespoons flour

1 teaspoon Lawry's
  seasoned salt
¼ teaspoon Lawry's
  seasoned pepper
1 garlic clove, minced
1½ cups milk

Cook the spinach according to the package directions. Drain well. Fry the bacon and the onions together until the onions are tender—about 10 minutes. Remove from heat. Add the flour, seasoned salt, seasoned pepper, and garlic. Blend thoroughly. Slowly add the milk, return to heat, and stir until thickened. Add the spinach and mix thoroughly.

BUTTERNUT SQUASH WITH PARMESAN

Publick House
Sturbridge, Massachusetts

3 butternut squash
Salt and pepper, to taste

3 tablespoons butter
Parmesan cheese, grated

Butternut squash has sweet orange flesh. Cut the squash in half, lengthwise, and scoop out the seeds and the stringy part. Leave the rind on. Parboil for 15 minutes in boiling salted water. Remove and drain thoroughly. Season well with salt and pepper, dot with small bits of butter, and sprinkle generously with grated Parmesan cheese.

Bake for 20 to 30 minutes or till done in a moderate oven (375°).

CALABACITAS CON CREMA

Cafe La Margarita
Chicago, Illinois

1 pound young, tender, summer squash, sliced
4 bell peppers, sliced
1 small onion, finely chopped
1 pint fresh cream

3 tablespoons butter
Salt and pepper to taste
4 tablespoons Parmesan cheese, grated (optional)

Slice the summer squash and peppers as thin as possible and finely chop the onion. Melt the butter in a porcelain pot, pour in the vegetables and cook until tender, without a drop of water. Add the cream, stir, and serve. As a tempting extra, it is interesting to add grated Parmesan cheese.

OCEAN HEARTH TOMATO

Ocean Hearth Restaurant
Boca Raton Sun and Surf Beach Club
Boca Raton, Florida

1 cup instant rice
1 cup white sauce
  (including whole egg)
6 hollowed out tomato
  halves
½ teaspoon sweet basil
1 bay leaf

Salt and pepper to taste
Oregano to taste
¾ cup mayonnaise
3 tablespoons bread crumbs
3 tablespoons Parmesan
  cheese

Cook instant rice, and add to it 1 cup of medium white sauce prepared with the whole egg. While blending, add sweet basil, bay leaf, salt and pepper to taste, and two pinches of oregano. Put mixture in a hollowed out half tomato, and cover with mayonnaise. Mix bread crumbs and Parmesan cheese together and sprinkle over stuffed tomatoes. Put under broiler and brown.

TURNIP CASSEROLE

Bacon Farm Inn
Barnstable Village, Massachusetts

2½ pounds turnips
3 tablespoons brown sugar
1 teaspoon salt
¼ teaspoon allspice
¼ teaspoon white pepper

3 tablespoons butter
½ cup cream
1 egg, well beaten
Bread crumbs

Cook, peel and mash turnips. Add all ingredients together and put into buttered baking dish. Sprinkle with bread crumbs. Bake in slow oven 1 to 1½ hours.

VEGETABLE SOUFFLÉ

The Coquina Club
Ormond Beach, Florida

½ cup green beans,
  finely chopped
½ cup carrots,
  finely chopped
¼ cup almonds,
  finely chopped
¼ cup celery,
  finely chopped

¼ cup spinach,
  finely chopped
¼ cup green onions,
  finely chopped
1½ cups cream sauce
3 eggs, separated
Salt, pepper to taste

Prepare cream sauce. Stir in vegetables, add egg yolks, stirring constantly. Season with salt and pepper. Cool mixture and fold in well beaten egg whites. Bake the soufflé in a greased baking dish in 350° oven for about 40 minutes.

ZUCCHINI CASSEROLE AT BARROWS HOUSE

Barrows House
Dorset, Vermont

2 pounds fresh, firm
  Zucchini, peeled and
  sliced in ¾-inch squares
1 small onion, chopped
1 small green pepper,
  chopped

½ cup sugar
Salted water
12 Ritz crackers, crumbled
Heavy cream

Put sliced zucchini in salted water to cover and boil a few minutes until about half done. Drain very thoroughly and put in small flat roasting pan. Add onion, pepper and sugar and mix together. Then add about half an inch of very heavy cream (half an inch on the bottom of the pan). Mash about 12 Ritz crackers into crumbs and sprinkle over top of casserole. Bake in 350° oven (preheated) for 45 to 60 minutes. It is important that the Zucchini be thoroughly drained and very heavy cream is absolutely necessary.

SALADS AND SALAD DRESSINGS

STUFFED ARTICHOKE SALAD

Mark Thomas Inn
Monterey, California

6 medium artichokes
¾ cup vinegar
4 tablespoons olive oil
Salt
1 pound fresh crab meat

1 cup Thousand Island
   dressing
Juice of 1 lemon
12 white asparagus tips
Garnish: parsley, sliced
   eggs, pickled red beets

Cook artichokes in salted water with vinegar and oil until tender. Pull out the fuzzy portion from the heart of the artichoke. Sprinkle artichoke bottom with lemon juice. Stuff with crab meat. Place the artichoke on a plate with a lettuce leaf and shredded lettuce and garnish with lemon, asparagus, parsley, sliced eggs and pickled beets. Serve Thousand Island dressing on side.

VAN'S FAMOUS BEAN SALAD

Van's Cafe
Brainerd, Minnesota

1 cup cut canned green
   beans
1 cup dark brown
   kidney beans
1 cup cut wax beans
1 clove garlic

½ cup onion, chopped fine
½ cup celery, chopped
   fine
½ cup French dressing
½ cup mayonnaise
1 head lettuce

Drain juices off and chill beans thoroughly. Rub mixing bowl with garlic. Add onion and celery, to the mixed beans in bowl. Mix with equal parts of French dressing and mayonnaise. Serve on chilled lettuce leaves.

CAESAR SALAD

The Clipper Room
Yankee Clipper Hotel
Fort Lauderdale, Florida

Salt
1 clove fresh garlic
4 tablespoons salad oil
4 tablespoons anchovies, finely chopped
2 tablespoons wine vinegar
Juice of ½ lemon
2 dashes Worcestershire Sauce
½ teaspoon English mustard
1 egg, coddled 1½ minutes
2 heads Romaine lettuce
Freshly ground black pepper, to taste
2½ tablespoons Parmesan cheese, grated
3 tablespoons garlic-croutons

Sprinkle wooden salad bowl with salt, then mash clove of garlic in bowl and remove all garlic from bowl. Pour salad oil in bowl; add finely chopped anchovies and mash anchovies into oil. Add vinegar, lemon juice, Worcestershire Sauce, mustard and coddled egg. Mix all together well.

Use two heads of romaine lettuce. Remove all outside leaves, wash well and chop into 2 inch pieces. Dry with towel and put in refrigerator to crisp and cool.

Add chopped romaine to the dressing, mix well and then add fresh ground pepper to taste, Parmesan cheese and garlic croutons. Blend salad very carefully and serve at once.

CAESAR SALAD

Gaucho Steak House
Americana Hotel
Bal Harbour, Florida

4 tablespoons olive oil
1 clove garlic, minced
1 teaspoon salt
½ teaspoon freshly ground black pepper
12 anchovies (1 12-ounce can) drained
Juice of 2 lemons
2 tablespoons red-wine vinegar
2 bunches romaine lettuce
1 cup garlic flavored croutons (½ inch cubes)
2 tablespoons Parmesan cheese, grated
2 coddled eggs*

To olive oil, add garlic, salt and pepper. Let stand at room temperature several hours. Put anchovies into wooden salad bowl and crush into a paste. Add the oil, lemon juice, and vinegar. Beat mixture with fork until thoroughly blended. Cut romaine into strips ½ inch wide; place in salad bowl. Mix with 2 forks until each piece of romaine is lightly coated. Add croutons and sprinkle with cheese. Add eggs and toss. Serve on chilled plates.

*Pour boiling water over eggs. Cover; let stand 2 minutes.

Chef's hints: "Don't be afraid to add salt, even though recipe has anchovies . . . Add eggs the very last moment so the cheese will cling to the lettuce and look attractive . . ."

CUCUMBER SALAD

Yamato Sukiyaki Restaurant
San Francisco, California

3 medium cucumbers, peeled, thinly sliced
½ cup cider vinegar
4 tablespoons sugar
1 teaspoon salt
1 teaspoon Ac'cent

Salt cucumbers. Cover and refrigerate several hours. Squeeze out excess liquid. Mix together remaining ingredients. Pour a little over cucumbers; squeeze out excess liquid. When ready to serve, add the remainder of the dressing to the cucumbers.

PEPPER CABBAGE

Haag's Hotel
Shartlesville, Penna.

1 medium head cabbage, finely shredded
1 carrot, shredded
1 medium green pepper, cut fine
1 medium red pepper, cut fine

3 stalks celery, chopped
½ cup cider vinegar
½ cup water
½ teaspoon salt
½ cup sugar

To cabbage add carrot, peppers and celery. Mix the vinegar, water, salt and sugar. This should be sweet-sour. Pour mix over the cabbage-carrot-pepper-celery mixture. Place in refrigerator to blend and cool. Serve cold.

CABBAGE SALAD

The Lark Restaurant
Tiffin, Iowa

Salad

1 small white cabbage, finely shredded
1 small red cabbage, finely shredded

3 carrots, chopped fine
½ cup celery, diced

Dressing

1 cup heavy cream, whipped stiff
¾ cup sugar
⅛ cup vinegar

¼ teaspoon salt
1 cup mayonnaise
1¼ teaspoons celery seed
Juice from 1½ lemons

Garnish

Tomato wedges   Ripe olives
Lettuce

Place shredded and chopped vegetables in a mixing bowl.
Whip cream until stiff. Add remaining dressing ingredients slowly, and blend well. Pour over shredded cabbage
and vegetable mixture.

Arrange tomato wedges on lettuce leaves. Form ball of
cabbage on top. Garnish with ripe olives.

COLE SLAW

Shoyer's Restaurant
Philadelphia, Pennsylvania

1 head cabbage, finely   1½ cups salad oil
  shredded   ½ cup white vinegar
White pepper, to taste   4 tablespoons sugar
Salt, to taste

Cut out and discard center core of cabbage. Shred cabbage and wash in cold water. Drain well. Place cabbage in
mixing bowl and add all the ingredients. Mix ingredients
thoroughly through the cabbage. This blending will cause
liquids to rise out of and cover cabbage. Allow cole slaw
to remain in refrigerator over night to soak and blend
completely.

SWEET 'N' SOUR COLE SLAW

Testa's Restaurant
Palm Beach, Florida

1 medium head cabbage,   ¼ teaspoon salt
  finely shredded   1 tablespoon olive oil
2 large carrots, finely   3 tablespoons vinegar
  shredded   3 tablespoons sugar

The object of the dressing is to create a sweet and sour taste so you want a lot of sugar and a lot of vinegar, just a little salt (to break the flatness) and just a little oil. Mix dressing and grated vegetables well and place in refrigerator at least an hour before serving. Mix well again just before serving.

OLD FASHIONED SWEET AND SOUR COLE SLAW

Brookville Hotel
Brookville, Kansas

1½ pounds green cabbage, shredded
1 teaspoon salt

⅔ cup sugar
1 cup heavy cream
⅓ cup vinegar

Place shredded cabbage in covered dish in refrigerator for several hours. Mix ingredients in order given 30 minutes before serving. Chill and serve.

GUACAMOLE

Arizona Inn
Tucson, Arizona

4 ripe avocados, peeled and mashed
2 tablespoons chopped onions
1 cup mayonnaise

1 cup sour cream
1 tablespoon lemon juice
1 teaspoon salt
1 teaspoon white pepper
Few drops of Tabasco sauce

Mix all ingredients together and serve with crackers or toast. Makes 1 quart.

HOT GERMAN POTATO SALAD

Mac's Restaurant
Jamestown, North Dakota

4 pounds potatoes
3 medium onions,
   coarsely chopped
¾ cup sugar
Salt and pepper to taste

½ pound bacon, diced
¾ cup very hot water
¾ cup cider vinegar
Hard boiled eggs and
   greens for garnish

Boil potatoes until tender; pare and slice while still warm. Heap chopped onion in center of potatoes. Top with sugar, salt and pepper. Fry diced bacon until crisp. Skim bacon from frying pan and set aside. Add water and vinegar to bacon grease and bring to a boil. Pour over potatoes and onions and toss lightly to mix well. Add bacon and garnish with hard boiled eggs and greens. Serves 8.

BON TON SALAD

Farm Fare
Lucerne, Colorado

6 romaine lettuce leaves
18 large white asparagus
   tips

6 slices vertically sliced
   tomato

Arrange on a small plate Romaine lettuce leaf. Place a slice of tomato on it and over the tomato the asparagus tips. Serve with any dressing.

SALAD MAX

*Imperial House
Chicago, Illinois*

Salad

8 heads of limestone
2 large tomatoes cut into
6 equal sections
3 ounces hearts of palm,
sliced

2 hard cooked eggs,
sliced
1 avocado, sliced
6 carciofini (baby Italian
or California artichokes)

Clear French Dressing

Generous ¼ cup wine
vinegar
Generous ½ cup olive oil
1 tablespoon prepared
mustard

Few drops Worcestershire
sauce
Salt and pepper to taste
8 filets of anchovies,
puréed

Croutons

3 slices white bread, toasted
2 tablespoons butter

1 clove garlic

Cut toasted bread into ½ inch squares. Sauté in butter
with garlic. Remove garlic.

Mix salad greens with tomatoes, hearts of palm, eggs,
avocado, and cold cooked artichokes. Pour French dressing
over all and sprinkle with croutons.

CANLIS' SPECIAL SALAD

*Canlis' Charcoal Broiler Restaurant
Seattle, Washington*

Salad

2 heads romaine, sliced
2 peeled tomatoes, peeled
and cut in eighths

2 tablespoons olive oil
Salt, to taste
Large clove garlic

Condiments

¼ cup green onion,
  chopped
½ cup Romano cheese,
  freshly grated

1 pound rendered bacon,
  finely chopped
1 cup croutons

Dressing

⅜ cup olive oil
Juice of 2 lemons
½ teaspoon fresh ground
  pepper

¼ teaspoon fresh mint,
  chopped
¼ teaspoon oregano
1 egg, coddled 1½
  minutes

Salad

Into a large bowl (wooden) pour approximately 2 table-spoons olive oil, sprinkle with salt, and rub firmly with large clove of garlic. (The oil will act as a lubricant and the salt as an abrasive.) Remove garlic and in the bottom of the bowl first place the tomatoes cut in eighths, add romaine, sliced in 1-inch strips. You may add other salad vegetables if you choose, but remember to put the heavy vegetables in first with romaine on top. Add condiments.

Dressing

Into a bowl pour the olive oil, lemon juice and seasonings. Add coddled egg and whip vigorously.

When ready to serve, pour dressing over salad. Add croutons last. Toss generously.

PARRY LODGE SALAD

*Parry Lodge
Kanab, Utah*

1 head cauliflower,
  broken into flowerettes
1 cup black olives,
  drained and chopped
1 cup tiny green onions,
  finely chopped
1½ cups mayonnaise

Salt, to taste
1 green pepper, sliced
  into rings
6 pimento slices
2 tomatoes, cut into
  wedges

Grate raw cauliflower buds. Add black olives and tiny green onions. Mix all together with mayonnaise and salt to taste. Serve with pepper ring, pimento slice and tomato wedge. This is a very rich salad and can be served in small amounts. It has a rather nutty flavor and excites a good deal of curiosity as to the ingredients. Chill before serving.

LOUIS PAPPAS' FAMOUS GREEK SALAD

*Louis Pappas' Riverside Restaurant
Tarpon Springs, Florida*

1 large head lettuce
3 cups potato salad
12 sprigs watercress
2 tomatoes cut into
  6 wedges
1 cucumber, peeled and
  cut lengthwise into
  8 fingers
1 avocado, peeled and
  sliced
6 portions Feta cheese
  (a Greek cheese)
1 green pepper, cut
  into rings

6 slices of cooked beet
6 shrimp, cooked and
  peeled
6 anchovy filets
12 black olives
6 radishes
12 medium hot Salonika
  peppers
½ cup white vinegar
¼ cup each olive and
  salad oil, blended
Orégano

Line large platter with the outside lettuce leaves, and place potato salad in a mound in center of platter. Cover with remaining shredded lettuce. Arrange watercress on top. Place tomato wedges around edge of salad, place cucumber wedges in between tomatoes, making a solid base of the salad. Place avocado slices around outside. Slices of Feta cheese should be arranged on top of salad, with green pepper slices over all. On very top, place sliced beets with a shrimp on each beet slice and anchovy filet on the shrimp. Arrange as desired: olives, radishes, peppers and green onions. Sprinkle entire salad with vinegar and blended oil. Sprinkle orégano over all.

INDIAN HOT CHUTNEY SALAD

*The Hotel Pierre
New York City*

13 ounces mixed greens—
  1 head romaine or
  lettuce, endive,
  watercress
2 large onions, finely
  chopped
2 green peppers, chopped
2 tablespoons parsley,
  chopped

2 cloves garlic, crushed
6 radishes, sliced
Salt and pepper to taste
1 cup oil and vinegar
  dressing
1 teaspoon chile pepper,
  crushed

Mix together and serve.

VEGETABLE BUJJIA (SALAD)

The Hotel Pierre
New York City

1 onion, chopped
2 cloves garlic
1 cup oil
1 cauliflower
½ pound lima beans
½ pound cut string beans
2 carrots, sliced
3 large potatoes, diced
2 tablespoons curry
  powder
½ tablespoon ground
  cumin
½ tablespoon tumeric
2 tablespoons tomato
  purée
Water to cover
1 tablespoon paprika
1 teaspoon salt

Smother onion and garlic in oil for five minutes. Add vegetables and potatoes. Simmer for five more minutes. Sprinkle curry, cumin, tumeric, paprika and salt over all. Add tomato purée and cover with water. Cook for 35 minutes, until vegetables are barely tender. Remove the vegetables, strain the sauce and cook over low flame until reduced to half the quantity. Pour sauce over vegetables. Chill before serving.

ROMAINE SALAD

La Avenida Restaurant
Coronado, California

3 to 4 heads romaine,
  chilled crisp
1½ cups crisp croutons
4 tablespoons garlic oil
Salt to taste
Black pepper
1 tablespoon
  Worcestershire sauce
6 heaping tablespoons
  Romano cheese, freshly
  ground
1 egg, coddled 1½ minutes
6 tablespoons lemon juice
12 cloves garlic
1 quart olive oil

Use only pale green heads of romaine. Remove outer leaves. Wash thoroughly, shake out and place in refrigerator until crisp. Cut or tear in size preferred and place in salad bowl.

Add croutons. Combine garlic oil, lemon juice, Worcestershire sauce, egg, salt and pepper and stir vigorously. Pour over salad and toss. Sprinkle with cheese. Romano cheese is readily available. Italian Parmigiano cheese is better, if obtainable.

Garlic Oil

Chop garlic cloves and put into quart bottle filled with oil. Keep at kitchen temperature. Oil absorbs the flavor of garlic. Pass through cheesecloth before using.

RAW MUSHROOM SALAD JULIENNE WITH PICADILLY DRESSING

The John Bartram Hotel
Philadelphia, Pennsylvania

Salad

12 large fresh white mushrooms, thinly sliced	2 hearts of celery, cut julienne
	1 head lettuce
	½ teaspoon salt

Remove all the leaves from the celery heart. Wash celery in cool water with salt, drain well, add mushrooms and serve on a bed of lettuce.

Dressing

2 hard cooked eggs	½ teaspoon parsley flakes
½ cup olive oil	2 cloves garlic, chopped fine
¼ cup white vinegar	½ teaspoon sugar
1 whole red pimento, finely minced	Salt, pepper, to taste
1 teaspoon ground horseradish	

Separate the white and yolks of the hard-cooked eggs. Pass through a tea strainer. Mix the oil and vinegar together and add the rest of the ingredients. Sprinkle the salad with the white and yolks of the eggs.

ORLEANS ROOM SPECIAL SALAD

Hotel Blackstone
Omaha, Nebraska

1 large tin anchovy filets, cut in pieces
1 tablespoon Worcestershire sauce
Lawry's salt
1 teaspoon mustard
4 tablespoons olive oil
2 tablespoons wine vinegar

Mixed greens—lettuce, watercress, spinach, beet tops, Belgian endive, romaine, may be used
Whole peppers
3 tablespoons Roquefort cheese, crumbled

Marinate for 1 hour anchovy filets in Worcestershire sauce, with a dash of Lawry's salt, mustard, olive oil and vinegar added. Blend well and pour over mixed greens in bowl. Add a few whole peppers for flavor. Sprinkle Roquefort cheese on top.

ASHEVILLE SALAD

King's Inn
Highlands, North Carolina

1 cup condensed tomato soup
½ pound cream cheese, whipped
2 tablespoons gelatin
½ cup cold water

1 cup mayonnaise
1½ cups celery, chopped
1 green pepper, chopped
1 small onion, chopped
¼ teaspoon salt
Olives, nuts (optional)

Bring soup to boiling point, add cheese, stirring until smooth. Dissolve gelatin in cold water and add to soup mixture. When mixture is perfectly cold, add mayonnaise, vegetables, and salt. Chopped olives and nuts may be added if desired. Pour in individual wet molds, and set in refrigerator to jell. Unmold on shredded lettuce.

CRAFTWOOD SALAD

Craftwood Inn
Manitou Springs, Colorado

1 package lemon Jello
½ cup marshmallows, diced
¾ small can crushed
  pineapple (drained)
½ cup longhorn or mild
  cheddar cheese, grated

½ pint heavy cream,
  whipped
½ cup Tokay grapes
  (optional)
1 head lettuce

Dissolve Jello according to directions on package. Let set until slightly thick, then whip. Add remaining ingredients. Pour into wet mold, chill until firm. For fancier salad add ½ cup Tokay grapes. Unmold on lettuce leaves.

MOLDED CIDER SALAD

Hotel Racine
Racine, Wisconsin

½ cup seedless raisins
1 envelope plain gelatin
2 tablespoons lemon juice
1¾ cups apple cider
Dash salt

1 large red apple, cored
  and diced
¼ cup celery, diced
Salad greens
Mayonnaise
Commercial sour cream

Rinse the raisins, cover with water and boil 5 minutes. Drain and cool. Soften gelatin in lemon juice. Heat cider to boiling, and dissolve gelatin in it. Blend in salt. Cool until slightly thickened. Fold raisins, apples and celery into gelatin. Spoon into individual molds and chill until firm. Unmold on crisp salad greens. Serve with dressing made by blending equal parts of mayonnaise and commercial sour cream.

JADE MOLD SALAD

Carriage House Restaurant
Norfolk, Virginia

1 package lime gelatin
2 cups boiling water
1 cup cucumber, grated
¼ cup onion, grated
1 cup cottage cheese

1 cup mayonnaise
1 cup heavy cream,
  whipped
1 head lettuce, shredded

Dissolve gelatin in boiling water and cool it until it begins to set. Fold remaining ingredients into gelatin and pour into ring mold. Chill in refrigerator until set. Unmold and serve on lettuce.

STRAWBERRY JELLO SALAD

Bar X Bar Ranch
Crawford, Colorado

1 package strawberry
  Jello
1½ cups boiling water
1½ cups heavy cream,
  whipped

1 cup crushed pineapple
1 cup nuts, pecans or
  walnuts, chopped
1 head lettuce

Mix Jello and boiling water together and let set, then whip until foamy in electric mixer. Add whipped cream, fruit and nuts. Pour into molds or shallow dish. Let set in refrigerator about 3 hours. Serve on bed of lettuce.

ZIPPY MOLDED PINEAPPLE SALAD

Hickory Stick Farm
Laconia, New Hampshire

1 small package lemon
    jello (3 oz.)
1 small package lime
    jello (3 oz.)
2 cups boiling water
1 #2 can crushed
    pineapple
1 can evaporated milk

1 small package cottage
    cheese (1 pound)
¾ cup mayonnaise
2 tablespoons horseradish
Few crushed walnuts
Watercress or 1 head
    lettuce, shredded

Dissolve jello in the boiling water, stirring until dissolved. Add rest of the ingredients. Mix well, pour into molds, and place in refrigrator. Chill until firm. Unmold and garnish to taste with watercress or shredded lettuce.

ORANGE AND ONION SALAD

Saddleback Inn
Santa Ana, California

3 sweet oranges, peeled and thinly sliced
3 yellow onions, peeled and thinly sliced
French dressing

Peel and slice sweet oranges. Peel yellow onions, slice into paper thin slices and wash them in cold water. Drain the onions.

Combine a layer orange slices and a thin layer onion. Pour a thin thread French dressing over the oranges and onions. Excellent served with chicken.

TROPICAL FRUIT SALAD

Hotel Valley Ho
Scottsdale, Arizona

3 pineapples, cut in half
  lengthwise
1 pineapple, cut into
  slices
Peaches, cut bite size
Pears, diced
Apricots, halved

Figs
Prunes, halved and pitted
Apples
Tangerines, cut into
  sections
Cherries
Rainbow sherbet

Cut 3 pineapples in half. Remove the flesh. In each pineapple half place an assortment of peaches, pears, apricots, figs, prunes. Slice red Delicious apples thin and set in pears for wing and tail feathers. Surround with pineapple rings decorated with tangerine section and cherries and fill the center with a scoop of rainbow sherbet. In order to make it resemble a Bird of Paradise, cut the center of one pineapple half with a cutter in the shape of a bird's head.

CALIFORNIA FRESH FRUIT PLATE

Pine Cone/Branding Iron Restaurant
San Jose, California

For each two servings, use any or all fruits

2 scoops of sherbet, ice
  cream or cottage cheese
2 slices fresh pineapple
5 strawberries
8 boysenberries
4 slices orange
6 cherries
6 wedges apple
4 wedges cantaloupe
Boston lettuce or fig
  leaves garnish

½ nectarine, sliced
2 wedges watermelon
½ pear, sliced
½ peach, sliced
1 small bunch grapes
½ banana
¼ cup crème de menthe
  marshmallow dressing
2 slices orange nut bread

On a large round plate, place lettuce or fig leaf garnish. In the center of the plate, put the scoop of sherbet, ice cream or cottage cheese. Arrange fruit as you desire. Top with crème de menthe marshmallow dressing and serve with nut bread slices.

Marshmallow Dressing

1 cup large marshmallows, cut in pieces	¼ cup water
½ cup sugar	1 egg white, beaten stiff
	Crème de menthe, to taste

Boil sugar and water for 5 minutes. Add marshmallows. Stir well and pour slowly over egg white. Beat until well blended. Chill and add crème de menthe.

FROZEN FRUIT SALAD

The Hearthstone Restaurant
Fort Mitchell, Kentucky

1 cup flour	1 small can crushed pineapple
½ cup sugar	Juice of two lemons
½ cup butter	½ cup chopped pecans (optional)
1 #2 can pineapple juice (mixed fruit juice may be used)	1 cup heavy cream, whipped
1 #2 can fruit cocktail	

Blend flour, sugar, butter and juice until smooth, and cook in double boiler until thick. Cool. Add fruit cocktail, crushed pineapple, lemon juice and chopped nuts. Blend well and fold in whipped cream, gently. Pour into freezing trays. Freeze. Cut into squares and serve with cream dressing.

Cream Dressing

½ cup heavy cream, whipped
1½ cups mayonnaise

Beat cream until stiff. Slowly stir in mayonnaise.

COTTAGE CHEESE MOLDED SALAD

The Glockenspiel
Fleetwood, Pennsylvania

1 package lemon gelatin
2 cups hot water
1 cup cold water
¼ cup lemon juice

Rind of 2 lemons, grated
4 cups sieved cottage
cheese

Dissolve gelatin in hot water, then add cold water, lemon juice and grated lemon rind. Chill until partially set then add cottage cheese. Chill until firm in small wet molds or one large wet mold. Unmold and serve with a lemon whipped cream dressing. Garnish with fresh strawberries or blueberries.

Lemon Whipped Cream Dressing

1 cup heavy cream, whipped
¼ teaspoon salt
4 tablespoons lemon juice

Beat cream until stiff. Slowly beat in salt and lemon juice.

ZIPPY CHEESE SALAD

Colonial Room
Peabody Hotel
Memphis, Tennessee

1 can tomato soup
2 3-ounce packages
Philadelphia cream cheese
1 tablespoon Knox gelatin
½ cup water
1 cup celery, finely
chopped
½ cup bell pepper,
finely chopped

⅓ cup pecans, chopped
1 cup mayonnaise
1 small onion (juice only)
1 teaspoon
Worcestershire Sauce
1 dash Tabasco
1 head lettuce

Dissolve Philadelphia cream cheese in hot tomato soup. Cool.

Dissolve gelatin in water. Blend together the cream cheese and gelatin. Add remaining ingredients. Pour into wet molds. Chill and unmold on lettuce.

SALADE YAM YAM

Restaurant Laurent
New York City

3 heads Boston lettuce,
   shredded
1½ cups tongue,
   cut Julienne
1½ cups ham, cut Julienne
1½ cups celery roots,
   cut Julienne

12 artichoke hearts,
   split in half
1½ cups boiled chicken,
   cut in small pieces
Capers
Chives, finely chopped

Mix first six ingredients, sprinkle with capers and chives. Mix thoroughly with Louis Dressing.

Louis Dressing

1½ cups mayonnaise
¾ cup tarragon
   French dressing
½ cup chili sauce

4 tablespoons olives,
   chopped
2 teaspoons
   Worcestershire sauce
Salt and pepper to taste

CHICKEN SALAD ALA JACQUES

Jacques French Restaurant
Chicago, Illinois

5 large chicken breasts,
   cooked and chilled
1 cup mayonnaise
½ cup heavy cream,
   whipped
2 cups celery, diced
1 teaspoon salt
Dash pepper
Crisp lettuce cups
4 teaspoons capers, drained

1 10-ounce package frozen,
   cooked (or 1 one-pound
   can) French style green
   beans, drained and chilled
½ cup Italian dressing
12 tomato slices
12 ripe olives
3 hard cooked eggs,
   quartered

Cut 6 thin slices from chicken; set aside. Cube remaining chicken. Fold ½ cup mayonnaise into whipped cream. Fold in diced chicken, celery, salt, and pepper; chill. To serve, spoon salad into crisp lettuce cups. Top with reserved chicken slices and a dollop of mayonnaise; sprinkle with capers. Toss green beans with Italian dressing; arrange on platter with salad. Garnish with tomato slices, ripe olives, and hard-cooked eggs.

STRONGBOW TURKEY SALAD

Strongbow Turkey Inn
Valparaiso, Indiana

1½ pounds breast of
   turkey meat
2 celery hearts, chopped
   medium fine
½ cup French dressing
1 head lettuce
3 hard cooked eggs

3 tomatoes, peeled and
   cut in wedges
Parsley
2 tablespoons mayonnaise
Almonds, toasted and
   slivered

Cut breast of turkey into half-inch cubes. Mix with celery. Marinate in French dressing for at least one hour before serving.

Place large lettuce cup on salad plate. Pack ¾ cup for each serving with turkey salad and turn out on lettuce. Decorate with ½ egg quartered and four wedges tomato. Garnish with parsley. Top each serving with 1 teaspoon mayonnaise and sprinkle with almonds.

HERRING OR COMBINATION SALAD

Ola Restaurant
Boston, Massachusetts

6 large herring fillets
3 large apples, peeled and cored
2 large dill pickles
2 thick slices cold, cooked meat
5 cold boiled potatoes
1 onion, peeled

Brine from herring
1 cup pickled beets, chopped
3 hard cooked eggs, finely chopped
2 dill pickles, sliced
8 pickled beets, sliced

Put through coarse grinder herring fillets, apples, dill pickles, meat (meat loaf or any kind of cold, cooked meat on hand except ham), boiled potatoes and onion. Add brine from your pickled herring and mix thoroughly. Shape like a big round cake on a round platter. Garnish with pickled beets and hard-cooked eggs, alternating eggs and beets in pie-shaped segments. Edge platter with round slices of dill pickles and sliced pickled beets.

Sauce for Herring Salad

1 cup mayonnaise
½ cup heavy cream, whipped
2 teaspoons Worcestershire sauce

2 tablespoons juice from pickled beets
Pinch salt and pepper

To mayonnaise add whipped cream and other ingredients. Stir carefully so as not to make sauce too thin. This sauce may also be used for vegetable salad of any kind.

SHRIMP BOAT SALAD

Hotel Astor
New York City

2 heads romaine,
    quartered lengthwise
36 cooked jumbo shrimp
6 slices pineapple,
    cut in half
1½ cups mayonnaise

6 stuffed olives, sliced
3 tomatoes, cut in
    quarters
3 deviled eggs, cut in
    quarters
½ bunch watercress

Cut romaine in quarters lengthwise. Place one quarter on each dinner plate, wedge side up.

Line up shrimp across wedge of romaine. Place ½ slice pineapple at each end of wedge. Place ¼ cup mayonnaise across top of shrimp. Garnish with sliced olives.

On each side of shrimp boat place a wedge of tomato and two quarters deviled egg. Garnish plate with crisp watercress.

CREOLE PRAWN SALAD, NEW ORLEANS

Carson City Nugget
Carson City, Nevada

Salad

2½ cups boiled rice,
    cold and dry
1½ pounds cooked cleaned
    prawns (large shrimp)
    cut into 4 pieces
1 cup raw cauliflower,
    cut in pieces a little
    larger than rice
½ cup green peppers,
    chopped

1 cup stuffed olives,
    chopped
1 teaspoon white pepper
1 tablespoon salt
1 cup garlic dill pickles,
    chopped
Juice of ½ lemon
1 teaspoon Tabasco sauce
1 cup mayonnaise

Garnish

Lettuce leaves
Tomatoes
  3 hard cooked eggs,
    sliced
Parsley
Lemon wedges

Cook rice and cool. Then combine all ingredients and toss lightly. Chill well and serve on lettuce. Garnish with tomato, sliced eggs, parsley and lemon wedges.

LONDON GRILL CRAB SALAD

London Grill
Portland, Oregon

6 cups crab meat and
  legs (Dungeness)
6 tablespoons celery,
  diced
6 teaspoons horseradish
6 tablespoons mayonnaise
3 teaspoons lemon juice

Salt and pepper to taste
  6 abalone shells
  1 head lettuce
  6 stuffed eggs
 12 cherry tomatoes
 12 black olives
  6 radish roses
Crab legs

Mix crab meat, celery, horseradish, mayonnaise, lemon juice and seasonings and put in half sphere shape in abalone shells lined with lettuce leaves.

Garnish each shell with eggs, cherry tomatoes, small black olives, radish rose, parsley, crab legs.

PENNSYLVANIA DUTCH BACON DRESSING

Walps Restaurant
Allentown, Pennsylvania

1 whole egg
1 cup sugar
1 teaspoon salt
1½ cups sour cream
¼ cup cider vinegar
1 cup milk

¼ pound bacon,
  fried and chopped,
  plus bacon drippings
½ cup flour
¼ cup cold milk

Combine egg, sugar, salt, sour cream, vinegar, 1 cup of milk, and bacon and drippings. Bring to boil, stirring constantly. Combine flour and ¼ cup milk, add to first mixture and bring again to boil, stirring constantly. Cook for 15 minutes over low flame. Serve dressing warm.

This dressing is excellent over chopped lettuce, endive, dandelion, or spinach, or combination of all.

PANDL'S BACON DRESSING

Pandl's Whitefish Bay Inn
Milwaukee, Wisconsin

¼ pound bacon
  (6 or 7 strips)
3 cups water
1½ cups sugar
¾ cup vinegar
¼ teaspoon salt

1 teaspoon chicken
  soup base (optional)
½ teaspoon white pepper
½ cup onion, chopped
½ cup flour

Chop bacon and fry until brown and crisp.

Combine water, sugar, vinegar, salt, soup base and pepper. Heat to boiling. Skim out bacon into water mixture. Fry onions in remaining bacon fat until soft but not brown. Add flour, let it bubble up 2-3 minutes. Add this roux to hot water mixture. Stir until smooth. Simmer 5 minutes.

Serve hot over lettuce, green or wax beans. Or use as sauce in German Potato Salad.

DEDEK'S SPECIAL BLUE CHEESE DRESSING

Dedek's Thunderbird Restaurant
North Wildwood, New Jersey

4 tablespoons imported
blue cheese
2 cups sour cream
⅓ cup buttermilk
¼ cup milk
3 tablespoons distilled
white vinegar

Dash Worcestershire
sauce
½ teaspoon coarse
ground black pepper
¼ teaspoon garlic salt
¼ teaspoon salt

Combine blue cheese and mix all ingredients well. Store in refrigerator. Sauce improves after one or two days.

BLACKHAWK BLUE CHEESE-CREAM CHEESE DRESSING

Blackhawk Restaurant
Chicago, Illinois

¼ pound cream cheese
2½ ounces blue cheese
½ cup water

Blend cream cheese and blue cheese with water and mix until smooth and creamy. This dressing should be stored in the refrigerator but served at room temperature.

PRINCESS COLE SLAW DRESSING

Sid's Restaurant
Algonac, Michigan

2 cups white vinegar
1½ cups light corn oil
1 cup super fine sugar
2 teaspoons salt
(approximately)

1 teaspoon white pepper
1 teaspoon garlic powder
1 teaspoon onion powder

Blend vinegar and oil together. Add sugar, mixing until sugar is dissolved. Add all remaining ingredients, blend well. Store in container in refrigerator. Shake well before using.

CUCUMBER DRESSING

Colonial Room
Peabody Hotel
Memphis, Tennessee

1 large cucumber, peeled,
   seeded and grated
1 medium onion, grated
1½ cups mayonnaise

½ cup tarragon vinegar
½ teaspoon salt
1 teaspoon sugar
½ teaspoon dry mustard

After blending all ingredients, tint lightly with green. This is most popular over wedged lettuce.

FOX HILL DRESSING

Fox Hill Restaurant
Ridgefield, Connecticut

2 egg yolks
1 tablespoon English
   mustard
1 tablespoon Spanish
   paprika
1 teaspoon
   Worcestershire Sauce

1 tablespoon lemon juice
¾ teaspoon salt
¼ teaspoon black pepper
½ cup wine vinegar
1½ cups oil

Mix egg yolks. With wire whisk blend in all ingredients except the oil. Slowly pour in oil, stirring constantly. If dressing thickens too quickly, add a little water, then stir in the remaining oil.

FRENCH DRESSING

Strongbow Turkey Inn
Valparaiso, Indiana

1 clove garlic
1 teaspoon salt
¾ teaspoon freshly
  ground white pepper

½ cup pure vinegar
1½ cups olive oil

Place small clove garlic, slightly crushed, into bottle in which French Dressing is to be made. Add salt, pepper and vinegar. Let stand or shake until salt dissolves. Add olive oil. Close bottle and refrigerate. Shake well before using.

FRENCH HERB SALAD DRESSING

Old Adobe Patio Restaurant
Tucson, Arizona

1¼ cup olive oil
1 cup wine vinegar
½ cup apple cider
  vinegar
2 teaspoons
  Worcestershire sauce

1 teaspoon lemon juice
2 teaspoons salt
2 teaspoons sugar
Dash of black pepper
½ teaspoon paprika

Herbs (see below)
    Season with garlic powder or crushed clove of garlic, rosemary, and sweet basil.
    Mix all ingredients in bottle, filling bottle only ¾ full. Shake well and chill. When ready to use, shake again.

SOUR CREAM DRESSING

Wisconsinaire
Hazelhurst, Wisconsin

1 cup commercial
    sour cream
1 tablespoon onion,
    chopped
4 tablespoons cider
    vinegar
¼ teaspoon salt

¼ teaspoon black pepper
1 teaspoon sugar
½ cup mayonnaise or
    salad dressing
4 ounces cream cheese,
    whipped

Mix all ingredients together until thoroughly blended. Chill before serving.

VINAIGRETTE SALAD DRESSING

Fleur de Lys
San Francisco, California

Dash of salt
Dash white pepper
Imported white wine
    mustard, to taste
⅔ cup imported
    olive oil

⅓ cup red wine vinegar
Freshly ground black
    pepper, to taste
Herbs: Plenty (preferably
    fresh gathered from your
    neighbor's garden)

Combine salt, pepper and mustard. Beat in oil slowly. Add vinegar and continue beating. Add black pepper and herbs and mix.

Prepare no more than ten minutes before you intend to use it. Add salad and mix. Mix again.

SWEET AND SOUR DRESSING

Doc's Airpark Restaurant
Quincy, Illinois

½ can tomato soup
1 cup sugar
1 cup vinegar
1 cup mazola oil
1 teaspoon salt

1 teaspoon Ac'cent
1 medium green pepper, minced
1 medium onion, minced

Mix all ingredients together and stir until well blended.

SALAD DRESSING A LA PARADOR

El Parador Cafe
New York City

⅔ can condensed tomato soup
2 teaspoons salt
1 teaspoon paprika
1 teaspoon onion powder
1 teaspoon garlic powder
½ teaspoon pepper
½ teaspoon dry mustard

½ teaspoon confectioners' sugar
1 tablespoon Louisiana hot sauce or 1 teaspoon Tabasco
½ cup wine vinegar
1 cup olive oil

Combine ingredients, except vinegar and oil; mix thoroughly. Beat in vinegar and oil alternately, beginning with vinegar; mix thoroughly. Store in refrigerator. Yield: 1 pint.

RED LION SALAD DRESSING

Red Lion Inn
Hackensack, New Jersey

¾ cup sugar
3 cloves garlic, finely chopped
1 teaspoon paprika
1½ cups white vinegar

Pinch black pepper
¼ teaspoon dry mustard
1 teaspoon salt
2 cups oil

Thoroughly mix sugar, garlic, paprika, vinegar, black pepper, dry mustard and salt. Then blend in slowly the salad oil. Shake well before using.

LEMON DRESSING

Le Chateau Richelieu
New York City

⅔ cup olive oil
⅓ cup lemon juice

1 teaspoon salt
¼ teaspoon black pepper

Combine olive oil, preferably French because it is finer, and lemon juice. Season with black pepper and salt. Mix well.

This dressing is superb served on Belgian endive that has been split into quarters and placed on plate with slices face up.

BUD BIGELOW'S GREEN GODDESS DRESSING

Bud Bigelow's Restaurant
Houston, Texas

1 small clove garlic
3 tablespoons anchovies
(boneless, skinless)
3 tablespoons chopped
green onions, tops and all
⅓ cup parsley
(no heavy stems)

1 tablespoon lemon juice
3 tablespoons tarragon
wine vinegar
1 cup mayonnaise
½ cup commercial
sour cream
Salt and pepper to taste

If you don't have a blender, chop the first four ingredients on a board until they are very, very fine, and then combine as directed.

Using a blender, place garlic, anchovies, onions, parsley, lemon juice and vinegar in the blender. Turn on blender until well mixed.

Combine mayonnaise with commercial sour cream. Add the blended ingredients and mix well. Add salt and pepper to taste. Easy on the salt, the anchovies are salty. Makes one pint.

GOLDEN PARROT SALAD DRESSING

Golden Parrot Restaurant
Washington, D. C.

1 can condensed tomato
   soup
½ cup salad oil
1½ cups white vinegar
1 tablespoon sugar

1 teaspoon salt
1 teaspoon mustard
1 teaspoon
   Worcestershire sauce
½ teaspoon garlic powder

Blend thoroughly with mixer and store in refrigerator until used. Shake well before using.

RUSSIAN SALAD DRESSING

Latchstring Inn
Savoy, South Dakota

1 cup catsup
½ cup salal oil
½ cup vinegar
½ cup sugar

1 onion, grated
1 teaspoon salt
Juice of 1 lemon
Paprika

Mix all together and blend thoroughly.

SID'S ROQUEFORT CHEESE DRESSING

Sid's Restaurant
Algonac, Michigan

4-inch wedge Roquefort
   cheese
1 cup salad dressing
   (your favorite)
Black pepper, to taste
4 tablespoons fresh
   lemon juice

Dash Worcestershire
   sauce
4 tablespoons parsley,
   chopped
¼ cup heavy cream
4 tablespoons
   Parmesan cheese
Dash Tabasco sauce

Break down cheese in one-half inch pieces in mixing bowl. Do not mash to paste. Blend in salad dressing. Blend next seven ingredients together. Add all ingredients together, stirring only until well blended. Store in covered stone crock. Keep in refrigerator.

ROQUEFORT DRESSING

Gourmet House
Mandan, North Dakota

8 tablespoons blue cheese
2 cups heavy cream, whipped stiff
2 tablespoons green onion, chopped

Dash Tabasco sauce
Dash Worcestershire sauce
Dash Garlic salt

Mix all ingredients well in mixer.

PASTA, RICE, EGGS, CHEESE NOODLES

NOODLES

Augustine's Restaurant
Belleville, Illinois

3 cups flour
1 teaspoon salt
2 eggs

½ cup spinach
(puréed baby food)

Place 2 cups flour in mixing bowl, sprinkle in salt. Combine eggs and spinach purée in separate bowl, mix well. Add all at once to flour and with hands place the remaining flour on a board and knead well, until all flour has been worked in. Form into 2 balls, wrap in waxed paper, and let stand at room temperature for one hour. Roll out on lightly floured board about 16″ x 14″. This dough is quite stiff, so this will take a few minutes. Sprinkle lightly with flour. Starting from narrow side, roll like a jelly roll and cut into ¼″ slices. Repeat with other ball. Unroll slices and place on lightly floured dry towels. Let stand for several hours. This will make about one pound of noodles. (For regular noodles, omit the spinach purée and add 2 eggs in its place).

BUTTERED ALMOND NOODLES

Win Schuler's Restaurant
Marshall, Michigan

2 cups water
2 cups egg noodles

½ pound almonds,
blanched and slivered
4 tablespoons butter

Bring well salted water to a boil. Add egg noodles and cook until noodles are tender (12 to 15 minutes). Blanch and sliver almonds. In a skillet, sauté almonds in butter until they just begin to turn golden in color. Fold noodles into butter and almonds and sauté until hot. Serve noodles as a garnish for a casserole.

ALSATIAN NOODLES WITH CREAM

Fleur de Lys
San Francisco, California

1 pound noodles
3 ounces butter
Salt, pepper, dash
   nutmeg powder

6 ounces heavy cream
4 ounces Swiss cheese,
   grated

Cook noodles in salted boiling water for 8 minutes. Strain and dry. Separately break in small pieces a handful of uncooked noodles and sauté them in 1 ounce of butter in a frying pan unil dark brown. Heat cream and add it to cooked noodles. Season with salt, pepper, nutmeg and cook additional 10 minutes, stirring occasionally.

Add to the cooked noodles the brown fried pieces, 2 ounces additional butter and the cheese. Mix together and serve hot.

FETTUCINI
(Egg Noodles)

Camillo Restaurant
New York City

1 pound egg noodles
¼ pound butter
1 cup cream
1 hard cooked egg
   (chopped very fine)

Parmesan cheese, grated
Freshly ground pepper
Pinch salt

Boil ¼ inch wide egg noodles until soft. Dry very well. Melt butter in flat skillet. Add cooked noodles. Add hard cooked egg and cream. Cover with grated cheese, add freshly ground pepper and pinch of salt. Toss until butter, cream and cheese adhere to noodles. Serve piping hot.

FETTUCCINE ALA AUGUSTINE'S

*Augustine's Restaurant
Belleville, Illinois*

½ pound Fettuccine
 noodles
¼ pound soft butter
1 cup heavy cream

Freshly ground black
 pepper
¼ pound freshly grated
 Parmesan cheese

Cook noodles in boiling salted water until tender, about 8 minutes. Drain well and place in a chafing dish or large electric skillet. (If neither is available, place in regular skillet large enough to toss noodles freely.) Place over low heat. Add butter, in several pieces, to noodles, stirring gently until butter coats the noodles as it melts. Stir in cream and grind a generous amount of pepper over this mixture. Continue stirring and tossing noodles until the cream thickens and clings to noodles. Add cheese, mix well until cheese also melts. Be careful not to burn. Serve dish immediately.

FETTUCINE A GIOIA

*Mercurio Restaurant
New York City*

1 pound medium flat
 egg noodles
2 tablespoons butter
1 clove garlic, crushed
6 slices Prosciutto ham,
 cut Julienne style
2 tablespoons Pesto
 (Genoese flavoring)

1 ounce truffle paste or
 sliced truffle
½ cup tomato sauce
5 tablespoons Parmesan
 cheese, grated
Black pepper
½ cup plain consomme
1 tablespoon parsley,
 chopped

Cook noodles according to package directions. While noodles are cooking, prepare sauce as follows:

Melt butter and lightly brown crushed garlic. Add Prosciutto, sauté for 1 minute. Add Pesto, truffles paste and sauté for another minute. Add tomato sauce and simmer 1 minute. In the meantime, drain noodles and add to skillet, Sprinkle Parmesan cheese on noodles, tossing noodles lightly. Add crushed black pepper and, if desired, add consomme and cook for 1 minute. Sprinkle with parsley and serve very hot. If dry dish is preferred, omit consomme.

SPAGHETTI WITH ANCHOVIES

Valerio's Italian Restaurant
San Antonio, Texas

1 pound thin Italian
  spaghetti
½ cup olive oil
1 clove garlic

12 anchovy filets, cut up
Salt, pepper to taste
½ cup Parmesan cheese,
  grated

Cook spaghetti in 4 quarts rapidly boiling salted water until tender. Drain. Fry garlic in hot oil 5 minutes. Remove garlic. Cut anchovies in ½ inch pieces and add to hot oil. Cook for 2 minutes, stirring constantly. Add a little white pepper and salt very sparingly (anchovies are salty). Pour over spaghetti. Sprinkle with grated Parmesan cheese.

LASAGNETTE VERDI

Terry & Jerry's O Solo Mio
Bay City, Michigan

6 eggs
4 cups flour
1 cup frozen spinach,
  cooked, strained and
  chopped

Boiling water
Salt
Parmesan cheese, grated
Sweet butter

Work and knead with the hands eggs, spinach and flour to a smooth fine dough. Roll into two balls. The dough should be very stiff—add more flour if necessary. Place in uncovered dish in refrigerator for twenty minutes. Remove dough one ball at a time to a floured board and roll as thin as possible, lifting from time to time and flouring board so it does not stick. Keep dough floured. Fold dough over two times like a jelly roll. With a sharp knife cut noodles to desired thickness, shake out to length and dry for an hour before using. Have large sauce pan of boiling, salted water (one teaspoon salt to one quart of water). Boil about 15 to 20 minutes until done. Drain noodles, place in warm casserole, toss lightly with grated Parmesan cheese and sweet butter.

PASTA CON VONGOLI
(Spaghetti with Clams)

Tony's
St. Louis, Missouri

1 onion, chopped
1 glove garlic, chopped
¼ cup olive oil

2 pounds fresh clams, chopped
¼ cup parsley, chopped
Pepper to taste

Sauté onion and garlic in olive oil, but do not brown; add clams and cook very slowly for 30 minutes (do not cook too fast as clams will become tough). Add parsley and pepper. Stir and cook for 5 minutes. Pour over freshly cooked spaghetti. Serve with tossed crisp green salad, hot garlic bread and chilled white wine.

LASAGNE

Villa Venice
Tulsa, Oklahoma

½ pound beef, chopped
¼ pound lean pork, chopped
1 egg, slightly beaten
1 clove garlic, minced
2 tablespoons parsley, finely chopped
1½ tablespoons Parmesan cheese, grated
4 tablespoons olive oil

3 slices stale French bread
1 pound Lasagne
1 #2 can Italian plum tomatoes
1 small can tomato paste
1 bay leaf
1½ cups Mozzarella
1 Italian sausage
2 cups Ricotta cheese
1½ cups Parmesan cheese

Combine chopped beef and ground lean pork with egg,

clove garlic, finely chopped parsley, grated Parmesan cheese, and olive oil. Soak sliced stale French bread in water for 5 minutes, squeeze out and blend in beef mixture. Form the mixture into small balls and fry in hot oil until brown on all sides.

Make sauce by combining Italian plum tomatoes, tomato paste, bay leaf, salt and pepper to taste. Simmer for 1½ hours, until fairly thick. Remove the bay leaf.

In a large pot of rapidly boiling salted water, cook 1 pound Lasagne noodles until tender. Add a tablespoon of oil to prevent noodles from sticking while they cook. Drain.

Place a layer of lasagne into a baking dish, then a layer of finely sliced Mozzarella. On the cheese arrange a layer of thinly sliced sausage and meatballs. Over the meatballs spread a layer of Ricotta cheese and sprinkle generously with grated Parmesan cheese. Pour a layer of tomato sauce over all.

Repeat the layers until all the ingredients have been used, ending with tomato sauce and a layer of grated Parmesan.

Bake the dish in a moderate oven 350° for 20-25 minutes. Serve piping hot.

MAMA'S LASAGNE

*Locante's
Pittsburgh, Penna.*

2 pounds Lasagne noodles
Tomato Sauce
¾ pound ground beef
1 tablespoon oil
2 hard cooked eggs, sliced

¼ pound Italian sausage,
 sliced thin
½ pound mushrooms,
 sliced
Mozzarella cheese

Boil Lasagna noodles for 20 minutes. Prepare a deep baking dish by covering the bottom with tomato sauce. Add a layer of noodles. Cook ground meat by sautéing in oil.

Then place ground pre-cooked beef, slices hard cooked egg, sliced Italian sausage, mushroom slices, and a layer mozzarella cheese. Top with more tomato sauce, and start over again with another layer of noodles, etc. until casserole is filled. Bake one hour at 350°.

CREAMED MACARONI AND LOBSTER MONSIGNOR

*The Parker House
Boston, Massachusetts*

½ pound medium
  size macaroni
3 ounces butter (solid)
1 pound lobster meat,
  cut in cubes
1 tablespoon paprika
4 ounces sherry wine

1 quart light cream sauce,
  hot
Salt and white pepper to
  taste
2 ounces Parmesan cheese,
  grated
1 ounce butter, melted
Boil and drain macaroni

Place butter in a sauce pan, sauté lobster meat and paprika for a few minutes, add sherry wine and simmer till lobster is flavored. Add the hot cream sauce and cooked macaroni— blend everything well. Add salt and white pepper to taste.

Place in casserole, sprinkle top with Parmesan cheese and melted butter and bake in 325° oven until golden brown, about 30 minutes.

ZITE A LA BECHAMEL
(Macaroni Francaise)

*Renato Restaurant
New York City*

1 pound butter
6 tablespoons flour
2 cups milk
½ teaspoon grated nutmeg
½ pound zite (macaroni)

1 cup cream
1 cup Parmesan cheese,
  grated
4 ounces cooking sherry
Salt and pepper to taste

Melt butter, add flour, pour in warm milk, salt, pepper, nutmeg. Cook and stir continuously for 15 minutes. Add sherry and cream. Boil zite, strain, put in flat pan, pour the whole sauce on, sprinkle with cheese, and bake in 325° oven until brown, 25 to 35 minutes.

MACARONI MOUSSE

King's Inn
Highlands, North Carolina

2 cups macaroni, broken
  in two-inch pieces
1½ cups scalded milk
1 cup soft bread crumbs
¼ cup melted butter
1 pimento, chopped
1 tablespoon parsley,
  chopped

1 tablespoon onion,
  chopped
1½ cups American cheese,
  grated
⅜ teaspoon salt
⅛ teaspoon pepper
Dash paprika
3 eggs, well beaten

Cook the macaroni in boiling salted water, blanch in cold
water and drain. Pour the milk over the bread crumbs. Add
butter, pimento, parsley, onion, grated cheeese and seasonings.
Add the well-beaten eggs. Put the macaroni in a heavily
buttered loaf pan and pour the milk and cheese mixture over
it. Bake about 50 minutes in a slow oven, 275°, or until the
loaf is firm and will hold its shape when turned out on a
platter. Serve with mushroom sauce.

STUFFED RIGATONI
(large ribbed pasta)

Locante's
Pittsburgh, Penna.

1 pound rigatoni (pasta)
1 pound ground beef
3 tablespoons olive oil
1 pound frozen spinach,
  chopped
2 eggs, well beaten

½ cup Romano cheese,
  grated
Pinch garlic powder
Salt, pepper to taste
Tomato sauce

Boil rigatoni macaroni (medium size). Brown ground
beef in oil. Boil frozen chopped spinach until done. Mix beef
and spinach together after each has been cooled. Add eggs,
grated Romano cheese, pinch garlic powder, black pepper

and salt to taste. Mix all ingredients together well. Add more spices if desired. Take cooked rigatoni and stuff them well. Place in casserole into which tomato sauce has been added about ⅛-inch deep in bottom. Bake for 25 minutes in 375° oven. Serve very hot.

PIROJSKI

Embassy Club and Knight Box
Sheraton-East Hotel
New York City

½ pint lukewarm water	3½ cups flour
1 package yeast	½ teaspoon salt
1 cup milk	¼ teaspoon sugar
8 ounces butter, melted	Fat for deep frying
2 egg yolks	

Dissolve yeast in water. Bring milk to boil, cool and add softened yeast. Add half the flour and beat until smooth. Cover and let stand about one half hour. Add melted butter, egg yolks, salt, sugar and enough remaining flour to make soft dough. Cover and let rise until double in bulk. Roll out to ¼ inch thickness and cut into egg-sized pieces. Place filling in center. Roll into a ball the size of a good-size plum and deep fry in hot fat for 6 minutes. Drain on absorbent paper.

Meat Filling for Pirojski

1 pound lean beef, chopped	3 tablespoons cream sauce
1 medium onion, chopped	3 tablespoons brown sauce
2 tablespoons parsley, chopped	Salt and pepper
2 hard cooked eggs, chopped	

Brown the chopped meat with onion, grind once more in grinder; add parsley, eggs, sauces, salt and pepper. Mix well and fill center of Pirojski.

FRUIT DUMPLINGS

Vasata Restaurant
New York City

1 cup warm milk
2 packages yeast
1 teaspoon + 1 tablespoon
  sugar

1¼ cups sifted flour
1 teaspoon sweet butter,
  softened
1 egg yolk
Pinch salt

Fruit for filling: plums, apricots, peach halves or cherries (all pitted) Cinnamon sugar (optional)

Combine ⅓ cup warm milk with yeast and 1 teaspoon sugar and let the mixture stand for 15 minutes.

In a large bowl, combine the yeast mixture with flour, the remainder of the warm milk, 1 tablespoon sugar, butter, egg yolk and salt. Knead the dough thoroughly. Cover the bowl with a towel and let the dough stand in a warm place for 30 minutes, or until it is almost double in bulk. Roll the dough out ½ inch thick and cut it into small squares.

In the center of each square place 1 plum (or 1 apricot, ½ peach or 4 cherries) and fold over the edges to form round balls. Put the dumplings on a board or table, cover them with a towel, and let them stand for 30 minutes, turning them over once.

Fruit Dumplings

Drop the dumplings, one at a time, into boiling salted water, lower the heat, and simmer them, covered, for about 10 to 15 minutes, turning them once. Remove the dumplings with a slotted spoon and drain them in a colander. With a fork make a small opening in the center of each dumpling. Sprinkle the dumplings with sugar and pour over them melted clarified butter. Serve sprinkled with cinnamon sugar, if desired, or cottage cheese.

BREAD DUMPLINGS

Vasata Restaurant
New York City

½ loaf stale white   ½ teaspoon salt
   bread, cubed   1 cup milk
2 tablespoons butter   ½ cup cold water
4 cups flour   3 eggs

Fry cubed bread in butter until golden and let cool. Sift flour with salt in a large mixing bowl. Combine milk, water and eggs and pour mixture slowly into flour, stirring with a large wooden spoon. Then beat dough with the same spoon until very smooth and medium thick. Stir in fried bread and let stand ½ hour. Divide dough into two parts.

Shape into two long dumpling rolls (look like small loaves of French bread) and slip them into boiling salted water. Boil 30 minutes turning once with a wooden spoon. Cut dumplings while hot with a very sharp thin knife. Slices should be about ½ inch thick. Left-over dumplings can be reheated by steaming. Dumplings are served with meat and gravy.

JAPANESE BOILED RICE

Yamato Sukiyaki Restaurant
San Francisco, California

3 cups rice, washed and
   well drained
3¼ cups water

Bring rice and water to boil. Turn heat down, cover, and simmer 15 minutes. Turn off heat and let rice stand, covered, for 15 minutes.

RICE PILAF

London Chop House
Detroit, Michigan

½ cup butter
1 clove garlic, finely
   chopped
1 small onion,
   finely chopped

4 cups beef broth
Tabasco sauce
1 teaspoon salt
2 cups rice

Melt butter in heavy skillet. Add garlic clove and onion. Cook over low heat until transparent. Add rice and sauté until browned. Add broth, salt, pepper, Tabasco sauce. Cover the pan and do not touch rice. Simmer until rice has absorbed all the liquid.

WILD RICE

Le Chateau Richelieu
New York City

1 cup wild rice
2 cups beef consommé
3 tablespoons butter
1 onion, finely chopped

Bacon, minced
Ham, minced
Salt, pepper

Wash rice several times until thoroughly clean.

Combine wild rice with consommé in a sauce pan. Cover, but allow a vent for the steam to escape. Sauté in butter onion, chopped very fine, minced bacon and ham, until tender. Then combine with the wild rice. Season with salt and pepper. Stir occasionally and allow to cook over low heat for 25 to 35 minutes, till liquid is absorbed and rice is tender.

WILD RICE WITH MUSHROOMS AND CHEESE

Hotel Racine
Racine, Wisconsin

1 cup wild rice	2 tablespoons flour
½ pound mushrooms, sliced	1 cup light cream
2 tablespoons butter	¼ pound cream cheese

Cook the wild rice in rapidly boiling salted water until done, about 30 minutes. Then drain. Sauté mushrooms in one tablespoon butter for five minutes. Melt the remaining butter in the top of a double boiler and stir the flour smoothly into it. Gradually add cream and stir until thickened. Add the cheese and stir until it melts. Then add the mushrooms. Butter a one-quart casserole and place alternate layers of the rice and mushroom mixture in it. Bake in a slow oven, 325°, for one hour.

WILD RICE À LA PLACE PIGALLE

Place Pigalle
San Francisco, California

2 cups wild rice	4 slices crisp bacon, reserve fat
1 cup onion, minced	½ teaspoon thyme
1 cup celery, minced	1 bay leaf
2 cups very thin consommé	Salt and pepper to taste

Thoroughly wash and clean wild rice and soak in cold water for at least ½ hour.

Sauté onion and celery in ½ cup bacon fat. Add hot consommé, thyme and bay leaf. Add wild rice.

Place in shallow baking dish and cover with buttered brown paper. Cook in moderate oven, 350°, for one hour.

(If desired, serve topped with mushroom sauce)

WILD RICE DRESSING

Gourmet House
Mandan, North Dakota

1½ cups wild rice
¼ pound butter
½ pound mushrooms—
    either sliced or stems and
    pieces will do

¼ cup chives, chopped
4 tablespoons chicken stock
1 teaspoon salt
Pinch cayenne pepper

Wash wild rice and drain. Fill a large saucepan ¾ full with water and set to boil. When water comes to a boil add rice and salt. Cook rice until tender, but not too soft. When rice is done drain, and rinse with warm water to remove all the starch.

In another large pan, melt the butter. Add the mushrooms and chives and sauté about 10 minutes. Add chicken stock and cayenne pepper. Add the cooked rice and mix well. Heat and serve.

WILD RICE DRESSING

London Grill
Portland, Oregon

1 cup wild rice
¼ pound cooked giblets,
    chopped
3 tablespoons onions,
    chopped
1 large garlic clove,
    chopped

2 strips bacon, chopped
½ cup celery, chopped
¼ cup butter
4 ounces croutons
3 cups chicken stock
Salt and pepper

Wash the wild rice and blanch it in boiling water for 10 minutes. Cool under running cold water and drain. Chop the onions, garlic, celery, bacon and giblets, and sauté them all together in butter over a hot fire for 5 minutes, stirring constantly. Add the wild rice, croutons, salt and pepper and blend together. Cover with chicken stock and bake in 350° oven for 25 minutes.

WILD RICE FOR STUFFING

Junco's Stone Ends Restaurant
Glenmont, New York

½ cup wild rice
  1 cup chicken stock or
    bouillon

2 mushrooms, sliced
1 small onion, diced fine
Salt, to taste

Wash wild rice in warm water and let soak for 5 minutes. Rinse and cover with cold water (⅓ cup), add chicken stock, raw sliced mushrooms, onions and salt to taste. Cook over low fire until rice is tender and absorbs all liquid. Keep covered while cooking.

INDIAN RICE

East Indian Kitchen
Hotel Pierre
New York City

Ball of saffron
  1 cup cold water
¼ pound butter
  3 cups rice

1 onion, chopped
1 teaspoon salt
3 cups hot water

Soak saffron about the size of a teaball in cold water for about two hours. Melt butter and add raw rice and onion and salt. Add the liquid from the saffron to the rice and butter, and put it in a hot oven, and stir every ten minutes until the rice is very dry. Then add 3 cups of hot water and stir. Keep covered for 15 minutes. Then remove from fire and keep in a warm place until ready to serve.

RICE À LA PUNJAB

Punjab Restaurant
New York City

1 clove garlic, minced	2 tablespoons vegetable oil
1 large onion,	2 cups rice
chopped fine	Ac'cent, salt, pepper to taste
½ pound butter	Chicken stock to cover

In a saucepan sauté garlic and onions until soft in butter and vegetable oil. Add rice, stir until rice absorbs ingredients. Add Ac'cent, salt and pepper to taste, and stir. Add chicken stock, stir and let boil. When boiling, lower flame and cover. Stir occasionally as rice and broth thicken. Cook over low flame until desired softness of rice is reached.

BAHAMIAN PEAS AND RICE

Emerald Beach Hotel
Nassau, Bahamas

1 large onion, chopped fine	½ cup tomato puree
1 tablespoon butter	2 sprigs thyme
1½ cups rice	4 cups chicken stock
1 tin pigeon peas	Salt and pepper
(must be from Nassau)	

Chop onions fine and cook lightly in butter. Add remaining ingredients. Cook 20 to 25 minutes or until rice is tender. A little chopped bacon or ham may be added to enhance the flavor. Watch liquid carefully, adding more if necessary to prevent buring.

Note: Canned cooked pigeon peas are available.

RISOTTO ALA AUGUSTINE'S
Rice, Milanese Style

Augustine's Restaurant
Belleville, Illinois

3 tablespoons butter	1 teaspoon salt
½ cup onion, finely chopped	4½ cups boiling chicken broth
2 tablespoons beef marrow (optional)	2 tablespoons parsley, minced
2 cups raw long grain rice	½ cup Parmesan cheese, grated
¼ cup dry white wine	

Melt 2 tablespoons butter in a saucepan; add the onions and marrow, if used. Cook over low heat until onions are soft and yellow. Stir in the rice, cooking until it is yellow. Add the wine and salt; cook until absorbed. Add 1 cup broth, cover and cook until absorbed. Continue adding 1 cup broth at a time, until rice is tender but firm. Stir in the remaining butter, then the parsley and cheese. Remove from heat and let stand covered 5 minutes before serving.

SOPA DE ARROZ
(Rice in Soup Stock)

Cafe La Margarita
Chicago, Illinois

½ pound dry rice	2 cloves garlic, mashed
2 tablespoons corn oil	Salt and pepper
1 small onion, chopped	1 quart soup stock

Sauté the dry rice in oil over a low flame for five minutes. Add the onion and garlic and sauté for another five minutes. Add salt, pepper and soup stock. Cover tightly and finish cooking over your lowest heat for 30 to 45 minutes until dry.

SPANISH RICE

Saddleback Inn
Santa Ana, California

2 tablespoons bacon fat
2 onions, sliced fine
2 bay leaves
1 teaspoon sweet basil
½ cup green peppers, minced

1 cup uncooked rice
1½ cups tomato juice
1 cup boiling water or stock, if necessary
Salt, pepper to taste

Sauté onions in bacon fat until soft. Add bay leaves, sweet basil and green pepper. Add rice, tomato juice and bring to a boil. Add stock or water if rice becomes too dry. Stir well, cover, and bake in 375° oven until rice is tender, 35 to 45 minutes.

RICE VALENCIA

Mediterrania Restaurant
Beverly Hills, California

1 onion, diced
1 bell pepper, diced
8 fresh mushrooms, diced
4 ounces butter
1 clove garlic, crushed
1 teaspoon paprika
2 cups rice

4½ cups chicken broth
3 teaspoons salt
1 teaspoon monosodium glutamate
1 pimiento, diced
½ cup peas

Sauté onions, peppers, mushrooms in 2 ounces butter, until limp. Add crushed garlic and paprika. Stir and add rice. Stir well until kernels of rice are coated with butter. Add chicken broth and seasonings. Bring to boil, cover, and place in 350° oven. When rice is tender (approximately 20 minutes) remove from oven, add pimiento, peas, and dot with remaining butter. Blend and serve.

HAM FRIED RICE

Kahiki Supper Club
Columbus, Ohio

2 tablespoons butter
½ yellow onion, chopped
1 cup cooked diced ham
2 cups precooked rice

Soy sauce mixture
  (see recipe below)
2 eggs, beaten
2 stalks scallions,
  chopped

Melt butter in heavy skillet and sauté onion and ham. Add rice and soy sauce mixture. Add eggs. Mix well. Add chopped green onions. Serve piping hot.

Soy Sauce Mixture

¼ teaspoon salt
1 teaspoon sugar

2 tablespoons soy sauce
Mix ingredients well.

POACHED EGGS SUNSET

The Beverly Hills Hotel
Beverly Hills, California

6 eggs
2 tablespoons salt
2 tablespoons white
  vinegar

3 tomatoes
Salt and pepper, to taste
Dill, to taste

Put water in skillet, add vinegar and salt. Bring to a boil. Reduce heat and poach the eggs in hot water. Leave them soft. Remove eggs from water with slotted spoon and drain on absorbent paper.

Cut tomatoes in half, season with salt, pepper and dill, and broil a few minutes. Put an egg on top of each tomato half and glaze with Hollandaise sauce (see Sauces).

FRENCH OMELET

Publick House
Sturbridge, Massachusetts

For Each Omelet

3 eggs	Pinch salt
1 tablespoon water	Butter for cooking

The pan should be of heavy metal and at least 6 inches across for an individual omelet. Preheat the pan for about 10 minutes over very low heat.

For each omelet beat eggs, water and a little salt with a fork until well blended, but not frothy. When ready to make the omelet, turn up the heat under the pan. The pan should be hot enough to make butter sizzle but not brown.

Put butter in the pan and when it is melted, pour in the eggs. Leave for maybe 30 seconds, until the bottom starts to set a little, then shake the pan with one hand and stir the eggs lightly with a fork with the other. While the omelet is still soft and creamy, let it stand for a few seconds, then tilt the pan at right angles toward a hot plate or omelet dish, and with the same fork, fold the omelet over and turn out.

Serves two.

RED CAVIAR OMELET WITH SOUR CREAM

Publick House
Sturbridge, Massachusetts

See French Omelet recipe for same restaurant.

Garnish top of a folded French omelet with a band of red caviar (as much as you can afford). Beside it, spoon on a band of snowy sour cream. Trim plate with parsley sprigs.

ROQUEFORT OMELET

Fleur de Lys
San Francisco, California

12 eggs
4 ounces butter
Salt, pepper

½ cup heavy cream
½ pound Roquefort
cheese, grated

Separate yolks and whites. Beat up whites firmly. To the yolks add salt, pepper and 1 ounce melted butter. Mix together and fold in whites. In large frying pan, melt butter and pour in egg mixture. Cook 3 to 4 minutes, then cover with the grated cheese and let cook until cheese is melted in the omelet.

Roll on hot platter. Garnish top with Roquefort cheese.

HIGHLAND FARMHOUSE EGGS

Royal Scots Grill
Pick-Congress Hotel
Chicago, Illinois

3 cups breadcrumbs
¾ pound Cheddar or
Cheshire cheese, grated

6 eggs
1 pint medium cream
Salt and pepper to taste

Cover the bottom of a casserole with breadcrumbs; then cover the crumbs with a layer of grated cheese, Cheddar or Cheshire. Break eggs into the dish. Cover with another layer of breadcrumbs and cheese. Carefully pour over the cream. Sprinkle with a thick layer of breadcrumbs and cheese. Season each layer with salt and pepper. Place in a slow oven, 325°, and cook until eggs are set and the crumbs and cheese are browned.

EGGS À LA TURK

Brennan's French Restaurant
New Orleans, Louisiana

4 tablespoons butter
6 to 7 shallots, finely
  chopped
1½ pounds chicken livers
2 tablespoons flour

1½ cups chicken stock
1 cup Burgundy wine
1 pound mushrooms,
  sliced thin
12 eggs

Sauté shallots and chicken livers in butter. Blend in flour and chicken stock. Add Burgundy wine and fresh mushrooms. Let boil 10 to 15 minutes to reduce sauce. Put a tablespoon of sauce in 6 individual casseroles. Break two eggs in each and bake in moderate oven, 350°, for 12 to 15 minutes. Cover eggs with remainder of sauce and serve.

HUEVOS RANCHEROS

Cafe La Margarita
Chicago, Illinois

6 tortillas
Oil for frying
1 onion, chopped
1 garlic clove, minced
2 cups tomato sauce
6 eggs

2 small, green, piquant
  chili peppers or
2 tablespoons chopped
  bell pepper with 2 drops
  Tabasco sauce

Fry the tortillas quickly, but do not allow them to become hard or crisp. Sauté the onion, garlic, and peppers and add tomato sauce. Cook for five minutes. Fry the eggs sunnyside up, place each one on a tortilla, pour the tomato sauce over the top, and serve. Sliced avocado and cheese goes very well with this dish.

EGGS HUSSARDE

Brennan's French Restaurant
New Orleans, Louisiana

12 large thin slices of ham,
   grilled
12 Holland rusks
¼ cup Marchand de Vin
   Sauce (recipe below)
   for each portion

12 slices tomato grilled
12 eggs, soft poached
¼ cup Hollandaise Sauce
   (recipe below) for each
   portion
Paprika

Lay a slice of ham across each rusk and cover with
Marchand de Vin Sauce. Cover next with tomato and then
egg. Top with Hollandaise Sauce. Garnish with sprinkle of
paprika.

Marchand de Vin Sauce (about 2 cups)

¾ cup butter
⅓ cup mushrooms,
   finely chopped
½ cup minced ham
⅓ cup shallots, finely
   chopped
½ cup onions, finely
   chopped

2 tablespoons garlic,
   minced
2 tablespoons flour
½ teaspoon salt
⅛ teaspoon pepper
Dash cayenne
¾ cup beef stock
½ cup red wine

In a 9-inch skillet, melt butter and lightly sauté the
mushrooms, ham, shallots, onion and garlic. When onion is
brown, add the flour, salt, pepper and cayenne. Brown well
(7 to 10 minutes). Blend in the stock and the wine and
simmer over low heat for 35 to 45 minutes.

Hollandaise Sauce (about 1½ cups)

4 egg yolks
2 tablespoons lemon juice,
   or to taste

½ pound butter, melted
Salt and pepper to taste

In top half of double boiler, beat egg yolks and stir in lemon juice. Cook very slowly in double boiler over low heat, never allowing water in bottom pan to come to a boil. Add butter a little at a time, stirring constantly with a wooden spoon. Add salt and pepper. Cook slowly until thickened.

EGGS FOO YOUNG

Nankin Cafe
Minneapolis, Minnesota

6 eggs, well beaten
6 scallions, finely chopped
½ pound mushrooms, peeled and sliced
2 stalks celery, peeled and sliced
1 cup water chestnuts, sliced

1 cup cooked meat or fish, finely cut up
2 tablespoons oil
Salt, pepper to taste
Fat, peanut oil or lard for frying
Soy sauce

Sauté scallions, mushrooms, celery, water chestnuts and meat or fish in oil over a low flame. Season to taste. Drop mixture, ½ cup at a time (to form small omelets) into hot fat, 350°, and fry to crisp brown. Drain on absorbent paper. Serve with soy sauce.

EGGS SARDOU

Brennan's French Restaurant
New Orleans, Louisiana

1½ pounds spinach, cooked, chopped, creamed
2 artichoke bottoms for each serving

2 poached eggs for each serving
Hollandaise Sauce

On a base of creamed spinach, place 2 artichoke bottoms. Fill these with poached eggs and cover all with Hollandaise Sauce.

HIGHLAND FARMHOUSE EGGS

Royal Scots Grill
Pick-Congress Hotel
Chicago, Illinois

1½ cups bread crumbs
1½ cups cheese, cheddar
   or cheshire, grated

6 eggs
1½ cups cream
Salt, pepper to taste

Cover the bottom of a casserole with stale breadcrumbs. then cover the crumbs with a layer of grated cheese. Break six eggs into the dish, cover with another layer of breadcrumbs and cheese. Carefully pour over 1½ cups cream. Sprinkle with a thick layer of breadcrumbs and cheese. Season each layer with salt and pepper. Place in a slow oven, 325° F., and cook until eggs are set, and the crumbs and cheese are browned.

CHEESE SOUFFLE

J. A. C. Cafeteria
Columbia, Missouri

1½ cups milk
⅛ pound butter or
   margarine
¼ cup flour
4 to 5 eggs, beaten
   separately (must be at
   room temperature)

½ pound American cheese,
   grated
½ teaspoon salt
2 drops Tabasco sauce
½ teaspoon prepared
   mustard

Heat milk in double boiler. Melt butter or margarine in sauce pan and blend in flour. Add hot milk, constantly stirring and bring to a hard boil while stirring. Have egg yolks beaten until thick and lemon colored. Remove sauce from heat and stir in yolks, one spoon full at a time. Add cheese, seasonings, and ¼ teaspoon salt, and stir until cheese is melted. Beat egg whites with remaining salt until very stiff. Carefully fold beaten whites into cheese mixture. Place in souffle dish and bake in 325° oven for 35 to 45 minutes, or until done in center. Serve with tomato or mushroom sauce.

QUICHE LORRAINE

Empress Hotel Dining Room
Victoria, British Columbia

3 ounces bacon
1 ounce mushrooms, chopped
2 ounces Gruyere cheese, in small cubes
3 ounces Old Canadian cheese, in small cubes
1 medium onion, diced

2 teaspoons parsley, chopped
Dash of garlic salt, white pepper and nutmeg
1 pint light cream
4 beaten eggs
9-inch unbaked pie shell

Sauté bacon, onion, mushrooms and parsley, draining off any excess fat, and let cool. Fill the bottom of the pie shell with the cheese and sautéed ingredients. Combine cream, beaten eggs and seasoning and pour into pie shell. Bake in 400° oven for 10 minutes, reduce heat to 350° and continue baking for another 30 minutes. Serve warm. Serves 6.

QUICHE LORRAINE

The Greenbrier
White Sulphur Springs, West Virginia

3 eggs, well beaten
1 pint light cream
½ cup Swiss cheese, grated
Salt, pepper, cayenne to taste
½ cup onions, chopped

½ cup ham, diced
½ cup melted butter
½ cup crisp bacon, crumbled
½ cup Swiss cheese, diced
1 9-inch pastry shell

Mix eggs, cream, grated cheese and seasoning.
Sauté onions and ham in butter. Add bacon and diced

cheese and spread evenly on bottom of 9-inch pastry shell (pie form or French tart).

Pour egg mixture on top, filling to rim of shell.

Bake in 375° oven for approximately 40 minutes, or until custard is set and top is brown.

QUICHE LORRAINE

The Harrison Hotel
Vancouver, British Columbia

Puff Pastry

4 cups sifted flour	1 teaspoon salt
1¼ cups water	14 ounces butter

Spread flour in a circle and add water, mixed with salt, in the middle. Work water and flour to make a firm, slightly sticky dough and roll out ½ inch thick, keeping it square. Place butter in middle and fold dough from both sides over it (like making a package). Roll out the dough again, fold it like a book and let it rest in refrigerator for 10 minutes. Repeat this procedure four times to make dough crisp when baked.

Filling

½ pound bacon, cut in small strips	1 teaspoon paprika
	Dash nutmeg and pepper
½ onion, diced	1 teaspoon Knorr Aromat
5 medium mushrooms, cut in small strips	Salt to taste, remembering salt in bacon
Parsley, finely chopped	10 ounces Parmesan and Swiss cheese, mixed
2 eggs, well beaten	
2 cups milk	1 glass white dry wine

Sauté bacon, chopped onion and mushrooms in frying pan. Add chopped parsley when bacon and mushrooms are nearly cooked. Remove from heat. In separate bowl, beat eggs and mix with milk, spices and salt to taste. Add the eggs and milk mixture, then the cheese and wine to the frying pan. Lay out 12 to 15 muffin forms with ⅛-inch rolled out puff pastry. Fill shells and bake in 350° oven for 20 to 30 minutes. Serve hot.

WELSH RAREBIT

Chowning's Tavern
Williamsburg, Virginia

¼ cup butter
½ cup flour
3 cups milk
½ teaspoon salt
½ tablespoon Tabasco
   sauce

1 teaspoon prepared
   mustard
½ tablespoon
   Worcestershire Sauce
½ cup beer or ale
1 pound sharp Cheddar
   cheese, diced

Melt butter, add flour; stir until smooth. Add milk and continue cooking and stirring for about 5 minutes over hot water. Add cheese and seasonings; continue cooking until cheese melts. Add beer, stirring well. Serve bubbling hot over toast triangles.

CHEESE FONDUE

Swiss Chalet Restaurant
Washington, D. C.

8 ounces Switzerland
   Swiss cheese
8 ounces Gruyère cheese
2 cups dry white wine
1 clove garlic

3 tablespoons Kirsch
1 teaspoon cornstarch
Salt and pepper
French bread cut in cubes
   with crust on each cube.

Rub cooking pot with garlic first. Pour in wine. Set over low heat. When air bubbles rise to surface, add cheese, stirring constantly with wooden spoon until melted. Add cornstarch blended with Kirsch, stirring until the mixture is thickened and creamy. Add salt and pepper.

Serve bubbling hot, spearing bread cubes with fork and dunking into fondue.

SWISS CHEESE FONDUE

The Greenbrier
White Sulphur Springs, West Virginia

1 clove garlic, peeled
2 cups Neuchâtel wine
1 pound Gruyère cheese,
  shredded
½ teaspoon flour

2 tablespoons Kirschwasser
Freshly ground pepper,
  salt, nutmeg
1 loaf French bread

Rub an earthenware casserole with garlic. Add the wine and heat slowly over chafing dish burner. Lightly mix the cheese with the flour. When the bubbles in the wine rise to surface (do not boil), add cheese mixture, a handful at a time, stirring until each handful melts and continue until all the cheese is melted. Add seasoning and Kirschwasser; stir well. Turn heat low but keep fondue slowly bubbling.

Cut French bread into cubes, leaving one side of crust on each. Provide long-handled forks. Each guest impales a bread cube and dunks it into the fondue, stirring it around as he does. If fondue becomes too thick, add a little hot wine (never cold).

NIPPY CHEESE AND SALMON FONDUE

Hotel Blackhawk
Davenport, Iowa

12 slices white bread,
  crusts removed
9 slices American cheese
1½ pound can Red
  Salmon, flaked

1½ cups milk
3 eggs beaten
2 teaspoons lemon juice
Salt, white pepper,
  paprika, to taste

Place 6 slices trimmed white bread in a casserole; cover with sliced American Cheese. Separate and sprinkle Red Salmon over the cheese. Place 6 slices of white bread over this and crisscross with American Cheese. Add a mixture of 1½ cups milk, the beaten eggs, lemon juice and seasonings.

Set the casserole in a pan of hot water and bake in 350° oven until a knife inserted in center comes out clean.

MARGARET WAHLGREN'S TOMATO, CORN AND CHEESE PIE

Hotel Racine
Racine, Wisconsin

4 slices buttered white
  bread, crusts removed
1 egg white, slightly
  beaten
4 tablespoons dry bread
  crumbs
1 can whole tomatoes
1 small can drained whole
  kernel corn

Salt and pepper
1 teaspoon sugar
2 tablespoons grated onion
1¼ cup cheddar cheese,
  grated
2 eggs, well beaten
1 cup milk

Preheat oven to 350°. Butter a 9-inch pyrex pie pan. Line the pan with slices of buttered bread, the buttered side down. No crusts on, please!

Cut buttered strips to fit around the outside just as you do with pie crust. Buttered sides next to the glass. Brush bread surfaces with beaten egg white and sprinkle with dry bread crumbs.

Drain the tomatoes, slice, and lay on crumbs. Cover with the drained, whole kernel corn. Sprinkle with salt, pepper, sugar and grated onion. Sprinkle grated cheese evenly over the top. Beat eggs and milk together and pour over the cheese.

Bake for ½ hour at 350°. Serve with broiled sausage or Canadian bacon.

SUN VALLEY CHEESE TART

Sun Valley Inn
Sun Valley, Idaho

5 strips bacon, diced
1 onion, diced
Pinch salt
1 pint milk
4 eggs, lightly beaten

Pinch red pepper
Pinch nutmeg
2 ounces flour
1 cup Swiss cheese, diced
Butter

Sauté bacon until crisp. Remove from skillet and crumble. Cook onions in bacon grease until transparent. Mix salt, milk, eggs, red pepper, nutmeg and flour. Strain, set aside.

Line a 9-inch pie mold with pie dough. Fill with diced Swiss cheese, onions and bacon. Pour custard over the top until full. Place a small pat of butter on top and bake at 350° until a knife inserted in center comes out clean. Serve at once.

This is served as an appetizer at Sun Valley, but makes an excellent main course for luncheon.

ARROZ CON CAMARONES

Cafe La Margarita
Chicago, Illinois

4 tablespoons butter
2 tablespoons flour
2 cups milk
Salt and pepper
1 teaspoon curry powder
2 tablespoons onion, grated

½ cup chopped mushrooms
1 pound small shrimp, cooked and peeled
Juice of ½ lime
3 cups Sopa de Arroz (see separate recipe under "Vegetables")

Heat the butter in a ceramic vessel and dissolve the flour. Add milk and stir constantly until it thickens into a white sauce. Sprinkle in salt, pepper and curry and simmer a minute. Add the onion and mushrooms and stir. Cook for ten minutes. If the sauce is too thick add more milk. Drop in the shrimp, stir a minute and remove from the fire. Add lime juice, but do not return to heat once the citrus is in. The rice, made from the Sopa de Arroz recipe, is then served on a platter with the shrimp sauce poured over it.

BREADS

GARLIC CROUTONS

The Pantry
Portland, Oregon

Day-old bread
1 clove garlic

1 quart corn oil
Salt to taste

Dice ½ loaf day-old bread into inch squares. French fry in garlic oil, deep fat, at 375°. Drain the croutons on paper towels. Sprinkle with salt.

Garlic oil is made by soaking 1 clove of garlic in 1 quart of corn oil, overnight.

APRICOT BREAD

Johnny Cake Inn
Ivoryton, Connecticut

1½ cups dried apricots,
   cut fine
1 cup hot water
2 cups sugar
2 eggs

4 tablespoons melted
   butter
1 cup orange juice
3½ cups flour
1 teaspoon baking soda
1 teaspoon salt

Cut apricots finely, add hot water. Add sugar, mix well. Add eggs one at a time, beating well. Add melted butter and orange juice. Sift flour three times with salt and baking soda. Add to apricot mixture. Mix well.

Spoon into two buttered loaf pans, 3½ x 7¼ or equivalent. Bake at 350° for 50 to 60 minutes. When cool, wrap in foil. Stays fresh one week.

BOSTON BROWN BREAD

Red Lion Inn
Cohasset, Massachusetts

1 cup rye meal
1 teaspoon salt
1 cup corn meal
1 cup graham flour

¾ teaspoon baking soda
1¾ cup sweet milk
¾ cup molasses

Mix and sift first five ingredients. Add milk and molasses, stir until well mixed. Place in covered, greased molds, or covered baking powder tins, ⅔ full. Place molds on a rack in deep kettles. Add boiling water half the height of the mold. Set over heat and steam for 2½ to 3 hours. Keep water boiling, adding more as needed.

DATE NUT BREAD

The Lord Jeffery Inn
Amherst, Massachusetts

¾ cup dates
2 tablespoons butter
¾ cup boiling water
2 cups flour, sifted
1 teaspoon baking powder
1 teaspoon soda

1 teaspoon salt
¾ cup sugar
1 cup nut meats, chopped
1 egg, well beaten
1 teaspoon vanilla

Pit the dates. Put them into a large mixing bowl with the butter, pour boiling water over them, and let stand for 20 minutes. Then mash dates a little with a fork.

Sift dry ingredients together, add chopped nuts. Add beaten egg and vanilla to the date mixture. Then add the dry ingredients and mix just until the flour is all dampened. Place in a greased 9 x 4 x 2½ inch loaf pan. Bake for 60 to 70 minutes in a moderate, 350°, oven.

BANANA BREAD

The House by the Road
Ashburn, Georgia

½ cup shortening
1 cup sugar
3 bananas, well mashed
2 eggs, beaten
2 cups flour

1 teaspoon soda
1 teaspoon salt
1 cup pecans or
   walnuts, cut up
8 dates, cut in small pieces

Cream shortening and sugar. Stir in beaten eggs; add bananas which have been mashed fine, and stir well. Sift dry ingredients and quickly stir into banana mixture. Add nuts and dates. Turn into greased loaf pan, let stand 20 minutes. Then bake in moderate oven, 350°, for 50 to 60 minutes.

KAUAI SURF BANANA BREAD

The Kauai Surf Hotel
Nawiliwili, Hawaii

1 cup shortening
2 cups sugar
6 ripe bananas, mashed
4 eggs, well beaten

2½ cups cake flour
1 teaspoon salt
2 teaspoons baking soda

Cream together shortening and sugar. Add mashed bananas and beaten eggs. Sift three times cake flour with salt and baking soda. Blend wet and dry ingredients together. Do not overmix—when traces of flour disappear, stop mixing. Bake at 350° for 50 to 60 minutes. Bakes two 1 lb. 4 oz. loaves.

HOT BREAD

Lambertville House
Lambertville, New Jersey

1½ cups milk, lukewarm
½ cup water, lukewarm
1 cake yeast
1 tablespoon salt

1 tablespoon sugar
2 tablespoons vegetable
shortening
7 to 7½ cups flour

Crumble yeast into lukewarm milk and water. Add sugar, salt, and shortening. Stir in enough flour to make dough workable on board, add flour in small quantities and knead until mix becomes elastic. Place in bowl in a warm, draft-free place, cover with a towel and let rise until double in bulk. Cut into five equal portions and shape into loaves and place in greased loaf pans. Cover again and let rise in warm place until double in bulk. Bake for about 30 minutes at 375° until golden brown. Makes five 8-ounce loaves.

LEMON BREAD, BLUEBERRY HILL

Blueberry Hill Farm
Brandon, Vermont

6 tablespoons butter
1 cup sugar
2 eggs
½ cup milk
Rind of 1 lemon, grated
1½ cups flour

1 teaspoon baking powder
¼ teaspoon salt
1⅓ cups walnuts or
pecans, finely chopped
⅓ cup sugar
Juice of 1 lemon

Cream together butter and sugar, beating with an electric mixer until rich and creamy. Add and continue beating the eggs, milk and grated lemon rind. Grate just the yellow, not the white, as the white is bitter.

Sift flour, baking powder and salt together. Add dry ingredients to butter-sugar mixture quickly, using a spoon. Also add the chopped nuts. Combine wet and dry ingredients with a light touch. As soon as you have a batter without flour specks, stop! Spoon the batter into a well-greased regulation bread pan and bake 60 to 65 minutes in 350° oven. Remove from oven.

Immediately after removing bread from oven, pour over it a mixture of ⅓ cup sugar and the juice of the one lemon. This juice will soak quickly into the bread. Cool the bread in the pan.

HONEY BREAD

Old Mill Inn
Bernardsville, New Jersey

2 cups milk	2 tablespoons honey
1 tablespoon salt	1 cake compressed yeast
2 tablespoons shortening	6 to 6½ cups flour

Scald milk and cool to lukewarm. Add salt and shortening. Put honey and yeast in mixing bowl. Let stand until yeast is softened. Add milk and half the flour. Beat thoroughly. Gradually add enough flour to make a soft dough. Turn out on floured board and knead until smooth and elastic. This requires about eight minutes. Place in a slightly greased bowl and let rise until double in bulk. Punch down lightly and let rise again. Form into loaves. Place in greased pans. Allow to rise until double in bulk. If baked in individual loaves (one pound) bake 40 minutes at 425°.

OATMEAL BREAD

Wilson's
Moosehead, Maine

1 cake yeast	1 tablespoon lard
½ cup warm water	½ cup molasses
2 cups milk, scalded	1 teaspoon salt
1 cup rolled oats	3 to 4 cups flour

Add yeast to water and let it dissolve.

Scald milk. While milk is hot, add rolled oats, lard and remove from stove. Cool to lukewarm. Add molasses, salt and dissolved yeast cake. Thicken with 3 to 4 cups flour, until dough is quite stiff. Let rise until double in size. Knead down and let rise again until double. Turn into greased bread pan. Let rise 1½ hours more. Bake in 400° oven for 15 minutes, then reduce heat to 350° and bake until done, 20 to 25 minutes more.

ORANGE BREAD

Latchstring Inn
Savoy, South Dakota

Peelings of 3 oranges, cut into small pieces	2 eggs, well beaten
½ cup water	1 cup sugar
½ teaspoon salt	1 teaspoon salt
1½ cups sugar	1 cup milk
3 tablespoons water	3½ cups flour
	2 teaspoons baking powder

First make a syrup: Boil orange peelings in ½ cup water with ½ teaspoon salt for 10 minutes. Drain; add 1½ cups sugar and 3 tablespoons water and boil 5 minutes, stirring occasionally to prevent burning. Let cool.

Beat eggs well; beat in sugar and salt. Stir in milk. Sift together flour and baking powder and stir into egg mixture. Add the batter to cooled syrup. Bake in two small, well-greased bread pans for 45 to 50 minutes at 350°.

SPOON BREAD

Valley View Inn
Hot Springs, Virginia

¾ cup white corn meal	1 teaspoon salt
¾ cup boiling water	1 tablespoon sugar
3 cups sweet milk	2 eggs, separated
2 tablespoons butter	1 teaspoon baking powder

Scald corn meal with boiling water.

Scald milk; add corn meal and cook, over low heat, 30 minutes, stirring frequently. Cool. Add butter, salt, sugar and beaten egg yolks. Mix well. Add baking powder and mix. Fold in stiffly beaten whites. Place mixture in a well greased casserole. Bake in 375° oven 35 to 40 minutes.

FAMOUS PARKER HOUSE ROLLS

Parker House
Boston, Massachusetts

1 ounce yeast	1 egg
1½ cups lukewarm milk	2 teaspoons butter
2 tablespoons sugar	5 cups flour
2 teaspoons salt	

Dissolve yeast in ½ cup milk. Put sugar, salt, egg, butter and remaining milk in a pan, add the dissolved yeast and the flour and mix everything thoroughly until the dough does not stick to the bowl. Place dough in a well-greased pan and let stand in a warm place about 35 minutes. (It should now have doubled in volume.)

Shape into balls and brush top with melted butter. Let stand on table for 15 minutes more. With handle of a wooden spoon, press the balls through the center almost cutting them in half. Brush one half with butter, fold other half over and press together like a pocketbook. Put them in a well-greased pan and allow to rise again for 20 minutes. Bake in a 425° oven for 15 to 20 minutes. Brush tops with butter after baking and serve hot. Makes 24 rolls.

CLOVER LEAF ROLLS

A. Q. Chicken House
Springdale, Arkansas

2 cups lukewarm milk	2 eggs, well beaten
2 teaspoons salt	½ cup melted butter
½ cup sugar	7½ to 8 cups flour, sifted
2 cakes compressed yeast	

Mix together milk, salt and sugar. Crumble yeast into milk mixture and stir until yeast is dissolved. Stir in eggs and butter until well blended. Mix in flour, first with spoon, then with hands. Knead dough on floured board. Cover with clean cloth and let rise till doubled in bulk.

Divide dough into small balls. Place three in each greased muffin cup and let rise again until light, 15 to 20 minutes. Bake in hot, 425°, oven 15 to 20 minutes.

GRANDMOTHER STEWART'S BISCUITS

Camelback Inn
Phoenix, Arizona

2 cups flour, sifted
4 teaspoons baking powder
½ teaspoon salt
½ cup sugar

2 cups raisins
½ cup margarine or butter
½ cup heavy cream
Milk

Sift dry ingredients together. Add raisins and cut in shortening. Add cream, mix, and knead lightly on a floured board. Roll out and cut out biscuits. Paint tops of biscuits with milk and sprinkle with sugar. Bake at 425° for 10 to 15 minutes.

CREAM OF TARTAR BISCUITS

Wilsons
Moosehead, Maine

3 cups flour
1 teaspoon salt
2 teaspoons cream of
   tartar

1 teaspoon baking soda
¼ cup shortening
¾ cup milk

Sift first four ingredients together twice. Add shortening at room temperature and work into sifted mixture. Then add milk gradually. Put on floured board and knead as little as possible. Roll. Cut out biscuits and bake in hot oven, 450°, until golden brown, 8 to 10 minutes.

RISEN BISCUITS

The Wilbur Hotel
Corbin, Kentucky

2½ cups flour
½ teaspoon soda
  3 rounded tablespoons
    shortening
  1 tablespoon sugar

½ teaspoon salt
½ cake yeast, dissolved in
1 cup buttermilk at room
  temperature

Mix everything together and roll to thickness of ¼ inch on floured board. Cut with biscuit cutter. Dip in melted butter. Place one biscuit on top of the other (stacked two high). Let rise about 1½ or 2 hours. Bake at 375° for 15 minutes.

BAKING POWDER BISCUITS

Dewey's Restaurant
Lebanon, Tennessee

  2 cups sifted flour
  3 teaspoons baking powder
  1 teaspoon salt

6 tablespoons shortening
⅔ cup sweet milk

Sift flour with baking powder and salt. Cut in shortening until mixture resembles coarse crumbs. Add milk all at once and mix just until dough follows fork around bowl. Turn onto floured surface and knead gently ½ minute. Roll ½ inch thick and cut. Bake in 450° oven 10 to 12 minutes until browned.

LAMBERTVILLE HOUSE HOT BREAD

Lambertville House
Lambertville, New Jersey

1½ cups milk, scalded
½ cup water, lukewarm
½ cake yeast
  1 tablespoon salt

1 tablespoon sugar
2 tablespoons vegetable
  shortening
2 pounds flour

Crumble yeast into lukewarm milk and water. Add sugar, salt, and shortening. Stir in enough flour to make dough workable on a board; add flour in small quantities and knead until mix becomes elastic. Place in bowl in a dark draft-free place, cover with a towel and let rise until double in bulk.

Cut dough into five equal portions and shape into loaves and place in greased loaf pans. Cover again and let rise in warm place until double in bulk. Bake for 30 minutes at 375° until golden brown. This recipe will make 5 8-ounce loaves.

PENN-DAW CORNSTICKS

Penn-Daw Restaurant
Alexandria, Virginia

2 cups cornmeal
½ cup flour, sifted
1 tablespoon baking
  powder
1 cup milk
½ cup shortening
Salt to taste
1 egg

Mix flour and meal. Add remaining ingredients, adding the egg last. Mix well and whip. Turn into well-greased bread stick pans. Bake at 400° for 25 to 30 minutes.

YANKEE CORN STICKS

Publick House
Sturbridge, Massachusetts

1⅓ cups sifted flour
⅔ cup corn meal
2 teaspoons baking powder
½ teaspoon salt
3 tablespoons sugar
1 egg, well beaten
⅔ cup cream-style corn
  (canned)
1 cup milk
2 tablespoons cool melted
  shortening or salad oil

Sift together the flour, corn meal, baking powder, salt and sugar, into a large mixing bowl. Blend well the beaten egg with cream-style corn, milk and melted shortening. Add to the dry ingredients and stir just until all the flour is moistened—do not beat. Fill or pipe into well-greased, heated, corn-stick pans. Bake in a hot oven, 425°, about 20 minutes, or until golden brown. Bakes 12 corn sticks.

DAVY CROCKETT HUSH PUPPIES

Davy Crockett Restaurant
Walnut Ridge, Arkansas

2 cups corn meal	1 egg
1 tablespoon flour	3 tablespoons onion,
1 teaspoon baking powder	finely chopped
1 teaspoon salt	1 cup buttermilk

Mix all dry ingredients together. Add onion, then milk, and then the beaten egg. Form into finger-shaped patties. Drop into hot bacon fat in which fish has been or is being fried. Fry to a golden brown. Drain on paper.

BLUEBERRY MUFFINS

Craftwood Inn
Manitou Springs, Colorado

2 cups flour	1 cup milk
4 tablespoons sugar	4 tablespoons melted
4 teaspoons baking powder	shortening
½ teaspoon salt	1 cup fresh or frozen
1 egg, well beaten	blueberries, well drained

Sift dry ingredients and add blueberries. Combine egg, milk, and melted shortening, and pour into dry ingredients. Stir just enough to combine. Place in greased muffin pans and bake 20 to 25 minutes in a 400° oven.

BLUEBERRY HILL MUFFINS

Blueberry Hill Farm
Brandon, Vermont

3 tablespoons butter
½ cup sugar
½ teaspoon salt
2 eggs
1 cup sour cream

2 cups flour
1 teaspoon soda
¼ teaspoon nutmeg, grated
½ to 1 cup blueberries

Cream butter, sugar and salt with electric mixer at high speed. Beat for 3 minutes, until smooth and creamy. Make a hole in the middle of the batter and add eggs. Beat well, until thoroughly combined and a light lemon color. Add sour cream. Beat well.

In another bowl, mix with a fork flour, soda and nutmeg. Grease muffin pans. Combine wet and dry ingredients quickly. As soon as dry ingredients are thoroughly moist, stop. Fold in blueberries which have been lightly floured. Fill pans ½ full. Bake at 400° 20 to 25 minutes.

Sprinkle each muffin with ¼ teaspoon sugar, or, if you like, use cinnamon-sugar. Let cool for 2 minutes, then loosen from pans. Serve piping hot. Makes about 24 two-inch muffins.

BRAN MUFFINS

Craftwood Inn
Manitou Springs, Colorado

4 teaspoons sugar
4 tablespoons melted shortening
1 egg, slightly beaten
1 cup flour
2 teaspoons baking powder
½ teaspoon baking soda

Dash of salt
Dash of cinnamon, optional
1 cup bran
1 cup raisins
½ cup honey

Mix together sugar, shortening and egg. Sift together flour, baking powder, soda and salt, and cinnamon, if used.

Add bran and raisins. Stir bran mixture into shortening mixture, alternately with honey. Fill greased muffin tins ⅔ full. Bake at 400° 20 to 25 minutes, or until muffins are nicely browned. Makes 12 medium sized muffins.

ORANGE MUFFINS

Chateau Laurier Hotel
Ottawa, Ontario

2 cups flour
2 tablespoons sugar
2 teaspoons baking powder
1 teaspoon salt
1 egg, well beaten
1 cup milk

3 tablespoons melted butter
½ teaspoon grated orange rind
¼ cup orange juice
½ cup seedless raisins

Sift dry ingredients together. Mix remaining six ingredients together, then add to the flour mixture all at once and mix only enough to moisten the flour. Do not beat.

Pour the batter into well greased muffin tins being sure to fill only ⅔ full. Bake at 375° for 20 to 25 minutes. Makes 12 medium sized muffins.

DOROTHY'S PUMPKIN MUFFINS

Dorothy's Oven
San Diego, California

1½ cups flour
½ cup sugar
2½ teaspoons baking powder
¾ teaspoons salt
1 teaspoon cinnamon
1 teaspoon nutmeg

2 teaspoons mixed pumpkin spices
⅓ cup Mazola oil
½ cup seedless raisins
1 egg, well beaten
⅓ cup milk
½ cup pumpkin

Mix together flour, sugar, baking powder, salt and spices. Pour in raisins. Beat egg and add. Add oil, milk and pumpkin to the flour mixture, stirring only until the flour is moistened. Batter will be lumpy. Pour into greased muffin pans. Bake in 400° oven for 18 to 20 minutes. Makes 10 to 12 muffins.

HALEKULANI POPOVERS

Halekulani Hotel
Honolulu, Hawaii

4 eggs
2 cups milk
2 cups flour

½ teaspoon salt
1 ounce melted butter

Beat eggs and milk together. Fold in flour and salt that has been sifted together three times. Add butter and turn into hot, generously greased muffin tins, filling them ½ full. Bake 20 minutes in 450° oven. Reduce heat to 350° and bake 20 minutes longer. Serve at once. Makes 12 large popovers.

RUM ROLLS, SEAFARE

The Seafare
Nags Head, North Carolina

1 cup sweet milk,
  lukewarm
½ cup sugar
2 tablespoons shortening
1 teaspoon salt
1 cake compressed yeast
1 egg, well beaten

2 teaspoons rum extract
3 cups sifted flour
3 tablespoons butter or
  melted margarine
1 cup seeded raisins,
  cut fine

Pour scalded milk over ¼ of the sugar, shortening and salt. Cool to lukewarm and crumble yeast into it. Beat with rotary beater until smooth. Add egg and rum extract. Add flour gradually, beating with rotary beater. Then knead. Cover with clean towel and let rise in a warm place (80°–85°) until double in bulk. Roll dough into strips 12″ long, ½″ thick and 4″ wide. Brush top with melted butter and sprinkle with sugar and raisins. Roll up, pulling dough out at edges to keep uniform. Strips should be 15″ long when rolled. Cut rolls in crosswise slices ¾-inch thick. Place in greased muffin tins, cover with a clean towel and let rise in a warm place until double in bulk. Bake in moderately hot oven, 400° for 15 to 20 minutes, until well browned. As soon as rolls are removed from oven, cover with icing. Makes 18 rolls.

Icing for Rum Rolls

1 cup confectioners sugar   2 tablespoons rum extract
2 tablespoons hot water

Add liquids to sugar, beat with small spoon until smooth.

GOUGÈRE CLASSIQUE
(Gruyère Pastry)

Four Seasons Restaurant
New York City

1 cup water   4 eggs
½ cup butter   1 cup Gruyère cheese,
½ teaspoon salt   grated
2 cups flour   Pinch cayenne pepper

Place water, butter and salt in saucepan; bring to a boil and remove from heat. Stir in flour; mix thoroughly until dough forms ball in center of pan. Cool a few minutes.

Stir in 2 eggs, mix thoroughly, stir in 2 more eggs, mix thoroughly and set aside to cool. Add 1 cup grated Gruyère cheese (bought in bulk), pinch cayenne pepper, and mix well.

Arrange on baking sheet in ring shape (about 8 inches in diameter with a 3-inch hole in center). Bake 35 to 40 minutes at 375° or until ring becomes puffed, dry and brown. Slice to go with wine or serve alone as luncheon bread.

NISU
Finnish Coffee Bread

Bacon Farm Inn
Barnstable Village, Massachusetts

2 packages dry yeast	2 cups lukewarm milk
¼ cup water	¾ cup soft butter
1 cup sugar	15-20 cardamon seeds,
3 eggs	pounded
2 teaspoons salt	8 cups flour, sifted

Dissolve yeast in ¼ cup water. Mix sugar, eggs, salt, milk, butter, and cardamon seeds and small amount of flour; beat smooth. Add yeast and remaining flour, knead with hands until firm and smooth. Cover with clean towel and let rise in warm place until doubled in bulk, about two hours. Turn onto bread board and knead until smooth.

To shape coffee bread:

Take half the dough, divide it into three parts and cut each part into three pieces of equal size. Roll with hands into long ropes and braid. Place on buttered baking sheet, cover and let rise. Brush with slightly beaten egg. Sprinkle with sugar and chopped almonds and bake in moderate oven, 375°, 25 to 30 minutes.

BEVERAGES

MAI TAI

Halekulani Hotel
Honolulu, Hawaii

For each serving

1 small lime	2½ ounces light rum
½ teaspoon simple syrup	½ ounce dark rum
½ teaspoon Orange Curacao	Garnish of mint leaves and pineapple stick

For each serving, fill a 14-ounce glass with shaved ice. Squeeze in one small lime, and drop in half the shell. Add ½ teaspoon simple syrup, ½ teaspoon Orange Curacao and 2½ ounces light rum. Float ½ ounce dark rum on top. Garnish with sprig of mint leaves and a pineapple stick. Float a vanda orchid (optional).

CHAMPAGNE PUNCH

The Garden Seat
Clearwater, Florida

½ cup lemon juice	½ cup brandy
¼ pound powdered sugar	½ cup Curaco
½ cup Maraschino	1 fifth champagne

Mix all ingredients except the champagne. Chill well and just before serving add chilled champagne. If desired, soda may be substituted for some of the champagne. Six to eight servings.

MULLED CIDER

Stagecoach Inn
Manitou Springs, Colorado

1 quart apple cider   2 whole cloves
1 small stick cinnamon

Place cinnamon, cloves into cider and heat. Remove spices and serve piping hot.

HOT CRANBERRY PUNCH

Publick House
Sturbridge, Massachusetts

2 tablespoons whole cloves   ¼ teaspoon salt
1 tablespoon whole   4 cups pineapple juice
   allspice   (canned, unsweetened)
12 inches stick cinnamon,   2 1-pound cans (4 cups)
   broken   jellied cranberry sauce
¼ cup brown sugar   Few drops red food coloring
4 cups water   Few bits butter
                               Cinnamon sticks

Tie whole cloves and allspice in small piece of cheese-cloth. In a saucepan, combine the spice bag, cinnamon pieces, brown sugar, 1 cup water and salt. Bring slowly to a boil. Add pineapple juice and 3 cups water. Crush cranberry sauce with a fork and add. Bring to a boil again and simmer for 5 minutes; remove spices. Add a few drops of red food coloring. Pour into a heated punch bowl. Add a few bits of butter. For trim, float clove-studded orange slices, cut in half. Simmer in mugs with cinnamon as stirrers. Makes about 10 to 12 cups.

COFFEE DELIGHT

The Inn Unique
Hart's Location, New Hampshire

6 cups strong coffee
8 tablespoons minute
    tapioca
⅔ cup raisins
1 cup sugar

½ teaspoon salt
2 envelopes Drene
2 tablespoons vanilla
Whipped cream, if desired

Bring coffee, tapioca, raisins to boil. Simmer until clear, stirring constantly. Take from heat. Add sugar, salt, mix thoroughly. Let stand until cool. Then fold in two envelopes of beaten Drene, and vanilla. May be served with a dot of whipped cream, if desired.

CAFE BRULOT

Brennan's
New Orleans, Louisiana

Peel of one lemon
Peel of one orange
4 to 6 cloves
4″ stick of cinnamon

6 cubes of sugar
2 ounces curacao
4 ounces brandy
3 cups black coffee

Put small slices of the lemon and orange peel in a chafing dish. Add cloves and cinnamon stick and sugar cubes, and stir them. Then add the curacao, followed by brandy and heat. Now the mixture is ready to be flamed; ignite the brandy and then pour in the coffee slowly. Serve while hot, in demitasse cups.

COFFEE WELLINGTON

London Grill
Portland, Oregon

For each cup use:
 2 teaspoons coconut syrup
4½ ounces coffee
 1 ounce Bacardi light dry
 rum

1 tablespoon whipped
 cream flavored with
 instant coffee

We use 7 ounce Hall china cups. Put coconut syrup in bottom of the cup. Pour piping hot coffee over it, stir until coconut syrup is dissolved. Add the rum and top with whipped cream.

IRISH COFFEE

The Gourmet Restaurant
Terrace Hilton Hotel
Cincinnati, Ohio

6 teaspoons brown sugar
6 jiggers Irish whiskey
6 cups coffee—very strong,
 very hot

1½ cups whipped cream
3 teaspoons of
 Kaluah liquor

Into each of six hot goblets, put 1 teaspoon brown sugar, 1 jigger of whiskey, coffee, topped with whipped cream and a half teaspoon Kaluah liquor. Serve immediately.

DESSERTS

ANGEL PIE

Palmer Lodge
Keene, New Hampshire

Meringue

4 egg whites   1 cup sugar
¼ teaspoon cream of tartar

Beat egg whites until stiff. Sift cream of tartar and sugar together, add to egg whites, 2 tablespoons at a time, and continue beating. Be sure that all sugar is dissolved. Grease 9-inch pie plate and pour meringue mixture into it. Spread meringue higher on the sides. Preheat oven to 300° and bake 1 hour.

Filling

4 egg yolks   1 teaspoon each lemon and
½ cup sugar   orange rind
4 tablespoons orange juice   1 cup heavy cream,
2 tablespoons lemon juice   whipped

Beat egg yolks, add sugar, orange and lemon juice, and the grated rinds. Cook in double boiler for 9 minutes. When cold, put in center of cold meringue shell. Let stand in refrigerator 24 hours. Serve with whipped cream.

APPLE PIE

Chowning's Tavern
Williamsburg, Virginia

1¼ to 1½ cups sugar,
  to taste
⅛ teaspoon salt
¾ teaspoon cinnamon
½ teaspoon nutmeg

Pie crust for a double
  crust pie
6 to 8 apples, peeled and
  sliced
2 tablespoons lemon juice
½ teaspoon lemon rind

1 heaping tablespoon butter

Mix sugar, salt, cinnamon, nutmeg and flour together. Line a pie pan with your pastry. Place sliced apples in the pan, lining them in a row around the pan and working toward the center until the pan is covered—continue until the pan is filled. Sprinkle the sugar mixture over the apples and follow this with the lemon juice and rind. If the apples are very tart, omit the lemon juice. Dot with butter. Wet the edge of the under crust. Put on the top crust. Trim to ½ inch larger than pie pan and press the edges together. Bake at 500° for 6 to 8 minutes. Reduce oven to 350° and cook until the apples are soft (about 1 hour).

Note: Cinnamon and nutmeg may be increased or decreased according to taste.

APPLE NUT PIE

Hickory Stick Farm
Laconia, New Hampshire

¼ cup shortening
1 cup sugar
1 egg
1 cup flour
1 teaspoon soda

½ teaspoon nutmeg
½ teaspoon cinnamon
1 teaspoon vanilla
3 cups sliced apples
½ cup chopped nuts

Cream together shortening, sugar and egg. Add remaining ingredients. Mix all together well. Spread into greased 9-inch pie pan. Bake in 350° oven for 45 minutes.

FRESH APPLE PIE WITH HOT RUM SAUCE

Santa Maria Inn
Santa Maria, California

4 or 5 tart apples, peeled
and cored and cut into
eighths
1 cup sugar
¼ teaspoon grated nutmeg

Pinch salt
1 teaspoon lemon juice
Few gratings lemon rind
2 teaspoons butter

Line pie plate with pie crust, put row of apples around plate ½ inch from edge, and work toward center until plate is covered. Then pile on remainder.

Mix sugar, nutmeg, salt, lemon juice and grated rind and sprinkle over apples. Dot with pieces of butter.

Wet edges, cover with upper crust, and press edges together. Bake 10 minutes at 400°; reduce to 350° and bake 45 to 50 minutes until done. Serve with Hot Rum Sauce.

Hot Rum Sauce

¼ cup rum
1 cup boiling water

¼ cup rum

Make a syrup by boiling sugar and water for 5 to 10 minutes. Then add the rum. Serve hot.

BRAY-WOOD APPLE PIE

Bray-Wood Resort
Eagle River, Wisconsin

Make pie crusts with pure
lard
1 can comstock apples
¼ can water
1¾ cup sugar
Pinch salt
½ teaspoon cinnamon

¼ cup brown sugar
2 tablespoons flour
3 tablespoons butter,
cut in pieces
¼ cup melted butter
¼ cup granulated sugar

Mix apples with water, sugar, salt, cinnamon, brown sugar and flour. Place in uncooked 9-inch pie shell. Dot with butter. Then put on top pie crust and spread with melted butter and sugar on top. Bake 1 hour in 425° oven.

APRICOT PIE

Vick's Restaurant
Dallas, Texas

1 can apricots, halves or sliced
½ cup sugar

2 tablespoons corn starch
2 9-inch pie crusts

Mix sugar and corn starch together, add apricots and juice. Pour into pie plate lined with crust. Have another crust ready for topping. Bake in 400° oven 30 to 40 minutes until brown, and juice begins to bubble.

BLUEBERRY CHIFFON PIE

The Yardarm
Searsport, Maine

1 envelope gelatin
¼ cup cold water
½ cup sugar
¼ teaspoon salt
1⅓ teaspoons lemon rind, grated
¼ cup lemon juice

2 large eggs, separated
2 tablespoons sherry
1 8-inch baked pie shell
1 cup blueberries, frozen or fresh
¾ cup heavy cream, whipped

Soften gelatin in cold water. Mix sugar, salt, grated lemon rind and lemon juice in a saucepan. Add beaten egg yolks and cook over low heat, stirring constantly, until thickened.

Add softened gelatin and sherry. Chill until consistency of unbeaten egg whites.

Beat egg whites with ¼ cup sugar until stiff. Fold gelatin mixture into meringue.

Fold in blueberries, and pile into 9-inch baked pie shell. Scatter a few blueberries on top. Chill.

Garnish with whipped cream.

BOSTON CREAM PIE

Publick House
Sturbridge, Massachusetts

1 cup sifted cake flour	1 teaspoon grated lemon
1 cup sugar	peel
5 eggs, separated	1 tablespoon lemon juice
½ teaspoon salt	Pastry cream
	Chocolate glaze

Have all ingredients at room temperature. Add 4 tablespoons out of the cup of sugar to sifted cake flour and sift them together 4 times. Beat egg whites until foamy. Add ½ teaspoon salt and beat until the egg whites stand in peaks but are not dry. Beat in the remaining ¾ cup of sugar, 2 tablespoons at a time. With the same beater beat the yolks until very thick and lemon colored. Beat in grated lemon peel and lemon juice. Cut and fold the whites into the yolks. Sift about ¼ of the flour and sugar mixture over the top and gently fold it in. Repeat until all the flour and sugar mixture is blended in. Place carefully in two paper-lined 8-inch round cake pans and tap on the table once to break any large air bubbles. Bake in moderate oven (350°) about 25 minutes or until done. Cool in pans. Sandwich cake with Pastry Cream, top with Chocolate Glaze or sifted confectioners' sugar. (If layers slide, anchor with a few toothpicks.)

Pastry Cream

1½ cups milk	4 egg yolks
Vanilla bean—1-inch piece	¼ cup flour
½ cup sugar	

Scald milk with vanilla bean. Mix sugar and egg yolks until creamy and lemon colored. Add flour and gradually add scalded milk, stirring continuously. Cook mixture, stirring vigorously, until it reaches the boiling point. Remove vanilla bean. Strain and cool.

Chocolate Glaze

2 tablespoons shortening
2 squares chocolate

1 cup confectioner's
  sugar, sifted
2 tablespoons boiling water

Melt shortening and chocolate together. Stir in sugar and water and beat until smooth.

BLACKBOTTOM PIE

Pirate's House
Savannah, Georgia

Crust

1¼ cups chocolate cracker
  crumbs
4 tablespoons melted butter

Mix together until well blended and press into pie pan. Set aside in refrigerator to chill.

Filling

1¼ tablespoon plain gelatin
¼ cup cold water
2 cups milk
¾ cup sugar
1¼ tablespoon cornstarch
4 eggs (separated)
1½ squares bitter chocolate,
  melted

1 teaspoon vanilla
4 teaspoons rum
1 cup heavy cream,
  whipped
½ ounce shaved sweet
  chocolate

Soak gelatin in cold water. Set aside. Put milk in double boiler—combine ½ cup sugar and cornstarch, add to milk. Beat egg yolks, add to custard. Stir until custard coats spoon. Add chocolate and vanilla to one cup of custard and put into chocolate crust. Add gelatin to remaining custard and let cool. Add rum. Beat egg whites, adding 4 tablespoons of sugar slowly. When egg whites stand in peaks (not dry) fold into custard. Pour over chocolate custard. Chill about 3 hours. Decorate with whipped cream and shaved chocolate.

CHERRY PIE

Stagecoach Inn
Manitou Springs, Colorado

2½ cups fresh cherries,
  pitted
1 tablespoon flour
1½ cups sugar

2 rich pastry pie crusts
  (see below)
1⅓ tablespoons butter

Mix flour and sugar, then stir into cherries. Pour into pastry shell, dot with butter, and cover with pastry top. Bake in 350° oven for 45 minutes.

Rich Pastry Pie Crust

2½ cups sifted flour
1 teaspoon salt

¾ cup shortening
¼ cup water

Mix flour and salt. Cut shortening into it until pieces are size of a bean. Mix well with water until dough comes together and can be shaped into a ball. Divide into 2 parts and roll out crusts. Makes two 9-inch pie crusts.

CHOCOLATE PIE

The Coffee Pot
Luverne, Alabama

3 egg yolks
1 cup sugar
2 squares bittersweet
  chocolate, melted

1 pint milk
2 tablespoons cornstarch
2 tablespoons butter
9 inch pie shell, baked

Combine first six ingredients and cool in double boiler until mixture thickens. Cool and pour into pie shell. Cover with meringue.

Meringue

3 egg whites
3 tablespoons sugar

Pinch salt
1 teaspoon vanilla.

Have egg whites at room temperature. Beat until stiff, add sugar gradually, beating all the time, add salt and vanilla. Pour over chocolate filling and bake in 225° oven until meringue is brown, about 10 to 15 minutes.

CHOCOLATE PIE

The Pirate's House
Savannah, Georgia

1 baked pie shell
2 cups milk
2 squares chocolate, cut up

¾ cup sugar
3 eggs, separated
3 tablespoons cornstarch
1 teaspoon vanilla

Scald milk over low heat and add chocolate.

Mix sugar and cornstarch with egg yolks. Blend well. Add to milk and chocolate mixture and cook in double boiler until thick. Add vanilla. Pour into pie shell. Beat egg whites, adding 3 tablespoons sugar gradually. Cover pie with meringue. Bake for about 15 minutes in 350° oven.

CHOCOLATE CREAM PIE

Hotel Severin
Indianapolis, Indiana

2½ cups milk
¼ cup cornstarch
⅓ cup sugar
Pinch salt
4 egg yolks, beaten

¼ cup white corn syrup
2 squares chocolate, grated
1 teaspoon vanilla
1 baked 9-inch pie shell

Scald milk. Mix cornstarch, sugar, salt. Add egg yolks and corn syrup. Add hot milk slowly. Cook over medium heat, stirring constantly until thick. Add grated chocolate. Cool and add vanilla. Pour into baked 9-inch pie shell. Top with meringue.

Meringue

4 egg whites	1 teaspoon vanilla
¼ cup sugar	Chocolate sprinkles

Beat egg whites; add sugar gradually and vanilla. Spread on pie. Top with chocolate sprinkles. Brown in 375° oven 8 to 10 minutes.

CHOCOLATE CREAM PIE

Berry's On-the-Hill
Orangeburg, South Carolina

2 egg whites	¼ pound semi-sweet chocolate
⅛ teaspoon cream of tartar	1½ tablespoons powdered sugar
½ cup sugar	2 cups whipping cream, whipped
½ cup pecans, chopped	
1½ teaspoons vanilla	

Beat egg whites until foamy, add salt and cream of tartar. Beat until mixture stands in soft peaks. Add sugar gradually, beat until very stiff. Fold in chopped pecans and ½ teaspoon vanilla. Turn into lightly greased 8-inch pie plate. Make a nest-like shell, building up sides above edge of plate. Bake in 300° oven for 35 minutes. Cool.

Melt chocolate in double boiler; add 1½ tablespoons powdered sugar with 3 tablespoons hot water, blend. Cool. Add 1 teaspoon vanilla. Fold in half of whipped cream. Turn into meringue shell, chill. When ready to serve, cover top with rest of whipped cream. Serves 6.

CHOCOLATE CRISP PIE

The Yardarm
Searsport, Maine

3 eggs
1½ cups sugar
⅓ cup butter
2 squares baking chocolate

½ cup English walnuts or
pecans, broken into
pieces
¾ teaspoon vanilla
1 cup heavy cream,
whipped

Beat eggs, add sugar and blend well. Melt butter and chocolate together. Add to egg mixture with nuts and vanilla. Mix well. Pour into unbaked 8″ pieshell. Bake at 350° for 30 minutes. Serve with whipped cream.

HOTEL ROANOKE CHOCOLATE ICE CREAM PIE

Hotel Roanoke
Roanoke, Virginia

1¼ cup graham cracker
crumbs
3 tablespoons sugar
⅓ cup butter, melted
1 teaspoon cinnamon
1 quart chocolate
ice cream

½ pint heavy cream,
whipped
3 egg whites, beaten
½ cup sugar
Chocolate syrup

Blend cracker crumbs, sugar, butter and cinnamon thoroughly and place in bottom and on side of 9-inch pie plate. Refrigerate for 30 minutes.

Put softened chocolate ice cream in pie shell and place in freezer for 3 hours. Top this pie with whipped cream. Make meringue of egg whites and sugar, adding sugar gradually to beaten whites. Put meringue on top of pie with fluted tube and pastry bag. Place pie in very hot oven until meringue browns, approximately 1 minute. Return to freezer until ready to serve. Serve each slice with chocolate syrup.

COCONUT PIE

The Pirate's House
Savannah, Georgia

½ cup + 3 tablespoons   Pinch salt
    sugar   2 cups milk
3 tablespoons cornstarch   1 teaspoon vanilla
3 eggs, separated   1 cup coconut
    1 baked 8-inch pie shell

Mix sugar, cornstarch and egg yolks and salt. Add mixture
to milk. Heat, stirring continuously, until custard coats spoon.
Add vanilla and coconut and pour into baked pie shell. Beat
egg whites. Add 3 tablespoons sugar gradually. Top the pie
with egg white mixture and sprinkle with about ¼ cup coconut. Brown in 325° oven for about 15 minutes.

WILLOWS COCONUT CREAM PIE

The Willows
Honolulu, Hawaii

2 cups milk   ¼ cup fresh grated
½ cup sugar   coconut
Pinch salt   1 tablespoon butter
2 tablespoons cornstarch   Vanilla to flavor
4 eggs, separated   8-inch pie shell, baked

Combine milk, sugar and salt in sauce pan; let come to near
boil then stir in cornstarch and egg yolks. Let cook for a few
minutes, add grated coconut, butter and vanilla. Cool and fill
in pie shell. Top with meringue 4 inches high (see recipe
below) and put in oven to brown.

Meringue   ½ cup sugar
4 egg whites   ½ teaspoon cream of tartar

Beat well, spread over pie, being sure to cover all edges.

CREAM CHEESE PIE

The Pirate's House
Savannah, Georgia

Filling

2 eggs	12 ounces cream cheese
½ cup sugar	1 teaspoon milk
	¼ teaspoon vanilla

Use high speed on mixer and beat eggs for five minutes, adding sugar gradually. Divide cheese into two parts. Turn mixer to low speed and add part of cheese. Blend before remaining cheese is added. When well blended add milk and vanilla. Pour into 9-inch graham cracker pie shell and cook at 375° for 15 minutes. Allow to cool.

Pie Shell

1½ cups ground graham crackers	6 tablespoons sugar
	1 tablespoon cinnamon
	½ cup melted butter

Mix all ingredients well. Pat into bottom and sides of 9-inch pie tin and chill in refrigerator for 30 minutes before filling.

Topping

¾ cup sugar	¼ teaspoon vanilla
	1 cup sour cream

While pie is baking, blend sugar, vanilla and sour cream. Set in refrigerator. When pie is cool, top with sour cream mixture and return to oven for five minutes. Let set in refrigerator at least 8 to 10 hours before serving. Pie is also good when topped with strawberries or pineapple.

DUTCH APPLE CHEESE PIE

Water Gate Inn
Washington, D. C.

2 pounds apples, peeled
  and sliced
¾ cup sugar
¼ teaspoon nutmeg
¼ teaspoon cinnamon

⅛ teaspoon salt
1/6 cup butter
¼ cup cornstarch
¼ pound American cheese,
  grated

Cook the apples, sugar, spices, salt and butter until the apples are done. Add cornstarch and continue cooking until mixture thickens. Allow to cool and then fold in grated or shredded American cheese. Pour into unbaked 9-inch pie shell.

¼ pound brown sugar

¼ cup flour
2 tablespoons butter.

Mix the three ingredients and sprinkle over pie. Bake at 450° for about 45 minutes, or until top is dark brown and crust is done.

FLORIDA ORANGE GROVE PIE

The Tides Hotel
St. Petersburg, Florida

Meringue

4 egg whites
¼ teaspoon cream
  of tartar

1½ cups sugar
Walnuts, finely chopped

Heat oven to 275°. Beat egg whites until foamy, add cream of tartar and beat to stiff peaks. Gradually add sugar and continue beating to very stiff peaks. Spread just to the edge of a 9-inch pie plate which has been thoroughly greased. Sprinkle edge with finely chopped walnuts. Bake 1 hour. Cool.

Filling

4 egg yolks	⅛ teaspoon salt
½ cup sugar	2 Florida oranges, cut
2 tablespoons lemon juice	into small pieces
3 tablespoons orange rind, grated	1 cup heavy cream, whipped

Beat yolks slightly, add sugar, lemon juice, orange rind and salt. Cook over boiling water, stirring constantly until thick, about 10 minutes. Fold in oranges. Cool and fold in whipped cream. Pour into center of meringue. Chill 6 hours or longer in refrigerator.

GOLDEN LAMB BLACK BOTTOM PIE

*The Golden Lamb
Lebanon, Ohio*

Crust

1½ cups graham cracker crumbs	¼ cup sugar
6 tablespoons melted butter	½ teaspoon salt
	½ teaspoon plain gelatin (do not dissolve)

Mix all ingredients together. Press into a pie pan and chill.

Filling

4 eggs, separated	4 tablespoons cold water
1½ cups milk, scalded	¼ teaspoon cream of tartar
1½ tablespoons cornstarch	Rum, to taste
1 cup sugar	1 cup heavy cream, whipped
¼ teaspoon salt	½ square chocolate (thin shavings)
1½ squares unsweetened chocolate	
1 teaspoon vanilla	
1 tablespoon gelatin	

Slowly add beaten egg yolks to scalded milk. Mix together cornstarch, ½ cup sugar and ¼ teaspoon salt. Stir into egg mixture and beat to blend thoroughly. Cook in double boiler for 20 minutes until thick as custard. Remove from fire and take out 1 cup of mixture.

Add chocolate to the cup of custard and beat well. As custard cools add vanilla. Pour into crust and chill.

Blend thoroughly gelatin with cold water and add to remaining hot custard. Let cool but not thicken. Beat egg whites, gradually adding ½ cup of sugar mixed with cream of tartar, to make a meringue. Fold this into custard.

As soon as chocolate custard is set add rum to the second mixture and pour over chocolate. Chill until it is set. Spread whipped cream over top of pie and shave chocolate over pie.

FROZEN LEMON PIE WITH GRAHAM CRACKER CRUST

Nelson House
Poughkeepsie, New York

Graham Cracker Crust

½ cup butter   1½ cups graham crackers
¼ cup sugar   (ground)

Grind crumbs, combine with sugar. Add melted butter and blend well. With back of spoon, press mixture into the bottom and sides of a 9-inch pie tin. Chill well before adding filling.

Lemon Pie Filling

1 cup sugar   1 cup heavy cream,
⅛ teaspoon salt   whipped
Grated rind of ½ lemon   ⅓ cup (about 3) egg
⅓ cup fresh lemon juice   whites
2 egg yolks, well beaten

Combine sugar, salt, lemon rind, lemon juice and well beaten egg yolks. Cook over hot water until mixture is thick enough to hold its shape. Stir frequently while cooking. Remove from heat and thoroughly chill in pan of ice. Whip cream. Beat egg whites and fold into whipped cream. When lemon mixture is thoroughly chilled, fold in whipped cream mixture. Pour into graham cracker crust. Freeze and serve in frozen state.

SHADY NOOK LEMON PIE

Shady Nook Inn
Salmon, Idaho

Filling

1 cup sugar
1½ cups water
¼ teaspoon salt
3 tablespoons cornstarch
2 tablespoons flour, mixed
   with ⅓ cup water for
   paste

3 egg yolks (save the
   whites)
Juice of 1½ lemons
Grated rind of 1 lemon
1 tablespoon butter

Bring sugar, water and salt to rolling boil. Add cornstarch and flour paste. Stir until clear and smooth. Then add beaten egg yolks, lemon juice, grated rind and butter. Cook, stirring constantly, for 2 minutes. Cool. Pour into baked pie shell and top with meringue.

Pie Crust

½ cup shortening
1½ cups sifted flour

½ teaspoon salt
4 tablespoons ice water

Cut shortening into sifted flour and salt. Add ice water. Roll out on floured board. Line a 9-inch pie pan. Prick edges with fork. Bake at 450° for 15 minutes. Cool before filling.

Meringue

3 egg whites
Pinch salt

¼ teaspoon cream of tartar
6 tablespoons sugar

Beat egg whites with pinch salt until frothy. Add cream of tartar, beat until stiff. Add sugar gradually, ½ teaspoon at a time, beating all the while, till meringue holds its peaks. Spread over lemon filling. Be sure that meringue covers edges of pie crust (otherwise it pulls away when baking). Place in very hot oven ,450° for 2 or 3 minutes.

LEMON CHESS PIE

The Seafare
Nags Head, North Carolina

2 cups sugar
1 tablespoon water-ground white or yellow cornmeal
1 tablespoon flour
⅛ teaspoon salt
¼ cup melted butter

¼ cup milk
Grated rind of 2 lemons
Juice of 2 lemons
4 eggs
1 9-inch unbaked pie shell

Mix sugar, cornmeal, flour and salt in a fair-sized bowl. Mix melted butter and milk; add to sugar-cornmeal mixture. Add grated lemon rind, and when you perform this grating operation do it with the delicate touch so that you don't get any of the white part of the lemon skin. Add lemon juice. Add eggs, beat for a minute, and pour into an unbaked pie shell.* Bake at 350° for 40 minutes. The center should be just barely firm.

*Before filling, run the unbaked shell under the red-hot broiler for 1 minute. This will do wonders for the crust.

MACAROON PIE

Chez Bruchez
Daytona Beach, Florida

12 soda crackers, rolled fine
1 cup sugar
¼ teaspoon baking powder
3 egg whites, beaten stiff but not dry

12 dates, chopped fine
¼ cup pecans, chopped
1 teaspoon almond extract
½ cup heavy cream, whipped

Mix cracker crumbs, sugar and baking powder together. Fold egg whites into dry mixture. Add dates, pecans and flavoring. Pour into a well buttered 9-inch pie plate. Bake 30 minutes in 300° oven. Serve with whipped cream.

MACAROON PIE

Crystal Room
Pick-Fort Hayes Hotel
Columbus, Ohio

8 soda crackers, rolled fine
1 teaspoon baking powder
4 egg whites, beaten stiff

1 cup sugar
1 teaspoon vanilla
1 cup pecans, ground

To fine-rolled crackers, add baking powder, mix well. Beat egg whites stiff; fold in sugar gradually. Add vanilla. Add crackers to egg whites, then pecans. Put in 6 individual pie pans and bake at 325° for 40 minutes to 1 hour.

MAPLE BUTTERNUT PIE

The Little House and Pantry
Northfield, Vermont

¾ cup maple syrup
3 egg yolks, beaten
½ teaspoon salt
2 teaspoons gelatin
¼ cup cold water
3 egg whites, beaten

3 tablespoons sugar
½ cup heavy cream, whipped
½ cup butternut meats
1 baked pie shell

Heat maple syrup in double boiler, add egg yolks and return to double boiler; cook until mixture thickens. Add salt. Soak gelatin in cold water 5 minutes. Set it over hot water until it dissolves. Beat whites, add sugar gradually and beat until stiff but not dry. Fold in whipped cream. When first mixture begins to set, fold in cream and egg white mixture. Pour into baked pie shell and arrange butternut meats on top. Keep refrigerated. (If you do not live in butternut country, pecans may be used.)

CHATEAU MAPLE SYRUP PIE

Chateau Laurier Hotel
Ottawa, Ontario

2 tablespoons flour
1 tablespoon butter
2 egg yolks, beaten well
1 cup maple syrup
½ cup water

1 baked pie crust
½ cup heavy cream,
   whipped
Maple sugar shavings

Cream flour and butter; add beaten egg yolks and mix well. Add the maple syrup and water. Cook in double boiler until mixture begins to thicken. Pour into baked pie crust and allow to set. Top with whipped cream and sprinkle with maple sugar shavings.

MOLASSES-COCONUT PIE

Moselem Springs Inn
Moselem Springs, Penna.

¼ cup butter
9 tablespoons sugar
3 eggs, well beaten
½ cup molasses

¼ cup water
1 cup coconut, grated
1 unbaked 9-inch pie shell

Melt butter. Add remaining ingredients. Pour into unbaked shell and bake at 375° until center is set.

FRENCH MINT PIE

Craftwood Inn
Manitou Springs, Colorado

1½ squares unsweetened
   chocolate
1 cup powdered sugar
1 tablespoon butter

2 eggs, unbeaten
¼ teaspoon mint flavor
Graham cracker pie crust

Dissolve chocolate over hot water and let cool. Beat sugar and butter until smooth, add eggs one at a time. Beat until smooth; add chocolate, then mint. Spread into 9-inch pie tin lined with graham cracker crust. Place in refrigerator and chill for several hours.

OLD FASHIONED APPLE PIE

Durgin-Park
Boston, Massachusetts

6 large apples, peeled and finely sliced
1 cup sugar
⅛ teaspoon salt
⅛ teaspoon nutmeg (to taste)
¼ teaspoon cinnamon (to taste)
3 tablespoons butter
Juice of ½ lemon

Make your pie dough the way you usually do and line large pie plate. Peel and slice apples. Fill pie plate half full of apple slices. Put ½ cup of sugar, salt, a little nutmeg and cinnamon on top. Now add the rest of the apples, filling up pie plate roundfull. Add more cinnamon and nutmeg, another ½ cup of sugar, a large piece of butter cut in small pieces. Pour on a little lemon juice. Cover with pricked pie dough. Bake the pie 10 minutes in 450° oven; then reduce heat to 350° and bake 1 hour in all.

OLD SOUTH SUGAR PIE

Wilsons
Moosehead, Maine

1 unbaked 9″ pie shell
3 eggs
3 cups light brown sugar
½ cup milk
½ teaspoon salt
1 teaspoon vanilla
½ cup melted butter
½ cup pecans, cut up (optional)

Beat eggs, add brown sugar, milk, salt, vanilla and melted butter. Blend well. Pour in pastry lined pan. Bake in 450° oven for 10 minutes, reduce heat to 325° for 25 minutes. Add pecans before baking, if desired.

RHUBARB PIE

Parkway Restaurant
Waukegan, Illinois

9-inch unbaked pie shell	Salt
1½ cups sugar	⅛ teaspoon nutmeg
2 tablespoons flour	4 or 5 cups diced rhubarb
2 tablespoons tapioca	2 eggs, well beaten
	Butter

Blend sugar, flour, tapioca, salt and nutmeg together and add to diced rhubarb. Stir in eggs. Pour into pie shell. Dot with butter. Add lattice strips of crust. Bake the pie in 450° oven for 10 minutes. Reduce the heat to 350° and bake about 35 to 45 minutes.

RITZ CRACKER PIE

Mountain View Hotel
Gatlinburg, Tennessee

20 Ritz crackers	3 egg whites
¾ cup pecan meats, cut up	1 cup sugar
	½ pint heavy cream, whipped

Crush crackers fine, add ½ cup sugar and nuts, mix well. Beat egg whites stiff, add ½ cup sugar, then mix all ingredients. Bake in buttered pan or baking dish for 50 minutes at 300°. Cool. Cover with whipped cream and leave in refrigerator at least 6 hours or longer. Cut in squares or pie wedges.

RUM CHIFFON PIE

The Glockenspiel
Fleetwood, Pennsylvania

2 tablespoons gelatin
½ cup cold water
6 tablespoons sugar
½ teaspoon salt
½ cup milk
2 eggs, separated
3 tablespoons rum extract
1 teaspoon vanilla

1 cup heavy cream, whipped
¼ teaspoon cream of tartar
6 tablespoons sugar
Garnish of whipped cream, nuts, nutmeg
Graham cracker pie shell

Dissolve gelatin in cold water and set aside. Add sugar and salt to milk and heat slowly, stirring often. Lightly beat two egg yolks, then add a small amount of the heated milk. Stir the egg yolks into the milk mixture, then add gelatin and stir until it is dissolved. Chill until partially set. Beat until smooth; add rum extract and vanilla. Fold in whipped cream. Beat 2 egg whites with cream of tartar. Gradually add 6 tablespoons sugar. Fold meringue into egg yolk mixture. Pour into pie shell. Chill until firm. Garnish with whipped cream, chopped nuts and a sprinkle of nutmeg.

RUM CREAM PIE

Chez Bruchez
Daytona Beach, Florida

3 egg yolks
½ cup sugar
1½ teaspoons gelatin
¼ cup water
1 cup heavy cream, whipped

¼ cup rum
Bitter-sweet chocolate, grated
1 Graham cracker pie crust

Beat egg yolks and sugar until light. Dissolve gelatin in water, stirring until dissolved. Add to egg mixture, beating briskly. Let cool. Add cream whipped stiff and rum. Pour into graham cracker crust. Place in refrigerator to set. Grate bitter-sweet chocolate on top before serving.

SHERRY CHIFFON PIE

The Garden Seat
Clearwater, Florida

1 baked 9-inch pie shell
4 whole eggs
½ cup sugar
½ teaspoon salt
½ cup sherry
1 teaspoon lemon rind, grated

1 tablespoon unflavored gelatin
¼ cup water
4 egg whites
½ cup sugar
½ cup heavy cream, whipped

Beat whole eggs in a double boiler; add ½ cup sugar, salt, sherry and lemon rind. Cook and stir until thick.

Soften gelatin in water and add to above mixture. Place pan in a bowl of cracked ice and chill until mixture starts to set. Beat 4 egg whites until stiff, add ½ cup sugar gradually and fold into mixture. Fold in whipped cream and pour mixture into pie shell. Chill well, garnish with chopped maraschino cherries and serve.

SOUR CREAM RAISIN PIE

Arizona Inn
Tucson, Arizona

1 cup raisins
½ cup cold water
4 tablespoons brown sugar
⅔ cup granulated sugar
2 tablespoons light Karo syrup
¼ teaspoon salt
¼ teaspoon cinnamon
2 tablespoons cornstarch

4 tablespoons water
1 tablespoon lemon juice
1 tablespoon butter
1 cup sour cream
3 tablespoons powdered sugar
Vanilla flavoring to taste
1 unbaked pie shell

Prepare pie shell as for custard pie. In a saucepan, mix raisins, water, sugars, syrup, salt and cinnamon, bring to boil and simmer for 40 minutes. Thicken with cornstarch mixed with water; add lemon juice and butter. Let cool. Fill pie shell with the cold raisin mixture, and bake at 450° for 25 minutes. Let cool, then top pie with sour cream, sprinkled over with powdered sugar and vanilla. Put back in oven for 5 minutes at 500°.

PEACH PRALINE PIE

The Eagles Nest
Verona, Wisconsin

4 cups peaches, peeled
    and sliced
½ cup sugar
2 tablespoons quick
    cooking tapioca
1 teaspoon lemon juice

½ cup flour, sifted
¼ cup brown sugar
½ cup pecans, chopped
¼ cup butter
9-inch pie shell, unbaked

Combine peaches, sugar, tapioca, and lemon juice in large bowl. Let stand 15 minutes. Combine flour, brown sugar and pecans in small bowl, cut in butter until crumbly. Sprinkle ⅓ over pastry shell. Cover with peach mixture, sprinkle remaining pecan mixture over peaches. Bake at 450° for 10 minutes, then reduce to 350° and continue baking for 20 minutes or until peaches are tender and topping is brown.

PECAN PIE

King's Arms Tavern
Williamsburg, Virginia

3 eggs, well beaten
⅔ cup sugar
Vanilla to taste
2 tablespoons butter,
    melted
1 cup corn syrup (dark)

½ cup Vermont maple
    syrup
1 cup pecans, broken into
    pieces
Pastry for 9″ pie

Beat eggs and sugar together. Add vanilla to butter and then add to egg-sugar mixture. Add syrups and pour over pecans. Fill pastry shell and bake at 350° for 40 to 45 minutes, or until filling is set.

PEANUT PIE

Blanchard's Restaurant
Lumberton, North Carolina

20 Ritz crackers, rolled out fine
½ cup sugar
¾ cup roasted peanuts, chopped
3 egg whites, beaten stiff

¼ teaspoon cream of tartar
½ cup sugar
1 teaspoon vanilla
½ cup heavy cream, whipped
Bitter chocolate, grated

Roll crackers out fine and mix with sugar and chopped peanuts. Beat egg whites stiff, add and beat in cream of tartar, sugar and vanilla. Fold cracker mixture into egg white mixture. Bake in pie tin for 20 minutes at 350°. Let cool. Top with whipped cream and grated bitter chocolate. Refrigerate 3 to 4 hours before serving.

STRAWBERRY PIE

The Golden Lamb
Lebanon, Ohio

1 quart cleaned strawberries
1 cup sugar
4 tablespoons cornstarch

1 9-inch baked pastry shell, or 9-inch graham cracker crust
½ cup heavy cream, whipped

Take one half of the strawberries and mash. Cook until thick with sugar and cornstarch. Cool and then add the rest of the strawberries. Put mixture in crust and top with whipped cream.

STRAWBERRY ICE CREAM PIE

*The Homestead Inn
Lake Placid, New York*

16 marshmallows
2 tablespoons crushed
  strawberries
Red food coloring
2 egg whites
¼ cup sugar

¼ teaspoon salt
1 9-inch baked pastry shell
1 quart vanilla ice cream
1 cup fresh strawberries,
  sliced

Heat marshmallows with crushed strawberries, folding over and over until marshmallows are half melted. Remove from heat and continue folding until mixture is smooth and spongy. Add a few drops of red food coloring and cool. Beat egg whites until nearly stiff, then beat in sugar slowly. Add salt. Fold into cooled marshmallow mixture. Place vanilla ice cream in a 9-inch baked pastry shell or graham cracker crust. Cover with fresh, sliced strawberries. Top with marshmallow meringue. Brown quickly under broiler for 30 seconds.

STRAWBERRY CHIFFON PIE

*Wisconsinaire
Hazelhurst, Wisconsin*

1 box strawberry gelatin
  (3 ounces)
⅔ cup boiling water
⅛ teaspoon salt
2 tablespoons lemon juice

1 box frozen sliced
  strawberries, thawed
  (10 ounces)
3 egg whites
⅓ cup sugar
Ladyfinger or graham
  cracker crust

Dissolve gelatin in boiling water. Add salt, lemon juice and strawberries. Chill until thickened but not firm. Beat egg whites until foamy, gradually adding sugar, and beat until stiff but not dry. Fold into gelatin. Pile in crust. Chill until firm.

FRENCH STRAWBERRY PIE

*Century Inn
Scenery Hill, Pennsylvania*

1 3-ounce package
 Philadelphia cream
 cheese
½ cup powdered sugar
1 teaspoon vanilla
2 cups heavy cream,
 whipped
1 baked 9-inch pastry
 shell

1 quart fresh
 strawberries,
 washed and stemmed
¾ cup granulated sugar
2 tablespoons cornstarch
½ cup water
Few drops red food coloring

Combine cream cheese, powdered sugar and vanilla. Beat until blended. Whip cream and fold into mixture. Spread on the bottom of the pastry shell. Cover with half of the fresh strawberries. Cut remaining berries in half.

Combine sugar and cornstarch. Add water, stirring until well blended. Add remaining strawberries and cook until thickened, stirring constantly. Add red food coloring; mix well. Pour immediately over the strawberries in the pastry shell. Chill. Decorate with whipped cream and fresh strawberries.

GLAZED STRAWBERRY PIE

*The Thomas Jefferson Inn
Charlottesville, Virginia*

1 quart ripe, firm
 strawberries
Transparent glaze
 (see recipe below)

1 cup heavy cream,
 whipped
10-inch pie shell, baked

Brush a thin coating of hot glaze over the bottom of the pie shell. Arrange strawberries in the shell and brush only enough glaze on berries to cover their exposed surface. When the pie has cooled, border or strip with whipped cream.

Transparent Glaze

1 cup sugar
⅔ cup water
2⅔ teaspoons glucose or
white corn syrup

Red food coloring
2⅔ tablespoons tapioca
flour

Bring sugar, water, glucose or corn syrup and food coloring to a boil. Hold out enough water to dissolve tapioca flour. When sugar mixture has come to full boil, add the dissolved flour, stirring constantly until thick. Let this mixture return to a full boil. It is best to use the glaze while hot.

STRAWBERRY-BANANA PIE

The Ranchhouse Restaurant
Estes Park, Colorado

2 pints frozen strawberries,
thawed
1 cup sugar
3 tablespoons cornstarch
2 teaspoons lemon juice

2 large bananas
½ cup heavy cream,
whipped
1 9-inch baked pie crust

Strain the juice from strawberries and bring juice to a rolling boil. Dissolve cornstarch in cold water and add cornstarch, sugar and lemon juice to the boiling strawberry juice. Let boil until it thickens. Pour the thickened juice over the strawberries. Slice the bananas in a pie crust and put the strawberry mixture over them. When cool top with whipped cream.

SHOO-FLY PIE

Haag's Hotel
Shartlesville, Pennsylvania

1¼ cups flour
½ cup light brown sugar
½ cup butter
¼ teaspoon salt
1 teaspoon cinnamon,
(optional)

¾ cup molasses
¾ cup hot water
½ teaspoon soda
1 9-inch pie shell

Rub flour, sugar, butter, salt and cinnamon between fingers to form coarse crumbs. Dissolve soda in hot water and mix with molasses. Into pie shell, pour one layer liquid, then crumbs, then liquid, then crumbs. Bake at 350° for about 45 minutes.

VICTORIA PIE

*Rickey's Studio Inn
Palo Alto, California*

Almond Filling

4 ounces almond paste	5 large apples,
½ cup sugar	sliced
6 egg yolks	½ cup water
⅓ cup cream	½ cup raisins

Beat almond paste, sugar and egg yolks together until stiff. Add cream. Cook sliced apples with water until soft. Add raisins. Add sugar and cinnamon to taste. Roll out pie crust (see recipe below), place in 10-inch pie plate, and fill with the apple filling. Bake in hot oven, 400° for 15 minutes, until the crust is partly baked. Then add the almond filling on top of the apples, and bake again for 10 minutes at 350°.

Pie Crust

2 cups pastry flour	Pinch salt
¾ cup shortening	½ cup water

Cut shortening into flour and salt, till lumps form the size of peas. Sprinkle over water, and quickly form into ball. Roll out on floured board.

CHRISTMAS TREE PIE

Stagecoach Inn
Manitou Springs, Colorado

2 cups milk
3 eggs, separated
1 cup sugar
1 envelope plain gelatin
1 tablespoon rum extract

Red and green candied
   cherries, cut up
Almonds, blanched and
   slivered
Graham cracker pie crust

Scald milk in double boiler. In separate bowl, mix egg yolks, ½ cup sugar and gelatin. Add to milk and cook until it coats spoon. Set aside and cool. Beat egg whites, add ½ cup sugar, rum extract and stir into soft custard. Pour half of mixture into graham cracker pie shell. Sprinkle with cut up red and green cherries. Add rest of custard and sprinkle with more cherries and almonds. Chill for two hours. Top with whipped cream and serve.

BLACK FOREST CAKE

London Grill
Portland, Oregon

A four-layer chocolate sponge cake, soaked with Kirsch Wasser, with rich fillings between each layer.

Sponge Cake

8 ounces chocolate
2 cups milk
8 eggs, separated
2 cups sugar

2 cups flour
½ teaspoon salt
Kirsch Wasser

Melt chocolate in milk. Separate eggs; beat whites until they stand up in soft peaks; add 1 cup sugar gradually, beating continuously. Beat yolks until thick. Gradually beat in 1 cup sugar and add chocolate mixture. Pour yolks over beaten whites and blend gently and thoroughly. Sift flour and salt together and fold into mixture. Pour into 4 9-inch layer cake pans and bake in 350° oven about 30 minutes.

First Layer

Circles of icing and red sour cherries, soaked in red wine, Kirsch, almond and orange flavor.

Second Layer

Chocolate mousse made out of whipped cream, Dutch or German sweet chocolate and Kirsch.

Third Layer

Whipped cream with vanilla flavor and gelatin.

Top the cake with shaved milk chocolate, powdered sugar, and maraschino cherries with the stems.

ANGEL FOOD CAKE WITH COCOA FILLING

Martha Washington Inn
Abingdon, Virginia

6 tablespoons cocoa
6 tablespoons sugar
⅛ teaspoon salt
1½ pints heavy cream

1 cup blanched almonds, slivered and toasted
1 large angel food cake

Mix first three ingredients with cream and chill for 1 hour. Whip until stiff. Fill the cavity of a large angel food cake with ⅓ of the cream mixture and ⅓ of the almonds. Frost with remaining cream mixture. Sprinkle remaining almonds over top and sides of cake. Chill for 2 or 3 hours before serving. (6 to 12 servings)

ANGEL FOOD CAKE WITH STRAWBERRY WHIPPED CREAM

*The Golden Lamb
Lebanon, Ohio*

Make your favorite angel food cake. After cake has been baked and cooled, split cake into three layers. Spread the filling between the layers and on top and sides of cake. Sprinkle slivered toasted almonds over the cake and chill.

Filling

1 pint ripe strawberries
1 cup sugar
1 tablespoon plain gelatin
1 cup water

¼ cup almonds, blanched, toasted and slivered
2 cups heavy cream, whipped

Cook strawberries and sugar to the boiling point. Dissolve plain gelatin in water and stir into strawberries. Let cool and fold in whipped cream.

HOT MILK SPONGE CAKE

*Whitney's
Jackson, New Hampshire*

½ cup milk
2 tablespoons butter
2 eggs
1 cup sugar

1½ cups flour
1 teaspoon baking powder
1 teaspoon vanilla or lemon extract (optional)

Heat to boiling milk and butter. Beat eggs until light and pale. Add sugar gradually, beating constantly. Sift flour with baking powder, fold into mixture, a small amount at a time. Fold in flavoring. Pour batter into a lightly buttered 8" x 8" pan and bake at 350° for about 30 minutes. Cake rises better if oven is not at its full heat when cake is set into it.

BUTTERNUT CAKE
With Maple Sugar Frosting

Publick House
Sturbridge, Massachusetts

2¾ cups sifted cake flour
¾ teaspoon salt
3½ teaspoon baking powder
½ cup soft butter
1 teaspoon vanilla

1⅓ cups sugar
3 eggs, separated
1 cup milk
1 cup chopped butternuts
or walnuts

Have all the ingredients at room temperature. Preheat oven to 375°. Prepare two 9-inch layer cake pans.

Sift together sifted cake flour, salt and baking powder. Cream soft butter or vegetable shortening thoroughly. Add vanilla and blend well. Add sugar, a tablespoon at a time, beating well after each addition. Continue beating after all the sugar is added until very light and fluffy. (This step is the secret of success with this method. Beating air into the mixture makes the cake light and gives it a good texture. It is almost impossible to overbeat, quite easy to underbeat— and an electric mixer expedites matters considerably.)

Scrape the bowl often. Beat in egg yolks, one at a time, again beating well. Use a low speed on the mixer for the next step, or use a large wooden spoon. Add the dry ingredients alternately with milk, beginning and ending with the dry ingredients, and adding about ¼ at a time, and ⅓ cup of milk. Add chopped butternuts to last addition of flour. Last, fold in stiffly beaten egg whites.

Fill immediately into the cake pans. Drop the pans gently on a table or run a knife through the batter to break any large air bubbles. Bake about 25 to 30 minutes in a moderate oven (375°), until a toothpick inserted in the center comes out dry. Let stand for at least 10 minutes, then turn out on a cake rack to cool. Frost with Maple Sugar Frosting when cool. Sprinkle top and sides with additional butternuts (extra good if toasted lightly at first).

Maple Sugar Frosting

½ pound maple sugar or
1 cup brown sugar
⅓ cup boiling water
1 egg white, beaten stiff

⅛ teaspoon cream of
tartar
½ teaspoon vanilla

Mix sugar and water. Stir until dissolved and boil for 10 minutes. Add cream of tartar to egg white. Beat until stiff and dry. Pour hot syrup into beaten white and continue beating until right consistency to spread.

BLACK MIDNIGHT CAKE

Emerson's Smorgasbord
Newcastle, Maine

½ cup cocoa
1 cup boiling water
½ cup shortening
1½ cups sugar
2 eggs

1 teaspoon vanilla
1⅓ cups cake flour, sifted
1 teaspoon soda
¼ teaspoon baking powder
¾ teaspoon salt

Mix together cocoa and water and cool slightly.

Cream together shortening and sugar and beat in eggs and vanilla. Add to cocoa mixture.

Sift together dry ingredients and add to creamed mixture. Bake in two well-greased 9-inch layer cake pans, at 350°, for 30 to 35 minutes. Remove from pans and when cool frost with Seven Minute Icing.

Seven Minute Icing

2 egg whites
1 cup sugar
⅓ cup Karo Syrup (dark
or light may be used)

¼ cup cold water
⅛ teaspoon salt
½ cup semi-sweet
chocolate bits

Place egg whites, sugar, syrup, water and salt in top of double boiler and beat with egg beater until blended. Place over boiling water and continue beating for seven minutes, or until mixture holds its shape. Ice cake between layers, top, and sides.

Melt semi-sweet chocolate bits and spread over icing. Let run over sides of cake.

CHIP AND DATE CAKE

The Glen
Pittsburgh, New Hampshire

1 package dates, chopped	1¾ cups flour
1 teaspoon soda	1 teaspoon baking powder
1 cup boiling water	1 tablespoon cocoa
½ cup butter	1 teaspoon vanilla
1 cup sugar	1 cup chocolate chips
2 eggs	½ cup pecans, chopped

Soak dates and soda in boiling water until soft. Cream butter and sugar together. Add eggs, one at a time, and beat until fluffy. Sift all dry ingredients together. Add alternately with date mixture to creamed mixture. Add vanilla. Mix two minutes at low speed. Add ½ cup chocolate chips. Spread in a 9 x 13 inch buttered pan. Sprinkle with remaining chocolate chips and pecans. Bake at 350° for 35 to 45 minutes.

GERMAN CHOCOLATE CAKE

The Greenbrier
White Sulphur Springs, West Virginia

¼ pound butter	½ pint warm water
14 ounces sugar	½ pint melted chocolate
10 eggs, separated	1 teaspoon vanilla
9 ounces cake flour	1 teaspoon salt
1 teaspoon soda	½ pint buttermilk

Cream butter and sugar until light and fluffy. Add egg yolks and beat in. Sift cake flour with soda. Mix water, melted chocolate, vanilla and salt. Add buttermilk.

Then add the sifted dry ingredients and the liquid

alternately to the creamed mixture, beating after each addition until batter is smooth. Beat egg whites and fold in by hand. Pour batter into two 10-inch cake pans. Bake at 350° for approximately 30 minutes.

Note: This recipe will make two 10-inch layers.

CHOCOLATE ICE BOX CAKE

El Charro Lodge
Phoenix, Arizona

½ pound German semi-
   sweet chocolate
3 tablespoons water
4 egg yolks
2 tablespoons
   confectioners sugar

½ cup walnuts or
   pecans, chopped
4 egg whites, stiffly beaten
1 cup heavy cream,
   whipped
12 to 16 lady fingers

Melt chocolate in double boiler. Add water and blend. Remove from fire. Add egg yolks, one at a time, beating vigorously until smooth and blended. Add confectioners sugar and nuts. Blend. Fold in stiffly beaten egg whites and whipped cream.

Line dish with lady fingers and pour in mixture. Let set 12 to 24 hours in refrigerator. Serve with whipped cream.

WHISTLING OYSTER FUDGE CAKE

The Whistling Oyster
Ogunquit, Maine

Cake

½ cup butter
2 cups brown sugar,
   sifted
2 eggs, well beaten
4 squares chocolate,
   melted

2 cups cake flour
1 teaspoon baking soda
1 cup milk
1 teaspoon vanilla

Cream shortening. Add sugar gradually and continue to cream. Add eggs. Add melted chocolate. Sift flour with baking soda. Add vanilla to milk. Add flour and milk alternately to creamed mixture. Bake in greased 8-inch layer cake tins in 350° oven for 20 to 30 minutes. Place chocolate filling (see recipe below) between layers. Frost with chocolate fudge icing (see recipe below).

Chocolate Filling

2 squares chocolate	2 tablespoons flour
1 tablespoon butter	1 tablespoon cornstarch
1 cup milk	¼ teaspoon salt
⅜ cup sugar	1 teaspoon vanilla

Melt chocolate and butter in top part of double boiler. Add milk gradually and beat continuously. Mix sugar, flour and cornstarch and salt; add some of the hot milk and chocolate mixture. Return all to double boiler. Add vanilla. Stir and cook until thickened.

Chocolate Fudge Icing

¼ cup butter	4 squares chocolate,
½ cup granulated sugar	melted
1½ cups confectioners sugar	

Cream butter, add sugar gradually. Add cooled melted chocolate. Beat until smooth.

LAKE BREEZE FUDGE CAKE

Lake Breeze Resort
Three Lakes, Wisconsin

Cake

1½ cups white sugar
2 cups flour
1 teaspoon soda
1 teaspoon baking powder
⅛ cup butter, softened
2 egg yolks, well beaten

1 teaspoon vanilla
4 ounces chocolate,
  melted in ⅓ cup
  boiling water
2 egg whites, stiffly beaten

Sift together sugar, flour, soda, baking powder and salt. Add butter, milk, egg yolks, vanilla and chocolate. Beat well. Carefully fold in egg whites. Pour into well greased 9-inch layer pans. Bake 30 to 35 minutes in 350° oven.

Frosting

⅓ cup milk
3 cups confectioners
  sugar

2 squares chocolate,
  melted with
2 tablespoons shortening
3 tablespoons butter

Boil milk and pour over confectioners sugar. Add other ingredients and beat well. Frosting will thicken as you beat.

CHOCOLATE ROLL

Valley View Inn
Hot Springs, Virginia

5 eggs, separated
½ cup sugar
3 tablespoons cocoa

2 tablespoons flour
1 teaspoon vanilla

Beat egg whites until stiff. Beat yolks until foamy. Add sugar gradually, beating all the time. Add cocoa, then flour, then vanilla. Last, fold in stiffly beaten whites.

Grease a cookie sheet, line with wax paper, grease wax paper. Pour in mixture and bake in 400° oven 12 to 15 minutes, or until tester comes out dry.

Turn onto wet cloth. Let cool. Peel off wax paper, roll; then unroll and fill with ice cream or flavored whipped cream, and roll up again.

CHOCOLATE ANGEL DELIGHT

Spring Lake Restaurant
Harrison, Arkansas

1 13-ounce Angel Food cake
12 ounces semi-sweet chocolate chips
3 tablespoons water
3 eggs, separated

Pinch salt
3 tablespoons sugar
1½ cups heavy cream, whipped
1 teaspoon vanilla
Vanilla ice cream

Melt chocolate chips and water in top of double boiler. Stir in egg yolks and salt. Beat egg whites until they are stiff. Add sugar gradually to egg whites and stir them into cooled chocolate mixture, and blend well. Whip cream, add vanilla, then fold into chocolate mixture. Break angel food cake into bite sized pieces and place in 9 x 14 baking dish. Cover with chocolate sauce. Chill in refrigerator at least 6 hours before serving. Serve cold in squares; top each portion with a dip of ice cream.

MOCHA REFRIGERATOR CAKE

The Shed
Santa Fe, New Mexico

1 12-ounce package chocolate bits
2 tablespoons instant coffee
2 tablespoons sugar
2 tablespoons water
7 eggs, separated

1 teaspoon vanilla
⅛ teaspoon salt
Thin chocolate wafers (Nabisco's Famous Chocolate Wafers)
½ cup heavy cream, whipped

Combine chocolate, coffee, sugar, water in saucepan or double boiler. If using saucepan, put on very low heat. Stir. Add egg yolks, vanilla, salt. Beat egg whites until stiff, fold in. Cover bottom of pan (9" x 9") with layer of chocolate wafers. Add one half mocha mixture and cover this with another thin layer of chocolate wafers. Place in freezer compartment for about 45 minutes to set. Remove. Add second half of mocha filling, topping with final layer of chocolate crumbs. Serve with whipped cream. Cake takes about 3 hours to set and will have moist, pudding-like consistency. Do not freeze.

MAGUIRE CAKE
With Mocha Filling

Chalet Suzanne
Lake Wales, Florida

10 egg whites	1 teaspoon almond extract
2 teaspoons cream of tartar	1 teaspoon lemon extract
1¼ cups sugar	Mocha filling (see recipe below)
1 cup sifted cake flour	Boiled white frosting
8 egg yolks	

Beat whites until foamy, add cream of tartar and beat until stiff. Gradually add ¼ cup sifted sugar. Sift remaining sugar and flour five times. Beat egg yolks until thick and lemon color. Beat in almond and lemon extract. Fold into egg white mixture. Fold in flour and sugar mixture. Bake in angel food pan in 325° oven for 1 hour and 15 minutes. Invert pan and cool. Cut into 2 layers and put together with mocha filling. Frost cake with boiled white frosting.

Mocha Filling

3 tablespoons butter	¼ cup strong coffee
2 cups confectioner's sugar, sifted	¾ cup toasted almonds, chopped

Mix ingredients together.

Boiled White Frosting

1 cup sugar	2 egg whites, beaten stiff
⅓ cup water	1½ teaspoons vanilla
⅓ teaspoon cream of	extract
tartar	

Boil sugar, water, cream of tartar until syrup spins a thread (242°). Pour hot syrup over egg whites, very slow, beating continuously. Add vanilla extract. Continue beating until of spreading consistency.

STAGECOACH CHOCOLATE MAYONNAISE CAKE

Stagecoach Inn
Manitou Springs, Colorado

3 cups sifted flour	1½ cups mayonnaise
1½ cups sugar	1½ cups hot water
6 tablespoons cocoa	1½ teaspoons vanilla
2¼ teaspoons soda	

Mix all dry ingredients together. Add mayonnaise, hot water and vanilla. Mix thoroughly. Pour mixture into two greased 8-inch or 9″ x 13″ cake pans; bake at 350° for 45 to 50 minutes.

BAHAMIAN COCONUT CAKE

Emerald Beach Hotel
Nassau, Bahamas

Sponge Cake

4 eggs	3 tablespoons butter,
1 cup sugar	melted
1 cup flour	

Warm eggs over hot water and beat until fluffy. Gently fold in sugar and flour; then gently fold in butter. Bake at 325° for 25 to 35 minutes, in a 9-inch ungreased tube pan. When done, remove pan from oven and invert it until cake is cold.

Custard

4 egg yolks
1 pint milk
1½ ounces cornstarch
5 ounces sugar

1 tablespoon melted
   butter
¼ cup cream, whipped

Mix yolks, part of milk and cornstarch. Bring remaining milk and sugar to a boil. Add yolk mixture and boil. Add butter and let cool. When custard is cold, add whipped cream.

Cut cake in three, fill with custard, and cover with boiled frosting (see recipe below). Cover top and sides with fresh grated coconut.

Boiled Frosting

2 egg whites
1½ cups sugar
¼ teaspoon cream of
   tartar

⅓ cup water
Fresh grated coconut

Place all ingredients, except coconut, in bowl over boiling water and whip till fluffy and mixture holds its shape. Spread over top and sides of cake and sprinkle liberally with fresh grated coconut.

GATEAU MALMAISON

Malmaison Restaurant
New York City

This dish consists of two pastes and two creams. The two pastes are Short Paste and Choux Paste. The two creams are St. Honore Cream and Whipped Cream.

Short Paste

½ pound flour   ½ teaspoon salt
¼ pound butter   1 cup water
1 ounce sugar

Place flour on board, making a well in center, to which all other ingredients should be added. Mix all ingredients and flour delicately with fingertips, but rapidly to avoid giving paste elasticity. Roll into ball and cover with a linen cloth. Let stand in cool place. Preparation of this paste the day before use will give the best results.

Choux Paste

½ to ⅔ cups flour   Pinch salt
¼ cup butter   2 eggs, unbeaten
½ teaspoon sugar   ½ cup water

Sift flour. Place water, salt, sugar and butter in a casserole and bring to a boil, and when all the butter is melted, pour in the sifted flour, stirring with a spatula, making a very thick paste. Remove from the stove and add the eggs, one by one. Stir well each time an egg is added. The resulting paste should be soft but not liquid.

St. Honore Cream

1 quart milk   1½ teaspoons vanilla
8 eggs, separated   extract, or 1 inch stick
1 cup sugar   vanilla bean
¼ pound flour

Whip egg yolks and sugar in a casserole and add flour. Bring milk to a boil, add egg mixture, then add vanilla. Beat egg whites stiff but not dry. Cool egg yolk mixture but while still warm, add beaten whites. Mix all ingredients together well.

Whipped Cream

1 cup heavy cream

Have cream very cold; whip until firm.

St. Honore Gateau (Gateau Malmaison)

Cut a slice of the short paste, about ¼ inch thick, the size of a large plate. Place Choux paste in pastry bag with large finger size tube and form an edge about ¾ inch thick around circle. Make 12 small balls and 12 small strips to form a swan's neck.

Bake in 425° oven for 10 minutes. Reduce to 300° and bake for 20 to 30 minutes. When cool, fill centers with St. Honore cream.

Cook 5 ounces of sugar to the crack stage, then plunge the small Choux Paste balls into it immediately. Place on the border of the cake, pasting them together. Place necks on top of Choux to form the swan.

Decorate cake with whipped cream. Keep in refrigerator at very cold temperature.

LEMON-FILLED DESSERT CAKE

Bacon Farm Inn
Barnstable Village, Massachusetts

4 eggs, separated	½ teaspoon baking
½ teaspoon salt	powder
1 teaspoon vanilla or	2 tablespoons water
almond flavoring	Bread crumbs
¾ cup sugar	Orange juice
¾ cup flour	

Beat egg whites with salt until stiff. Add flavoring, beat in sugar; gradually add egg yolks, flour sifted with baking powder, and water. Fold all gently together. Pour into 2 8-inch layer cake pans that have been well buttered and spread with bread crumbs. Bake in 350° oven 30 to 40 minutes. When cold, cut each layer in half, crosswise, making four layers in all; moisten layers with sweetened orange juice. Spread each layer with filling and cover top with whipped cream.

Topping

1 pint heavy cream

Chill cream thoroughly, whip until stiff. Spread over top of cake and swirl lightly over sides.

Filling

1 package lemon Jello
1 package fresh or frozen strawberries
3 bananas, sliced thin

Dissolve Jello into 2 cups boiling water; add strawberries and bananas. When cool spread between layers of cake.

HARLEQUIN PARTY CAKE
With Lemon Jelly Filling

Mirror Lake Inn
Lake Placid, New York

1 cup butter or oleo, creamed	½ teaspoon salt
2 cups sugar	3 egg yolks, beaten
3 cups sifted cake flour	1 cup milk
1 teaspoon cream of tartar	2 teaspoons vanilla
½ teaspoon soda	3 egg whites, beaten
	1 ounce chocolate, melted

Cream butter and sugar together. Sift cake flour with other dry ingredients. Combine beaten egg yolks, milk and vanilla. Add alternately with dry ingredients to the butter and sugar. Add beaten egg whites last, folding in carefully.

Divide into three equal parts. Put one part into one

buttered 8-inch cake pan. To the second part, add strawberry color and pour into 8-inch pan. To the third part, add melted chocolate, and pour into pan. Bake 25 minutes in a 350° oven.

When cool, put lemon jelly filling between layers, and cover sides and top with white mountain cream icing.

Lemon Jelly Filling

¾ cup sugar
¼ teaspoon salt
3 tablespoons corn starch

¾ cup water
1 tablespoon butter
⅓ cup lemon juice

Mix sugar, salt, cornstarch and water, and boil 1 minute. Add butter and lemon juice. Cool, then spread between layers of cake.

White Mountain Cream Icing

1 cup sugar
⅓ cup water
¼ teaspoon cream of
tartar

2 egg whites, well beaten
1 teaspoon vanilla
extract

Cook sugar, water and cream of tartar until it spins a long thread or until it shows 240° on thermometer. Pour boiling syrup gradually over the well beaten egg whites, beating until the syrup is all poured in. Add vanilla for flavor. Spread on top and sides of cake.

CARROT CAKE

Wisconsinaire
Hazelhurst, Wisconsin

½ cup flour
1 cup granulated sugar
½ teaspoon soda
1 teaspoon cinnamon
½ teaspoon salt

4 eggs, separated
½ cup Mazola corn oil
1 cup grated carrots
1 teaspoon vanilla

Sift together the flour, sugar, soda, cinnamon and salt. Add corn oil and egg yolks, beat well until blended. Add 1 cup of grated raw carrots and fold in stiffly beaten whites and vanilla. Bake in 350° oven for 40 to 45 minutes, until cake shrinks from the pan.

Frosting

3 ounces cream cheese
½ teaspoon butter

1 teaspoon vanilla
2 cups powdered sugar

Blend and beat until creamy.

FRUIT COCKTAIL CAKE

*Holiday Inn Restaurant
Harrison, Arkansas*

4 cups flour
2 cups sugar
2 teaspoons baking soda

1 No. 2½ can fruit
cocktail, undrained

Mix ingredients with a spoon, then pour into 9″ x 13″ greased pan. Before placing in oven, cover with topping below.

Topping

Combine: ½ cup light brown sugar; ½ cup coconut and ½ cup chopped pecans. Sprinkle on top of unbaked cake. Bake in 350° oven for 45 minutes, or until cake springs back at touch. While cake is still warm, spread on frosting below.

Frosting

Combine: 1 cup sugar; 1 small can evaporated milk; ½ cup butter and 1 teaspoon vanilla. Cook with medium fire until thick, then spread on warm cake.

ORANGE DELIGHT

*Old Adobe Patio Restaurant
Tucson, Arizona*

1 cup shortening
1¾ cups sugar
4½ teaspoons baking
  powder
½ teaspoon salt
3 cups cake flour

1½ cups orange juice,
  fresh or frozen
4 eggs
2 tablespoons grated
  orange rind

Cream (cream very well) shortening, sugar, baking powder and salt (3 minutes in mixer). Add flour and orange juice. Beat or mix another 3 minutes. Beat in one egg at a time. Beat or mix 3 minutes longer. Add rind. Bake at 325° to 350° in a large pan, approximately 12″ x 18″, for 30 to 40 minutes.

Orange Filling

½ cup cornstarch
1 cup sugar
½ teaspoon salt
1½ tablespoons lemon
  juice

2 tablespoons orange
  rind, grated
2 tablespoons butter
1½ cups orange juice
3 egg yolks, well beaten
2 cups orange segments

Blend well all ingredients except egg yolks and orange segments. Cook mixture until it thickens, stirring constantly. Add well beaten egg yolks and boil one minute. Remove from heat and add orange segments. Cool. Spread filling on cake.

Frosting

2 cups sugar
½ cup water
2 tablespoons corn syrup
½ teaspoon cream of
  tartar

¼ teaspoon salt
3 egg whites, beaten
½ teaspoon vanilla
Orange rind, grated

Put sugar, water, corn syrup, cream of tartar and salt in a kettle, stirring until sugar is dissolved. Boil this syrup to 240° or until it spins in a long thread.

Pour syrup gradually on the beaten egg whites, and continue beating until thoroughly blended and until stiff enough to stand up in peaks. Add vanilla.

With a spatula spread frosting on top of the orange filling. Sprinkle grated orange rind on the very top.

•

GATEAU PARADISE

Restaurant Laurent
New York City

Meringues

4 egg whites beaten stiff
Pinch salt
1½ cups sugar

⅓ cup almonds, finely ground

Whip egg whites with pinch of salt until stiff and then add, very gradually, sugar and finely ground almonds.

Cut out 4 rounds of paper about 8 inches in diameter. Spread each round of paper with meringue and bake on a baking sheet in a slow oven, 250°, for 20 to 25 minutes, or until the meringue is dry. Turn the layers over and continue to dry for about 5 minutes.

Filling

2 egg whites
½ cup sugar
2 tablespoons sweet cocoa

1 cup sweet butter, softened
¼ pound sweet chocolate, melted

In the top of a double boiler, over hot but not boiling water, beat egg whites until foamy. Beat in remaining ingredients, in order given, adding them gradually. Beat well, and remove from heat. When the filling is firm, spread it on 3 meringue layers and put them together, the fourth layer on top. Dust with confectioners sugar.

1000 ACRES CREAM CHEESE CAKE

1000 Acres Ranch Resort
Stony Creek, New York

1½ cups Zwieback crumbs
4 large egg whites
½ cup super fine sugar
1 teaspoon vanilla
1 teaspoon lemon juice

1½ pounds cream cheese, softened
1 cup sour cream
1 teaspoon vanilla
1 tablespoon sugar

Butter well 9″ x 3″ spring pan and line with crushed, sifted zwieback crumbs. Beat egg whites till they form a peak. Add to beaten whites super fine sugar, vanilla, lemon juice. Beat well, until it has the consistency of meringue. Fold soft cream cheese in evenly. Pour into prepared pan and bake in moderate oven, 350° for 40 minutes.

Mix together sour cream, vanilla and 1 tablespoon sugar. Remove cake from oven and pour sour cream mixture evenly over entire cake while hot. Return to hot oven, 400° for 4 or 5 minutes, until mixture sets. Remove cake from oven, let cool, then chill in refrigerator.

This cake may be served plain or with sliced sweet strawberries, blueberries or any topping of your own choice.

PAULINE'S REFRIGERATOR CHEESE CAKE

Rimrock Room
Hotel Palliser
Calgary, Alberta

2 envelopes unflavored gelatin
1 cup granulated sugar
¼ teaspoon salt
2 eggs, separated
1 cup milk

1 teaspoon lemon rind, grated
1 tablespoon lemon juice
3 cups cream cheese
1 cup heavy cream, whipped

Mix gelatin, ¾ cup sugar, salt in top of double boiler. Beat egg yolks; add milk. Add to gelatin mixture and cook over boiling water, stirring continuously until well blended and mixture thickens. Remove from heat. Add lemon rind and juice. Cool. Cream the cheese until smooth. Stir in the gelatin mixture, stirring occasionally. When slightly thickened fold in whipped cream and pour into 8-inch pan lined with crumb mixture (see recipe below). Chill well before serving.

Crumb Crust

¾ cup fine crumbs
2 tablespoons melted butter

¼ teaspoon cinnamon
1 tablespoon sugar

Mix together. Sprinkle half the crumbs on the bottom of pan and sprinkle top of cheesecake with remaining crumbs.

CHEESE CAKE MEDALLION

Cafe Medallion
St. Francis Hotel
San Francisco, California

¾ cup graham cracker crumbs
2 tablespoons butter, melted
2 8-ounce packages cream cheese
¾ cup sugar

2 eggs, separated
Rind of 1 lemon, grated
1 tablespoon unflavored gelatin
¼ cup cold water
1 cup heavy cream, whipped

Combine crumbs and butter; pat onto bottom of buttered 9-inch spring form pan. Bake in 350° oven for 5 minutes. Cool. Meanwhile, beat cheese until fluffy; add ½ cup sugar, egg yolks, and lemon rind, beating well. Beat egg whites until soft peaks form; gradually add remaining ¼ cup sugar and continue beating to stiff meringue. Set aside. Whip cream; set aside. Soften gelatin in the cold water; dissolve over low heat. Cool until syrupy, then stir into cheese mixture, beating well. Carefully fold meringue and whipped cream into cheese mixture. Pour into crust. Chill 8 hours, or overnight. With thin knife blade, loosen cheese cake; remove rim of spring form pan. Sprinkle fine graham cracker crumbs over top and pat onto sides of cake. Serve with sweetened fresh strawberries or Blueberry Sauce. (Make ahead and freeze, if desired.)

SCHIMMEL CHEESE CAKE

Hotel Blackstone
Omaha, Nebraska

Crust

1½ cups ground graham
  crackers
  6 tablespoons sugar

1 tablespoon cinnamon
½ cup melted butter

Blend ingredients together. Line spring form of 8″ layer cake pan 2 inches deep with crumb mixture.

Filling

2 eggs, well beaten
½ cup sugar
  6 ounces cottage cheese

6 ounces cream cheese
½ teaspoon salt
½ teaspoon vanilla

Beat eggs thoroughly, add sugar, cottage cheese, cream cheese and vanilla. Beat well.

Pour over graham cracker crust. Bake 20 minutes at 375°. Remove from oven. Cool 5 minutes; then add topping.

Topping

¾ pint sour cream
  2 tablespoons sugar
½ teaspoon vanilla

Mix well sour cream, sugar and vanilla. Pour over cake and return to oven for 5 minutes at 425°.

Chill cake overnight. Sprinkle with graham cracker crumbs before serving.

CRAFTWOOD CHEESE CAKE

Craftwood Inn
Manitou Springs, Colorado

1 package unflavored
    gelatin
2 eggs, separated
Juice of 1 lemon

1 pound cottage cheese,
    whipped
¾ cup crushed pineapple
1 cup whipped cream

Dissolve gelatin as directed. Beat egg yolks and add to gelatin. Add lemon juice. Bring to boil, then chill in refrigerator. Mix cottage cheese with pineapple. Whip egg whites and fold in, then add chilled gelatin mixture. Mix well. Add whipped cream. Put mix in graham cracker crust. Chill before serving.

Graham Cracker Crust

15 graham crackers,
    crushed
1 tablespoon sugar

½ teaspoon cinnamon
¼ cup butter, melted

Mix ingredients until crumbs are moistened. Press into pie pan.

CANADIAN GRILL CHEESE CAKE

Chateau Laurier Hotel
Ottawa, Ontario

Crust

5 ounces graham cracker
    crumbs
2 tablespoons sugar

2 tablespoons melted
    butter

Filling

¾ pound cream cheese
½ cup sugar
¼ teaspoon salt

¼ teaspoon grated lemon
rind
4 eggs
6 tablespoons sour cream

Topping

8 tablespoons sour cream
½ ounce sugar

¼ teaspoon vanilla
Canadian maple syrup

Combine cracker crumbs, sugar and melted butter. Mix well, and press mixture into the bottom and sides of a 9-inch pie pan.

Combine cream cheese, sugar, salt and lemon rind. Mix well. Add eggs, one at a time, mixing in slow speed and being sure to scrape down the sides of the bowl often. Add sour cream and mix slowly until well blended.

Fill cracker crust with cheese mixture and bake for 20 to 25 minutes in 350° oven.

Remove from oven, cool at room temperature for 10 minutes. Spread with topping, made by combining sour cream, sugar and vanilla. Return cake to oven for 5 to 10 minutes. Cool to room temperature before serving.

Serve with a generous helping of Canadian Maple Syrup.

SNOWBIRD CHEESE FLUFF CAKE

Snowbird Mountain Lodge
Robbinsville, North Carolina

1 9-ounce package of
cream cheese
1 13-ounce can evaporated
milk
35 graham crackers or
vanilla wafers

1 cup sugar
⅓ cup butter
3 tablespoons sugar
1 box lemon gelatin
1 teaspoon vanilla

Crush wafers or crackers very fine; put aside. Mix lemon gelatin with 1 cup boiling water, put aside to cool but do not let jell.

Put evaporated milk in empty ice tray and put into freezing compartment until milk freezes around the edges.

While milk is freezing, cream the 1 cup of sugar and cream cheese very well. Melt butter and add to ¾ of cracker crumbs and 3 tablespoons sugar. Pack into bottom of an angelfood loose tube pan or springform pan. When evaporated milk is ready, put into electric mixer bowl and beat well. Add vanilla. Pour into pan with cracker mixture. Sprinkle balance of crumbs on top. Place in refrigerator for at least 8 hours or overnight.

PINEAPPLE CHEESE CAKE

Gaucho Steak House
Americana Hotel
Bal Harbour, Florida

¾ cup graham cracker crumbs
1½ pounds cream cheese
1½ cups sugar
2½ tablespoons cornstarch
¼ teaspoon salt
3 eggs
3 egg yolks
⅜ cup light cream
Grated peel of 1 lemon
Juice of 1 lemon
¼ teaspoon vanilla
Canned pineapple rings
Maraschino cherries
Apricot jam

Reserve ½ cup of the crumbs. Press remaining crumbs onto bottom and 2 inches up the sides of *generously* buttered 7-inch spring form pan. Stir cream cheese to soften; beat until fluffy. Mix sugar, cornstarch and salt; gradually blend into cheese. Add eggs and yolks, one at a time, beating well after each; be sure there are no lumps. Stir in remaining ingredients for filling, cream, lemon rind and juice, and vanilla. Pour into the crumb-lined pan. Bake in slow oven, 325°, 1 hour and 20 minutes, or until done.*

Cool in pan about 2 hours. Remove sides of pan and arrange pineapple rings and maraschino cherries on top of cake. Glaze by spreading with sieved apricot jam. Sprinkle sides with reserved crumbs. Chill.

*Cake will not be completely set in center and will have a slight depression on top.

PINEAPPLE ICEBOX CAKE

Williams Wayside Inn
Berthoud, Colorado

¼ pound butter
2 cups confectioner's sugar
4 eggs, separated
2 cups well drained crushed pineapple

2 cups vanilla wafers, crushed
½ cup nuts, chopped

Blend butter and sugar. Add beaten egg yolks and mix. Stir in pineapple and fold in beaten egg whites. Spread half of crumbs and nuts over bottom of 24″ x 12″ pan and pour pineapple mixture over them. Cover with remaining nuts and crumbs. Chill in refrigerator overnight, before serving.

PEDRO'S TATER CAKE WITH COCONUT FROSTING

South of the Border Restaurant
South of the Border, South Carolina

1½ cups cooking oil
2 cups sugar
4 eggs, separated
4 tablespoons hot water
2½ cups sifted cake flour
3 teaspoons baking powder
¼ teaspoon salt

1 teaspoon ground nutmeg
1 teaspoon cinnamon
1½ cups raw sweet potato, grated
1 cup nuts, chopped
1 teaspoon vanilla

Combine oil and sugar; beat until smooth; add egg yolks and beat well. Add water and then dry ingredients that have been sifted together. Stir in potatoes, nuts, vanilla; beat well. Beat egg whites until stiff and fold into mixture. Turn into three 8-inch greased and floured layer cake pans and bake in 350° oven 25 to 30 minutes. Cool and frost with Coconut Frosting.

Coconut Frosting

1 cup evaporated milk
1 cup sugar
½ cup butter
3 egg yolks

1 teaspoon vanilla
1½ cups flaked coconut
1 cup nuts, chopped
(optional)

Combine milk, sugar, butter, egg yolks and vanilla in saucepan. Cook over medium heat about 12 minutes, stirring constantly, until mixture thickens. Remove from heat and add coconut and nuts. Beat until cool and of spreading consistency. Spread between layers and on top of cake.

PRUNE CAKE

Valley View Inn
Hot Springs, Virginia

½ cup Wesson oil or
  vegetable shortening
1½ cups sugar
3 eggs, beaten
1 cup buttermilk
2 cups flour
1 teaspoon soda
1 teaspoon allspice

1 teaspoon cloves
1 teaspoon nutmeg
1 teaspoon cinnamon
½ teaspoon salt
1 cup prunes, cooked and
  chopped
1 cup nuts, chopped

Cream oil and sugar; beat eggs and add to creamed mixture. Sift flour with soda, spices and salt and stir into creamed mixture. Finally add chopped prunes and nuts. Bake in a greased pan, 9″ x 13″, for 35 to 45 minutes in 350° oven.

PRUNE CAKE

Hart's Moose Lake Coffee House
Moose Lake, Minnesota

1 large tablespoon
  shortening, rounded
  (all butter, or half butter
  and half lard)
1 cup sugar
1 egg yolk
2 level teaspoons soda
1½ teaspoon baking
  powder

1 pinch salt
1 teaspoon cinnamon
2 cups sifted flour
1 cup milk
1 cup cooked prunes,
  chopped
1 tablespoon prune juice
1 teaspoon vanilla

Cream butter, sugar and egg yolk. Mix soda, baking powder, salt and cinnamon with sifted flour. Add milk and flour alternating to the creamed mixture. Add prunes, prune juice and vanilla. Bake in two 8-inch layer cake pans in 350° oven for 25 to 30 minutes. Spread chocolate filling between layers (below). Frost with white frosting (below).

Chocolate Filling

2 squares chocolate
1 tablespoon butter
1½ tablespoons corn
  starch

½ cup sugar
¼ teaspoon salt
1 cup milk
½ cup walnuts, chopped

Melt chocolate and butter together. Mix dry ingredients together, then add to chocolate mixture and heat until smooth. Add gradually 1 cup milk and cook 5 minutes or until thick, stirring constantly. Add nuts and spread between layers.

Frosting

1 cup sugar
⅓ cup water

⅓ teaspoon cream of
  tartar
2 egg whites

Bring first three ingredients to brisk boil. Put egg white in small bowl of electric mixer. Add boiling syrup to unbeaten egg white and start beating at high speed. Continue beating until spreading consistency is reached. Frosting should stand up in peaks.

APPLE BUTTER SPICE COFFEE CAKE

Dorothy's Oven
San Diego, California

½ cup butter	1 teaspoon soda
¾ cup sugar	1 cup sour cream
2 eggs	1 cup apple butter
2 cups flour	1 teaspoon vanilla
1 teaspoon baking powder	

Cream butter and sugar. Add eggs. Beat well. Sift dry ingredients and add alternately with sour cream and apple butter. Add vanilla. Add topping (below) and bake 30 to 35 minutes at 350° in well greased pan.

Topping

½ cup brown sugar	½ teaspoon nutmeg
½ cup white sugar	1 cup cut up walnuts
1 teaspoon cinnamon	

Mix sugars and nutmeg. Stir in walnuts.

BLUEBERRY COFFEE CAKE

Saddleback Lake Lodge
Rangeley, Maine

⅓ cup soft margarine	1 teaspoon vanilla
1¼ cups granulated sugar	2½ teaspoons baking powder
1 egg	1 teaspoon salt
1¾ cups sifted flour	1½ cups blueberries
⅔ cup milk	

Cream margarine, add sugar and mix until creamy. Beat in egg and vanilla. Add milk alternately with dry ingredients which have been sifted together. Gently stir in 1 cup blueberries. Spread in greased 8 x 10 pan. Sprinkle remaining blueberries on top, and add crumb topping (below). Bake in 375° oven 30 to 40 minutes.

Crumb Topping for Blueberry Coffee Cake

½ cup brown sugar
⅓ cup all purpose flour
Dash of salt

½ teaspoon cinnamon
3 tablespoons soft margarine

Mix together sugar, flour, salt and cinnamon. Add margarine and blend well until like crumbs. Sprinkle on cake.

DANISH SULTANA LOAF CAKE

Arne Nissen's Tivoli
Toledo, Ohio

½ pound margarine (do not use butter)
1 cup sugar
3 eggs, well beaten
¼ teaspoon baking powder
1 teaspoon salt
1¾ cups cake flour
½ cup mixed candied fruit, chopped

¼ cup seedless raisins, chopped
⅓ cup nut meats, chopped
1 to 2 tablespoons flour (for dusting fruits and nuts)

Mix margarine and sugar together, blend until smooth and creamy. Add eggs and blend well. Sift baking powder, salt and flour and gradually add to above mixture; mix well. Fold in candied fruit, raisins and nuts which have been lightly dusted with flour. Pour into loaf pan and bake 75 to 90 minutes at 350°. Icing is not recommended.

SUNDAY COFFEE CAKE

Whitney's
Jackson, New Hampshire

¾ cup sugar
2 cups flour
3 teaspoons baking powder
½ teaspoon salt

2 eggs
2 tablespoons melted shortening
1 cup milk

Place all ingredients in a bowl and beat together. Put in a 7" x 13" pan and top with topping (see recipe below). Bake 30 minutes in 350° oven.

Topping

2 tablespoons flour
4 tablespoons sugar

¼ teaspoon cinnamon
1 teaspoon soft butter

Mix all ingredients and scatter over the unbaked cake.

SWEDISH CHRISTMAS COFFEE CAKE
"Jule Kaga"

The Knudson House Norge
Ephraim, Wisconsin

2 tablespoons dry yeast
1½ cups lukewarm water
⅔ cup shortening (half butter, half vegetable shortening)
⅔ cup sugar
1½ teaspoons salt

1 teaspoon cardamon seeds
1 cup mashed potatoes
2 eggs, beaten
5 to 6 cups flour
1½ cups mixed fruits and nuts, chopped

Dissolve yeast in lukewarm water. Let stand 5 minutes. Cream together shortening and sugar and salt. Add cardamon seeds, mashed potatoes and beaten eggs. Then add yeast and water mixture. Add sifted flour to make a medium dough.

Let rise to double. Knead in mixed fruits and nuts. Form into two rings or cut into strips and braid. Let rise again to double size. Bake in a 375° oven, about 30 minutes. Cool. Frost with butter frosting and decorate with red and green cherries.

Butter Frosting

⅛ pound butter
2 cups confectioners sugar

2 teaspoons lemon extract
3 tablespoons warm water

Soften butter. Place in top of double boiler with 1 cup sugar. Blend well. Add extract and water and 1 cup sugar. Let simmer over simmering water 12 to 15 minutes. Remove from heat and beat well until cool and of spreading consistency.

ALBEMARLE HUGUENOT TORTE

Evans Farm Inn
McLean, Virginia

4 eggs
1 cup sugar
1 teaspoon baking powder
½ teaspoon salt
1 cup tart cooking apples, chopped

1½ cups pecans or walnuts, chopped (reserve ½ cup for topping)
1 teaspoon vanilla
Whipped cream

Beat whole eggs in electric mixer or with rotary beater until very frothy and lemon-colored. Add other ingredients in order listed. Pour into two well-buttered baking pans about 8″ x 12″. Bake in 325° oven about 45 minutes or until crusty and brown. To serve, scoop up with pancake turner (keeping crusty part on top), pile on large plate and cover with whipped cream and a sprinkle of nuts.

HONEY NUT TORTE

The Keys
Indianapolis, Indiana

6 eggs, separated
1 cup sugar
½ teaspoon salt
2 tablespoons baking powder
1 teaspoon cinnamon

2 cups zwieback crumbs
2 cups nuts, ground
2 teaspoons vanilla
1 cup heavy cream, whipped

Beat egg whites. Cream egg yolks and sugar together. Mix together salt, baking powder, cinnamon, zwieback crumbs and ground nuts; add to creamed mixture, then fold in beaten egg whites. Add vanilla. Place in well-greased baking pan and bake in 350° oven 30 to 35 minutes. Remove torte from oven. Pour honey topping (see recipe below) over while still hot, cover top with chopped nuts and let set. Serve with whipped cream.

Topping

2 cups nuts, chopped
1 cup honey

2 cups sugar
4 cups water

Boil slowly for 30 minutes.

RIBISEL SCHNITTEN

Trapp Family Lodge
Stowe, Vermont

1 cup flour
½ cup butter
½ cup sugar
2 egg yolks
Rind of one lemon

1 pound Ribisel (red currants)
1 cup egg whites and 1 cup of sugar

Mix together the flour, butter, ¼ cup sugar, 2 egg yolks and lemon rind. Pour into baking pan and bake until light golden brown.

If using dry red currants, add approximately 1 cup of water, mix with ¼ cup sugar and bring to boil. Strain and place on top of baked bread mixture.

Beat 1 cup of egg whites until medium stiff. Add cup sugar while beating. Place on top of red currants and bread mixture and place in oven until golden brown. Serves 6.

SALLY LUNN

*King's Arms Tavern
Williamsburg, Virginia*

1 yeast cake	2 eggs, well beaten
1 cup warm milk	3½ cups flour
3 tablespoons shortening	1¼ teaspoons salt
3 tablespoons sugar	

Dissolve yeast cake in warm milk. Cream together shortening and sugar. Add eggs and mix well. Sift in flour and salt which have been sifted together, alternately with the milk and yeast mixture. Beat well. Let rise in warm place to about double in bulk. Knead lightly. Put into well greased Sally Lunn mold.* Let stand in a warm place and rise again until double in bulk. Bake at 350° for about 40 to 45 minutes, until golden brown and crusty.

*A 3-½" x 10" ring mold or an angel food cake tin may be used.

APPLE PANCAKE

*Sun Valley Inn
Sun Valley, Idaho*

1 cup flour, sifted	4 whole eggs
½ teaspoon salt	3 large tart apples, peeled, cored and thinly sliced
2 teaspoon sugar	
1½ cups milk	¼ cup lemon juice
4 tablespoons butter, melted	

Sift together sifted flour, salt and sugar. Stir in milk and butter. Add eggs, one at a time, beating continuously. Marinate apple slices in lemon juice. Fold sliced apples into batter. Fry pancake on one side in large frying pan, in butter. Turn it over on a buttered baking dish and brown in moderate oven, 350°, 4 to 6 minutes.

ADIRONDACK FLAPJACKS

Mirror Lake Inn
Lake Placid, New York

4 egg yolks, beaten
2 tablespoons sugar
½ teaspoon salt
2 cups milk

6 tablespoons melted
  butter
2 cups flour
2 teaspoons baking powder
4 egg whites, beaten stiff

Beat all the above ingredients together thoroughly. Add whites of egg, beaten stiff, last. Fry on hot griddle. When brown, turn and brown on other side. Serve well-buttered with hot maple syrup or shaved maple sugar as preferred and top with whipped cream. If a flame is desired, a sugar cube may be saturated with lemon extract and lit at the last minute. A bright red cherry is decorative, too. Serve as dessert.

These flapjacks can be used at breakfast. When used as a main course at lunch or dinner, make them a little larger, and eliminate the whipped cream, cherry and flame. Then serve with crisp bacon, sugar-cured ham or country sausage.

GERMAN PANCAKE

The Red Star Inn
Chicago, Illinois

½ cup milk
½ cup flour
3 eggs, beaten
1 tablespoon sugar
Dash salt

Butter
3 tablespoons sugar
¼ teaspoon cinnamon
Juice of ½ lemon

In a bowl, mix milk, flour, eggs, 1 tablespoon sugar and a dash of salt. Butter generously the inside of a 10-inch pan so the pancake will not stick to the sides when it rises. Pour in the batter and bake in a 450° oven for 8 minutes. Reduce heat to 375° and when nearly done powder with sugar mixed with cinnamon. Put some small bits of butter on top, and put back in oven until brown. Before serving sprinkle lemon juice over pancake.

Glaze any kind of fruit in butter and sugar for fruit pancake.

PANDL'S FAMOUS GERMAN PANCAKE

Pandl's Whitefish Bay Inn
Milwaukee, Wisconsin

½ cup all-purpose flour   Pinch salt
½ cup milk   1 pat butter
4 large eggs, well beaten   1 pat shortening

Mix flour, milk and salt until smooth. Add eggs and mix well. Pour into large frying pan which has been greased with a pat of butter and an equal amount of lard or shortening. (Fry pan with sloping sides is best). Fry until golden brown, turn with a spatula. Make 4 criss-cross cuts (2 each way) with spatula. Bake in hot, 425°, oven for about 12 minutes. (Pancake will not begin to rise until about 7 or 8 minutes.) Serve immediately with maple syrup, powdered sugar, jelly, bacon, or any other accompaniment you prefer.

PECAN WAFFLES

Chowning's Tavern
Williamsburg, Virginia

3 eggs, separated   2 teaspoons baking powder
1½ cups milk   1¾ cups flour
½ teaspoon salt   ½ cup butter, melted
1 tablespoon sugar   Pecans, cut into pieces

Beat yolks, and add milk, salt, sugar and baking powder, mixing well with flour. Beat egg whites until peaks form and fold into batter with melted butter. Add pecan pieces to batter. Bake for about 3 minutes in hot waffle iron. Makes 8 waffles.

SPOTTED DOG

The Fort
Morrison, Colorado

¼ pound butter	2 cups cooked apples, cut up
2 loaves dry bread, broken into 1-inch cubes	2 cups applesauce
2 cups Longhorn or sharp Cheddar cheese, grated	2 pounds dark brown sugar
¼ pound pinon nuts, pignatoles, or slivered almonds	1 quart water
	Cream
2 cups raisins, cut up	½ to 1 ounce dark rum

Heat butter and sauté bread cubes. When slightly toasted, mix with cheese, nuts, raisins, apples, apple sauce. Melt sugar in water, bring to a boil and add cinnamon. Place pudding mixture in large, flat baking dish about 3 inches deep. Pour brown sugar syrup over all and bake for 40 minutes at 300°. Serve with cream and dark rum.

Called Spotted Dog by the mountain men, this dish's proper name is "capirotada." It is typically New Mexican. Because of pronunciation difficulties, and due to its raisins, it received the name Spotted Dog.

BRITISH TRIFLE, PRINCE EDWARD

Royal Scots Grill
Pick-Congress Hotel
Chicago, Illinois

8 ounces sponge cake	2 cups custard sauce
½ cup strawberry jam	1 cup fresh strawberries
2 cups whipped cream	¼ cup candied cherries
½ cup sweet sherry	2 ounces angelica, cut up

Cut sponge cake in pieces, and make a layer of sponge in the bottom of a serving dish. Top with jam and half the whipped cream. Pour sherry over it. Add a second layer of cake. Pour custard over all. Cool. Top with remaining whipped cream and garnish with strawberries, cherries and angelica.

Custard Sauce

3 to 4 egg yolks
¼ cup sugar
⅛ teaspoon salt

2 cups milk, scalded
Flavor to taste
(vanilla or rum)

Beat egg yolks, add sugar and salt. Place in top of double boiler over hot water. Add milk to egg yolk mixture, stirring constantly, and continue stirring until mixture begins to thicken. Add flavor.

SWEDISH RAISIN PUFFS

*O'Quinn's Dining Room
La Mesa, California*

1½ cups raisins
1 cup boiling water
2 teaspoons baking soda
½ cup shortening
¾ cup brown sugar

¼ cup white sugar
2 eggs
2 cups flour
½ teaspoon salt

Soak raisins in soda and hot water for four hours or overnight. Drain, reserving water and raisins. Blend shortening and sugar together and beat in eggs. Sift flour and salt and add one-half of this to the creamed mixture. Add juice from raisins and remaining flour to batter. Add raisins last, folding in gently. Drop by small spoonfuls on a greased baking tin. Bake in 400° oven about 20 minutes or until golden brown and light. Makes 36 puffs.

TEA CAKE, BLUEBERRY CAKE AND CORN BREAD

Durgin-Park
Boston, Massachusetts

Tea Cake

¾ cup sugar
2 eggs, beaten well
3 cups flour
1 tablespoon baking powder

¾ teaspoon salt
1 tablespoon butter, melted
1½ cups milk

Mix sugar with beaten eggs. Sift flour, baking powder and salt together. Add melted butter and milk. Beat up quickly and bake in large buttered pan in very hot oven, 425° about 25 minutes.

Blueberry Cake

Add 1 cup blueberries, well drained, last.

Corn Bread

Substitute one cup granulated corn meal for one of the three cups of flour.

CREAM PUFF SHELLS

Chateau Laurier Hotel
Ottawa, Ontario

½ cup water
¼ teaspoon salt
¼ cup butter

½ teaspoon sugar
½ cup flour
2 eggs, unbeaten

Heat water with salt; pour over butter and stir until butter is melted. Add sugar and bring mixture to a boil. Add flour and beat with a wooden spoon until the batter leaves the sides of the pan. Allow to cool for 5 to 6 minutes; then beat in the eggs, one at a time. Pipe onto greased baking sheets, one third the desired size. Recipe will make 6 large cream puff shells. Bake at 400° for 10 minutes; reduce temperature to 300° and bake 30 to 45 minutes, until golden colored.

PECAN COCONUT ICING

The Greenbrier
White Sulphur Springs, West Virginia

1 cup evaporated milk	2 ounces butter, melted
⅔ cup brown sugar	½ cup pecans, cut up
2 egg yolks, slightly beaten	½ cup coconut, shredded

Place milk, brown sugar, egg yolks and butter in a large pan and cook until thick. Be sure to stir to keep from burning. Add pecans and coconut. Let cool. Frost top and between layers of cake.

MAPLE FROSTING

Publick House
Sturbridge, Massachusetts

1¾ cups maple syrup
½ cup egg whites (4 or 5 whites), stiffly beaten

Cook maple syrup to 242° (medium ball). Pour slowly over stiffly beaten egg whites, and continue to beat until very thick and marshmallowlike.

CREAMY CHOCOLATE FUDGE

Craftwood Inn
Manitou Springs, Colorado

2 to 3 tablespoons butter
2 cups sugar
1 cup evaporated milk
Dash salt
1 to 2 ounces chocolate
 chips

2 tablespoons marshmallow
 creme
1 cup pecans, broken
1 teaspoon vanilla

Put butter, sugar, milk and salt in a pan and bring to a boil. Cook gently to 236° on a candy thermometer. Stir constantly. Remove from heat and add chocolate chips and marshmallow creme. Stir until smooth. Add pecans and vanilla. Pour into buttered pans. Makes about 1¼ pounds of fudge.

CHOCOLATE MOUSSE

Doc's Airpark Restaurant
Quincy, Illinois

3 squares baking
 chocolate, melted
½ cup powdered sugar
1 cup milk
1 scant tablespoon
 unflavored gelatin

¼ cup cold water
¾ cup granulated sugar
Pinch salt
2 cups heavy cream,
 whipped

Bring chocolate, powdered sugar and milk to a boil.
Soak gelatin in cold water. Add to chocolate mixture. Stir until smooth. Add granulated sugar and pinch salt. Stir well. Chill (set pan in another pan containing ice cubes and water). When thick, beat until light in color with electric mixer. Add cream whipped stiff but not dry.
Butter well 1½ quart ring mold. Pour mixture into mold and set in refrigerator for at least 3 hours. Wipe with a hot cloth and invert on serving dish.
Mousse usually is frozen, but this one is not.

MOUSSE AU CHOCOLAT

Chez Bruchez
Daytona Beach, Florida

6 ounces Baker's chocolate (6 squares)
3 tablespoons water
½ cup sugar (¾ cup sugar may be used, if desired)
1 cup light cream

4 eggs, separated
1 tablespoon vanilla flavor
¾ cup heavy cream, whipped
Cherries, nuts, for garnish

Melt chocolate with water. Add sugar and mix. Mix cream with egg yolks and add to chocolate. Add vanilla. Whip egg whites until stiff. Add chocolate mixture. Stir lightly and pour into glass mold. Let chill. When ready to serve, top with whipped cream, candied cherries and nuts.

CHOCOLATE POTS DE CREME

Restaurant Laurent
New York City

Scald 2 cups cream with 1-inch piece of vanilla bean, 4 ounces melted sweet chocolate and ¼ cup sugar; cool slightly. Beat 6 egg yolks until light and lemon-colored, then add cream, stirring constantly. Strain mixture through fine sieve and pour into 6 small earthenware pots or custard cups. Set in pan of water, cover and bake in 250° oven for 15 minutes or until a knife inserted in the center comes out clean. Serve chilled. Serves 6.

CHOCOLATE SOUFFLE PUDDING

The Greenbrier
White Sulphur Springs, West Virginia

1 pint milk
4 ounces butter
1 cup flour
5 egg yolks

2 tablespoons sweet
chocolate, melted
5 egg whites
5 ounces granulated
sugar

Boil milk. Mix butter and flour, stirring continuously. Add milk and stir until the mixture is stiff; then remove from flame and add egg yolks, one at a time. After all the egg yolks are in, add melted chocolate and mix thoroughly.

Beat egg whites and sugar to meringue and fold carefully into chocolate mixture.

Pour mixture into a buttered and sugared soufflé dish or mold and bake at 350° for approximately 30 minutes. To prevent burning, place dish of soufflé in pan of water while baking.

Serve with Sabayon or vanilla sauce.

CHOCOLATE SOUFFLÉ

Monblason Inn
Pine Plains, New York

2 squares Baker's
unsweetened chocolate
⅓ cup superfine sugar
3 teaspoons instant coffee
⅓ cup hot water
2 tablespoons flour
4 tablespoons sweet butter

1 cup scalded milk
1 tablespoon vanilla
extract
4 egg yolks
7 egg whites
2 tablespoons superfine
sugar

Melt chocolate in double boiler, add sugar and stir, then mix in coffee mixed with hot water. Make a smooth white sauce with butter, flour and milk and combine with chocolate mixture. Cool until just warm and then stir in the egg yolks, mix well, and add the vanilla. Beat the egg whites until stiff, but not dry, add 2 tablespoons superfine sugar, beat one more minute and fold in the chocolate sauce. Pour in a well-greased 2½-quart soufflé dish. Bake 5 minutes in preheated 375° oven, then reduce heat to 350° and bake 20 minutes longer.

Seerve with "Creme Chantilly" (whipped cream with a little fine sugar and vanilla added).

SOUFFLE GRAND MARNIER

The Voisin Restaurant
New York City

6 eggs, separated
4 ounces granulated sugar
2 ounces flour

6 drops vanilla extract
1 pint milk
2 ounces Grand Marnier

Boil the milk. Mix the egg yolks and sugar and flour in a bowl. Pour the boiling milk into mixture, stirring continuously. Return mixture to the pan and bring to a boil. Add vanilla and Grand Marnier and cool mixture. Beat egg whites until very stiff and fold into the mixture. Pour into a well buttered soufflé dish and bake at 375° for 30 to 45 minutes. Serve immediately.

SOUFFLE AU KIRSCH

The Greenbrier
White Sulphur Springs,
West Virginia

½ cup powdered sugar
½ cup flour
4 eggs
1 pint milk, boiling

1 tablespoon sweet butter
3 tablespoons Kirsch
liqueur

Mix sugar and flour with one whole egg and the yolks of the other three eggs. Dilute with the boiling milk. Cook for 2 minutes, stirring constantly. Remove from fire and add butter. When cool, add Kirsch and 3 egg whites, whisked to a very stiff froth. Turn into a buttered baking dish. Bake in a moderate oven, 350°, about 30 to 45 minutes. Remove from oven and serve at once.

SOUFFLE A L'ORANGE

Quo Vadis
New York City

1 cup milk
3 ounces sweet butter
3 ounces flour
3 ounces sugar

1 orange
5 eggs, separated
3 ounces Grand Marnier
Preheat oven to 350°.

Grate orange rind, add to milk, heat milk in a pot with sugar. Cream butter, add flour. When milk is boiling, add flour-butter paste. Cook 3 minutes, remove from fire, add 4 egg yolks. Meanwhile beat the 5 egg whites to a stiff froth, then fold them into mixture. Fold in Grand Marnier. Pour batter into buttered souffle mold and bake for 25 to 35 minutes at 350°.

MRS. L. G. TREADWAY'S BLUEBERRY PUDDING

The Williams Inn
Williamstown, Massachusetts

4 cups blueberries
1 cup sugar
½ cup water

8 thin slices white bread
Softened butter
Cream or ice cream

This pudding is especially good when it is made with small ripe native blueberries rather than large cultivated ones. Bring the berries, sugar, and water slowly to a boil and simmer for 10 minutes. Remove the crusts from the bread and spread each slice with softened butter. If a small 9 x 4½ inch loaf pan is used, the bread will just fit, 2 pieces in each layer. Place the bread, buttered side down, in the pan and cover with hot berries. Continue these layers, ending with berries. Let stand until cool, then chill in the refrigerator. To serve, unmold on a platter and slice. Serve with cream or ice cream.

FAIRYLAND PUDDING

Brooks Hotel
Corvallis, Montana

1 medium sized angel
  food cake
2 cups crushed pineapple
1 pint milk
2 eggs, separated
¼ teaspoon salt
1½ tablespoons gelatin

8 tablespoons water
1 teaspoon vanilla
1 pint heavy cream,
  whipped
½ cup pecans, chopped
Maraschino cherries,
  chopped

Break angel food cake into small pieces and spread on bottom of shallow pan. Over this spread crushed pineapple.

In double boiler cook milk, egg yolks and salt until thick. Add gelatin which has been softened in cold water. Let cool until it begins to set, then fold in beaten egg whites, vanilla and whipped cream. Pour over cake and sprinkle with pecans and a few chopped maraschino cherries. Chill overnight and cut in squares.

BAKED INDIAN PUDDING

Durgin-Park
Boston, Massachusetts

½ cup yellow granulated
  corn meal
½ cup black molasses
¼ cup lard or butter

1 teaspoon salt
¼ teaspoon baking soda
2 eggs, well beaten
1 quart hot milk

Mix all the ingredients thoroughly with one half the hot milk and bake in very hot oven until it boils. Then stir in remaining half hot milk, and bake in slow oven, 325° for 2 to 3 hours. Bake in stone crock, well greased inside.

Delicious with a scoop of vanilla ice cream on top of piping hot pudding just taken from the crock.

BAKED INDIAN PUDDING

Olde Grist Mill
Kennebunkport, Maine

2 cups scalding milk	1 teaspoon salt
⅓ cup corn meal	1 teaspoon ginger or
½ cup molasses	cinnamon
½ cup sugar	2 cups cold milk
¼ cup butter	

Pour scalding milk on corn meal; cook in double boiler for 20 minutes. Add molasses, sugar, butter, salt and ginger or cinnamon. Pour hot mixture into buttered pudding dish, then pour in 2 cups cold milk. Do not stir.

Set in a pan of hot water and bake 3 hours in 250° oven. Top warm pudding with ice cream or with sweetened whipped cream. Serves 6 generously.

FLORENCE'S SWEET POTATO PUDDING

Purefoy Hotel
Talladega, Alabama

2½ cups raw sweet potatoes, pared and grated	½ teaspoon grated lemon rind
2 eggs, beaten until light	2 teaspoons lemon juice
1 cup sugar	½ teaspoon cinnamon
1½ cups rich milk	½ teaspoon nutmeg
¼ cup butter, melted	Cream (optional)
	Brown sugar (optional)

Put potatoes in mixing bowl; add eggs, mix well. Gradually beat in sugar; stir in milk, butter, lemon rind and juice. Add cinnamon and nutmeg. Mix thoroughly. Pour pudding in a greased baking dish. Bake in a moderate oven, 350°, for 30 to 45 minutes, or until light brown and well set. If desired, it can be served with cream; brown sugar sprinkled over the top is better.

NEW SALEM VILLAGE PUDDING

New Salem Lodge
Petersburg, Illinois

6 cinnamon rolls
1½ cups raisins
2 cups custard sauce
(see English Trifle
recipe)

Nutmeg, to taste
Lemon sauce, or cream,
optional

Slice cinnamon rolls horizontally into pieces about ¾ inch thick. Place the pieces in a pan approximately 3 inches deep and sprinkle generously with raisins. Over this, pour an egg custard, nearly filling the pan. This will cause the rolls to rise to the top. Sprinkle with nutmeg and bake in a medium oven, 350°. Serve with a lemon sauce or cream.

KNUDSON HOUSE RUM PUDDING

The Knudson House Norge
Ephraim, Wisconsin

3 eggs, separated
½ cup sugar
1½ tablespoons flour
Dash salt
2 cups milk, scalded
1 teaspoon gelatin

3 teaspoons cold water
Rum, to taste
1 cup heavy cream,
whipped (optional)
Candied fruit, cut up
(optional)

Beat egg yolks until creamy. Mix sugar and flour together and gradually add to egg yolks. Add salt and scalded milk to mixture. Cook in double boiler until thick. Add gelatin dissolved in water, to cooked mixture. When cool, add rum to taste. Add either three beaten egg whites or, for a richer pudding, whipped cream, and bits of fruit, if desired.

TIVOLI RUM PUDDING

Arne Nissen's Tivoli
Toledo, Ohio

3 egg yolks
6 tablespoons sugar
2 tablespoons rum
¼ teaspoon salt

1 tablespoon unflavored
  gelatin
¾ cup cold water
1 cup heavy cream,
  whipped to soft peak

Beat egg yolks and sugar well, add rum and salt. Soak gelatin in water and dissolve over hot water. Combine with egg mixture and as it thickens, fold in whipped cream. Pour into individual molds and chill. When ready to serve, top with lingonberry preserves (Swedish wild currant). A dash of rum or brandy may be added to the lingonberries for added flavor.

ALMENDRADO

Old Adobe Patio Restaurant
Tuscon, Arizona

1 envelope unflavored
  gelatin
¼ cup cold water
4 egg whites
½ cup sugar
Pinch of salt

3 drops almond flavoring
Red and green vegetable
  coloring
¼ pound blanched
  almonds, ground

Be sure egg whites are at room temperature.

Dissolve gelatin in cold water. Set over hot water to liquefy and then cool, stirring occasionally until it reaches the consistency of syrup. (If it is too hot the gelatin will thin egg whites too much.)

Whip egg whites until stiff. Gradually add sugar, salt, gelatin and flavoring.

Divide into three bowls. Color one part red or pink, one green and add the ground almonds to the remaining white.

Pour in layers into loaf shaped Pyrex dish, making the center layer white. (Makes one think of the Mexican flag, doesn't it?)

Place in refrigerator. When firmly set, slice like brick ice cream and serve the custard sauce over each portion.

Delectable with Mexican food!

Custard Sauce for Almendrado

2 egg yolks	1½ cups scalded milk
¼ cup sugar	¼ teaspoon almond
⅛ teaspoon salt	flavoring

Beat egg yolks slightly with a silver fork; add sugar and salt. Add milk gradually, stirring constantly.

Cook and stir in double boiler over hot, but not boiling, water until mixture coats the spoon, about 7 minutes.

Add the flavoring and chill.

NATILLA

El Parador Café
New York City

1 cup sugar	5 eggs, well beaten
3 tablespoons cornstarch	2 tablespoons butter
¼ teaspoon salt	1 teaspoon vanilla extract
1 quart milk	Cinnamon

Combine sugar, cornstarch, and salt. Stir in ¼ cup milk to make a smooth paste. Add eggs and stir until smooth. Scald remaining 3¾ cups milk in top of double boiler. Add egg mixture slowly. Place over boiling water and stir constantly with wooden spoon until mixture thickens slightly and spoon becomes coated. Stir in butter and vanilla. Pour into individual serving dishes. Chill. Before serving, sprinkle on cinnamon.

BAVARIAN MINT DESSERT

Hilltop House
Omaha, Nebraska

½ pound butter
2 cups powdered sugar
6 egg yolks
5 squares semi-sweet
    chocolate, melted

2½ teaspoons peppermint
    extract
6 egg whites, stiffly beaten
Vanilla wafer crumbs

Cream together the butter and powdered sugar. Add egg yolks, melted chocolate and peppermint extract. Fold in egg whites. Pour mixture into pan approximately 7 x 12. Cover with vanilla wafer crumbs. Place in refrigerator until firm, 1 to 3 hours.

MAMMY LOU CARAMEL CUSTARD

Evans Farm Inn
McLean, Virginia

4 eggs
½ cup sugar
⅛ teaspoon salt

2 cups milk
1 teaspoon vanilla

Beat eggs well, add sugar, salt, then milk and vanilla. Place small amount of caramel syrup in bottom of mold or other oven-proof custard cups. Pour custard mixture over caramel. Place custard cups in pan half filled with water. Bake at 300° for 30 to 40 minutes. When a silver knife comes out clean, the custard is done. Do not let water boil or the custard will curdle.

Caramel Syrup

½ cup sugar

Melt sugar over low heat, in a heavy skillet, stirring constantly, until the sugar melts and turns light brown.

BAKED ALASKA

Century Inn
Scenery Hill, Pennsylvania

1 loaf cake (your favorite)	5 egg whites
1½ quarts ice cream, brick or bulk (very hard)	½ teaspoon cream of tartar
	⅔ cup sugar

Slice cake in half lengthwise. Use the bottom half. Cover a bread board, large enough to hold the cake, with white paper or aluminum foil. Place the cut cake on the paper. Then pile ice cream on the cake. Make sure the cake extends about one inch beyond the ice cream.

Just before serving, beat egg whites until foamy, then add cream of tartar. Beat until smooth. Gradually add the sugar. Continue beating until meringue is stiff and glossy.

Completely cover ice cream and sides of cake with a thick covering of the meringue. Place in preheated 450° oven. Just as soon as meringue is golden brown, remove.

Slip dessert from bread board to serving platter and serve immediately.

SEA FOAM FLEET

The Careless Navigator Restaurant
Treasure Island, Florida

1 pint heavy cream, whipped	Grated rind of 1 orange
1 tablespoon powdered sugar	Grated rind of ¼ lemon
1 ounce Triple Sec (or other orange flavored liqueur)	2 oranges, sectioned
	Graham cracker crust with chocolate

Line six champagne glasses with graham cracker crust. Whip cream and fold in powdered sugar. Add Triple Sec. Add half of grated rinds. Place in pastry bag, squeeze generous amount into each glass on top of crust. Pyramid 4 orange sections on top of each and swirl remaining whipped cream mixture on top. Sprinkle each with remaining rind and freeze for 24 hours.

BISCUIT DE SAVOIE AUX FRAISES AND SAUCE A LA RITZ

The Penrose Room
The Broadmoor Hotel
Colorado Springs, Colorado

8 egg yolks	⅔ cup potato starch
1½ cups sugar	½ teaspoon salt
2 tablespoons powdered	½ teaspoon vanilla
sugar	extract
1 cup flour, sifted	8 egg whites
1 pint strawberries	

Combine egg yolks and sugar in mixing bowl. Place in hot water and beat by hand for 20 minutes or until mixture reaches 98° on candy thermometer. Remove bowl from hot water and beat with electric mixer until fluffy and cold. Add powdered sugar, flour, potato starch, and salt which have been mixed together. Add vanilla extract and last fold in the stiffly beaten egg whites. Bake in buttered and floured ring mold in slow oven, 325°, until cake shrinks from sides of the pan.

When serving Biscuit, fill center with strawberries sprinkled with sugar. Serve on the side Sauce a la Ritz.

Sauce a la Ritz

1 cup heavy cream,	1 cup purée of raspberries
whipped	Triple Sec, to taste

Mix ingredients together, gently, but thoroughly. Chill until ready to serve.

SUGAR COOKIES

Lake Breeze Resort
Three Lakes, Wisconsin

1¼ cups flour, sifted
¼ teaspoon baking
  powder
¼ teaspoon soda
¼ teaspoon salt

¼ cup butter
¼ cup lard
2 large eggs
¾ cup sugar
1 teaspoon vanilla

Sift flour, baking powder, soda and salt together. Blend in butter and lard as for piecrust.

Combine eggs, sugar and vanilla. Beat till thick and fluffy. Add to dry ingredients and shortening. Mix well.

Roll out thin and cut with cookie cutter on lightly floured board. Place on greased pan. Bake in 400° oven, 7 to 10 minutes, until light brown.

SELF-FROSTING COOKIES

Whitney's
Jackson, New Hampshire

½ cup butter or oleo
1 cup sugar
1 egg and 1 egg yolk,
  well beaten
1½ cups all-purpose flour,
  sifted
¼ teaspoon salt

1 teaspoon baking powder
1 tablespoon milk
½ teaspoon vanilla
1 egg white
1 cup brown sugar
½ cup nuts, chopped

Mix together butter and sugar. Add whole egg and egg yolk. Sift together flour, salt and baking powder and stir into butter mixture. Add milk and vanilla. Place into a 9 by 9-inch buttered tin. Beat egg white, add brown sugar. Spread over cookie mixture. Sprinkle with chopped nuts. Bake 30 minutes in 325° oven. Cut in squares.

CRANBERRY CRUNCH

Menemsha Inn
Menemsha, Massachusetts

1 cup uncooked oatmeal	½ cup butter
½ cup flour	1 can jellied cranberry
1 cup light brown sugar	sauce

Mix oatmeal, flour and brown sugar. Cut in butter to make a crumb mixture. Spread half of mixture in well greased 8 x 8 baking pan. Cut jellied cranberry sauce in slices and place over mixture. Cover with balance of the mixture. Bake 35 to 40 minutes in 350° oven. Serve at room temperature with vanilla ice cream.

APPLE FRITTERS

Moselem Springs Inn
Moselem Springs, Pennsylvania

2 eggs	1 cup flour, sifted
1 cup milk	2 tablespoons sugar
1 tablespoon butter, melted	1 teaspoon baking powder
¼ teaspoon salt	3 medium size apples

Beat together eggs, milk and butter. Add sifted flour, re-sifted with salt, sugar and baking powder. Peel and core apples. Slice ⅓ inch thick. Dip in batter and fry in deep hot (370°) fat from 3 to 5 minutes. Drain on absorbent paper. Sprinkle with powdered sugar.

DATE BARS

Waioli Tea Room
Honolulu, Hawaii

Date Mixture

2 cups dates, cut up
½ cup brown sugar
1 cup water

1 tablespoon flour
2 teaspoons vanilla

Cook dates with sugar, water and flour slowly until thick but soft. Let cool, then add vanilla to mixture.

Dry Mixture

1¼ cups flour, sifted
½ teaspoon baking soda
1 teaspoon salt

2 cups rolled oats
(old fashioned)
1 cup brown sugar
¾ cup butter, melted

Stir butter and sugar together. Sift together flour, soda and salt and add to butter mixture. Add rolled oats and mix well.

Press half of dry mixture into an 8 x 8 inch pan. Pour the date mixture over the dry layer. Press the rest of the dry mixture over the date layer. Bake at 400° for 30 to 35 minutes, until light brown. While warm, cut into bars.

CAMELBACK INN BARS

Camelback Inn
Phoenix, Arizona

First Part

½ cup butter
¼ cup granulated sugar
1 egg
4 tablespoons cocoa

2 cups graham wafer
crumbs
1 cup coconut
½ cup chopped nuts

Mix butter, sugar, egg and cocoa. Set over boiling water and stir until mixture resembles a custard. Combine crumbs, coconut and nuts. Blend well with custard mixture. Spread and press tightly in 9 by 9 inch pan.

Second Part

¼ cup butter	2 cups powdered sugar, sifted
3 tablespoons milk	
2 tablespoons vanilla custard powder	4 squares semi-sweet chocolate, melted
	1 tablespoon butter

Cream butter, milk, custard powder and powdered sugar. Spread over mixture in pan. Melt the chocolate over hot water, add butter, and blend well. Spread over the icing mixture and let it set. Cut into small bars.

Very rich!

APPLE DUMPLING, VANILLA SAUCE

Lake Mohonk Mountain House
New Paltz, New York

6 medium size baking apples	3 teaspoons cinnamon
6 tablespoons sugar	3 teaspoons butter
	1 recipe rich pie crust

Peel and core medium size baking apples. Roll a rich pie crust into a 12-inch square, cut out 4-inch circles, cover the bottom half of the apple with the crust; fill the center of apple with cinnamon, sugar and dot with a little piece of butter. Put another circle of crust over the top of apple, join crusts together by moistening edges with a little water. Bake in moderate oven, 350° for 45 minutes or until brown.

Vanilla Sauce

¾ cup milk	1 tablespoon cornstarch
½ cup sugar	2 teaspoons vanilla

Bring milk to boil. Mix sugar and cornstarch together and add to milk, stirring until smooth. Cool for one minute, add flavoring, put apple dumpling in dish, cover with sauce and serve.

COTTAGE CHEESE AND ALMOND PUFFS

Chateau Laurier Hotel
Ottawa, Ontario

2 cups cottage cheese
1 teaspoon lemon juice
½ cup seedless raisins
½ cup toasted almonds, slivered

¼ teaspoon salt
12 cream puff shells
Assorted fruits for garnish

Combine cheese, lemon juice, raisins, almonds, and salt. Split cream puff shells, line bottom with lettuce leaf, place a generous scoop of cheese mixture on top of lettuce and cap with other half of cream puff.

Serve accompanied with sliced pineapple, peaches, pears, cluster of grapes or bing cherries.

PECAN CONFECTIONS

King's Arms Tavern
Williamsburg, Virginia

1 egg white
1 cup brown sugar
Pinch salt

1 tablespoon flour
1 cup pecans, chopped

Beat egg white to a stiff froth. Add, gradually, the brown sugar, salt, flour. Stir in chopped pecans, and drop on greased tins by small spoonsful far apart. Bake in a very slow oven, 250°, 15 minutes. Remove from tin when partly cooled. Makes 2 dozen.

OLD FASHIONED FREEZER ICE CREAM

Brookville Hotel
Brookville, Kansas

2 eggs	1½ cups heavy cream
1 cup sugar	2 teaspoons vanilla
1 teaspoon salt	1 quart milk

Beat eggs until very light. Gradually add sugar and salt. Beat mixture well. Then add cream and vanilla. Add milk last. Allow about 2½ inches for swelling in freezer can. Freeze in dash type old fashioned ice cream freezer. Makes 2 quarts of delicious vanilla ice cream.

ROSETTES WITH CHOCOLATE SAUCE OR FRESH STRAWBERRIES

Ola Restaurant
Boston, Massachusetts

Rosettes

1 cup flour	½ teaspoon salt
1 cup milk	2 tablespoons sugar
2 eggs	Shortening or lard for frying

Beat flour, milk, eggs, salt and sugar for a few minutes with an egg beater. Fry in shortening at 375°, using rosette iron. Drain rosettes on absorbent paper.

Filling for Rosettes

Place in center of each rosette 1 tablespoon whipped cream. Cover with chocolate sauce. Crushed strawberries mixed with a little sugar, or sliced peaches may be used also. Do not put sugar into whipped cream. The sauce makes the filling sweet enough.

ENGLISH TAFFEE

The Eagles Nest
Verona, Wisconsin

1 cup vanilla wafers, crushed	1½ squares unsweetened chocolate, melted
1 cup walnuts, chopped	½ teaspoon vanilla
¼ pound butter	1 cup heavy cream, whipped
1 cup powdered sugar	
3 eggs, separated	

Mix crushed wafers and chopped nuts. Spread ½ of mixture over bottom of buttered 9″ x 9″ pan. Cream butter and sugar. Add beaten egg yolks, melted chocolate and vanilla. Fold in beaten egg whites. Pour over wafers and spread remaining wafers-nut mixture on top. Refrigerate overnight. Cut in squares and serve with whipped cream.

APPLE CRISP

Cobb's Mill Inn
Weston, Connecticut

4 cups tart apples, sliced	¾ cup flour
½ cup water (less if the apples are very juicy)	1 cup sugar
1 teaspoon cinnamon	½ cup butter

Arrange apples in deep baking dish. Add water. Blend cinnamon, flour, sugar and butter with fork. Add to apples and bake at 350° until the apples are half done. Take out of oven.

Make biscuit dough using two cups of good commercial biscuit mix and the proportionate amount of water indicated in the package plus a little additional water to make the dough lighter. Spread unevenly on the apples.

Topping

½ cup flour
⅓ cup butter
1 cup sugar
½ teaspoon cinnamon

Ice cream or
¾ cup heavy cream,
   whipped

Mix ingredients and crumble together. Spread on top of the biscuit mixture. Put the pan back in the oven and continue baking at 350° until the biscuit dough has risen and the crumbs are golden brown.

Serve with ice cream or whipped cream.

Note: The baking time depends on the type of apples used.

APPLE BEIGNET

*Barberian's Steak House
Toronto, Ontario*

3 large apples
2 eggs
1½ teaspoon sugar
1 cup milk
1 cup flour, sifted
½ teaspoon salt

½ teaspoon vanilla
1 tablespoon melted
   butter
Cinnamon sugar
Walnuts, crushed
Ice cream

Peel apples, remove cores and slice ¼ inch thick. Prepare batter as follows:

In a mixing bowl, beat eggs, add sugar, milk, vanilla and melted butter. Add flour and salt. Stir together until batter is fairly thick. If not thick enough, add more flour.

Dip apple slices in batter. Fry in hot deep fat at 350° until golden brown. Remove from fat and drain well on absorbent paper. Cover with sugar and cinnamon mixture. Sprinkle with crushed walnuts and serve with ice cream.

BRANDIED FRUIT THAIS

The Caribbean Room
The Pontchartrain Hotel
New Orleans, Louisiana

Use assorted fruits, such as peaches, apricots, pears, pineapple, bananas, and pitted Bing cherries or use drained canned fruit. Arrange fruits in layers in a baking dish. Sprinkle each layer with brown sugar, dabs of butter and shredded blanched almonds. Pour one half cup sherry over all and cover the top with crushed macaroon crumbs. Bake 20 minutes and serve hot.

The amounts to be used vary according to individual taste and the size of the baking dish.

BRANDIED FRUIT

Corinne Dunbar's
New Orleans, Louisiana

1 cup each peach slices, apricot slices and pineapple chunks (canned)
12 red maraschino cherries, chopped
12 green maraschino cherries, chopped
1 pinch cinnamon
3 ounces brandy

Pour off all fruit juices and save for sauce. Dissolve cinnamon in a bit of water and add to juices. Add brandy and stir. Pour mixture back over fruit and marinate overnight. Serve in parfait glasses.

Note: The addition of fresh strawberries in season is an interesting variation.

BANANAS FOSTER

Brennan's
New Orleans, Louisiana

6 bananas	¼ cup rum
¼ pound butter	2 tablespoons creme de
1 cup brown sugar	banana
2 teaspoons cinnamon	Vanilla ice cream, to taste

Cut bananas into 4 lengthwise strips each. Brown butter with brown sugar and cinnamon. When the sugar has melted and the mixture begins to thicken, place bananas in the pan and cook until soft. Just before serving, add rum and creme de banana. Ignite and serve while hot, either plain or over vanilla ice cream.

SHERRIED BANANAS

Corinne Dunbar's
New Orleans, Louisiana

6 half-ripe bananas	3 cloves
½ cup butter	½ lemon, sliced
1 cup sugar	2 tablespoons sherry
2 cups water	

Cut bananas in half, lengthwise. Fry in ¼ cup butter until golden brown and remove from skillet. Brown sugar in skillet. Add water and cook until it forms a thick syrup. Add cloves, lemon, remaining butter and sherry and simmer 10 minutes. Add bananas and simmer 5 to 10 minutes more.

BANANAS FLAMBÉE À LA CARIBIENNE

The Red Onion
Aspen, Colorado

6 bananas
2 oranges, peeled and
cut into sections
Juice of 1 orange
4 tablespoons butter

¾ cup sugar
¼ cup dark rum
¼ cup cream
½ pint vanilla ice cream
¼ cup Grand Marnier

Peel bananas and slice in half lengthwise. Peel oranges carefully and cut rind into thin strips. Pour the juice of the orange over the bananas. Sprinkle chafing dish with sugar and heat until sugar is caramelized. Then add butter and orange sections and mix well. Add banana halves. After the orange juice has evaporated, flambé with rum. Next add cream and let simmer for a few minutes, until bananas are cooked. Place bananas on serving dish with one spoon of vanilla ice cream. Cook glacé sauce until of syrup consistency. Add Grand Marnier and pour over the bananas and ice cream.

ORANGES MOROCCO

Quorum
Denver, Colorado

6 oranges
2 tablespoons butter
2 tablespoons granulated
sugar
2 tablespoons brown sugar

½ cup almonds, blanched
and shredded
¾ cup dates, shredded
¼ cup brandy
Ice cream or orange sherbet

Peel and thinly slice oranges. Heat butter in a chafing dish; add granulated and brown sugar and allow to dissolve being careful not to burn the sugar. Place the oranges in the sugar-butter mixture and cook for 2 to 3 minutes. Add almonds and dates and heat; pour over the brandy and flame; when the fire has gone out, spoon over ice cream or orange sherbet.

STRAWBERRY CHANTILLY

El Chorro Lodge
Scottsdale, Arizona

1 cup strawberry purée	2 tablespoons water
12 tablespoons sugar	2 cups heavy cream,
Pinch salt	whipped
1½ teaspoons gelatin	Meringue layers
	(see recipe below)

Rub strawberries through a sieve to make 1 cup purée. Add sugar and pinch of salt. Soak gelatin in 2 tablespoons water. Dissolve over hot water and add to strawberry purée. Beat cream until stiff and fold in the strawberry mixture. Put 1 meringue layer in tray. Cover with strawberry mixture. Top with meringue and freeze.

Meringue Layers

4 egg whites	¼ teaspoon vanilla
¾ cup sugar	5 teaspoons sugar

Beat egg whites until stiff. Add ¾ cup sugar gradually and vanilla. Fold in 5 teaspoons sugar and shape on tin sheet covered with letter paper, in four portions the size of freezer tray. Bake about 30 minutes at 250°. Turn over and remove paper by laying a damp cloth over it for a few minutes.

BEIGNETS DE FRAISES IMPERIAL HOUSE

Imperial House
Chicago, Illinois

Beignets

1½ cups flour	1½ cups milk
⅓ teaspoon salt	2 tablespoons butter,
2 teaspoons sugar	melted
3 eggs	1 quart strawberries

Combine flour, salt and sugar. Beat eggs with milk and melted butter. Add the liquid to the dry ingredients, stirring constantly to make a rather thin batter. Roll perfect washed and hulled strawberries in granulated sugar and dip them into the batter. Fry the "Beignets" lightly in deep hot fat (370°), drain them on absorbent paper, and sprinkle them lightly with powdered sugar. Serve at once with a sauceboat of Sauce Sabayon (see below).

Sabayon

6 egg yolks
½ cup granulated sugar

¼ cup Marsala or Sherry
¼ cup dry white wine
2 tablespoons brandy

Whip egg yolks and granulated sugar until the mixture is light and almost white in color. Stir in Marsala or Sherry and dry white wine and the brandy. Cook in the top of a double boiler over hot water (not boiling water) or in the blazer of a chafing dish, stirring constantly, until the mixture has quadrupled in bulk and is very foamy.

PECHE MACERE AU COGNAC

*The John Bartram Hotel
Philadelphia, Pennsylvania*

1 pint water
6 fresh Alberta peaches
6 tablespoons honey
1 orange cut in four,
with skin left on

6 tablespoons maple syrup
4 cloves
2 cinnamon sticks
3 to 4 ounces cognac
French vanilla ice cream

Boil water with peaches, honey, orange, syrup, cloves and cinnamon sticks, for 10 minutes. Remove peaches. When cool, remove skin from peaches, split peaches and remove the stones. Strain the juice. Place peaches and juice in a chafing dish. Allow to simmer for 2 minutes. Add cognac for flaming. Place peaches on top of ice cream and add the flaming remains.

PESCE IMBOTTITI IN MARSALA
(Baked Stuffed Peaches in Marsala Wine)

Terry and Jerry's O Solo Mio
Bay City, Michigan

12 canned peach halves, drained	4 walnuts, chopped fine
6 macaroons, crumbled	2 ounces Cream de Almond
4 almonds, chopped fine	½ teaspoon almond extract
	½ cup sweet Marsala wine

Mix macaroons, nuts, extract and cordial; fill cavity of peaches. Place in baking pan. Pour Marsala over peaches and bake in 350° oven for 15 minutes.

HALEKULANI BAKED PINEAPPLE IN FLAMES

Halekulani Hotel
Honolulu, Hawaii

1 ripe pineapple	Brandy
Powdered sugar	Rum
Kirsch	Vanilla ice cream
1 tablespoon cornstarch	1 cup heavy cream,
2 tablespoons pineapple juice	whipped

Remove the top from one ripe pineapple, cutting it about 1 inch down the green leaves. Remove the meat from the pineapple, leaving about ½ inch of the flesh all around. Cut meat into cubes, marinate in powdered sugar and Kirsch. Thicken with cornstarch which has been diluted with a little pineapple juice. Cook the above mixture in a saucepan until the pineapple cubes are partly cooked. Refill shell. Cover, and bake in oven at 375° for 2 minutes. Pour in a little brandy and rum. Ignite and keep pineapple mixture in flames for a few minutes.

On each serving plate, place vanilla ice cream (brick) with a ring of whipped cream topped with the baked pineapple cubes.

FRAISES MIMOSA

*The Baroque Restaurant
New York City*

1 quart strawberries
3 oranges, peeled and
sliced

Kirsch and sugar to taste
2 cups heavy cream,
whipped
2 tablespoons sugar

Clean strawberries thoroughly. Slice oranges. Mix strawberries and sliced oranges with Kirsch and sugar. Whip cream; add sugar while whipping.

Mix ⅔ of the whipped cream with the strawberries and oranges and place in serving bowl. Add a little red color to remainder of whipped cream (this is optional) and cover the contents of bowl; decorate to taste.

ORANGES MOROCCO

*Quorum
Denver, Colorado*

6 oranges
2 tablespoons butter
2 tablespoons granulated
sugar
2 tablespoons brown sugar

½ cup almonds, blanched
and shredded
¾ cup dates, shredded
¼ cup brandy
Ice cream or orange sherbet

Peel and thinly slice oranges. Heat butter in a chafing dish; add granulated and brown sugar and allow to dissolve being careful not to burn the sugar. Place the oranges in the sugar-butter mixture and cook for 2 to 3 minutes. Add almonds and dates and heat; pour over the brandy and flame; when the fire has gone out, spoon over ice cream or orange sherbet.

CARAMEL POPCORN

Bar X Bar Ranch
Crawford, Colorado

3 quarts popped corn	1 tablespoon butter
1 cup white sugar	1 teaspoon soda
1 cup dark syrup	½ teaspoon salt
½ cup water	

Pop corn; set aside. Mix sugar, syrup and water; cook until mixture forms hard ball (252° on candy thermometer) when small amount is placed in cold water. Add butter, soda and salt and mix well. Pour over popped corn, stirring until all corn is coated.

CRÊPES SUZETTE

The Gill Hotel
Fort Lauderdale, Florida

Batter	*Sauce*
¾ cup flour, sifted	2 ounces sweet butter
2 eggs	15 small sugar cubes
1 egg yolk	Juice of 1 orange
1 ounce sugar	Juice of ¼ lemon
1 cup milk	2 tablespoons Curacao
1 pinch salt	Liqueur
½ teaspoon vanilla extract	3 tablespoons Grand
½ ounce butter	Marnier Liqueur
¼ pound butter for	3 tablespoons Cognac
cooking	

You will need two small French frying pans, 5-inch diameter, and a chafing dish.

Place into a mixing bowl the eggs, egg yolk, sugar and salt and mix with a wire whip. Add the sifted flour and beat until smooth. Add slowly, while stirring, lukewarm milk, vanilla extract, and blend thoroughly. Place ½ ounce butter in a frying pan and heat until light brown and add this butter to the batter while hot. Blend well. This amount of batter will make 30 five-inch, very thin crêpes.

To fry, first prepare some clarified butter made by placing ¼ pound butter in a sauce pan and melting it slowly. Let stand for 10 minutes. Pour off the clarified butter into another utensil and discard the milky mixture.

Then preheat pan on moderate heat, place small amount of hot butter into pan and pour excess butter back into the utensil. It is important that the pan is thoroughly buttered, but that there is not too much butter in the pan. Hold pan in left hand at a slight angle and pour approximately 2 tablespoons batter into the pan, swinging the pan in a circular motion to distribute the batter evenly. Fry the crêpes quickly, to golden brown on both sides, remove to a platter and save until needed.

To prepare sauce, place butter in the top pan of chafing dish and add the sugar cubes which have been previously rubbed against the skin of the orange. Crush the sugar with a fork and while stirring constantly, cook this mixture until slightly golden. Add the orange and lemon juice, Curacao and Grand Marnier to this mixture. Bring to a boil and simmer slowly while stirring until the sauce becomes slightly oily in texture. Place the crêpes in this sauce, four at a time, and cook approximately ½ minute on each side, then fold each crêpe in quarters and move to the side of the pan while continuing with the remaining crêpes.

After all the crêpes are done, pour the Cognac over them and ignite by tilting the pan, so the flame can reach the edge of the pan. Serve 6 crêpes per person after the flame has died.

CRÊPES FOURREES ALSACIENNES
(Alsatian Pancakes)

Fleur de Lys
San Francisco, California

18 pancakes (use your
   own pancake recipe, or
   use basic crêpes recipe)
1 quart vanilla ice cream
1½ pounds jubilee cherries
   (approximately 18
   cherries to a person)

½ cup granulated sugar
4 ounces butter
Peel of 1 orange, grated
6 ounces Kirsch
   (cherry brandy)

Heat pancakes (three to a person) in a frying pan with butter. Sprinkle with sugar and grated orange peel. When hot, fill each pancake with vanilla ice cream and six cherries. Roll pancakes and place in frying pan. Pour Kirsch brandy over and flame. Serve hot.

CRÊPES WITH BUTTERSCOTCH

Acapulco Hilton
Acapulco, Mexico

Crêpes

1 pound flour
5 eggs
10 ounces granulated sugar
Peel of 1 orange, grated

Peel of 1 lemon, grated
1 pint milk
3 ounces butter
3 ounces powdered sugar

In a bowl place flour, eggs, granulated sugar, orange and lemon peels. Mix well; then add milk. Batter must have consistency of a thickish cream.

Heat two or three small frying pans, special for pancakes (thick bottom). Put batter in pan and coat sides and bottom. Pour batter on hot pans. The crêpes must cook quickly. Brown on one side, turn, and brown on other side.

Fill pancakes with heated butterscotch cream (see recipe below) and fold twice. Sprinkle powdered sugar on top and heat under broiler for a few minutes. Can also be served flamed with rum.

Butterscotch Cream

1 cup brown sugar
6 tablespoons flour
Pinch salt
1 cup hot milk

1 egg yolk, beaten
1 tablespoon butter
1 teaspoon vanilla

In top of a double boiler, place sugar, flour, salt. Slowly stir in milk and egg yolk and cook, stirring constantly until cream is thick and smooth. Cover, lower flame, and cook 10 minutes longer. Remove from fire, stir in butter and vanilla.

CRÊPES FITZGERALD

Brennan's
New Orleans, Louisiana

4 ounces cream cheese
Enough sour cream to
  make thick paste

2 cups strawberries
  soaked in liqueur
3 ounces brandy
Crêpes (see basic recipe)

Thin Philadelphia cream cheese with sour cream to make a thick paste. Put mixture in center of thin pancake and fold ends of pancake toward middle.

In pan, put 2 cups strawberries in liqueur. Cook until strawberries are tender. Use strawberry juice sparingly. Add brandy. Add crêpes and flame.

Spoon strawberry mixture over crêpes (or pancakes) and serve.

SOUFFLÉ GRAND MARNIER

The Voisin Restaurant
New York City

1 pint milk
6 egg yolks, lightly beaten
½ cup granulated sugar
3 tablespoons flour

6 drops vanilla extract
1 pony Grand Marnier
6 egg whites, beaten stiff

Boil the milk. Mix the egg yolks, sugar and flour in a bowl. Pour the boiling milk into mixture while stirring well. Return mixture to the pan and bring to a boil. Add vanilla extract and Grand Marnier and cool mixture. Beat egg whites until very stiff and fold into the mixture. Pour into a well buttered soufflé dish and bake at 400° for about 25 to 30 minutes. Serve immediately.

SOUFFLE ROTHSCHILD

Le Chateau Richelieu
New York City

3 ounces candied fruit,
   finely diced
Dantzig Gold Wasser
   brandy
3 tablespoons butter
3 tablespoons flour

1 cup milk, scalded
4 eggs, separated
Garnish of fine strawberries,
   or halves candied
   cherries

Steep the candied fruit in Dantzig Gold Wasser brandy containing plenty of gold leaf spangles. Melt the butter, add flour and stir continuously until blended. Add milk and stir vigorously until mixture thickens. Remove from heat. Beat in egg yolks, one at a time. Combine cream souffle preparation with candied fruit. Beat egg whites stiff and fold into mixture. Pour into 2-quart souffle dish and bake in 375° oven 35 to 45 minutes. Border with strawberries or candied cherry halves.

SOUFFLE À LA SAUCE D'ABRICOT

Restaurant Laurent
New York City

3 tablespoons butter
2 tablespoons flour
1 cup milk, scalded
1-inch piece vanilla bean
    or
½ teaspoon vanilla extract

5 egg yolks
3 tablespoons sugar
6 egg whites
1 tablespoon sugar

Melt butter, add flour and cook, stirring, until the roux just starts to turn golden. Add scalded milk and a 1-inch piece vanilla bean (or add vanilla extract after the mixture has cooked). Cook the sauce, stirring constantly until it thickens, and then continue cooking, stirring for 5 minutes longer. Remove the vanilla bean or add the extract. Beat egg yolks well with 3 tablespoons sugar and combine them with the batter. Beat egg whites stiff, adding 1 tablespoon sugar during the last minutes of beating. Fold thoroughly and carefully into the mixture one-fourth of the beaten egg whites and add the remaining egg whites, cutting them in lightly but completely by raising and folding the mixture over and over. Pour the batter into a buttered and lightly sugared souffle mold and bake the souffle in a moderately hot oven (350°) for 35 to 40 minutes. Serve at once with apricot sauce.

Apricot Sauce

½ pound dried apricots
Water to cover

½ cup sugar
Peach liqueur to taste

Wash dried apricots, soak them in water to cover for several hours, and simmer them in the same water until they are soft. Rub the fruit through a sieve, add ½ cup sugar, and stir the purée over heat for a few minutes. Flavor the sauce to taste with peach liqueur. This sauce will keep indefinitely in the refrigerator.

ORANGE PANCAKES WITH ORANGE SYRUP

Colonial Room
Peabody Hotel
Memphis, Tennessee

1 egg, beaten
1 cup light cream

1 6-ounce can frozen
   orange concentrate
1 cup pancake mix

Combine egg, cream and ¼ cup of the orange concentrate (reserve remainder). Add pancake mix, stirring to remove most of the lumps. Bake on hot griddle, turning once. Serve with warm orange syrup.

Orange Syrup for Pancakes

½ cup melted butter
1 cup sugar
Frozen orange concentrate (remaining from pancake batter)

Combine melted butter, sugar and orange juice concentrate. Heat just to boiling. Makes 1½ cups.

FLOATING ISLAND

Malmaison Restaurant
New York City

3 cups milk
½ pound sugar
Vanilla extract, to taste

6 egg whites
½ cup almonds, blanched,
   toasted and sliced

Simmer milk together with 3 tablespoons sugar and a drop of vanilla extract. Beat egg whites until stiff and very gradually add 5 tablespoons sugar. When firm, mould the egg whites out with an ice cream scoop and drop them into the simmering milk. After a few minutes turn them gently around and when firm at the finger's touch, place them on cloth napkins to drain.

Sauce

6 egg yolks
¾ pound sugar
Milk in which egg whites have poached

Place egg yolks and sugar in a bowl and mix with a wooden spoon. Pour milk in which the whites have been poached over the egg yolk mixture, then return mixture to the pan. Heat and stir; do not let milk boil. When the mixture becomes thick enough to coat the end of the spoon, remove from fire. Cool.

Pour the chilled sauce into a glass bowl. Float the poached egg whites (Oeufs à la neige) on top and sprinkle generously with toasted almonds.

SAUCES—FOR MEAT, FISH & VEGETABLES

DEMI-GLACE SAUCE

Add chopped stems and peelings of 6 mushrooms to ⅓ cup sherry. Cook until reduced to ½ original quantity. Add 2 cups brown sauce and 1 tablespoon meat extract. Bring to boil, reduce flame and simmer for 15 to 18 minutes. Strain.

STEAK SAUCE

Restaurant Embassy
Mexico City

1 cup mushrooms, sliced
1 cup oil
3 cloves garlic,
    finely chopped
3 cups red wine
½ cup brandy

¾ cup tomato purée
½ cup parsley, chopped
1 dash marjoram
1 dash thyme
1 small laurel leaf

Cook the mushrooms 5 minutes in oil. Add all other ingredients and boil for 15 minutes, stirring frequently.

MUSHROOM SAUCE

King's Inn
Highlands, North Carolina

1½ cups milk
½ cup liquor drained
    from mushrooms
2 tablespoons butter
2 tablespoons flour

1 small can mushrooms
¼ teaspoon salt
⅛ teaspoon pepper
Dash paprika

Make a sauce of the milk, mushroom liquor, butter, flour and seasonings. When thick, add mushrooms.

MADEIRA SAUCE

The Pickfair Tavern
Toronto, Ontario

2 tablespoons butter
1 tablespoon ham,
  finely minced
1 small onion,
  finely minced
1 small carrot, chopped
1 stalk celery, chopped
1 garlic clove
2 tablespoons flour

1 quart beef broth
2 tomatoes, chopped
1 sprig parsley, chopped
1 sprig thyme, chopped
¼ bay leaf
3 peppercorns, whole
1 cup Madeira wine
Salt to taste

Melt the butter in a thick bottomed sauce pan, add ham and cook for a few minutes. Add onions, carrot, celery and garlic and fry briskly until light brown. Stir in flour until lightly brown, add the beef broth and all remaining ingredients except the wine. Add salt and simmer for 30 minutes. During the cooking, fat will come to the surface. Remove it with a spoon, then strain. This sauce should have the consistency of cream. Add the wine last and season to taste.

BROWN SAUCE

Beverly Hilton Hotel
Beverly Hills, California

4 tablespoons butter
2 tablespoons of green
  onions, finely chopped
1 can beef gravy

1 teaspoon lemon juice
Dash Tabasco sauce
Freshly ground black
  pepper

Melt butter in a large saucepan and cook shallots or green onions until transparent. Add the beef gravy and season with lemon juice and Tabasco sauce. Add freshly ground black pepper to taste.

BROWN SAUCE

Ernie's Restaurant
San Francisco, California

Note: This brown sauce is highly recommended by Ernie's. It is usually prepared in large quantities and refrigerated for later use. This is an excellent basic sauce for any recipe.

2 pounds veal shank bone
2 onions, chopped
2 carrots, coarsely
   chopped
1 tablespoon tomato paste
1 stalk celery
2 tablespoons flour
1 quart consomme
2 quarts water

Brown the cut shank bone in oven for 20 minutes. Add 2 chopped onions (don't chop them too fine), put in carrots and celery and brown for an additional 10 minutes. Add 2 tablespoons flour, tomato paste. Brown 10 minutes more, stirring occasionally. Cover with consomme and 2 quarts of water. Let cook 2 hours.

SAUCE CHASSEUR

Ernie's Restaurant
San Francisco, California

2 tablespoons butter
2 tablespoons olive oil
¾ pound mushrooms
   and stems, sliced
1 teaspoon shallots,
   chopped
1 clove garlic, chopped
1 glass white wine
½ glass Marsala or port
1 cup brown sauce
1 cup consomme
½ cup chopped tomatoes
Salt and pepper to taste
1 bay leaf
1 tablespoon fresh
   parsley, chopped

Sauté mushrooms in butter and olive oil. Add shallot and garlic. Let mushroom mixture brown slightly. Add white wine and Marsala (or port if preferred). Let the wine reduce until half the volume. Add brown sauce, consomme and tomatoes, and season to taste. Add bay leaf. Let cook 20 to 25 minutes. When ready to serve add chopped fresh parsley.

SAUCE BEARNAISE

Club Domino
San Francisco, California

5 egg yolks
2 ounces Burgundy
1 teaspoon beef extract
1 tablespoon tarragon
vinegar
1 teaspoon tarragon,
chopped fine

¼ cup sweet butter, melted
½ cup butter, melted
1 teaspoon onion, chopped
1 large mushroom,
chopped
Pinch salt

In a double boiler, beat egg yolks, add Burgundy wine, beef concentrate, tarragon vinegar and tarragon, chopped fine. Beat all over boiling water until very fluffy. Then add melted sweet and salt butter, and the onion-mushroom mixture. Season. Fold all together to make a rich sauce.

BEARNAISE SAUCE, PLACE PIGALLE VERSION

Place Pigalle
San Francisco, California

2 tablespoons vinegar
Dash ground black pepper
Pinch salt
1 teaspoon shallots,
chopped very fine
1 tablespoon fresh
tarragon, chopped
very fine

5 egg yolks
1 tablespoon Sauterne
wine
½ pound butter
2 teaspoons strong,
jellied beef stock
Dash Tabasco

Put vinegar in top of double boiler, add ground black pepper, salt, shallots and tarragon. Reduce over direct heat until vinegar is absolutely dry. Remove from fire and wait until pan is cold. Add egg yolks and wine and whip. Put pan over lower part of double boiler and continue whipping until eggs start to thicken and reach proper consistency. Whip in melted butter which is only slightly warm. Remove from fire. Add beef stock and Tabasco.

MORNAY SAUCE

The Penthouse Club
New York City

1 cup béchamel sauce
½ cup hollandaise or
  mayonnaise

½ cup heavy cream,
  whipped
3 tablespoons Cheddar
  cheese, grated

Mix all ingredients lightly, until blended.

PERIGOURDINE SAUCE

The Baroque Restaurant
New York City

2 cups veal stock
⅓ cup Madeira
1 truffle chopped

Truffle liquid
1 tablespoon butter

Cook veal stock until it is reduced to 1 cup. Add Madeira. Bring to boiling point, but do not let it boil. Add truffle and a little truffle liquid. Bit by bit add butter, stirring so butter mixes into sauce.

MARCHAND DE VIN SAUCE

Brennan's French Restaurant
New Orleans, Louisiana

¾ cup butter
½ cup mushrooms,
  finely chopped
½ cup minced ham
⅓ cup shallots,
  finely chopped
½ cup onions, finely
  chopped

2 tablespoons garlic,
  minced
2 tablespoons flour
½ teaspoon salt
⅛ teaspoon pepper
Dash cayenne
¾ cup beef stock
½ cup red wine

In a 9-inch skillet melt butter and lightly sauté the mushrooms, ham, shallots, onion and garlic. When the onion is golden brown, add the flour, salt, pepper and cayenne. Brown well, about 7 to 10 minutes. Blend in the stock and wine, and simmer over low heat for 35 to 45 minutes. Yield: 2 cups.

MARCHAND-DE-VIN SAUCE

Brennan's
New Orleans, Louisiana

6 tablespoons butter	4 ounces ham, chopped
½ bunch scallions,	fine
chopped fine	Pepper to taste
1 small onion, chopped	½ cup consomme
fine	¾ cup red wine
	Salt and pepper to taste

Heat 4 tablespoons butter until hot. Over low flame, cook scallions and onion until wilted. Add ham and pepper to taste. Add the consomme and reduce the liquid to ¼ cup. Add red wine and the remaining butter, bit by bit, stirring gently. Season to taste.

BARBEQUE SAUCE

Ye Olde Lantern
Tucson, Arizona

½ cup tomato purée	1 tablespoon barbeque
½ cup tomato juice	spice
1 cup tomato catsup	1 teaspoon garlic salt
2 teaspoons black pepper	4 tablespoons cider
¼ cup Worcestershire	vinegar
sauce	½ cup liquid smoke
½ teaspoon salt	

Combine ingredients, mix thoroughly, and stir over a low flame, until the sauce thickens. Serve very hot.

BÉCHAMEL SAUCE

The Penthouse Club
New York City

2 tablespoons butter
2 tablespoons flour
1 cup milk

Salt
Freshly ground pepper

Melt butter over medium heat. Add flour and stir until well blended. Add milk. Heat on low flame for 10 minutes, stirring constantly. Season to taste with salt and pepper.

SHISH KEBAB SAUCE

London Grill
Portland, Oregon

½ bunch parsley
3 large onions
½ medium bunch celery
1 green pepper
½ pound mushroom stems
1 large fresh ginger root
1 whole clove garlic
½ cup olive oil
1 heaping tablespoon turmeric
1 heaping tablespoon Madras curry
½ heaping tablespoon crushed peppercorns

½ heaping tablespoon Sweet Basil
½ heaping tablespoon marjoram
¼ tablespoon thyme
¼ tablespoon oregano
¼ tablespoon cloves
¼ cinnamon stick
Tiny pinch saffron
Tiny pinch crushed juniper berries
1 large bay leaf
½ tablespoon Rosemary
½ cup red wine
1 cup dry sauterne

Shish Kebab Sauce

1 quart rich veal brown gravy
Salt to taste

3 drops Angostura bitters
1 quart tomato puree

Mince the parsley, onions, celery, pepper, mushroom stems and ginger root and garlic fine in food chopper and sauté in olive oil. Do not brown. Add the spices and herbs and blend well.

Combine the red wine, sauterne, gravy, salt, Angostura and tomato puree and add to first mixture. Simmer over low flame for at least 30 minutes.

RAGOUT FIN SAUCE

Sun Valley Inn
Sun Valley, Idaho

3 tablespoon butter
7 tablespoons flour
1 quart chicken stock

3 ounces white wine
Salt and pepper to taste
1 cup cream

Make a supreme sauce by making a butter roux of the butter and flour. Stir this until it is a golden—not dark—brown. Add the remaining ingredients, and blend well.

Julienne (cut in thin strips) whatever you have in the refrigerator—spiced veal, ham, tongue, turkey, sweetbreads, roast beef. Pour the sauce over and simmer for 15 minutes. Serve in a small patty shell as an hors d'oeuvre or a larger shell as a luncheon dish.

GIBLET GRAVY

Young's Restaurant
Akron, Ohio

¾ pound chicken gizzards
  and hearts (equal number
  of each)
1 medium onion, chopped
1 garlic cove, minced
3 tablespoons shortening

3 cups water
1 tablespoon paprika
½ cup flour
1 cup water
½ cup thick sour cream
Salt and pepper to taste

Clean and wash gizzards. Sauté onion and garlic in shortening, and giblets (gizzards and hearts) and 3 cups water. Simmer until tender. Add paprika, then simmer 7 to 10 minutes. Beat flour with 1 cup water until smooth before blending in sour cream; beat mixture until fluffy. Stir sour cream mixture into giblets; cook over low flame for 20 minutes. Season to taste.

SAUCE PARADIS

Antoine's
New Orleans, Louisiana

¼ cup butter
¼ cup flour
 2 cups double strength veal stock
½ cup Madeira wine

2 tablespoons red currant jelly
2 cups seedless white grapes
2 large truffles, sliced

Melt butter, add flour and stir until smooth. Add veal stock and cook, stirring constantly, until slightly thickened. Add wine and jelly and stir until jelly is melted. Add grapes and truffles. Makes about 4 cups. Chicken stock may be substituted for veal stock.

SPICED CRANBERRY SAUCE

Publick House
Sturbridge, Massachusetts

1 cup water
1¼ cups brown sugar
¾ cup white sugar
½ cup vinegar
 2 teaspoon whole cloves

2 sticks cinnamon (6 inches)
4 cups fresh cranberries (1 pound)

Combine water, sugars, vinegar and spices in a saucepan and simmer for 5 minutes. Remove the cloves and the cinnamon. Add cranberries and cook over moderate flame until cranberries burst open. Cool. Makes about 3½ cups of sauce.

MEAT SAUCE

Caprioni's
Cincinnati, Ohio

10 ounces lean beef
4 ounces veal
6 ounces lean pork
1 strip bacon
½ cup parsley
1 small stalk celery
(cut off leaves)
4 ounces fresh mushrooms
1 large onion
2 large cloves garlic

½ cup butter
½ cup olive oil
1 6-ounce can tomato paste
2 #2½ can Italian peeled
tomatoes
Pinch ground allspice
Pinch oregano
1 tablespoon salt
1 teaspoon pepper

Grind meats, bacon, parsley, celery, mushrooms, onion and garlic together, using medium blade. Sauté this mixture in butter and olive oil until golden brown. Now add tomato paste and blend well. Then add remaining ingredients. Simmer slowly for at least two hours.

The sauce can be used in combination with almost any kind of spaghetti or with any of the larger macaroni shapes.

SPAGHETTI SAUCE

Bray-Wood Resort
Eagle River, Wisconsin

1 pound spareribs
3 tablespoon olive oil
2 cans tomato paste
(standard small cans)
3 cans water
1 garlic clove

1 large can peeled Italian
tomatoes
1 green pepper, diced fine
Pinch salt
Pinch sugar

Sauté spareribs until brown in olive oil. Add all other ingredients and simmer slowly, uncovered, for two hours until the sauce is thick.

SAUCE FOR FISH

East Indian Kitchen
Hotel Pierre
New York City

½ cup oil
4 onions, chopped
2 tablespoons curry powder
1 teaspoon paprika
1 teaspoon black pepper

1½ tablespoons salt
½ to 1 cup tomato sauce
 (depending upon taste)
3 to 4 cups hot water
3 pounds fish filet

Heat oil in stew pan. Add onions, curry powder, paprika, pepper and salt, and brown together. Then add tomato sauce. Cook until almost dry, stirring constantly to avoid burning. When almost dry, add hot water. Boil about 20 minutes. Add fish to sauce and cook slowly until tender, about 15 minutes. Do not stir after adding fish.

TARTAR SAUCE, MISSISSIPPI STYLE

Michael's Fine Food
Cleveland, Mississippi

½ bottle capers
1 large onion
2 tablespoons lemon juice
2 tablespoons vinegar

1 pint mayonnaise
Dash Tabasco
Salt to taste
Paprika to taste

Grind capers and onion, mix with seasonings and mayonnaise. Chill.

EPICUREAN SAUCE

The Coquina Club
Ormond Beach, Florida

excellent with fried sea food

1 cup heavy cream,
  whipped stiff
6 tablespoons mayonnaise
2 teaspoons prepared
  mustard

2 tablespoons prepared
  horseradish
Salt, to taste

Beat cream until stiff, then slowly stir in mayonnaise, mustard, horseradish, and salt to taste. Blend well. Serve cold.

ALMOND BUTTER SAUCE

Christiana Campbell's Tavern
Williamsburg, Virginia

½ cup butter
Generous ½ cup almonds,
  blanched and sliced
1 teaspoon onion juice
1 teaspoon chives,
  finely chopped

1 teaspoon green pepper,
  finely chopped
1 teaspoon lemon juice.
Salt, pepper, to taste
Dash nutmeg

Melt butter in a small saucepan. Add blanched, sliced almonds and cook over a low flame, stirring occasionally, until the almonds are slightly browned. Stir in onion juice, chives, green pepper and lemon juice. Heat to the boiling point, stirring gently. Season the sauce to taste with salt, pepper and a dash of nutmeg. Pour over fish.

SWEET AND SOUR SAUCE

Carson City Nugget
Carson City, Nevada

1 cup green peppers,
    chopped in half-inch
    squares
1 onion, chopped in half-
    inch squares
2 tablespoons oil
½ teaspoon ground cloves

¼ teaspoon ginger
1 cup pineapple juice
6 pineapple slices, diced
½ cup vinegar
½ cup brown sugar
Salt and pepper to taste
2 tablespoons cornstarch

Sauté peppers and onion in oil until half done. Add all remaining ingredients and simmer. Thicken to desired consistency with about 2 tablespoons cornstarch, stirring constantly. This makes about 2½ to 3 cups.

Use this sauce with spareribs, tenderloin slices, meat balls, pork chops, diced pork, chicken, and prawns.

SHRIMP OR LOBSTER SAUCE

The Flame Steakhouse
Pittsburgh, Pennsylvania

1½ cups diced shrimp or
    lobster meat
½ cup butter
½ cup flour
2 cups milk, scalded

2 cups cream, scalded
¼ cup sherry wine
Salt and white pepper
    to taste

Sauté lobster meat or shrimp in butter over low heat, just enough to heat through. Blend in flour. Add scalded milk and cream. Cook on low heat, constantly stirring, until sauce is smooth. Just before serving, stir in the wine and season to taste. Serve over rice.

LAMAZE SAUCE

The Warwick Hotel
Philadelphia, Pennsylvania

1 cup mayonnaise
¼ cup India relish
1 cup chili sauce
2 teaspoons prepared
  mustard
1 teaspoon chives,
  chopped

1 hard-cooked egg,
  chopped
Salt, to taste
Black pepper, to taste
Dash of A-1 sauce

Pre-chill mayonnaise, chili sauce, relish, chopped egg. Use well-chilled bowl for mixing.

Mix well in following order: mayonnaise, India relish, chili sauce, prepared mustard, chives, boiled egg. Add salt and pepper to taste. Dash A-1 sauce over dressing when serving. (This sauce must be kept in refrigerator at all times until served.)

CURRY SAUCE

The Willows
Honolulu, Hawaii

2 tablespoons butter
3 cloves garlic
1 inch slice ginger root
  (fresh)
1 small onion, finely
  chopped
1 teaspoon salt

1 tablespoon sugar
1 tablespoon curry powder
  (Spice Island preferred)
4 tablespoons flour
1 quart coconut milk
  (see below)

Melt butter; add garlic, ginger root and onion finely chopped; add salt, sugar, curry powder and flour. Mix thoroughly. Add coconut milk a little at a time, stirring to a smooth thickness, and cook for 20 minutes (until it boils). Let sauce stand for several hours. Strain before using.

Can be used with chicken, jumbo shrimp, crab, lamb, turkey or veal.

Coconut Milk

2 cups boiling water or
  hot milk
Meat of 2 coconuts, grated

Add boiling water or hot milk to grated coconut meat. Allow to stand for 20 minutes and squeeze through cheesecloth.

HOLLANDAISE SAUCE

The Beverly Hills Hotel
Beverly Hills, California

3 egg yolks   Salt, pepper to taste
4 ounces butter   Pinch cayenne pepper
1 tablespoon water   Juice of ¼ lemon

Melt the butter; it should only be lukewarm. Place egg yolks and water in top of a double boiler and beat with a whisk over hot but not boiling water until thick and foamy. Remove from heat and add the butter gradually, in small quantities, stirring constantly with the whisk and making sure that the whey is left behind.

Season with salt, pepper, a pinch of cayenne pepper and the lemon juice, and strain through a muslin cloth. Whip lukewarm, since the sauce curdles at higher temperatures.

CHEDDAR CHEESE SAUCE

Public House
Sturbridge, Massachusetts

A tempting, smooth golden sauce to ladle over steaming-hot boiled onions, or broccoli, or cauliflower.

2 tablespoons butter   1 cup Cheddar cheese,
2 tablespoons flour   grated
1 cup milk   1 egg, slightly beaten
             Salt and pepper

Melt butter and blend in flour. Pour in milk; cook and stir continuously until the mixture comes to a boil. Remove from heat. Add Cheddar cheese and stir until the cheese is melted. Stir in egg and cook, stirring all the while, for a minute or two. Season to taste with salt and pepper.

SPICY OR DEVILED BUTTER SAUCE

Yankee Inn
Holyoke, Massachusetts

1 pound butter
4 cloves garlic,
  chopped fiine
3 shallots, chopped fine
Dash cayenne pepper
1 teaspoon salt

¼ cup olive oil
¼ cup wine vinegar
Juice of ½ lemon
1 tablespoon chopped
  parsley

In mixer, add all dry ingredients, plus butter, then add liquid ingredients slowly. When fully incorporated, add parsley. Refrigerate until ready to use.

MUSTARD SAUCE

Parker House
Boston, Massachusetts

1 tablespoon onion,
  minced
3 tablespoons butter
2 tablespoons cider vinegar

2 teaspoons dry mustard
  (English)
¼ bay leaf
2 cups brown gravy

Sauté minced onion in butter. Add cider vinegar and simmer 5 minutes. Moisten dry mustard with water and blend, then add brown gravy and bay leaf. Simmer a few minutes, season to taste, and strain. Serve very hot.

AVOCADO SAUCE

Restaurant Embassy
Mexico City

2 ripe avocados
1 cup onion, minced
1 teaspoon coriander
　leaves, minced
2 teaspoons chili peppers,
　minced
Dash Tabasco sauce

1¼ pounds green tomatoes,
　cooked and mashed
Juice of ½ lemon
　2 tablespoons oil
Salt and pepper to taste
1 teaspoon cream

Force avocados through a sieve. Place onion in mixing bowl. Using beater at low speed add the coriander, chili, Tabasco sauce, oil, green tomatoes, lemon juice and salt and pepper. Add avocados. Add cream last. Will keep in refrigerator for 8 days.

Note: The green tomatoes should be boiled in water until soft, then mashed with potato masher.

CHERRY WINE SAUCE FOR BAKED HAM

The Mohawk
Old Forge, New York

Juice of 2 oranges
½ teaspoon grated
　orange rind
Juice of 1 lemon
½ teaspoon grated
　lemon rind
1 tablespoon cornstarch
¼ teaspoon powdered
　cloves

½ cup currant jelly
2 tablespoons butter
2 cups canned Bing
　cherries, pitted and
　drained
⅓ cup Marsala
⅓ cup sherry

Grate needed amount of rind from orange and lemon and reserve. Squeeze orange and lemon juice, add cornstarch, cloves and currant jelly. Heat in double boiler or heavy pan until jelly melts. Add butter, cherries and the reserved rind.

Just before serving, add Marsala and sherry. Serve hot over slices of baked ham.

MARSHMALLOW FRUIT SAUCE

Hoffman House
Madison, Wisconsin

¼ cup fresh orange juice
¼ cup lemon juice
¼ cup pineapple juice
2 tablespoons cornstarch
10 tablespoons sugar
1 tablespoon mustard

3 whole eggs, well beaten
15 marshmallows, cut in pieces
1½ cups heavy cream, whipped stiff

Heat all juices, but do not boil. Mix cornstarch, sugar, mustard with eggs. Add juices, stirring constantly. Add marshmallows. Stir until thoroughly blended. Allow to cool. Whip cream and fold into juice mixture.

SAUCES FOR DESSERTS

SABAYON SAUCE

The Greenbrier
White Sulphur Springs, West Virginia

6 egg yolks
⅔ cup sugar

1 cup Grand Marnier or
Curacao

Place egg yolks and sugar in the top of a double boiler over hot (not boiling) water and beat until fluffy.

Continue beating until sauce thickens. Stir in Grand Marnier or Curacao liqueur. Serve hot.

Note: *Always* make this sauce at the last minute.

BUBBLING RUM SAUCE
(for apple pie)

J. A. C. Cafeteria
Columbia, Missouri

1 cup light brown sugar
1 cup honey, strained
½ cup water

½ cup butter
½ cup rum, golden

Combine all ingredients, except rum, in a saucepan. Gradually heat to the boiling point, stirring constantly. Remove from heat, cover and cool to room temperature. Stir in the rum. Cover and keep at room temperature. Serve over apple pie, three or four tablespoons per serving. Put under boiler and heat until bubbling, and serve at once.

FOAMY SAUCE

*The Lord Jeffery
Amherst, Massachusetts*

¼ pound butter
 1 cup confectioners sugar
 1 egg, well beaten
Dash salt

¼ cup hot water
 1 teaspoon flavoring—
    sherry, vanilla or rum

Cream butter and sugar, then gradually add egg, salt and hot water. Heat over hot water until smooth and light. Add flavoring. Serve hot, over steamed puddings.

HARD SAUCE

*The Lord Jeffrey
Amherst, Massachusetts*

¼ pound butter
 1 pound confectioners
    sugar

1 egg
Vanilla or liquor

Cream butter and sugar; then blend in egg. Add enough vanilla or liquor to bring to desired consistency and flavor. Heat over hot water until thick. Serve hot.

CHERRY RHUBARB SAUCE

*Knott's Berry Farm
Buena Park, California*

 2 pounds cherry rhubarb
2¼ cups water
1½ cups sugar

Wash, but do not peel, cherry rhubarb and cut into 1½ inch pieces. Add water and sugar. Cook in open kettle one or two minutes after it boils; time will depend on condition of rhubarb. If lid is put on kettle, rhubarb will mash. Let stand a few hours before serving, so that rhubarb will absorb sugar from the juice. Serve chilled.

ORANGE SAUCE

Hoffman House
Madison, Wisconsin

6 oranges, peeled and
   diced
2 ounces butter
2 cups orange drink

½ teaspoon ground
   allspice
¼ cup brown sugar
1½ teaspoons cornstarch
¼ cup water

Remove orange rinds and dice. Dice the orange meat.
Sauté both the rinds and meat of oranges in butter until
tender. Add orange drink, allspice and brown sugar and
simmer for ten minutes. Dilute cornstarch with cold water
add to sauce and bring to rolling boil until slightly thickened.
Cook out any cornstarch taste.

MISCELLANEOUS

CLARIFIED BUTTER

To clarify butter, cut it into pieces. Place in a saucepan over moderate heat. When the butter has melted, skim off the foam. Strain the clear yellow liquid into a bowl, leaving the milky residue in the bottom of the pan to be used for soups or sauces.

DUXELLES

La Strada Restaurant
San Francisco, California

¾ pound fresh mushrooms, peeled and finely chopped
6 ounces calf brains, uncooked
2 ounces prosciutto ham
1 teaspoon shallots, chopped fine
1 medium size onion, chopped fine
1 medium size green pepper, chopped fine
1 small clove garlic
1 teaspoon fresh garden herbs (thyme, rosemary, oregano, marjoram, basil)
2 tablespoons olive oil
1 cup sherry wine
1 tablespoon Worcestershire sauce
2 tablespoons tomato catsup
Salt and pepper to taste
12 oysters in shells
Hollandaise sauce
Parmesan cheese, grated

Chop all ingredients very fine. Sauté in olive oil. Add wine, Worcestershire sauce, and catsup. On low flame, reduce to a firm consistency. Fill oyster shells with mixture, placing oysters whole on top. Cover with Hollandaise sauce. Sprinkle with Parmesan cheese. Bake in 375° oven until brown.

CRÊPES HENRI IV

King Henri IV
New York City

Batter for 6 crêpes:

3 tablespoons flour
1 whole egg
Pinch of salt

⅔ cup milk
2 teaspoons butter

Mix flour and egg with wire whisk and add salt and milk. Mix well. Strain through a fine sieve. In a small frying pan, heat small piece of butter (2 teaspoons). Pour in batter and tilt pan so that bottom is covered with a thin layer of batter. Cook the crêpe quickly on one side, turn over and cook on other side.

Stuffing for crêpes:

6 ounces filet of sole, diced
¼ cup dry white wine
1 chopped shallot
2 ounces chopped, cooked lobster meat or shrimp

2 ounces flaked crabmeat
Pinch of salt
1 tablespoon each flour and melted butter

Dice filet of sole and poach in white wine, to which shallots and a little water have been added; season, and cook a few minutes. Add lobster or shrimp and crabmeat, bring to a boil. Mix thoroughly flour and melted butter and add to fish mixture. Bring to boil again to thicken. Place fish mixture in center of each crêpe and roll.

Mornay Sauce

1 tablespoon butter
1 tablespoon flour
¾ cup milk or light cream
Salt and pepper to taste

1 large or 2 small egg yolks, slightly beaten
4 tablespoons grated cheese, Parmesan or Swiss

Melt butter, add flour and cook over low flame, stirring constantly. Boil milk or cream and add gradually, stirring constantly with wire whisk to avoid lumps. Season and cook a few minutes until thickened. Remove from heat, add egg yolk and 3 tablespoons cheese. Stir briskly.

Cover crêpes with sauce, sprinkle with 1 tablespoon grated cheese and brown lightly under broiler.

CRÊPES LAURENT

Restaurant Laurent
New York City

6 French pancakes—thin (see basic recipe for crêpes)
½ cup crabmeat
½ cup lobster meat
1 dozen shrimp, finely chopped
4 tablespoons butter

2 tablespoons sherry
¼ teaspoon curry powder
Salt, pepper, Ac'cent, to taste
6 teaspoons cream sauce (see recipe below)
Parmesan cheese, grated

Sauté seafood in butter. Add sherry and curry powder. Season with salt, pepper and Ac'cent to taste. Roll 1 tablespoon into each pancake and place on serving platter. Add 1 teaspoon cream sauce, pouring it over each pancake. Sprinkle a little grated cheese on top. Place under broiler until slightly brown.

Cream Sauce

2 tablespoons butter
2 tablespoons flour
1 cup milk
1 egg yolk

2 tablespoons Parmesan cheese, grated
¼ cup heavy cream, whipped

Melt butter, blend in flour and slowly stir in milk, cooking until thickened. Add 1 egg yolk, beaten, grated Parmesan cheese and whipped cream.

BEUREK A LA TURQUE

The Red Knight
San Francisco, California

6 8-inch crêpes
  (see basic crêpes recipe)
1½ cups chicken, cooked
  and minced
¾ cup Velouté sauce
  (cream sauce)
Salt, pepper to taste

Flour for dredging
 2 eggs, slightly beaten
Bread crumbs
Fat for frying
Brown wine sauce
  (see recipe below)

Prepare 8-inch crêpes; set aside. For stuffing, mix minced chicken with Velouté sauce and seasonings; stuffing should be firm enough to hold shape. Place mixture on each crêpe, and roll crêpes into cylinders. Dip into flour, then beaten eggs, then roll in bread crumbs. Deep fry at 375° for 5 minutes, until light brown. Drain. Serve with a brown wine sauce gravy.

Brown Wine Sauce

2 cups brown sauce
⅓ cup dry white wine

Cook brown sauce until reduced to about 1½ cups. Add white wine; bring to a boil and simmer for 5 to 8 minutes.

STUFFED CRÊPES A LA FOX HILL

Fox Hill Restaurant
Ridgefield, Connecticut

3 pound roasting chicken
Basic cream sauce
  (see recipe below)
½ cup Sherry
3 egg yolks

½ pint heavy cream,
  whipped
Parmesan cheese, grated
Crêpes—see basic recipe

Boil roasting chicken until tender, about 40 minutes. Let cool. Remove meat and dice very fine. Blend diced chicken with about ½ cup basic cream sauce (see recipe below). Stir in Sherry wine.

Put 2 tablespoons of chicken mixture on each crêpe and roll up. Place rolled crêpes in a chafing dish. Make a sauce by mixing 3 egg yolks into 1 pint cream sauce. Blend in whipped cream. Pour sauce over rolled crêpes, sprinkle with grated cheese and place under broiler until lightly browned.

Basic Cream Sauce

2 tablespoons butter	½ cup milk
2 tablespoons flour	3 egg yolks, beaten

Melt butter, blend in flour. Gradually stir in milk. Pour a little of the hot mixture into beaten yolks, then return to butter-flour-milk mixture.

CRÊPES DE POULET MAYFAIR

Mayfair Farms
West Orange, New Jersey

Crêpes (see basic recipe)	½ cup dry white wine
Butter	1 cup heavy white cream
2 shallots, chopped	sauce
Diced cooked chicken—	Salt and pepper
about 1½ chickens of a	Mornay sauce
2½ pound size	(see recipe below)

Prepare crêpes. Set aside. Melt butter in pan, add chopped shallots and sauté for three minutes. Then add diced cooked chicken and sauté for about 5 minutes. Add white wine and let mixture boil. Add cream sauce and season with salt and pepper. Mixture should be thick. Place in crêpes, and roll.

Spread Mornay sauce over top of crêpes and glaze in broiler.

Mornay Sauce

1 cup white cream sauce
1 tablespoon cheese, grated
2 tablespoons Hollandaise sauce (or substitute 2 egg yolks)

4 tablespoons whipped cream
Salt and pepper to taste

To cream sauce add all other ingredients, stirring gently until well blended.

CRÊPES QUO VADIS

*Quo Vadis
New York City*

Crêpes

1⅛ cups sifted flour
1½ cups milk
3 eggs, well beaten
Dash salt

2 tablespoons melted butter

Sift flour and salt into bowl. Stir eggs into milk. Combine egg and milk mixture with dry ingredients and stir until batter is smooth. Batter should coat a spoon. This makes 24 crêpes in 5 to 6 inch pan.

Filling

Shrimp, diced
Lobster meat, diced
Scallops, diced

Crab meat, diced
Butter
Light curry sauce

Sauté diced seafood in butter; add a light curry sauce and boil for 5 minutes.

Glacing

Light cream sauce
2 eggs yolks

4 tablespoons whipped cream

Add beaten egg yolks to cream sauce and blend together. Fold in whipped cream.

Fill pancake with seafood, roll; pour glacing over it and brown under flame over broiler.

VIRGINIA PECAN PANCAKES

Williamsburg Lodge
Williamsburg, Virginia

3 egg yolks
1½ teaspoons salt
¼ cup maple syrup
3 cups pastry flour, sifted

2 tablespoons baking powder
2¼ cups milk
½ cup shortening
½ cup pecans, roasted and chopped

Beat egg yolks and salt until light. Add maple syrup and beat. Sift flour with baking powder. Then add flour and milk alternately. Melt shortening and add to batter. Add pecans to batter. Bake on griddle. Serve with Wild Mountain Blackberry Syrup.

WAFFLES

The House by the Road
Ashburn, Georgia

1¾ cups cake flour, sifted
2 teaspoons baking powder
2 teaspoons sugar
1 teaspoon salt
3 eggs, separated

1½ cups sweet milk
6 tablespoons melted butter
Butter
Syrup

Sift together flour, baking powder, sugar and salt. Beat egg yolks well and add milk and butter. Combine sifted ingredients with liquid. Beat egg whites stiff and fold into batter. Grease a hot waffle iron and pour in batter. Bake 4 to 5 minutes. Serve hot with butter and syrup.

SOURMILK WAFFLES

*The Wilbur Hotel
Corbin, Kentucky*

1⅓ cups flour	1 teaspoon sugar
½ teaspoon salt	¼ cup melted shortening
½ teaspoon baking soda	1 cup sour milk
3 eggs, separated	1 cup sweet milk

Sift flour, measure, and resift with salt and baking soda. Beat egg yolks until light and foamy. Add sugar and shortening. Mix well. Add milk, alternately with sifted dry ingredients, to egg mixture. Fold in stiffly beaten egg whites. Bake in hot waffle iron.

ENVUELTOS DE AGUACATE

*Cafe La Margarita
Chicago, Illinois*

18 tortillas	1 tablespoon chili powder
4 tablespoons chopped onions	4 average avocados
Corn oil for deep frying	Salt
2 cans tomato sauce	2 tablespoons lime juice

Sauté two tablespoons onions in 1 tablespoon oil until soft but uncolored. Stir in tomato sauce and chili and cook for five minutes. Mash the avocado meat to a uniform paste and stir in salt, two tablespoons chopped onion and lime juice. In hot, deep cooking oil drop each tortilla, turning immediately and removing. Tortillas should brown lightly but remain soft. Fill each tortilla with avocado sauce, double over and pour the tomato sauce on top.

SUBGUM CHOW MEIN

New China Inn
Baltimore, Maryland

4 tablespoons cooking oil
Salt and pepper to taste
2 cups fresh pork, diced
1 cup bamboo shoots, diced
1 cup water chestnuts, diced
1 cup Bok Toy (Chinese vegetables) diced
1 cup celery, diced
1 cup mushrooms, diced
½ cup green peas

2 cups chicken broth or stock
2 tablespoons cornstarch
½ teaspoon Gourmet powder
2 tablespoons soy sauce
1 tomato, diced
½ cup almonds, blanched and toasted
½ cup barbecued pork, diced

Heat skillet and oil over moderate flame. Put in salt and pepper, fresh pork, and stir 2 minutes. Then add bamboo, water chestnuts, Bok Toy, celery, mushrooms and peas. Mix thoroughly. Add broth; cover and cook 10 minutes.

In the meantime, dissolve cornstarch in ¼ cup water and put in Gourmet powder and soy sauce. When ingredients are done, add tomato and cornstarch seasoning. Stir about 1 minute until mixture thickens. Pour mixture over noodles and top it with almonds and barbecued pork.

Note: For chicken Subgum Chow Mein, use diced chicken in place of fresh pork and barbecued pork. For Shrimp Subgum Chow Mein, use shrimp instead of pork.

CHOW CHOW

Haag's Hotel
Shartlesville, Pennsylvania

Vegetables

1 pint celery, cut in short
   lengths
1 pint lima beans
1 pint carrots, sliced
1 pint green string beans,
   cut in short lengths

1 pint yellow string beans,
   cut in short lengths
1 pint cauliflower
1 red pepper, diced
1 green pepper, diced
1 pint small pickles
1 cup small onions

Juice

3 cups apple cider vinegar
3 cups water

3 cups sugar
1 tablespoon salt

If vinegar is strong, more water may be added. Also, more or less sugar may be added to vinegar solution according to taste. The juice should be sweet-sour.

Season vegetables with salt and precook until almost tender the lima beans, carrots, green and yellow string beans and cauliflower. Mix all of the vegetables with the juice and boil the entire mixture 10 minutes. Let stand in cool place for several hours. Place in refrigerator to blend and chill. Serve cold.

Boiling mixture may be put in sterile jars and sealed.

LAKE BREEZE CASSEROLE SANDWICH

Lake Breeze Resort
Three Lakes, Wisconsin

6 slices toast, crusts
   trimmed
6 thick slices tomato,
   peeled
12 strips bacon, cooked
6 large slices white
   meat of turkey

2 cups medium white
   sauce
⅜ pound sharp Cheddar
   cheese, grated
½ teaspoon
   Worcestershire sauce
Paprika and/or grated
   Parmesan cheese

Place each slice of toast in individual casserole. Top with tomato slice. Cover with cooked bacon slices, then turkey slice. Add cheese to white sauce, stir till melted. Add Worcestershire sauce. Spoon sauce over turkey slices. Sprinkle with paprika or Parmesan, or both. Bake at 350° for 10 to 15 minutes, or until sauce is bubbly.

Serve as a main luncheon dish with a green salad.

BAKED PINEAPPLE HAWAIIANA

Hawaiian Village
Honolulu, Hawaii

1½ cups cream
¾ cup coconut milk
3 tablespoons butter,
   melted
3 tablespoons flour
2 cups white meat of
   chicken, diced and
   cooked

3 teaspoons almonds,
   blanched and slivered
Salt and pepper to taste
3 tablespoons sherry
1½ cups diced fresh
   pineapple (3 fresh
   pineapples)

Cut 3 medium-size pineapples in half, cut out center to make a pocket, dice the pineapple that has been scooped out and set aside.

Heat cream and coconut milk. Make a roux by blending the melted butter and flour together. Cook for 1 minute, whisking continually. Remove from stove. Add hot cream and coconut milk. Put back on stove, whisking briskly until sauce comes to a boil. Fold in the diced chicken, almonds and pineapple, salt and pepper and sherry. Spoon the ingredients into the pineapple shells and set aside.

The Glaze—Hollandaise Sauce, Plain

3 egg yolks
3 teaspoons hot consomme
⅜ pound butter, melted

Beat egg yolks with hot consomme in glass or stainless steel bowl over hot water bath, until the consistency of a light mayonnaise. Remove bowl from over hot water, and beating continually, slowly add warm melted strained butter, until all is blended together. Then add ½ cup of the cream sauce, mix well, and spoon over the chicken in the pineapple. Put under broiler and glaze to a golden color. Serve at once.